LENNON AND McCARTNEY

Even when they were collaborating in The Beatles (left), Lennon and McCartney had very different ways of working.

LENNON AND McCARTNEY
together alone

a critical discography of their solo work **JOHN BLANEY**

LENNON AND McCARTNEY: TOGETHER ALONE

A critical discography of their solo work

JOHN BLANEY

A Jawbone Book
First Edition 2007
Published in the UK and the USA by Jawbone Press
2a Union Court
20-22 Union Road
London SW4 6JP
England
www.jawbonepress.com

ISBN: 978-1-906002-02-2

EDITOR Tony Bacon
DESIGN CONCEPT Paul Cooper Design
DESIGN Lisa Tai
JACKET Balley Design Ltd

Printed by Colorprint Offset Ltd (Hong Kong)

1 2 3 4 5 11 10 09 08 07

contents

together alone

'LOVE IN THE OPEN AIR'

McCARTNEY'S first solo project outside of The Beatles was a commission to write incidental music for a film made by the Boulting Brothers. Set in the north of England, *The Family Way*, as it was eventually titled, was a piece of lightweight social realism. Although it became Paul's project, it was originally reported as a joint Lennon and McCartney venture. *NME* reported in October: "When he returns from filming in Spain next month, John Lennon will help his songwriting partner Paul McCartney to score the new Hayley Mills film, *All In Good Time*. ... The picture's alternative working title of *Wedlocked* has now been dropped, the producers having settled on *All In Good Time*. Paul is believed to be already working on the music."

However, when Lennon returned home he had other plans. So had McCartney, who, far from knuckling down to the job, had to be pressured by George Martin to write something. Although he had provided Martin with the film's title theme, it wasn't enough for an entire soundtrack. Speaking to *NME* in December, Martin said: "I went to America for a time and, on returning [probably November 21st], realised we needed a love theme for the centre of the picture, something wistful. I told Paul and he said he'd compose something. I waited, but nothing materialised, and finally I had to go round to Paul's house and literally stand there until he'd composed something. John was visiting and advised a bit, but Paul created the tune and played it to me on guitar. I listened and wrote it down. It is a fragile, yet compelling, melody. I arranged it for woodwinds and strings, and we called it 'Love In The Open Air'. It's quite haunting."

With two McCartney themes to work with, George Martin wrote 13 variations, to be recorded by session musicians. Work progressed at lightning speed. Martin wrote the arrangements, hired the session musicians, led by Neville Marriner, and recorded the music – all within three weeks.

Although he had to be cajoled by Martin, McCartney wrote two contrasting themes that illustrate his instinctive sense of melody. Each has a distinctive mood conveyed with graceful eloquence. 'Love In The Open Air' is mellifluous and romantic; 'The Family Way' is brazen and resolute. Arranged by Martin, they proved to be remarkably adaptable and won McCartney an Ivor Novello Award for Best Instrumental Theme.

'Love In The Open Air' data

Decca were contracted to issue the recordings as an LP, but they also planned to issue a single (F12536). Martin objected, arguing that the versions recorded for the Decca LP were not commercial enough. He insisted that they be re-recorded and made plans to issue his own recordings as a single (UP 1165). Decca were forced to postpone the release of the LP until Martin had recorded his own versions. Both recordings were released on Friday January 6 1967. To add to the confusion, the American pressing of Martin's single (UA 50148) offered an alternative edit and B-side ('Bahama Sound', a Martin composition).

In Britain, Decca issued *The Family Way* LP in stereo (SKL 4847) with blue and silver labels and in mono (LK 4847) with red and sliver labels. In America, London issued *The Family Way* LP in stereo (MS 82007) and in mono (M 76007). The London LP was issued in a cover different to the British edition. Some copies of the London LP were issued with stickers fixed to the front cover to denote that they were demonstration copies, not for sale. *The Family Way* soundtrack was issued in Canada on CD by Disques XXI-21 Records on July 22 2003, but the original 1966 recordings

'LOVE IN THE OPEN AIR' / 'THE FAMILY WAY'
GEORGE MARTIN & HIS ORCHESTRA
UK RELEASE December 6 1966; United Artists UP 1165; failed to chart.

'LOVE IN THE OPEN AIR' / 'BAHAMA SOUND'
GEORGE MARTIN & HIS ORCHESTRA
US RELEASE April 24 1967; United Artists UA 50148; failed to chart.

- **'Love In The Open Air'** (McCartney)
- **'The Family Way'** (McCartney)

Both with George Martin (conductor), The George Martin Orchestra (violins, violas, double bass).
Both probably recorded at Abbey Road Studios, London, England. Both produced by A.I.R. (London).

'LOVE IN THE OPEN AIR' / 'THE FAMILY WAY'
THE TUDOR MINSTRELS
UK RELEASE December 6 1966; Decca F 12536; failed to chart.

- **'Love In The Open Air'** (McCartney)
- **'The Family Way'** (McCartney)

Both with Neville Marriner (conductor), The Tudor Minstrels (drums, basses, guitars, organ, trumpets, trombones, flutes, oboes, violins, violas, cellos). Both recorded at CTS Studios, London, England. Both produced, supervised, and orchestrated by George Martin.

THE FAMILY WAY
ORIGINAL SOUNDTRACK RECORDING
UK RELEASE January 6 1967; Decca LK 4847 (mono), SKL 4847 (stereo); failed to chart.
US RELEASE April 24 1967; LP London M 76007 (mono), MS 82007 (stereo); stereo reel-to-reel tape LPL-70136 (Ampex black box); 4-track cartridge LFX 17136 (white shell, front and back artwork); 8-track cartridge LE 72136 (white shell, front and back artwork); failed to chart.

appear to have been mastered from a vinyl source (there are bonus recordings added by Carl Aubut and the Quatuor La Flute Enchantee, recorded in 1995 and 1998 respectively).

TWO VIRGINS

A LOT had happened in the two years since the release of McCartney's music for the film *The Family Way*. In 1968, Beatlemania had forced the group into the studio and distanced them from their audience. Entrenched at Abbey Road, they developed new ways of writing and recording that transformed their music and enthralled their listeners. A thirst for knowledge and a delight in experimentation ensured that The Beatles embraced new ideas faster than Marshall McLuhan could say "the medium is the message". By the time the public had caught up with them, The Beatles had moved on.

The group were absorbing complex ideas and incorporating them into their work with remarkable speed and ease. Although their music had become more sophisticated and, at times difficult to understand, a new record by The Beatles was always eagerly awaited. What new direction had their music taken? What had they to say? If, by the mid 1960s, their music and message had grown increasingly oblique, there were still legions of fans eager to hear it.

What then would Lennon have to say with the release of his debut solo album? Whatever it was, surely it would be worth hearing? After all, hadn't it been Lennon who, with McCartney, had written some of the most insightful songs of the 1960s? Obviously The Beatles had changed. No longer mop-tops, they had grown and matured. Few would have expected Lennon's debut to contain twee boy-meets-girl ballads. But when Lennon eventually issued his debut album, what listeners heard came as a complete shock.

Two Virgins was as far removed from pop music as one could get. Inspired by the avant-garde and musique concréte recordings that supplied London's art scene with its soundtrack, Lennon was partnered by a relatively obscure Japanese artist, Yoko Ono, whom he'd met in November 1966.

Ono was exhibiting at the Indica Gallery in central London and Lennon was invited to the preview. "I'd been going around to galleries a bit on my days off in between records," he recalled. "I got the word that this amazing woman was putting on a show next week, and there was going to be something about people in bags, in black bags, and it was going to be a bit of a happening and all that. So I went down to a preview of the show. There was an apple on sale there for 200 quid. I thought it was fantastic: I got the humour in her work immediately. But there was another piece which really decided me for or against the artist: a ladder which led to a painting which was hung on a ceiling. It looked like a blank canvas with a chain and a spyglass hanging on the end of it. I climbed the ladder, looked through the spy glass, and in tiny little letters it said, "Yes". So it was positive. I felt relieved.

"I was very impressed, and [gallery owner] John Dunbar sort of introduced us; neither of us knew who the hell we were. And Dunbar had been sort of hustling her, saying, 'That's a good patron, you must go and talk to him or do something,' because I was looking for action. John Dunbar insisted she say hello to the millionaire, you know what I mean? And she came up and handed me a card which said 'breathe' on it, one of her instructions, so I just went [pant!]. This was our meeting!"

Having established contact, Ono asked Lennon if he would consider giving a manuscript of one of his songs to avant-garde composer John Cage for his 50th birthday. Ono had originally asked McCartney, but he turned her down. Lennon obliged and donated a multicoloured manuscript that he and McCartney had created for their song 'The Word'. Lennon probably didn't know it at the time but his gift was significant, especially for Ono.

By the time Ono met Lennon, she had been a professional artist for several years. Like Lennon, she began her career in the late 1950s. Working in New York City, she developed a conceptual and performance practice that drew on Zen Buddhism, Haiku poetry, and philosophy. She shared these interests with a number of artists, including Cage, who was then teaching at the New School for Social Research. His scores were often written as instructions: his most famous, '4' 33"', directs the performer(s) to make no sounds. As with many of Ono's pieces, the audience play an important role in the piece. The intention was for the audience to create something, either real or in their imagination, thereby establishing a reciprocal dialogue that blurred the barrier between artist and spectator, art and life.

Ono met Cage through her first husband, Toschi Ichiyanagi. He too was an avant-garde composer, whom she met while attending the Julliard School of Music in New York. Ichiyanagi studied at the New School for Social Research, where a number of visual artists interested in music were working with Cage. This small circle, which included George Brecht, Dick Higgins, Allan Kaprow, and Mac Low, would eventually have a considerable impact on the contemporary New York art scene. Ichiyanagi returned to Japan in 1960, but Ono stayed in New York to continue working as an artist.

One of the events Ono produced, a series of concerts organised with composer La Monte Young, became the catalyst for these artists, who formed themselves into a group, Fluxus. George Maciunas, an ardent promoter of Fluxus, suggested that artists should produce work that evoked a sense of flux. (The Lennons would work on several projects with Maciunas when they moved to New York in the early 1970s.) As Fluxus scores or performances often involved audience participation, they could never be performed the same way twice. They could, therefore, evoke a sense of liquidity that Maciunas's 'Fluxus Manifesto' described as a "continuous moving on or passing by, as of a flowing stream: a continuous succession of changes".

This notion of fluidity is clearly audible in the music that Lennon and Ono created. Their collage of made and found sounds flows from one improvised motif to another. Lennon's stream-of-consciousness utterances and Ono's vocalisations oscillate from visceral to contrived. Both were well versed in the kind of spontaneous creativity needed to produce this kind of music: Ono through her work as a multimedia artist; Lennon through his studio experimentation with The Beatles.

Thanks to their producer George Martin, The Beatles developed a healthy appetite for audio experimentation that found its way onto their records. As early as the 1950s, Martin used the recording studio as a sound laboratory, where sounds were dramatically manipulated. Working with The Goons and on his own Ray Cathode recordings, Martin took the art of recording to new areas. Within a few years, the recording techniques he'd developed were influencing and being used by The Beatles on their own records. Backwards tapes first appeared on 'Rain', the B-side of 'Paperback Writer', while sound effects and sound collages were scattered throughout *Sgt. Pepper's Lonely Hearts Club Band*. Once The Beatles discovered what could be done with tape, a few studio tricks, and a lot of imagination, there was no stopping them.

With The Beatles no longer committed to touring, the group had more time to take in London's burgeoning avant-garde scene and develop ideas of their own. While McCartney embraced London's artistic milieu, Lennon viewed it with a cynical eye. Although The Beatles had incorporated pioneering ideas into their music, Lennon had long been suspicious of the avant-garde. It was he who famously said that avant-garde was "French for bullshit".

Unlike McCartney, Lennon remained ambivalent towards the movement. "I'd get very upset about it being intellectual or all fucking avant-garde, then I'd like it, then I wouldn't," he explained. Nevertheless, it had a huge effect on the pair, who began experimenting with sound recordings at their respective home studios. Inspired by the work of Cardew, Cage, and Stockhausen, McCartney produced a number of tape loops that were superimposed onto Lennon's 'Tomorrow Never Knows'. While some of McCartney's experiments made it onto Beatles records, most of Lennon's did not. However, as unsuccessful as Lennon's experimental recordings were, they revealed that he too was thinking beyond the pop envelope, long before he met Yoko Ono.

Although Lennon and Ono had met on several occasions, it had always been in public and never as a couple. Lennon had sponsored the *Yoko Plus Me* exhibition at the Lisson Gallery in September 1967, but as far as the media were concerned, he was still happily married to Cynthia. In truth, the marriage had been failing for some time. By the time Lennon returned from India in early 1968, it was all but over. Ono maintained contact with Lennon through a series of letters and notes that intrigued and infuriated him. He was smitten, and later, while Cynthia was on holiday in Italy, he invited Ono to his house for the evening. To break the ice, he suggested that they retire to his attic studio, where he could play her some of his experimental recordings. Ono was impressed and suggested that they make a recording together. Their collaboration was significant. Not only did it mark the beginning of a long and fruitful career together, it also marked the beginning of the end of The Beatles. For *Two Virgins* was a powerful statement that effectively distanced Lennon from his cute mop-top image.

As George Melly noted, The Beatles and their contemporaries turned "revolt into style". But by the mid 1960s there was too much style and not enough revolt. The Establishment quickly absorbed The Beatles by bestowing gifts of MBEs. The teenage consumer revolt, spearheaded by The Beatles, was turning sour and losing impetus. Consumerism was becoming a drag, and where it had once been fashionable to care passionately, by 1967 it was time to drop out and bite the hand that fed you. The teenage revolution that started with rock'n'roll in the 1950s had done little to change things. There may have been more freedoms, but there was also more oppression. The Cold War raged, as did the war in Vietnam, and by 1968, with riots spreading across America and Europe, the West was in turmoil.

A culture of dissent emerged, with its roots in the late 1950s and the establishment of CND and civil protest. One way of showing your displeasure with the status quo was through public demonstration, and the artistic community was quick to respond. In 1962, George Maciunas published a *Fluxus Policy Newsletter* in which he advocated civil disruption. For many artists within the group, Maciunas's suggestion went too far. For them, art should be less interventionist and more consciousness changing. By the mid 1960s, a growing number of artists were committed to this idea and, like them, Lennon and Ono wanted to expand artistic perimeters and pursue a socially-engaged public art. They believed that anything could be considered art, including avant-garde recordings, and that this art had the potential to change society for the better.

On Saturday August 24 1968 they appeared on the British television programme *Frost On Saturday* to explain their ideas. Speaking to the presenter, David Frost, Lennon and Ono suggested that anything that could be sensed could be considered art. They went on to point out that, as individuals, we are all works of art and that, when the body and mind come together to make something creative, it should be considered as art, in the same way as a critic might consider a painting or sculpture. Their argument was that the world is one vast gallery, one enormous art exhibition, that sends out vibrations which, they believed, could create positive changes. They attempted to explain to Frost what vibrations were and how they might work.

FROST: What do you mean by vibration?
ONO: Um, a message. Just smiling is a nicer message than, um, scorning or something ...
LENNON: A vibration is ... if somebody's happy, if we're sitting in your house or something, and we're feeling depressed, and somebody who doesn't feel depressed can come in and cheer us up, just by his vibration – or, his attitude ...
ONO: ... Presence!
LENNON: ... Whatever. His presence ...
ONO: ... Aura!
LENNON: ... If you say words, something happens, it just doesn't drop onto the floor or something, it's like radio waves, whatever I'm saying now goes on, ad infinitum, wherever it goes, because it's a wave form or a pattern, you know – it sets up a vibration. So everything you do or think, does this too!

If everyone was an artist, then anyone could add to Lennon and Ono's 'Unfinished Music'. If it was possible for an individual to transform a work of art in this way, it was possible for them to transform their life and those of others for the better. At least that was the thinking. The idea was to create a "revolution in the head" that would act as an engine for change.

Speaking in December 1968, Lennon responded to an article in *Black Dwarf* magazine that claimed he was as revolutionary as *Mrs. Dale's Diary*, a rather dull and predictable BBC radio soap opera. Speaking less than a week after the release of *Two Virgins*, Lennon explained how he thought the music he'd made with Ono could bring about positive change. "You can change people, you know, change their heads. A lot of people have changed my head, just with their records. I believe you can change, that's what Yoko and my singing is, to change it like that. All I'm saying is I think you should do it by changing people's heads, and they're saying, 'Well, we should smash the system.' Now the system-smashing scene has been going on forever, you know. The Irish did it, the Russians did it, and the French did it, and where's it got them? It's got them nowhere. That's the same old game."

For Lennon, *Two Virgins* spoke in bold terms of new beginnings. The album certainly loosened his bond with The Beatles and did much to debunk the myth of celebrity. A year earlier, he attempted to destroy his ego with LSD. Now, intent on reworking his public image, he released what many considered an unlistenable album with an unflattering naked image plastered over its front cover.

The photograph was taken at 34 Montagu Square in central London, in a flat that Lennon shared with Ono. Tony Bramwell, an Apple employee, set up the camera before leaving Lennon to take the photograph. "We were both a bit embarrassed when we peeled off for the picture, so I took it myself with a delayed action shutter," Lennon explained. "The picture was to prove that we are not a couple of demented freaks, that we are not deformed in any way, and that our minds are healthy. If we can make society accept these kind of things without offence, without sniggering, then we shall be achieving our purpose."

UNFINISHED MUSIC NO. 1: TWO VIRGINS
JOHN LENNON AND YOKO ONO
SIDE 1 'Two Virgins 1', 'Together' (De Silva, Brown, Henderson), 'Two Virgins 2', 'Two Virgins 3', 'Two Virgins 4', 'Two Virgins 5'.
SIDE 2 'Two Virgins 6', 'Hushabye, Hushabye', 'Two Virgins 7', 'Two Virgins 8', 'Two Virgins 9', 'Two Virgins 10'.
UK RELEASE November 29 1968; Apple APCOR 2 (mono), SAPCOR 2 (stereo); failed to chart.
US RELEASE January 6 1969; LP Apple T 5001 (stereo); 4-track cartridge (distributed by Tetragrammation) Apple TNX-45001 (white shell and slip cover) or (distributed by GRT) Apple 473 5001; 8-track cartridge Apple TNM-85001; 8-track cartridge Tetragrammation 873 5001; chart high No.124.

• **'Two Virgins'** (Lennon, Ono)
John Lennon (various instruments), Yoko Ono (voice). Recorded at Home Studio, Kenwood, Wood Lane, St George's Hill Estate, Weybridge, Surrey. Produced by John Lennon and Yoko Ono.

Lennon then asked another Apple employee Jeremy Banks (assistant to Derek Taylor) to get the film processed. Apple's Neil Aspinall took up the story: "John had just given Jeremy a roll of film and said, 'Get that developed please.' And when he got it back and saw the nude pictures he said, 'This is mind-blowing.' Everything was always 'mind-blowing' to Jeremy, but – just that one time – he was actually right. He couldn't believe it."

It wasn't as if male and female nudes hadn't been depicted before, but few, if any, had appeared on the cover of a long-playing record. Most nudes are perfect, idealised representations of the human form, not "two flabby bodies naked", which is how George Harrison described them. By 1968, a growing number of artists, including Yoko Ono, had taken to using their bodies to make art. Ono's *Cut Piece*, for example, involved members of the audience cutting off her clothes. She also made *Film No. 4 (Fluxfilm 16)*, consisting of naked bottoms, which the British Board of Film Censors banned by refusing to issue it with a certificate.

Ono considered the *Two Virgins* album cover as part of her artistic endeavours and an important statement. "From my point of view, I was in the artistic community, where a painter did a thing about rolling a naked woman with blue paint on her body on a canvas; nakedness was part of the event 'happening' kind of thing that was going on at the time. The only difference was that we were going to stand together, which I thought was very interesting, instead of always exploiting women's bodies. This was: we are together, man and woman. And also it wasn't a sexy scene; it was just standing straight. I liked that concept. And that's why I had this filmic idea about us standing naked and being filmed in a way that was part of nature or something like that. But John's idea about putting it on an album cover, wow! That was very good."

The unglamorous image was another way for Lennon to break the illusion of his celebrity. The Beatles were the epitome of glamour, the Four Kings of EMI, who mixed with the cream of London's swinging hipsters. By presenting himself in as unglamorous a manner as possible, he asked his audience to question the entire celebrity-making machine. "We felt like two virgins, because we were in love, just met, and we were trying to make something. And we thought to show everything. People are always looking at people like me, trying to see some secret. 'What do they do? Do they go to the bathroom? Do they eat?' So we just said, 'Here.' What we did purposely is not have a pretty photograph; not have it lighted so as we looked sexy or good. There were a couple of other takes from that session where we looked rather nice, hid the little bits that aren't that beautiful; we looked good. We used the straightest, most unflattering picture just to show that we were human."

Two Virgins data

Although Lennon owned a share in Apple Records, when it came to releasing *Two Virgins* he ran into problems. EMI had no problem manufacturing the record, but they would not distribute it. Lennon appealed to Sir Joseph Lockwood, chairman of EMI, but even though he was part of the company's greatest asset, EMI refused to distribute the album with the cover he wanted. Apple overcame the problem by employing some fans, known as "Apple scruffs", to put the records in the covers. Jack Oliver, an Apple employee, explained: "I had a bunch of Apple scruffs sleeve the record in the basement of the old Apple shop and then Track picked them up to distribute to the shops." While *Two Virgins* was due for release on November 29, the distribution problems may have caused this date to slip. Speaking to John Peel on BBC Radio 1 on December 11 1968, Lennon not only gave the LP's catalogue number, which he cited as SAPCOR 12093, but he also said that the LP had sold 700 copies on its first day of release, December 10.

In Britain, the LP was issued in mono and stereo. The mono edition (APCOR 2) has the title and composer credit in two lines above the spindle hole and the artist credit and publisher in three lines below the spindle hole. The stereo edition (SAPCOR 1) has the title above the spindle hole, and the track listing in four lines followed by publisher and artist credits below the spindle hole. The stereo edition also has Track Records' logo and catalogue number (603012) in the top right corner above the Apple catalogue number. Technik printed the cover, which differs from its American counterpart in that the quote from McCartney and the album title appear on the rear.

Tetragrammaton Records, a company co-owned by US entertainer Bill Cosby, handled distribution of the album in America. As in Britain, the release date was held up because of problems with the cover. The scheduled release date of November 11 slipped, and the album was not issued until January 6 1969. The LP was issued in stereo, with Apple labels with title and composer credits in two lines above the spindle hole and artist credit and publisher below.

Although Capitol had nothing to do with the album, it distributed promotional blank picture discs of *Two Virgins* in a moulded plastic cover to its employees at their annual sales meeting in June 1969. Because the album was deleted quickly, counterfeit copies of *Two Virgins* were manufactured in America. Original Tetragrammaton pressings were issued in a brown paper outer cover, sealed with a circular white sticker; counterfeits do not have the white paper seal. Original pressings have glossy Apple labels; counterfeits have matt Apple labels.

In America, *Two Virgins* was issued by Apple on 8-track cartridge. It was originally distributed by Tetragrammaton and later GRT (General Recording Tape) for Tetragrammaton. The cartridge itself was manufactured by Ampex, North American Leisure Corp, and GRT.

In 1991, Rock Classics issued *Two Virgins* on CD (SSI 9999). A semi-legal CD, it was obviously dubbed from a vinyl source. Rykodisc issued the CD (RCD 10411) on June 3 1997. Taken from the original master tapes, it removes the last 30 seconds from side two of the album. It does, however, have a bonus Yoko Ono track, 'Remember Love', originally the B-side of 'Give Peace A Chance'.

ASPEN FREE DISC

IF THE Lennons' first collaborative recording reached a relatively small audience, their second was heard by even fewer people. Issued as part of *Aspen Magazine* No.7, the recordings were made on a portable cassette recorder at Queen Charlotte's Maternity Hospital in London.

Aspen magazine was the brainchild of Phyllis Johnson, a former editor of *Women's Wear Daily* and *Advertising Age*. Johnson got the idea to publish a multimedia magazine while on holiday in Aspen, Colorado. Each issue would employ a different designer in order to capture a certain period, point of view, or person. Abandoning the traditional magazine format, which Johnson thought too restrictive, *Aspen* would consist of a variety of communication media, including print, film, and sound recordings.

The first two issues looked at the Aspen festival scene, but the magazine's scope was broadened with No.3, a Pop Art issue designed by Andy Warhol and David Dalton and devoted to New York's art and counterculture scenes. Issue 7, designed by John Kosh (who would also design The Beatles' *Get Back* book), explored new voices in British arts and culture. This issue arrived in a hinged box measuring 10 by 9½ by 1¼ inches, shipped flat, designed by Richard Smith. Besides contributions from the Lennons, the magazine featured offerings from several of Britain's leading artists, writers, and designers including Ossie Clark, Edward Lucie-Smith, J. G. Ballard, Eduardo Paolozzi, Peter Blake, and David Hockney.

Issued on an 8-inch square 33⅓ rpm 'flexi' record, the recordings were made under difficult circumstances. Ono was expecting their first child and had been admitted to Queen Charlotte's because her pregnancy was not going well. Only weeks earlier, on October 18 1968, Lennon's flat had been raided by the Scotland Yard Drug Squad. Headed by Detective-Sergeant Norman Pilcher, who had already busted several members of Britain's rock aristocracy, the 12-strong squad discovered a small quantity of cannabis resin and arrested Lennon and Ono, who were taken to Paddington Green police station. Charged with possession of cannabis and wilfully obstructing the police in the execution of their search warrant, the two were ordered to appear at Marylebone Magistrates Court the following day. Lennon took full responsibility, pleading guilty to save Ono from a criminal record – a decision he would live to regret. Released on bail, they had to battle through a 300-strong crowd and the waiting press.

Lennon subsequently claimed that the cannabis had been planted in his flat. Pilcher was seeking promotion by busting high-profile individuals and was not beyond planting evidence to ensure a conviction. However, Lennon's drug consumption was legendary, and had Pilcher bothered to search the flat he would surely have found what he was looking for without having to plant it. Years later, Pilcher was imprisoned for perjury and Lennon was forced to fight a long battle with the US authorities because of his criminal record.

This high-profile drugs bust did little to improve Ono's health. Several months' pregnant, she was admitted to hospital for observation. Lennon, of course, insisted on being by her side. To begin with, he slept in the bed next to hers, but when that bed was needed, he slept on the floor in a sleeping bag. A Conservative Member of Parliament thought Lennon's presence in the hospital ward an invasion of privacy and raised the matter in Parliament. Although it says more about prevailing attitudes to the presence of men during childbirth than it does about Lennon's desire to be with Ono, that his presence should be remarked upon in Parliament says much about the couple's media profile. Besides being recorded in a hospital room, these recordings are made all the more remarkable as an indication of the pair's unquenchable desire to document every moment of their life together.

Aspen songs

Ono began writing 'Song For John / Let's Go Flying' before she met her future husband. She was already looking for a record deal and recalled that 'Song For John' was originally destined for what would have been her debut album. "A record company had suggested I do an album of my sort of freak-type freestyle things,

ASPEN MAGAZINE NO. 7 THE BRITISH ISSUE
FREE DISC WITH *ASPEN* MAGAZINE
JOHN LENNON 'Radio Play'.
YOKO ONO 'Song for John / Let's Go On Flying', 'Snow Is Falling All The Time', 'Mum's Only Looking For Her Hand In The Snow'.
YOKO ONO & JOHN LENNON 'No Bed For Beatle John'.
US RELEASE magazine published spring/summer 1969 by Roaring Fork Press, New York City, with 8-inch square flexible plastic record, 33⅓ rpm, mono; edited by Mario Amaya; designed by John Kosh.

• **'Song For John / Let's Go On Flying', 'Snow Is Falling All The Time'** (Ono)
Yoko Ono (voice).
• **'Mum's Only Looking For Her Hand In The Snow'** (Lennon, Ono)
Yoko Ono (voice), John Lennon (guitar).
• **'No Bed For Beatle'** (Lennon, Ono)
Yoko Ono (voice), John Lennon (voice).
• **'Radio Play'** (Lennon, Ono)
Yoko Ono (voice), John Lennon (voice, radio).
All recorded at Queen Charlotte Hospital, Second West Ward, Room 1, London. All produced by John Lennon and Yoko Ono.

one of which was 'Song For John'. When I was writing it, I was thinking about wanting to meet somebody who could fly with me. Then suddenly, [Lennon] came into the picture and was the first person who listened to the demo – so I felt a sentimental reason for the name to be John."

Several of Ono's early works employ the sky as a metaphor for intellect and transcendence. Besides writing scores and songs that referred to the sky, she made several 'paintings', intended as conceptual pieces, to act as conduits for transcendence.

'Song For John' was later reworked and re-recorded for her album *Approximately Infinite Universe*.

'Snow Is Falling All The Time' is reminiscent of a nursery rhyme and, if anything, is even more fragile than the first two parts of this recording. It was later reworked into 'Listen, The Snow Is Falling', issued as the B-side of 'Happy Christmas (War Is Over)'.

For 'Mum's Only Looking For Her Hand In The Snow', Lennon improvises some bluesy riffs on a nylon-string acoustic guitar to back Ono on an early version of 'Don't Worry Kyoko (Mummy's Only Looking For Her Hand In The Snow)'.

'No Bed For Beatle' finds Ono singing in the style of Gregorian chant, with Lennon in the background, intoning lines from newspaper articles about their stay in hospital and the impending release of the *Two Virgins* album. It's another example of their desire to document almost everything they did and said, and would not be the last.

'Radio Play' is an attempt at John Cage-like avant-garde composition, using nothing other than a radio. It sounds like the kind of early electronic music produced by the BBC's Radiophonic Workshop – without the tunes. A series of truncated blips eventually become recognisable as spoken and sung word fragments, which nevertheless remain the briefest of segments and unrecognisable. Meanwhile, in the background, Lennon and Ono have a conversation and Lennon makes a telephone call. As with several of Ono's pieces, it evokes a sense of absence, balance, and unity. Absence – the missing fragments of speech – are balanced by their conversation, and combined they create a whole. Ironically, this is an edited version of the complete recording, a longer version of which would be made available on the album *Life With The Lions*.

LIFE WITH THE LIONS

LENNON and Ono's second album of avant-garde music appeared in early 1969 on Apple's new and shortlived imprint Zapple. The original intention was for Zapple to issue budget-price spoken word and avant-garde albums by the likes of Lenny Bruce, Richard Brautigan, Allen Ginsberg, and Charles Bukowski. The label was intended to respond quickly to cultural changes; the records would only be listened to once or twice and then disposed. Barry Miles, owner of the Indica gallery and bookshop, was made label manager and told to compile a list of releases. Besides approaching literary figures, Miles also intended to record world leaders such as Mao Tse Tung and Fidel Castro for the label. Although several writers including poet Charles Olon, Fugs drummer Ken Weaver, and author Lawrence Ferlinghetti were recorded for Zapple, only albums by Lennon and Geroge Harrison were issued.

Zapple was launched on February 3 1969, with a press release explaining what it intended to issue and that some of its albums would sell at budget prices – UK LPs were intended to retail for 15/-, 21/- and 30/6 (75p, £1.05, £1.52) and US albums would sell for $1.98 and $4.98. However, by the time Zapple was up and running, Beatle manager Allen Klein had slashed funding, and what would have been a memorable series of recordings was shelved. When Zapple did issue records, they were little more than self-indulgent solo projects by George Harrison and John and Yoko, and sold at full price.

Life With The Lions documents two significant events in the life of Lennon and Ono. Side 1 was recorded at the couple's first concert performance together; side 2 features recordings made at Queen Charlotte's Hospital, London, some of which had already been issued by *Aspen* magazine (see previous entry). The album's title was a reference to a BBC radio programme, *Life With The Lyons*, that ran from 1951 to 1960. It was unique in that it featured a real family and real events, albeit exaggerated for comic effect. It isn't clear whether Lennon chose to name this album after the programme because of its documentary quality or simply because he remembered it from his childhood. What is clear is that the records and films he and Ono made were a very public diary. "I'm trying to get over as quickly as I can what exactly is happening to me at this given time, and so we collect photos, tape it, or make films of what's happening," he explained.

Some people were open to what the pair were attempting to do with their music; others were less receptive to their ideas. Writing for *Rolling Stone* magazine, Edmund Ward had nothing but contempt for the album. "*Life With The Lions* is utter bullshit, and perhaps a bit in poor taste. There is absolutely nothing on it to justify the expenditure of four bucks. Oh, wait – there is, too. One of the cuts on side 2 is called 'Two Minutes Silence,' and it is just that. Not only is it a much needed respite from the rest of the record, but it is also useful for checking the amount of rumble caused by your turntable's motor. See any hi-fi manual for instructions." The album was never going to sell to a mainstream audience, and Ward should have taken that into consideration. Although his criticism is a little harsh, it's true that *Life With The Lions* is hard-going. It's unlikely that it was, or will ever be, a turntable favourite, but it is, nevertheless, an important historical document.

Life With The Lions songs

Only weeks after recording what would become *Let It Be*, Lennon made his first solo live appearance in support of Yoko Ono. The event was a free jazz concert at Cambridge University's 500-seat Lady Mitchell Hall. Ono was no stranger to events such as these, having performed a similar concert at the Albert Hall on February 29 1968 with jazzman Ornette Coleman. Although Lady Mitchell Hall was somewhat smaller than the Albert Hall, this time Ono was second on the bill to jazz pianist Chris McGregor. The concert had been booked long before Ono teamed up with Lennon, and she had intended to cancel, but Lennon insisted that she should go ahead with the concert.

Ono explained: "Cambridge asked me to come and do it before they knew about John and me. When we got together, there's a few appointments I missed because we were so involved with each other. But John was saying, 'Call them back, call them back,' so I said, 'OK, I'll call back,' and I said, 'Yes, I will come.' And then John was saying, 'Say that you'll bring your own band.' OK. 'I'm bringing my own band.'"

Tickets for the concert were priced at a reasonable 16/- (80p, about $2 then), and the audience were urged to bring their own "voice, flute or little shaker". The first act took to the stage at approximately three o'clock in the afternoon and immediately set the tone for what was to follow. Maggie Nichols, backed by two pianos, two basses, a trumpet, three woodwind instruments, and two drum kits, performed an ambitious free-form improvisation.

Nichols' vocalisations echoed those of Ono's and were described by Douglas Oliver of *The Cambridge Evening News* as "epic wailing, weird pulses of sound, or cries – almost – of help".

After a short break, Yoko Ono strolled on stage followed by her accompanist, John Lennon. Positioning himself in front of a large Fender amplifier, he sat with his back to the audience throughout the entire performance. Dressed in black and standing behind two microphones – one for the PA, the other for recording – Ono announced timidly: "This is a piece called 'Cambridge 1969'." Then, without any further word of warning, she let out a long, sustained note, joined a few seconds later by ear-splitting guitar feedback. This atonal aural assault, formless and without melody or rhythm, continued for 26 minutes. Towards the end of the piece, saxophonist John Tchicai and percussionist John Stevens joined them on stage. After a few minutes of squawking saxophone and thumping percussion, Lennon and Ono left the stage and, one suspects, a traumatised audience behind them.

Whatever the audience thought of the performance, Lennon certainly found the experience liberating. "I just turned my guitar on and blew my mind out. She blew hers out, and you either get it or you don't. Just pure feedback and whatever is on that track," said Lennon. "If you hear it, it's just pure sound, because what else can you do when a woman's howling, you know, you just go along with it, right? ... Yoko and I went to Cambridge, did the show and I discovered more about the guitar than I did for all these years. I enjoyed it!"

Just as the cover of *Two Virgins* had freed Lennon from the restrictions of being a Beatle, so performing with Ono freed him creatively. Here he was, one half of the world's greatest songwriting team, abandoning all the musical rules and concepts that had placed him at the top of his profession. He walked away from the concert a changed man. Ono's total abandonment of her classical training gave him the confidence to experiment. "What she did for guitar playing was to free it, the way she'd freed her voice from all the restrictions," Lennon explained.

Clearly, he was intent on destroying barriers, and performing with Ono was one way of doing so. Interviewed by B.P. Fallon for the *NME* around April 1969, he said: "All the musicians talk about no barriers between music and poetry. Yet most of them show it. We're doing it. Yoko will make pop records with me to show 'em."

Their quest for artistic freedom would not be an easy one. The music they produced was often unsettling, for not only did it mirror their own feelings of pain and frustration but also the troubled atmosphere of the period. The *Cambridge Evening News* reviewer recognised the nexus that their music established between art and life. "The concert was strange and chilling. Not in a bad sense, but because there was so much unusual texture. At no time did the music become comforting. It was an extraordinary experience."

While at Queen Charlotte's with Ono, Lennon recorded the sound of their unborn baby's heartbeat. Sadly, the baby, named John Ono Lennon II, was stillborn. Lennon took the recording he'd made, looped it, and produced this recording. In light of Ono's miscarriage, issuing 'Baby's Heartbeat' was a very public reminder of their loss and a brave statement. It was not the first time Ono had alluded to child mortality in her work. The subject first appeared in a work from 1960, *A Grapefruit In The World Of Park*, and would reappear in later work such as 'Greenfield Morning I Pushed An Empty Baby Carriage All Over The City' from *Yoko Ono/Plastic Ono Band*.

'Baby's Heartbeat' is followed by 'Two Minutes Silence'. Whether they intended it as a memorial for their lost baby is not clear. Programming it to follow the recording of their lost child certainly strengthens the sense of loss and makes the baby's heartbeat seem all the more fragile.

It was also a sly reference to John Cage, but with one significant difference. As Ono explained, the piece was conceived as a tribute to the avant-garde composer. "In 'Two Minutes Silence', we sent a tribute to John Cage in a way. Cage did '4' 33"', and the title was the timing, the time. And he was saying the music is the sound that comes in, the sounds that come in during the silence, like environmental sounds, that was the music. So we were going to make a piece called 'Two Minutes Silence', and we were giggling, because we did the opposite, which was we made it

UNFINISHED MUSIC NO. 2: LIFE WITH THE LIONS
JOHN LENNON AND YOKO ONO
SIDE 1 'Cambridge 1969'.
SIDE 2 'No Bed For Beatle John', 'Baby's Heartbeat', 'Two Minutes Silence', 'Radio Play'.
UK RELEASE May 2 1969; Zapple ZAPPLE 01; failed to chart.
US RELEASE May 26 1969; LP Zapple ST 3357; 8-track cartridge Zapple 8XT-3357; chart high No.179.

• **'Cambridge 1969'** (Lennon, Ono)
John Lennon (guitar), Yoko Ono (voice), John Tchicai (saxophone), John Stevens (percussion).
Live recording at Lady Mitchell Hall, Cambridge University, Cambridge, England. Produced by John Lennon and Yoko Ono.
• **'Baby's Heartbeat'** (Lennon, Ono)
Yoko Ono and John Lennon.
Recorded at Queen Charlotte Hospital, Second West Ward, Room 1, London, England. Produced by John Lennon and Yoko Ono.
• **'Two Minutes Silence'** (Lennon, Ono)
No personnel.
Recording location unknown but probably Abbey Road Studios, London, England. Produced by John Lennon and Yoko Ono.
OTHER TRACKS see *Aspen* flexi, previous entry.

totally dead silence! Like, this is the real silence, baby! So we were just being rebellious."

Unfortunately, the joke falls a bit flat: like Cage's piece, 'Two Minutes Silence' does consist of extraneous sounds. Pressed on vinyl, there were inevitably static pops and clicks to interrupt the silence and, of course, the same external environmental sounds that Cage's '4' 33"' had set out to incorporate. Not content with borrowing Cage's idea wholesale, the pair even had the gall to copyright the silence and claim it as their own (and John would later do the same with his 'Nutopian International Anthem'). But when composer Mike Batt tried the same thing in July 2002, Cage's publishers sued for infringement of copyright. Batt had placed one minute's silence on his CD *Classical Graffiti* and credited it as a Batt/Cage composition. Because Batt jokingly claimed to have written the piece in collaboration with Cage, he was forced to pay the American composer's publishers a six-figure sum. In claiming it for their own, the Lennons got away with it.

Life With The Lions data

This time, EMI and Capitol manufactured and distributed the album – not that it made much difference to a poor sales performance. Original pressings came with a white paper inner sleeve printed with song titles and details of who played on which track. Zapple also issued the album in Japan (AP-8782), where it appeared with and without the Zapple logo printed on the label. Promotional copies of the LP issued in Japan were pressed on low-noise red vinyl. The Japanese reissue (EAS-80701) came with a four-page lyric sheet rather than a printed inner sleeve. Rykodisc issued the album on CD (RCD10412) on June 3 1997 with enhanced packaging and two bonus tracks, 'Song For John' and 'Mulberry'.

'GIVE PEACE A CHANCE'

LENNON and Ono arrived in Toronto, Canada on May 25 1969 to begin their second bed-in for peace. The following day, the couple and their entourage moved into room 1742 of La Hotel Reine Elizabeth in Montreal. Inviting the world's media into their suite, the pair spent the week discussing peace.

Their original plan had been to stage the bed-in in America, but Lennon's conviction for possession of cannabis was already causing problems and he was denied a visa. With no direct access to American media networks, Lennon tried The Bahamas. But this location proved to be unsuitable. The next logical location was Canada, as it shared a border with the USA.

The Lennons had staged their first bed-in in Suite 902 at the Amsterdam Hilton from March 25 to 29. Besides publicly celebrating their honeymoon – they were married on Gibraltar on March 20 – Lennon and Ono designed the 'event' as part of a growing peace campaign that would occupy them for the best part of ten months. The world's media were invited and were again baffled by the couple's antics. How could staying in bed for a week contribute to world peace? As usual they missed the point.

The bed-ins were part of a massive multimedia advertising campaign that was intended to get people, including world leaders, talking about peace rather than war. Speaking to David Frost, Lennon explained: "We're trying to sell peace, like a product, you know, and sell it like people sell soap or soft drinks, [because it's] the only way to get people aware that peace is possible and it isn't just inevitable to have violence; not just war – all forms of violence. People just accept it and think, 'Oh they did it,' or, 'Harold Wilson did it,' or, 'Nixon did it,' they're always scapegoating people. And it isn't Nixon's fault: we're all responsible for everything that goes on, you know, we're all responsible for Biafra and Hitler and everything. So we're just saying 'sell peace,' anybody interested in peace just stick it in the window, it's simple but it lets somebody else know that you want peace too. Because you feel alone if you're the only one thinking, 'Wouldn't it be nice if there was peace and nobody was getting killed.' So advertise yourself that you're for peace if you believe in it."

Bed-ins were only part of the marketing strategy. Poster campaigns, films, radio, television, and of course records all played their part in getting the message across. Lennon's first solo single was intended as part of the campaign and became the most successful element in his multimedia armoury.

Although this was his first solo single, it was not issued under John Lennon's name. The release of 'Give Peace A Chance' established another Fluxus-inspired concept, Plastic Ono Band. The band would have an ever changing line-up, echoing the Fluxus ideas of conceptualisation and fluidity: advertisements for the band's first single stated: "You Are The Plastic Ono Band."

The group was launched with a press reception at Chelsea Town Hall on July 3. Lennon and Ono should have attended the event, but they had been injured in a car accident and were hospitalised. Ringo and Maureen Starr took their place and Perspex boxes containing recording equipment represented the band.

The Beatles' press officer, Derek Taylor, told *Disc*: "The band was made in Perspex in Hoylake, in Cheshire (where Selwyn Lloyd and I were brought up separately) by an inventor I know called Charles Melling. It was Yoko's idea, with John, made to her specifications; four pieces – like John, Paul, George, and Ringo, three taller and one shorter. Two rectangular, one cylindrical, and a cube. One column holds a tape recorder and amplifier, another a closed-circuit TV set with live camera, a third a record player with amplifier, and the fourth has a miniature lightshow and a loudspeaker. But they could hold anything; they are as adaptable as The Beatles. The Perspex columns were fitted with their equipment by Apple electronics under the direction of [Magic] Alexis Mardas, and here ends the first and last technological press release you will have from me."

Taylor also remarked upon the group's Fluxus credentials and their fluid nature. "The band may be the property of Apple, but it also belongs to everyone because what it represents is freedom, freedom for performers to be themselves, taking no heed of who they are or what they look like or where they have been or what their music is supposed to be. It could be children in a playground screaming their release from the bondage of the classroom or it could be John and Yoko screaming their love for one another. It could be anything. The band will tour – the British band will tour here, and in the US another band is to be built, built to withstand the long hauls across that amazing continent and maybe beyond, maybe far beyond one day. Who knows, any more?" Taylor's predictions were spot on: the band went through many changes on both sides of the Atlantic. The only thing he didn't get right was Lennon's commitment to touring. The Plastic Ono Band never did tour America and their live performances were few and sporadic.

'Give Peace A Chance' was recorded in room 1742 at La Hotel Reine Elizabeth, Montreal, on the night of May 31 and was completed in the early hours of June 1 1969. The Lennons had spent all week speaking with the media about peace and their message was simple: "All we are saying is give peace a chance," a phrase Lennon used during an interview he gave on arrival in Toronto on May 25. In the days that followed, he fleshed out his chorus with a simple verse, and on the final day of the Montreal bed-in he decided to record it.

While the song was credited to Lennon–McCartney, Paul McCartney played no part in its composition. Although Lennon was growing apart from The Beatles, he still felt obliged to stand by his original agreement with McCartney and split songwriting credits with him.

Taylor was asked to arrange for some recording equipment to be set up in the hotel room and contacted a local studio proprietor to provide it. André Perry got a call from Capitol asking him to provide 4-track recording gear, which he hired from RCA Victor because his own equipment was already in use, and deliver it to the hotel. As soon as everyone had been assembled, there was time for a quick rehearsal and soundcheck before the recording proper.

Perry, who engineered the session, recalls that the song was captured in one take. Although Lennon was happy with the take, Perry was not so sure, as conditions in the room were far from ideal. Perry noted that the recording was suffering from distortion, so the following day he overdubbed additional vocals to mask these defects. Back in his studio, Perry transferred the 4-track tape to 8-track and invited some friends and singers to contribute to the recording. Lennon approved of Perry's work and the tape was sent back to the UK for mastering, and it was issued as Lennon's debut

'GIVE PEACE A CHANCE' / 'REMEMBER LOVE'
PLASTIC ONO BAND
UK RELEASE July 4 1969; Apple APPLE 13; chart high No.2 (re-enters January 24 1981, chart high No.33).
US RELEASE July 21 1969; Apple APPLE 1809; chart high No.14.

- **'Give Peace A Chance'** (Lennon, McCartney)
John Lennon (vocals and guitar), Yoko Ono (vocals), Tommy Smothers (guitar), Allen Ginsberg, Dr Timothy Leary, Petula Clark, Rosemary Woodruff, Derek Taylor, Murray The K, Dick Gregory, Abraham Feinberg, the Canadian chapter of the Radha Krishna Temple (hand drums, finger cymbals), unknown others (backing vocals).
- **'Remember Love'** (Ono)
John Lennon (guitar), Yoko Ono (vocals).
Both recorded at Room 1742, La Hotel Reine Elizabeth, Montreal, Canada. Both produced by John Lennon and Yoko Ono.

solo single a few weeks later.

'Give Peace A Chance', with just two chords, the stream-of-consciousness verses, and a simple repeated chorus, was deliberately simple. A mantra for peace, it was undeniably catchy and gave the peace movement something to sing besides 'We Shall Overcome'. While it's not considered one of his finest compositions, it is one of Lennon's best-known songs and has become a present-day folk song.

Although it was rumoured that Ringo Starr added percussion to the track, Perry insists that no further overdubs were added to the tape other than those he applied in Montreal. The later release of an excerpt from a rehearsal of 'Give Peace A Chance', on *John Lennon Anthology*, features the unnamed percussionist, proving that Starr did not overdub percussion at a later date. What the rehearsal take highlights is Ono's off-key singing, which was placed well down in the final mix.

Having completed 'Give Peace A Chance', Lennon and Ono turned to recording what would be the record's B-side. Written by Ono, 'Remember Love' took about four hours to make. Recording started at about one o'clock in the morning of June 1 and finished around five. Unlike her earlier avant-garde recordings, 'Remember Love' is a gentle ballad that borrowed from another recent Lennon composition, 'Sun King'.

'Give Peace A Chance' data

Apple issued 'Give Peace A Chance' in Britain with generic Apple labels and a picture sleeve. Three label variations were produced. The first has a dark green Apple label, is without 'Sold in U.K. subject to resale price conditions, see price lists', has 'Mfd. in U.K.' and song publishers 'Northern Songs NCB', and has a Parlophone catalogue number, R 5795, printed below the Apple catalogue number.

The second has a dark green Apple label, with 'Sold in U.K. subject to resale price conditions, see price lists', 'Mfd. in U.K.', and song publishers 'Northern Songs.' The third has a light green Apple label without 'Sold in U.K. subject to resale price conditions, see price lists' but with 'Mfd. in U.K.' and song publishers 'Northern Songs'.

In America, Apple also issued the single with generic Apple labels and a picture sleeve. The American single lacks the introductory count-in, which appears on the British version. An alternative colour picture sleeve, with different machines in the Perspex tubes, was created for the American market. Although proofs were printed, the alternative design was never produced commercially. The image was, however, used to advertise the band's *Live Peace In Toronto* album.

American pressings were produced with two label variations. The first has a dark green Apple label with song title at nine o'clock, with composer credits and 'STEREO' below. Catalogue number and artist credit appear at three o'clock. This variant has thin text. The second has a dark green Apple label with song title at ten o'clock and composer credits below. 'STEREO' is at two o'clock and catalogue number at three o'clock, with artist credit centre bottom. This version has bold text.

'Give Peace A Chance' was produced as a 4-inch flexi-disc Pocket Disc by Americom. This company began working with Capitol in late 1968 and produced three Beatles singles in the new format. The discs were intended as an affordable alternative to the more expensive 7-inch single and originally aimed at the very young, although later research showed that they were being bought by people who rarely purchased pop records. The flexi-discs were printed with silver text and a line drawing of Apple A- and B-side labels. The Pocket Disc single was issued with two catalogue numbers, one assigned by Capitol, 1809P (the 'P' standing for Pocket Disc), the other M-435A, which was the Americom catalogue number. The discs were not issued in picture sleeves but in blue or red generic card sleeves.

Capitol's Special Markets Division produced gold-plated copies of 'Give Peace A Chance' in 1994 with purple Capitol labels (S7-17783). About 100 copies escaped the plating and found their way into the collectors' market.

'Give Peace A Chance' was issued as a 12-inch single (1C052-90372YZ) in Germany in 1981 with a picture sleeve based on an illustration from the *Shaved Fish* album cover. In Britain, EMI reissued 'Give Peace A Chance' (G 45 2) on March 12 1984 coupled with a new B-side, 'Cold Turkey', and a picture sleeve.

'THE KYA 1969 PEACE TALK'
FEATURING JOHN LENNON OF THE BEATLES WITH KYA'S TOM CAMPBELL AND BILL HOLLEY
US RELEASE 1969; KYA Records 1259; failed to chart.

KYA 1969 PEACE TALK

THE LENNONS' second bed-in was intended to reach an American audience. However, John was unable to enter the country so they went to Canada; he spent hours on the telephone speaking to American radio stations from Montreal. His interview with KYA in San Francisco was issued as a 7-inch single.

Interviewed by Tom Campbell and Bill Holley, Lennon sounded lively and engaging. Although he was primarily promoting peace, he was happy to answer questions on everything from the bed-in to The Beatles' latest single.

'COLD TURKEY'

JOHN Lennon had to have a drug of one kind or another. He admitted as much. "I've always needed a drug to survive. The others, too, but I always had more, more pills, more of everything, because I'm more crazy probably." By 1969, his drug of choice was heroin. It was a drug that he and Ono used to alleviate their pain. Although he appeared to have everything, Lennon suffered a lot in the late 1960s.

The root of his problem was the reaction of others to the woman he loved. Above all else, Lennon wanted his friends to accept Ono as he did. But The Beatles and their circle were a tight unit. They didn't accept outsiders and never approved of Ono, whose presence they barely tolerated. Worse still, the media openly criticised Lennon for his relationship with her. At the time, women, particularly those married to rock stars, were meant to be glamorous and subservient. Ono was neither of these. Furthermore, she was an Oriental, a weird Japanese artist who made films of people's bottoms.

Naturally, Lennon felt troubled by the private and public reaction to his relationship with Ono. His troubles were compounded by a high-profile drugs bust, a conviction for possession of cannabis, Ono's miscarriage and the loss of their child, a divorce from his wife of six years, a growing discontent with The Beatles, a worsening relationship with McCartney, and vicious press coverage that labelled him and Ono as freaks. All this consolidated Lennon and Ono's misery. Outcasts, their only escape was through drugs. Speaking about his drug problem, Lennon said: "It just was not too much fun. I never injected it or anything. We sniffed a little when we were in real pain. ... And we get into so much pain that we have to do something about it. And that's what happened to us. We took H because of what The Beatles and others were doing to us."

It has been suggested that Ono dabbled with heroin while Lennon was in India and that Lennon had been a user before meeting Ono. But it doesn't matter who took heroin first – what mattered was the grip it had on the couple. The most commonly consumed drugs in the 1960s were amphetamines, cannabis, and LSD. Heroin was new and dangerous. At first, Lennon was attracted to the drug's reputation as an artistic indulgence, but he quickly grew horrified at how difficult it was to kick it. Determined to rid himself of the monkey on his back, so he could father a child with Ono, Lennon decided on total abstinence. Rehab clinics were almost unheard of and hospitalisation would have attracted more adverse publicity, so Lennon had no other choice than to go cold turkey. Withdrawing from heroin is a little like having a bad bout of flu. Symptoms begin six to eight hours after the last dose and peak between 48 and 72 hours later. The symptoms include chills, goose bumps (hence the name), stomach cramps, and vomiting, and usually subdue after seven days.

Lennon had written songs about drugs before 'Cold Turkey'. Even some of his songs that had absolutely nothing to do with drugs were assumed to allude to them. He wasn't the first to write about his drug experiences and he wouldn't be the last, but he was perhaps the most honest. 'Cold Turkey' was another reading from Lennon's personal diary that he was determined to make public. Documenting his withdrawal from heroin, the song's bleak warning was a disturbing wake-up call to those naive about the danger of hard drugs.

The song was demoed in the summer of 1969. Lennon backed himself on acoustic guitar, which he then double-tracked. To this he added an acoustic lead guitar and a second vocal (and the result was issued later on *John Lennon Acoustic*). The tape was then spooled back to the start for Ono to add her contribution. Although it was only intended as a demo recording, the acoustic setting failed to complement Lennon's startling lyric. The song failed to convince when it was performed at the Toronto Rock & Roll Revival festival on September 13 1969 (see the *Live Peace In Toronto* album featured later in this chapter). Still in embryonic state, it sounded no more shocking than any of the old rockers that Lennon performed that night.

Before its Toronto debut, Lennon offered 'Cold Turkey' to The Beatles, suggesting that they issue it as their next single. The offer was made prior to his performance in Toronto, as it was during that trip that he decided to leave the group. With The Beatles having turned it down, Lennon recorded it with Plastic Ono Band. As Clapton and Voormann knew the song from the Toronto show, they were asked to play on the studio recording. And although he had decided to quit The Beatles, Lennon invited Ringo Starr to play drums.

Convening at Abbey Road Studios on the evening of September 25, this line-up recorded 26 takes before calling it quits. Lennon was obviously unhappy with the results because the group were recalled to remake the song at Trident Studios on the 28th. Things went better this time, and the tape was mixed the following evening at Abbey Road. On October 5 more overdubs were added at Abbey Road and the final mix completed.

'COLD TURKEY' / 'DON'T WORRY KYOKO (MUMMY'S ONLY LOOKING FOR A HAND IN THE SNOW)'
PLASTIC ONO BAND
UK RELEASE October 24 1969; Apple APPLES 1001; chart high No.14.
US RELEASE October 20 1969; Apple APPLE 1813; chart high No.30.

- **'Cold Turkey'** (Lennon)
John Lennon (vocals, guitar), Eric Clapton (guitar), Klaus Voormann (bass), Ringo Starr (drums).
Recorded at Abbey Road Studios and Trident Studios, London, England. Produced by John and Yoko (BAG).
- **'Don't Worry Kyoko (Mummy's Only Looking For A Hand In The Snow)'** (Ono)
Yoko Ono (vocals), John Lennon (guitar), Eric Clapton (guitar), Klaus Voormann (bass), Ringo Starr (drums).
Recorded at Studio A, Lansdowne Studios, Lansdowne Road, London, England. Produced by John and Yoko (BAG).

The finished product is a raw, stark confessional, almost as harrowing to listen to as the experience of going cold turkey. Voormann's bass pounds like blood pulsing in the ear, while Clapton's guitar howls like a banshee, or a junkie suffering the pain of withdrawal. It's little wonder that several radio stations banned the record. It would have frightened the living daylights out of most listeners.

On November 26, Lennon returned his MBE in protest against Britain's involvement in Nigeria, its support of America's war in Vietnam – and because 'Cold Turkey' was slipping down the charts. Legitimate protest that it was, Lennon's humorous reference to his latest single's decline was controversial. It was, of course, all part of a carefully planned publicity stunt to benefit the Lennons' peace campaign. It also gave Lennon the opportunity to distance himself from the Establishment and stake a claim as counterculture politico, a persona he would embrace wholly in the early 1970s.

Recorded by the same line-up that played on the A-side, Ono's 'Don't Worry Kyoko (Mummy's Only Looking For A Hand In The Snow)' had appeared in embryonic form on the *Aspen* magazine flexi-disc. The song would also appear on her double album, *Fly*, issued as a companion to Lennon's *Imagine*.

'Cold Turkey' data

Apple issued 'Cold Turkey' in Britain in a picture sleeve and generic Apple labels with "PLAY LOUD" printed in large bold type in the centre of both the A- and B-side labels.

American pressings were issued with two label variants. The first has a dark green Apple label and thin text, the song title at ten o'clock with the composer credits below, and "STEREO" at eight o'clock. "PLAY" appears at twelve o'clock and "LOUD" at six o'clock. The artist's name appears centre bottom. The second type has a light green Apple label with bold text, song title at ten o'clock, and artist's name at eight o'clock. "STEREO" appears at two o'clock, with the catalogue number and producer credits on the right-hand side of the label.

THE WEDDING ALBUM

LENNON and Ono's third album of avant-garde recordings was a celebration of their honeymoon and, by implication, their art. Side two of the record was a montage of recordings made during the Lennons' first bed-in in Amsterdam. Knowing that the media would report their honeymoon whether they wanted the publicity or not, Lennon and Ono decided to use the occasion to promote world peace. Turning their honeymoon into a Fluxus based 'event', they blurred the boundary between art and life. Speaking at the time, Lennon said: "Our life is our art. That's what the bed-ins were. When we got married, we knew our honeymoon was going to be public, anyway, so we decided to use it to make a statement."

The Lennons' honeymoon was the perfect Fluxus event. It transgressed the boundaries of art and life; it confounded the media and the public alike; and as a mass media event it was available to all for the price of a newspaper. For those who wanted a more substantial and lasting reminder of the event, the couple issued a lavishly packaged album.

They entered Abbey Road Studio Two on Tuesday April 22 1969 to record a new avant-garde composition they named after themselves, 'John And Yoko'. The piece consisted of their heartbeats, over which they called each other's names. The recording was influenced by Ono, who had previously used bodily sounds for her avant-garde compositions. For one of her early pieces she attached microphones to people so that when they moved the amplified sounds were transformed into a bizarre form of music. John Cage, who had a strong influence on Ono, argued that all sound could be considered as music, but she was one of the first composers to use bodily noises and sounds that exist outside our normal range of hearing as a medium for generating music.

Although the Lennons had previously issued the sound of their unborn child's heartbeat, this was the first time they had recorded the sound of their own bodies to create music. Writing in *Melody Maker*, Richard Williams acknowledged the musical nature of the piece. He contended that "the rhythm of the heartbeats, constantly colliding and separating, resembles (albeit accidentally) the playing of African drummers, and in the middle, when the voices quieten, the metabolic sound surges through with considerable strength".

As simple as it is, this avant-garde piece had as many nuances as music made with conventional instruments. It was a challenging piece of experimentation, but Ono's use of unconventional sounds expressed universal emotions. The heart traditionally symbolises love; the sound of two heartbeats coming together created an equally powerful metaphor. If the sound of their unborn baby's heartbeat could represent loss, then the sound of their own heartbeats could stand as a metaphor for the intimacy of their relationship.

The session began at 11:00pm and continued until 4:30 the following morning. Five days later, on Sunday April 27, the pair returned to Abbey Road and remade the track. This time, recording and mixing was completed between 3:00 and 8:00pm. The piece was completed on May 1, when Lennon combined elements from both recordings. Three attempts were made to create the finished stereo mix, which he took away with him at the end of the session.

'Amsterdam' is a collage of songs, soundbites, and interviews recorded during their Amsterdam bed-in. Although the title suggests a specific location, parts of the recording were probably made in London after the event, as the bed-in is often discussed in the past tense. The musical content is similar to that found on the *Aspen* flexi-disc, although this time the mood was more up-beat.

THE WEDDING ALBUM
JOHN LENNON AND YOKO ONO
SIDE 1 'John And Yoko'.
SIDE 2 'Amsterdam'.
UK RELEASE November 14 1969; Apple SAPCOR 11; failed to chart.
US RELEASE October 20 1969; LP Apple SMAX 3360; 8-track cartridge Apple 8AX-3360; chart high No.178.

• **'John And Yoko'** **(Lennon, Ono)**
John Lennon (vocals, heartbeat), Yoko Ono (vocals, heartbeat).
Recorded at Abbey Road Studios, London, England.
• **'Amsterdam'** **(Lennon, Ono)**
John Lennon (vocals, guitar), Yoko Ono (vocals).
Recorded at Room 902, The Hilton Hotel, Amsterdam, Netherlands.
Both produced by John Lennon.

The Wedding Album data

Apple issued *The Wedding Album* as a boxed set that included a booklet of press cuttings, a poster of drawings by Lennon and Ono, a large poster of black-and-white photographs taken on their wedding day, a postcard, a strip of passport photographs, a photograph of a slice of wedding cake, a plastic bag (not included in the Japanese reissue), and a copy of their marriage certificate. Because the packaging was so extravagant, the album was issued a good six months after the event it was intended to celebrate.

Richard Williams's review of the album for *Melody Maker* earned him a place in rock history. He was sent two one-sided test pressings of the LP, each including a blank side on the reverse containing nothing but an engineer's test signal. Assuming that the album was a double, and the 'tones' a couple more of Lennon and Ono's minimalist pieces, Williams reviewed the blank sides. He suggested that "constant listening reveals a curious point: the pitch of the tones alters frequency, but only by microtones or, at most, a semitone. This oscillation produces an almost subliminal, uneven 'beat' which maintains interest. On a more basic level, you could have a ball by improvising your very own raga, plainsong, or even Gaelic mouth music against the drone." Lennon loved the review and sent Williams a personal thank-you.

Rykodisc issued a CD (RCD10413) on June 3 1997 with three bonus Yoko Ono tracks, 'Who Has Seen the Wind?' (originally the B-side of 'Instant Karma!'), 'Listen, The Snow Is Falling' (originally the B-side of 'Happy Xmas War Is Over') and 'Don't Worry, Kyoko (Mummy's Only Looking For Her Hand in the Snow)' (the *Aspen* magazine version, where it had the working title 'Mum's Only Looking For Her Hand In The Snow').

'YOU KNOW MY NAME'

BY SEPTEMBER 1969, John Lennon had decided to quit The Beatles. He'd already formed a new band for solo projects and by mid 1969 issued two singles. Despite the decision to quit, he was determined to issue two offbeat recordings he'd made with The Beatles. Apple announced the release of Plastic Ono Band's third single on Friday December 5. It was mastered and test pressings made – one acetate was inscribed 'Look Up The Number Johnny' – but commercial copies failed to materialise. As the record was effectively a new Beatles single, it was put on permanent hold. What would have been the A-side was eventually issued as the B-side of The Beatles' last UK single, 'Let It Be'.

'You Know My Name (Look Up The Number)' began to take shape on Wednesday May 17 1967, when 14 takes of the first part of the song were recorded at Abbey Road. Work on the song began again on Wednesday June 7, when overdubs were applied to take 9. The rest of the evening was spent improvising on the song's main theme. The Beatles returned to the song the following evening, at which point Brian Jones of The Rolling Stones added his saxophone parts. The Beatles returned to the song the next evening, Friday June 8, to record another rhythm track (lasting 6:08). And that is were The Beatles left the song.

Twenty-two months later, on Wednesday April 30 1969, Lennon and Paul McCartney returned to the song to add their vocals. It was mixed at the end of the session, with three mono mixes completed, the third marked 'best'.

'YOU KNOW MY NAME (LOOK UP THE NUMBER)' / 'WHAT'S THE NEW MARY JANE'
PLASTIC ONO BAND
UK PROPOSED RELEASE December 5 1969; Apple APPLES 1002; not issued.

- **'You Know My Name (Look Up The Number)'** (Lennon, McCartney)
John Lennon (vocals, guitar, maracas), Paul McCartney (vocals, piano, bass), George Harrison (backing vocals, guitar, vibes), Ringo Starr (vocals, drums, bongos), Mal Evans (spade in gravel), Brian Jones (alto saxophone).
Recorded at Abbey Road Studios, London, England. Produced by George Martin.
- **'What's The New Mary Jane'** (Lennon, McCartney)
John Lennon (vocals, piano), George Harrison (vocals, acoustic guitar), Yoko Ono (vocals), Mal Evans (?) (handbell).
Recorded at Abbey Road Studios. Produced by George Martin / Geoff Emerick / John Lennon.

Recorded in a marijuana haze during the summer of love, 'You Know My Name (Look Up The Number)' is little more than a throwaway. It consists of the title sung to different musical settings, but is nevertheless one of the funniest records The Beatles ever recorded. Often cited by McCartney as one of his favourite Beatles recordings, it recalls the work of Lennon's heroes The Goons and the group's own Christmas records.

Lennon booked Abbey Road Studio Two on Wednesday November 26 1969 with the intention of producing finished masters for both 'You Know My Name (Look Up The Number)' and 'What's The New Mary Jane'. A copy was made of the mono mix of 'You Know My Name' from April 30 and edited down from 6:08 to 4:19. Lennon then turned his attention to 'What's The New Mary Jane'.

When interviewed for *NME* in May 1969, Lennon suggested he had written 'Mary Jane' with Alex Mardas. Magic Alex, as he was known, was employed by Apple as their resident mad inventor and head of Apple Electronics. Lennon claimed: "There was a mad thing I wrote half with our electronics genius, Alex. It was called 'What A Shame Mary Jane Had A Pain At The Party', and it was meant to be on the last Beatles album. It was real madness, but we never released it. I'd like to do it again."

Why would Lennon collaborate with the amateur Mardas when he had his pick of the world's greatest musicians? It does seem unlikely that Mardas helped with the song: he certainly wasn't credited as co-author and he didn't appear on the finished recording. Probably Lennon just threw in the comment during the interview simply to promote Apple Electronics – which, as it was failing to produce anything of worth, needed all the publicity it could get.

What is certain is that John Lennon, George Harrison, Yoko Ono, and Mal Evans recorded 'What's The New Mary Jane' at Abbey Road on Wednesday August 14 1968. Four takes were recorded, the final take being overdubbed with additional guitar, piano, and vocals. At the end of the session the track was mixed to mono, and that's how it remained until November 1969. On November 26, Lennon and Ono added more overdubs to a 2-track stereo master produced 15 months earlier. Once they had completed the overdubs, the tape was edited and several versions produced. The final master was selected from the many Lennon made that night.

'What's The New Mary Jane' is a darkly disturbing recording that lacks the natural humour of 'You Know My Name'. As harrowing to listen to as any of John and Yoko's avant-garde recordings, it would have been best left in Abbey Road's tape archive.

LIVE PEACE IN TORONTO

THIS is perhaps the defining moment in Lennon's career. While travelling to Toronto for this show, he decided the time was right to leave The Beatles.

The Toronto Rock'n'Roll Revival festival may have featured some of the biggest names from the 1950s playing alongside newcomers like the Doors and Chicago Transit Authority but, with only a couple of days to go, the event was far from sold-out. On the afternoon of September 12, in an act of desperation, concert promoter John Bower contacted Lennon at his London office to ask if he might consider acting as compère for the event. Lennon's reply was typically spontaneous. Not only would he attend, he would also perform. The only problem was that Plastic Ono Band existed in name only. This didn't bother Lennon. Wheels were set in motion and the trip arranged.

The next task was to assemble a band. Not that difficult a job, if you're John Lennon. George Harrison was asked if he wanted the gig, but he turned it down. Lennon's next choice was Eric Clapton. He was somewhat harder to contact and claimed to know nothing of the concert until the morning of September 13, the day of the concert. Klaus Voormann was invited to play bass and Alan White drums.

The next morning, the 13th, the Lennon entourage, which included Beatles roadie Mal Evans and Lennon's personal assistant Anthony Fawcett, convened at London Airport. There was, however, no sign of the Lennons or Clapton. It appears that no one had been able to contact Clapton, who was unaware of the plans. Fawcett made a frantic call to Tittenhurst Park, only to be told by the cook that Lennon and Ono were still in bed. When Lennon eventually made it to the telephone, he told the hapless Fawcett that the gig was off. Fawcett claims that it was he who persuaded Lennon to keep his promise, but Bower tells it differently.

Bower claims that Fawcett called him to explain that Lennon and Ono weren't coming, and that during their exchange he persuaded Fawcett to give him Eric Clapton's home phone number. Clapton had by now agreed to perform, but had been unable to get to the airport to make the first flight. Bower called Clapton and said: "Eric, you may not remember me, but I'm the promoter who lost $20,000 on your Blind Faith show last month. Please call John Lennon, and tell him he must do this or I will get on a plane, come to his house, and live with him, because I will be ruined." Clapton's call to Lennon worked. Lennon respected the guitarist and was apparently ashamed at having "pissed him off so much". The gig was back on, and the entourage eventually left England on Air Canada flight 124 for Toronto.

Lennon, Ono, and Clapton boarded the aircraft and headed for first class and something to eat. The rest of the group sat in the back and waited for Lennon and Clapton to join them for a brief rehearsal. Once in flight, the group managed a rehearsal of sorts and finalised a set-list.

"Now we didn't know what to play, because we'd never played together before, the band," Lennon explained. "And on the aeroplane we're running through these oldies, so the rehearsal for the record, which turned into not a bad record, was on the plane, with electric guitars ... not even acoustic, you couldn't hear."

More importantly, it was during the flight that Lennon decided to leave The Beatles. The writing had been writ large for some time. Ringo and George had left the band, only to return, and Lennon had made his discontent known through his recent solo projects. The concert in Toronto proved beyond doubt to Lennon that he no longer needed The Beatles. "I announced it to myself and the people around me on the plane – Klein came with me – I told Allen, 'It's over.' When I got back, there were a few meetings, and Allen said, 'Well, cool it, cool it.' There was a lot to do, business-wise, you know, and it would not have been suitable at the time."

At 30,000 feet over the Atlantic, Lennon called time on the greatest band the world had ever known.

By the time the Lennon entourage landed at Toronto airport, a crowd of fans had gathered to welcome them. Having cleared immigration, there was a slight problem because Ono didn't have the necessary vaccinations. The group were driven to Varsity Stadium where they holed up in the dressing room. Here they had another rehearsal before taking to the stage around midnight.

Live Peace In Toronto songs

Once on stage, the band ripped through several oldies, a track from the *White Album*, and two new Lennon compositions. Carl Perkins recorded his 'Blue Suede Shoes' for Sun Records in 1955, and it became his signature tune and a massive hit, both for Perkins and Elvis Presley, who recorded the song not long after. While Perkins' recording, issued by Sun on January 1 1956, was a hit in the USA, where it sold over a million copies, Presley's take on the song was a hit in the UK. That two of Lennon's heroes should record the song must have influenced his decision to perform it when he appeared at Toronto. That and the fact he seemed able to remember lyrics to his favourite rock'n'roll songs better than his own.

Although The Beatles recorded several Perkins songs for their early albums, they did not formally record 'Blue Suede Shoes'. They did rehearse it while filming *Let It Be* in early 1969, but this was little more than an impromptu, ragged jam.

Having decided that he would open the Toronto show with the Perkins classic, Lennon was insistent that Plastic Ono Band play the correct arrangement. Speaking to Shelley Germeaux of *Daytrippin*, drummer Alan White recalled Lennon urging the band to follow Perkins' original. "I remember one conversation in particular, because he wanted to play the Carl Perkins version, not the [Elvis Presley], of *Blue Suede Shoes*, because it's one beat shorter. 'One for the money – da-da-da – two for the show…' It was very funny because he was insistent that we stick to that version for the show."

Barrett Strong recorded 'Money (That's What I Want)' in 1958. A hit for Anna Records in America, it was issued by London-America in the UK. The Beatles first recorded the song on January 1 1962. Auditioning at Decca Records' London studio, the group, with Pete Best on drums, ran through highlights from their concert repertoire, selected for them by their manager, Brian Epstein. Their arrangement at Decca lacked the drive that made the version recorded at Abbey Road Studios on July 18 and 30 1963 eclipse Barrett's original. That version appeared on the group's second album, *With The Beatles*. They also recorded the song six times for broadcast by BBC radio. The Plastic Ono Band's performance lacks the verve of The Beatles' version; instead they produce a grungy, garage-band reading that is as loose as The Beatles' take is tight.

The Beatles also recorded a version of the Larry Williams rocker 'Dizzy Miss Lizzy', at the request of Capitol Records. The group's American label needed additional material for what would become the sixth US album, *Beatles VI*. By holding back a couple of tracks from the British albums and by including B-sides, Capitol managed to expand the group's catalogue by several albums.

Convening at Abbey Road on the evening of May 10 1965, The Beatles cut two Williams songs, 'Dizzy Miss Lizzy' and 'Bad Boy', both of which had been in the group's pre-fame concert repertoire. Mono and stereo mixes were completed at the end of the session and sent to Capitol, who issued them five weeks later. British fans had to wait until Friday August 6 before they could hear 'Dizzy Miss Lizzy', issued on *Help!* (PMC 1255/PCS 3071), and 19 months before they could hear 'Bad Boy', issued on December 9 1966 on *A Collection Of Beatles Oldies* (PMC 7067/PCS 7016).

The Beatles also recorded 'Dizzy Miss Lizzy' for the BBC at the Piccadilly Theatre, London, a little over two weeks after recording it for EMI. This version, recorded on May 26 1965, was later issued on *The Beatles At The Beeb* (8 31796 2). Finally, a live version recorded at the Hollywood Bowl on August 30 1965 was issued on *The Beatles Live At The Hollywood Bowl* (EMTV 4) on May 6 1977. The Plastic Ono Band's reading is looser than the Beatles take, but they drive Williams' moronic riff home like proto-headbangers.

A parody of the British blues boom, Lennon wrote 'Yer Blues' while studying transcendental meditation with the Maharishi Mahesh Yogi in Rishikesh, India in 1968. On their return from Rishikesh, The Beatles convened at George Harrison's house to record demos of what they had written while in India, including 'Yer Blues'. Recording proper began at Abbey Road Studios on Tuesday August 13.

PLASTIC ONO BAND – LIVE PEACE IN TORONTO 1969

PLASTIC ONO BAND

SIDE 1 'Blue Suede Shoes', 'Money (That's What I Want)', 'Dizzy Miss Lizzy', 'Yer Blues', 'Cold Turkey', 'Give Peace A Chance'.

SIDE 2 'Don't Worry Kyoko (Mummy's Only Looking For Her Hand In The Snow)', 'John John (Let's Hope For Peace)'.

UK RELEASE December 12 1969; Apple CORE 2001; failed to chart.

US RELEASE December 12 1969; LP Apple SW 3362; 8-track cartridge Apple 8XT-3362; stereo reel-to-reel tape Apple L-3362; chart high No.10.

- **'Blue Suede Shoes'** (Perkins)
- **'Money (That's What I Want)'** (Bradford, Gordy)
- **'Dizzy Miss Lizzy'** (Williams)
- **'Yer Blues'** (Lennon, McCartney)
- **'Cold Turkey'** (Lennon)
- **'Give Peace A Chance'** (Lennon, McCartney)
- **'Don't Worry Kyoko (Mummy's Only Looking For Her Hand In The Snow)'** (Ono)
- **'John John (Let's Hope For Peace)'** (Ono)

All with John Lennon (vocals, guitar), Yoko Ono (vocals), Eric Clapton (guitar, backing vocals), Klaus Voormann (bass), Alan White (drums), except 'Don't Worry Kyoko' and 'John John' with Yoko Ono (vocals), John Lennon (guitar), Eric Clapton (guitar), Klaus Voormann (bass), Alan White (drums).
All recorded live at Varsity Stadium, Toronto, Canada.
All produced by John and Yoko (Bag Productions).

In an attempt to introduce some spontaneity to the recording process (Harrison's 'Not Guilty' had gone to more than 100 takes), The Beatles moved out of their home-from-home, Studio Two, and into a small annexe to that studio's control room. Recording in what for them were cramped conditions, they set up their equipment, turned up the volume, and recorded 14 takes of the basic track. Two reduction mixes and one edit piece were then made. Finally, the beginning of take 17 was edited onto the end of take 16 – the edit is clearly audible at 3:17. This was done on the original 4-track master, an unusual and radical decision. The following evening, Lennon returned to the song, overdubbing a second vocal and mixing the track to mono. Finally, Ringo's count-in was recorded on Tuesday August 20 and edited onto the previous mono mix. The stereo mix was created on Monday October 14.

Lennon performed the song again on December 10 1968, not with The Beatles but with a spur-of-the-moment band, The Dirty Mac, which consisted of Lennon (vocals, guitar), Keith Richard (bass), Eric Clapton (guitar), and Mitch Mitchell (drums). Lennon was invited to perform for the Rolling Stones film project *Rock'n'Roll Circus*, and he chose to do so without The Beatles, an early sign of his growing dissatisfaction with the group. Lennon's performance would remain unreleased for almost 27 years (it was eventually issued in 1996). Rehearsals for the Stones film took place on December 10; filming, which took place before an invited audience, was completed the following night.

Lennon also chose to perform 'Yer Blues' at Toronto. At least two of the musicians involved knew the song from the *Circus* date, and its authentic blues shuffle made it easy for the rhythm section to fall into place. The irony of having Eric Clapton playing guitar on a song that parodied the genre he was most associated with can't have been lost on Lennon, who gives a spirited performance.

The world premiere of 'Cold Turkey' – Lennon's account of his withdrawal from heroin addiction – was a truly public event. In keeping with his manifesto of blurring the boundaries between art and life, Lennon came out of the closet to over 20,000 people and admitted his addiction to the drug. No doubt Lennon's intention was to offer a warning to those members of the audience who might similarly be tempted into trying anything stronger than cannabis. Yet much of the song's shock value was lost. Had there been sufficient rehearsal time, Plastic Ono Band could no doubt have turned in a vicious aural assault to equal Lennon's purpose. Unfortunately, because the song was as new to the band as it was to the Toronto audience, this was little more than a fumbling, rudimentary public rehearsal for the genuinely unsettling studio recording made a little over two weeks later.

Lennon would perform the song again on December 15 at the Lyceum Ballroom in central London with an extended line-up of Plastic Ono Band. This recording, eventually issued on the double album *Some Time In New York City*, has a vicious potency that the Toronto performance lacks. Lennon also chose to perform the song when he gave two concerts at Madison Square Garden in New York City on August 30 1972.

What was by far the simplest song in Plastic Ono Band's repertoire appeared the most difficult to perform convincingly. The band struggle through 'Give Peace A Chance' as if wading through treacle. What Lennon had managed to capture with two acoustic guitars and a room full of people proved simply impossible to replicate with the standard rock line-up of two guitars, bass, and drums. Ono didn't help by singing off key, but at least Lennon had the good sense to bury her deep in the mix. However, Lennon wasn't there to give a stunning performance; he was there to spread the good gospel of peace – and this was *the* peace anthem. Did it matter that he couldn't remember the verses, or that the band sounded like a group of amateurs? No. In this instance it was the message, rather than the medium, that was important, and Lennon was determined to deliver it in whatever way he could

After that, it was Ono's turn. Crowd reaction to her two songs was muted. The Toronto audience's reaction to Plastic Ono Band was mixed from the outset, but there were reports of booing during her performance. Lennon had chided them for being less than enthusiastic; now they were verging on hostility. After all, they had come to listen to good ol' rock'n'roll, not a Japanese woman screaming at the top of her voice. After their appearance, the Lennon entourage were driven to Thor Eaton's country retreat, where they spent a relaxing weekend before heading back to London.

On 'Don't Worry Kyoko (Mummy's Only Looking For Her Hand In The Snow)', Lennon and Clapton trade blues riffs over which Ono improvises a message of reassurance to her estranged daughter. An early version of the song had appeared on the *Aspen* flexi-disc and part of the lyric formed one of Ono's instruction pieces first published in her book *Grapefruit*. The same line-up recorded a studio version of the song a few weeks after this performance, issued as the B-side of 'Cold Turkey'.

While one could at least get into the groove of 'Don't Worry Kyoko', Ono's second song of the evening was pure avant-garde noise. 'John John (Let's Hope For Peace)' first appeared on side two of *The Wedding Album*, but this 12-minute version is devoid of either melody or rhythm – the very antithesis of what the audience had come to experience. You have to be either brave or stupid to perform this kind of material in public, particularly to a festival audience. Lennon and Ono obviously thought that their audience were intelligent enough to 'get' the message they were attempting to convey. However, all the audience could do was stand and wonder. Had the song been performed at an art event, it would probably have gone down a storm. As it was, by the time this atonal, feedback-drenched attack on the senses finished, the audience were all but stunned into silence.

Almost two weeks later, on September 25 1969, Lennon mixed

the 8-track tapes of the Toronto concert at Abbey Road. Working from 10:00am to 1:45pm, he produced the finished stereo master. Then, on October 20, he produced a new stereo mix of Yoko's 'Don't Worry Kyoko' to replace the previous one.

Thankfully, Lennon removed most of Yoko's caterwauling from his songs. A wise move, for had they remained, they would have spoilt an otherwise enjoyable set. The film soundtrack reveals just how invasive Ono's vocals were. (D. A. Pennebaker's film of the concert was later released as *Sweet Toronto* both on video and DVD, the DVD claiming to have a 5.1 soundtrack created from the original two-track mix.) Some of Eric Clapton's equally flat backing vocals were also removed. The album was cut at Apple's new cutting room at 3 Savile Row in central London and issued on December 12.

Even though this album was more mainstream than Lennon's previous solo efforts, Capitol Records were still not happy about issuing the disc. Speaking to Andy Peebles in December 1980, Lennon recalled: "We tried to put it out on Capitol, and Capitol didn't want to put it out. They said, 'This is garbage, we're not going to put it out with her screaming on one side and you doing this sort of live stuff.' And they just refused to put it out. But we finally persuaded them that, you know, people might buy this. Of course, it went gold the next day.

"And then, the funny thing was – this is a side story – Klein had got a deal on that record that it was a John and Yoko Plastic Ono record, not a Beatles record, so we could get a higher royalty, because the Beatles' royalties were so low – they'd been locked in '63 – and Capitol said, 'Sure you can have it,' you know. Nobody's going to buy that crap. They just threw it away and gave it us. And it came out, and it was fairly successful and it went gold. I don't know what chart position, but I've got a gold record somewhere that says … . And four years later, we go to collect the royalties, and you know what they say? 'This is a Beatle record.' So Capitol have it in my file under Beatle records. Isn't it incredible?"

Live Peace In Toronto data

In Britain, the LP was issued with a unique catalogue number, CORE 2001, that didn't follow Apple's customary APCOR/SAPCOR mono/stereo numbering system. Issued in a minimalist Yves Klein blue cover with a wispy white cloud bottom left, *Plastic Ono Band – Live Peace In Toronto 1969* was supplied with a 13-month John and Yoko calendar, of which three different versions were produced: stapled; wire spiral bound; or plastic comb bound. Both the wire and plastic comb styles were placed inside the LP jacket with the spines toward the opening. However, because the metal spines were found to be damaging the records, some American copies of the album were issued with a card that could be posted to Apple, who sent a copy of the calendar by return post. American pressings (SW 3362) erroneously state that the album was recorded in England.

The LP was issued with two label variants. Labels printed in Los Angeles were produced with or without SW prefixing the catalogue number and with either 'MFD. BY APPLE RECORDS' or 'MFD. BY CAPITOL RECORDS' etc. in the perimeter. Labels manufactured at Capitol's Scranton factory have an alternative layout, with the band's name on the first line and the album title *Live Peace In Toronto 1969* on the second. The album was reissued in America in 1982 with purple Capitol labels and in 1986 with black/colour-band Capitol labels.

The album was also issued in America on 8-track (8XT-3362) and 7-inch reel-to-reel tape (L-3362).

When issued on CD (CDP 7904282), the album was remixed from the original 8-track tapes at Quad Recording Studios, New York. The new mix by Rob Stevens differs considerably from the original LP version, with Ono placed even lower in the mix on some songs but heard more prominently on others. EMI issued the new mix on CD, complete with an updated version of the John and Yoko calendar, on May 1 1995. Capitol issued the CD ten weeks later, on July 18. The CD was issued by MFSL Original Master Recordings on April 4 2006.

BASF

together alone

1970-79

'INSTANT KARMA!'

JOHN Lennon wrote 'Instant Karma!' on January 27 1970, constructing the melody around a simple three-chord pattern that many have argued he borrowed from the nursery rhyme 'Three Blind Mice'. Melinde Kendall, wife of Yoko Ono's ex-husband Tony Cox, provided the lyrical theme. The Lennons had spent Christmas with the Coxes and the phrase "instant karma" had turned up in conversation.

Lennon would have been well aware of the basic concept of karma. The Beatles studied Hinduism, largely under George Harrison's influence, with the Maharishi Mahesh Yogi. They weren't alone in developing an interest in Eastern spirituality. Hippies cherry-picked from a number of sources, including Eastern spirituality, absorbing and changing ideas for their own ends. Borrowing from Eastern religions, in an attempt to circumvent what they considered corrupt Western influences, they trivialised the notion of karma to mean a deserved fate, good or bad. The idea that one could somehow obtain 'instant karma' was nothing more than an absurd Western contradiction.

Lennon, of course, loved the idea of 'instant karma'. Like many of us, he was hooked on instant gratification. Whether it was emotional, sexual, or creative pleasure, Lennon may not have always known what he wanted, but he knew when he wanted it. And more often than not he wanted it now. But instant satisfaction is more often than not a hollow experience, its delights fleeting. Lennon didn't trust immediate enlightenment any more than he trusted those who embraced it.

'Instant Karma!', then, is both a plea for mankind to take responsibility for its fate and a warning against the quick fix. It also finds Lennon questioning the idea of stardom and suggesting that everyone has the potential within them to achieve greatness. 'Instant Karma!' also signalled a move away from simple sloganeering to a more sophisticated political critique. This was Lennon developing his own brand of egalitarianism, an ideal he sustained throughout his solo career.

Typically, Lennon decided to record and issue the song as quickly as possible (and it was released by Apple just a few weeks before Paul McCartney called time on The Beatles). Lennon said: "I wrote it in the morning on the piano, and I went into the office and I sang it many times, and I said, 'Hell, let's do it,' and we booked the studio and Phil (Spector) came in and said, 'How do you want it?' And I said, '1950s,' and he said, 'Right,' and BOOM! I did it in about three goes: he played it back and there it was. The only argument was I said a bit more bass, that's all, and off we went. He doesn't fuss about with fucking stereo or all that bullshit, just 'does it sound all right?' then, 'Let's have it!' It doesn't matter whether something's prominent or not prominent, if it sounds good to you, as a layman, or as a human, take it – just take it, and that suits me fine."

Lennon was working so quickly that Geoff Emerick, who began engineering the session before being asked to leave as it was making Spector "edgy", claims that the song was not mixed properly. Emerick has said that 'Instant Karma!' received only a rough mix and that Spector marked the tape box "Do Not Use".

Phil Spector had been called in to salvage The Beatles' ill-fated *Let It Be* album, which had been intended to see the group return to its rock'n'roll roots. He was also working for George Harrison, producing his *All Things Must Pass* album. As Harrison recalled, he asked Spector to produce the 'Karma!' session for Lennon. "John phoned me one morning in January and said, 'I've written this tune and I'm going to record it tonight and have it pressed up and out tomorrow – that's the whole point: 'Instant Karma!', you know." So I was in. I said, 'OK, I'll see you in town.' I was in town with Phil Spector and I said to Phil, 'Why don't you come to the session?' There were just four people: John played piano, I played acoustic guitar, there was Klaus Voormann on bass, and Alan White on drums. We recorded the song and brought it out that week, mixed – instantly – by Phil Spector."

Although Spector moved the *Let It Be* project away from McCartney's original idea, adding layers of orchestration to the group's simple backing tracks to create his 'wall of sound', his production style was exactly what Lennon wanted for 'Instant Karma!'.

The eccentric American took Lennon's song and transformed it into an echo-drenched hypnotic masterpiece. Alan White's drums deliver a barrage of fills in place of lead guitar lines, and Klaus Voormann's bass supplies a thunderous bottom-end rumble over which heavily sustained keyboards hover like sheets of quicksilver. A crowd of nightclubbers, recruited by keyboardist Billy Preston from a nearby nightspot, provided the backing

'INSTANT KARMA!' / 'WHO HAS SEEN THE WIND?'
LENNON/ONO WITH PLASTIC ONO BAND
UK RELEASE February 6 1970; Apple APPLES 1003; chart high No.5.
US RELEASE February 20 1970; Apple APPLE 1818; chart high No.3.

• **'Instant Karma!'** (Lennon)
John Lennon (vocals, guitar, electric piano), Yoko Ono (vocals), George Harrison (guitar, piano), Klaus Voormann (bass, electric piano), Billy Preston (organ), Mal Evans (handclaps, chimes), Alan White (drums, piano), Allen Klein and unknown others (backing vocals). Recorded at Abbey Road Studios, London, England. Produced by John and Yoko and Phil Spector.
• **'Who Has Seen The Wind?'** (Ono)
Yoko Ono (vocals, recorder), John Lennon (guitar), John Barham (harpsichord). Recorded at Trident Studios, London, England. Produced by John Lennon.

vocals. The finished result was startling. At last Lennon had produced a musical statement that defined him as a solo artist. (On the B-side, Ono's 'Who Has Seen The Wind?' is a gentle acoustic ballad that draws on several ideas that first appeared among her 'instruction pieces', which were like small poems with instructions.)

'Instant Karma!' data

As with the Lennons' previous single, this one was issued with generic Apple labels with 'PLAY LOUD' printed in large bold type in the centre of the A-side label and 'PLAY QUIET' printed in the same bold text on the B-side.

Issued in America two weeks later than in Britain, 'Instant Karma!' was the first solo Beatle single to sell one million copies there. As Apple's American office had a few weeks rather than a few days in which to produce a picture cover, the US sleeve featured photographs of Lennon and Ono. One other difference between American and British pressings is that the US single was credited to John Ono Lennon with no mention of Plastic Ono Band.

American pressings were issued with eight label variations. The first has a dark green Apple label, with song title at 10 o'clock with composer credit below and 'STEREO' at 9 o'clock. 'PLAY' is at 12 o'clock and 'LOUD' at 6 o'clock, with the artist's name 'JOHN ONO LENNON' centre bottom.

The second has a dark green Apple label with song title on five lines at 9 o'clock and composer credit below. 'PLAY' and 'LOUD' are in slightly larger text at 12 and 6 o'clock. Artist's name 'JOHN ONO LENNON' is centre bottom.

The third variation has a medium dark green Apple label, with song title on four lines at 10 o'clock and composer credit below. A small 'PLAY' and 'LOUD' are at 12 and 6 o'clock, 'STEREO' at 2 o'clock, and artist's name 'JOHN ONO LENNON' centre bottom.

Fourth has a light green Apple label, song title on four lines at 10 o'clock with composer credit and 'STEREO' below; 'PLAY' and 'LOUD' at 12 and 6 o'clock; catalogue number and producer credit on the right side of the label; artist's name 'JOHN ONO LENNON' centre bottom.

Fifth has a light green Apple label, song title on four lines at 10 o'clock, with composer credit and 'STEREO' below; 'PLAY' and 'LOUD' at 12 and 6 o'clock; catalogue number and producer credit on the right side of the label; artist's name 'JOHN ONO LENNON (with the Plastic Ono Band)' centre bottom.

The sixth US label variation has a light green Apple label with song title on five lines at nine o'clock and composer credit below; 'PLAY' and 'LOUD' at 12 and 6 o'clock; 'STEREO' at 2 o'clock; artist's name 'JOHN ONO LENNON' centre bottom.

Seventh has a medium dark green Apple label with song title on four lines at 10 o'clock and composer credit below; small 'PLAY' and 'LOUD' at 12 and 6 o'clock; 'STEREO' at 2 o'clock; artist's name 'JOHN ONO LENNON (with the Plastic Ono Band)' centre bottom.

The eighth and last variation has a medium dark green Apple label with song title on five lines at 9 o'clock with composer credit below; 'PLAY' and 'LOUD' at 12 and 6 o'clock; artist's name 'JOHN ONO LENNON' with 'Recorded in England' centre bottom.

To promote the 'Instant Karma!' single in Britain, Lennon and Ono appeared on the BBC TV chart show *Top Of The Pops*. Lennon was the first Beatle to appear on it since The Beatles' only 'live' appearance in 1966. Two different performances were filmed on February 11 for broadcast on the 12th and 19th. Lennon sang a live vocal to a pre-recorded backing track, while Alan White, Klaus Voormann, B. P. Fallon, Mal Evans, and Ono mimed with varying degrees of success. Both performances have since been issued. The 'cue card' version appeared on the *John Lennon Collection* video, the 'knitting' version, with an extended and remixed soundtrack, on the *Lennon Legend* DVD. This recording was also issued on the CD single *Happy Xmas (War Is Over)* (CDR 6627), released in Britain on December 8 2003.

A two-song CD single (8800492) of 'Instant Karma!' backed with 'Oh My Love' was issued in The Netherlands in July 1992. Copies were given free with initial copies of the *John Lennon Collection* video. A four-song version of the CD single, with 'Karma!' plus 'Bless You', 'Mother', and 'Oh My Love', was released in the rest of Europe (excluding Britain).

'THE SHORT RAP' / 'THE LONG RAP'

LENNON and Ono's second visit to Canada began on December 16 1969. The trip, part of the couple's peace campaign, included talks with John Brower (who had persuaded Lennon to perform in Toronto earlier that year) to plan a massive free peace festival. The Lennons' headquarters were at the home of singer Ronnie Hawkins, from where Lennon gave radio interviews, signed copies of his *Bag One* lithographs, and relaxed by listening to Hawkins' new album. Lennon was impressed by the record and promised to record a brief message to promote it. Back in England, he made good on his promise by recording a brief promo that was issued as the B-side of promotional copies of Hawkins' single 'Down In The Alley'.

For the 'The Long Rap', Lennon says: "This is John 'O' Lennon here just muttering about Ronnie Hawkins, and how on our last trip to Canada, somehow it was arranged that we stay at his house. I had a great time, and of course I knew him from way back on record, 'Forty Days' and all that. I didn't know anything about him but he turned out to be a great guy, and it just so

'THE SHORT RAP', 'DOWN IN THE ALLEY' / 'THE LONG RAP'
JOHN LENNON ON RONNIE HAWKINS / JOHN LENNON
US RELEASE February 1970; Cotillion PR-105; promotional record, no commercial release.

• **'The Short Rap'/ 'The Long Rap'** (Lennon)
John Lennon (spoken word).
Recording location unknown. Producer unknown.

happened, as it were, that he'd just made an album. He's about the only person that doesn't try and greet you, as they say, and he played us this album, but he didn't want to play it, he was shy like most musicians or artists are shy, you know. I don't like playing my record to people. I have to do it because you have that need. I hope this isn't too long for a promo? Anyway, I was signing these 20-million lithographs, and this album was going on. And I was listening to most of it and still signing, until this track came on 'Down In The Alley', and it really sort of buzzed me, you know? And it sounded like now and then, and I like that. So let's hear it."

McCARTNEY

RELEASED a mere seven days after McCartney announced that he was leaving The Beatles, his eponymous debut was recorded as the most influential band in the world disintegrated around him. By the time *McCartney* was begun in September 1969, the end of The Beatles was nigh. Harrison and Starr had both quit the band but were coaxed back. As we've seen, Lennon had made his dissatisfaction known through a series of solo projects that included peace events, concerts, avant-garde records, and films. He'd even announced his intention to leave the band at an Apple board meeting but was persuaded to keep quiet by manager Allen Klein, who was renegotiating The Beatles' contract with EMI.

Brian Epstein's death in 1967 marked the beginning of the end of The Beatles. It started power struggles and infighting that dogged the group until its end and beyond. Lennon had been the driving force, but as his relationship with Yoko Ono developed, he became increasingly distanced from the group. With Lennon committed to projects outside of The Beatles, McCartney took control of the group and began directing its output. Eleven weeks after completing the mammoth *White Album*, The Beatles began work on another McCartney-influenced project, the back-to-basics *Get Back/Let It Be*. Intended to pull The Beatles together, it effectively tore them apart. Coming too soon after the lengthy *White Album* sessions, *Get Back/Let It Be* was a disaster waiting to happen. It was described by George Harrison as "the low of all-time" and by John Lennon as "the shittiest load of badly recorded shit, with a lousy feeling toward it, ever". To say that The Beatles weren't getting on is an understatement.

Aligned with this ill feeling were growing business and management concerns. Apple, a conglomerate of companies designed to ease The Beatles' tax burden, was launched in 1968 as a kind of hippie business utopia. Needless to say, this egalitarian dream quickly turned sour. The group's desire to combine counterculture values (artistic freedom) with modern business practices opened up a financial black hole that all but swallowed them whole. Derek Taylor, friend of The Beatles and Apple press officer, recalled: "They took on a lot with Apple. They took on business and pleasure and funding the arts, and did try to live up to some of their personal promises. There was a high quotient of sincerity in there, as well as a bit of madness."

Apple quickly metamorphosed from hippie utopia into chaotic business dystopia. Attempting to save their empire from ruin, Lennon called in notorious American businessman Allen Klein, who made drastic cutbacks in an attempt to stop the outward flow of cash. McCartney, however, was having none of this – not because he didn't want to put Apple on a stable business footing, but because he insisted on having his father-in-law, Lee Eastman, manage his business affairs.

In their search to find a replacement for Brian Epstein, Lennon and McCartney were divided. Lennon had Klein recommended to him; McCartney wanted Linda's father, Lee Eastman, a successful show-business lawyer who represented some of America's leading songwriters, television personalities, and artists. Klein became the manager.

By late summer 1969, McCartney had had enough and began recording his own solo album. Initially, he recorded at his London home using a Studer 4-track tape recorder borrowed from EMI (and with Robin Black engineering the sessions at Morgan). He opted for home recording for the privacy it afforded him and because he wanted to keep the album a secret from Apple and Klein. "It was in the middle of all the Beatles wrangles," McCartney explained. "And so what we had to do was we had to keep it all out of Apple in case somebody burned the negatives or burned the tapes. It was a bit political at the time. So we just kept it all out. Just booked the studios ourselves, didn't show anyone at Apple the cover. Got another guy in, a mate of ours, to do the cover. Linda shot that nice cover with the baby and the jacket and cherries on the other side."

When McCartney did record outside his home studio (at Morgan and Abbey Road in London), sessions were booked either by Linda or using the pseudonym Billy Martin. "For two reasons, really: fun and privacy," he recalled. "I think there's a big character in American baseball called Billy Martin, so that's where the name came from."

The Beatles revelled in spontaneity, and much of what

McCARTNEY
PAUL McCARTNEY
SIDE 1 'The Lovely Linda', 'That Would Be Something', 'Valentine Day', 'Every Night', 'Hot As Sun – Glasses', 'Junk', 'Man We Was Lonely'.
SIDE 2 'Oo You', 'Momma Miss America', 'Teddy Boy', 'Singalong Junk', 'Maybe I'm Amazed', 'Kreen–Akore'.
UK RELEASE April 7 1970; LP Apple PCS 7102; 8-track cartridge Apple 8X-PCS 7102; mono reel-to-reel tape Apple TA-PMC 7102; chart high No.2.
US RELEASE April 20 1970; LP Apple STAO-3363; 8-track cartridge Apple 8XT3363; stereo reel-to-reel tape Apple L-3363; chart high No.1.

• **'The Lovely Linda'** (McCartney)
Paul McCartney (vocals, guitar, bass, hand slaps).
Recorded at home studio, Cavendish Avenue, London, England.
• **'That Would Be Something'** (McCartney)
Paul McCartney (vocals, guitar, bass, tom tom, cymbal).
Recorded at home studio, Cavendish Avenue; mixed at Abbey Road Studios, London, England.
• **'Valentine Day'** (McCartney)
Paul McCartney (vocals, guitar, bass, drums).
Recorded at home studio, Cavendish Avenue; mixed at Abbey Road Studios.
• **'Every Night'** (McCartney)
Paul McCartney (vocals, guitar, bass, drums).
Recorded at Abbey Road Studios.
• **'Hot As Sun / Glasses'** (McCartney)
Paul McCartney (guitar, bass, keyboards, maracas, bongos, wineglasses, vocal, piano, drums). Recorded at Morgan Studios, London, England.
• **'Junk'** (McCartney)
Paul McCartney (vocals, guitar, bass, xylophone, drums, Mellotron, piano), Linda McCartney (backing vocals).
Recorded at home studio, Cavendish Avenue and Morgan Studios.
• **'Man We Was Lonely'** (McCartney)
Paul and Linda McCartney (vocals, guitar, steel guitar, bass, drums), Linda McCartney (backing vocals).
Recorded at Abbey Road Studios.
• **'Oo You'** (McCartney)
Paul McCartney (vocals, guitar, bass, aerosol, percussion, drums).
Recorded at home studio, Cavendish Avenue and Morgan Studios.
• **'Momma Miss America'** (McCartney)
Paul McCartney (vocals, guitar, bass, piano, drums).
Recorded at home studio, Cavendish Avenue.
• **'Teddy Boy'** (McCartney)
Paul McCartney (vocals, guitar, bass, drums), Linda McCartney (backing vocals).
Recorded at home studio, Cavendish Avenue and Morgan Studios.
• **'Maybe I'm Amazed'** (McCartney)
Paul McCartney (vocals, piano, keyboards, guitar, bass, drums), Linda McCartney (backing vocals).
Recorded at Abbey Road Studios.
• **'Kreen-Akore'** (McCartney)
Paul McCartney (vocals, guitar, piano, organ, bow & arrow, percussion, drums), Linda McCartney (backing vocals).
Recorded at Morgan Studios.
All produced by Paul McCartney.

McCartney committed to tape was improvised in this spirit. But his instinctive outbursts of creative energy, combined with the album's understated production, seemed out of character. Coming off the back of *Abbey Road*, the rough simplicity of *McCartney* was surprising. Many people thought McCartney would carry on where The Beatles had left off, but he never envisaged his solo album as *Abbey Road Part Two*. "When *McCartney* came along I had all these rough things," he said, "and I liked them all and thought, well, they're rough, but they've got that certain kind of thing about them, so we'll leave it and just put it out."

The album wasn't exactly thrown together, but because he'd provided songs for The Beatles, Mary Hopkin, and Badfinger, McCartney was forced to rework unfinished songs and improvise others. Consequently, songs chosen for *McCartney* spanned more than a decade, and some were of questionable quality. He said: "They were almost throwaways, you know? But that's why they were included. They weren't quite throwaways. That was the whole idea of the album: all the normal things that you record that are great and have all this atmosphere but aren't that good as recording or production jobs. Normally that stuff ends up with the rest of your demos, but all that stuff is often stuff I love."

He let previous high standards slip, and his debut marked the beginning of a creative roller-coaster ride that fuelled accusations of creative decline. The problem was that after years working in a creative maelstrom like The Beatles, he had no one other than himself to turn to. Years after his split with Lennon, he admitted that he missed having someone to bounce ideas off. "I definitely did miss a collaborator, because even if you've written a thing on your own, it's handy to just take it along to someone. They only have to tell you it's great – that's all the collaboration you need sometimes. Whereas otherwise you're just still wondering if it's any good. It's always good to have a little check, [a] second opinion."

Scheduled for release on April 17 1970, *McCartney* was set to conflict with The Beatles' *Let It Be*, due for release on May 8. This created more tension within the group when McCartney was asked to postpone his album for the good of the group. Ringo Starr was dispatched to McCartney's London home with the request and was duly sent away with a flea in his ear. McCartney wasn't going to change the release date of his album for anyone, particularly as he planned to upstage The Beatles' release with a surprise statement. Seven days before *McCartney* was issued, he announced that he was leaving The Beatles.

Advance copies of the album distributed to the British media contained a questionnaire in which Paul made it clear that he and The Beatles had parted company.

Q: Is this album a rest away from The Beatles or the start of a solo career?
A: Time will tell. Being a solo album means 'the start of a solo career' ... and not being done with The Beatles means it's a rest. So it's both.
Q: Are you planning a new album or single with The Beatles?
A: No.
Q: Is the break with The Beatles temporary or permanent, due to personal differences or musical ones?
A: Personal differences, business differences, musical differences, but most of all because I have a better time with my family. Temporary or permanent? I don't know.
Q: Do you foresee a time when Lennon-McCartney becomes an active songwriting partnership again?
A: No.

McCartney songs

The album opens with 'The Lovely Linda', an uncompleted fragment that he suggested was "a trailer to the full song, which will be recorded in the future". Recorded as an experiment "with more concern for testing the [tape] machine than with anything else", it was issued as it stood, unfinished. McCartney simply never got around to finishing it. But when interviewed in 2001, he admitted: "I was always going to finish it, and I had another bit that went into a Spanish song, almost mariachi, but it just appeared as a fragment and was quite nice for that reason."

The next track, 'That Would Be Something', was also recorded at McCartney's London home and finds its author evoking the force of nature as a metaphor for his relationship with Linda. Watching her symbolically cleansed by "the falling rain", he imagines a moment of transcendence where Linda, the personification of natural beauty, becomes one with nature.

On 'Valentine Day', working on his own again, McCartney was forced to revisit a recording practice he first explored while making the *White Album*. McCartney, Lennon, and Harrison developed a way of using multi-track tape to record their own backing tracks without the assistance of the others. McCartney took the practice a stage further and developed it as a way of writing. Improvising without a preconceived melody or arrangement in mind, he could write and record new compositions on the spot. Letting his subconscious run free, he layered random impressions onto the multi-track tape, shaping his music without knowing where it would lead him.

Explaining the process later to Paul Gambaccini, he said: "What I did was to just go into the studio each day and just start with a drum track. Then I built it up a bit without any idea of how the song was going to turn out. It's like a reverse way of working. After laying down the drum track I added guitars and bass, building up the backing track." Like Lennon, McCartney was exploring a form of creativity developed by earlier generations of artists, writers, and composers. However, unlike Lennon's adventures with the avant-garde, McCartney's remained melodic and accessible. Improvised at home, 'Valentine Day' was an exploration of nonconformist creative techniques, influenced by an interest in the avant-garde and the restraints under which it was recorded.

McCartney busked 'Every Night' while filming *Let It Be* at Twickenham Studios in January 1969 and finished it while on holiday in Greece. A love song inspired by Linda, it finds McCartney struggling with his personal demons. Attempting to reconcile conflicting emotions, he considers his options. The easy choice, drink and drugs, is rejected in favour of the infinitely more fulfilling alternative, domesticity and Linda. Attempting to deal with his traumas, McCartney increasingly turned to songwriting as catharsis. Writing 'Every Night' transformed his neurosis into creative energy. Revealing a troubled mind, it hints at an increasing reliance on Linda as a stabilising presence in his life.

To relieve their boredom while making *Let It Be*, The Beatles often revisited their early repertoire, which was peppered with instrumentals like 'Hot As Sun'. Ad-libbing the piece while filming *Let It Be,* McCartney performed it in a droll Hawaiian style. He later recorded it at Morgan Studios, cross-faded to two unrelated pieces at the end: playing wine glasses, he created the atmospheric instrumental 'Glasses'; then, as a teaser, he edited onto the end an uncredited fragment of 'Suicide', a song written with Frank Sinatra in mind.

"I wrote this song called 'Suicide' which was very cabaret," he explained. "It was murder! Horrible song!" Sinatra rejected it. "Apparently he thought it was an almighty piss take. 'No way!' he's supposed to have said to one of his people. 'Is this guy having me on?'" Bootleg recordings of the piano demo have since surfaced, but the brief nine-second snippet on *McCartney* is all that has been made commercially available. (McCartney eventually debuted 'Suicide' on the BBC's *Michael Parkinson Show*, recorded at BBC Television Studios, London, on December 2 1999 and broadcast the following day on BBC One.)

'Junk' was written during The Beatles' Indian sojourn at Rishikesh in the Himalayan foothills. On their return to Britain, they gathered at George Harrison's Esher home and made demo recordings of the songs they'd written while in India. Although McCartney intended to use 'Junk' for *Abbey Road*, it remained unused until resurrected for *McCartney*. (The Beatles' attempt at the song – almost identical to McCartney's solo version – was released in 1996 on The Beatles' *Anthology 3*.) He recorded two versions at home before adding more instrumentation at Morgan. Take one appeared without vocals as 'Singalong Junk'; take two had vocals. Its inclusion as an instrumental is superfluous and points to McCartney's struggle to find enough material to complete the album.

As concise a piece of self-analysis as anything Lennon wrote for his *Plastic Ono Band* album, McCartney's 'Man We Was Lonely' was, like Lennon's 'Hold On', influenced by the pain he experienced at the break-up of The Beatles. While it was born out of trauma, he nevertheless sees a resolution to his anxieties. His life-affirming refrain echoes Lennon's cries of self-realisation and suggests independence. Unlike Lennon, who exposed his vulnerability to the world, McCartney masks his with bravado and an upbeat musical support, which nevertheless reveals an exposed sensibility.

Part self-analysis, part defiant response, 'Man We Was Lonely' was a forthright piece of self-assurance, a celebration of having weathered the storm. As a considered message of intent, which informed the world (but more importantly Lennon and Ono) that Paul and Linda were doing just fine on their own, the song was a result of McCartney's alienation. Yet he turned this to his advantage, steeling his resolve to succeed and strengthen his relationship with Linda. Speaking to *Life* in April 1971, he said: "As a married couple, Linda and I've really become closer because of all those problems, all the decisions. It's been very real what I've been through, a breath of air, in a way, because of having been through very inhuman things." According to its author, 'Man We Was Lonely' "was written in bed at home, shortly before we finished recording the album". Twelve takes were attempted at Abbey Road on February 25 1970, with McCartney completing overdubs and mixing at the same seven-hour session.

'Oo You' was improvised at home and, originally an instrumental, was "given lyrics one day after lunch". McCartney added the newly acquired lyric to his basic track when he moved to Morgan Studios. While there, he copied his 4-track tape onto 8-track so that he could make more overdubs. With the extra space this made available, he added guitar, percussion, and an aerosol spray (panned hard right). The addition of lyrics gives the piece substance, but 'Oo You' remains little more than a well-disguised throwaway.

'Momma Miss America' too was ad-libbed at home and consists of two separate pieces joined together, with a sloppy edit marking the join. Like the other improvised instrumentals recorded for *McCartney*, it's proficient but not inspired. While recording *Get Back/Let It Be*, The Beatles churned out this kind of improvised material by the hour, and almost all of it remains unreleased – with good reason.

While they were filming *Let It Be*, Lennon, McCartney, and Harrison showcased a number of songs that later appeared on their solo albums. Lennon performed songs that later appeared on *Imagine*. Harrison played songs destined for *All Things Must Pass*. McCartney previewed songs that later appeared on *McCartney* and *Ram*. Like much of McCartney's material recorded for the ill-fated project, 'Teddy Boy' was sabotaged by Lennon. Programmed by Glyn Johns for The Beatles' *Get Back* album, the song was dropped from the running order when Phil Spector was called in to salvage the project. Never completed to McCartney's satisfaction, it remained unreleased until reactivated for this album. Recorded at home and overdubbed at Morgan, the solo version is taken at a slightly faster tempo and benefits from a considered vocal arrangement.

'Maybe I'm Amazed' would have made a stunning debut single, but for some reason it was overlooked. "Sometimes we're a bit daft here," McCartney explained. "We have a bit of a funky organisation, you know, which isn't that clued into picking up tracks off albums. At the time we thought 'Maybe I'm Amazed' was a good track and maybe we should do that as a single, which it probably should have been. But we never did." Nonetheless, McCartney may have considered releasing the song as a single, because a promotional film by Charlie Jenkins was screened on British and American TV on April 19 1970.

When asked how he came to write the song, he said he couldn't particularly remember. "I know what it was about in my own mind, you know? It was about just getting married, I suppose, and just sort of saying, you know ... the sort of doubt kind of thing of it all is what, I suppose, I was trying to sum up."

He was obviously feeling troubled when he wrote 'Maybe I'm Amazed'. For much of 1969/70, he'd felt isolated, insecure, and worried; even his relationship with Linda, it appears, worried him. Yet it was Linda who shouldered the burden of his depression, hauling him out of his despondency by encouraging him to write. Although he found the music business disheartening, with Linda's help he turned to music as therapy. "It's worked for you before, you know," she is alleged to have told him.

A paean to self-realisation and Linda's indomitable spirit, 'Maybe I'm Amazed' finds McCartney exploring the deepest corners of his fragile psyche. It is an attempt at understanding his melancholia and coming to terms with it. If previously he appeared confident, even arrogant, privately McCartney was an emotional wreck. But at least he had an escape route that bypassed the usual slow descent into drink and drug abuse. 'Maybe I'm Amazed' is a song of deliverance and self-realisation. Even if McCartney felt he couldn't overcome his insecurities, at least he could recognise and write about them – and that was half the battle won.

'Maybe I'm Amazed' was completed in one productive session on February 22 1970 at Abbey Road. McCartney began the session with the intention of mixing 'That Would Be Something' and 'Valentine Day' to stereo. But he did that quicker than anticipated, so he remade 'Every Night' and then recorded 'Maybe I'm Amazed'. Its release as a single in 1977, seven years too late, meant that one of McCartney's finest songs failed to achieve the commercial success it deserved.

'Kreen-Akore' is an improvised instrumental recorded at Morgan. McCartney was inspired by a television programme about the Kreen-Akrore Indians, who live in the Brazilian jungle.

The documentary, *The Tribe That Hides From Man*, shown by ITV, revealed how the Indians' way of life was being altered by European settlers. With the programme fresh in his mind, he began work on the track. "The next day, after lunch, I did some drumming," he recalled. Improvising, McCartney added percussion, which included the unusual application of a guitar case, to simulate a stampede. He then overdubbed some heavily compressed breathing, which becomes increasingly frantic and oppressive as the tempo and textures develop. It's an unusual track, which manages to combine both melodic and rhythmic elements with startling effect, and his decision to programme the piece directly after 'Maybe I'm Amazed' was a daring, provocative way to close his first solo album.

McCartney data

Apple issued the album with generic labels, with the title in a customised font, in a black paper inner sleeve. A striking abstract photograph by Linda graced the front cover, with a photograph of Paul, Linda, and daughters Heather and Mary on the back. Gordon House and Roger Huggett designed the cover, which originally had a reversed gatefold sleeve – and the record was placed in the front pocket rather than the rear.

EMI reissued *McCartney* in the mid 1970s with black and silver Capitol 'dome' labels. It was reissued for a second time on April 2 1984 by EMI's FAME imprint (FA 413100-1) with generic Apple labels.

American pressings were issued with generic Apple labels with several variations. The first has the title, *McCartney*, and 'Paul McCartney' printed on separate lines, with song titles in two columns on the B-side label. The second has the title and 'Paul McCartney' on separate lines, and the song titles in one column on B-side label.

The third US label variation has the title and 'Paul McCartney' printed on separate lines, with 'MFD. BY CAPITOL RECORDS' etc and Capitol logo perimeter print on the B-side. A fourth variation has the Apple label with only the title *McCartney*, in a custom font, and catalogue number SMAS-3363.

The gatefold sleeve was manufactured with three minor variations: with Apple's New York address on the back cover; with Apple's California address on the back cover; and with Apple's New York address and 'an abkco managed company' on the back cover. Capitol reissued McCartney with generic black and silver 'dome' labels in the mid 1970s. It was reissued by Columbia in the early 1980s with generic red labels (JC-36478, FC-36511, and PC-36478).

McCartney was issued on 8-track both in Britain (8X-PCS-7102) and the USA (8XT 3363). Columbia reissued the 8-track (JCA-36478) in the early 1980s. The album was also issued as a 7-inch reel-to-reel tape in the USA (Apple/Ampex L-3363) and in the UK (Apple/EMI TA-PMC 7102). The British reel-to-reel tape was in mono and remained on EMI's stock list until 1975.

JOHN LENNON/PLASTIC ONO BAND

HAVING spent most of 1969 preoccupied with their peace campaign, Lennon and Ono spent much of 1970 in isolation. As every action has an equal and opposite reaction, the Lennons retreated from their frantic schedule of public appearances and immersed themselves in one another. Speaking in 1980, Lennon recalled: "We stopped talking to the press, we became 'recluses'. … I was calling myself Greta Hughes or Howard Garbo."

Locked away in their Berkshire mansion, they spent every waking minute together. However, as the weeks turned into months, they sank into a deep depression. Lennon wasn't the only ex-Beatle suffering at the group's break-up. McCartney was equally affected. However, while Paul and Linda seemed to draw strength from their troubles, John and Yoko's relationship began to flounder. Although Lennon's love for Ono remained constant, Anthony Fawcett, the couple's personal assistant, recalled the atmosphere at Tittenhurst as tense. "Living with them became harder day by day," he said. "Beside Val, the cook, I was the only person around, and I was acutely aware of the rapid deterioration of their relationship."

Salvation came in the form of a book. Dr. Arthur Janov's *The Primal Scream – Primal Therapy: The Cure for Neurosis* arrived out of the blue and had a dramatic affect on Lennon and Ono. Typically, Lennon took to the book and the promise it offered like a zealot.

Janov argues that neurosis is caused by repressed pain that divides the subject in two. "Coming close to death at birth or feeling unloved as a child are examples of such Pain," he suggests. "The Pain goes unfelt at the time because the body is not equipped to experience it fully and deal with it. When the Pain is too much, it is repressed and stored away. When enough unresolved Pain has occurred, you lose access to your feelings and become neurotic."

Janov's definition of neurosis describes perfectly Lennon's childhood and his addictive personality. He had lost his mother, Julia, not once but twice. When his parents separated, he was sent to live with his aunt and uncle. Although his mother lived only a few streets away, his contact with her was minimal. It was only as a teenager that he developed a relationship with Julia. And then, just as they were getting to know one another, Julia was killed in a road accident. He never came to terms with the pain his mother's death caused him; instead, he repressed it.

Inevitably he turned to drugs, and as the years passed the drugs became harder. By the time Janov entered their lives, Lennon and Ono had already endured heroin addiction. But heroin just dulled the pain, it didn't remove it. Lennon obviously recognised as much, as he had already warned of the pitfalls of short-sightedness ('Instant Karma!') and the pain of heroin withdrawal ('Cold Turkey'). If anyone was ripe for Janov's primal therapy, it was Lennon.

Contact was made and Janov agreed to fly to England and treat his high-profile patients in their own home. But before treatment could begin, Janov insisted that Lennon and Ono separate for 24 hours. For the first time in over two years, they were physically cut off from one another. Ono stayed in the master bedroom, while Lennon moved into his new recording studio. "We did a lot of it in the recording studio, while they were building it," recalled Janov. "That was kind of difficult. But it went very, very well. John had about as much pain as I've ever seen in my life. And he was a very dedicated patient. Very serious about it. When I said to him, 'You've got to come to LA now, I can't spend the rest of my life in England,'" he said, "'Fine,' and he came."

However, before they decamped to California, Lennon and Ono moved into separate hotels in London for further treatment. After three weeks in Janov's care, they left England in late April 1970 for the Primal Institute in California and four months of intensive therapy.

Between their sessions with Janov, they relaxed at a rented Bel Air house, watching television and writing songs. Lennon had already started work on two compositions, 'Mother' and 'Isolation', which he completed in California. Several others were written from scratch during their stay. Not only did Janov's treatment have a powerful effect on Lennon's mental wellbeing, but also it influenced the music he was making, which reflected the pain he experienced while in therapy. When interviewed by Jann Wenner for *Rolling Stone*, both Lennon and Ono used the word mirror when describing their experiences of primal therapy. But primal therapy did more than reflect their pain, it allowed them to see beyond it.

"Janov showed me how to feel my own fear and pain; therefore I can handle it better than before, that's all," said Lennon. "I'm the same, only there's a channel." Coming close to an epiphany, Lennon found that primal therapy offered him a means by which he could transform pain into creative energy. It informed his writing, and the resulting songs were raw, emotive, personal, powerful, and sometimes shocking.

The anger that surfaced in Lennon's songs was equalled by the musical settings he recorded on his return to England. He stripped the songs of any artifice by recording them as a three-piece. Employing Ringo Starr and Klaus Voormann as his rhythm section, Lennon eschewed complex arrangements and overdubs. This was primal rock'n'roll, straight from the gut. All of the songs were performed live in the studio with the emphasis on attitude rather than perfection. Voormann told *Rolling Stone* how Lennon's candid approach spilled over into the studio. "The playing itself, to him, was not that important. It was more important to capture the feeling. We did mostly one or two takes. There's a lot of mistakes on [the album] and timing changes, but it was just like a pulse, exactly what John wanted. He loved it."

JOHN LENNON/PLASTIC ONO BAND

JOHN LENNON

SIDE 1 'Mother', 'Hold On', 'I Found Out', 'Working Class Hero', 'Isolation'.

SIDE 2 'Remember', 'Love', 'Well Well Well', 'Look At Me', 'God', 'My Mummy's Dead'.

UK RELEASE December 11 1970; LP Apple PCS 7124; 8-track cartridge Apple 8X-PCS 7124; chart high No.11.

US RELEASE December 11 1970; LP Apple SW 3372; 8-track cartridge Apple 8XW-3372; stereo reel-to-reel tape Apple M-3372; chart high No.6.

- **'Mother'** (Lennon)
John Lennon (vocals, piano), Klaus Voormann (bass), Ringo Starr (drums).
- **'Hold On'** (Lennon)
John Lennon (vocals, guitar), Klaus Voormann (bass), Ringo Starr (drums).
- **'I Found Out'** (Lennon)
John Lennon (vocals, guitar), Klaus Voormann (bass), Ringo Starr (drums).
- **'Working Class Hero'** (Lennon)
John Lennon (vocals, guitar).
- **'Isolation'** (Lennon)
John Lennon (vocals, piano), Klaus Voormann (bass), Ringo Starr (drums).
- **'Remember'** (Lennon)
John Lennon (vocals, piano), Klaus Voormann (bass), Ringo Starr (drums).
- **'Love'** (Lennon)
John Lennon (vocals, acoustic guitar), Phil Spector (piano).
- **'Well Well Well'** (Lennon)
John Lennon (vocals, guitar), Klaus Voormann (bass), Ringo Starr (drums).
- **'Look At Me'** (Lennon)
John Lennon (vocals, guitar).
- **'God'** (Lennon)
John Lennon (vocals), Billy Preston (piano), Klaus Voormann (bass), Ringo Starr (drums).
- **'My Mummy's Dead'** (Lennon)
John Lennon (vocals, guitar).

All recorded at Abbey Road Studios, London, England, except 'My Mummy's Dead' recorded at house on Nimes Road, Bel Air, California.

All produced by John & Yoko and Phil Spector.

Stripping the band of its finesse, Lennon created a potent, raw sound that echoed the way in which primal therapy had stripped him of his neurosis. Lennon, Starr, and Voormann cut through the flabby flesh of pop to reveal the hard, white bone of rock'n'roll. Performing a vocal with each take, Lennon had rarely sounded so commanding. Greil Marcus was moved to remark that "John's singing on the last verse of 'God' may be the finest in all of rock".

The pain that Lennon hoped to express and disavow was not solely the result of his childhood pain or Janov's therapy. It had been building in him for years. Freed of The Beatles and all they stood for, he told the world exactly how he felt about the way it had treated him. Speaking to Jann Wenner just after the album's release, Lennon revealed just how frustrated he had become with the music business. "One has to completely humiliate oneself to be what The Beatles were, and that's what I resent. ... And that's what I'm saying on this album – I remember what it's all about now, you fuckers – fuck you! That's what I'm saying, you don't get me twice."

John Lennon/Plastic Ono Band was more than invective, it was catharsis. Lennon named and laid bare his pain to free himself of it. This was Lennon scaled to the bone. Stripping away the phoney veneer that for too long he had hidden behind, he offered instead truth and honesty. With this in mind, his choice of producer seemed perverse.

Phil Spector is best known for overblown productions that bury the singer under a trademark 'wall of sound'. Spector may be credited as co-producing this album, but Lennon suggested that he had most of the sounds before he asked the producer to help complete the record. This is confirmed by the demo recordings Lennon made in California in the summer of 1970. Nevertheless, he thought that Spector brought a lot of energy to the project and taught him a lot. Ono confirmed that Lennon produced most of the album himself and that Spector was only called in to assist with technical aspects. She was, however, unhappy with Spector's exact nature; she was, after all, more interested in ambiguity than certainty. Spector worked quickly, mixing songs as they were completed. Typically, he mixed several tracks to mono (despite the label of the issued record stating that they are in stereo). Compared to his work on The Beatles' *Let It Be* or George Harrison's *All Things Must Pass*, Spector has a peripheral presence on *John Lennon/Plastic Ono Band*, audible only in the copious amounts of echo he applied to Lennon's otherwise dry mixes.

Between recording Lennon's songs, the band worked on Ono's companion album, *Yoko Ono/Plastic Ono Band*. Previously, she had been given space on the B-side of John's singles, but with these two albums, Lennon and Ono established a practice of issuing complementary solo albums – a practice that continued through to *Double Fantasy*, which would find them sharing the same album for the first time since 1972's *Some Time In New York City*.

John Lennon/Plastic Ono Band songs

As we've seen, Lennon began writing 'Mother' in England and completed it in California. While still in therapy, he recorded a number of guitar-based demos. Even at this early stage, he had developed a sound to match his mood. Plugging his pickup'd acoustic guitar into an amplifier with the tremolo turned up to ten, he produced a sound that oscillates between shimmering clean highs and dirty distorted lows. Upon entering Abbey Road Studios, he recorded a guitar-based version, later issued on the *John Lennon Anthology*. Taken at a slightly faster tempo and without the heavily sustained piano chords of the finished master, it lacks the primal quality that Lennon was searching for.

Abandoning the guitar, he turned to the piano and remade the song. The menacing piano chords are prefigured by four tolls of a church bell, slowed down to sound even more funereal. Lennon got the idea while watching a horror film on television and decided to use the tolling of bells to open the album. Speaking to Wenner, Ono said that the church bells were an allusion to Lennon's childhood, as he often spoke to her of hearing church bells on a Sunday. Lennon also implied that they were, perhaps, an attempt to evoke the loneliness he associated with Sundays. (The track was edited when issued as a single and the recording correctly designated as being in mono. The Japanese pressing, AR 2734, was issued in stereo. Lennon performed the song at both shows he gave at Madison Square Garden on August 30 1972.)

Described by Andy Grey of *NME* as "sombre", 'Hold On' is in fact a beacon of light in what is otherwise a dark, moody album. It is a song of reassurance, both a personal epistle of hope and a plea for harmony. Addressing himself, Ono, and the world in general, Lennon has a simple message: hold on and everything is gonna be all right. As he explained to Wenner: "It's only going to be all right ... now, at this moment it's all right ... . That's how we're living now, but really like that and cherishing each day, and dreading it too. I'm really beginning to cherish it when I'm cherishing it."

But stoicism alone is not the answer: individuals, communities, and countries must all come together to build the utopia that Lennon implies is within our reach. His aspiring lyric is matched by warm, shimmering guitars and minimal backing from Starr and Voormann. Between takes, the three musicians jammed on old rock'n'roll songs from the 1950s (one of which, 'Long Lost John', was later issued on the *John Lennon Anthology*). During one lull in proceedings, they tried an up-tempo take of 'Hold On', a 44-second extract of which was later issued on the *John Lennon Anthology*.

For 'I Found Out', Lennon turns up the distortion on his amplifier and the vitriol in his voice, and decries the false idols and causes he had mistakenly let into his life. If George Harrison was the great seeker of spirituality, then Lennon was the great seeker of truth. 'I Found Out' sees him rejecting the things that divert him from the truth – whatever that is. It's not clear if it took Janov's primal therapy for Lennon to discover that he had been let down by almost everyone from his parents to Paul McCartney. Like Dylan before him, Lennon suggests that we avoid following leaders. The only path to political, social, or religious enlightenment lies within, not in abstract systems devised by others. He puts himself forward not as a leader but as an example of someone who has made mistakes only to discover that enlightenment comes from within.

Before recording properly, Lennon made demo recordings in California. Working through the song, he made changes to the arrangement and lyric; changing the tense from the third to first person and in the last verse substituting neurosis for religion.

Although Voormann remembers Lennon breaking down while making the album, outtakes from the sessions confirm that he was often in buoyant mood and enjoying the experience. Instructing Starr and Voormann about how they should work, Lennon said: "Just play how you feel, you know, cos it is Carl Wolf," an allusion to heroes Carl Perkins and Howlin' Wolf. A slightly longer take of the song reveals Lennon's intentions. As the band play on, he breaks into Carl Perkins' 'Gone Gone Gone'.

'Working Class Hero' was influenced as much by contemporary left-wing thinking as by Janov's primal therapy. Like several left-wingers of the time, Lennon argues that the only way to overcome a system that ensures conformity is not through organised revolution but through revolution of the self. He had already commented on the growing political unrest and student riots of 1968 with 'Revolution' and 'Revolution 9'. His political commitment increased apace the following year with a far-reaching peace campaign.

Aligning himself with the New Left, Lennon restates their central belief in 'Working Class Hero': "the personal is the political". Like the New Left, he argues that it is what you do and not some external theory that informs your political stance. What was needed was a 'new man', a working class hero, who would refuse to be co-opted by a repressive system. The song may not be couched in intellectual terms, but it expresses these beliefs more precisely than the lengthy political screeds published at the time.

Speaking to Wenner about the song, he said: "I just think its concept is revolutionary, and I hope it's for the workers. ... I think it's for the people like me who are working class, whatever, upper or lower, who are supposed to be processed into the middle classes, or in through the machinery, that's all. It's my experience, and I hope it's just a warning to people."

He had hopes that his song might bring about the kind of revolution in the head that the New Left were dreaming of. He hoped it would be taken up in the same way as 'Give Peace A Chance'. For him, it was a revolutionary piece of work and the ideal New Left anthem.

Speaking to Robin Blackburn and Tariq Ali less than two months after the album's release, Lennon stressed the political beliefs that he had put forward in 'Working Class Hero'. He said: "I was very conscious of class – they would say [I had] a chip on my shoulder – because I knew what happened to me and I knew about the class repression coming down on us – it was a fucking fact, but in the hurricane Beatle world it got left out, I got farther away from reality for a time." He continued: "But nothing changed except that we all dressed up a bit, leaving the same bastards running everything. The continual awareness of what was going on made me feel ashamed I wasn't saying anything. I burst out because I could no longer play the game any more, it was just too much for me."

While Lennon would be constantly chided for preaching from an ivory tower, with 'Working Class Hero' he acknowledged the limitations he laboured under and the effect it had upon him. For all his attempts to break free of the system, he concedes that he remained defined by a set of terms as narrow as his attempts to escape them were broad.

Recorded entirely solo by Lennon at Abbey Road, 'Working Class Hero' drew comparisons with early Dylan, whom he disavows in another song on the album, 'God'. "Anyone that sings with a guitar and sings about something heavy would tend to sound like Dylan," Lennon explained. "I'm bound to be influenced by that because that is the only kind of real folk music I listen to. So in that way I've been influenced, but it doesn't sound like Dylan to me."

Because of its simplicity, the commercial version was issued in mono. It also features an obvious edit at 1:25. Lennon admitted to Wenner that he had missed a verse, which he had to drop in later. An alternative version, issued on the *John Lennon Anthology*, features a complete, unedited take of the song. Because the lyrics include the word 'fucking', crude edits to remove the expletive were made to the song for Australian pressings of the album. The lyrics were also censored for all countries when printed on the record's inner sleeve.

'Isolation' finds Lennon caught in a moment of existential doubt. Laying open his angst, he reveals that he is as helpless and alienated as anyone else. For someone who needed to belong as much as he did, this admission of isolaphobia sees him stripping away another layer of fiction and exposing the reality behind. Despite his success and popularity, Lennon reflects on his own limitations and proffers an epistle of acceptance and forgiveness. Despite everything he has said and done, nothing has changed. The world remains as irrational as ever; the insanity we construct and inhabit results in nothing but anxiety or despair; our search for meaning within our lives remains illusive and ultimately alienating.

Lennon recorded 'Remember' on October 9, his 30th birthday, and the song finds him in a nostalgic mood. If primal therapy required the subject to confront the pain experienced in childhood, it also brought back more pleasurable memories. Lennon presents the listener with these conflicting emotions. Tinged with disappointment, at phoney heroes and the illusion of a stable family life, 'Remember' has Lennon looking through rose-tinted glasses at a youth spent without regret. He was as nostalgic as the next person, but not at the expense of ignoring the realities of the present, or the consequences of his actions. Remember the past by all means, but don't forget today.

The version presented on *Plastic Ono Band* was edited down from a much longer take. The full version lasts 8:15 and featured an organ overdub. Lennon told Wenner that the reference to the

5th of November was an ad lib, influenced by his singing sounding like Frankie Laine. Somehow this led him to sing the opening lines from a nursery rhyme about Guido Fawkes, who attempted to blow up London's Houses Of Parliament in November 1605. Having decided to keep the take, Lennon edited an explosion on the end as a joke and further reference to the celebrated event.

'Love' dispels the myth that Lennon was an angry rocker incapable of writing tender ballads. While his up-tempo songs were often written as catharsis or out of guilt, his love songs were real expressions of devotion that held their meaning long after he dismissed other songs as "self-conscious poetry". Lennon defines what love means to him and, in keeping with the rest of the material written for the album, he does so with simple, honest precision.

He recorded a version of the song while in California, backing himself with amplified acoustic guitar treated with copious amounts of tremolo. Back at Abbey Road he repeated the process, recording an equally plain acoustic version, which appeared on the *John Lennon Anthology*. With his guitar and vocal in the bag, he asked Spector to overdub a delicate piano part to complete the arrangement. In 1982, the song was remixed for release as a single, when it was issued in territories outside of the USA to promote the *John Lennon Collection*. The introduction and ending were increased in volume, in an attempt to make the song 'radio-friendly'.

On 'Well Well Well', a pounding rhythm section and piercing guitar support a penetrating Lennon vocal that shifts from tender to savage. He recalls intimate moments with Ono over a pulsing rhythm track that echoes the beating hearts of 'John And Yoko', and he contrasts this with intense screams of painful emotional release.

Spector mixed the commercial version to mono, although an early rough mix appears in stereo. When the album was remixed in 2000, the track was given a much wider stereo picture, which reveals a second guitar part that is almost inaudible on the original. Lennon's remarks about cramp at the end of the song are also clearly audible. The song would be performed live just twice, at the matinee and evening shows of the 1972 One To One charity concert in New York.

'Look At Me' was written during The Beatles' Indian sojourn and reveals that even by early 1968 Lennon was struggling to come to terms with what he'd become. The Beatles may have had the world on a plate, but they were all feeling the pressures of fame and had discovered the unsettling truth that money doesn't make things better. Influenced by George Harrison, they looked to Eastern spirituality for an answer and thought they had found it in the Maharishi Mahesh Yogi. Looking for a spiritual answer to their problems worked for Harrison but not the others. Lennon came away from India as confused and cynical as he'd always been. The many letters that Ono sent him only contributed to his sense of unease and they undermined what was left of his relationship with Cynthia.

'Look At Me' finds Lennon addressing himself, hoping to discover who he is and what it is that makes him whole. Meditating on what it is to be, Lennon concludes that only his lover can answer the question and complete him.

He recorded two demos of the song, in 1968 and 1970, played fingerpicking-style and almost identical to the finished master, but made well before he recorded it for *John Lennon/Plastic Ono Band*. An alternative studio version issued on the *John Lennon Anthology* differs from both the demos and the master recording, with Lennon strumming his guitar and captured in stereo; the commercial release is in mono. When his *Plastic Ono Band* album was remixed in 2000 for reissue on CD, 'Look At Me' was at last issued in stereo.

Back in the summer of 1966, Lennon gave an interview to Maureen Cleave of *The Evening Standard*, a London newspaper, in which he attempted to explain his views on contemporary Christianity. His line about The Beatles being "bigger than Jesus" went almost unnoticed in Europe but, taken out of context, caused a wave of anti-Beatle behaviour to unfold across America. Bowing to pressure from his manager, Brian Epstein, Lennon apologised for having made the remark but also tried to make himself better understood. "I'm not anti-God, anti-Christ or anti-religion," he explained. "I was not saying we are greater or better. I believe in God, but not as one thing, not as an old man in the sky. I believe that what people call God is something in all of us."

His ideas didn't change much in the years that followed. For Lennon, God was something abstract that formed part of the human condition. Speaking to David Wigg in June 1969, he said: "God is a power, which we're all capable of tapping. We're all light bulbs capable of tapping energy. You can use electricity to kill people or light the room. God is that. Neither one nor the other but everything." He continued the conversation with Dr. Janov the following year. Janov recalled: "He would say, 'What about religion?' and I would say something like, 'People in pain usually seek out religion.' And he would say, 'Oh, God is a concept by which we measure our pain.'"

Combining his own beliefs with what he'd discovered while in primal therapy, Lennon constructed 'God' in three parts to illustrate his feelings. It opens with his bold statement about God, which he repeats to validate his claim. He then introduces a second musical theme, in which he presents the listener with a litany of things he no longer believes in. The list began spontaneously and developed into a disavowal of everything once held precious. "It was just going on in my head and *I Ching* and *Bible* and the first three or four just came out, whatever came out," he explained.

Developing the list, he includes several cultural and religious icons that three years earlier appeared on the cover of *Sgt. Pepper's Lonely Hearts Club Band*. It was as if the past held too many painful memories that had to be effaced. What mattered was to experience reality as it appeared now. He dismissed ideas and things that had previously defined as phoney relics from the past. The problem was: how to end the list? "I thought, where do I end? Churchill," he said. "And who have I missed out? ... It got like that, you know, and I thought I had to stop. ... I was going to leave a gap and just say fill in your own, you know, and put whoever you don't believe in."

Lennon ends the song with the biggest illusionists of them all. His disavowal of The Beatles distanced him from the group and the past, and it also announced a new beginning for all. The dream was over, the time had come to get real. Like David Bailey's book *Goodbye Baby & Amen*, 'God' was a farewell to the 1960s and everything it stood for. It was also Lennon's way of affirming what he now believed in. The closing refrain says it all: "I was the walrus but now I'm John." And as if to reinforce his belief, Lennon delivers one of the finest vocals of his career.

He recorded several versions of the song while in California. The first take finds him mumbling his way through his litany of fakes and phoneys. By the second and third takes his list was pretty much finalised. All of these early recordings end by returning to the opening refrain, as the song's closing statement had yet to be written. When he came to record the song at Abbey Road, he tried to replicate his guitar-based demo recording with help from Starr and Voormann. However, as with other songs originally written on guitar, he turned to the piano and employed the skills of Billy Preston to capture the definitive performance. Although the song received substantial radio play on some liberal American radio stations, it was not issued as a single. (It was, however, issued as a one-track promotional CD single, PE 98030, in Spain in 1998.)

Recalling the harrowing recordings that Lennon and Ono made at Queen Charlotte's Maternity Hospital, 'My Mummy's Dead' is a concise expression of Lennon's primal experience. Its simple construction, based on 'Three Blind Mice', combined with his monotone delivery, suggests an absence of emotion. The cries of pain that Lennon employed on 'Mother' are gone; all that remains is blank acceptance. The ghostly sound of the recording evokes a sense of Lennon's long-held emptiness, and this simple, childlike song of sorrow seems to emerge as if from the distant past, a spectral reminder of a long repressed event. Like many of the songs on *John Lennon/Plastic Ono Band*, 'My Mummy's Dead' is stripped of illusion. Influenced by the precision of Japanese Haiku poetry, Lennon's lyric reveals a chilling reality. Two takes of the song were recorded, the best being selected to close the album.

John Lennon/Plastic Ono Band data

The album was issued with custom Apple labels and a printed inner sleeve. British and American label designs differ. The British label offered a plain white silhouette of an apple on a black background with copyright perimeter print. American labels were based on a similar 'white apple' label, but rather than a silhouette the apple has the illusion of depth. The 'white apple' may have been an allusion to Yoko's contemporary artworks, many of which were painted white.

It was reissued by Capitol in 1978 with purple Capitol labels that had a large Capitol logo, in 1982 with black/colour band Capitol labels, and again in 1988 with purple Capitol labels.

The album was issued as an 8-track cartridge in Britain (8X-PCS 7124) and the USA (8XW-3372). In America it was also issued as a 7-inch reel-to-reel tape by Apple/Ampex (M-3372).

The album was scheduled for release on CD by EMI on July 20 1987 but delayed for several months due to problems with the original master tapes allegedly caused by Lennon and Spector's unorthodox recording techniques. The CD was put on hold for nine months while EMI worked on improving the sound quality. It was eventually issued in Britain and the USA on April 5 1988.

John Lennon/Plastic Ono Band was remixed and remastered at Abbey Road under Ono's supervision in spring/summer 2000 and issued by EMI with two bonus tracks and a new booklet on October 9 2000. MFSL Original Master Recordings also issued the remixed version, as an Ultradisc II 24 kt. gold CD in January 2004 (UDCD-759).

'MOTHER'

ISSUING 'Mother' as a single was a bold move. The recording is as harrowing to listen to as 'Cold Turkey', and it's hard to believe that many, if any, radio stations gave it primetime airplay. Nevertheless, Lennon was convinced that it was a commercial record, but conceded that if he could sell more records by singing about love than about his mother he would. So he was more interested in making a statement with this single than he was in selling records.

When issued as a single, the bells were removed and the song trimmed to 3:55. Unlike the album version, which is in stereo, the single is in mono. Japanese pressings, however, use the unedited album version and are in stereo.

'MOTHER' / 'WHY'
JOHN LENNON / YOKO ONO PLASTIC ONO BAND
US RELEASE December 28 1970; Apple APPLE 1827; chart high No.43.

• **'Why'** (Ono)
Yoko Ono (vocals), John Lennon (guitar), Klaus Voormann (bass), Ringo Starr (drums).
Recorded at Abbey Road Studios, London, England. Produced by John & Yoko.

The antithesis of Lennon's stately A-side, Ono's 'Why', from her companion *Plastic Ono Band* album, was selected for the record's B-side. A raucous conflation of avant-gardism and rock'n'roll, it features her free-form vocalising and some of Lennon's most explosive guitar playing. He said in interviews that Ono's singing had influenced his playing, and here the two are fused perfectly. Lennon's guitar howls like a banshee, matching the vocal perfectly. Speaking to Andy Peebles in 1980, Lennon recalled the song with some pride. "The fascinating thing is, even we didn't know where Yoko's voice started and where my guitar ended on the intro."

In the late 1970s, younger musicians who formed part of the emerging punk/new wave scene were discovering Ono's work for the first time. The B-52s owed much to her vocal style, and Lennon was quick to endorse them, but later bands, such as The Pixies, must have been influenced by his extraordinary playing on this record. Jimi Hendrix may have turned guitar playing into an art form, but Lennon's work on this track eclipses anything produced by Hendrix or any other guitar hero.

'Mother' data

The American issue had five label variations. The first has a light green Apple label; song title at 11 o'clock with composer credit below; '(From the Apple LP "John Lennon/Plastic Ono Band" SW-3372)' at 8 o'clock; 'Recorded in England' at 2 o'clock; and the artist's name 'John Lennon/Plastic Ono Band' centre bottom. The second variant has a dark green Apple label with identical text layout, and the third has the light green Apple label with identical text but a black star at 9 o'clock.

The fourth US label variant has a dark green Apple label; 'Recorded in England' at 10 o'clock; '(From the Apple LP "John Lennon/Plastic Ono Band" SW-3372)' at 9 o'clock; song title at 7 o'clock with composer credit below; artist's name 'John Lennon/Plastic Ono Band YOKO ONO/PLASTIC ONO BAND' centre bottom.

The fifth variant has a light green Apple label; 'MONO' at 11 o'clock; song title at 10 o'clock with composer credit below; '(From the Apple LP "John Lennon/Plastic Ono Band" SW-3372)' at 8 o'clock; artist's name 'John Lennon/Plastic Ono Band' at 2 o'clock.

'ANOTHER DAY'

WHILE John and Yoko were recovering from their primal therapy, Paul and Linda were busy recording in New York City. 'Another Day' was recorded during the sessions for *Ram* but had been previewed two years earlier while filming *Let It Be*. Although it had been written speculatively for The Beatles, as a solo single it provided a clear indication of what was to follow.

For the first time, the McCartneys' distinctive harmonies featured prominently. It was a deliberate attempt to create a unique McCartney style, a musical identity outside of The Beatles. "I wanted *our* sound," McCartney explained. "I wanted the amateur approach, something we could make ourselves and then work on. We've been writing many more songs and we're developing as a harmony team." He was pushing for Linda to play an active role in his career. He taught her to play keyboards and encouraged her as she had encouraged him a few months earlier. But his claim that she co-wrote 'Another Day' didn't wash with his publisher.

McCartney wasn't alone in wanting his wife to share songwriting credits and royalties: Lennon insisted that Ono had co-written some of his songs. As The Beatles' finances were in the hands of the official receivers, claims by McCartney and Lennon that their wives were contributing to their songs was little more than a ploy to double income from publishing. However, Sir Lew Grade, the new owner of Northern Songs, who published the Beatle catalogue, was having none of it.

McCartney told *Rolling Stone*: "Lew Grade suddenly saw his songwriting concessions – which he'd just paid an awful lot of money for, virtually to get hold of John and I – he suddenly saw that I was now claiming that I was writing half of my stuff with Linda, and that if I was writing half of it she was entitled to a pure half of it, no matter whether she was a recognised songwriter or not. I didn't think that that was important; I thought that whoever I worked with, no matter what the method of collaboration was, that person, if they did help me on the song, should have a portion of the song for helping me."

The lawsuit was settled with McCartney agreeing to make a programme for Grade's television company. The embarrassment of *James Paul McCartney* aside, Grade's lawsuit had at least one positive outcome: it encouraged Linda to write. Her first attempt at songwriting would be 'Seaside Woman', the result of pressure from both Grade and McCartney. "I did a song, 'Seaside Woman', right after we'd been to Jamaica," she recalled. "That's when ATV was suing us saying I was incapable of writing, so Paul said, 'Get out and write a song.'"

Behind its glossy facade, 'Another Day' is an acute examination of isolation and social alienation. In one brief verse and chorus, McCartney records the sense of repetition that overshadows the daily routine of the suburbanite. His epistle to social estrangement documents a daily treadmill of tedium determined by economic interest and sexual compulsion and reveals the obsessive nature of fantasies that we all engage in to obliterate time. The only escape is to hope and dream of the perfect lover, but even when the dream becomes reality, it's fleeting and ultimately frustrating. A song that maps the modern human condition, 'Another Day' comments on the loss of individualism and the way we vainly attempt to impose order on the chaotic reality of life.

'ANOTHER DAY' / 'OH WOMAN, OH WHY'
PAUL McCARTNEY
UK RELEASE February 19 1971; Apple R 5889; chart high No.2.
US RELEASE February 22 1971; Apple 1829; chart high No.5.

• **'Another Day'** (Mr & Mrs McCartney)
Paul McCartney (vocals, guitar, bass), Linda McCartney (backing vocals), Dave Spinoza or Hugh McCracken (guitars), Denny Seiwell (drums).
• **'Oh Woman, Oh Why'** (McCartney)
Paul McCartney (vocals, bass), Linda McCartney (backing vocals), Dave Spinoza or Hugh McCracken (guitars), Denny Seiwell (drums).
Both recorded at Columbia Studios, New York City, NY, USA. Both mixed at Sound Recorders, Los Angeles, CA, USA. Both produced by Paul and Linda McCartney.

Remarkably, it wasn't McCartney who selected 'Another Day' for release as a single but studio assistant Dixon Van Winkle. "We were sitting in Studio A2 one day listening to the takes and Paul asked me to pick the single," he recalled in *Mix*. "I had definite feelings about the record and was in love with 'Another Day'. Paul said, 'OK. 'Another Day' it is.' I mixed the track and David Crawford cut about 100 copies of it in a back room at A&R for the radio stations. The next day, when I heard it on the air, I realised it was a disaster. We got carried away with the bass part, and when it hit the radio station's compressor, it pumped like crazy. I learned that lesson real quick! But we never remixed the song, and Paul never said anything about it."

McCartney turns up the heat with 'Oh Woman, Oh Why', a tense, blusey rocker with a rip-roaring vocal. Economical basslines combine with Seiwell's thunderous drumming to establish a solid foundation upon which tight guitar lines interweave. McCartney's gritty vocal is one of his best and provides some raw and convincing authenticity to this blues-based rocker. Unusually for McCartney, 'Oh Woman, Oh Why' sees him questioning rather than celebrating womanhood. Rarely has he sounded so aggressive, which is particularly notable in light of the song's subject matter.

'Another Day' data

Apple issued 'Another Day' in Britain in generic Apple labels and a black paper sleeve. There were two label variants. Some copies have '*Joint interest claimed by McCartney Music Inc.' printed below the 'Northern Songs NCB' publishing credit; others have an additional claim '*Copyright also claimed by Maclen (Music) Ltd.' Apple issued demonstration copies with a large 'A' at 10 o'clock and 'DEMO RECORD NOT FOR SALE' on three lines above the spindle hole. When the single was reissued in the mid 1970s with black and silver Capitol 'dome' labels, the publishing was claimed by 'McCartney Music by arrangement with ATV Music Ltd'.

Several label variations were produced in America. The first has a dark green Apple label; bold type with 'STEREO' at 10 o'clock; 'Recorded in England' at 8 o'clock; song title and artist name centre bottom; publisher information, catalogue number, and producer's name on the right of the label. The second variant has a dark green Apple label; song title and composer credits at 10 o'clock; 'STEREO' at 8 o'clock; artist name and 'Recorded in England' centre bottom.

The third US label variant has a dark green Apple label; song title and composer credits at 11 o'clock on one line; 'STEREO' at nine o'clock; artist name and 'Recorded in England' centre bottom. The fourth has a light green Apple label; 'STEREO' at 9 o'clock; a black star at 8 o'clock; song title, songwriter, artist name, and 'Recorded in England' centre bottom. The fifth and last variant has a light green Apple label; song title and composer credits at 11 o'clock; 'STEREO' at 9 o'clock; artist name and 'Recorded in England' centre bottom.

Unique mono mixes of both A and B-side were produced for American AM radio stations and issued as a demonstration single (PRO-6193). Demonstration copies were issued with light green Apple labels with a black star, 'PROMOTIONAL RECORD' at 11 o'clock, and 'NOT FOR SALE' at 8 o'clock. The single was also issued in mono in France (2C006-04758M). Copies of the single manufactured in America with black and sliver Capitol 'dome' labels have 'Manufactured By MPL Communications, Inc.' added to the label perimeter text.

'POWER TO THE PEOPLE'

WHILE the McCartneys were in New York City, Lennon and Ono spent much of January 1971 in Japan, only returning to England at the insistence of the lawyers dealing with McCartney's High Court action to dissolve The Beatles. Upon their return, Lennon and Ono were interviewed for *Red Mole*, a left-wing magazine edited by Tariq Ali and Robin Blackburn.

Educated at Oxford, Ali became the face of British left-wing political activism. A vigorous protester against the war in Vietnam, he helped form the Vietnam Solidarity Campaign, eventually becoming its figurehead. Under his direction, the VSC became a highly visible protest group. He was inspired by what had been happening in America and focused on large-scale public demonstrations to voice opposition to the war. Unlike the Lennons, who championed non-violent means of protest, Ali advocated taking to the streets and if necessary engaging in violence.

Ali wrote in *The New Revolutionaries: A Handbook Of The*

International Radical Left: "The new revolutionaries were quite open about their aims: it was hypocritical to protest against violence at home while justifying it in Vietnam; we were not pacifists, and if a policeman hit us we would defend ourselves. Our violence was defensive – a response to the repressive violence of the state machine."

By the late 1960s, public demonstrations were becoming increasingly confrontational and violent. The VSC organised a protest on March 17 1968 that culminated outside the American Embassy in Grosvenor Square, London, and was the most violent to take place in Britain for years and probably decades. This was the type of protest the Lennons had spoken out against during their peace campaign. Yet two years later their whole political and philosophical outlook had changed. Now they embraced active intervention and endorsed the radical New Left.

Lennon had never fully engaged with politics, let alone thoughts of revolution. When he wrote and recorded 'Revolution' for The Beatles' *White Album* he was unable to commit to the idea. From the comfort of Abbey Road Studios, he told the world that when push came to shove they could "count me out/in". Yet by the time he was interviewed by Ali and Blackburn, his ambivalence appeared to have deserted him.

But Lennon was no fool. He knew how to manipulate the media and he told Ali and Blackburn exactly what they wanted to hear, which was not necessarily what he believed. Speaking to David Sheff in 1980, Lennon confessed that 'Power To The People' was his way of gaining their acceptance. "I felt I ought to write a song about what [Ali] was saying. That's why it didn't really come off. I was not thinking clearly about it. It was written in a state of being asleep and wanting to be loved by Tariq Ali and his ilk, you see. I have to admit to that so I won't call it hypocrisy. I couldn't write that today."

'Power To The People' openly contradicted his earlier role as peacemaker. But whether Lennon was acting hypocritically or not, he took to his new political commitments unreservedly. He donated money to worthy causes and attended several protest rallies. Yet, years later, Lennon felt troubled by his involvement with the New Left and described it as based on guilt. He told Andy Peebles in 1980: "Tariq Ali had kept coming round wanting money for the *Red Mole* or some magazine or other and I used to give anybody ... money kind of out of guilt. ... I kind of wrote 'Power To The People' in a way as a guilt song, you know."

The day after his interview with *Red Mole*, Lennon set about constructing a musical manifesto that he hoped would become a new people's anthem. As with 'Give Peace A Chance', the chorus is based on a simple slogan, ambiguous enough to be used by any group that wanted it. The verses offer nothing new or revolutionary; Lennon simply reinforces the old revolutionary war-cry by calling on the exploited to rise up and overthrow their oppressors. There is a concession to the emergent feminist movement, but despite Ono's presence, Lennon's feminism fails to convince.

Moving to the studio, Lennon began to develop the song, but it wasn't until Phil Spector intervened that it came alive. Early takes have all the basic elements in place; what Spector did was to exaggerate them. Essentially, he reworks the model he'd created for 'Instant Karma!'. The gospel-style backing vocals were developed into a full-blown choir. Bobby Keys' saxophone took the place of Alan White's dominant drumming. And with Spector's help, Lennon added an authoritative vocal, smothered in tape echo, that he'd been unable to capture on earlier takes. Spector's tour de force was to record the group's marching feet. This not only created a unique percussion effect but also evoked the sound of a street rally. If all this sounds unbearably heavy, it isn't. Spector took Lennon's rather pedestrian setting and transformed it into a funky groove, as suited to the street as it was the disco.

'Power To The People' was Lennon's first British single since 'Instant Karma!', released over a year earlier. The record should have been available in Britain on March 5 but was held up a week because of problems with Ono's B-side. Philip Brodie, managing Director of EMI, thought the lyrics to that song "distasteful" and requested that they be changed. For the US release, 'Open Your Box' was replaced with 'Touch Me', from *Yoko Ono/Plastic Ono Band*, which delayed the release until March 22.

With the prospect of having another song banned by their own record company, Lennon and Ono reworked 'Open Your Box' to mask Ono's apparently distasteful lyric. Although it's been suggested that she re-recorded her vocal, the offending words were simply hidden under washes of echo. Issued on her album *Fly*, where it was titled 'Hirake', the song's offending lyrics were clearly audible. EMI didn't seem too concerned about it appearing on an expensive double album – or perhaps they were fooled into believing it was a new composition. Either way, the Lennons also managed to have the offending lyrics printed on the inner sleeve, albeit backwards.

They each had their own ideas as to why the song came in for so much criticism. Lennon thought it was because of the ambiguous nature of the word 'box'. "I don't know what the hell 'box' means in America," he said. "Apparently it means crotch, or whatever."

Ono thought it was because the male-dominated music business simply could not accept this kind of song from a woman. "This song has been banned and I believe it is because I am a woman. One of the reasons is because the word 'box' has many different meanings, especially in America, where it refers to a certain part of a woman's body. If a man makes a statement like that, he can easily get away with it. I think the fact that it was a woman supposedly making an obscene statement [was what] really shocked people. Men sing about legs a lot. ... The song is not

'POWER TO THE PEOPLE' / 'OPEN YOUR BOX'
JOHN LENNON / YOKO ONO PLASTIC ONO BAND
UK RELEASE March 12 1971; Apple R 5892; chart high No.7.

'POWER TO THE PEOPLE' / 'TOUCH ME'
JOHN LENNON / YOKO ONO PLASTIC ONO BAND
US RELEASE March 22 1971; Apple APPLE 1830; chart high No.11.

- **'Power To The People'** (Lennon)
John Lennon (vocals, guitar, piano), Klaus Voormann (bass), Alan White (drums), Billy Preston (piano, keyboards), Bobby Keys (saxophone), Rosetta Hightower and unknown others (backing vocals).
Recorded at Abbey Road Studios, London, England. Produced by Phil Spector and John & Yoko.
- **'Open Your Box'** (Ono)
Yoko Ono (vocals), John Lennon (guitar), Klaus Voormann (bass), Jim Gordon (drums).
Recorded at Trident Studios, London, England. Produced by John & Yoko.
- **'To7uch Me'** (Ono)
Yoko Ono (vocals), John Lennon (guitar), Klaus Voormann (bass), Ringo Starr (drums).
Recorded at Abbey Road Studios. Produced by John & Yoko.

really that crude, and then it's banned, just like that. 'Box' is a very philosophical song, about opening everything up: minds, windows, your country, it's sort of like 'We're All Water'."

The Plastic Ono Band attempted to record 'Open Your Box' while working on the *Plastic Ono Band* albums. A slower, looser alternative seven-minute version was issued on the Rykodisc reissue of *Yoko Ono/Plastic Ono Band*. It's an early take, recorded at Abbey Road, but lacks the raw power that Plastic Ono Band captured with their remake.

Recorded at Trident Studios, the remake transformed Ono's provocative song into an avant-garde powerhouse. Lennon's guitar stutters over a tight, funky rhythm section like a needle being dragged across a record. He has disposed of the blues-based riffing that usually provided him with a musical crutch. In its place there's a freeform vortex of sound. Ricocheting frenziedly, his playing somehow locks into the rhythm track and perfectly complements the unique vocal.

'Open Your Box' would be performed at Lennon's 1972 One To One concert with Elephant's Memory during both matinee and evening shows, but live readings of the track have yet to appear commercially.

'Open Your Box' was one of several songs that Ono revisited and updated with a contemporary remix. The reworked version proved to be even more successful than the original, spending seven weeks in the *Billboard* Club Play charts. Remixed by the Vermont collective Orange Factory, it was issued in Britain by Parlophone (CDMIND001) on June 24 2002. In the USA it was issued by Mind Train Records as a 12-inch single (MTR 001) in 2001.

The original US B-side, 'Touch Me', was taken from Ono's *Plastic Ono Band* album and finds Lennon, Starr, and Voormann exploring a jazz-rock fusion, their investigations into group dynamics producing a wave of sound to support Ono's vocal modulations. These early Plastic Ono Band compositions sound improvised – which they were. For Ono, the creative impulse is bound to the idea of reciprocity and incompleteness. It's difficult to imagine her having much time for the word 'closure'. She is more interested in openings.

Improvisation was merely the first step in Yoko Ono's creative praxis. The listener is supposed to extend the creative process by adding to the work. Speaking to *Mojo* magazine in July 2002, she commented: "I called it Unfinished Music, which meant that you were supposed to put your own thing on, in the same way that remixers do today." This 'additional act' was intended to elicit positive reciprocity. By extending this idea to other areas of their lives, people could contribute to and improve the world for the better.

'Power To The People' data

British pressings were issued with a monochrome picture sleeve with red text. Initial pressings featured the full green Apple A-side label on both sides of the record. Two variants were issued: the first version features a dark green Apple label with 'Copyright also claimed by Maclen (Music) Ltd.'; the second has a light green Apple label but without 'Copyright also claimed by Maclen (Music) Ltd.'

Later pressings assigned the A-side label to Ono and the white sliced B-side label to Lennon. A full-colour version of the picture cover was used for the American release and four label variations were issued. The first has a light green Apple label; song title at 11 o'clock with composer credit below; 'STEREO' at 9 o'clock with a black star below; artist's name 'JOHN LENNON PLASTIC ONO BAND' centre bottom with 'Recorded in England' below. The second has a dark green Apple label with song title top centre and composer credit below right; publisher credits at 9 o'clock and 'STEREO' below; artist's name 'JOHN LENNON PLASTIC ONO BAND' centre bottom.

The third US label variant has a light green Apple label, with song title at 10 o'clock with composer credit below; 'STEREO' at 9 o'clock; artist's name 'John Lennon/Plastic Ono Band' centre bottom with 'Recorded in England' below. And the fourth variant has a light green Apple label, with song title at 11 o'clock and composer credit below; 'STEREO' at 9 o'clock; artist's name 'John Lennon/Plastic Ono Band' centre bottom with 'Recorded in England' below.

RAM

ALTHOUGH Lennon and McCartney may have considered themselves as alike as chalk and cheese, they had more in common than they might have cared to admit. Like John and Yoko, Paul and Linda withdrew from the public gaze. They moved into a small, ramshackle cottage on the west coast of Scotland. Rejecting bachelorhood and a bohemian lifestyle, McCartney wrote about the simple pleasures he found there. His move not only marked a break with cosmopolitanism, it offered temporary escape from Apple and The Beatles. So great was the pressure on him from the break-up of The Beatles that McCartney suffered a physical and mental breakdown. "I was going through a bad time, what I suspect was almost a nervous breakdown," he recalled. "I remember lying awake at nights shaking, which has not happened to me since. I had so much in me that I couldn't express, and it was just very nervy times, very difficult."

Like Lennon, McCartney wrote about his experiences and feelings. His songs reflected both the pleasure and pain he perceived in the months after the Beatles split. They also expressed a growing discontentment with his former bandmates and in particular John Lennon.

Lennon and McCartney had been sniping at one another for months. They used the music press to rail at one another, and their petulant squabbling inevitably found its way into their songs and onto their albums. The early 1970s found all four Beatles using their songwriting skills to comment on the others. Ringo recorded 'Back Off Boogaloo', which was also apparently aimed at Paul, and George included 'Sue Me Sue You Blues', a wry comment on The Beatles' business troubles, on his *Living In The Material World* album. Along with Lennon's *Imagine* album ('How Do You Sleep?' was a barbed critique of McCartney), *Ram* marked a low point in the ex-Beatles' relationship. Voicing their feelings in public was not the best way to manage the situation. Although each used songwriting as therapy, it was far from curative.

McCartney was in a bullish mood (or should that be ramish?). He was intent on telling his side of the story, and nobody was going to stop him. For him, the album's title, *Ram*, summarised exactly how he felt. "Ram seemed like a good word," he explained, "cos it not only meant ram forward, press on, be positive, that aspect of it. I also, as a lot of people probably know, am well into sheep, and have been for a number of years," he laughed, "since I got my Scottish farm and inherited a flock. So the ram being the male sheep was kind of good and sort of male and that kind of stuff."

To showcase his new approach, McCartney issued 'Another Day' as a standalone single. While this found favour with the public, the album received less than favourable reviews from the critics. Of the ex-Beatles, they preferred Lennon's raw primitivism to McCartney's urbane pop. Only months before McCartney released *Ram*, Lennon issued his *Plastic Ono Band* album and 'Power To The People' single, both of which offered intense, gutsy rock'n'roll. McCartney's welcoming pop, described by one critic as "suburban rock'n'roll", was the antithesis of Lennon's intense, angst-ridden primitivism. McCartney characteristically shrugged off negative criticism, saying: "I still read the notices and stuff and they're usually bum ones when you're expecting them to be great. Like after *Ram*." Not every review was negative. Lon Goddard, writing in *Record Mirror*, gave the album a favourable notice and suggested that Paul and Linda's harmonies were on a par with those of The Everly Brothers.

Although Linda had contributed to the *McCartney* album, *Ram* was her baptism of fire. "God, I tell you I worked her on the album," McCartney recalled. "Because she hadn't done an awful lot, so it was a little bit out of tune. I was not too pleasant to live with, I suppose, then. She was all right; she took it. She understood that it had to be good and you couldn't let any shit through. I gave her a hard time, I must say, but we were pleased with the results; it just meant we really forced it. [We] worked on all the harmonies even if they were hard harmonies – just stuck on it. Elton John later said somewhere that he thought it was the best harmonies he'd heard in a long while."

Dixon Van Winkle, who worked on the *Ram* sessions as a studio assistant, recalled how the pair worked on their harmonies. "The interplay between Paul and Linda was sweet, especially when they were on-mic. Linda actually came up with some parts on her own – the entire backing vocals on 'Uncle Albert/Admiral Halsey' consists of the two of them – but when she needed a hand, Paul was great with her."

Linda's reward for all her hard work was equal billing – the record was credited to Paul And Linda McCartney. She also received co-author credits for several songs. As McCartney explained: "Linda and I have been writing songs together – and my publishers are suing because they don't believe she wrote them with me. You know: suddenly she marries him and suddenly she's writing songs. 'Oh, sure (wink, wink). Oh, sure, she's writing songs.'"

While Sir Lew Grade saw this as an infringement of his agreement with McCartney, George Martin thought Linda's influence was adversely affecting Paul's writing. "I don't think Linda is any substitute for John Lennon," he remarked. Obviously, Linda couldn't compete with Lennon as a writer, musician, or collaborator. Nevertheless, she fulfilled the key roles of performer and muse. But whether this justified a co-author credit is questionable.

Paul, Linda, and family few to New York City on January 3 1971 to begin work on the album. Auditions began two days later in one of the less glamorous parts of Manhattan. Everyone, no matter what their reputation, was up for audition. Guitarist Dave Spinoza was apparently none too pleased at having to audition; his reputation as one of New York's top session players was normally enough to secure any job. However, McCartney was taking no chances, and reputation alone was not enough. As well as acquiring Spinoza, he secured the services of guitarist Hugh McCracken and drummer Denny Seiwell, who stayed with the McCartneys until late 1973.

Recording began on January 10 1971 with McCartney quickly establishing a professional, workmanlike atmosphere. According to David Spinoza, he instigated a regime of set hours. "In the studio, he's very businesslike. He came in at nine every morning. We'd listen to what we'd done the day before, then it was eight hours of just playing." Keeping to this routine, the group reportedly recorded 21 songs between January and March 1971. Of those, two were released as a standalone single ('Another Day' / 'Oh Woman Oh Why?'), 12 featured on *Ram*, and two would appear on *Red Rose Speedway* ('Get On The Right Thing' and 'Little Lamb Dragonfly'). 'Little Woman Love' appeared as the B-side of 'Mary Had A Little Lamb', 'A Love For You' was issued on the *In-Laws* soundtrack, while 'Sunshine Sometime', 'Rode All Night', and 'Hey Diddle' remain unreleased.

Basic tracks were recorded as a three-piece with McCartney usually playing piano, Seiwell drums, and Spinoza guitar. McCartney then overdubbed additional instrumentation on to the basic track before adding his and Linda's vocals. After recording at A&R Studios, where the bulk of the album was made, they moved to Columbia Studios, also in New York, for additional overdubs, mainly the orchestral parts. Final mixing and programming was completed in Los Angeles at Sound Recorders.

Ram songs

The album begins with two words directed at John Lennon: "Piss off." McCartney explained: "Yeah. Piss off, cake. Like, a piece of cake becomes piss off cake, and it's nothing, it's so harmless really, just little digs." His tirade didn't go unnoticed and, unsurprisingly, Lennon took 'Too Many People' as a personal attack. Although some suggested that this was just another case of Lennon's paranoia – he had good reasons to be paranoid – one look at the song's first verse confirms his suspicions.

McCartney later admitted that his lyric, every bit as vitriolic as Lennon's later 'How Do You Sleep?', was indeed aimed at his former partner. "I remember there was one little reference to John

RAM
PAUL AND LINDA McCARTNEY
SIDE 1 'Too Many People', '3 Legs', 'Ram On', 'Dear Boy', 'Uncle Albert/Admiral Halsey', 'Smile Away'.
SIDE 2 'Heart Of The Country', 'Monkberry Moon Delight', 'Eat At Home', 'Long Haired Lady', 'Ram On', 'The Back Seat Of My Car'.
UK RELEASE May 21 1971; LP Apple PAS 10003; 8-track cartridge Apple 8X-PAS 10003; chart high No.1.
US RELEASE May 17 1971; LP Apple SMAS-3375; 8-track cartridge Apple 8XW3375; chart high No.2.

• **'Too Many People'** (McCartney)
Paul McCartney (vocals, bass), Linda McCartney (backing vocals), Dave Spinoza or Hugh McCracken (guitars), Denny Seiwell (drums).
• **'3 Legs'** (McCartney)
Paul McCartney (vocals, bass), Linda McCartney (backing vocals), Dave Spinoza or Hugh McCracken (guitars), Denny Seiwell (drums).
• **'Ram On'** (McCartney)
Paul McCartney (piano, keyboards, ukulele, vocals), Linda McCartney (backing vocals).
• **'Dear Boy'** (Paul and Linda McCartney)
Paul McCartney (vocals, bass, piano), Linda McCartney (backing vocals), Dave Spinoza or Hugh McCracken (guitars), Denny Seiwell (drums).
• **'Uncle Albert / Admiral Halsey'** (Paul and Linda McCartney)
Paul McCartney (vocals, bass), Linda McCartney (backing vocals), Dave Spinoza or Hugh McCracken (guitars), Denny Seiwell (drums), The New York Philharmonic Orchestra.
• **'Smile Away'** (McCartney)
Paul McCartney (vocals, keyboards, bass), Linda McCartney (backing vocals), Dave Spinoza or Hugh McCracken (guitars), Denny Seiwell (drums).
• **'Heart Of The Country'** (Paul and Linda McCartney)
Paul McCartney (vocals, bass, guitar), Linda McCartney (backing vocals), Dave Spinoza or Hugh McCracken (guitars), Denny Seiwell (drums).
• **'Monkberry Moon Delight'** (Paul and Linda McCartney)
Paul McCartney (vocals, piano, bass), Linda McCartney (backing vocals), Dave Spinoza or Hugh McCracken (guitars), Denny Seiwell (drums).
Recorded at Columbia Studios. Mixed at Sound Recorders.
• **'Eat At Home'** (Paul and Linda McCartney)
Paul McCartney (vocals, bass), Linda McCartney (backing vocals), Dave Spinoza or Hugh McCracken (guitars), Denny Seiwell (drums).
• **'Long Haired Lady'** (McCartney)
Paul McCartney (vocals, keyboards, bass), Linda McCartney (backing vocals), Dave Spinoza or Hugh McCracken (guitars), Denny Seiwell (drums), The New York Philharmonic Orchestra.
• **'The Back Seat Of My Car'** (McCartney)
Paul McCartney (vocals, piano, bass), Linda McCartney (backing vocals), Dave Spinoza or Hugh McCracken (guitars), Denny Seiwell (drums), The New York Philharmonic Orchestra.
All recorded at Columbia Studios, New York City, NY, USA, except 'Uncle Albert / Admiral Halsey', 'Long Haired Lady', and 'The Back Seat Of My Car' recorded at Columbia Studios (tracking) and A&R Studios (orchestra), New York City, NY, USA. All mixed at Sound Recorders, Los Angeles, CA, USA.
All produced by Paul and Linda McCartney.

in the whole thing," he explained. "He'd been doing a lot of preaching, and it got up my nose a little bit. I wrote 'Too many people preaching practices' I think is the line. I mean, that was a little dig at John and Yoko. There wasn't anything else on it that was about them. Oh, there was 'Yoko took your lucky break and broke it in two.'"

More than a "little dig", this was McCartney at his most acerbic. Thankfully, he had the good sense to alter his original reference to Yoko, otherwise he may never have spoken with Lennon again. Lennon replied in kind. His *Imagine* album would include the cutting 'How Do You Sleep?' and a postcard depicting him grappling with a pig – a parody of the *Ram* cover.

After the opening 'Too Many People' on *Ram* comes '3 Legs', a song loaded with ambiguous metaphors, which could be read as a commentary on the break-up of The Beatles and a thinly veiled attack by McCartney on his former bandmates. While his lyric seems to address his feelings about The Beatles' fall from grace, it also alludes to freedom and redemption, which he'd found in the wilds of Scotland. Like much of what he'd written for *Ram*, it finds him attempting to reveal his innermost feelings while at the same time concealing them in metaphors and encrypted symbolism.

Guitarist Spinoza recalled working on the song and shed some light on McCartney's recording technique. "There's one track, which is a cute thing, a blues tune, which I had fun doing. '3 Legs', it's called. We both played acoustic and sometimes Paul played piano but never played bass while we were there. He overdubbed the bass later. It was a bit weird, because bass, drums, and guitar would have been more comfortable."

In 'Ram On', McCartney reflects on the here and now and suggests that he/we should live for the moment. Discarding the florid piano introduction in favour of a simple strummed ukulele, recalling the music hall tradition of simpler times, his arrangement suggests a rejection of flamboyance in favour of a simpler lifestyle.

'Ram On' fades midway and returns on side 2, thereby establishing what would become a long-standing practice for McCartney of bookending albums with a reprised musical theme to create an impression of continuity.

At the time, some read 'Dear Boy' as yet another critique of Lennon, and at first glance the lyric appears to confirm this. But McCartney later said: "'Dear Boy' wasn't getting at John, [it] was actually a song to Linda's ex-husband: 'I guess you never knew what you had missed.' I never told him that, which was lucky because he's since committed suicide. And it was a comment about him, cos I did think, 'Gosh, you know, she's so amazing, I suppose you didn't get it.'"

'Dear Boy' is, of course, as much about Paul and Linda as it is about her ex-husband, and in its own way it's as autobiographically revealing as McCartney gets. As with several songs from the earlier *McCartney*, 'Dear Boy' reveals that, post-Beatles, McCartney's mental well-being remained fragile and that it was only Linda's stabilising presence that pulled him from the abyss of despair.

Turning to his family for inspiration, McCartney called on his Uncle Albert, a colourful relation who, he recalled, "used to quote the Bible to everyone when he got drunk". 'Uncle Albert/Admiral Halsey' was fashioned from several unfinished tunes – the song has 12 distinct motifs – that were combined to complete the song. McCartney was well versed in this practice and often fused unfinished fragments when unable to complete a composition. He had taken this to its logical conclusion when various unfinished songs were brought together to form the 'long medley' on *Abbey Road*. Like the 'long medley', 'Uncle Albert/Admiral Halsey' has enough melodic twists and turns to keep the listener engaged, and the restrained use of the New York Philharmonic Orchestra, arranged by George Martin, further enhances the song's Beatle-esque qualities.

Guitarist Hugh McCracken had recorded several songs with McCartney, always under his direct supervision. However, when he came to record the basic tracks for 'Uncle Albert/Admiral Halsey', McCartney let the guitarist write his own parts. "This song represented a breakthrough in our musical relationship," McCracken recalled in *Mix*. "Paul is a genius. He sees and hears everything he wants, and would give specific instructions to me and the drummer. But he didn't know what he wanted the guitar part to be like on this song. I asked him to trust me, and he did. After I came up with the parts, he was very pleased. For the rest of the record, Paul let me try things out before making any suggestions."

In 'Smile Away' McCartney examines the apparent hypocrisy of his adversaries (Klein and the other ex-Beatles) and finds them wanting. While each would claim otherwise, the McCartney-Lennon nexus was stronger than either of them cared to accept. When it came to slagging one another off, each expressed himself in remarkably similar ways. McCartney often attempted to conceal this side of his personality, but 'Smile Away', like Lennon's 'How Do You Sleep?', reveals that he was as capable of vitriol as his former partner.

'Heart Of The Country' finds McCartney re-examining the symbolic divide between town and country, a subject he had explored before in 'Mother Nature's Son'. The notion of getting back to the country in order to 'get it together' was adopted by many musicians in the late 1960s and early 1970s. The Beatles, who could afford it more than most, became increasingly aware of the need to escape the pressures of fame, and they sought fulfilment through spiritual rather than material means. Presented in a breezy country style, 'Heart Of The Country' adumbrates McCartney's belief in that notion. A mini manifesto, it documents the changes and benefits to his mental and physical wellbeing brought forth by a bucolic lifestyle. Delighting in his new-found facility, McCartney employs a jazz-styled bridge, complete with scat singing, to drive the point home.

He was motivated to write 'Monkberry Moon Delight' through a fascination with his children's malapropisms and a fondness for the songsmiths Leiber and Stoller. As he explained: "When my kids were young they used to call milk 'monk' for whatever reason that kids do – I think it's magical the way that kids can develop better names for things than the real ones. In fact, as a joke, Linda and I still occasionally refer to an object by that child-language name. So, monk was always milk, and monkberry moon delight was a fantasy drink, rather like 'Love Potion No. 9,' hence the line in the song 'sipping monkberry moon delight.' It was a fantasy milk shake."

It's a light-hearted romp of a song, full of surreal imagery, its antecedents lying in The Beatles' delight with chance and instantaneity. From the mid 1960s, Lennon and McCartney's lyrics began to read like surrealist poetry. Jumbled allusions to sensory experiences ('Strawberry Fields Forever') and multiple self-referencing ('Glass Onion') crept into their songs. Like the Surrealists before them, they delighted in playing games to generate random coincidences, which they would use to leap from one idea to another.

'Monkberry Moon Delight' was written in the same spontaneous way. McCartney used his children's words as a springboard for free association. Look for meaning if you wish, but his lyric was intended to confuse. His imagery defies logic; disparate and incongruous, it is pure automatism. The Beatles knew that almost everything they wrote would be analysed until every last drop of meaning had been squeezed from it. The cross-referencing they fed into their lyrics was a game they played to see how much meaning could be read into something that resulted from chance. McCartney replays that game here, with obvious delight.

Much of what McCartney chose to write about in the immediate post-Beatles period focused either on Linda or on family life. So why shouldn't he write about the delights of home cooking? Well, that's exactly what he did, almost. 'Eat At Home' finds him once again extolling the virtues of domestic bliss and, of course, the love of a good woman. Influenced by his hero, Buddy Holly, McCartney's upbeat slice of retro-pop was so popular in some territories that it was issued as a single.

'Long Haired Lady' was written as a tribute to Linda but fails to match earlier love songs dedicated to her. When Lennon wrote about Yoko or Harrison about Patti, both managed to avoid the overt sentimentality of McCartney's heartfelt but insipid lyric. If the best he could do was to describe Linda as his "sweet little lass" (patronising) or "long haired lady" (superficial), then George Martin was right: Paul's songwriting could be uninspired.

'The Back Seat Of My Car' may have been intended for *Abbey Road* as it was one of several new compositions that McCartney previewed while filming *Let It Be* at Twickenham Studios. However, like many songs presented at this time, it was held back for a solo project.

McCartney's early readings of the song were peppered with jokey allusions to The Beach Boys, which he developed while recording the song in New York. A homage to the fictionalised fantasy America of his youth, 'The Back Seat Of My Car' is an idealised expression of teenage love: its visual counterpart is the squeaky-clean, formulaic, romantic comedies that populated 1950s cinema.

Explaining the song, he said: "'The Back Seat Of My Car' is the ultimate teenage song, and even though it was a long time since I was a teenager and had to go to a girl's dad and explain myself, it's that kind of meet-the-parents song. It's a good old driving song. And obviously 'back seat' is snogging, making love." However, unlike the lightweight films to which it alludes, 'The Back Seat Of My Car' has substance and weight. A song on a grand, elegant scale, its sweeping range gives it a celebratory feel. Its repeated refrain, "We believe that we can't be wrong", supports this upbeat theme. Unsurprisingly Lennon read it as another personal slight. His reply was typical. "Well," he said, "I believe that you could just be wrong." Although it had little to do with their feuding, that Lennon could read it as such says much about the state of their relationship at the time.

Ram data

In Britain, *Ram* was issued by Apple with generic Apple A and B-side labels, in a gatefold sleeve designed by McCartney. American pressings were issued with light or dark green Apple labels in three variations: credited to 'Paul and Linda McCartney', Apple label with small Capitol logo within perimeter print on B-side; credited to 'Paul and Linda McCartney', Apple label with 'MFD BY APPLE RECORD INC' perimeter print on B-side; or unsliced Apple B-side labels on both sides of the record.

The LP was reissued in the mid 1970s with black and silver Capitol 'dome' labels, in Britain and America. In the early 1980s, Columbia reissued the LP (JC-36479 and PC-36479).

Capitol/Apple issued *Ram* on 8-track in Britain (8X-PAS 10003) and the USA (8XW 3375). When Columbia obtained the rights to McCartney's back catalogue in the 1980s it reissued the 8-track (JCA 36479). Apple/Ampex issued *Ram* in America as a stereo 7-inch reel-to-reel tape (L-3375).

EMI issued the album on CD in Britain on its Capitol imprint on April 25 1987 and issued a remastered edition (CDPMCOL2) on July 7 1993. In America, Capitol issued the CD (CDP 7 46612 2) on January 17 1988 and DCC Compact Classics issued a gold CD (GZS-1037) in 1993.

To promote *Ram*, Apple issued mono pressings of the LP (MAS-3375) to American radio stations. The promotional album was mastered from an alternative mono mix of the album, which has yet to be made commercially available. (The LP was issued in mono in Brazil, although this was more probably a simple mono reduction of the stereo master rather than the McCartney-sanctioned mono mix used for the American promo LP.) However, it has been widely bootlegged, although all unofficial sources have been dubbed from a vinyl source.

Apple also issued a promotional 12-inch single (SPRO 6210) to US radio stations. The disc featured 15 versions of 'Now Hear This Song Of Mine', which was written specifically to promote the album. The disc was issued with two letters from McCartney Productions in either the commercial LP cover or a plain white cover. Original copies of the disc were banded evenly and each song 'paused' at the end for radio convenience. Counterfeit copies were manufactured with uneven spacing and played straight through (and some were on coloured vinyl).

BRUNG TO EWE

WHILE working on *Ram*, Paul and Linda recorded 'Now Hear This Song Of Mine', an extended jingle designed to promote the album. Fifteen versions of the song, ranging in length from 30 seconds to just over a minute, were issued on a 12-inch promotional record. Unlike Britain, which at the time had only one national radio station playing rock music, the USA had hundreds, all clamouring for exclusive material. It would have been impossible for the McCartneys to visit them all, so issuing a promotional record through MPL's New York office got round the problem of supply and demand. The 12-inch one-sided record, titled *Brung To You By*, was issued either in the commercial *Ram* LP cover or in a plain white sleeve. It was accompanied by two letters, one from Paul and Linda, the other from their production company.

'GOD SAVE US'

OZ MAGAZINE was a mainspring of the British underground press, along with *International Times* (which received financial assistance from McCartney). *Oz*'s mixture of satire and 'underground titbits' blossomed to take in more substantial issues such as feminism. Under the psychedelic eye of art director Martin Sharp, who designed many of the magazine's more colourful covers, it defined the counterculture scene and its values. As the magazine's layout grew increasingly psychedelic and difficult to read, it wasn't so much what it said but how it said it that was important. Because of its alternative views, the authorities soon took an interest in the magazine, but it wasn't until issue 28, the *School Kids* issue, that the magazine finally felt the full weight of the law.

BRUNG TO EWE BY
PAUL AND LINDA McCARTNEY
US RELEASE Apple 12-inch promotional record SPRO-6210.

• **'Now Hear This Song Of Mine'**
Various personnel.
Recorded at A&R Studios and Columbia Studios, New York City, NY, USA, and Sound Recorders, Los Angeles, CA, USA.
Produced by Paul and Linda McCartney.

The editor, Richard Neville, felt that the magazine had grown boring. With the intention of introducing some new blood, he placed an open invitation in issue 26 to anyone under the age of 18 interested in editing an issue of the magazine. It should be made clear that the *School Kids* issue was made by kids, not for them. Consequently, these adolescent editors, who were given the freedom to do whatever they liked, produced a magazine full of typical sixth-form toilet humour. The *School Kids* edition hit the streets in April 1970 with scarcely a ripple of interest from the powers that be.

However, two months later and the *Oz* offices were visited by the Obscene Publications Squad. Then, on August 18, *Oz* was served with a summons for "publishing an obscene magazine". The '*Oz* Three' – Richard Neville, Jim Anderson, and Felix Dennis – were prosecuted in what became the longest obscenity trial to be held in Britain. The three editors were found guilty on four charges, fined, and given prison sentences of varying lengths. However, they spent little time in prison before being granted bail. Their convictions were overturned on appeal, but the Establishment won the day. Although *Oz* limped on for another two years, by prosecuting the magazine the government had effectively hammered another nail in the counterculture coffin.

To help pay their legal costs, the magazine organised the Friends Of *Oz* to create press kits, hold benefits, and raise money. Stan Demidjuk was one of those entrusted with running the fund, and he knew John Lennon. Like Tariq Ali and Robin Blackburn before him, Demidjuk approached Lennon for help. Typically, Lennon's support was generous, and he agreed to write and record a song, donating all royalties to *Oz*, as well as attending a march in support of the 'Oz Three' and recording a special message of encouragement.

Lennon told *Sounds*: "Stan and some people from *Oz* rang up and said, 'Will you make us a record?' and I thought, 'Well, I can't' because I'm all tied up contractually and I didn't know how to do it. So then we got down to would I write a song for them? I think [Yoko and I] wrote it the same night, didn't we? We wrote it together and the B-side. First of all we wrote it as 'God Save Oz', you know 'God Save Oz from it all', but then we decided they wouldn't really know what we were talking about in America so we changed it back to 'us'."

Lennon fashioned a song that, lyrically at least, reiterated much of what he'd said with 'Power To The People'. He began by recording a rough demo, fleshing out his unfinished lyric with ad libs. Having completed the song, he set about recording both sides of the record at his newly built recording studio, jokingly named Ascot Sound Studios (ASS), in his Tittenhurst Park home near Ascot in Berkshire. Some confusion surrounds exactly who played what on the recording, as several people from *Oz* magazine augmented Lennon's choice of professional musicians.

As usual, Lennon recorded the basic track live in the studio, laying down a guide vocal with each take before it was replaced by another singer. Magic Michael, a regular on the hippie benefit circuit, was the first choice, but he was replaced by Bill Elliot because, as Lennon explained, "We got one singer in, and he was all right but he'd never had much experience recording – or singing actually, because he needed some experience singing and holding vaguely round the note. I can't hold a note – all my songs are all sung out of tune, but I can get fairly near it sometimes. This guy was way off, but it didn't work, so then I sang it just to show him how to sing it, how it should go, and we got this guy that Mal [Evans] had found in a group called Half-breed or something, and he sounded like Paul. So I thought, 'That's a commercial sound,' – it would have been nice to have Paul's voice singing 'God Save Us' – but the guy imitated more my demo, so he sounds like himself because he doesn't sound like me really, but he doesn't sound like Paul either."

Lennon's guide-vocal version of the song was later released on the *John Lennon Anthology*. Bill Elliot found fame a few years later as one half of Splinter, who recorded for George Harrison's Dark Horse label.

'Do The Oz' is a lazy remake of the old 'Hokey Cokey' dancing song. Lennon may have based his song on it as a sly reference to the *School Kids* edition of *Oz*. But like the *School Kids* issue, 'Do The Oz' was not intended for kiddies. The hokey cokey never sounded like this. Lennon changed the original lyric, but only slightly. Besides instructing the listener to put their left arm in and right arm out, Lennon urges us to vote the left-wing in and take the right-wing out.

Lennon's nightmarish B-side is as dark and menacing as the A-side is bright and auspicious. This was music for a new, disturbing dance craze, a counterculture remake of the original, intended to freak-out the Establishment.

Speaking to *Rolling Stone*, Ono recalled: "John and I actually once were thinking, 'Why don't we create a dance, you know, a dance movement, and put the instructions of how to do this new dance on the back of an album.' And he started to roll on the floor, trying to find a unique kind of action. But it just didn't happen. It was a bit difficult."

'Do The Oz' was included as a bonus track on the reissue of *John Lennon/Plastic Ono Band* released in 2000.

'God Save Us' data

Although this was Lennon's project, to avoid the impression that it was his official follow-up to 'Power To The People', the record was credited to Bill Elliot & The Elastic Oz Band. Singer Bill Elliot not only received top billing but appeared on the front cover of the picture sleeve. The group photograph on the reverse of the sleeve is of various individuals associated with *Oz* magazine. They are (left to right) back row: Sue Miles, Jim Anderson, Stan Demidjuk, Felix Dennis; front row: Debbie Knight, Bill Elliot.

Unlike previous singles, there is little difference between British and American releases. However, American pressings were issued with three label variations. The first has a dark green Apple label; song title at 10 o'clock on three lines with composer credit below; 'STEREO' at 8 o'clock; artist's name 'BILL ELLIOT AND ELASTIC OZ BAND' centre bottom in small upper case text.

The second variant has a dark green Apple label with song title in bold at 11 o'clock with composer credit below; 'STEREO' at 9 o'clock; artist's name 'BILL ELLIOT AND ELASTIC OZ BAND' in bold centre bottom. And the third label variant has a light green Apple label with 'STEREO' at 9 o'clock; song title with composer credit below and artist's name 'BILL ELLIOT AND ELASTIC OZ BAND' centre bottom.

In the USA, Apple issued promotional copies with light green Apple labels with 'NOT FOR SALE' at 10 o'clock; 'STEREO' at 9 o'clock; 'PROMOTIONAL RECORD' at 7 o'clock; a black star appears at 2 o'clock; and the song title with composer credit below and artist's name 'BILL ELLIOT AND ELASTIC OZ BAND' centre bottom.

'GOD SAVE US' / 'DO THE OZ'
BILL ELLIOT & THE ELASTIC OZ BAND
UK RELEASE July 16 1971; Apple APPLE 36; failed to chart.
US RELEASE July 7 1971; Apple APPLE 1835; failed to chart.

- **'God Save Us'** (Lennon, Ono)
Bill Elliot (vocals), John Lennon (guitar), Klaus Voormann (bass), Ringo Starr (drums), Bobby Keys (saxophone), Diane (keyboards).
Recorded at Ascot Sound Studios, Tittenhurst Park, Sunninghill, near Ascot, England. Produced by John, Yoko, Mal Evans, and Phil Spector.
- **'Do The Oz'** (Lennon, Ono)
John Lennon (vocals, acoustic guitar), Klaus Voormann (bass), Ringo Starr (drums), Bobby Keys (saxophone), Michelle (acoustic guitar), Charles Shaar Murray (acoustic guitar).
Recorded at Ascot Sound Studios.
Produced by John, Yoko, and Phil Spector.

'UNCLE ALBERT'

ISSUED by Apple as a single in the USA, 'Uncle Albert/Admiral Halsey' went to number 1 on all the major singles charts. Issued with generic Apple labels and a black paper sleeve, the single was manufactured with six label variations.

Variant one has a light green Apple label; bold type with 'STEREO' at 9 o'clock; song title and writer's credit at 10 o'clock; artist's name and 'Copyright also claimed by McCartney Music, Inc,- BMI' centre bottom.

Variant two has a medium green Apple label; bold type with 'STEREO' at 1 o'clock; song title and writer's credit at 10 o'clock; 'Copyright also claimed by McCartney Music, Inc, BMI' at 8 o'clock; artist's name centre bottom.

Variant three has a dark green Apple label; plain type with 'STEREO' at 9 o'clock; song title and writer's credit at 10 o'clock; artist's name and 'Copyright also claimed by McCartney Music, Inc,- BMI' centre bottom.

Variant four is as three but with a full dark green Apple A-side label on both sides.

Variant five has a dark green Apple label; bold type with 'STEREO' at 9 o'clock; song title top centre; writer's credit at 10 o'clock; 'Copyright also claimed by McCartney Music, Inc,- BMI' at 8 o'clock; artist's name centre bottom.

Variant six is as five but with a full dark green Apple A-side label on both sides.

Demonstration copies of the single (PRO-6279) were manufactured with mono mixes of the A and B-side. The single was reissued in the mid 1970s with black and silver Capitol 'dome' labels.

'UNCLE ALBERT / ADMIRAL HALSEY' / 'TOO MANY PEOPLE'
PAUL AND LINDA McCARTNEY
US RELEASE August 2 1971; Apple 1837; chart high No.1.

'THE BACK SEAT OF MY CAR'

RELEASED as a single in Britain rather than 'Uncle Albert/Admiral Halsey', 'The Back Seat Of My Car' failed to match the commercial success of its US counterpart, barely making it into the Top 40. The fact that McCartney had been in the most popular and influential band in the world counted for little; long gone were the days when anything The Beatles did, whether as a group or as individuals, immediately shot to the top of the charts. Ironically, it would be Ringo Starr, the least prolific songwriter in the group, who in the early 1970s would have a better hit-to-release ratio than either Lennon or McCartney.

The single may have suffered from the restructuring then taking place at Apple Records. After Allen Klein moved back to New York City, the British side of the business all but ceased trading. By the time 'The Back Seat Of My Car' came out, most of Apple's releases were being co-ordinated through the company's American office. This could account for the success of 'Uncle Albert/Admiral Halsey' in the USA and the relative failure of 'The Back Seat Of My Car' in Britain.

'THE BACK SEAT OF MY CAR' / 'HEART OF THE COUNTRY'
PAUL AND LINDA McCARTNEY
UK RELEASE August 13 1971; Apple R 5914; chart high No.39.

'The Back Seat Of My Car' data

Issued with generic Apple labels and black paper sleeve, this release was exclusive to Britain: most of Europe went with 'Eat At Home'. The single was issued in the mid 1970s with black and silver Capitol 'dome' labels. Publishing credits for the B-side, 'Heart Of The Country', were changed from 'Northern Songs NCB Copyright also claimed by McCartney Music Inc' to 'McCartney Music Ltd by arrangement with ATV Music Ltd.'

IMAGINE

UNLIKE the last album, *John Lennon/Plastic Ono Band*, which was written quickly to capture the experience of primal therapy, *Imagine* was a considered collection of themes and songs that had occupied Lennon for some time. From sweeping utopian anthems to scathing attacks on his former songwriting partner, confessions of self-doubt, and songs of devotion, *Imagine* was a richly textured collection that showed how little and how much he had changed. The album mixed personal introspection with the political in equal measures. Lennon claimed that the album was every bit as political as anything he'd produced. However, this time the edge was missing. He had learnt to be subversive and hid his radicalism under Phil Spector's lush production and sugar-coating.

According to contemporary accounts, Lennon was in awe of the American producer, but not to the point of sycophancy. His working relationship with Spector may have developed to the extent that he allowed him to sweeten certain songs with the addition of strings, but he was careful to keep the producer's excesses in check. Explaining how they worked together, Lennon said: "Phil doesn't arrange or anything like that – and [Ono] and

Phil will just sit in the other room and shout comments like, 'Why don't you try this sound,' or 'You're not playing the piano too well, try that,' something like that. I'll get the initial idea and say, 'Nicky [Hopkins], you get on piano, and someone else get on that,' and then Phil will suggest three acoustic guitars strumming somewhere, and we'll just find a sound from it. It's quite easy working with him."

While he was content to defer some production duties to Spector, Lennon turned to Ono for advice. He may have admired Spector, but he trusted Ono, whom he relied on to 'A&R' his songs. However, despite her intervention, Alan White claimed that no one, apart from perhaps John, took much notice of her. One example caught on film found Ono complaining to Lennon that the band were improvising. He tells the band to "stop jamming", but as White explained: "We didn't take notice of that, cos you know what? We'd do it again, and do it the same way, and she didn't know the difference. He knew that we knew what she was doing, and he'd just get on with it. He knew we were doing the right thing, but it's just the wife, doing her thing. We knew the music."

Basic tracks were recorded at the new 8-track studio Lennon had installed at his Tittenhurst Park home. Sessions appear to have begun in late May, as Steve Peacock, who interviewed Lennon at Tittenhurst for *Sounds* on May 22, reported that recording was well underway at the time of his visit. In the same interview, Lennon suggested that all of the backing tracks were completed over a nine-day period. If Peacock is correct, then the backing tracks were completed by early June, not early July as is often stated.

The sessions were relaxed affairs. Recording usually began in the late morning and ended in the early evening. White recalled: "We used to start warming up around 11 in the morning, and we'd go have lunch at 1 or 2 in the afternoon, and then see if we could get something down, or at least get to a point where it was sounding good. Sometimes we'd record things late in the evening. But mostly we recorded in the afternoon – we usually recorded [then], if we got a really good take, [and] we'd finish and have dinner around 6:30, 7:00."

With the musicians gathered around him, Lennon would rehearse the song they were about to record, teaching them the chords and working on a rough arrangement. They would then play through the song until Lennon, Ono, or Phil Spector was happy with it. Lennon always sang a guide vocal with each take, which he replaced with an overdub.

For this album, Plastic Ono Band were augmented by a number of seasoned professionals, who were drafted in to assist with the recording. George Harrison turned in some stunning performances, as did Nicky Hopkins, who played piano alongside Lennon on the album's title track. Guitarists Joey Molland and Tom Evans from Badfinger contributed to the album, as did keyboard player John Barham, who had recently worked on George Harrison's *All Things Must Pass* album.

Overdub sessions took place at the Record Plant East, New York City, in early July. Torrie Zito, who had worked with Frank Sinatra and Quincy Jones, wrote the album's dramatic string arrangements, which were recorded there by "some Philharmonic people", whom Lennon dubbed The Flux Fiddlers. The reference to the Fluxus group alluded to the use of toy violins, supplied by Joe Jones, that were employed for the string section. It was also during these NYC sessions that King Curtis added his saxophone to the multi-track tape.

The album produced three outtakes: a studio version of 'Well (Baby Please Don't Go)', 'I'm The Greatest', later given to Ringo Starr for his *Ringo* album, and a spontaneous rendition of 'San Francisco Bay Blues'. The sessions also produced several tracks used for Ono's companion album, *Fly*.

The Tittenhurst sessions were filmed for a feature-length documentary, *Imagine*, that was first screened on American television on December 23 1972. An edited version of this film was issued on video in 1985 and a revamped version, which paid greater attention to the recording sessions, was issued on DVD as *Gimme Some Truth* in 2000.

Imagine songs

Lennon had signed off *John Lennon/Plastic Ono Band* by stating that the dream was over. *Imagine* opens with the offer of a new dream, every bit as idealistic as the one he previously condemned. Inspired by Ono's book *Grapefruit*, which the couple were promoting while recording the *Imagine* album, Lennon composed 'Imagine'. Years later, he admitted his debt to Ono. Speaking to Andy Peebles about 'Imagine', he said: "Well, actually that should be credited as a Lennon/Ono song. A lot if it – the lyric and the concept – came from Yoko, but in those days I was a bit more selfish, a bit more macho, and I sort of omitted her contribution, but it was right out of *Grapefruit*."

Grapefruit was a collection of Ono's instruction pieces, many of which encouraged the reader to 'imagine' certain events they could hold in their memory. For her, the book wasn't important. In fact, she suggested that it be burnt once it had been read. The important part was the visualisation of ideas that could be stored in the reader's imagination. At around the same time, Lennon received a prayer book from Dick Gregory which, like *Grapefruit*, championed the power of imagination. He combined both ideas and wrote a humanistic paean for the people.

Recalling Ono's early Fluxus scores and instruction pieces, Lennon's lyric asks us to imagine a world without the three main concepts that give our lives meaning – religion, nationhood, and possessions. He was responding to real anxieties caused by the failure of these systems to sustain our belief in them. He asks us to picture a world without these controlling systems, encouraging us to think of ourselves as citizens of the world, not as individuals defined by them. (Lennon would embrace this idea to the end – original pressings of *Double Fantasy* were inscribed "One World, One People".)

Lennon contends that global harmony is within our reach, but only if we reject the mechanisms of social control that restrict human potential. What he hoped to do was raise self-awareness, emphasise self-creation, and compel individuals to question their own abstract relationship with the institutions that order our lives. However, he offers no answers, only hypotheses. All Lennon had to offer were possibilities that may occur.

Although Lennon argues for a world without grand, all-encompassing themes, when asked about the song in 1971, he stressed what he thought was the song's overriding left-wing ideology. "'Imagine', which says: 'Imagine that there was no more religion, no more country, no more politics,' is virtually the Communist manifesto, even though I'm not particularly a Communist and I do not belong to any movement."

Lennon's thinking seems a little nebulous. He expects us to imagine a world without systems, while proposing a system akin to Communism. Somehow his form of Communism was as nice and fluffy as the real thing was unpleasant and harsh. Speaking to the *NME* about his philosophy, he said: "It might be like Communism, but I don't really know what real Communism is. There is no real Communist state in the world; you must realise that. The socialism I speak about is a British Socialism, not the way some daft Russian might do it. Or the Chinese might do it. That might suit them. Us, we should have a nice Socialism here. A British Socialism."

This sounds very isolationist, and not at all like the inclusive global oneness he envisions with 'Imagine'. Lennon seemed more than a little confused. Indeed, the song seems riddled with contradictions. Its hymn-like setting sits uncomfortably alongside its author's plea for us to envision a world without religion. And how could a millionaire pop star's appeal for us to imagine a world without possessions be taken seriously? But that is to miss the point. Lennon knew he had nothing concrete to offer, so instead he offers a dream, a concept to be built upon.

Melodically, Lennon hints at the possibilities on offer with a simple motif that cries out to be developed and extended. The sense of indeterminacy evoked by his apparently incomplete melodic sketch offers a number of possible interventions and interpretations for the listener to complete. Like many Fluxus artists, Lennon encourages the listener to add to the piece, if only in their imagination. By offering the listener the opportunity to add to his composition in this way, he hints at the sense of global progress and change that his lyric calls for. The Fluxus credo of reciprocity and participation made itself felt even here, the most unlikely Fluxus manifestation in Lennon's canon.

At the time of writing, no demo recordings of 'Imagine' have come to light. What has been issued are numerous alternative takes. Before recording 'Imagine', Lennon gathered the musicians around an upright piano to play them his new song. This rehearsal recording was issued on *Imagine: John Lennon* (CDP 7 90803 2). At the end of this rehearsal take, Klaus Voormann suggested using the white baby grand piano situated in the Lennons' 'white room'. Several takes were attempted there but, because Spector was unhappy with the room's acoustics, the session was abandoned.

When work on the song continued, the main concern was how best to capture the piano sound that Lennon had in mind. Some takes featured him and Nicky Hopkins playing the same piano in different registers. Others were augmented by harmonium, played by John Barham. Take one, which features Barham's harmonium, was issued on the *John Lennon Anthology*. The final master features Lennon on piano and a string overdub recorded in New York.

Next on the album comes 'Crippled Inside'. Blending idioms borrowed from American popular music, it swings like the goodtime music that inspired it. But behind the vitality of Nicky Hopkins's honky-tonk piano and the fluidity of George Harrison's down-home dobro lurks a lyric dripping with cynicism. The song seems to attack 'straight' society for creating falsehoods. Outwardly, Lennon's acutely observed lyric appears to attack many of the social conventions we hide behind to mask our inadequacies. However, it's as self-critical as anything from *John Lennon/Plastic Ono Band* and could easily be an expression of the guilt he felt at the fiction he himself propagated. Lennon had addressed similar issues with 'I'm A Loser', but having matured considerably and with the experience of primal therapy behind him, he wrote a song that recalls but also pokes fun at the seriousness of his previous attempts at self-analysis.

Lennon wrote the melody for 'Jealous Guy' in India in 1968. At that time, the song was called 'Child Of Nature' and reflected the hippie ethos The Beatles were then enjoying. On their return to England, The Beatles recorded 'Child Of Nature' in demo form at George Harrison's house before Lennon abandoned it. By 1971, he had rewritten the lyrics to express his growing desire to become more trusting.

Lennon's attitude to women changed little over the years, as he explained to *Playboy*. "I was a very jealous, possessive guy. Toward everything. A very insecure male. A guy who wants to put his woman in a little box, lock her up, and just bring her out when he feels like playing with her." Although 'Jealous Gu'y finds Lennon expressing a desire to reject the male chauvinist values he had grown up with, in reality little had changed. As footage from the *Imagine* film reveals, Lennon relied on Ono for more than inspiration and creative advice. Despite her independence and professed feminism, she still served his meals and mended his clothes.

During the making of the *Imagine* album, Lennon and Ono were interviewed for the BBC radio programme *Woman's Hour* about attitudes to love and sex, and Lennon revealed how possessive he was. "When you actually are in love with somebody, you tend to be jealous and want to own them and possess them 100 percent, which I do. But intellectually, before that, I thought right, owning a person is rubbish, but I love Yoko, I want to possess her completely. I don't want to stifle her, you know? That's the danger, that you want to possess them to death. But that's a personal problem, you know?"

'Jealous Guy' finds Lennon acknowledging that he had a problem and attempting to do something about it, even if it were only to write a song about it. It wasn't the first time that he'd written on the subject and it would not be the last. At around the time he wrote the lyrics for 'Jealous Guy', he wrote a song titled 'Call Your Name', which formed the basis of 'Aisumasen (I'm Sorry)' on 1973's *Mind Games* album. Both songs point to a shift in Lennon's songwriting, documenting a transition from arrogant bravado to a passive acceptance of his own shortcomings.

Joey Molland from Badfinger helped record 'Jealous Guy' with bandmate Tom Evans. Molland was somewhat star-struck at meeting Lennon, but also a little surprised at his no-nonsense attitude. As usual, Lennon played the song to the group before moving to the studio and was obviously keen to get the session started. As Molland recalled: "He was really brusque with us, really almost rude, but not rude. ... Then he sits down on the stool and starts playing 'Jealous Guy'. ... So we recorded acoustic guitars on that and John said, 'You can fuck off now if you'd like.' Of course, he wasn't being like, 'Fuck off.' It was like, 'Do what you like.' So they started playing 'I Don't Wanna Be A Soldier' and me and Tommy were just hanging out. We just started to play along because we weren't about to move and let somebody throw us out. We didn't play it, we just started this 'doodley-do' kind of Bo Diddley strumming, because the song didn't seem to settle into any particular rhythm. And it ended up on the record. One of the most exciting nights of me life."

Rough mixes of 'Jealous Guy' placed Molland and Evans's acoustic guitars high in the mix, but by the time Spector had finished work on the song, he'd buried them well down in the mix. Their playing is more audible on 'I Don't Want To Be A Soldier', where Spector placed them much higher in the balance. Alan White also played on the track. Because the studio was small, he found himself

IMAGINE
JOHN LENNON AND PLASTIC ONO BAND (WITH THE FLUX FIDDLERS)
SIDE 1 'Imagine', 'Crippled Inside', 'Jealous Guy', 'It's So Hard', 'I Don't Want To Be A Soldier'.
SIDE 2 'Give Me Some Truth', 'Oh My Love', 'How Do You Sleep?', 'How?', 'Oh Yoko!'.
UK RELEASE October 7 1971; LP Apple PAS 10004; quadraphonic LP Apple Q4PAS 10004 released June 1972; 8-track cartridge Apple 8X-PAS 10004 released November 1971; quadraphonic 8-track cartridge Apple Q8-PAS 10004 released March 1972; chart high No.1.
US RELEASE September 9 1971; LP Apple SW 3379; stereo reel-to-reel tape Apple L-3379; 8-track cartridge Apple 8XW-3379; quadraphonic 8-track cartridge Apple Q8W-3379; chart high No.1.

• **'Imagine'** (Lennon)
John Lennon (vocals, piano), Klaus Voormann (bass), Alan White (drums), The Flux Fiddlers (strings).
• **'Crippled Inside'** (Lennon)
John Lennon (vocals, electric guitar), George Harrison (dobro), Nicky Hopkins (piano), Ted Turner (acoustic guitar), Rod Lincon (acoustic guitar), John Tout (acoustic guitar), Klaus Voormann (bass), Steve Brendell (upright bass), Alan White (drums).
• **'Jealous Guy'** (Lennon)
John Lennon (vocals, acoustic guitar), John Barham (harmonium), Alan White (vibraphone), Joey Molland (acoustic guitar), Tom Evans (acoustic guitar), Mike Pinder (tambourine), Klaus Voormann (bass), Jim Keltner (drums), The Flux Fiddlers (strings).
• **'It's So Hard'** (John Lennon)
John Lennon (vocals, guitar), Klaus Voormann (bass), Jim Gordon (drums), King Curtis (saxophone), The Flux Fiddlers (strings).
• **'I Don't Want To Be A Soldier'** (Lennon)
John Lennon (vocals, guitar), George Harrison (slide guitar), Nicky Hopkins (piano), Joey Molland (acoustic guitar), Tom Evans (acoustic guitar), Klaus Voormann (bass), Jim Keltner (drums), Mike Pinder (tambourine), Steve Brendell (maracas), The Flux Fiddlers (strings).
• **'Give Me Some Truth'** (Lennon)
John Lennon (vocals, guitar), George Harrison (lead guitar), Nicky Hopkins (piano), Rod Linton (acoustic guitar), Andy Davis (acoustic guitar), Klaus Voormann (basses), Alan White (drums).
• **'Oh My Love'** (Lennon, Ono)
John Lennon (vocals, piano), George Harrison (guitar), Nicky Hopkins (electric piano), Klaus Voormann (bass), Alan White (drums, Tibetan cymbals).
• **'How Do You Sleep?'** (Lennon)
John Lennon (vocals, piano), George Harrison (slide guitar), Nicky Hopkins (piano), John Tout (piano), Ted Turner (acoustic guitar), Rod Linton (acoustic guitar), Andy Davis (acoustic guitar), Klaus Voormann (bass), Alan White (drums).
• **'How?'** (John Lennon)
John Lennon (vocals, piano), Nicky Hopkins (piano), John Barham (vibraphone), Klaus Voormann (bass), Alan White (drums), The Flux Fiddlers (strings).
• **'Oh Yoko!'** (Lennon)
John Lennon (vocals, guitar, mouth organ), Phil Spector (backing vocals), Nicky Hopkins (piano), Rod Linton (acoustic guitar), Andy (acoustic guitar), Klaus Voormann (bass), Alan White (drums), The Flux Fiddlers (strings).
All recorded at Ascot Sound Studios, Tittenhurst Park, Sunninghill, near Ascot, England, except 'Imagine', 'Jealous Guy', 'It's So Hard', 'I Don't Want To Be A Soldier', and 'How?' recorded at Ascot Sound Studios and at The Record Plant East, New York City, NY, USA.
All produced by John & Yoko and Phil Spector.

playing in a bathroom next to the studio. He said: "I was playing vibraphone in the bathroom. There was a door in the corner, with a bathroom back there, and we couldn't have the vibes out in the room where the drums were, cos it would go all over the mics, so they put me in the bathroom."

'It's So Hard' summarises Lennon's daily struggle with life and the problems it put in his way. Respite from his troubles wasn't far from hand. Unsurprisingly, he finds comfort in Ono's presence.

To test his new studio, Lennon gathered a small band around him and recorded a stomping, gritty rocker. He claimed that at the time his studio was so new that certain pieces of equipment – limiters and equalisers – hadn't even been installed. With only three musicians involved in recording the basic track, little could go wrong and, despite the lack of equipment, the basic track of 'It's So Hard' was captured successfully.

What in other hands could have been a maudlin song of self-pity was averted by a bouncy arrangement that features some snappy rhythm/lead guitar, played by Lennon. Basic tracks completed, the song was set aside while the rest of the album was recorded. It was not worked on again until Lennon and Spector supervised overdub sessions at the Record Plant East in New York City. First they added strings and then, on July 4, Lennon called on the services of saxophonist King Curtis, who added his masterly playing to the track.

Curtis played on some of the greatest R&B records to come out of America and supported The Beatles on their 1965 American tour. Lennon was thrilled to have him on the track, so much so that he recorded the overdub session for posterity. Lennon's instructions to Curtis were vague; his only suggestion was that he wanted something like 'Honky Tonk', a 1956 hit for The Bill Doggett Combo. Lennon played through his song a few times, ad-libbing the melody he wanted Curtis to play. A few takes later and Curtis had the overdub in the bag.

On *John Lennon/Plastic Ono Band*, 'God' had found Lennon listing the things he no longer believed in. A little over a year later, 'I Don't Want To Be A Soldier' saw him reworking his litany to include the things he didn't want to be. He was constantly repositioning himself, changing his identity and beliefs to suit his circumstances. 'Soldier' was Lennon's way of acknowledging how precarious a grip he had on his own identity. For him to sustain acceptability within his social circle, he had to expel all that was considered inappropriate and 'straight'. By disavowing the things that operate on the periphery of his life, he establishes a claim for authenticity. Instead of using the power of imagination to rid himself of these things, he performs a symbolic exorcism to unburden himself of their influence. By symbolically disowning the things that threaten to de-centre him, Lennon was able to define and control them. Yet, by articulating his fears, he drew himself further into the world he abhorred. He may not have wanted to be a soldier, but a few months after recording the song he was dressing in army fatigues. True, he was fighting for the 'people', but by adopting the image of a soldier he had become the very thing he disdained.

Musically, 'I Don't Want To Be A Soldier' is unadventurous. Lennon indulged in this kind of improvisation while filming *Let It Be*. Little more than an extended jam, it would have been dull indeed without Spector's magic touch. As it was, Spector transformed the song by adding layers of echo that lend it an eerie texture. The track also benefits from King Curtis's playing, which adds to the recording immeasurably.

Described by Lennon as "one of those moany songs", 'Give Me Some Truth' was started while in India in early 1968. A year later, The Beatles attempted some half-hearted rehearsals of the song while filming *Let It Be*, but it didn't get past that stage. In this context, Lennon's pleas for truth may have been directed at his fellow bandmates.

Relations within The Beatles then had disintegrated to the point where each felt alienated from the others. Ringo Starr recalled for the later *Anthology* project how troubled everyone felt at the time. "I left the group because I felt two things: I felt I wasn't playing great; and I also felt that the other three were really happy and I was an outsider. I went to see John, who had been living in my apartment in Montagu Square with Yoko since he moved out of Kenwood. I said, 'I'm leaving the group because I'm not playing well and I feel unloved and out of it, and you three are really close.' And John said, 'I thought it was *you three*!'" Lennon felt just as anxious, but rather than leave the group he turned to heroin to repress his feelings. The Beatles were in trouble, but rather than face the truth, they took to hiding behind a mask of deceit to conceal what was actually happening. The truth was there, but no one wanted to face it.

By the time he came to record 'Give Me Some Truth' for *Imagine*, Lennon had rewritten some of the lyrics to include references to US President Richard Nixon. 'Tricky Dicky' Nixon became the bane of Lennon's life. It was Nixon's government who tapped his phone, watched his every move, and tried to deport him from America. But Lennon had it in for Nixon long before Nixon had it in for him. With the escalating war in Vietnam, Nixon was marked by most as Public Enemy Number One. After years of campaigning for peace, Lennon was growing tired of the lack of progress. If anything, the situation had grown worse. Thanks to Nixon's intervention, the war in Vietnam had intensified and the prospect of a world at peace seemed as remote as ever. Although 'Give Me Some Truth' appears to signal despair at the lack of political progress and the intransigence of world leaders, Lennon remained committed to politics and increased his political activity.

The next song on *Imagine* also dates from 1968. 'Oh My Love' is a tender love song that Lennon wrote at the start of his relationship with Ono. It's an intense expression of affection that finds him in the grip of infatuation, experiencing the world anew. If 'Give Me Some Truth' suggested a mind clouded by untruths, here Lennon confesses to a clarity of vision restored by the purity of his love. Fittingly, Ono received a co-author credit, and her influence can be clearly heard in the song's lyric. The allusions to natural elements such as the wind and clouds are typical of her instruction pieces.

Lennon's innocent lyric is supported by the most delicate of melodies, performed with a lightness of touch as gentle as his expression of devotion is honest. George Harrison's hauntingly beautiful guitar figure offers the perfect complement to Lennon's vaguely Oriental sounding melody. Harrison started the session on dobro but quickly moved to his Gibson Les Paul, its rich, warm tones complementing the intimate nature of the recording perfectly. Lennon's own playing is enhanced by Nicky Hopkins's delicate piano motif, which adds a rococo sparkle to the arrangement.

Not content with calling each other names over the boardroom table and in the pages of the British music press, John Lennon and Paul McCartney had turned to songwriting to badmouth one another. McCartney's *Ram* album was littered with snipes at his former partner. Songs like 'Too Many People' and 'The Back Seat Of My Car', with its refrain "We believe that we can't be wrong", really galled Lennon.

"I heard Paul's messages in *Ram* – yes there are dear reader!" Lennon told *Crawdaddy*. "Too many people going where? Missed our lucky what? What was our first mistake? Can't be wrong? Huh! I mean Yoko, me, and other friends can't all be hearing things. So to have some fun, I must thank Allen Klein publicly for the line 'just another day'. A real poet! Some people don't see the funny side of it. Too bad. What am I supposed to do, make you laugh? It's what you might call an 'angry letter', sung – get it?"

When Lennon and McCartney channelled their rivalry in a common cause, it was a positive power for good. When channelled at one another, it was only destructive. Never one to take things lying down, Lennon couldn't resist replying to McCartney's jibes. On 'How Do You Sleep?' he attacks McCartney for breaking up The Beatles and claims that he is a spent force. Alluding to the myth that McCartney had died in 1966 and been replaced with a double, Lennon suggests that the "freaks" who promulgated these fictions were right and that McCartney had died, at least creatively.

Although Lennon took sole credit for writing the song, at least two others contributed to the lyrics. When Lennon first played the song to Harrison, the lyrics appeared finished. But as Spector noted at the time, Lennon was apt to change lyrics right up to the last take. Felix Denis of *Oz* magazine recalled that Ono contributed to the song. "Yoko wrote many of the lyrics. I watched her racing into the studio to show John, and they'd burst out laughing. The mood there wasn't totally vindictive – they were taking the piss out of the headmaster."

Allen Klein told *Playboy* that he got Lennon to change a potentially libellous line about McCartney plagiarising his song 'Yesterday'. Klein said the original couplet was "The only thing you done was yesterday / You probably pinched that bitch anyway" and that he thought it too strong, offering "Since you've gone you're just another day" as an alternative for that second line.

The song was obviously written in the heat of the moment and intended to irk McCartney, but Lennon claimed that he simply used his former partner as a catalyst. "It was like Dylan doing 'Like A Rolling Stone', one of his nasty songs," said Lennon. "It's using somebody as an object to create something. I wasn't really feeling that vicious at the time, but I was using my resentment towards Paul to create a song. Let's put it that way. It was just a mood. Paul took it the way he did because it, obviously, pointedly refers to him, and people just hounded him about it, asking, 'How do ya feel about it?' But there were a few little digs on *his* album, which he kept so obscure that other people didn't notice 'em, you know? But I heard them. So, I thought, 'Well, hang up being obscure! I'll just get right down to the nitty-gritty.'" Lennon was clearly out to get McCartney, but also intent on having fun. He may have been enjoying himself but at least one ex-Beatle thought he was going too far. Ringo Starr, who was visiting the studio at the time, was upset by the song and reportedly told Lennon, "That's enough, John."

Starr was right: Lennon had gone far enough. 'How Do You Sleep?' effectively ended Lennon and McCartney's public squabbling. As a form of catharsis it allowed Lennon to rid himself of the anger and frustration he experienced at the break-up of The Beatles, and it was shocking enough to silence McCartney, whose follow-up to *Ram*, *Wild Life*, all but ignored the situation. Instead, McCartney turned in 'Dear Friend', a ballad that pointed to the reconciliation that was to come. Similarly, Lennon never directly attacked McCartney through song again. Ironically, within a few years Lennon and Ono were engaged in and relishing the kind of cosy domesticity they'd lambasted the McCartneys for enjoying. By the mid 1970s, Lennon had become a 'house husband', besotted with his son Sean and, like McCartney before him, writing cosy pop songs about his newly found joy.

Post-primal therapy, Lennon appeared as racked with doubts as he had before Janov entered his life. Primal therapy, it seems, had emptied Lennon of all emotion. The experience made him a hollow vessel, struggling to find meaning in his life. If nothing else, The Beatles had given its members' lives meaning and held them together, both physically and mentally. With the group's dissolution, all four struggled to find meaning and establish solo voices. 'How?' finds Lennon staring into an existential void and attempting to make sense of who he was becoming. He sees no meaning to his life, only choices that fill him with anxiety. Caught in abeyance, Lennon had reached a defining moment where the choices he made would shape his future in countless ways. The closing verse, sung in the third person, suggests that all of us share similar feelings and fates, but are unwilling to face them. Like 'Imagine', 'How?' asks listeners to take control of their life and consider a future better than the one they inhabit.

As a confession of insecurity, 'How?' could have sat comfortably alongside anything on *John Lennon/Plastic Ono Band*.

Its hesitant pauses underline a mood of uncertainty, but the glorious middle eight and Zito's string arrangement lift it from the slough of despair. Lennon took several takes to capture his vocal, but the effort paid off and he delivered one of his best.

Imagine closes with the jubilant 'Oh Yoko!'. The song has little more to say than I love you, but Lennon's tender-heartedness was also a plea for reassurance. Speaking in 1980, he said: "It's a message to Yoko. Because I couldn't say it in real life. Maybe, I don't know." Lennon's ambivalence was reflected in the different approaches he took to the song before recording it properly. An early version, recorded in June 1969 while Lennon and Ono were very much a love-struck couple, has the same buoyant mood as the album version. However, when Lennon returned to the song a little over a year later, in November 1970, it had taken on a melancholy air. Performed on piano, the demo recording reveals just how primal therapy had affected Lennon. Recorded a few weeks after completing *John Lennon/Plastic Ono Band*, it finds him reeling from its effects and close to the edge of an emotional abyss. When it came time to record 'Oh Yoko!' for the *Imagine* album, Lennon reverted to its original up-beat arrangement.

Imagine data

Imagine was the first Apple album issued in quadraphonic, a shortlived four-channel system that provided an early form of surround-sound. In Britain, the quadraphonic mix was issued on LP (Q4PAS 10004) and 8-track cartridge (Q8-PAS 10004) but in the USA was available only on 8-track (Q8W-3379). The quadraphonic mix produced only one noticeable anomaly: the sound of the orchestra warming up was removed from the beginning of 'How Do You Sleep?'. In America, the album was issued on reel-to-reel tape (L 3379) by Apple/Ampex.

Apple issued *Imagine* in Britain two days before John's 31st birthday, but it had appeared in America almost a month earlier. Customised Apple labels were used for both British and American editions, which were issued with a printed inner sleeve, poster, and postcard. Ono took the cover photograph, after the original design – a photograph of Lennon with his eyes replaced by clouds – was abandoned. George Maciunas, a central figure within the Fluxus movement, was commissioned to design the inner sleeve and the typography used on the front cover.

The most commercially successful of Lennon's albums, *Imagine* has been reissued several times. EMI reissued it on November 17 1997 (LPCENT27) as a special limited-edition release to celebrate the company's centenary. The album featured original packaging, 180-gram virgin vinyl, analogue cutting from analogue tape, and heavy quality cover. The LP was reissued again in 2000 when it was remixed, remastered, and reissued by EMI/Parlophone (5248571) on February 14 2000. This pressing featured generic Apple labels with slightly altered credits: 'I Don't Want To Be A Soldier' was suffixed with 'Mama'. Unlike original pressings, it was issued with a gatefold cover and card inner sleeve.

When Capitol repressed *Imagine* in 1978, it replaced the custom Apple labels with purple Capitol labels with a large Capitol logo. Capitol issued the LP again in 1986, this time with black/colour band Capitol labels. In 1987, Capitol issued the album with black/colour band Capitol labels; this version has 'Digitally Remastered' printed at the top of the front cover. In 1988, Capitol issued the album with purple Capitol labels with a small Capitol logo.

The album was remastered in 1984 by MFSL Original Master Recordings, which issued a half speed master version of the album (MFSL-1-153). In February 2004, MFSL issued a 180-gram GAIN 2 Ultra Analog half speed master vinyl pressing of the 2000 remix (LMF277).

The album was issued on coloured vinyl in two countries. Original Japanese pressings of the LP (AP-80370) were issued on red vinyl, and in France the LP was issued on blue vinyl (2C 064-4914).

Imagine was issued on 8-track in Britain (8X-PAS 10004) and America (8XW-3379). A quadraphonic mix was also issued on 8-track: Q8-PAS 10004 in the UK and Q8W-3379 in the USA.

Imagine was first issued on CD by EMI in Britain on May 26 1987 (CDP 7 46641 2). As was the practice at the time, EMI manufactured the CDs in Japan and matched them with covers made in Britain. In America, Capitol issued the CD on March 17 1988. The Japanese CD (CP32-5451) featured a mono version of 'How Do You Sleep?'. On February 14 2000, EMI/Capitol issued a remixed and remastered edition of *Imagine* on CD (524 8582). It was also issued on August 22 2003 by MFSL Original Master Recordings as an Ultradisc II 24 kt. gold CD (UDCD-758).

Several live versions of the title track, 'Imagine', have appeared over the years, and the earliest was taped not long after the *Imagine* album had been issued. On December 17 1971, Lennon and Ono appeared at the Apollo Theatre, New York City. Backed by a hastily-formed band, Lennon performed the song with acoustic guitar rather than piano. This recording was eventually issued on the *John Lennon Anthology*. A version recorded with Elephant's Memory on January 27 1972 for US TV's *The Mike Douglas Show* was issued in mono on *Lennon In His Own Words* (no catalogue number), a CD included with copies of James Henke's book *Lennon Legend*. The One To One concert on August 30 1972 produced another live version, which was issued on *John Lennon Live In New York City*. Capitol issued this recording as a 12-inch promotional record (SPRO-9575). Finally, an instrumental version of 'Imagine' found its way onto the *Lennon Legend* DVD and was issued on the *Happy Christmas (War Is Over)* CD single (CDR 6627) in 2003.

Lennon also played 'It's so Hard' at the matinee and evening performances of the 1972 One To One concert. Both performances have since been issued: the matinee recording is available on *John Lennon In New York City*; the evening recording on the *John Lennon Anthology*.

'IMAGINE'

'IMAGINE' / 'IT'S SO HARD'
JOHN LENNON AND PLASTIC ONO BAND (WITH THE FLUX FIDDLERS)
US RELEASE October 11 1971; Apple APPLE 1840; chart high No.3.

ISSUED as a single two days after John Lennon's 31st birthday, 'Imagine' was his first solo single not to feature one of Ono's songs on its B-side. 'It's So Hard' was the B-side in most countries, with the exception of Britain, where the single was backed with 'Working Class Hero'.

The single was issued with a white Apple label, similar to those used for the *John Lennon/Plastic Ono Band* LP, and came in a generic Apple sleeve. Two label variations were issued. Both have identical text layout, but one has 'MFD. BY APPLE, RECORDS INC', the other 'MFD. BY APPLE, RECORDS INC UNAUTHORISED DUPLICATION IS A VIOLATION OF APPLICABLE LAWS'. The single was reissued with purple Capitol labels in 1978 and with black/colour band Capitol labels in 1983. It was reissued in 1988 with purple Capitol labels.

In 1992, Capitol's Special Markets Division issued the record with a new catalogue number (S7-17688). These records were intended to be gold-plated for presentation sets, but approximately 1,000 copies escaped the electro-plating process and found their way onto the open market.

WILD LIFE

MUSICALLY, *Wild Life* is to McCartney as *Plastic Ono Band* is to Lennon. But where the bite of Lennon's *Plastic Ono Band* resulted from a desire to express the pain of primal scream, the coarseness of *Wild Life* resulted from expedience. McCartney was eager to work with a band and, in line with the back-to-basics philosophy he'd developed since leaving The Beatles, he wanted to keep it simple. Keen to get back on the road, he assembled a new band rather than form a supergroup. Starting from scratch, he acquired drummer Denny Seiwell, who had worked on *Ram*, and guitarist Denny Laine, late of The Moody Blues. Guitarist Hugh McCracken was also asked to join but, although he attended rehearsals, he decided against joining the group.

This as-yet unnamed band rehearsed at Rude Studio (a small 4 track demo studio in a wood-lined, stone-walled building on McCartney's farm in Scotland). Working in this intimate setting, they fashioned material for their debut album before moving to London and Abbey Road Studios.

Pleased with their first sessions, McCartney introduced his new band to the press on August 3 1971. He'd toyed with various bandnames, including Turpentine (still a favourite), but eventually found the right one on September 13 while Linda gave birth to their third daughter, Stella. Complications with the birth meant that Stella was born by Caesarean section, which ensured that McCartney was not present when his daughter entered the world. Ushered into a waiting room, he thought of the name Wings. "I sat next door in my green apron praying like mad ... [and] the name Wings came into my head," he recalled. Wings Mk.1 – Paul, Linda, Denny Laine, and Denny Seiwell – were born.

Explaining why he recorded the album so quickly, McCartney said: "I was inspired by Dylan, the way he just comes in the studio and everyone just falls in and makes a track."

Just as with the *McCartney* album before it, some of the songs were literally 'made up' on the spot. Production was kept to a minimum and five of the eight tracks were apparently first takes. *Wild Life* was a valiant attempt to capture moments of epiphany that spontaneity occasionally delivers. Unfortunately, the 'magic' that McCartney was hoping for simply never materialised. Nevertheless, *Wild Life* captured a moment of becoming that was both brave and startlingly honest. Intended as a beginning, it made public what most bands do in private – but most people quite simply weren't ready for this kind of unabashed openness, at least not from McCartney.

Promoted with a party at the Mecca Ballroom on London's Leicester Square on November 8 1971, *Wild Life* had a lot to live up to. Expectations were high and comparisons inevitable, but when styli began hitting plastic, there was a shock. Savaged by the critics, the album nevertheless has much to offer. Although some of the songs are obvious throwaways, it has several McCartney compositions that are as good as anything he's written. *Wild Life* is a breath of fresh air: crude, uncomplicated, and often wanting, it nonetheless has bags of character.

Wild Life songs

'Mumbo' opens the album. Written during jamming with the band, it appears to be little more than a throwaway. However, its raw energy more than makes up for what it lacks in lyrical content (most of the lyrics are incomprehensible, so perhaps McCartney should have called it 'Mumble'). It's almost as if McCartney is unable to express or define the pent-up feelings he was still coming to terms with. Those feelings are too intense to be expressed rationally, so he resorts to pure emotion to express himself.

There was another reason for writing like this: it provided material quickly, and Wings desperately needed new material. It also gave McCartney the opportunity to check out his new band and promote a sense of collective purpose and responsibility through group participation. He encouraged this process of bonding from the band's conception.

Proof that Wings were working at lightning speed can be heard in McCartney's opening remarks. Addressed to engineer Tony Clarke – best known for his work with The Moody Blues – "Take it, Tony" was intended to ensure that Clarke captured the song on tape. McCartney latter admitted: "I think, in fact, [that] often we never gave the engineer a chance to even set up a balance."

A mid-tempo rocker, *Bip Bop*, follows, and while this has the advantage of proper lyrics, it still fails to match the work McCartney was capable of producing. The author himself wasn't that impressed with his efforts, saying: "It just goes nowhere; I still cringe every time I hear it." Could this really have been composed by the same person who a few years previously had written a string of urbane, considered, intelligent pop songs? Unfortunately, the answer is yes.

'Love Is Strange' had already proved successful for Mickey & Sylvia and later The Everly Brothers, providing them with a British hit in 1965. Before Wings began recording, Paul and Linda spent some time in Jamaica, where they enthusiastically investigated the local music scene. The couple returned home with a quantity of reggae singles, to which Linda added a copy of the recently released *Tighten Up* compilation, which she played incessantly.

By the early 1970s, the popularity of reggae had grown considerably. Jamaican musicians were not only producing hits, they were expanding musical perimeters and influencing European musicians. Inspired by what they heard, the McCartneys decided to record a reggae-influenced instrumental. By chance, the lyrics for 'Love Is Strange' happened to fit with Wings' newly recorded backing, and so the two were fused together to complete the track.

Rather than go for a retro feel, which would have been in keeping with his original intention for the album, McCartney gave the song a 'reggae' arrangement because, he explained, "reggae is the newest and best beat around. There are more possibilities with reggae than anything at the moment". Suitably inspired, McCartney applied an extended reggae arrangement to this pop ballad and made it his own.

On the surface, 'Wild Life' appears to be a song about animal rights, and as such could mark the beginning of the McCartneys' long engagement with the cause. Certainly at this time, the McCartneys were beginning to embrace vegetarianism. But when John Mendelsohn reviewed the song for *Rolling Stone*, he suggested that it might be a subtle parody of Lennon's political critique, bolstering his argument by pointing at McCartney's vocal, which at times hints at the kind of primal screaming that Lennon employed for much of his *Plastic Ono Band* album.

If, as Mendelsohn suggests, 'Wild Life' criticises left-wing activism – and there are signs that this might be the case – then it represents as astute a piece of political analysis as anything Lennon or any left-wing intellectual ever conceptualised. Then again, of course, it could still just be a song about saving the planet.

Dating from the summer of 1969, 'Some People Never Know' was written while the McCartneys holidayed in Barbados. A typically melodic ballad, it could easily have appeared on any of The Beatles' later albums and not sounded out of place. Resigned to the fact that others will never know what it means to love, McCartney uses music as a metaphor to explore his relationship with Linda. This may sound sentimental, but any bathos is dispelled by the obvious tenderness of his lyric. Like much of the material on *Wild Life*, 'Some People Never Know' relies on understatement to underline content.

Songs obviously mean a lot to McCartney, so it made perfect sense to employ the concept as a metaphor for his relationship with Linda. 'I Am Your Singer' is sung as a duet as McCartney calls on the reciprocity of singer and song to represent their relationship. Each enhances the other and neither can work successfully on its own.

Once again, this may sound like the kind of unbearably sentimental fetish that lovers indulge in, but any sentimentality in the song is effectively effaced by a strong melody, an honest lyric, and simple but effective instrumentation that focuses attention on the vocal interaction between husband and wife. A sincere expression of requited love, its allusions to freedom and escape prefigure themes McCartney would explore on *Band On The Run*.

'I Am Your Singer' is followed by the first of two brief instrumentals. The first, 'Bip Bop Link', is a simple acoustic guitar doodle; the second, 'Mumbo Link', which comes at the very end of the album, is a brief jam – probably recorded while studio engineers were balancing recording levels. Both were credited to the McCartneys, although the second sounds more like a spontaneous jam involving Seiwell and Laine – Linda doesn't appear to be involved. The two pieces originally appeared untitled and were only named when the album was eventually released on CD.

'Tomorrow', another song about Paul and Linda's relationship, reveals how far things had changed. A year previously, McCartney had bemoaned his loss of confidence; even Linda couldn't draw him out of his melancholia. Now in buoyant mood, he expressed his rediscovered self-confidence with a bright, breezy melody that is uplifting and self-assured. Yet despite an equally optimistic lyric, it's obvious that he was still reliant on Linda's support. If 'I Am Your Singer' suggested emotional reciprocity, 'Tomorrow' hints at his fears of future rejection and his reliance on Linda to get him through his dark nights of the soul. If the McCartneys' world wasn't perfect, 'Tomorrow' suggests that at least their future looked rosy.

'Dear Friend' finds McCartney contemplating his relationship with Lennon. As subtle a piece of writing as he's produced, its sensitive lyrics and emotive melody evoke a sense of resignation that mirrored his feelings about his former partner. Long after Lennon's death, McCartney said: "'Dear Friend' was written about John, yes. I don't like grief and arguments, they always bug me. Life is too precious, although we often find ourselves guilty of doing it. So after John had slagged me off in public, I had to think of a response, and it was either going to be [to] slag him off in public – some instinct stopped me, which I'm really glad about – or do something else. So I worked on my attitude and wrote 'Dear Friend', saying, in effect, let's lay the guns down, let's hang up our boxing gloves."

McCartney conveniently appears to have forgotten that he had spent some of *Ram*, not to mention what he said in the press, slagging off Lennon. However, 'Dear Friend' does point to a reconciliation, even if both would have rejected the possibility as nonsense.

Wild Life data

No singles were taken from the album either in Britain or in the USA, although Odeon in Venezuela did issue 'Wild Life', split into two parts, as a single (278 - A [YEX 871]). An edit of 'Love Is Strange' lasting 4:07 was scheduled for release as a single in Britain (Apple R 5932) and white label copies were manufactured with 'I Am Your Singer' on the B-side, but it never appeared. Wings recorded a 'blues instrumental', 'Great Cock And Seagull Race', intended for a proposed maxi-single, but it too failed to materialise. 'Love Is Strange' was issued in Mexico on a four-song EP (EPEM-10604) that included 'Love Is Strange', 'I Am Your Singer', 'Tomorrow' (prefixed by 'Bip Bop Link'), and 'Mumbo'. The EP was issued in mono with generic Apple labels and picture sleeve.

Original copies of the LP were issued with customised labels featuring photographs that Paul and Linda had taken of one another, in a yellow paper inner sleeve. The cover, printed on thick card (an oblique reference to the rock'n'roll albums of McCartney's youth), was as uncompromising as the music. At a time when rock was becoming increasingly sophisticated and urbane, Wings positioned themselves as fervent ruralists diametrically opposed to the emergent glam rock scene then sweeping the country.

Because the cover did not feature the band's name or album title, in America Capitol placed a 4-inch by 2-inch rectangular sticker to the front cover with 'WINGS "WILD LIFE"' in yellow. A second white rectangular sticker with 'Paul McCartney and Friends' in blue was produced for later editions.

EMI re-released *Wild Life* in the mid 1980s on its budget FAME imprint (FA 416101-1) with generic black and silver Parlophone labels and a plain white inner sleeve. In America, Columbia reissued the album with generic red labels (FC-36480 and PC-36480).

The album was issued on 8-track cartridge in Britain (8X-PCS 7142) and America (8XW 3375). The American edition of the 8-track was issued without an Apple logo on the cover but with the text '© McCartney Productions, Inc 1971' printed below the Apple's address. Columbia reissued the 8-track (JCA 36480) in the early 1980s.

EMI issued *Wild Life* on CD (CD-FA 3101) on its FAME imprint on October 5 1987 and reissued a remastered edition on Parlophone (CDPMCOL3) on June 20 1989. Capitol issued the CD (CDM 7 52017 2) on the same day in 1989.

WILD LIFE
WINGS
SIDE 1 'Mumbo', 'Bip Bop', 'Love Is Strange', 'Wild Life'.
SIDE 2 'Some People Never Know', 'I Am Your Singer', 'Bip Bop Link', 'Tomorrow', 'Dear Friend', 'Mumbo Link'.
UK RELEASE November 15 1971; LP Apple PCS 7142; 8-track cartridge Apple 8X-PCS 7142 released January 1972; chart high No.8.
US RELEASE December 6 1971; LP Apple SW-3386; 8-track cartridge Apple 8XW 3386; chart high No.10.

- **'Mumbo'** (Paul and Linda McCartney)
Paul McCartney (vocals, bass), Linda McCartney (keyboards, backing vocals), Denny Laine (guitar), Denny Seiwell (drums).
- **'Bip Bop'** (Paul and Linda McCartney)
Paul McCartney (vocals, bass), Linda McCartney (backing vocals), Denny Laine (guitar), Denny Seiwell (drums).
- **'Love Is Strange'** (Smith, Baker)
Paul McCartney (vocals, bass), Linda McCartney (keyboards, backing vocals), Denny Laine (guitar), Denny Seiwell (drums).
- **'Wild Life'** (Paul and Linda McCartney)
Paul McCartney (vocals, bass), Linda McCartney (keyboards, backing vocals), Denny Laine (guitar), Denny Seiwell (drums).
- **'Some People Never Know'** (Paul and Linda McCartney)
Paul McCartney (vocals, piano), Linda McCartney (backing vocals), Denny Laine (guitar), Denny Seiwell (drums).
- **'I Am Your Singer'** (Paul and Linda McCartney)
Paul McCartney (vocals, recorder, bass), Linda McCartney (vocals), Denny Laine (guitar, recorder), Denny Seiwell (drums).
- **'Bip Bop Link'** (Paul and Linda McCartney)
Paul McCartney (guitar).
- **'Tomorrow'** (Paul and Linda McCartney)
Paul McCartney (vocals, piano), Linda McCartney (backing vocals), Denny Laine (guitar), Denny Seiwell (drums).
- **'Dear Friend'** (Paul and Linda McCartney)
Paul McCartney (vocals, piano), Linda McCartney (backing vocals), Denny Seiwell (drums).
- **'Mumbo Link'** (Paul and Linda McCartney)
Paul McCartney (vocals, bass), Denny Laine (guitar), Denny Seiwell (drums).

All recorded at Abbey Road Studios, London, England.
All produced by Paul and Linda McCartney.

'GIVE IRELAND BACK TO THE IRISH'

McCARTNEY could hardly be accused of playing it safe with the release of this Wings debut single (the first by the Mk.2 line-up: Paul, Linda, Laine, and Seiwell, plus new guitarist Henry McCullough).

Written in response to the Bloody Sunday Massacre that occurred in Northern Ireland on January 30 1972, it was as politically committed as anything Lennon issued. But where Lennon used the old trick of turning a cliché on its head to make a satirical comment ('The Luck Of The Irish' on *Sometime In New York City*), McCartney's appraisal of the situation was less successful. Speaking to *Sounds* about the song, he said: "Our government happened to be shooting Irish people, and I thought that was real bad news, and I felt I had to say something about it. I'm glad I did because, looking back, I could have just sat through it and not have said anything. But it was just that it got so near home on that particular day I felt I had to say something."

Written, recorded, and released at high speed, 'Give Ireland Back To The Irish' saw McCartney reintegrate himself, in spirit at least, with the political counterculture. However, this was more a one-off statement of disgust than an attempt to align himself with the radical left as Lennon was doing in New York City. Commenting on his decision to release the song and the political pressure Lennon was experiencing for expressing similar beliefs, McCartney said: "I always used to think, god, John's crackers doing all those political songs. I always used to think it's still cool not to say anything about it, because it's not going to sell anyway and no one's going to be interested. So I tried it, it went to number 1 in Ireland, and, funnily enough, it was number 1 in Spain, of all places. I don't think Franco could have understood." On its release, the song was immediately banned from the British airwaves, which didn't help the record's sales but added to its credibility.

'Give Ireland Back To The Irish' was still causing problems almost 30 years after its original release. When McCartney wanted to include it on *Wingspan – Hits And History*, EMI asked for it to be removed. "I support the idea of Ireland being free and being handed back," explained McCartney. "I feel that, like a lot of people; but I don't support [the IRA's] methods. I certainly don't want to be in support when a bomb goes off in London and people are killed. I would have a hard time supporting that. So when EMI rang me up and said, 'Look, you know, we're pretty nervous and you don't have much time on the album. We should pull that one,' that was really why it got pulled."

'Give Ireland Back To The Irish' lacks the melodic invention associated with McCartney and fails to convince as a rocker. Superior live recordings exist and suggest that, had Wings been given the opportunity to fine-tune their arrangement and performance, the song would have emerged from Abbey Road in better shape than it did. (The B-side was an instrumental version, emulating a practice of vocal/instrumental releases favoured by reggae bands.)

'GIVE IRELAND BACK TO THE IRISH' / 'GIVE IRELAND BACK TO THE IRISH (VERSION)'
WINGS
UK RELEASE February 25 1972; Apple R 5936; chart high No.16.
US RELEASE February 28 1971; Apple 1847; chart high No.21.

- **'Give Ireland Back To The Irish'** (McCartney, McCartney)
- **'Give Ireland Back To The Irish (Version)'** (McCartney, McCartney)

Both with Paul McCartney (vocals, bass), Linda McCartney (keyboards, backing vocals), Denny Laine (guitar), Henry McCullough (guitar), Denny Seiwell (drums).
Both recorded at Abbey Road Studios and Island or Apple Studios, London, England. Both produced by The McCartneys.

'Give Ireland Back To The Irish' data

The single was released with customised labels featuring five shamrocks (symbolic of the new five piece line-up?) in a generic yellow Wings sleeve.

British pressings exist with two label variations. Original pressings have 'Northern Songs Ltd' as the publisher, with 'Copyright also claimed by Kidney Punch Music'. The single was reissued in 1976, by which time the publishing credit had changed to 'McCartney Music Ltd by arrangement with ATV Music Ltd'. These pressings also include the legend 'EMI Records Ltd' printed below the band's name.

American singles were issued with the same label design as British pressings and in yellow Wings sleeves with the addition of the song's lyrics. Reissued in 1976, the single was manufactured with black and silver Capitol labels.

'WOMAN IS THE NIGGER OF THE WORLD'

LENNON the dreamer. Lennon the peacemaker. Lennon the activist. All these facets of his persona were believable. But Lennon the feminist? By the time 'Woman Is The Nigger Of The World' was issued, his sloganeering was wearing thin. When he wrote from the heart, there were few who could match him. But when he let his head rule his heart, as he did here, the result was hollow at best.

Lennon was no longer writing for himself, but for others. Where once he had led, now he followed. This song stretched the theme of revolutionary change he'd been exploring to breaking point. It wasn't as if the subject hadn't been tackled before. Sandy Posey wrote 'Born A Woman' in 1966, Loretta Lynn composed several proto-feminist songs, including 'Don't Come Home A' Drinkin' (With Lovin' On Your Mind)' and 'The Pill'. Even Helen Reddy wrote 'I Am Woman', for which she received a Grammy in 1972. Lennon may not have been the first songwriter to tackle the problem of sexual inequality, but he was probably one of the first male songwriters to do so.

Of course, the idea was Ono's. Lennon's feminist anthem was inspired by something she said in a *Nova* magazine interview in 1969. Although he was keen to promote the idea that the two of them were equals, he was the typical male artist. Speaking with Robert Enright in 1994, Ono recalled how the London music scene drove her to make the remark. "When I went to London and got together with John that was the biggest macho scene imaginable. That's when I made the statement 'woman is the nigger of the world'." Ono's remark was more a cry of frustration than a considered feminist statement. While speaking to Enright, she confirmed that when she had said it, she had "no notion of feminism". But when the Lennons transformed themselves into hip New York activists, her comment on rock's macho posturing was recycled and used as a feminist slogan, intended to change the 'heads' of people like her husband.

Lennon, of course, was a typical male chauvinist. But Ono is a strong woman and her impact on him was considerable. Without her, it's doubtful that he would have written a song like 'Woman Is The Nigger Of The World'. Talking to Roy Carr in 1972, he admitted her influence. "She changed my life completely. Not just physically ... the only way I can describe it is that Yoko was like an acid trip or the first time you got drunk. It was that big a change, and that's just about it. I can't really describe it to this day."

She opened his eyes to a world of possibilities, not least of which was personal freedom. By the early 1970s, the Lennons' plea for global harmony had become more focused. The only way to achieve revolution on a global scale was through a revolution of the self, and an important part of this was to attain sexual equality. Lennon spoke to *Red Mole* of women's liberation and his growing awareness of sexual inequality. "The women are very important too, we can't have a revolution that doesn't involve and liberate women. It's so subtle the way you're taught male superiority. It took me quite a long time to realise that my maleness was cutting off certain areas for Yoko. She's a red hot liberationist and was quick to show me where I was going wrong, even though it seemed to me that I was just acting naturally. That's why I'm always interested to know how people who claim to be radical treat women."

Lennon was right. A lot of Ono's work was about liberation and freedom from sexual oppression. But despite what he said to *Red Mole*, in reality he and his fellow male activists had changed little. Lennon was hip to this, and 'Woman Is The Nigger Of The World' was his way of criticising the macho attitudes that male left-wing activists were perpetuating. Activists Jerry Rubin and Abbie Hoffman may have had 'radical' ideas, but what of their attitude to women? The truth was that, like Lennon, they were typical male chauvinists.

Besides borrowing the title of his song from Ono, Lennon appropriated the chord sequence from The Platters' 'Only You' to kick-start the writing process. He recorded solo acoustic demos in late 1971 before recording began with Elephant's Memory in February '72. Phil Spector was called in to work his magic on the track, but even he struggled to breathe life into what was one of Lennon's weaker songs. Stan Bronstein's sax fills echo those on 'Power To The People', and Lennon delivered another electrifying vocal that outstrips Spector's echo-laden backing with confident ease – even if he wasn't a full-blown feminist, his performance just might convince you that he was. Yet despite everyone's best efforts the track failed to convince.

'Woman Is The Nigger Of The World' received its live debut on US TV's *The Dick Cavett Show* on May 11 1972, as did Ono's B-side – but it made little difference to the record's chart placing. One reason the record didn't sell was because radio stations refused to play it. The 'N' word was a big turn-off, but the record's chances weren't helped by Apple's failure to promote the single.

Pete Bennett, Apple's American promotion manager, hated the record and refused to promote it. Although Lennon and Ono thought they had a sure fire Number 1 with the single, Bennett knew better. "I told [Lennon] that I wouldn't promote it. So John says to me, 'Well, you're our promotions man, you have to listen to us, we pay you ... I'm the President of Apple.' I said, 'John, I don't care what the story is. I don't want the record – I'm not going to promote it. If I don't like it I won't promote it.' So John says, 'I'll tell you what – I'll promote it, and if I make this record Number 1, that means you're not the number one promotions man in the business.' I said, 'John, you got a deal ... but if the record doesn't happen, I want you to kiss my butt and double my salary and expenses.' So he says, 'You got a deal ... but I'm gonna make it Number 1.'

Bennett continued: "But without John knowing, I checked out all the radio stations and they said they weren't going to play it. So John called all of the stations himself and he tried to do a promo job. He was so happy and he came back to me and said, 'We still got that bet?' and I said, 'John, God bless you, we still have that bet and you better kiss my butt if you lose, and if you win, you can tell me, Peter, you're shit, and if you don't want me to work with you any more, that's it.' 'Well, you're gonna lose,' he told me, because he had called Chicago, he called San Francisco, and he talked to the Program Directors, and they were so nice to him, they took interviews with him. The thing was, the stations put him on tape, and while they played the record in the studio, they never put it on the air. What happened was that a few idiots played it on FM – but at that time FM was nothing, it couldn't sell two records – and all the top stations wouldn't play it. Apple sent out 30,000 records and about 15,000 came back."

'Sisters, O Sisters', Ono's open letter to her oppressed sisters, marked a dramatic change in her work. Previously, she and Lennon had encouraged their listeners to use the power of positive projection to bring about radical change. Here, she encourages direct intervention. As praiseworthy as her message was, if she'd couched it as a metaphor it would have had considerably more weight. As it stood, 'Sisters, O Sisters' had all the power of second-hand political cant.

It also reveals the effect that Lennon was having on her work. 'Sisters, O Sisters' was a conventional rock song with a 'reggae' twist. Musically, at least, she was moving away from the avant-garde into the mainstream. Her next album, *Approximately Infinite Universe*, a two-record set, contained no avant-garde music at all. Speaking to Roy Carr in 1972, she said: "Rock is a whole new field for me, and I get inspired so much that I find that now a lot of songs are coming out of me. Also, I think I was getting to a point where I didn't have too much competition. John was always with boys who were working together and therefore in direct competition." Ironically, Yoko was writing more songs, and better songs, than her husband.

Working with Elephant's Memory had its limitations. Lennon, like McCartney, was greatly influenced by reggae and wanted to record 'Sisters, O Sisters' in that idiom. The problem was that these musicians hadn't a clue, and the only reggae lick Lennon had to teach them with was Desmond Dekker's 'Israelites'. Talking to Andy Peebles in 1980, Lennon described how difficult it was to get them to play what he wanted. "I remember that session, Elephant's Memory, all New York kids, you know, saying they don't know what reggae was, I'm trying to explain to them all ... so if you listen to it you'll hear me trying to get them to reggae." He never did get them 'to reggae', and all the attempt produced was an uncomfortable juxtaposition of two contrasting styles. Better to have let them rock out and pretend to be the MC5, which is probably what they wanted.

'WOMAN IS THE NIGGER OF THE WORLD' / 'SISTERS, O SISTERS'
JOHN LENNON/PLASTIC ONO BAND WITH ELEPHANT'S MEMORY AND THE INVISIBLE STRINGS / YOKO ONO/PLASTIC ONO BAND WITH ELEPHANT'S MEMORY AND THE INVISIBLE STRINGS
UK RELEASE December 5 1972; Apple R 5853; withdrawn.
US RELEASE April 24 1972; Apple APPLE 1848; chart high No.57.

- **'Woman Is The Nigger Of The World'** (Lennon, Ono)
John Lennon (vocals, guitar), Stan Bronstein (saxophone), Gary Van Scyoc (bass), Adam Ippolito (piano, organ), Wayne 'Tex' Gabriel (guitar), Richard Frank Jr. (drums, percussion), Jim Keltner (drums).
- **'Sisters, O Sisters'** (Ono)
Yoko Ono (vocals), John Lennon (guitar), Stan Bronstein (saxophone), Gary Van Scyoc (bass), Adam Ippolito (piano, organ), Richard Frank Jr. (drums, percussion), Jim Keltner (drums).

Both recorded at The Record Plant East, New York City, NY, USA.
Both produced by John & Yoko and Phil Spector.

'Woman Is The Nigger Of The World' data

Issued with the Lennon and Ono 'merging heads' label and in a picture cover, 'Woman Is The Nigger Of The World' was the first and only single lifted from the Lennons' forthcoming album, *Some Time In New York City*. Despite Lennon's claims that the record was "banned" because it featured the word nigger, it was more successful than the Lennons' previous single, but still failed to enter the Top 40.

The single was due to be issued in Britain on December 5 1972 but was withdrawn. White-label test pressings were made, but commercial copies of the record were not produced. The record may have suffered the same fate as the Lennons' previous British single, which was postponed because of their dispute with Northern Songs over Ono's claim as co-author. By the time it had been cleared for release, the album it was intended to promote had already been issued and had flopped. The songwriting dispute that held up the British release of 'Woman Is The Nigger Of The World' must have been resolved by December 1972, as 'Happy Xmas (War Is Over)' was issued in Britain in November that year. It obviously made more commercial sense to go with that seasonal song rather than issue a single that had failed to enter the American Top 40.

'MARY HAD A LITTLE LAMB'

FROM political slogans to nursery rhymes: McCartney makes another about-turn. While 'Give Ireland Back To The Irish' had been written out of frustration and revulsion, Wings' second single was inspired by the McCartneys' children. The contrast may have been baffling, but it was certainly surprising. When asked why a nursery rhyme, McCartney said: "I'm a Gemini, and I know that one minute I might be doing 'Ireland' and the next I'll be doing

'MARY HAD A LITTLE LAMB' / 'LITTLE WOMAN LOVE'
WINGS
UK RELEASE May 5 1972; Apple R 5949; chart high No.9.
US RELEASE May 29 1972; Apple 1851; chart high No.28.

• **'Mary Had A Little Lamb'** (McCartney, McCartney)
Paul McCartney (vocals, piano), Linda McCartney (backing vocals), Heather and Mary McCartney (backing vocals), Denny Laine (bass), Henry McCullough (mandolin), Denny Seiwell (drums).
Recorded at Olympic Sound Studios, Barnes, England. Produced by The McCartneys.
• **'Little Woman Love'** (McCartney, McCartney)
Paul McCartney (vocals, piano), Linda McCartney (backing vocals), Dave Spinoza or Hugh McCracken (guitars), Milt 'The Judge' Hinton (bass), Denny Seiwell (drums).
Recorded at Columbia Studios, New York City, NY, USA. Produced by The McCartneys.

'Mary Had A Little Lamb'. I can see how that would look from the sidelines, but the thing is we're not either of those records, but we are both of them."

However, his attempt to negate categorisation failed to contradict suggestions that 'Mary Had A Little Lamb' was an expression of contempt aimed at the censors who had banned his previous single, and it did little to appease either critics or public, who were becoming disenchanted with his catholic taste.

As he explained it, his reasons for writing 'Mary Had A Little Lamb' were less involved and more prosaic. "Now, you know, I've just got three kids over the last few years, and when I am sitting at home playing at the piano my audience a lot of the time is the kids." His daughter Mary enjoyed hearing her name mentioned in song, so dad wrote one for her. Or rather he wrote a new melody to accompany an existing verse. "I just wrote that one up, the words were already written, you know? I just found out what the words to the nursery rhyme were, wrote a little tune up around it, [and] went and recorded it." He later admitted that the record might have disappointed fans. "I see now … that it wasn't much of a record," he confessed. True, with no middle eight or solo, the song tends to drag, but its chorus is infuriatingly catchy.

When he recorded 'Mary Had A Little Lamb' at Olympic Sound Studios, McCartney involved his band and his family. Beside Wings, the McCartneys' two eldest daughters, Heather and Mary, were invited to sing backing vocals.

'Little Woman Love', inspired by Linda, is a breezy rocker with upfront slap bass played by jazz ace Milt Hinton and a rolling piano lick that gives it a cute rockabilly feel. Recorded in New York City while they worked on *Ram*, this typically slick McCartney recording wouldn't have sounded out of place on *Red Rose Speedway*, which would feature another two outtakes from the *Ram* sessions.

'Mary Had A Little Lamb' data

Apple issued 'Mary Had A Little Lamb' in Britain and the USA with customised labels and in a picture cover. In America, Capitol manufactured two variants of the picture cover: one with 'Little Woman Love' printed on it, the other without.

The record was reissued by EMI and Capitol in the mid 1970s with black and silver Capitol 'dome' labels and MPL production credits rather than an Apple Records credit. To promote the single in America, Capitol issued white-label demonstration copies with black text and the artist credit 'Paul McCartney'.

SOME TIME IN NEW YORK CITY

IF YOU want to know what John Lennon and Yoko Ono were doing and thinking in late 1971/'72, listen to *Some Time In New York City*. Although they were based in England for most of '71, they made frequent visits to New York City. They were there in June that year, attempting to gain custody of Ono's daughter Kyoko. During that trip, they joined Frank Zappa on stage on June 6, and they issued the joint performance on *Some Time In New York City*. They returned again in July to record overdubs for *Imagine*. During that visit, Lennon and Ono made contact with political activist Jerry Rubin, before returning to England on July 14 to continue work on *Imagine* and promote Ono's book, *Grapefruit*. And on August 31, in another attempt to obtain custody of Kyoko, they returned to New York City; this time to stay.

Explaining his reasons for moving to New York, Lennon told Ray Coleman: "It's the Rome of today, a bit like a together Liverpool. I always like to be where the action is. In olden times I'd like to have lived in Rome or Paris or the East. The 1970s are going to be America's."

The 1960s had certainly been Britain's. The Beatles had seen to that. Although the 1970s had barely started, it was obvious that Britain was changing and not for the better. Lennon had grown dissatisfied with the offhand way the British press treated the work that he and Ono did and thought, mistakenly as it happened, that America would embrace him with open arms.

"It's Yoko's old stamping ground," he explained, "and she felt the country would be more receptive to what we were up to." Ironically, America, or more precisely the Nixon led American government, was far from welcoming. Lennon's desire to play an active role in what was already an ebbing counterculture brought him into conflict with the authorities in ways that would never have happened had he remained in Britain.

By the time he decided to make the move to New York City permanent, he had already committed himself to political activism. He'd spoken of 'British socialism', supported the Oz

Three, namechecked the Yippies in 'Give Peace A Chance', attacked the Nixon government in 'Give Me Some Truth', and issued 'Power To The People' and 'Imagine', both powerful political statements. The 'radical' views that Lennon put so much effort into promulgating were tolerated in Britain, but proved too much for Nixon's paranoid government.

By the time he decided to make the move to New York permanent, Lennon had already committed himself to political activism. He'd spoken of British socialism, supported the Oz Three, name-checked the Yippies in 'Give Peace A Chance', attacked the Nixon government in 'Give Me Some Truth', and issued 'Power To The People' and 'Imagine', both powerful political statements. The 'radical' views that Lennon put so much effort into promulgating were tolerated in Britain, but were too much for Nixon's paranoid government.

The Nixon administration attempted to deport Lennon by using his criminal record as their main objection to his US residency. In reality, the US government considered Lennon – who was freely associating with members of the radical New Left – a potential threat to political stability. A memo in official government files stated that "radical New Left leaders plan to use Mr Lennon as a drawing card to promote the success of rock festivals, to obtain funds for a 'dump Nixon' campaign". Senator Strom Thurmond suggested to Attorney General John Mitchell that if rapid action were taken against Lennon they would avoid "many headaches". The FBI began tapping Lennon's telephone, attending his concerts, and studying his lyrics in an attempt to gather enough evidence to deport him. However, the US authorities could not deport him for his political beliefs, no matter how 'radical' they were. Instead, it was suggested that he "be arrested, if at all possible, on a possession of narcotics charge". Lennon's US visa expired on February 29 1972, an extension was granted that led to an appeal against deportation, and so began his long struggle to remain in the USA.

The American authorities may not have welcomed the Lennons with open arms, but the counterculture did. David Peel, a fervent campaigner for the legalisation of cannabis, made a big impression on Lennon, who loved his irreverent songs and unique brand of street politics. Lennon was so infatuated with Peel that they shared a stage and band at the John Sinclair Freedom Rally. They appeared together again when the Lennons recorded a TV appearance for *The David Frost Show* on December 16. Lennon went on to name-check Peel in *New York City*, produce Peel's third album, *The Pope Smokes Dope*, and invite him to take part in the 'Give Peace A Chance' encore at Lennon's One To One concert.

More important, but more damaging for Lennon, was his association with Jerry Rubin. Rubin had spent much of his adult life harassing the Establishment. He was instrumental in organising protests against the Vietnam War, which became increasingly sophisticated, theatrical, and media-orientated. Along with Abbie Hoffman, Rubin founded the Youth International Party, the 'Yippies', who were vehemently anti-Establishment and trouble bound.

The apotheosis of Yippie activity took place in Chicago in 1968, when they organised a massive rally, the Festival Of Life, in opposition to the National Democratic Convention, also being held there. The Festival Of Life was intended to give those opposed to the Establishment a voice. A Yippie announcement proclaimed that the event would "be a contrast in lifestyles. Ours will be an affirmation of life; theirs is d-e-a-t-h". Thanks to heavy-handed policing, the festival turned violent, and when Rubin and several others, including the singer and fellow Yippie activist Phil Ochs, attempted to nominate a pig for President, Rubin was arrested. He was prosecuted for conspiracy and intent to encourage a riot.

The trial of the Chicago Seven became one of the most infamous in American legal history. The Establishment were out to destroy the counterculture and would have done so had it not been for the high-handed attitude taken by Judge Julius Hoffman, who caused outrage with his treatment of Bobby Seale, an American civil rights activist, co-founder, chairman, and national organiser of the Black Panther Party, whom he ordered gagged and bound. Although Hoffman found them guilty, the Chicago Seven had their convictions overturned by the Supreme Court, who found that the Judge had used unscrupulous tactics in handling the case.

The experience left Rubin depressed and disillusioned with the interventionist style of politics he'd helped to spearhead. But salvation, in the form of a song from the *John Lennon/Plastic Ono Band* album, was just around the corner. When Rubin heard 'Working Class Hero' it turned his life around. On discovering that the Lennons were in New York, all it took was a phone call to secure a meeting with them. Rubin arranged to meet them at Washington Square Park, from where they moved to Abbie Hoffman's apartment to discuss business. Both parties hit it off immediately, and Rubin was made the Lennons' 'political advisor' and a member of their ad hoc band.

It's no surprise that Rubin and Hoffman felt an affinity with Lennon. Lennon informed them that he planned to tour America with a political travelling circus and give the money generated to good causes. "We want to go around from town to town, doing a concert every other night for a month, at least," said Lennon. The funds he hoped to raise with his tour would be used for "disruptive activities". The final concert was due to take place in San Diego, California, and coincide with the Republican National Congress. It would be Chicago all over again, with Lennon in the lead. What self-respecting activist wouldn't be impressed by such a generous patron?

The Lennon-Rubin partnership was made in heaven. Lennon's desire to be recognised as a bona fide political activist was complete and Rubin acquired a readymade spokesman whom he could manipulate for his own political gain. Rubin wasn't slow to use Lennon for the revolutionary cause. There was, however, one small problem. The Lennons could not obtain work permits, which limited their plans to tour or promote their work and political views. But Rubin had a cunning plan. Where no payment was made to the artist, work permits were not required. The Lennons were only too pleased to give their services for free, particularly when it was in the name of radicalism.

The first charity event they attended was the John Sinclair Freedom Rally, a star-studded event held at the Crisler Arena in Ann Arbor, Michigan. Sinclair had managed the MC5 and was minister of information for the White Panther Party, whose war cry was 'Everything free for everybody!' At the time, Sinclair was serving a ten-year prison sentence for selling a couple of joints to some undercover cops. The concert was part of a Yippie-led campaign to free him.

The audience waited hours to see Lennon and anticipation was running high. But when Lennon and Ono eventually ambled onto the stage in the early hours of the morning of December 11, their four-song performance was a heroic anticlimax. New York's *Village Voice* expressed an opinion that many in the crowd must have shared: "The audience was slightly stunned. John and Yoko had performed for 15 minutes, urged political activism and support for John Sinclair, and split. ... It was depressing."

His appearance at the Sinclair rally hadn't impressed, but Lennon had filmed and recorded the event and planned to issue his four-song performance as an EP. However, as Sinclair was

SOME TIME IN NEW YORK CITY

JOHN & YOKO/PLASTIC ONO BAND WITH ELEPHANT'S MEMORY AND INVISIBLE STRINGS

SIDE 1 'Woman Is The Nigger Of The World', 'Sisters, O Sisters', 'Attica State', 'Born In A Prison', 'New York City'.
SIDE 2 'Sunday Bloody Sunday', 'The Luck Of The Irish', 'John Sinclair', 'Angela', 'We're All Water'.
LIVE JAM: JOHN & YOKO/PLASTIC ONO BAND
SIDE 3: 'Cold Turkey', 'Don't Worry Kyoko'.
SIDE 4: 'Well (Baby Please Don't Go)', 'Jamrag', 'Scumbag', 'Aü'.
UK RELEASE September 15 1972; LP Apple PCSP 716; 8-track cartridge Apple 8X-PCSP 716; chart high No.11.
US RELEASE June 12 1972; LP Apple SVBB 3392; 8-track cartridge Apple 8XW 3393 and 8XW 3394; chart high No.48.

• **'Attica State'** (Lennon, Ono)
Yoko Ono (vocals), John Lennon (vocals, guitar), Stan Bronstein (saxophone), Gary Van Scyoc (bass), Adam Ippolito (piano, organ), Richard Frank Jr. (drums, percussion), Jim Keltner (drums).
• **'Born In A Prison'** (Ono)
Yoko Ono (vocals), John Lennon (vocals, guitar), Stan Bronstein (saxophone), Gary Van Scyoc (bass), John La Bosca (piano), Richard Frank Jr. (drums, percussion), Jim Keltner (drums).
• **'New York City'** (Lennon)
John Lennon (guitar), Stan Bronstein (saxophone), Gary Van Scyoc (bass), Adam Ippolito (piano, organ), Richard Frank Jr. (drums, percussion), Jim Keltner (drums).
• **'Sunday Bloody Sunday'** (Lennon, Ono)
John Lennon (guitar), Stan Bronstein (saxophone), Gary Van Scyoc (bass), Adam Ippolito (piano, organ), Richard Frank Jr. (drums, percussion), Jim Keltner (drums).
• **'The Luck Of The Irish'** (Lennon, Ono)
John Lennon (vocals, guitar), Stan Bronstein (flute), Gary Van Scyoc (bass), Adam Ippolito (piano, organ), Richard Frank Jr. (drums, percussion), Jim Keltner (drums).
• **'John Sinclair'** (Lennon)
John Lennon (vocals, guitar), Gary Van Scyoc (bass), Adam Ippolito (piano, organ), Richard Frank Jr. (drums, percussion), Jim Keltner (drums).
• **'Angela'** (Lennon, Ono)
John Lennon (vocals, guitar), Stan Bronstein (saxophone), Gary Van Scyoc (bass), Adam Ippolito (piano, organ), Richard Frank Jr. (drums, percussion), Jim Keltner (drums).
• **'We're All Water'** (Ono)
Yoko Ono (vocals), John Lennon (guitar), Stan Bronstein (saxophone), Gary Van Scyoc (bass), Adam Ippolito (piano, organ), Richard Frank Jr. (drums, percussion), Jim Keltner (drums).
• **'Cold Turkey'** (Lennon)
John Lennon (vocals, guitar), Yoko Ono (vocals, bag), George Harrison (guitar), Eric Clapton (guitar), Klaus Voormann (bass), Billy Preston (organ), Delaney Bramlett (guitar), Bonnie Bramlett (percussion), Bobby Keys (saxophone), Jim Price (trumpet), Andy White (drums), Jim Gordon (drums), Keith Moon (drums), Nicky Hopkins (piano overdub).
• **'Don't Worry Kyoko'** (Yoko Ono)
Yoko Ono (vocals, bag), John Lennon (guitar), rest as 'Cold Turkey'.
• **'Well (Baby Please Don't Go)'** (Ward)
John Lennon (vocals, guitar), Yoko Ono (vocals), Frank Zappa (vocals, guitar), Mark Volman (vocals), Howard Kaylan (vocals), Ian Underwood (woodwind, keyboard, vocals), Aynsley Dunbar (drums), Jim Pons (bass, vocals), Bob Harris (keyboard, vocals), Don Preston (Minimoog).
• **'Jamrag'** (Lennon, Ono)
Personnel as 'Well (Baby Please Don't Go)'.
• **'Scumbag'** (Lennon, Ono, Zappa)
Personnel as 'Well (Baby Please Don't Go)'.
• **'Aü'** (Lennon, Ono)
Personnel as 'Well (Baby Please Don't Go)'.
All recorded at The Record Plant East, New York City, NY, USA and produced by John & Yoko and Phil Spector, except: 'Cold Turkey' and 'Don't Worry Kyoko' recorded live at Lyceum Ballroom, London, England and produced by John & Yoko; 'Well', 'Jamrag', 'Scumbag' and 'Aü' recorded live at Filmore East, New York City, NY, USA and produced by John & Yoko and Phil Spector.

released from prison early, plans to issue the record were scrapped. Two songs from the show, 'The Luck Of The Irish' and 'John Sinclair', were later issued on the *John Lennon Anthology*.

Lennon and Ono's next appearance was at the Apollo Theatre on December 17. The Attica State Benefit was intended to raise money for the families of prisoners who had been killed during the riot at the Attica Correctional Facility. Lennon appeared with a stripped-down acoustic band, performing two songs, 'Attica State' and 'Imagine', both recorded and issued later on the *John Lennon Anthology*. The rough and ready Sinclair and Attica State live recordings are of historical interest but not comparable to the studio versions – while they are of interest to the completist, the casual listener may find them disappointing.

Lennon's ad hoc group were adequate enough for the kind of low-key hit-and-run performances he gave in late 1971, but if he wanted to record and tour, which is what he was planning to do, something more professional was required. Once again, Rubin provided the solution by suggesting that Lennon check out a group of hairy rockers. Although Rubin played a part in bringing the two parties together, Rick Frank, drummer with the band, recalled that Lennon first heard them on the radio, when they played a live show for a Long Island radio station, WLIR.

Lennon was impressed by what he heard and invited Frank to audition for him. Frank: "He had me play on material that had no drum tracks recorded. … I walked into the Record Plant and I saw an engineer we had worked with, so I connected with him right away. I was never a Beatles fan, so the awe-struck aspect of it … it was there, but it was not like I had some fanatical desire to meet John Lennon, or his lovely wife. But I connected with Lennon and he asked me to put drums on these songs." Lennon made his mind up there and then, offering Frank and his bandmates the gig and a contract with Apple records. Rehearsals began almost immediately. Within weeks Lennon had dropped the acoustic folk style and adopted a harder edge with Elephant's Memory.

Stan Bronstein and Rick Frank had formed Elephant's Memory in 1967, developing an outrageous stage routine along the lines of The Who and The Move's loud, destructive performances. The group's first album was issued in 1969 and included two songs that later featured on the soundtrack of *Midnight Cowboy*, but their next record marked a change in direction. Influenced by Detroit-area bands such as MC5 and The Stooges, the Elephants were now producing in-your-face rock. Their second album also revealed a radical political bent. *Take It To The Streets* saw the band engage in Yippie sloganeering.

Danny Adler, who played guitar with the band for a while in the early 1970s, recalled that they were "laying the revolution stuff on with a shovel". Their songs were, he continued, "very standard hippie/Yippie anthems and sloganeering, expensively produced, blindingly loud, and ridiculously extravagant," which is exactly what Lennon wanted. Lennon made only one change to the band: he added a second drummer. Jim Keltner, who had played on *Imagine*, was drafted in to add extra weight to the rhythm section.

Despite the fact that they were backed by big money, Elephant's Memory were committed to overthrowing the very system that supported them. They were, then, the perfect complement to Lennon's own mixed-up political programme. The band was also under FBI surveillance, which gave it real street credibility but did little to help Lennon and his plan to stay in America. Re-christened Plastic Ono Elephant's Memory Band, their first job was to back the Lennons during their week-long residency on TV on *The Mike Douglas Show*. Their performance of 'Imagine' was later issued on a CD that accompanied the *Lennon Legend* book.

The Lennons' appearance on the *Douglas* show was part of a concerted campaign to establish themselves as serious artists and political activists. Besides promoting Ono's art, they premiered clips from the *Imagine* film and performed material destined for their soon-to-be-released *Some Time In New York City* album. They made their political views known by inviting various activists onto the show, giving them unprecedented primetime exposure on American television. Naturally, Rubin was interviewed to explain his political ideas. He also performed with Plastic Ono Elephant's Memory Band, as did actress and film director Barbara Loden.

Now that Lennon had a new band, recording began in earnest. Studio time was booked at the Record Plant East, with Phil Spector co-producing. Sessions began in February and continued into March. The album was completed on March 20, the Lennons' third wedding anniversary. However, two weeks before that, their visas expired. They were both granted extensions, but on March 6 their visas were suddenly cancelled. Lennon and Ono had officially outstayed their welcome. Nixon's government wanted these troublemakers gone – and John Lennon's battle to reside in America had begun.

When it was released, *Some Time In New York City* was universally slammed. Stephen Holden's review for *Rolling Stone* summed up critical reaction to the album. "Throughout their artistic careers, separately and together, the Lennons have been committed avant-gardists. Such commitment takes guts. It takes even more guts when you've made it so big that you don't need to take chances to stay on top: the Lennons should be commended for their daring. What is deplorable, however, is the egotistical laziness (and the sycophantic milieu in which it thrives) that allows artists of such proven stature, who claim to identify with the 'working class hero', to think they can patronise all whom they would call sisters and brothers."

British critics were equally perturbed by what they saw as Lennon's patronising tone. Tony Tyler's review for the *Melody Maker* criticised Lennon for the way he presented his songs, as well as the songs themselves. Although Tyler praised the musicianship, he singled out the lyrics, describing them as "Insulting, Arrogant, Rigid, Dogmatic … in short, the effect achieved was the opposite of the effect desired (I hope)".

Perhaps one reason *Some Time In New York City* fails to satisfy is because it features just two songs written by Lennon. Everything else was either co-written with Ono or an Ono solo composition. Ono's earlier avant-garde work had forced Lennon to explore new modes of self-expression. But as she moved closer to the mainstream, her music became more influenced by his. Their relationship was changing, and it wouldn't be long before they separated.

They also seemed content to follow where once they had led. The result was that John slipped into autopilot, quoting secondhand slogans set to reworked melodies. Perhaps if Lennon had concentrated his writing skills on his own problems, rather than those of which he had no real knowledge, he might have had something interesting to say. As it was, critics and public alike all but ignored the album.

Both Lennon and Ono were at their best when their work remained unresolved, ambiguous, open to multiple interpretations. For all its apparent opaqueness, *Two Virgins* was more radical and potentially life-changing than all the sloganeering on *Some Time In New York City*. When Lennon asked the world to "imagine", anything was possible. By simply repeating hackneyed slogans, he limited the number of possibilities to those prescribed by a handful of left-wing political activists, thereby alienating anyone who didn't share his view. Furthermore, as politically correct as Lennon's songs were, they only addressed those who shared or were convinced by his view. The songs on *Some Time In New York City* did little to make people think or persuade anyone to change their position.

Critical reaction to the album hit Lennon hard. Perhaps he never fully recovered from it. From now on he would always doubt the quality of his work. None of the albums he recorded in the wake of *New York City* captured the brilliance of his first two solo records. That's not to say that they were artistic failures, it's just that the magic sparkle that permeated *Plastic Ono Band* and *Imagine* had been largely effaced.

The opening track on *Some Time In New York City* has its roots in an event on September 13 1971, when a riot broke out at Attica Correctional Facility in upstate New York, up towards Lake Ontario. Around 1,200 prisoners, mostly African-Americans, took control of the prison and took 50 hostages. Their demands were simple – better conditions and terms for amnesty. Rather than give in to the prisoners' demands, the police and army moved in and shot 32 prisoners and 11 guards.

A few weeks after the riot, Lennon started to fashion his response. On the night of October 9, he celebrated his 31st birthday at the Syracuse hotel with an impromptu singalong with some friends. During the party, he sang what he had of 'Attica State', which was little more than a chanted chorus. He finished the song a few weeks later, fleshing out his idea and recording a rough demo with Ono on percussion. The song received its world premiere on December 10 at the John Sinclair Freedom Rally. Lennon performed it again six days later on *The David Frost Show*.

During the *Frost Show*, Lennon was criticised by members of the audience, who argued that he was glorifying prisoners. He responded by quoting his own lyrics: "The song says, '43 widowed wives.' That means guards' wives as well as prisoners' wives." He repeated his belief that all that the prisoners needed was "love and care". What he didn't mention was his and Ono's desire to "free all prisoners everywhere", something they were actively planning to do with funds from their proposed tour. Although Lennon and Ono managed to avoid explicit support for the prisoners during the TV show, their appearance at the Attica State Benefit at the Apollo Theatre the following day, December 17, would seem to confirm it (the live recording made at the Apollo was issued years later on the *John Lennon Anthology*).

Some Time In New York City songs

Recorded for *Some Time In New York City*, 'Attica State' featured honking saxophone and aggressive slide guitar. It also took on a thuggish backbeat that made it particularly suited for use on protest marches. As if to prove that they were equally committed to the cause, Lennon and Ono share the lead vocal. Listened to today, 'Attica State' betrays its origins while the pair were engaged in radical politics, and seems craftsman-like but uninspired.

Ono's 'Born In A Prison' comes next, reworking earlier pleas for personal freedom by removing the abstract metaphors and replacing them with simple leftist dogma. If Ono had once been able to imagine a better world, here she seems weighed down by the meaninglessness of human existence and broken on a wheel of despair. She does offer some hope of escape from futility, but the allusions to change she offers fail to counterbalance the all-embracing darkness of the verses. All the positive vibrations that the Lennons had attempted to share with the world were erased with this negative commentary on the human condition. (They performed the song at the One To One concert, and footage of their performance was included on the video *John Lennon Live In New York City*, but it was not programmed for the 1986 album of the same name.)

The move to New York City energised Lennon in many ways, one of which was his return to gutsy rock'n'roll. Speaking to Ron Skoler in September 1971, he explained how the city had influenced him. "It's the hippest place on earth, and that's why it's really inspiring to be here, and it just makes you wanna rock like crazy." Influenced by the place and the people he encountered there, Lennon wrote 'New York City', a rough and tumble rocker to record what had happened to him since setting foot in the Big Apple.

Within a few weeks of establishing himself there, Lennon had written the bare bones of the song but had yet to complete more than its first verse, which he reworked later. An early version featured in the soundtrack of Lennon and Ono's film *Clock*, filmed in September 1971. Further demo recordings followed, with

Lennon fleshing out his lyric with more recent experiences. An acoustic demo recorded late in 1971 appears on the *John Lennon Anthology*. With the song finished and Elephant's Memory installed, Lennon cut a dense, exciting street rocker that was the highlight of the album. Unsurprisingly, he chose to open his One To One concert with the song (and the matinee performance appears on the *John Lennon In New York City* album).

Like many, including Paul McCartney, Lennon was appalled by the Bloody Sunday Massacre that took place in Northern Ireland on January 30 1972. And like his former partner he decided to express his feelings in song. "Most other people express themselves by shouting or playing football at the weekend," he explained. "But me, here I am in New York and I hear about the 13 people shot dead in Ireland, and I react immediately. And being what I am, I react in four-to-the-bar with a guitar break in the middle. I don't say, 'My God, what's happening? ... We should do something.'"

'Sunday Bloody Sunday' was, like much of what appeared on *Some Time In New York City*, an instant response to a politically charged event, and typically partisan. Lennon may have felt compelled to set down in song his feelings about the killings, but his song was also a piece of pro-Republican propaganda that ignored the historical facts in favour of emotional blackmail. The 'Irish problem' was a political issue that encompassed state oppression, sectarianism, violent conflict, and terrible killings. In short, everything the Lennons had campaigned against. Lennon's pro-Republican agenda did little to bring either side together and was somewhat hypocritical. Hadn't he spent many, many hours preaching pacifism and peaceful revolution? The Irish Republican movement that Lennon supported had a long history of violent protest, something he was well aware of.

Speaking in September 1971 about his apparent hypocrisy, he said: "I understand why [these people are] doing it, and if it's a choice between the IRA or the British army, I'm with the IRA. But if it's a choice between violence and non-violence, I'm with non-violence. So it's a very delicate line ... . Our backing of the Irish people is done, really, through the Irish Civil Rights, which is not the IRA. Although I condemn violence, if two people are fighting, I'm probably gonna be on one side or the other, even though I'm against violence."

Lennon's disgust merged with an awareness of his own Irish roots. Liverpool had a large Irish population and both Lennon and McCartney had family ties with the country. Speaking with Ron Sloler, again in September 1971, Lennon spoke of his link to Ireland. "I'm a quarter Irish or half Irish or something, and long, long before the trouble started, I told Yoko that's where we're going to retire, and I took her to Ireland. We went around Ireland a bit and we stayed in Ireland and we had a sort of second honeymoon there. So I was completely involved in Ireland."

When he came to write 'Sunday Bloody Sunday', Lennon made his bond with Ireland all the more personal by aligning himself with the oppressed. Singing "When Stormont bans *our* marches" he associates himself with the Irish people and their struggle. Not only did he give the Civil Rights Movement the oxygen of publicity, he donated his songwriting royalties as well. "On the *Some Time In New York City* LP, the royalties of 'Sunday Bloody Sunday' and 'The Luck Of The Irish' are supposed to go to the Civil Rights Movement in Ireland and New York," he explained.

Lennon was obviously thinking about his roots and the political situation in Ireland long before the events of January 30 1972. He wrote 'The Luck Of The Irish' in the autumn of 1971. He began by recording two demos of the unfinished song, which reveal he had yet to complete either the melody or lyric. He returned to the song on November 12 1971, recording more acoustic guitar demos for a film by John Reily, also called *The Luck Of The Irish*. A month later, Lennon performed the song at the John Sinclair Freedom Rally, and four days later he gave it a brief reading on *The David Frost Show*. He performed it again on television, in full, on *The Mike Douglas Show* on January 28 1972.

Lennon's referencing of traditional folk music may have been an attempt to allude to Republican protest songs; it may also have been a way of connecting the melody with the subject matter. He was certainly familiar with traditional music, and both he and Ono considered themselves 'folk' artists who were writing songs that could be taken up by 'the people' and used to political ends. When they were criticised for performing overtly simplistic music at the John Sinclair Freedom Rally, Ono replied with a considered defence. Arguing that they were writing to encourage audience participation, she said: "Both in the West and the East, music was once separated into two forms. One was court music, to entertain the aristocrats. The other was folk songs, sung by the people to express their emotions and their political opinions. But lately, folk songs of this age, pop song, is becoming intellectualised and is starting to lose the original meaning and function. Aristocrats of our age, critics, reviewed the Ann Arbor rally and criticised the musical quality for not coming up to their expectations. That was because they lost the ears to understand the type of music that was played there. That was not artsy-craftsy music. It was music alongside the idea of: message is the music.

"We went back to the original concept of folk song, like a newspaper," Ono continued. "The function was to present the message accurately and quickly. And in that sense, it was funky music, just as newspaper layout could be called funky. Also, it is supposed to stimulate people among the audience and ... make them think, 'Oh, it's so simple, even I could do it.' It should not alienate the audience with its professionalism but ... communicate to the audience the fact that they, the audience, can be just as creative as the performers on the stage, and encourage them to make their own music with the performers rather than to just sit back and applaud."

Lennon and Ono had been trying to engage people in the

creative process from the very start of their partnership. Their early avant-garde albums were attempts to establish a reciprocal creative relationship with their audience. But by abandoning avant-gardism in favour of instinctual sloganeering, they were no nearer to reaching their goal. After the euphoria of their protests had worn off, Lennon and Ono quickly realised that their activism had been in vain. Speaking to Peter Hamil in 1975, Lennon revealed how disillusioned he had become with writing protest songs. "It became journalism and not poetry. And I basically feel that I'm a poet. ... I'm not a formalised poet, I have no education, so I have to write in the simplest forms, usually. And I realised that over a period of time – and not just cos I met Jerry Rubin off the plane, but that was like a culmination. I realised that we were poets but we were really folk poets, and rock'n'roll was folk poetry – I've always felt that. Rock'n'roll *was* folk music.

"Then I began to take it seriously on another level, saying, 'Well, I am reflecting what is going on, right?'" Lennon continued. "And then I was making an effort to reflect what was going on. Well, it doesn't work like that. It doesn't work as pop music or what I want to do. It just doesn't make sense. You get into that bit where you can't talk about trees, cos, y'know, y'gotta talk about 'corruption on 54th Street!'. It's nothing to do with that. It's a bit *larger* than that. It's the usual lesson that I've learned in me little 34 years: as soon as you've clutched onto something, you think – you're always clutchin' at straws – *this is what life is all about*."

'The Luck Of The Irish' was planned as the lead single from the album, backed with 'Attica State' (Apple 1846), and may have been well intentioned, but it was fundamentally flawed and ultimately impotent. Its plodding metre, rose-tinted lyric, and uninspired vocal (Lennon's and Ono's) make it an unwelcome aberration in Lennon's oeuvre.

John Lennon and John Sinclair had more in common than a forename: both shared an interest in political activism and each had convictions for possessing cannabis. Although Lennon's drug bust caused problems with American immigration, all he received by way of punishment was a slap on the wrist. Sinclair, however, received a ten-year prison sentence, but he did have a history of drug-related convictions. He was arrested for possessing marijuana in late 1964. A second arrest took place in 1965, when Sinclair was sentenced to six months in the Detroit House of Correction for "sales and possession of marijuana". Four years later, in July 1969, he was sentenced to prison for nine to ten years for possession of two reefers. Convinced that Sinclair's harsh prison sentence was further evidence of the Establishment's draconian use of drug laws to silence the counterculture, Lennon wrote an impassioned song of protest to be performed at the John Sinclair Freedom Rally.

Lennon wrote 'John Sinclair' in late 1971 and recorded a demo accompanying himself on dobro at about the same time as he recorded demos of 'Luck Of The Irish' and 'Attica State'. The song was finished in time for it to be performed at the John Sinclair Freedom Rally on December 10. By the time Lennon performed the song again, on *The David Frost Show* on December 16, Sinclair had been released from prison and the song made redundant. Rather than abandon the song, as they abandoned Sinclair, the Lennons decided to record it for *Some Time In New York City*. The Lennons dropped their radical crusading as quickly as they had adopted it. Once they realised that associating with leftist radicals was jeopardising their chances of remaining in the USA, they sidelined Sinclair and his contemporaries.

Not long after he arrived in America, Lennon began writing what would become his next album, *Some Time In New York City*. Some of the songs he composed were directly influenced by the political process he was involved in, others less so. Among the batch of songs he recorded while staying at the St. Regis Hotel in November 1971 was 'JJ', an unfinished ballad that evolved into another political tirade, 'Angela'.

Angela Davis was a talented academic and a member of the Student Non-violent Co-ordinating Committee (SNCC), the Black Panther Party, and the American Communist Party. Removed from her teaching position at UCLA as a result of her social activism, she made national headlines when guns allegedly registered in her name were used in an attempted prison escape, during which four people were killed. Even though she was nowhere near the scene, Davis was placed on the FBI's Ten Most Wanted list and driven underground. An articulate speaker, Davis had argued that the state used the threat of prison to control politically active African-Americans. Ironically, when she was arrested and charged with kidnap, conspiracy, and murder, that is exactly where she found herself.

When asked to contribute to the 'Free Angela Davis' campaign, Lennon returned to the unfinished 'JJ' and with Ono wrote a new set of lyrics. The song had already been re-worked as 'People', but the third set of lyrics were obviously influenced by Ono, as her aphorisms are scattered throughout. Lines like "Angela, there's a wind that never dies" leads one to suspect that it was Ono who wrote most of the words. The fact that she takes the lead vocal, with Lennon adding harmonies on the chorus, confirms this.

Water fascinates Ono and featured in some of her earliest work. For her, water has magical properties and subversive qualities that potentially can bring about physical change or social unity – a consistent theme that runs throughout her work. For her *This Is Not Here* exhibition at the Everson Museum in Syracuse, New York, in October 1971, the audience was encouraged to submit a water sculpture to which Ono would contribute. The water event was intended to promote unity by symbolically establishing a relationship between the artist and audience. With this event foremost in her mind, Ono revisited the notes she wrote to accompany her *half-A-wind* exhibition at the Lisson Gallery, London. Reworking a piece called *Water Talk*, Yoko fashioned a lyric for 'We're All Water' that emphasised similarities rather than differences. (Backed by Elephant's Memory, she performed the song at 1972's One To One concert, but it does not appear on either the album or video of that event.)

To launch their 'War Is Over' poster campaign, the Lennons gave a performance at the Lyceum Ballroom, London, on December 15 1969 in aid of the United Nations Children's Fund. Alan White, who played drums with the band that night, has suggested that Lennon was initially unhappy about playing the concert. He said: "I remember going to Apple first, and [Lennon was saying to] Allen Klein: 'Why are you making me do this?' It was something contractually that he signed up for, or something like that, without knowing, and he had to do it. But in the end it became a really great evening, and he enjoyed it."

Lennon originally intended to perform with the same line-up that had backed him in Toronto a few months earlier, with the addition of Billy Preston on keyboards. But in keeping with the fluid nature of Plastic Ono Band, it was a much larger 'supergroup' that took to the stage. Eric Clapton and George Harrison arrived with Delaney & Bonnie Bramlett's band in tow, some of whom were invited to join Plastic Ono Band for the night.

The band walked on stage at midnight to a less than capacity crowd. According to contemporary reports, the 2,000-capacity ballroom was only half full. Most of the audience sat on the floor for the performance, which lasted a little under 30 minutes.

Plugging in their instruments, the band ripped through the first number of the night, 'Cold Turkey'. For a band that had barely rehearsed, Plastic Ono Supergroup delivered a stunning reading of Lennon's anti-drug anthem. However, because the ensemble had grown to twice its original size, the 4-track tape machine booked to record the concert was unable to capture all the musicians successfully. Billy Preston's performance was lost, so Nicky Hopkins was called on to overdub electric piano to replace the lost organ part. Hopkins's overdub was recorded in New York in 1971.

Although 'Cold Turkey' had been a sizeable hit, some in the audience were a little disappointed with Lennon's choice of material. One concert-goer said: "Why couldn't they have done stuff like 'Blue Suede Shoes', 'Dizzy Miss Lizzy', or 'Roll Over Beethoven'? Music is supposed to release the emotions. All I felt was depressed." Lennon was moving faster than his audience, many of whom still thought of The Beatles as cute mop-tops. Speaking after the show, Lennon took another step towards distancing himself from The Beatles as he explained how he saw Plastic Ono Band developing. "I'm sorry people get disappointed – but that's rock'n'roll! I'm not The Beatles anymore. The Plastic Ono Band is an impromptu thing. We could play 'Blue Suede Shoes' or Beethoven's 9th. It depends on how we feel."

Following the six-minute reading of 'Cold Turkey', Ono led the band through a 15-minute rendition of 'Don't Worry Kyoko'. With everyone locked into the song's hypnotic riff, the problem was how to bring the song to a close. Alan White had the solution.

White recalled: "One thing I had learned at a very early age is when something's just going on and on and on, how do you get out of the song? Because nobody knows who's doing what. So I taught myself to just start speeding the song up. So I started speeding the song up, and everybody went with me. [Then you] speed it up so fast that nobody [can] play any more," White laughed. "It was so fast, so it was like *nee-nee-nee*, and it becomes one note, and then you slow it down, and go bomp and finish it. ... It's going faster and faster and faster, and it gets so fast, nobody can play that fast any more, and then you can slow it down and – oh, it's finished."

There were more live recordings on *Some Time In New York City* beyond the two Lyceum cuts, but from a different event. While in New York to overdub strings on the *Imagine* album, Lennon and Ono were introduced to Frank Zappa by journalist Howard Smith. The introductions took place at Zappa's hotel, and Smith suggested that the Lennons might join Zappa on stage.

Zappa recalled the meeting with casual indifference. "The day before the show, a journalist in New York City woke me up – knocked on the door and is standing there with a tape recorder, and goes: 'Frank, I'd like to introduce you to John Lennon,' you know, waiting for me to gasp and fall on the floor. And I said, 'Well, OK, come on in.' And we sat around and talked, and I think the first thing [Lennon] said to me was, 'You're not as ugly as I thought you would be.' So anyway, I thought he had a pretty good sense of humour, so I invited him to come down and jam with us at the Filmore East. We had already booked in a recording truck because we were making the *Live At The Filmore* album at the time. After they had sat in with us, an arrangement was made that we would both have access to the tapes. He wanted to release it with his mix and I had the right to release it with my mix – so that's how that one section came about."

The Lennons joined Zappa on stage at about 2:00am for the band's final encore. After a brief introduction, Lennon backed by The Mothers Of Invention turned in a convincing performance of The Olympics' 'Well (Baby Please Don't Go)'. It was marred only by the band's inability to bring the song to a proper conclusion. (If only Alan White had been available.) Consequently, the sloppy ending was edited from the record. While Lennon alluded to the fact that he hadn't sung the song since his days at the Cavern, he had in fact only recently recorded it. He cut a version while making *Imagine* that didn't make that album but would later be made available on the *John Lennon Anthology*. (The Zappa event was also filmed, and although it has yet to be commercially released, it does circulate among video collectors.)

Having got things rolling with a blast from the past, Lennon, Ono, and Zappa set about confounding the audience with some reworked and improvised 'music'. 'Jamrag' was in fact a revised take of Zappa's composition 'King Kong'. Lennon and Ono contributed nothing to the piece, but, nevertheless, claimed the song as their own. Zappa, naturally, was less than happy. "The bad part is," he explained, "there's a song that I wrote called 'King

Kong' which we played that night, and I don't know whether it was Yoko's idea or John's idea, but they changed the name of the song to 'Jamrag', gave themselves writing and publishing credit on it, stuck it on an album, and never paid me. It was obviously not a jam-session song – it's got a melody, it's got a bassline, it's obviously an organised song. [That was a] little bit disappointing."

There are two more live cuts from the Zappa concert. 'Scumbag', an improvised song consisting of the title sung over and over again, is marginally better than what follows. On 'Aü', Ono wails, guitars feed back, and another evening with Lennon and Ono comes to an anticlimactic end. Lennon was so bored that he left the stage and Ono was trapped in her ever-present bag.

Some Time In New York City data

The album was issued in America by Apple on June 12 1972. Released as a two-record set in a gatefold jacket, it included printed inner sleeves, a postcard, and a petition. Initial pressings have a hand-etched message in the dead wax: "John and Yoko forever, peace on earth and good will to men 72" and carry 'merging heads' labels.

The LP was reissued by Capitol records in the late 1970s with purple labels with a large Capitol logo. This variant of the album was issued with both records placed in the rear pocket of the gatefold cover, the front pocket being glued shut.

British pressings were similar to those issued in the USA, but did not include the petition. Like the previous two singles, the British release of *Some Time In New York City* was held up because of the Lennons' dispute with Northern Songs. Despite the fact that the British release date was delayed by three months, it made a better impression on the charts there than it had in America.

The album was issued as a double 8-track in Britain (8X-PCSP) and the USA (8XW 3393/94), with both cartridges fitting into a card sleeve.

Some Time In New York City was issued as a two-CD set in Britain and America on August 10 1987 (CDS 7 46782 8). The album was remixed, remastered, and reissued in November 2005 as a single CD (0946 3 40976 2 8) with several of the 'Live Jam' cuts and the studio versions of 'Listen, The Snow Is Falling' and 'Happy Xmas (War Is Over)'.

'HAPPY XMAS (WAR IS OVER)'

THE ORIGINS of 'Happy Xmas (War Is Over)' stretched back to Lennon and Ono's 'War Is Over' poster campaign, launched on December 15 1969 in 12 cities around the world. The simple white posters proclaimed: "War Is Over! If You Want It. Happy Christmas from John & Yoko." With this germ of an idea in place, the pair wrote a seasonal song, developing the theme of peaceful revolution that Lennon had argued for with 'Imagine'.

'HAPPY XMAS (WAR IS OVER)' / 'LISTEN THE SNOW IS FALLING'
JOHN LENNON & YOKO ONO/PLASTIC ONO BAND WITH THE HARLEM COMMUNITY CHOIR / YOKO ONO AND PLASTIC ONO BAND
UK RELEASE November 24 1972; Apple R 5870; chart high No.4 (re-enters January 4 1975, chart high No.48; re-enters December 20 1980 chart high No.2; re-enters December 19 1981 chart high No.28; re-enters December 25 1982 chart high No.56; re-enters December 24 1983 chart high No.92; re-enters December 22 1984 chart high No.92; as R 6627 re-enters December 20 2003 chart high No.33).
US RELEASE December 1 1971; Apple APPLE 1842; failed to chart.

- **'Happy Xmas (War Is Over)'** (Ono, Lennon)
John Lennon (vocals, guitar), Yoko Ono (vocals), Hugh McCracken (guitar), Chris Osbourne (guitar), Teddy Irwin (guitar), Stuart Scharf (guitar), Nicky Hopkins (piano, chimes, glockenspiel), Jim Keltner (drums, sleigh bells), The Harlem Community Choir (backing vocals).
- **'Listen, The Snow Is Falling'** (Ono)
Yoko Ono (vocals), John Lennon (guitar), Hugh McCracken (guitar), Nicky Hopkins (piano, chimes), Klaus Voormann (bass), Jim Keltner (drums).

Both recorded at The Record Plant East, New York City, NY, USA.
Both produced by John & Yoko and Phil Spector.

He often 'borrowed' motifs from other songs to kick-start his own. He'd based 'Come Together' on Chuck Berry's 'You Can't Catch Me', but the first few bars of 'Happy Xmas (War Is Over)' were appropriated from The Paris Sisters' 'I Love How You Love Me' – at least, that's what Phil Spector claimed. Spector had produced the Paris Sisters record, so he should have known. Also, Lennon instructed the producer that he wanted the record to sound like the one he'd just produced for his wife, Ronnie Spector, 'Try Some, Buy Some'. Spector obliged by having the assembled guitarists play a mandolin-like riff to complement the song's main musical motif.

As Klaus Voormann's flight to New York was delayed, one of the guitarists was called on to play bass. Basic tracks and instrumental overdubs were completed in one evening. A rough mix was produced at the end of the session, perhaps the one that appears on the *John Lennon Anthology*, which the Lennons took away with them. The Harlem Community Choir added their contribution to the record two days later, on October 31.

A Christmas classic with a timeless melody and intelligent lyrics, 'Happy Xmas (War Is Over)' was produced to perfection by Phil Spector. Sadly, it is as relevant today as when it was written.

Ono's 'Listen, The Snow Is Falling' predated by almost a year the 'War Is Over!' poster campaign that influenced Lennon's A-side. Her song first surfaced as 'Snow Is Falling All The Time' on the Aspen flexi-disc recorded in late 1968. It restates an idea used for another B-side, 'Who Has Seen The Wind?'. For Ono, natural elements have the power to connect people. 'Listen, The Snow Is Falling' combines her fascination with natural elements, such as wind and water, with her desire for global harmony and unity.

Recording the song should have been simple, but Ono grew increasingly frustrated with the musicians, who she thought weren't taking her work seriously. First she couldn't agree with Lennon on the song's tempo. She wanted it fast, but all that happened was that the band started to rock out, which wasn't what she wanted. Nicky Hopkins' playing came in for criticism, and when Klaus Voormann and Hugh McCracken began to develop some riffs to enhance the melody, she got into a shouting match with Voormann over where they should go. It was only Lennon's intervention that stopped the bass player from walking out of the session. The studio atmosphere may have been tense, but the recording sounded as relaxed and graceful as her earlier recordings had sounded tense and feral.

'Happy Xmas (War Is Over)' data

Apple issued 'Happy Xmas (War Is Over)' in the USA on December 1 1971. The British release was held up by almost a year because of Ono's claim as co-author. The Lennons, like the McCartneys, were having problems with their music publishers, who were unhappy at Lennon's claim that he was writing with his wife. Lennon's British publishers, Northern Songs, were refusing to accept the fact that Ono had contributed to the composition of 'Happy Xmas (War Is Over)'. Consequently, the British single was not released until the dispute was resolved.

American pressings were issued on green or black vinyl with a picture cover and two label variations. Copies were issued with a bespoke 'merging heads' label, based on photographs of Lennon and Ono taken by Ian Macmillan, or generic Apple labels.

Seven-inch white-label promotional copies of the single (S-45X-47663) were manufactured in very limited numbers for US radio stations. The American Apple label variant was issued with three typographical variations. The first has a light green Apple label with song title on three lines at 11 o'clock and composer credit below; 'STEREO' at 9 o'clock; publisher credits at 2 o'clock; artist's name 'JOHN & YOKO and the LENNON PLASTIC ONO BAND with THE HARLEM COMMUNITY CHOIR' centre bottom.

The second variant has a light green Apple label with song title on four lines at 11 o'clock and composer credit below; 'STEREO' at 9 o'clock; artist's name 'JOHN & YOKO and the LENNON PLASTIC ONO BAND with THE HARLEM COMMUNITY CHOIR' bottom left. And the third has a light green Apple label with song title on two lines at 11 o'clock and composer credit below; 'STEREO' at 9 o'clock; artist's name 'JOHN & YOKO and the LENNON PLASTIC ONO BAND with THE HARLEM COMMUNITY CHOIR' centre bottom.

By the mid 1980s, Capitol had manufactured the single with several label variations. They reissued the single in 1976 with orange Capitol labels; in 1978 with purple Capitol labels; in 1983 with black/colour band labels (these can be found with or without 'Under License From ATV Music'); and in 1988 with purple Capitol labels with the publishing credited to 'Ono Music / Blackwood Music Inc. Under License From ATV Music (Maclen)-BMI.'

In 1986 Capitol produced two different white vinyl 12-inch pressings for promotional use. The first of these (SPRO-9929) was limited to 2,500. Pressed with a silver and white variant of the 'merging heads' label, it was packaged in a transparent vinyl sleeve with a large silver sticker depicting one of Lennon's drawings. The second white vinyl 12-inch (SPRO-9894) was issued with black/colour band labels and a custom cover. The record featured 'Happy Xmas (War Is Over)' on both sides of the disc and was issued in a picture cover, which was hand numbered. Released in an edition of 2,000, this promotional record was produced to benefit the Central Virginia Foodbank charity.

In 1996, Capitol's Special Markets Division reissued 'Happy Xmas (War Is Over)' as a jukebox single (S7-17644) on green vinyl with purple Capitol labels. Between 20,000 and 22,000 copies of this edition of the single were manufactured and distributed.

Geffen Records reissued the single in November 1982, to promote the *John Lennon Collection*. The commercial 7-inch single (7-29855) was issued with a new picture cover and B-side, 'Beautiful Boy (Darling Boy)' from *Double Fantasy*. Geffen also produced a 12-inch promotional single (PRO-A-1079) issued to radio stations.

British pressings of 'Happy Xmas (War Is Over)' were only issued with the 'merging heads' label. Initial copies were pressed on opaque green vinyl (American pressings use transparent green vinyl). Because of the single's success in Britain, the initial batch of green vinyl pressings was quickly exhausted and the record was reissued on black vinyl.

In Britain the single was re-promoted almost every year after its original release, but it was not until 1980, when the record was re-promoted in the wake of Lennon's murder, that the picture cover was reinstated. The only difference between original 1972 covers and the 1980 reissue is that originals are made from heavier card.

The single was reissued, rather than re-promoted, in 2003 with a new B-side, 'Imagine'. That issue (R 6627) used a newly remastered version of 'Happy Xmas (War Is Over)' produced for the *John Lennon Legend* DVD. This single was also issued on green vinyl with a black Parlophone label in a revised picture cover with additional information about the *John Lennon Legend* DVD and CD. An enhanced CD single (CDR 6227) accompanied the vinyl release.

Promotional CD singles were issued to promote both the *Lennon Legend* and *Anthology* albums. A one-track CD single (IMAGINE 002) was manufactured by Parlophone/EMI for British radio stations to promote *Lennon Legend*. A two-track CD single (LENNON 002) of the rough mix of 'Happy Xmas (War Is Over)' backed with 'Be-Bop-A-Lula' was produced by Capitol to promote the *Anthology/Wonsaponatime* albums.

Ono also used 'Happy Xmas (War Is Over)' to promote the reissue of her back catalogue by Rykodisc. Issued as a CD single (VRCD-ONO) in 1991 with a Christmas message from her, the single was issued with a custom sleeve in a PVC wallet. In 1997, she had a limited number of CD singles of 'Listen The Snow Is Falling' / 'Happy Xmas (War Is Over)' produced as Christmas presents for friends. These privately produced CDs came with a picture cover depicting a burning match and instructions for her *Lighting Piece*.

'HI, HI, HI' / 'C MOON'
WINGS
UK RELEASE December 1 1972; Apple R 5973; chart high No.5.
US RELEASE December 4 1972; Apple 1857; chart high No.10.

• **'Hi, Hi, Hi'** (Paul and Linda McCartney)
Paul McCartney (vocals, bass), Linda McCartney (keyboard, backing vocals), Denny Laine (bass), Henry McCullough (guitar), Denny Seiwell (drums).
• **'C Moon'** (Paul and Linda McCartney)
Paul McCartney (vocals, piano, marimba), Linda McCartney (backing vocals, percussion), Denny Laine (bass), Henry McCullough (drums), Denny Seiwell (cornet, xylophone).
Both recorded at Morgan Studios, London, England.
Both produced by Paul McCartney.

'HI, HI, HI'

A REAL sex and drugs and rock'n'roll record, 'Hi, Hi, Hi' created more trouble with the censors but gave a real boost to Wings' street credibility. Some, particularly those at the BBC, thought 'Hi, Hi, Hi' might be taken to endorse the use of drugs – and McCartney's recent run-in with the authorities, for possession of marijuana, must have coloured official reaction to the song.

On August 10 1972, immediately after Wings' performance at the Scandinavium Hall in Gothenburg, Sweden, Paul, Linda and Denny Seiwell were arrested for possession of marijuana. Customs officials had intercepted a parcel addressed to McCartney containing seven ounces of the dreaded weed. When questioned, all three denied any knowledge of either the parcel or the drugs. However, after around three hours of questioning, they confessed that drugs were being sent to them on a regular basis so they could avoid going through Customs with the drugs themselves.

John Morris, the band's tour manager, made a statement to the press on their behalf. "Paul, Linda, and Dennis did admit to the Swedish police that they used hash. At first they denied it, but the police gave them a rough time and started threatening all sorts of things. The police said they would bar the group from leaving the country unless they confessed." The musicians were released after paying around £1,000 in fines (about $2,500 at the time) and given the option of either leaving the country or continuing with the tour. They continued, as planned, with a concert in Lund.

Less than a month later, police inspected McCartney's farm in Scotland and found several marijuana plants. He was charged with knowingly cultivating the plants and ordered to appear in court the following March. Pleading guilty to possessing and having control of cannabis, once again McCartney claimed that the seeds had been sent to him through the post by a fan. McCartney was fined £100 ($250), but as this was his second bust in just over a month, he obviously expected a harsher sentence. Interviewed outside the court he joked: "I was planning on writing a few songs in jail."

He wrote 'Hi, Hi, Hi' in Spain for the band's upcoming tour. Whether he was being deliberately rebellious or just plain naive, he thought "the 'Hi, Hi, Hi' thing could easily be taken as a natural high, could be taken as a booze high and everything. It doesn't have to be drugs, you know, so I'd kind of get away with it. Well, the first thing they saw was drugs, so I didn't get away with that." Although his references didn't go undetected, having the record banned did little harm to either his reputation or the record's sales. In the short-term, McCartney's conviction for possession of cannabis made headline news and provided much needed publicity. One unnamed member of Wings allegedly said: "The police action against us was an excellent advertisement. Our name flies now all over the world." In the long-term it caused problems with immigration authorities, particularly those in the USA, as they could refuse admission to any person with a conviction of this type.

If McCartney thought he could fool the censors into believing that 'Hi, Hi, Hi' was unrelated to any form of drug-induced high, the song's sexual innuendoes proved to be just as provocative. Due to no fault of his own, radio stations received incorrect copies of the lyrics. He said: "I just had some line, 'Lie on the bed get ready for my polygon.' The daft thing about all of that was our publishing company, Northern Songs, owned by Lew Grade, got the lyrics wrong and sent them round to the radio station, and it said, 'Get ready for my body gun,' which is far more suggestive than anything I put. 'Get ready for my polygon' – watch out baby. I mean it was suggestive, but abstract suggestive, which I thought I'd get away with. Bloody company goes round and makes it much more specific by putting 'body gun' – better words, almost."

A classic McCartney rocker, 'Hi Hi Hi' has everything going for it: controversial lyrics, a rock solid performance, and a false ending that's as ripped as a speed freak's adrenaline rush.

'C Moon' finds Wings in reggae mode, and to keep things fresh the band swapped instruments. McCartney played piano and marimba, Linda tambourine and backing vocals, Henry McCullough drums, Denny Laine bass, and Denny Seiwell cornet. Although 'C Moon' seemed innocuous, it too had a message. It was McCartney's coded way of saying everything was cool. Explaining the lyric to *Sounds*, he said: "Remember Sam The Sham and 'Woolly Bully'? Well, there's a line in that that says 'Let's not be L 7' – and at the time everyone was saying 'What's L 7 mean?' Well, L 7, it was explained at the time, means a square – put L and 7 together and you get a square. So I thought of the idea of putting a C and a crescent moon together to get the opposite of a square. So C Moon means cool."

'Hi, Hi, Hi' data

'Hi, Hi, Hi' / 'C Moon' was released in the UK by Apple Records as a double A-side single with customised red labels and a generic yellow Wings sleeve. Original British pressings have on the label 'An Apple Record (P) 1972 The Gramophone Company Ltd. An EMI Recording' and publishing credits 'McCartney Music Limited Northern Songs Ltd'. Demonstration copies were issued with a large black 'A' at 2 o'clock and 'DEMO RECORD NOT FOR SALE' on three lines above the spindle hole.

When the single was reissued in the mid 1970s, the publishing credits were changed to 'McCartney Music Ltd by arrangement with ATV Music Ltd' and the reference to Apple Records replaced with '(P) 1972 MPL Communications Inc'. The reissue was manufactured with two label variations: red labels with black text, or black labels with silver text.

American pressings (issued with generic Apple sleeves) utilise the same label design as British pressings. The US reissue was manufactured with black and silver Capitol 'dome' labels. Apple did not prepare demonstration singles for the American release.

'MY LOVE'

WHILE Lennon was writing about American politics and recording with a hard-nosed band of rough and tumble rockers, McCartney had been busy crafting twee pop songs and honing Wings' studios skills to perfection. 'My Love' marked the beginning of Wings' mature period. Its restrained sensitivity, absent from much of the band's early material, indicated a growing self-assurance. For perhaps the first time Wings worked as a group, rather than a collective of individuals.

'My Love' featured some of the best ensemble playing that Wings Mk.2 ever recorded and was proof, if needed, that they were capable of creating work on a par with that of The Beatles. Unfortunately, this was to be the exception rather than the rule; inconsistencies dogged the forthcoming *Red Rose Speedway* album, as they would much of McCartney's solo career.

'MY LOVE' / 'THE MESS'
PAUL McCARTNEY AND WINGS
UK RELEASE March 23 1973; Apple R 5985; chart high No.9.
US RELEASE April 9 1973; Apple 1861; chart high No.1.

- **'My Love'** (McCartney)
Paul McCartney (vocals, electric piano), Linda McCartney (backing vocals), Denny Laine (bass), Henry McCullough (guitar), Denny Seiwell (drums). Recorded at AIR Studios or Abbey Road Studios, London, England.
- **'The Mess'** (McCartney)
Paul McCartney (vocals, bass), Linda McCartney (keyboards, backing vocals), Denny Laine (guitar), Henry McCullough (guitar), Denny Seiwell (drums). Live recording at Congresgebouw, The Hague, Netherlands.
Both produced by Paul McCartney.

Taken from *Red Rose Speedway*, 'My Love' marked a return to form and showcased some outstanding ensemble playing by Wings. It was recorded live in the studio, with a full orchestra, and features a sublime guitar solo by Henry McCullough. Yet despite his excellent performance, McCullough struggled to capture his solo. Just before yet another take, he asked if he could try something a little different. Perhaps it was recording with a full orchestra, or simply the pressure of trying to meet McCartney's exacting standards, but, as McCullough recalled: "Whenever the orchestra struck up, I took fright." Speaking to Richard Skinner, McCartney said: "We'd worked it out and rehearsed it, and we had a full orchestra, it was ... played and sung live. We had the whole orchestra waiting ... for the downbeat and Henry McCullough, the Irish guitar player, comes over to me and says, 'Just a minute, do you mind if I change the solo?' And actually it's one of the best solos he ever played."

Revealing another facet of Wings, 'The Mess' was a fine example of McCartney's other strength: heads-down-no-nonsense rock'n'roll. Recorded live in The Hague, it was one of the better songs Wings showcased during their 1972 European tour. Several others, such as '1882' and 'Best Friend', were also recorded and prepared for release, but only 'The Mess' made it onto record. McCartney made attempts to record a studio version, but he was unhappy with the results and decided to overdub onto the live version and edit that for release.

'My Love' data

Apple issued Wings' forth single in Britain with customised 'Red Rose Speedway' labels. In Britain, the single was issued with a red paper sleeve and came with two label variations: the first has the artist credit 'Paul McCartney & Wings'; the second 'McCartney's Wings'. Demonstration copies of the single were issued with a large silver 'A' at 4 o'clock and 'DEMO RECORD NOT FOR SALE' on three lines above the spindle hole.

The single was reissued in the mid 1970s with customised 'Red Rose Speedway' labels but without reference to Apple Records and publisher credits altered to 'McCartney Music by arr. with ATV Music Ltd'.

American pressings of the single were issued with the same label design as the British single, with the addition of 'Recorded In England', in generic Apple sleeves. White-label promotional singles with the song title, composer credit, artist, and copyright information printed in black text were issued to radio stations.

The US single was reissued in the mid 1970s with black and silver Capitol 'dome' labels. When McCartney signed with Columbia in the USA, the company reissued several new couplings of classic McCartney/Wings songs on their Hall Of Fame imprint. 'My Love' was coupled with 'Maybe I'm Amazed' (13-33407) and issued with red Columbia labels and, later, with grey labels.

RED ROSE SPEEDWAY

RELEASED to coincide with Wings' 1973 British tour, *Red Rose Speedway* was better conceived, performed, and produced than their debut album. However, while Linda claimed that they had some 30 songs to choose from – the album was originally planned as a double – much of what McCartney decided to include was lightweight and pedestrian. Interviewed after its release, Linda said: "*Red Rose Speedway* was such a non-confident record … . We needed a heavier sound. … It was a terribly unsure period."

Still searching for a solo voice, McCartney was desperate to produce a defining statement that would establish Wings as a viable alternative to the Fab Four. Nevertheless, *Red Rose Speedway* failed to provide Wings with the grounding they required to compete with much of the contemporary competition, let alone The Beatles.

Recorded between March and October 1972, the original double album was to have included contributions from Denny Laine and Linda. Laine's 'I Would Only Smile' was later released on his solo album *Japanese Tears*. Linda's 'Seaside Woman' was also intended for the album (work on the song began at AIR Studios, London, in November 1972), but the song remained unreleased until issued as a single in America in 1977 and didn't appear in Britain until 1980.

Also recorded for the album were 'Night Out' – which was worked on throughout the 1970s – 'Jazz Street', 'Thank You Darling', and a cover of Thomas Wayne's 'Tragedy'. 'Night Out' and 'Tragedy' were later scheduled for the *Cold Cuts* album, which McCartney planned to release on several occasions until the bootleggers beat him to it, whereupon he lost interest in the project.

Rather than release an expensive and possibly less commercial double LP, a decision was made to condense *Red Rose Speedway* to a single album. According to McCullough, McCartney was persuaded to do this by business advisors. Speaking in 1994, McCullough recalled his disappointment at the album's final running order. "I'd been really delighted, because from what you heard on the album, there was another side to it that brought out the best in McCartney. And I thought, 'Great, at last he's doing something that my friends are going to like!' He was starting to rock out a little bit. But it only came out as a single and the rest was never released."

Red Rose Speedway songs

The opening track, 'Big Barn Bed', was recorded at Olympic Studios while making *Red Rose Speedway* but harks back to *Ram*. The opening stanza first appeared as the reprise of 'Ram On' and was recycled for this rambling contrapuntal composition. Recycling lyrics from old songs, whether his own or others, was a trick that McCartney used when he sketched in sections of a song that were proving difficult to finish. Talking to Miles about songwriting, he said: "Often you just block songs out and words just come into your mind, and when they do, it's hard to get rid of them. You often quote other songs too, and you know you've got to get rid of them, but sometimes it's very difficult to find a more suitable phrase than the one that had insinuated itself into your consciousness." Apparently unable to better the lyric borrowed from 'Ram On', McCartney stuck with his original idea. The result was that, lyrically, 'Big Barn Bed' remained little more than an undeveloped fragment that went nowhere.

McCartney had more than enough material for a double album but for some reason selected two outtakes from *Ram*, which, although slightly reworked, hardly improved things. 'Get On The Right Thing' is hippie heaven – oneness with nature, sunshine, the wife and kids, and love sweet love – and McCartney the proselytiser wants to spread the word. Unfortunately, we've heard it all before and better.

'One More Kiss' is a simple country song that failed to bring anything new to the album. Ironically, superior country-flavoured material recorded during these sessions appeared as future B-sides, which is where 'One More Kiss' should have been issued.

Before it was released on *Red Rose Speedway*, 'Little Lamb Dragonfly' had been pencilled in for an early version of McCartney's proposed Rupert Bear film. Recorded while making *Ram*, it may be marginally better than much of what Wings recorded for *Red Rose Speedway*, but it still fails to satisfy. His decision to revisit the song was perhaps a recognition that something needed to be done to revitalise a flagging project, but it was too little too late. 'Little Lamb Dragonfly' is too cute for its own good and merely confirms the earlier observation that McCartney was trying to be all things to all men, women, and little lambs.

'Single Pigeon' found the band swapping instruments as they had with 'C Moon'. McCartney plays piano and sings lead, Laine plays drums, and Seiwell bass guitar; McCullough is absent as no guitar part was required. This song was far from inspired and eventually fell into the category of 'post-Beatles stuff' that McCartney all but disowned. "The Beatles were possibly the hardest act of all to follow," he recalled. "So Linda and I fell in with everyone else's opinion of it – which was that it was not as good as The Beatles, therefore it was no good at all. I hated a lot of the songs from that period."

When writing for others, particularly early in his career, McCartney turned out some particularly asinine lyrics – 'One And One Is Two,' mainly written by McCartney and given to The Strangers with Mike Shannon, is an example. Thankfully, few of the songs he chose to record himself have been quite as senseless. Unfortunately, the same cannot be said for much of what appeared on *Red Rose Speedway*, including 'When The Night', which is fatuous in the extreme.

'Loop (1st Indian On The Moon)' is laboured and undistinguished, sounding like a bad Pink Floyd outtake. The band chant block harmonies, guitars are smothered in echo, organs hum, and the whole thing plods along aimlessly. Some experimentation with group dynamics takes place midway before it lurches back into full swing (or should that be full plod?), but even this ploy fails to lift this dull instrumental from its spiritless slumber. Nobody gets a decent solo, and it's almost as if McCartney is deliberately holding the band back – which in the light of McCullough's exceptional solo on 'My Love' seems strange indeed.

The album closes *Abbey Road*-style with a long medley. However, unlike the *Abbey Road* medley, which gives the impression of totality, the *Red Rose Speedway* medley simply emphasises the disparate nature of McCartney's song fragments. In fact, it's probably better to consider the four 'songs' – 'Hold Me Tight', 'Lazy Dynamite', 'Hands Of Love', and 'Power Cut' – as individual compositions rather than a homogenised whole. Why McCartney bothered to construct a medley from these fragments – he already had superior completed songs to

RED ROSE SPEEDWAY

PAUL McCARTNEY AND WINGS

SIDE 1 'Big Barn Bed', 'My Love', 'Get On The Right Thing', 'One More Kiss', 'Little Lamb Dragonfly'.

SIDE 2 'Single Pigeon', 'When The Night', 'Loop (1st Indian On The Moon)', 'Medley: Hold Me Tight/Lazy Dynamite/Hands Of Love/Power Cut'.

UK RELEASE May 3 1973; LP Apple PCTC 251; 8-track cartridge Apple 8X-PCTC 251 released June 1973; chart high No.4.

US RELEASE April 30 1973; LP Apple SMAL-3409; 8-track cartridge Apple 8XW 3409; chart high No.1.

• **'Big Barn Bed'** (McCartney)
Paul McCartney (vocals, piano, bass), Linda McCartney (backing vocals), Denny Laine (guitar, backing vocals), Henry McCullough (guitar, backing vocals), Denny Seiwell (drums).

• **'Get On The Right Thing'** (McCartney)
Paul McCartney (vocals, bass, piano), Linda McCartney (backing vocals), Dave Spinoza (guitar), Denny Seiwell (drums).

• **'One More Kiss'** (McCartney)
Paul McCartney (vocals, guitar), Linda McCartney (electric harpsichord), Denny Laine (bass), Henry McCullough (guitar), Denny Seiwell (drums).

• **'Little Lamb Dragonfly'** (McCartney)
Paul McCartney (vocals, bass), Linda McCartney (dingers, backing vocals), Denny Laine (backing vocals), Hugh McCracken (guitar), Denny Seiwell (drums).

• **'Single Pigeon'** (McCartney)
Paul McCartney (vocals, piano), Linda McCartney (backing vocals), Denny Laine (drums), Henry McCullough (guitar), Denny Seiwell (bass).

• **'When The Night'** (McCartney)
Paul McCartney (vocals, piano), Linda McCartney (piano, backing vocals), Denny Laine (guitar, backing vocals), Henry McCullough (guitar, backing vocals), Denny Seiwell (drums, backing vocals).

• **'Loop (1st Indian On The Moon)'** (McCartney)
Paul McCartney (bass, guitar, Moog, chant), Linda McCartney (organ, chant), Denny Laine (guitar, chant), Henry McCullough (guitar, chant), Denny Seiwell (drums, chant).

• **'Medley: Hold Me Tight/Lazy Dynamite/Hands Of Love/Power Cut'** (McCartney)
Hold Me Tight: Paul McCartney (bass, piano, vocals), Linda McCartney (backing vocals), Denny Laine (guitar, backing vocals), Henry McCullough (guitar, backing vocals), Denny Seiwell (drums, backing vocals); Lazy Dynamite: Paul McCartney (bass, piano, Mellotron, vocals), Denny Laine (harmonica), Henry McCullough (guitar); Hands Of Love: Paul McCartney (guitar, vocals), Linda McCartney (backing vocals), Denny Laine (guitar), Henry McCullough (percussion), Denny Seiwell (drums, percussion); Power Cut: Paul McCartney (piano, celeste, Mellotron, vocals), Linda McCartney (electric piano), Denny Laine (guitar, backing vocals), Henry McCullough (guitar, backing vocals), Denny Seiwell (drums).

All recorded at Olympic Sound Studios, Barnes, England, except: 'Get On The Right Thing' and 'Little Lamb Dragonfly' recorded at A&R Studios and Columbia Studios, New York City, NY, USA; and 'One more Kiss' recording location unknown. All produced by Paul McCartney.

choose from – is a mystery. Perhaps it was an attempt to recapture the magic of *Abbey Road* – McCartney's favourite moment from that album was the long medley – but it was an attempt destined to fail.

'Hold Me Tight' consists of little more than the title repeated over a pleasant but uninspired tune. 'Lazy Dynamite' is slightly better, but only just. Only McCartney, McCullough, and Seiwell, who adds harmonica, play on the track; although drums are present, the drummer is uncredited. Essentially a solo recording, 'Lazy Dynamite' simply repeats the previous song's formula, in other words repeating the title – a lot.

Using an old trick from *Abbey Road*, 'Lazy Dynamite' is segued with 'Hands Of Love'. A guitar fanfare links the two, but this was accomplished with more panache on *Abbey Road*, where a similar approach was used to join 'Mean Mr Mustard' with 'Polythene Pam'. Deployed here for a second time it appears clumsy and amateurish. Rather than bridging both songs seamlessly, it acts only to establish the disparate qualities of each fragment.

The medley ends with 'Power Cut', cross-faded from 'Hands Of Love'. As Wings toured Britain in 1973, the country was in the grip of large-scale industrial unrest. A three-day working week had been introduced, with the result that the country often suffered power cuts. When interviewed for *Billboard* magazine in 2001, McCartney suggested that 'Power Cut' was written in response to these disruptions. Finally, in an attempt to create some form of musical unity, the main motifs from the previous three songs are repeated to bring the medley, and the album, to an end.

Red Rose Speedway data

Red Rose Speedway was issued in Britain with customised labels featuring a 'Red Rose Speedway' logo, a gatefold jacket, and an elaborate six-page colour booklet featuring photos of Wings in concert and on a trip to Marrakech. McCartney also employed the talents of two of Britain's leading artists to create artwork for the booklet, Alan Jones and Eduardo Paolozzi (contemporaries of Peter Blake and Richard Hamilton, who created the *Sgt Pepper* and *White Album* covers).

Original sleeves featured a Braille message that read, 'We love ya baby', a tribute to the McCartneys' favourite singer, Stevie Wonder. And for the first time, the address of Wings Fun Club, which ran until 1998, was printed on the sleeve.

EMI reissued the LP on its FAME imprint (FA 3193) on September 5 1987 without the Braille message or booklet. Columbia also reissued the LP, as FC-36481 and PC-36481.

American pressings of the LP were also issued with 'Red Rose Speedway' labels but with the addition of the band's new logo. Capitol produced a 3¾-inch by 1⅞-inch rectangular blue label with 'PAUL McCARTNEY AND WINGS' and the track listing, which was stuck to the front cover.

The album was issued on 8-track in Britain (8X-PCTC 251) and the USA (8XW 3409). When McCartney signed with Columbia in the 1980s the new company reissued the 8-track (JCA 36481).

Red Rose Speedway was issued on CD by EMI on its FAME imprint on October 5 1987 (CD-FA 3193) and by Capitol in November 1988 (CDM 7 52026 2). EMI issued a remastered CD (CDPMCOL4) on July 7 1993 and DCC Compact Classics issued a gold CD (GZS-1091) in 1996.

'LIVE AND LET DIE'

RECORDED in October 1972 while completing *Red Rose Speedway*, 'Live And Let Die' demonstrated that Wings were more than capable of producing powerful, atmospheric, well-crafted songs that contrasted markedly with the lacklustre *Red Rose Speedway*.

The producer of the film, Albert 'Cubby' Broccoli, commissioned 'Live And Let Die' with the intention that McCartney write the song for another artist to perform. However, McCartney and George Martin had other plans. "George took it out to the Caribbean," said McCartney, "where they were shooting the movie, and the film producers found a record player. After the record had finished they said to George, 'That's great, a wonderful demo. Now when are you going to make the real track, and who shall we get to sing it?' And George said, 'What? This is the real track!'" Once this misunderstanding was rectified, Wings' performance featured in the film.

Attention-grabbing theme songs are an essential part of the Bond formula. The original James Bond theme, arranged by John Barry, provided a dynamic, electrifying introduction to Ian Fleming's action-packed spy thrillers. McCartney's theme not only captures the excitement of a Bond movie but also fits perfectly into the whole Bond genre.

Recalling how he came to write the song, McCartney said: "I read the *Live And Let Die* book on a Saturday, got the feel of it, and on the Sunday sat down at the piano and wrote the music. Linda and I dug around with the words for a bit, then I asked George Martin if he'd produce it, and we recorded it with Wings, all mixed all proper, as you hear it in the film." McCartney knew instinctively that Martin was the ideal producer to help realise the song. Martin's experience as an arranger and producer was unequalled: if anyone could write a score to compliment McCartney's dynamic song, it was him.

McCartney and Martin's arrangement uses the full dynamic range of orchestra and band to create a dramatic soundscape that encapsulates Bond's visual image. Beginning with a simple piano and vocal introduction, lulling the listener into a false sense of security, the music explodes with a monster riff that conveys all the excitement and action one would expect of a Bond movie. Linda even managed to put a 'reggae' middle eight into the song, which lightens the mood a little before the thunderous riff re-emerges with stunning effect. 'Live And Let Die' quickly became a live favourite and remained in McCartney's live set from the mid 1970s through to the *Back In The World* tour of 2003. It appears on all four of his live albums.

'I Lie Around' was written by McCartney but sung by Denny Laine and finds its author extolling the virtues of a bucolic lifestyle. The countryside is again seen as a place of escape, where troubles and anxieties can be forgotten. It was recorded during sessions for *Red Rose Speedway* and benefits from a sympathetic arrangement that compliments McCartney's musings on nature as a mental restorative.

'Live And Let Die' data

Apple issued 'Live And Let Die' with generic Apple labels rather than the now customary bespoke design. Perhaps, now that Klein had departed, McCartney felt more comfortable and more willing to associate himself with the label.

Three label variations were issued in America. The first has a light green Apple label with 'STEREO' at 9 o'clock and 'Recorded in England' below; title, '(from the United Artists film "Live and Let Die")', composer, and band name are centre bottom.

The second label variant has a light green Apple label; '(from the United Artists film "Live and Let Die") at 10 o'clock; 'STEREO' at 9 o'clock with the Intro. and Total running times printed below; title, composer, band name, and 'Recorded in England' centre bottom.

The third variant has a light green Apple label; '(from the United Artists film "Live and Let Die")' at 10 o'clock; 'STEREO' at 9 o'clock with the Intro. and Total running times printed below; title, composer, band name, and 'Recorded in England' centre bottom.

The single was reissued by EMI and Capitol in the mid 1970s with black and silver Capitol 'dome' labels.

'LIVE AND LET DIE' / 'I LIE AROUND'
WINGS
UK RELEASE June 1 1973; Apple R 5987; chart high No.9.
US RELEASE June 18 1973; Apple 1863; chart high No.1.

• **'Live And Let Die'** (McCartney)
Paul McCartney (piano, vocals), Linda McCartney (keyboards, backing vocals), Denny Laine (bass, backing vocals), Henry McCullough (guitar), Denny Seiwell (drums). Recorded at AIR Studios, London, England.
• **'I Lie Around'** (McCartney)
Paul McCartney (bass, backing vocals), Linda McCartney (backing vocals), Denny Laine (guitar, vocals), Henry McCullough (guitar), Denny Seiwell (drums). Recording location unknown.
Both produced by George Martin.

'HELEN WHEELS' / 'COUNTRY DREAMER'
PAUL McCARTNEY AND WINGS
UK RELEASE October 26 1973; Apple R 5993; chart high No.12.
US RELEASE November 12 1973; Apple 1869; chart high No.10.

• **'Helen Wheels'** (McCartney)
Paul McCartney (bass, drums, vocals), Linda McCartney (keyboards, backing vocals), Denny Laine (guitar, backing vocals). Recorded at EMI and ARC Studios, Lagos, Nigeria; mixed at Kingsway Studios, London, England.
• **'Country Dreamer'** (McCartney)
Paul McCartney (bass, vocals), Linda McCartney (backing vocals), Denny Laine (guitar, backing vocals), Henry McCullough (guitar), Denny Seiwell (drums).
Recording location unknown.
Both produced by Paul McCartney.

'HELEN WHEELS'

THIS was McCartney's ode to the road. A song about travelling from his home in Scotland to London, it was inspired by an unlikely source – his car. "'Helen Wheels is … a name we gave to our Land Rover, which is a trusty vehicle that gets us around Scotland," he explained. "It takes us up to the Shetland Islands and down to London. The song starts off in Glasgow, then it goes past Carlisle, goes to Kendal, Liverpool, Birmingham, and London. It's the route coming down from our Scottish farm to London. So it's really the story of a trip down."

However, the song is more than an account of a road journey. It's a metaphor for McCartney's desire to escape the pressures of fame and running a band, and it mirrors similar themes (movement, escape, freedom) that would be explored in greater detail on *Band On The Run*.

'Country Dreamer' is another song about the pleasures that McCartney found in the countryside, recorded late in 1972 during sessions for *Red Rose Speedway*. In light of that album's overworked production, the economic arrangement and sensitive production of 'Country Dreamer' proved to be refreshingly honest.

'Helen Wheels' data

Apple issued *Helen Wheels* with generic labels in a black paper sleeve. There were three label variations for US releases. The first has a light green Apple label with 'STEREO' at 9 o'clock and Intro and Total running times directly above; title, composer, band name, and producer credits are centre bottom. The second has a dark green Apple label with the same layout.

The third US label variant has a dark green Apple label with 'STEREO' at 9 o'clock; Intro. and Total running times printed on right side of label directly above catalogue number; title, composer, band name, and producer credits centre bottom.

Demonstration copies (PRO-6786) of the A-side (mono/stereo) were issued with light green Apple labels. The A-side label has 'MONO' at 9 o'clock with 'NOT FOR SALE' printed below. 'Country Dreamer' was also issued as a mono/stereo demonstration single (PRO-6787) with light green Apple labels with a black star at 7 o'clock. A third demonstration single, with stereo versions of both A and B-sides, was also issued (P-1869).

'Helen Wheels' / 'Country Dreamer' was reissued by EMI and Capitol in the mid 1970s with black and silver Capitol 'dome' labels.

'MIND GAMES'

ALTHOUGH it lacked the obvious political tendency of Lennon's previous singles, he originally conceived 'Mind Games' as a protest song in the same vein as 'Give Peace A Chance'. Lennon began work on the song as early as 1969, completing a working version titled 'Make Love, Not War' in 1970. Never one to waste a good tune, he used the melody as the basis for another song he was working on at the time, 'I Promise'. He recorded demos of both songs at his Tittenhurst home in 1970, and examples of both appear on the *John Lennon Anthology*.

'Mind Games' remained unfinished until Lennon began work on the follow-up album to 1972's *Some Time In New York City*. Aware that the aphorism 'make love, not war' was well past its sell-by date, he found the inspiration he needed to finish the song in a book. *Mind Games: The Guide To Inner Space* by Robert Masters and Jean Houston was about consciousness-raising – something the Lennons had been preaching for years. Their desire for revolutionary change was still present, only now it was tempered with a yearning for something more spiritual and lasting. The avant-gardism and in-your-face sloganeering of earlier works was replaced by an ambiguous mysticism.

Lennon's return to 'pop' confirmed his earlier acknowledgement that the public would only accept radical ideas if they were sugar-coated. Having ditched Elephant's Memory, Lennon found himself solo again. He stuck with New York musicians but this time employed a select handful of the city's top session players to create the lush pop soundscapes he now desired.

But Lennon created the hypnotic leitmotif of 'Mind Games' by himself. He told Andy Peebles in 1980: "The seeming orchestra on it is just me playing three notes on a slide guitar. And the middle eight is reggae. Trying to explain to American musicians what reggae was in 1973 was pretty hard, but it's basically a reggae middle eight if you listen to it."

Lennon chose to produce the record himself, breaking a two-year partnership with Phil Spector. Even without Spector, he managed to create a dense sonic soup that echoed the commercial sophistication of *Imagine* but which unfortunately masked some of the song's subtle nuances. This wasn't the end of their relationship – but Lennon's next project would be Spector was doomed from the start. 'Mind Games' was a positive, upbeat return to pop, a welcome respite from Lennon's political sloganeering of the pervious year.

Lennon wrote 'Meat City' soon after he and Ono moved to New York, and it chronicled a fascination with the city and his life-long love affair with rock'n'roll. The song began to take shape in late 1971 with the basic idea that rock'n'roll could either liberate or imperil. His first attempt had more than its fair share of improvised lyrics, but the melody was clearly taking shape. Just over a year later, he returned to the song, rewriting the lyrics and completing the melody.

'Meat City' reveals that Lennon was both fascinated and horrified by the events he describes. The total abandonment of reason that rock'n'roll could elicit from its audience – the hysteria that surrounded Beatlemania, for example – could be both exciting and disturbing. It created a culture of 'freaks' who played out a wild rock'n'roll fantasy of Lennon's making. Although he experienced the fantasy firsthand and still desired it, total abandonment appeared to disturb him. He may have poked and prodded at the boundaries of convention and indulged in sex and drugs, but unlike some of his contemporaries, complete abandonment to hedonism was never his scene.

Lennon develops the fantasy to take in China, which at this time still rejected Western values. China remained a distant, exotic land, which Lennon hoped to experience for himself. His desire to bring rock'n'roll to the Chinese was perhaps fuelled by the hope that it would emancipate the East in the same way it liberated the West. But it wasn't to be.

Two versions of 'Meat City' were issued, each with a unique backwards message. The single urges the listener to "check the album". The version on the album has a message that is more

'MIND GAMES' / 'MEAT CITY'
JOHN LENNON
UK RELEASE November 16 1973; Apple R 5894; chart high No.26.
US RELEASE October 29 1973; Apple APPLE 1868; chart high No.18.

- **'Mind Games'** (Lennon)
- **'Meat City'** (Lennon)

Both with John Lennon (vocals, guitar), Ken Ascher (keyboards), David Spinozza (guitar), Gordon Edwards (bass), Jim Keltner (drums), except add Rick Marotta (drums) on 'Meat City'.
Both recorded at Record Plant East, New York City, NY, USA.
Both produced by John Lennon.

explicit; referring to the song's backing vocals, the mystery voice intones: "Fuck a pig."

'Mind Games' data

Apple issued 'Mind Games' in Britain with generic Apple labels and a picture cover. In America, the single also came with generic Apple labels and in a picture cover identical to the British release.

American pressings were issued with two label variations. The first has a dark green Apple label; 'from the LP MIND GAMES SW-3414' on four lines at 11 o'clock; 'STEREO' at nine o'clock; song title, composer credit, and artist's name 'JOHN LENNON' centre bottom. The other variant has a medium dark green Apple label; 'from the LP MIND GAMES SW-3414' on three lines at 11 o'clock; 'STEREO' at 9 o'clock; song title, composer credit, and artist's name 'JOHN LENNON' and '(P) 1973 EMI Records Limited' centre bottom.

In the USA, Apple issued mono/stereo promotional copies (P-1868/PRO-6768) with light green Apple labels with a black star at 7 o'clock. 'Mind Games' was reissued by Capitol in 1978 with purple labels, and again in 1983 with black/colour band labels.

MIND GAMES

AS 1972 slipped into 1973, Lennon began to distance himself from the radical politics he'd been engaged in for much of the previous 18 months. The army fatigues of the radical-activist-cum-street-fighter were exchanged for less militant garb. Never one to procrastinate, he had wearied at the Left's lack of political success. He had another more personal reason for leaving the Yippies to carry on without him. He wanted to make the USA his home, and the only way he could do that was to be seen to reject activism and the radical Left.

If he was to stay in America he had to appease the US Immigration and Naturalisation Service and, of course, the FBI. He had already been instructed to leave the country and had successfully appealed against that order. Then, on March 23 1973, he was told to leave the country within 60 days. Again, he appealed. Lennon's fight with the US authorities dragged on until July 1976, by which time they relented and granted him a green card.

Lennon and Ono were still living in their cramped Greenwich Village apartment, and their marriage was going through a rough patch. In early May 1973, the Lennons made another symbolic move: leaving the Village, they relocated to a 12-room apartment in the Dakota building overlooking Central Park. Lennon had done little since *Some Time In New York City* other than write and demo a few songs for his next album, *Mind Games*. Ono, however, had busied herself with a number of recording and performance projects. By Lennon's own admission they were growing apart. "Now she knows how to produce records and everything about it, I think the best thing I can do is keep out of her hair," he told Chris Charlesworth of *Melody Maker*.

According to Ono, Lennon was going through a phase of soul-searching that led him to give her some more space – to the extent that he was happy to sit in the wings while she took centre stage. When she began recording her follow-up to *Approximately Infinite Universe*, she took complete control of the project. He turned up to a few sessions, playing guitar on 'Woman Power' and 'She Hits Back', but *Feeling The Space* was Ono's album from start to finish. Although he had little to do with her record, Lennon was impressed by the New York musicians she'd hired. So much so that he decided to use them for his own.

He knew he had to produce something to surpass the disappointing *Some Time In New York City*. Adverse criticism had shattered his confidence. His battle to stay in America was also weighing him down. The constant court appearances and FBI surveillance began to affect his work. "I just couldn't function, you know? I was so paranoid from them tappin' the phone and followin' me."

As his relationship with Ono disintegrated, he found himself adrift from everything that had grounded him. Where previously he'd used his suffering to drive his songwriting, now he eschewed it. Instead of channelling his pain, he put it to one side and wrote an album of well-crafted but uninspired songs. Lennon's disappointment at being treated like property had turned to anger on more than one occasion. Speaking in 1970, he had been adamant that he would never allow the music business to have the upper hand again. Now here he was producing an album simply to fulfil contractual obligations. Big business had beaten him, again. That Lennon should take an extended sabbatical as soon as his contract ended says much about his desire to escape an industry to which he felt shackled.

Faced with similar uncertainties, Paul McCartney forged *Band On The Run*, an album that many still argue is among his best. Even Ringo Starr, admittedly with the help of Lennon, McCartney, and Harrison, turned in a confident album packed full of classy pop songs. *Mind Games*, however, was an album of mixed emotions and themes. Its lack of consistency, something that even the dire *Some Time In New York City* possessed, reveals a troubled mind. From the cover depicting Lennon, bag in hand, walking away from Ono, to its syrupy over-production, *Mind Games* saw Lennon retreating from what had made his best work truly magnificent. Circumventing the passion he'd employed previously, Lennon played it safe. *Mind Games* was an album that he or, more likely, his record company thought the public wanted to hear. Ironically, the record was Lennon's first not to play mind games with his audience. Rather, it presented a picture of the artist as a conformist rather than a rebel.

Tony King, who was working for Apple in Los Angeles, suggested to Lennon that he play up this image. King encouraged him to get out and promote the record using tried and tested means. King helped promote the album by arranging for Lennon to be interviewed by trade magazines *Record World* and *Billboard*. "I started working on the *Mind Games* album," said King, "the promotion, fixing John up to do interviews, ... getting him to do stuff I thought he should be doing because he hadn't been doing these things. While he had been with Yoko he had been involved with all these semi-subversive activities, which had not given him a great reputation in America. He said to me at the time, 'Look, I've got this album, what do you think I should do?' I said, 'Honestly, you've just got to go out and make a few friends, because you've lost a bit of support because you've been involved with things of a controversial nature.' So he said, 'Fine, you organise it, I'll do it.' And he did."

Recording began in July and continued through August. As usual, Lennon recorded quickly, perhaps a little too quickly. The album was mixed over a two-week period, which left many of the production subtleties buried in his dense mix. (This was rectified when the album was remixed at Abbey Road in 2002. The remix revealed much that had been hidden by Lennon's rushed job.) The rough mixes that have surfaced on bootlegs and the *John Lennon Anthology* give the listener a glimpse of what the album might have sounded like had Lennon the confidence to let the songs stand on their own merits.

The album produced just one outtake. 'Rock And Roll People' had been in development for some time but was obviously not completed to Lennon's satisfaction. It would eventually be issued on the patchy *Menlove Ave.* album.

Mind Games songs

The album opens with 'Tight A$', the first John Lennon song in some time that really had little to say. Gone are the visions and diatribes; in their place: sex and drugs. And that's about as deep as it gets. The return to jokey wordplay was a timely reminder of what Lennon was capable of, but only served to reveal how sterile his work had become.

An early demo begins with the guitar riff that would, with a little more work, become the instrumental 'Beef Jerky'. Holed up in Record Plant East, Lennon led his team of crack session musicians through several extended takes of the song. Take four was deemed best and edited for use as the master.

'Aisumasen (I'm Sorry)' introduces a dramatic change in mood. Whereas Ono had once brought Lennon unbounded joy, which had inspired him to write some of his most beautiful and moving love songs, here she is the root of deep-seated depression. The Lennons were drifting apart, and by the time Lennon came to record *Mind Games* they were no longer a couple. Like most men, Lennon had a roving eye. But unlike most men, he was in the unique position of being able to draw on his fame, wealth, and status to seduce whomsoever he fancied. Lennon was also capable of gross insensitivity. One particular incident found him seducing another woman within Ono's earshot, and became a source of much regret.

'Aisumasen (I'm Sorry)' was a very public apology, but like several songs recorded for *Mind Games* it had a long gestation period. It began to take shape in 1971. Originally titled 'Call My Name', it featured Lennon in the role of comforter, but by the time he recorded it properly, the tables had turned. It was Lennon who now found himself in need of comfort but, despite his pleas, he wasn't about to get any from Ono. The break-up hit Lennon hardest, and 'Aisumasen (I'm Sorry)' reveals just how much he relied on her. Without her, he was incomplete and adrift. He quickly returned to his old ways. Drinking to obliterate his pain, he became the archetypical hedonistic rock star, a figure every bit as pathetic as the one in this song.

'One Day (At A Time)' is a good song spoilt by an uncharacteristic falsetto vocal, suggested by Ono. While recording the track, Lennon sang his guide vocals in his usual register, only adopting his falsetto when he came to deliver the vocal overdub. In its rough form, without Something Different's backing vocals (described by one journalist as sounding like "a dozen school girls from a church choir"), the song has a genuine honesty that would be masked by Lennon's saccharine production. In its naked form, it reveals exactly how Lennon felt about Ono, but when he dressed the song with layers of unnecessary overdubs, it became impossibly idealistic. He had sung about his devotion to Ono on several occasions, but never had he made his feelings for her appear this tired.

Dating from late 1971, 'Bring On The Lucie (Freeda Peeple)' saw Lennon return briefly to the kind of political commentary that, until *Mind Games*, had been his post-Beatle stock in trade. Written while he was fully engaged with radical politics, the song has more humour than anything that found its way onto *Some Time In New York City*, yet it retains real bite. Unfortunately, Lennon's band of super-slick New York session players were incapable of producing a musical backing to match his pungent lyrics, which cry out for a gritty setting. Despite Lennon's opening war cry, the band settle into a comfortable groove that misrepresents its author's original intent. Even Lennon manages to conceal his real feelings. Far from sounding angry, he gives the impression of weary resignation, an emotion that only months earlier he wouldn't have dared to contemplate.

The song began life as little more than a chorus, played on a newly acquired National guitar (a fragment from Lennon's composing tape would be included as a bonus track on the remastered CD of *Mind Games*). Working on his lyric, Lennon developed its simple political sloganeering into a well observed, even prophetic, lyric full of revolutionary zeal that echoes earlier pleas for social, political, and personal change, which he'd championed with 'Imagine' and 'Power To The People'.

Even though he was under FBI surveillance and threatened with deportation, Lennon sailed close to the wind with a personal attack on Nixon and his government. He was never one to pull his punches, and his critique of Nixon and his administration was as libellous as his remark about Mr. Justice Argyle, whom he called an "old wanker" when recording his message of support for *Oz* magazine.

The song closes with further evidence of state-sanctioned violence against both Americans and Vietnamese. Despite the fact that Henry Kissinger and Le Duc Tho had signed a ceasefire agreement, the Vietnam War still raged. Lennon's demand that they "stop the killing now" fell on deaf ears, but by early 1974 Richard Nixon had been impeached and his days as President were rapidly coming to an end, as was the war.

Some more Cage-like high jinx follow, with the six seconds of silence intended as the national anthem for a new country, Nutopia. In the spirit of Fluxus, the Lennons announced at a bizarre press conference on April 1 1973 the birth of their conceptual country and their citizenship of it. They based the concept for their imaginary country on an idea first proposed by Thomas Moore in 1516. His book *Utopia* took its name from a word that has its origins in modern Latin and means literally 'not place'. It was fitting, then, that Lennon's national anthem should consist of 'not sound' and that the country's flag should be plain white.

The theme was extended to the album's inner sleeve which carried a 'Declaration of Nutopia' that offered citizenship to anyone who could declare their awareness of Nutopia. Like the song 'Imagine', Nutopia offered boundless possibilities and freedoms that flew in the face of state-sanctioned laws concerning citizenship and national identity. While poking fun at the American authorities, it also raised public awareness of the Lennons' plight.

Lennon was often at his best when exploring the darker side of life. Whenever he addressed his addictions, neurosis, or paranoia, he had a knack of writing insightful and enlightening songs. However, when it came to celebrating his own genius and the miracle of life, he was less successful. Set to a bouncy cadence that underscores a self-congratulatory lyric, 'Intuition' seems somehow ill-fitting on an album that appears to celebrate the darker side of personal relationships. Given what he was going through, the line "It's good to be alive" seems as out of place as the song's contrived cheeriness, more readily associated with Tin Pan Alley than an artist of Lennon's calibre. He wrote the song on piano, recording rough demos on the instrument in early 1973. With the lyrics still unfinished, he included a few lines from two earlier songs, 'How?' and 'God', to fill in the gaps.

The next song on *Mind Games*, 'Out The Blue', is an exquisite ballad that ranks among Lennon's finest. From the graceful acoustic guitar introduction to the majestic piano motif and inventive McCartneyesque bass lines, it reveals more than a glimpse of Lennon's genius.

Not for the first or last time, he acknowledges the debt he owed Ono. Like many songs in his canon, it was driven by a powerful devotion that was often stretched but never broken. Lennon was the hardest hit by the trial separation. While Ono remained focused and controlled, he slipped into a drunken twilight zone of his own making. If previously he had written love songs to express his security, now he wrote them to remind Ono how insecure he was without her.

'Out The Blue' formed part of a very personal musical dialogue between two remarkably mercurial individuals. Although Lennon and Ono were happy to present themselves as the perfect couple, they were never afraid to admit their failures. Lennon's acknowledgement of emotional insecurity may have been an attempt to rebuild the bond with Ono that he'd temporarily lost. It was also an honest expression of self-doubt, the like of which he hadn't committed to tape since *John Lennon/Plastic Ono Band*.

'Only People' found Lennon reworking a theme that lay at the heart of his and Ono's personal philosophy. They both believed that collective change through self-realisation would beneficially transform the world. Speaking on *The Mike Douglas Show*, John had prefigured the song's message when he said: "Only people can save the world." Ono's rephrased statement, "Only people can change the world," which was more in line with their intended goal, was printed on the inner sleeve of *Mind Games*.

The pair had addressed many times the notion that socio-political change could be obtained through collective potential. Unlike their early avant-garde recordings, which proffered genuine alternatives to conventional models of being, their orthodox protest songs were less successful. Despite their immediacy, songs like 'Give Peace A Chance', 'Instant Karma!', and 'Imagine' all worked within the system that they wanted people to transcend. These songs may have aroused debate, but they failed to threaten the system of order and control that the Lennons seemed determined to undermine. Like the politically correct songs written for *Some Time In New York City*, 'Only People' merely appeals to those already swayed by Lennon's argument.

Lennon recognised that 'Only People' failed as a song. Talking to *Playboy* magazine, he said: "It was a good lick, but I couldn't get the words to make sense." Even if he'd managed to write a more considered lyric, it's difficult to believe that the song would have been taken up in the same way as 'Give Peace A Chance'. Its happy-clappy gospel feel may have been great to sing along to, but the track lacks the bite of 'Instant Karma!' or the pseudo religiosity of 'Imagine', which are the qualities that made those two songs so appealing.

The couple had travelled a long way in their short marriage, and much of the journey was recorded in song. 'Imagine' featured some of Lennon's most heartfelt and joyous love songs. It also had songs of self-doubt, but nothing as emotionally irresolute as 'I Know (I Know)'. A mere two years had passed since the *Imagine* album, and his love for Ono was as strong as ever – but how the

MIND GAMES
JOHN LENNON (WITH THE PLASTIC U.F.ONO BAND)
SIDE 1 'Mind Games', 'Tight A$', 'Aisumasen (I'm Sorry)', 'One Day (At A Time)', 'Bring On The Lucie (Freda Peeple)', 'Nutopian International Anthem'.
SIDE 2 'Intuition', 'Out The Blue', 'Only People', 'I Know (I Know)', 'You Are Here', 'Meat City'.
UK RELEASE November 16 1973; LP Apple PCS 7165; 8-track cartridge Apple 8X-PCS 7165 released January 1974; chart high No.13.
US RELEASE November 2 1973; LP Apple SW 3414; 8-track cartridge Apple 8XW-3414; chart high No.9.

• **'Tight A$'** (Lennon)
John Lennon (vocals, guitar), Ken Ascher (keyboards), David Spinozza (guitar), Gordon Edwards (bass), Jim Keltner (drums).
• **'Aisumasen (I'm Sorry)'** (Lennon)
John Lennon (vocals, guitar), Ken Ascher (keyboards), David Spinozza (guitar), Sneaky Pete (pedal steel), Gordon Edwards (bass), Jim Keltner (drums).
• **'One Day (At A Time)'** (Lennon)
John Lennon (vocals, guitar), Ken Ascher (keyboards), David Spinozza (guitar), Gordon Edwards (bass), Sneaky Pete (pedal steel), Michael Brecker (saxophone), Something Different (female backing vocals), Jim Keltner (drums).
• **'Bring On The Lucie (Freeda Peeple)'** (Lennon)
John Lennon (vocals, guitar), Ken Ascher (keyboards), David Spinozza (guitar), Gordon Edwards (bass), Sneaky Pete (pedal steel), Something Different (backing vocals), Jim Keltner (drums), Rick Marotta (drums).
• **'Nutopian International Anthem'** (Lennon)
No personnel.
• **'Intuition'** (Lennon)
John Lennon (vocals), Ken Ascher (keyboards), David Spinozza (guitar), Gordon Edwards (bass), Sneaky Pete (pedal steel), Michael Brecker (saxophone), Jim Keltner (drums).
• **'Out The Blue'** (Lennon)
John Lennon (vocals, guitar), Ken Ascher (keyboards), David Spinozza (guitar), Gordon Edwards (bass), Sneaky Pete (pedal steel), Something Different (backing vocals), Jim Keltner (drums).
• **'Only People'** (Lennon)
John Lennon (vocals, guitar), Ken Ascher (keyboards), David Spinozza (guitar), Gordon Edwards (bass), Michael Brecker (saxophone), Something Different (backing vocals), Jim Keltner (drums).
• **'I Know (I Know)'** (Lennon)
John Lennon (vocals, guitar), Ken Ascher (keyboards), David Spinozza (guitar), Gordon Edwards (bass), Jim Keltner (drums).
• **'You Are Here'** (Lennon)
John Lennon (vocals, guitar), Ken Ascher (keyboards), David Spinozza (guitar), Gordon Edwards (bass), Sneaky Pete (pedal steel), Something Different (backing vocals), Jim Keltner (drums).
All recorded at Record Plant East, New York City, NY, USA. All produced by John Lennon.

tone had changed. 'I Know (I Know)' suggests that Lennon was no more emotionally stable post-primal therapy than before. If he had learnt anything, it was to forgive and recognise his shortcomings. For 'I Know (I Know)' finds him in conciliatory mood, apologising, again, for his thoughtlessness. He acknowledges that he still has a lot to learn, but more importantly that he knows the cause of his insecurity.

The song features a delicate guitar figure that echoes the fingerpicking folk style that Lennon learnt from Donavan while in Rishikesh, India, in 1968. Employed sparingly throughout, it gives 'I Know (I Know)' an honesty that enhances his plea for his lover's absolution. However, its considered, reflective mood balances Lennon's feelings of angst with those of unbridled optimism. Working with a small band, he fashioned a musical setting that was the match for anything on *Imagine*. The rough mixes that have surfaced on bootlegs reveal the painstaking overdubbing process he employed to develop his arrangement.

The phrase "you are here" had haunted Lennon for some time. It first appeared as the title for his debut one-man show at the Robert Frazer Gallery, London. The show, which opened on 1 July 1968, was obviously influenced by Ono and Fluxus. Visitors were invited to contribute to the event, either by placing money in a hat, inscribed by Lennon "for the artist thank you", or by returning cards attached to helium-filled white balloons, which Lennon and Ono had released into the sky. Lennon intended to publish a book based of the replies he received; typically, he never got around to it. At the heart of the exhibition was a white circular canvas upon which he'd written "you are here". Lennon next had the words printed on T-shirts, which he and members of Elephant's Memory sported during the early 1970s.

By the time he came to shape the song, his original concept had taken on many different forms and meanings. From conceptual joke to installation art, from fashion statement to love song, it occupied him for over five years. As a song, 'You Are Here' combined two themes close to Lennon's heart – love and peace. While it was obviously a love song written for Ono, it was also about the coming together of individuals, countries, and cultures. Lennon imagines a world without differences, modelled on his own relationship with Ono. The global harmony he envisions is as graceful and beatific as the melody he fashioned to support his words. The song originally had an extra verse, edited from the completed master, that made further references to the differences and similarities between Japan and England. A version with the extra verse was issued on the *John Lennon Anthology*.

Mind Games data

Apple issued the album in the USA with generic Apple labels and in a printed inner sleeve. The album was reissued by Capitol in 1978 with purple labels with a large Capitol logo. In 1980, Capitol issued a budget-price version with a new catalogue number, SN-15968.

Apple issued the album in Britain with the same packaging as the American release. The album was reissued on November 27 1980 on EMI's budget MFP label (MFP 5058) with a new cover and generic MFP labels.

Mind Games was issued on 8-track in Britain (8X-PCS 7165) and America (8XW-3414).

EMI issued the album on CD in Britain on August 3 1987 (CDP 7 46769 2), and Capitol issued the CD in America seven months later, on March 22 1988. The album was remixed, remastered and reissued on CD with three bonus tracks on October 7 2002 (UK) and November 5 2002 (USA). MFSL Original Master Recordings issued the remastered CD on November 22 2004 and a vinyl edition (MFSL-1-293) in 2005.

While the rest of the world issued 'Mind Games' as a single, Venezuela went with 'Bring On The Lucie (Freeda Peeple)' backed with 'You Are Here' (4AP 1844).

BAND ON THE RUN

WITH the issue of *Band On The Run* just two weeks after Lennon's *Mind Games*, Liverpool's two most famous sons were competing for album sales and chart superiority. As Lennon had a hit single he should have had the advantage, but McCartney would eventually come out on top. Wings' first LP to reach Number 1 on both sides of the Atlantic, *Band On The Run* became the most successful album by any of the ex-Beatles. It spawned two Top 10 singles – three in America, where 'Helen Wheels' was included – and, in stark contrast to the withering disdain normally reserved for McCartney, it received glowing reviews.

Rolling Stone magazine made it album of the year and couldn't praise it enough. The magazine suggested that McCartney's new assuredness resulted from his "walking a middle ground between autobiographical songwriting and subtle attempts to mythologise his own experience through the creation of a fantasy world of adventure – perhaps remotely inspired by his having recently written 'Live And Let Die'. He does it by uniting the myth of the rock star and the outlaw, the original legendary figure On The Run."

Whether or not *Band On The Run* was a conscious attempt at self-mythologising isn't important: what made it so rewarding was the intriguing and romantic ways in which McCartney expressed himself. At last, he had broken out of a disheartening rut and into the glowing limelight of success.

Band On The Run might have articulated a sense of euphoria, but recording it was a nightmare. Just as things were looking up, disaster struck. On the eve of Wings' departure for recording in Lagos, Nigeria, guitarist Henry McCullough and drummer Denny Seiwell left the band. Neither saw a secure future with Wings. Speaking to *Melody Maker* in April 1973, McCullough said: "I don't suppose we'll be together forever; I'm sure Paul's got more of a tie to The Beatles than to Wings." As The Beatles' business troubles were being resolved, McCullough obviously thought that a reunion was a real possibility. He was also unhappy with his role in the band.

When he made his feelings known to *Disc*, the music paper ran the headline: "McCullough To Quit Wings?" The article suggested that he wanted to contribute more of his own ideas, something he felt was being denied him. McCartney's quest for perfection often led him to appear dictatorial, which McCullough felt overbearing. Recalling later his time with Wings, McCullough said: "It was like being in a show band – you played the exact same thing as the record, and you played it every night from there on in."

McCartney, despite his love of improvisation, demanded strict adherence to formal arrangements when Wings performed in front of an audience. McCullough, however, felt stifled; for him, playing live was the musical equivalent of flying by the seat of your pants. Linda's presence didn't help, either. As she would have been the first to acknowledge, her musical inexperience undoubtedly caused friction within the group, as did the fact that she was the boss's wife. McCullough is quoted as saying: "Trying to get things together with a learner in the group didn't work as far as I was concerned."

McCullough's departure was put down to musical differences, and McCartney was pragmatic about his departure. "I think Henry McCullough came to a head one day when I asked him to play something he really didn't fancy playing. We all got a bit choked about it, and he rang up later and said he was leaving. I said, 'Well OK.' That's how that happened. You know, with the kind of music we play, a guitarist has got to be adaptable. It was just one of those things."

Denny Seiwell also felt troubled by the prospect of a Beatles reunion. Speaking to *Record Mirror*, he said: "Now that the obstruction in the form of Allen Klein has gone, I should think that there's a strong possibility that they will all get together again." In April 1973, McCartney intimated that a Beatles reunion was a possibility. "The only thing that has prevented us from getting together again has been Klein's contractual hold over The Beatles' name; when he is out of the way, there is no real reason why we shouldn't get together again."

Denny Seiwell's departure was a bit more dramatic than McCullough's. He only informed the McCartneys he was leaving an hour before the flight to Lagos was due to depart. McCartney: "So our drummer didn't want to go to Africa. I don't know quite why. We're all going to Africa to record and if the drummer won't come, what do you do?"

McCullough and Seiwell's departure marked the end of Wings Mk.2, but signalled another rebirth from which a newly invigorated band would rise phoenix-like from the ashes. As Linda recalled: "That period was almost a relief for Paul. He finally had people with him who cared, those who showed up at the airport. We didn't even know if Denny (Laine) was coming." Wings Mk.3 were Paul, Linda, and Denny Laine.

It was too late to call off the project, and the set of recordings that resulted were not only a triumph of will over adversity, but, perhaps because of the pressure under which they were made, some of Paul, Linda, and Denny's most creative and commercial recordings.

The first of several McCartney/Wings albums recorded in 'exotic' locations, *Band On The Run* was made at EMI Studios in Lagos and AIR Studios, London. McCartney's desire to record in a foreign location was, nevertheless, tempered by the need for technical excellence, which he believed an EMI studio would offer. As he explained: "I was at EMI and I'd been used to recording at their places, so I thought that any studio that EMI built I'd be able to relate to, the condition would be OK." However, when Wings reached Lagos their expectations were shattered. The studio, which backed onto a noisy pressing plant, was still under construction. Far from meeting EMI's high standards, it was crude and cheaply built. There was no backup equipment, no acoustic screens (used to stop one instrument's sound bleeding into another microphone), and in fact there appeared to be no microphones at all, until some were discovered in a cardboard box hidden inside a cupboard. And to top it off, the mixing board was faulty. Yet the three-piece Wings made the best of a bad situation. McCartney had hedged his bets: he took ex-Beatles engineer Geoff Emerick with him to engineer the sessions, and Emerick's skills helped save the album from disaster. Emerick had acted as tape operator or engineer for many Beatles albums, eventually managed Apple's recording studio, and has since worked with McCartney on a number of solo projects.

McCartney's initial reason for recording in Lagos was a desire to bring the region's music to a wider audience. His good intentions were, however, viewed with suspicion by local musicians, who thought he only wanted to steal their rhythms and create a diluted, Westernised version of *their* music for commercial gain. Fela Kuti, in particular, suspected that McCartney was there to exploit indigenous music at the expense of local musicians.

McCartney recalled: "I think old Fela, when he found us in Lagos, thought, 'Hello, why have they come to Lagos?' And the only reason he could think of was that we must be stealing black music, black African music, the Lagos sound: we'd come down there to pick it up. So I said, 'Do us a favour, we do OK as it is, we're not pinching your music.'"

Although McCartney thought about employing African musicians, particularly a drummer to replace Denny Seiwell, he decided against it, realising that "it would have taken hours to tell

BAND ON THE RUN
PAUL McCARTNEY AND WINGS
SIDE 1 'Band On The Run', 'Jet', 'Bluebird', 'Mrs Vandebilt', 'Let Me Roll It'.
SIDE 2 'Mamunia', 'No Words', 'Helen Wheels' (US edition only), 'Picasso's Last Words (Drink To Me)', 'Nineteen Hundred And Eighty Five'.
UK RELEASE November 30 1973; LP Apple PAS 10007; 8-track cartridge Apple 8X-PAS 10007 released January 1974; chart high No.1.
US RELEASE December 3 1973; LP Apple SO-3415; 8-track cartridge Apple 8XZ3415; quadraphonic 8-track cartridge Apple Q8W-3415; chart high No.1.

• **'Band On The Run'** (McCartney)
Paul McCartney (bass, guitar, drums, vocals), Linda McCartney (keyboards, backing vocals), Denny Laine (guitar, backing vocals).
• **'Jet'** (McCartney)
Paul McCartney (bass, guitar, drums, vocals), Linda McCartney (keyboards, backing vocals), Denny Laine (guitar, backing vocals).
• **'Bluebird'** (McCartney)
Paul McCartney (guitar, vocals), Linda McCartney (backing vocals), Denny Laine (guitar, backing vocals), Remi Kebaka (percussion), Howie Casey (saxophone).
• **'Mrs Vandebilt'** (McCartney)
Paul McCartney (bass, guitar, drums, vocals), Linda McCartney (backing vocals), Denny Laine (guitar, backing vocals).
• **'Let Me Roll It'** (McCartney)
Paul McCartney (bass, guitar, drums, vocals), Linda McCartney (keyboards, backing vocals), Denny Laine (guitar, backing vocals).
• **'Mamunia'** (McCartney)
Paul McCartney (bass, guitar, vocals), Linda McCartney (backing vocals), Denny Laine (guitar, backing vocals).
• **'No Words'** (McCartney, Laine)
Paul McCartney (bass, guitar, drums, vocals), Linda McCartney (vocals), Denny Laine (guitar, vocals), Ian Horne & Trevor Jones (backing vocals).
• **'Picasso's Last Words (Drink To Me)'** (McCartney)
Paul McCartney (bass, keyboards, guitar, vocals), Linda McCartney (backing vocals), Denny Laine (guitar, vocals), Ginger Baker (percussion).
• **'Nineteen Hundred And Eighty Five'** (McCartney)
Paul McCartney (bass, piano, guitar, vocals), Linda McCartney (keyboards, backing vocals), Denny Laine (guitar, vocals).
All recorded EMI Studios, Lagos, Nigeria and AIR Studios, London, England and mixed at Kingsway Studios, London, except 'Jet' recorded at Abbey Road and AIR Studios, London, England.
All produced by Paul McCartney.

[a new musician] exactly what I wanted. I knew basically that I could do most of it".

If antagonism from local musicians wasn't enough, Paul and Linda were mugged one evening while on their way to Denny's rented house. The couple were followed by a kerb-crawling car, out of which emerged a gang of muggers. Speaking to the *The Daily Express* in 1977, McCartney said: "The doors flew open and they all came out (there were six of them) and one had a knife. Their eyes were wild and Linda was screaming: 'He's a musician! Don't kill him!' You know, all the unreasonable stuff you shout in situations like that." The McCartneys were lucky to lose only some money and cassettes containing demos of songs intended for the album; they could have lost their lives.

McCartney suffered another unsettling incident when he attempted to escape the oppressive atmosphere of the studio. Stepping into the Lagos night for a breath of air, he found that the atmosphere outside was more polluted than in the studio. A sharp pain spread across the right side of his chest and he collapsed. When he awoke, he discovered that a local doctor was treating his condition somewhat offhandedly. Ordered to bed for a few days, he thought he was dying. Thankfully, McCartney wasn't suffering from any serious illness and, after spending the weekend resting, returned to the recording studio to continue work on the album.

When they got back to England, Wings continued recording throughout September and October at AIR Studios in London, where the original 8-track tapes were transferred to 16-track to facilitate further overdubs, and Tony Visconti's orchestral arrangements were added. Compared with the band's previous album, sessions for which stretched over several months, *Band On The Run* was completed surprisingly quickly.

McCartney created confident, well-crafted songs for the album and bold musical settings that matched his mood. Whereas *Wild Life* and *Red Rose Speedway* represent opposing manifestations of taste and style, *Band On The Run* fused his talents into a near perfect whole that had one critic enthusing that it was "the best thing any of The Beatles have done since *Abbey Road*". *Band On The Run* consolidated McCartney's post-Beatles reputation, as *Imagine* had for Lennon. But Lennon had peaked early, and by 1973 he had hit a creative doldrums. As Lennon began to drift, McCartney focused and honed his career, to the extent that Wings would soon rival The Beatles in popularity.

Band On The Run songs

The album starts with the title track, a five-minute mini-opera with all the magnificence but none of the pretensions that too often trouble this particular rock genre, as McCartney explores his desire for freedom.

McCartney was inspired by a chance remark that George Harrison made at an Apple business meeting. "He was saying that we were all prisoners in some way, some kind of remark like that. 'If we ever get out of here,' the prison bit ... and I thought that would be a nice way to start an album." George's comment neatly summarised The Beatles' business predicament, but also had universal meaning. All of us are trying to escape reality for some imagined better place. McCartney simply took Harrison's offhand quip and turned it into a powerful metaphor for determination and deliverance.

He weaves together a number of melodic themes, examining contrasting responses to our attachment to freedom. First, we are confronted by despair at being incarcerated – perhaps in a prison of our own making. Then a dramatic tempo change signals a declaration of intent, and finally a triumphant orchestral ostinato and dramatic change in timbre signifies hope. However, unlike Lennon's meditations on the subject, McCartney's vision is racked by doubt. Haunted by a succession of authority figures – jailer man (the law), sailor Sam (the armed forces), and an undertaker (death) – McCartney neither sees nor offers a solution to the problem. For him the pot of gold will forever be at the end of a rainbow, always over the next horizon, always out of reach.

When McCartney released *Band On The Run*, he insisted that it would stand on its own merits and that no singles would be issued from it. Although it had been selling well, it wasn't until 'Jet' was selected for release as a single that the album established itself at the top of the album charts. Released in November 1973, the album didn't reach Number 1 in Britain until the first week of July 1974, some eight months after its release.

Persuaded by radio plugger Al Coury, McCartney conceded and issued 'Jet' as a single. He had written the song in Scotland after watching one of his dogs at play. "We've got a Labrador puppy who is a runt, the runt of the litter," he said. "She was a bit of a wild dog, a wild girl who wouldn't stay in. She came back one day pregnant. She proceeded to walk into the garage and have this litter. So, Jet was one of the puppies. We gave them all names, there was one puppy called Golden Molasses. I rather like that."

But this is where inspiration ends and invention begins. Make of the lyrics what you will: they were probably written to fit the melody without much consideration for meaning. Even the suffragette motif was, likely as not, arrived at fortuitously. "I make up so much stuff," McCartney revealed. "It means something to me when I do it, and it means something to the record buyer, but if I'm asked to analyse it I can't really explain what it is. 'Suffragette' was crazy enough to work. It sounded silly, so I liked it."

Just as he was unhappy about lifting any singles from the album, McCartney was also unhappy about having his songs edited. If any songs were to be released as singles, he wanted them issued as they stood. However, at just over four minutes, 'Jet' was too long for most radio stations, who refused to play anything much over two minutes in length. After much persuasion, a McCartney-sanctioned edit was issued to American radio stations (Apple PRO-6827) and the single duly hit Number 1. Pop songs don't get much better than this: 'Jet' is as exuberant and vital as the Labrador puppy that inspired it.

'Bluebird' continues the album's theme of personal and spiritual emancipation. McCartney wrote it while on holiday in Jamaica, fashioning a metaphor for the transcendent power of love and the liberation of the human spirit from mental and physical bondage. His lyric reflects his transformation from traumatised to revitalised individual and maps a dramatic change in his general disposition. Enhanced by Howie Casey's warm saxophone, 'Bluebird' is an island of serenity in an equally calm sea. ('Bluebird' was issued as a single in Germany [1 C 006-05 529].)

'Mrs Vandebilt' finds McCartney asking the question, "What's the use of worrying?" and answering himself, "No use." Advancing a rejuvenated and optimistic attitude, the song finds him casting off his mantle of despair and revealing a more confident, carefree persona. Recording during a power cut, Paul, Denny and Linda found themselves relying on a noisy EMI generator, which they hoped wouldn't leak onto the backing track.

McCartney wrote 'Let Me Roll It' at home on his farm in Scotland. It's a stark Lennonesque track with a stripped-down arrangement, heavy rhythm section, and jagged guitar riff, which led many to believe that McCartney was somehow criticising his former partner. Lennonesque it may be, but McCartney was adamant that any similarities were purely coincidental. "*Let Me Roll It* was not really a Lennon pastiche, although my use of tape echo did sound more like John than me," he explained. "But tape echo was not John's exclusive territory. And you have to remember that, despite the myth, there was a lot of commonality between us in the way we thought and the way we worked." Comparisons with Lennon were inevitable, as 'Let Me Roll It' resembles Lennon's inert musicality more than it does McCartney's lively melodicism. McCartney, however, loved it, and with some justification, for like almost every song on the album, it displays a strength and confidence that many found surprising.

McCartney wrote 'Mamunia' while visiting Marrakech with Wings in early 1973. While there, the band stayed at a hotel called Mamounia. The original Arabic meaning of that word – safe haven, or refuge – probably held great significance for McCartney, but rather than take a literal translation, he turned it into a metaphor for rebirth. The first song recorded in Lagos, 'Mamunia' was taped during a heavy tropical storm. (Issued in America as the B-side of 'Jet' (Apple 1871), 'Mamunia' was quickly replaced by 'Let Me Roll It', as there were plans to issue 'Mamunia' as an A-side. 'Mamunia' is a bright and breezy pop song, celebrating the good things in life and equally as delightful.

'No Words' was a McCartney-Laine composition, also dating from early 1973. It features all three members of Wings singing unison lead vocals, although Denny and Paul each share a solo spot. It allegedly features roadies Ian Horn and Trevor Jones on backing vocals, but if they are there, they're buried well down in the mix. The basic track was recorded in Lagos, while Tony Visconti's brief orchestration was overdubbed back in London.

While on holiday in Jamaica, the McCartneys had dinner with Dustin Hoffman and his wife. During the evening the subject of songwriting entered the conversation and Hoffman suggested that McCartney might write a song based on Pablo Picasso's last words.

As McCartney recalled: "We went back a couple of nights later, and he said, 'I've been thinking about this. I've seen a little article in *Time* magazine about Picasso, and it struck me as being very poetic. I think this would be very good set to music.' So he says there's a little story here. In the article [Picasso] supposedly said, 'Drink to me, drink to my health, you know I can't drink any more.' He went to paint a bit, and then he went to bed at three in the morning. He didn't wake up the next morning and they found him, dead. Dustin Hoffman thought, 'Drink to me, drink to my health, you know I can't drink any more' was a great passing remark. They were Picasso's last words. So he said, 'Could you write something like that?'"

When Wings recorded 'Picasso's Last Words (Drink to Me)', McCartney made a deliberate attempt to echo the artist's visual style with his arrangement. Constructing a collage of themes and melodies, he tried to replicate the painter's fragmented cubist surfaces in musical form. "We thought we'd do this Picasso number, and we thought we'd do it straight," he said. "Then we thought, Picasso was kind of far out in his pictures, he'd done all these different kinds of things, fragmented, cubism, and the whole bit. I thought it would be nice to get a track a bit like that, put it through different moods, cut it up, edit it, mess around with it – like he used to do with his pictures."

Alluding to Picasso's cubist style, Wings extended their usual palette of textures in a brave attempt to emancipate their music from a reliance on hackneyed conventions. McCartney's poetic juxtapositions evoke notions of thematic and temporal simultaneity comparable to the cubist's experiments with form and space. Emphasising structure and texture, McCartney refers us to the process of recording, as Picasso refers the viewer to the process of painting.

The album closes with 'Nineteen Hundred And Eighty Five', a piano-driven rocker with swirling Mellotron, melodic basslines, and a lengthy orchestrated coda. McCartney had the song for some time but couldn't progress any further than the first line. "You see, with a lot of the songs that I do, the first line is it," he said. "It's all in the first line, and then you have to go on and write the second. That's all I had of that song for months. 'No one ever left alive in nineteen hundred and eighty five.'"

Despite its lack of narrative, the song has enough melodic twists and turns to keep the listener engaged until its finale. A mesmerising orchestral climax conveys notions of movement, vitality, and a release of creative energy that echoes the album's extended theme of escape. A brief reprise of 'Band On The Run' neatly bookends the album by returning the listener to the beginning of their flight. By bringing us full circle, McCartney suggests that we are caught in an eternal, inescapable loop of desire and despair. But it's the journey rather than the destination that's important.

Band On The Run data

Band On The Run was issued with customised labels, an inner sleeve with printed lyrics, and a poster of Polaroid photographs taken by Linda in Lagos.

As important as the music was the cover. It was photographed by Clive Arrowsmith on October 28 1973 and reflects the album's concept of escape and freedom. Paul, Linda, and Denny were joined by a small group of mainly British celebrities, including Michael Parkinson (journalist and talk-show host), Kenny Lynch (singer and actor; he toured with The Beatles in 1963), James Coburn (actor), Clement Freud (politician and raconteur), Christopher Lee (actor), and John Conteh (light heavyweight boxing champion of the world).

Arrowsmith took the photograph in the grounds of Osterley Park, west London. The cover shoot was also filmed and later projected behind Wings during their 1975/76 world tour.

Because the cover did not feature the band's name, Capitol manufactured a circular blue sticker with 'PAUL McCARTNEY WINGS' in white, which was adhered to the front cover. A second 2½-inch by 1-inch rectangular sticker with 'INCLUDES THE HITS JET HELEN WHEELS' appeared on later US editions of the LP.

Band On The Run became the bestselling album of 1974 in Britain and the seventh bestselling album of the 1970s, just behind Pink Floyd's *Dark Side Of The Moon* and Mike Oldfield's *Tubular Bells*. The album's popularity was confirmed by the number of 'limited' pressings it received in the late 1970s and early 1980s, when coloured vinyl and picture discs became fashionable.

In America, Capitol released a picture disc version (SEAX-11901), also issued in Japan. France issued the LP on yellow vinyl (DC9/C 066 05 503) and in Belgium it was issued on magenta vinyl (5C 062-05503). Perhaps the rarest pressing was produced by Nimbus Records in 1984. Nimbus are British specialists in audiophile pressings produced to the highest quality. Gerald Reynolds, one of a select handful of Nimbus staff who master the company's 'Supercut' records, confirmed that they always tried to use a studio tape as close to the original as possible. The discs were cut as 'flat' as possible, meanning without any sound manipulation or compression, to ensure that reproduction was as close to the original source tape as possible. The records were pressed on special vinyl, made for Nimbus by ICI, to give a faithful reproduction of the original tape. Nimbus used covers provided by EMI but added a sticker to indicate that they were 'Supercut' pressings. They made 500 copies of the album initially, which were available exclusively through *Hi Fi Today* magazine. Also, a half-speed mastered edition of the album was issued by Columbia in 1981 (HC 46382).

The album was issued on 8-track cartridge in Britain (8X-PAS 10007) and the USA (8XZ 3415). Capitol also issued a quadraphonic mix on 8-track (Q8W 3415).

Columbia issued *Band On The Run* on CD (CK 36482) on February 29 1984 and Capitol reissued it on December 1 1988 (CDP 7 46055 2). EMI issued the CD in Britain on February 4 1985 and issued a remastered edition (CDPMCOL5) on July 7 1993. A 25th anniversary two-CD edition (4991762) was issued on March 15 1999.

'JET'

THE DAYS of issuing standalone singles, separate from any album, were rapidly coming to a close. Marketing departments now saw singles as another promotional tool that could substantially improve album sales. Recognising the increased importance of singles and bowing to growing pressure from his record company, McCartney said: "The companies here and in America, worldwide, would like a single on the album. It makes more sense merchandising-wise. But sometimes, I just have to remember that this isn't a record store I'm running; this is supposed to be some kind of art. And if it doesn't fit in, it doesn't fit in."

'Jet' data

Issued with generic Apple labels and black paper sleeve, 'Jet' reversed *Band On The Run*'s slow chart descent by sending it back to Number 2 in the British charts and to Number 1 for a further two weeks in the US charts.

'Jet' was issued in Britain with generic Apple labels and paper sleeve. Demonstration copies were manufactured with 'DEMO RECORD NOT FOR SALE' on three lines above the spindle hole and a large 'A' at 2 o'clock. EMI also arranged for contract pressings to be made by Pathe Marconi in France. These records have Apple labels with solid centres and 'Made in France by Pathe Marconi' in addition to the standard perimeter print.

American pressings of the single were issued with two different

'JET' / 'LET ME ROLL IT'
PAUL McCARTNEY AND WINGS
UK RELEASE February 18 1974; Apple R 5996; chart high No.7.

'JET' / 'MAMUNIA'
US RELEASE January 28 1974; Apple 1871; withdrawn
'JET' / 'LET ME ROLL IT'
US RELEASE February 18 1974; Apple 1871; chart high No.1.

B-sides and several label variations. The single was initially issued with 'Mamunia' as its B-side and was manufactured with three label variations. The first has a light green Apple label with 'STEREO' at 9 o'clock and '(from the LP "BAND ON THE RUN" SO-3415') at 10 o'clock; title, composer, and artist credits appear centre bottom in bold print.

The second US variant has a dark green Apple label with 'STEREO' at 9 o'clock and the Intro. and Total playing time directly above; song title, composer. and artist credit appear centre bottom in bold print. The third has a dark green Apple label with 'STEREO' at 9 o'clock with the Intro. and Total playing time (incorrectly listed as 2:49) directly above; '(from the LP "BAND ON THE RUN" SO-3415') at 10 o'clock; title, composer, and artist credits centre bottom.

That single with 'Mamunia' on the B-side was withdrawn, and a new US version issued three weeks later with 'Let Me Roll It' as the flip. A further three label variants were manufactured. The first has a light green Apple label with 'STEREO' at 9 o'clock but with the Intro. and Total playing time on the right side of the label directly above the catalogue number; song title and artist credit centre bottom in bold print; B-side has the title in bold on two lines at 11 o'clock. The second variant has a dark green Apple label with identical text layout to the first, but the B-side has the title on one line in thin print.

The third variant has a dark green Apple label with 'STEREO' just below 9 o'clock and the Intro. and Total playing time directly above; '(from the LP "BAND ON THE RUN" SO-3415') at 10 o'clock; song title and artist credit centre bottom in thin print; B-side has the title in thin print bottom left on two lines.

American radio stations were issued with demonstration copies of the single (P-1871) featuring a mono edit (A-side) and full-length stereo mix (B-side) of the song. These were issued with light green Apple labels with a black star at 7 o'clock. The song title and artist credit appear centre bottom in bold print.

'Jet' / 'Let Me Roll It' was reissued in the mid 1970s in both Britain and the USA with black and silver Capitol 'dome' labels. Columbia reissued 'Jet' (13-33408) in 1980 as part of its Hall Of Fame series with 'Uncle Albert/Admiral Halsey' on the B-side. This 1980 pressing was issued with red labels; reissued in 1985, it had grey labels.

'BAND ON THE RUN'

WITH *Band On The Run* still high in the album charts, the title track was released as a single. Another massive hit for McCartney, it reached the Top 5 in both Britain and America: it made Number 1 in the USA where it also won a Grammy for best pop vocal performance. The single sold over two million copies worldwide – over one million in America alone – and its release ensured that the album at last hit the Number 1 spot in Britain. It also pushed the album back to the top of the American charts for the third time.

'BAND ON THE RUN' / 'ZOO GANG'
PAUL McCARTNEY AND WINGS
UK RELEASE June 28 1974; Apple R 5997; chart high No.3.

'BAND ON THE RUN' / 'NINETEEN HUNDRED AND EIGHTY FIVE'
PAUL McCARTNEY AND WINGS
US RELEASE April 8 1974; Apple 1873; chart high No.1.

• **'Zoo Gang'** (McCartney)
Paul McCartney (bass, keyboards), Linda McCartney (keyboards), Denny Laine (guitar), Jimmy McCulloch (guitar), Davy Lutton (drums).
Recorded at EMI Odeon Studios, Paris, France.
Produced by Paul McCartney.

'Zoo Gang' was a British ATV television programme produced by Lew Grade, who asked McCartney to write the show's theme tune. After completing *Band On The Run* in December 1973, Paul, Linda and Denny, along with Davy Lutton (drums) and Jimmy McCulloch (guitar), visited Paris, primarily to work on some of Linda's songs. While there, they also recorded 'Zoo Gang', as McCartney put it: "Just to see how it'd feel playing with musicians on a loose no-strings-attached basis". 'Zoo Gang' was a product of these 'test' sessions and found its way onto the B-side of 'Band On The Run'.

In an attempt to benefit from the publicity created by the television series, 'Zoo Gang' was also recorded by a group of session musicians, Jungle Juice, and issued on May 25 1974 by Bradley Records (BRAD 7407). The group, which included Colin Frechter on keyboards, recorded a similar-sounding instrumental, 'Monkey Business', for the B-side. Both sides of the record were produced by Tony Hiller, who did such a good job at recreating Wings' original that it fooled many into believing that Jungle Juice was another pseudonym. In fact, neither McCartney nor Wings had anything to do with the Jungle Juice single.

'Band On The Run' data

In Britain, Apple issued demonstration copies of the single with edited and full-length versions of the A-side. White-label copies with the EMI box logo top centre and 'DEMO RECORD NOT FOR SALE' printed above the spindle hole were also issued. Commercial copies of the single were issued with the full-length version of 'Band On The Run', with generic Apple labels and paper sleeve.

The US pressing (Apple 1873) was backed with 'Nineteen Hundred And Eighty Five' rather than the Eurocentric

'Zoo Gang' and was manufactured with three label variations. The first has a dark green Apple label with 'STEREO' at 9 o'clock and the Intro. and Total playing time directly below; '(from the LP "BAND ON THE RUN" SO-3415') at 10 o'clock; song title, composer, and band credits bottom centre in bold.

The second variant has a dark green Apple label with 'STEREO' at 9 o'clock; '(from the LP "BAND ON THE RUN" SO-3415') at 10 o'clock; song title and composer credit top centre; band name bottom centre.

The third US variant has a light green Apple label with 'STEREO' at 9 o'clock and the catalogue number directly below; '(from the LP "BAND ON THE RUN" SO-3415') at 10 o'clock; song title, composer, and band name bottom centre; Intro. time on the right side of the label above 'Total-5:09'.

Two demonstration singles were issued to American radio stations. The first (P-1873) was issued with a mono edit on the A-side and the full-length stereo version on the B-side. The second (PRO 6825) was issued with mono and stereo edits of the A-side on either side of the record. These were issued with light green Apple labels with a black star at 7 o'clock and the song title, composer, and band name centre bottom in bold.

When it was reissued in the mid 1970s, 'Band On The Run' / 'Nineteen Hundred And Eighty Five' was manufactured in Britain and America with black and silver Capitol 'dome' labels. 'Band On The Run' was reissued by Columbia (13-33409) in 1980 as part of its Hall Of Fame series with 'Helen Wheels' on the B-side. The 1980 pressing was issued with red labels; the 1985 re-pressing with grey labels.

'WHATEVER GETS YOU THRU THE NIGHT' / 'BEEF JERKY'
JOHN LENNON
UK RELEASE October 4 1974; Apple R 5898; chart high No.36.
US RELEASE September 23 1974; Apple APPLE 1874; chart high No.1.

• **'Whatever Gets You Thru The Night'** (Lennon)
John Lennon (vocals, guitar), Elton John (piano, organ, vocal harmony), Jesse Ed Davis (guitar), Eddie Mottau (acoustic guitar), Ken Ascher (clavinet), Bobby Keys (saxophone), Klaus Voormann (bass), Arthur Jenkins (percussion), Jim Keltner (drums).
• **'Beef Jerky'** (Lennon)
John Lennon (guitar), Jesse Ed Davis (guitar), Klaus Voormann (bass), Arthur Jenkins (percussion), Little Big Horns: Bobby Keys, Steve Madaio, Howard Johnson, Ron Aprea, Frank Vicari (horns), Jim Keltner (drums).
Both recorded at Record Plant East, New York City, NY, USA.
Both produced by John Lennon.

'WHATEVER GETS YOU THRU THE NIGHT'

STRANGE how Lennon and McCartney's solo careers seem to mirror one another. McCartney had just had a Number 1 single with 'Band On The Run', and now it was Lennon's turn with 'Whatever Gets You Thru The Night'.

Lennon's first solo chart-topper had little to say that was profound but got those toes tapping. At the time he wrote the song, he was in the grip of what he called his 'lost weekend'. Emerging from an extended period of over indulgence and self-destructive chaos, Lennon wrote a lyric that was both permissive and a eulogy to self-preservation.

Despite that recent bout of hedonism, 'Whatever Gets You Thru The Night' represents Lennon's more balanced attitude to life and marked a change in his mood. The prescriptive tone of old was gone. If he still wanted change, it was with a more relaxed live-and-let-live attitude. Better to let people think and act for themselves rather than bludgeon them with radicalism. But just as importantly, 'Whatever Gets You Thru The Night' marked a return to form, propelling Lennon to the top of the American charts for the first and only time in his lifetime. Its pop-disco fusion made it the perfect antidote to the self-inflicted pity he had recently experienced.

The song was inspired by two sources: George McRae's 'Rock Your Baby', and a phrase heard on a late-night radio phone-in. "I heard someone saying it on the radio, on a late night talk show, talking to someone on a phone, saying, 'Well, whatever gets you through the night.' And there it was, the whole tune came to me in my head," Lennon explained.

The phrase may have inspired him, but demo recordings reveal that a considerable amount of effort went into shaping the song (a fragment from Lennon's composing tape would turn up later on the *John Lennon Anthology*). Early attempts found him experimenting with different chord changes and lyrics. His early demos also have a downbeat feel that Lennon took with him when he entered the Record Plant to rehearse the song with a band.

Speaking to Lisa Robinson of the *NME*, he confirmed that he'd been under considerable pressure of late: "I would say that I was under emotional stress – a manic depression, I would call it." Rather than retain the mood, Lennon rejected his original pessimistic arrangement and dramatically rearranged the song, transforming it into an upbeat rocker that caught the ear instantly. "It was going to be like 'Rock Your Baby', but I often have an idea what it is going to be like but it never turns out anything like it. It's a very loose track," Lennon said. "I call it the 'Crippled Inside' of the album, you know, or the 'Oh Yoko!' of the album, which are tracks I made which people say I should put out as a single, and I always fought it. But this time I swayed with the people who told me to put it out. I think they were right. It's almost the first or second take, and the musicians are ragged but swinging. We tried to cut it a few times again but it never got that feel."

Elton John helped complete the song with the addition of piano, organ and harmony vocal overdubs. "How the record came about was that Elton was in town and I was doing it and needed a harmony," Lennon explained. "He did the harmony on that and a couple more, and played beautiful piano on it."

Despite Elton's powerful presence on the record, Lennon was never completely happy with the song. However, Elton was convinced that it was going to be a hit and asked Lennon to return the favour by joining him on stage should it make Number 1. Not thinking that it would ever be a hit, Lennon agreed. Within weeks of 'Whatever Gets You Thru The Night' being issued, it was sitting at the top of the US charts and Lennon was committed to performing with Elton John at Madison Square Garden in New York City.

He joined Elton John on November 28 1974 for the first of two shows the pianist gave there. The two Johns performed 'Whatever Gets You Thru The Night', 'Lucy In The Sky With Diamonds', and 'I Saw Her Standing There'. Lennon returned to play tambourine on 'The Bitch Is Back'. The show was recorded, and 'I Saw Her Standing There' issued as the B-side of Elton John's 'Philadelphia Freedom' (DJM DJS 10354). All three tracks were issued as an EP in 1981 (DJM DJS 10965).

'Beef Jerky' was modelled on the R&B records that Lennon had grown up with. The riff-heavy instrumental was recorded in July and August 1974, helped by a snappy brass arrangement and clever production touches. Lennon used every trick in the book to instil some verve in this otherwise pedestrian instrumental. However, his decision to place the rhythm section well down in the mix effectively prevented it from really taking off. Although Lennon never claimed to be a great guitarist, his playing on this track was more than a match for guitar virtuoso Jesse Ed Davis.

'Whatever Gets You Thru The Night' data

Apple issued 'Whatever Gets You Thru The Night' in Britain with generic Apple labels and paper sleeve.

American pressings were issued with three label variants. The first has a dark green Apple label; song title with composer credit and artist's name 'JOHN LENNON WITH THE PLASTIC ONO NUCLEAR BAND' centre bottom; 'STEREO' at 9 o'clock; publisher, intro and total playing time, catalogue number, and producer credit on the right side of the label.

The second variant has a dark green Apple label with artist's name offset right centre top; song title in bold with composer credit centre bottom; 'STEREO' at 9 o'clock with intro and total playing time and publisher credit below; catalogue number at 3 o'clock; producer credit at four o'clock.

The third US variant has a medium green Apple label with song title and composer credit at 11 o'clock; 'STEREO' at 9 o'clock; artist's name centre bottom; publisher, intro and total playing time, catalogue number, and producer credit on right side of label.

American promotional copies of the single (P-1874) were issued with light green Apple labels with the song title and composer credit centre bottom, plus a black star and 'NOT FOR SALE' at 10 o'clock. The A-side was issued in mono, the B-side in stereo. British promotional copies replicate the commercial pressing with the addition of a large 'A' at 11 o'clock, 'DEMO RECORD NOT FOR SALE' in the centre of the label, and '(4.10.74)' at 3 o'clock.

WALLS AND BRIDGES

ON COMPLETING *Mind Games*, Lennon and Ono separated. Ono stayed in New York while Lennon headed west for Los Angeles with his personal assistant and new girlfriend, May Pang. No longer able to live together, Lennon and Ono found that they couldn't live apart either. While they were no longer collaborating, they nevertheless remained in constant communication. Although it's been suggested that it was Ono who made all the moves, the fact that Lennon should even bother to receive her calls indicates that he too was finding it hard to make a clean break.

However, once he was out of Ono's immediate control, Lennon reverted to type. Having moved from pop star to peacenik to activist, he now made the move back to wild rocker. Determined to enjoy his new-found freedom, he reacquainted himself with the old London Ad Lib club crowd. Keith Moon, drummer with The Who and all round wild man of rock, was in town, as were Ringo Starr and Harry Nilsson. With nothing better to do, this boorish 'wild bunch' hit the town and painted it red. Their drunken antics were legion and legendary. Suffice to say, Lennon was making headline news, but for all the wrong reasons.

In a vain attempt to bring some order back into his life, Lennon decided the time was right to return to the studio. Unfortunately, all that happened was that the madness moved with him. The first thing he did was to reunite with Phil Spector for an album of rock'n'roll oldies. With no one prepared to control either Lennon or Spector's ego, the sessions quickly degenerated into chaos. John and Phil's 'Back To Mono' sessions became the biggest, wildest, and most expensive party in rock's history. Everyone indulged Lennon, who, more often than not, was drunk. The sessions didn't fizzle out as one might have expected, but came to an abrupt halt when Spector disappeared with the tapes.

Faced with a lengthy delay, in March 1974 Lennon turned to

producing an album for Harry Nilsson. Recording with many of the musicians who'd worked on the *Rock'N'Roll* project wasn't a good idea. Sessions for Nilsson's *Pussy Cats* album quickly became as chaotic as those abandoned a few months earlier.

Despite the madness, Lennon kept up a steady work schedule that would have shamed lesser artists. Paul and Linda McCartney also happened to be in Los Angeles and decided the time was right to meet up with Lennon. They dropped by the studio for a jam. Relations between Lennon and McCartney had been improving slowly for some time, and while the pair were nowhere as close as they had been, relations had obviously improved to the extent that McCartney felt comfortable enough to visit Lennon and even record with him in the studio.

Speaking to Denis Elsas on September 28 1974, Lennon said: "Paul was here about a month ago and I spent a couple of Beaujolais evenings with him." Lennon described their relationship as "very warm". Interviewed in 1997, McCartney too recalled the informal session. "The main thing that I recall, apart from the fact that Stevie Wonder was there, is that someone said, 'What songs shall we do?' and John said, 'Anything before '63; I don't know anything after '63!' Which I understood, because the songs from your formative years are the ones that you tend to use to jam."

Although the session involved two ex-Beatles, Harry Nilsson, Stevie Wonder, Jesse Ed Davis, and Bobby Keys, the results were ramshackle, marred by the consumption of certain illegal stimulants. It may have been uninspired, but this turned out to be the only post-Beatles recording that Lennon and McCartney made together. More importantly, it indicated that they were well on the way to resolving their differences.

While working on Nilsson's *Pussy Cats* album, Lennon also recorded a demo of '(It's All Down To) Goodnight Vienna' for Ringo Starr and produced a proposed single for Mick Jagger ('Too Many Cooks'). He also managed to write a batch of new songs for his next solo album. Not bad for a self-confessed drunken fool.

The non-stop party atmosphere he experienced in Los Angeles was beginning to take its toll, and Lennon realised that for his own health and sanity he had to leave it behind. "In LA you either have to be down by the beach or you become part of that never-ending show-business party circuit," he explained. "That scene makes me nervous, and when I get nervous I have to have a drink, and when I drink I get aggressive. So I prefer to stay in New York. I try not to drink at all here."

Back in New York City, Lennon finished Nilsson's album and began writing. As usual, he recorded a number of simple home demos, fleshing out ideas, melodies, and lyrics as the songs progressed. He would later dismiss these songs as the uninspired work of a "semi-sick craftsman". Nevertheless, he gained some benefit from the work; unpacking his bundle of emotional baggage was cathartic.

Speaking just after the album's release, Lennon appeared relieved but also disappointed. "Let's say this last year has been an extraordinary year for me personally," he said. "And I'm almost amazed that I could get anything out. But I enjoyed doing *Walls And Bridges*, and it wasn't hard when I had the whole thing to go into the studio and do it. I'm surprised it wasn't just all blanunuggggghhhh. I had the most peculiar year. And ... I'm just glad that something came out. It's describing the year, in a way, but it's not as sort of schizophrenic as the year really was. I think I got such a shock during that year that the impact hasn't come through. It isn't all on *Walls And Bridges*, though. There's a hint of it there. It has to do with age and god knows what else. But only the surface has been touched on *Walls And Bridges*, you know?"

Although he thought the work lacked originality, the record had continuity and conviction – which couldn't be said for the last album, *Mind Games*. In the light of what had been happening to him, *Walls And Bridges* was a solid album and proof that he was still capable of flashes of greatness, even if he was growing tired of the music industry's demands.

Writing *Walls And Bridges* may not have been as cathartic an experience for Lennon as writing *John Lennon/Plastic Ono Band*, but at least he came through the episode with a better understanding of who he was and what he wanted from life. He remained a seeker, but what he sought now was not political change, global harmony, or an unobtainable utopia, but personal fulfilment. The quest to bring meaning to his life was slowly becoming a reality. *Walls And Bridges* points the way to Lennon's final musical statement, *Double Fantasy*. That, however, was six years away; for the moment, he had more pressing matters to deal with.

Once he was ready to record, Lennon called upon his usual pool of musicians and, to familiarise them with the new material, began rehearsing at New York City's Record Plant studio in early July. Typically, these sessions were recorded – and several songs taped at these rehearsals would later appear on the *Menlove Ave.* album and the *John Lennon Anthology* boxed set. Because the musicians had rehearsed the material Lennon wanted to record, working out their own 'head' arrangements, the recording progressed quickly. Unlike the Spector 'Back To Mono' sessions, these were a model of professionalism. Regular work hours were established and all stimulants banned from the studio.

Jimmy Iovine, who acted as overdub engineer on *Walls And Bridges*, confirmed that Lennon was a consummate professional. "The *Walls And Bridges* sessions were *the* most professional I have been on," he recalled. "He was [there] every day, 12 o'clock to 10 o'clock; go home; off [at] the weekends; eight weeks; done. John knew what he wanted, he knew how to get what he was going after: he was going after a noise and he knew how to get it. And for the most part he got it. What he explained, we used to get. ... His solo thing had an incredible sound to it. And he really had his own sound."

With the basic tracks in the can, Lennon started the process of adding overdubs. Ron Aprea, saxophonist with the newly recruited Little Big Horns, recalled that the brass section was added over a frantic two-week period. Although he was astonished to discover that none of the songs had formal arrangements written for them, he was pleasantly surprised to discover just how accommodating Lennon could be. "Since he had no formal training in arranging, he would sit in the control room and let us make up our own parts," said Aprea. "If he liked what we played, he would let us know and then ask us for our opinion. He would also ask if there were any 'secrets' [mistakes]. If we thought we could get it better, he would say 'go for it'."

Although the Record Plant was one of the most advanced and sophisticated recording studios in New York, Lennon's vocal overdubs were recorded with an old stage microphone. Iovine: "[It] was an old beat-up one that was in a bass drum for years, so it was dull in a way, but John's voice was so bright that it sounded incredible on it. It turned out to be a great vocal sound, like on '#9 Dream'."

Days before Lennon was due to start recording what would become *Walls And Bridges*, Capitol Records executive Al Coury recovered the Spector 'Back To Mono' tapes. At roughly the same time, the US authorities gave Lennon 60 days to leave the country. Once again, he appealed against the decision. In light of these problems, the album's title was an apt one. Lennon was facing numerous barriers and the title, *Walls And Bridges*, taken from a public service announcement, summed up his situation perfectly.

Walls And Bridges turned out to be Lennon's last album of original material until *Double Fantasy* in 1980 – but a follow-up was planned for late 1975. Apple executive Tony King has suggested that Lennon planned to follow *Walls And Bridges* with an album called *Between The Lines*. King also suggested that guitarist Carlos Alomar had been hired to recruit a band of black musicians and that Lennon had already written 'Tennessee' and 'Nobody Told Me' for the album. When interviewed by Bob Harris for BBC TV's *Old Grey Whistle Test* in 1975, Lennon confirmed that he was planning a new album and a one-off television show, but neither surfaced.

Walls And Bridges songs

Hardly the most auspicious way to start an album, 'Going Down On Love' set the tone for most of what followed. Its sexual innuendo apart, the song is a bleak confession of despair. The 'lost weekend' may have looked like fun from the outside, but from Lennon's perspective things could not have been worse. He really had hit the bottom, and with no end in sight and no evident escape, all he could do was attempt to come to terms with the situation.

Although he was down, he wasn't out. Lennon was often at his best when exploring the darker side of his psyche. Whether it was the traumatic experience of heroin withdrawal or the after affects of primal therapy, he often shone when all around him seemed gloomy. As raw and honest as anything he'd written, 'Going Down On Love' finds him in a rare moment of contrition, praying for redemption and forgiveness. With Ono no longer there to control him, Lennon must have felt completely lost. Without a guiding hand, he forgoes any attempt to strip away illusions or to analyse the cause of his suffering. Rather there is blind acceptance of the fact that there is no magic cure, no quick fix, but only the fleeting experience of human existence at its darkest.

Having formulated the bare bones of the song, Lennon recorded several demos, developing the lyrics, melody, middle eight, and arrangement as he went. Moving to the piano, he recorded a strident, pounding arrangement that, when he shifted to the studio, would be forsaken in favour of the muted tone of his earlier guitar-based demo recordings. Rehearsing at the Record Plant in early July, Lennon recorded a stripped-down version of the song with just guitarist Jesse Ed Davis, bassist Klaus Voormann, and drummer Jim Keltner in support. Without the gloss of overdubs, the rehearsal take reeks of melancholia and Lennon sounds audibly vulnerable. (Some of these rehearsals were issued later on the *Menlove Ave.* album.)

Between bouts of drinking, drugging, and trouble-making, Lennon and Harry Nilsson managed to stay sober long enough to write 'Old Dirt Road'. Lennon suggested that his collaboration with Nilsson was "just to write a song. You know, 'seein' as we're stuck in this bottle of vodka together, we might as well try and do something'." But he was being disingenuous. Lennon's admiration for the singer's talents was considerable – he wouldn't have offered to produce Nilsson had he not liked him and his work. Although 'Old Dirt Road' is not the best song in his oeuvre, Lennon was too quick to dismiss it. Perhaps he associated the song with a period in his life that he would rather forget and therefore dismissed it as a song written while he was not at his creative best. Although it is not explicitly about the 'lost weekend', it does capture an atmosphere of listless intoxication that must have permeated their days.

Speaking on BBC radio in 1990, Nilsson recalled how he helped Lennon finish the song. Remarkably, it was completed while discussing business with some 'suits'. Nilsson: "When you said something that was either clever or good, [Lennon] would just jump on it. When he was writing 'Old Dirt Road', he'd started the tune, and he was up past the first verse, I guess, and some 'suit people' came in, and he said, 'Harry, what's a good Americanism?' And why this came about [I don't know], it came into my mind, but it was like, 'Trying to shovel smoke with a pitchfork in the wind.' And he said, 'Oh great, great. Fantastic! You're burning man, go for it.' And he talked to the suits over the piano, and wrote another verse, and I'd check in with him every few minutes like a secretary, go back to the piano, and he'd be going, 'Yeah, yeah you're on fire now.'"

The rehearsal take, issued later on *Menlove Ave.*, is the most basic of sketches but allows the listener to eavesdrop on the session as the song takes shape. An outtake issued on the *John Lennon Anthology* is considerably more formed and, with the addition of acoustic guitar, closer to the finished master.

Next up is 'What You Got', a slice of New York funk inspired by The O' Jays' 'Money, Money, Money' and, despite its apparent joie de vivre, a rather sad lament. Lennon restates a lyrical theme beloved of blues singers – "you don't know what you got until you lose it" – and in the process expresses real fears. Acknowledging that his drunken capers with Nilsson were rapidly getting him a reputation as a 'drag', he nevertheless had the wherewithal to recognise the fact and do something about it. Not only were the hangovers becoming too much, but so was his separation from Ono. Delivered with an emotionally charged vocal, 'What You Got' may not have had much new to say lyrically, but it said it musically in the most fashionable way possible.

At the time, Lennon was listening to a lot of dance music and planned to record his next album with black musicians. Although disco came in for a lot of criticism, especially from the punk and new wave tribes, dance music was where it was at, and Lennon loved it. Apple executive Tony King remembers stocking Lennon's jukebox with contemporary disco records, and one in particular, 'Shame Shame Shame' by Shirley And Company, influenced his later contribution to David Bowie's *Fame*. Like much dance music, 'What You Got' appears up-beat, but scratch the surface and you'll find a song as honest and self-explanatory as anything Lennon had written.

Paul McCartney didn't have a monopoly on romantic ballads. Lennon was equally capable of writing tender love songs. Like McCartney's 'My Love' from the previous year, 'Bless You' was a heartfelt expression of love and every bit as romantic. But its writing was tempered with the knowledge that both parties had grown apart and could no longer be described as John-and-Yoko. While Lennon was in Los Angeles with May Pang, Ono was in New York City and, Albert Goldman later alleged, was infatuated with guitarist David Spinozza. The Lennons now seemed engaged in a very open relationship, and whereas Lennon would have once been filled with rage and jealousy, he now had the grace to bless his usurper.

Unlike earlier songs dedicated to Ono, which were in effect one-sided expressions of love, 'Bless You' reveals a subtle change in attitude, a recognition that love is not a static emotion but one that is experienced and expressed in many shades and hues. "In a way, it's about Yoko and I," he explained. "And in a way it's about a lot of couples or all of us who go through that (whatever it's called) love experience. You know, the way love changes, which is one of the surprises of life that we all find out: that it doesn't remain exactly the same all the time, although it's still love. It comes in mysterious forms, its wonders to perform. And 'Bless You' expresses one side of it."

As with some of Lennon's best work, 'Bless You' came to him quickly. Speaking just after the release of *Walls And Bridges*, he revealed that he hadn't laboured over it as he had others. "As a song, I think it's the best piece of work on the album, although I worked harder on some of the other tracks. In retrospect, that seems to be the best track, to me."

Lennon took considerable care in shaping it, transforming the song from a rather maudlin ballad to a shimmering statement of regret that bypassed schmaltz for simple honesty. Although he allowed the musicians to develop their own parts, he made himself clear when he heard something he didn't like. While rehearsing 'Bless You', Lennon chastised guitarist Jesse Ed Davis for playing a chord with too many notes in it, even if they were the right ones. After the over-production of *Mind Games* and the Spector 'Back To Mono' sessions, Lennon returned to a simpler recording practice that struck the right balance between artifice and honesty.

As honest and analytical as anything written for *John Lennon/Plastic Ono Band*, 'Scared' was the product of a deepening depression brought on by Lennon's separation from Ono. This wasn't the first time he'd experienced crippling feelings of isolation and alienation brought about by drink, drugs, and fragmenting relationships. He'd expressed similar fears in 'Help!', a literal cry for succour written during a similar bout of personal torment. Like 'Help!', 'Scared' is a distillation of the pain he was experiencing during its writing. "I am scared a lot of the time, I think we all are," he said, "but I'm not always scared. I do have vindictive sides as well."

Adrift from Ono and with little else to do other than hit the bottle, Lennon had plenty of time to contemplate the meaning of life, the universe, and everything. What he found was of little comfort. Had his life's work been in vain? Was he nothing more than an uncommitted phoney, afraid to practice what he preached? Redemption seemed unobtainable, and the questions Lennon asked remained unanswered until he was reunited with Ono.

Musically, Lennon restates what he had originally intended for 'Help!'. Unhappy with The Beatles' up-tempo treatment of 'Help!', he attempted a brooding remake in 1970 when he taped a piano-based home demo at his Tittenhurst home. He also spoke of re-recording the song professionally, but the nearest he got to it was the moody setting he fashioned for 'Scared'. Unadorned by overdubs, the rehearsal take (later issued on *Menlove Ave.*) wouldn't have seemed out of place on *John Lennon/Plastic Ono Band*. It also has slightly different lyrics. Alluding to Dylan's 'Rainy Day Women #12 & 35' and his own recent indulgences, Lennon sings "I'm stoned" in place of "I'm scared".

The ethereal '#9 Dream' began as a string arrangement that Lennon wrote for Harry Nilsson's recording of 'Many Rivers To Cross'. However, this melody was too good to use just once and then discard. Reworking the arrangement, Lennon developed a dreamlike motif that hovers like a veil between contrasting worlds of reality and fantasy. The phantasmagorical atmosphere Lennon created was inspired, in part, by a dream in which he heard the nonsensical phrase "Ah! böwakawa poussé, poussé" and two women (Yoko Ono and May Pang?) calling his name. Combining his skills as a lyricist and melodist, Lennon perfectly captured that moment between sleeping and awakening in which reality and fantasy merge. The lyric was his most poetic for some time, packed with romantic allusions that evoke the dream state that inspired them.

To many listeners, '#9 Dream' has all the hallmarks of a classic. However, when speaking with Andy Peebles in 1980, Lennon was quick to dismiss the song. "That's what I call craftsmanship writing, meaning, you know, I just churned that out," he said. "I'm not putting it down, it's just what it is, but I just sat down and wrote it, you know, with no real inspiration, based on a dream I'd had." If '#9 Dream' was nothing more than "craftsmanship writing", it was a remarkably skilled piece of work.

Lennon began by recording rough work-in-progress demos. But it was only when he took the song into the studio that it really came to life. Once he'd recorded the basic track, to which a lush orchestral arrangement by Ken Ascher and backing vocals were added, he began work on developing the song's dreamy texture, achieved with a great deal of post-production work. Jimmy Iovine recalled that a huge amount of effects were used to create the finished track. "On '#9 Dream', that's an incredible vocal sound. There's a lot of very interesting things done to that vocal sound to make it sound like that. There was so much echo on his voice in the mix, and doubling and tape delay." The results were spectacular. Washes of sound envelop the listener, drawing them into Lennon's narcoleptic dream world.

A song inspired by Lennon's new beau, 'Surprise, Surprise (Sweet Bird Of Paradox)' was written in New York City at the beginning of his relationship with May Pang. He had several affairs, and occasionally wrote about them – 'Norwegian Wood' being an early example – but few were as explicitly revealed as this. Compared with his recent musings on Ono, 'Surprise, Surprise (Sweet Bird Of Paradox)' brims with warmth and emotion. He was clearly besotted with his new sweetheart. Although Pang experienced Lennon at his most depraved, she too was deeply in love with him. However, no sooner had Lennon issued the song than he was back with Ono. What happened to make him abandon Pang so quickly and utterly has never been explained. Whatever it was, Lennon and Ono seemed to pick up their relationship as if nothing had happened. Within months of moving back to the Dakota, Ono was pregnant and Lennon bound for five years of househusbandry. (The Dakota was the apartment block in New York City to which the pair had moved from their Bank Street apartment in May 1973.)

WALLS AND BRIDGES

JOHN LENNON (WITH PLASTIC ONO NUCLEAR BAND/LITTLE BIG HORNS/AND THE PHILHARMONIC ORCHESTRANGE)

SIDE 1 'Going Down On Love', 'Whatever Gets You Thru The Night', 'Old Dirt Road', 'What You Got', 'Bless You', 'Scared'.

SIDE 2 '#9 Dream', 'Surprise, Surprise (Sweet Bird Of Paradox)', 'Steel And Glass', 'Beef Jerky', 'Nobody Loves You When You're Down And Out', 'Ya Ya'.

UK RELEASE October 4 1974; LP Apple PCTC 253; 8-track cartridge Apple 8X-PCTC 253; chart high No.6.

US RELEASE September 26 1974; LP Apple SW 3416; 8-track cartridge Apple 8XW-3416; quadraphonic 8-track cartridge Apple Q8W-3416; chart high No.1.

• **'Going Down On Love'** (Lennon)
Personnel as 'What You Got' except Ken Ascher (electric piano).

• 'Old Dirt Road' (Lennon, Nilsson)
John Lennon (vocals, piano), Jesse Ed Davis (guitar), Eddie Mottau (acoustic guitar), Ken Ascher (electric piano), Nicky Hopkins (piano), Klaus Voormann (bass), Harry Nilsson (backing vocal), Jim Keltner (drums).

• **'What You Got'** (Lennon)
John Lennon (vocals, guitar), Jesse Ed Davis (guitar), Eddie Mottau (acoustic guitar), Ken Ascher (Clavinet), Nicky Hopkins (piano), Klaus Voormann (bass), Arthur Jenkins (percussion), Little Big Horns: Bobby Keys, Steve Madaio, Howard Johnson, Ron Aprea, Frank Vicari (horns), Jim Keltner (drums).

• **'Bless You'** (Lennon)
John Lennon (vocals, acoustic guitar), Jesse Ed Davis (guitar), Eddie Mottau (acoustic guitar), Ken Ascher (piano, Mellotron), Klaus Voormann (bass), Arthur Jenkins (percussion), Jim Keltner (drums).

• **'Scared'** (Lennon)
Personnel as 'What You Got' except Ken Ascher (electric piano).

• **'#9 Dream'** (Lennon)
John Lennon (vocals, acoustic guitar), Jesse Ed Davis (guitar), Eddie Mottau (acoustic guitar), Ken Ascher (Clavinet), Nicky Hopkins (electric piano), Bobby Keys (saxophone), Klaus Voormann (bass), Arthur Jenkins (percussion), The 44th Street Fairies: May Pang, Lori Burton, Joey Dambra (backing vocals), Jim Keltner (drums).

• **'Surprise, Surprise (Sweet Bird Of Paradox)'** (Lennon)
John Lennon (vocals, acoustic guitar), Elton John (vocal harmony), rest as 'What You Got'.

• **'Steel And Glass'** (Lennon)
John Lennon (vocals, acoustic guitar), rest as 'What You Got'.

• **'Nobody Loves You (When You're Down And Out)'** (Lennon)
John Lennon (vocals, acoustic guitar), Jesse Ed Davis (guitar), Klaus Voormann (bass), Little Big Horns: Bobby Keys, Steve Madaio, Howard Johnson, Ron Aprea, Frank Vicari (horns), Jim Keltner (drums).

• **'Ya Ya'** (Robinson, Lewis, Dorsey)
John Lennon (vocals, piano), Julian Lennon (drums).
All recorded at Record Plant East, New York City, NY, USA.
All produced by John Lennon.

'Surprise, Surprise' began as little more than an extended exploration of what became the song's middle eight. Accompanying himself on electric guitar, Lennon recorded a demo based on this motif. This early version seemed to question the strength of his relationship with Pang rather than celebrate it. Next he reworked the song to the point where it resembled the finished composition. He made a demo recording of the reworked song, this time accompanying himself with an acoustic guitar. Both demos feature musical elements that were discarded once he moved to the Record Plant. When proper recording began, the track took on a lighter tone – a version issued later on the *John Lennon Anthology* reveals just how far the song had developed once the band began work on it. With the backing track complete, Lennon began adding overdubs, which included a vocal contribution from Elton John.

'Steel And Glass' was Lennon's attempt to update 'How Do You Sleep?', and many believed that on this occasion his target was his ex-manager, Allen Klein. By the mid 1970s, Lennon's infatuation with Klein had waned considerably, to the extent that neither he nor Harrison nor Starr wanted Klein to manage their affairs any longer. Although Klein had probably made more money for them than Brian Epstein ever did, by 1974 Lennon, Harrison, and Starr were back in the courts attempting to disentangle themselves from his managerial grip. More than anything else, it was this litigation that caused Lennon to attack Klein with such obvious pleasure. Lennon and Klein may have been battling it out in the courts, but that didn't mean that they couldn't still be friends.

Even as Lennon was writing 'Steel And Glass', he was happy to visit and stay with Klein at his Westhampton home. But when asked about the song, Lennon refused to admit that it had anything to do with Klein, only that he may have used him as inspiration to write something nasty. "It actually isn't about one person in particular," he said, "but it has been about a few people and, like a novel writer, if I'm writing about something other than myself, I use other people I know or have known as examples. If I want to write a 'down' song, I would have to remember being down, and when I wrote 'Steel And Glass' I used various people and objects. If I had listed who they were, it would be a few people, and you would be surprised. But it really isn't about anybody. I'm loathe to tell you this, because it spoils the fun. I would sooner everybody think, 'Who's it about?' and try and piece it together. For sure, it isn't about Paul and it isn't about Eartha Kitt."

Before taking it to the studio, Lennon recorded a pounding piano demo with different lyrics to the finished song. He had a habit of rewriting lyrics, often making changes right up to the moment before recording his final vocal. A rehearsal take, recorded at the Record Plant and issued later on *Menlove Ave*, has Lennon abandoning the piano for an acoustic guitar, slowing the tempo, and leading his small band through a version of the song that still lacked a finished lyric.

If the 'lost weekend' had a signature tune, it was 'Nobody Loves You (When You're Down And Out)'. Written during Lennon's first few weeks in Los Angeles, it is an honest and revealing exploration of his fragile mental state. His feelings of rejection and alienation are etched deep into this song. Battered by critics, abandoned by Ono, cheated by the music industry, and ignored by the public, Lennon had come a long way from being the toppermost of the poppermost, and 'Nobody Loves You (When You're Down And Out)' reveals the effect this had on him.

From where he was standing, it seemed that he'd been abandoned. Derelict and depressed, Lennon muses that he will only be truly valued when he's "six foot in the ground". Exhausted by the demands placed upon him, Lennon found himself staring into a black hole of despair that threatened to swallow him whole. Like his ex-partner Paul McCartney, he'd suffered many dark nights of the soul, but he had survived and was looking for a way out.

Early versions of the song reveal the depth of Lennon's depression. From the earliest of home demos to the group rehearsals held before proper recording, Lennon sounds world-weary and fragile. The rehearsal take issued later on *Menlove Ave.* is dark and melancholic. Lennon's introductory whistling lends the song a sense of lonely isolation, but when guitarist Davis exacts palpable moans and cries of despair from his instrument, the song moves deeper into the shadows. An alternative take issued later on the *John Lennon Anthology* features extra musicians, second guitar, keyboards, and percussion not present on the rehearsal take and runs close to the finished master.

Lennon included a cover of 'Ya Ya' in an attempt to appease music publisher Morris Levy, who was suing over an alleged breech of copyright. It didn't work. Levy wanted something more than an ad-libbed 59-second snippet for him to drop legal proceedings. Lennon's next album, *Rock'N'Roll*, would settle the matter once and for all. (See that entry, later, for more details.) Although it was probably tagged on to the album as an afterthought, 'Ya Ya' captures a rare moment of intimacy between Lennon and his first son, Julian (who'd stayed with his mother, Cynthia, when she divorced his father in the late 1960s).

The album sessions produced one outtake. 'Move Over Ms L' was intended to sit between 'Surprise Surprise' and 'What You Got', before Lennon decided to alter the track listing. 'Move Over' was released six months later as the B-side of the single 'Stand By Me'. It was also given to drinking buddy Keith Moon, who recorded a version for his debut and only solo album, *Two Sides Of The Moon.*

Walls And Bridges data

Apple issued *Walls And Bridges* with generic Apple labels and a unique fold-over cover. Lennon had intended to use the paintings he made as a boy for the cover of his 'oldies' album, but as that was postponed he told Roy Kohara to base the design for *Walls And Bridges* on the images already supplied. The package also included a printed inner sleeve and eight-page full colour booklet.

British pressings appear to have been manufactured from masters supplied by Capitol, as the album's US catalogue number, SW 3416, appears crossed out in the dead wax.

American copies of the LP were produced with three label variations. The first has a medium green Apple label; bold text with the first song title above the spindle hole; B-side label with title at 10 o'clock; artist credit at two o'clock. The second has a medium green Apple label; plain text with all song titles below the spindle hole; B-side label with title and artist credit on two lines at 10 o'clock. And the third has a medium green Apple label; bold text with all song titles below the spindle hole; B-side label with title and artist credit on three lines at 10 o'clock.

The album was reissued in America by Capitol in 1978 with purple Capitol labels and again in 1982 with black/colour band Capitol labels. In 1989, Capitol reissued the album with purple Capitol labels with a small Capitol logo. In 1999, EMI released *Walls And Bridges* as a limited-edition 'Millennium' 180 gram audiophile vinyl LP (4994641).

The album was issued in the USA on 8-track cartridge in both stereo (8XW-3416) and quadraphonic (Q8W-3416). In Britain, the 8-track was issued in stereo only (8X-PCTC 253).

Walls And Bridges first appeared on CD in Britain in July 20 1987 (CDP 7 46768 2) with an eight-page booklet. The CD was issued in the USA on April 19 1988. The album was remixed, remastered, and issued by EMI/Capitol with three bonus tracks and revised cover and label artwork on November 22 2005.

The album's respectable chart placing was achieved by Lennon's willingness to engage in promotional duties; he made guest appearances on several American radio stations, and an array of promotional material appeared included badges, stickers, posters, press kits, and photographs, all with the theme 'Listen To This'. Additionally, a 59-second 'Listen To This Radio Spot', featuring both Lennon and Ringo Starr, was distributed to American radio stations. In Britain, EMI issued an interview single (PSR 369), which it gave to its sales reps. The interview with Bob Merger was produced by Lennon and issued as a white-label 7-inch with the EMI logo and the legend 'An Apple record'. The interview was eventually issued as a bonus track on the 2005 remastered CD.

'WALKING IN THE PARK WITH ELOISE' / 'BRIDGE OVER THE RIVER SUITE'
THE COUNTRY HAMS
UK RELEASE October 18 1974; EMI EMI 2220; failed to chart.
US RELEASE December 2 1974; EMI EMI 3977; failed to chart.

• **'Walking In The Park With Eloise'** (James McCartney Senior)
Paul McCartney (bass), Chet Atkins (guitar), Floyd Cramer (piano), Geoff Britton (drums), Denis Good, Bobby Thompson, Bill Puitt (saxophones), Don Sheffield (trumpet). Recorded at Sound Shop Studios, Nashville, TN, USA.
• **'Bridge Over The River Suite'** (McCartney)
Paul McCartney (bass, washboard), Linda McCartney (keyboards), Jimmy McCulloch (guitar), Denny Laine (guitar), Davy Lutton (drums), Bill Puitt (saxophone), George Tidwell, Barry McDonald (trumpets), Norman Ray (baritone saxophone), Dale Quillen (trombone), Thaddeus Richard (saxophone). Recorded at EMI Odeon Studios, Paris, France and Sound Shop Studios, Nashville.
Both produced by Paul McCartney.

'WALKING IN THE PARK WITH ELOISE'

HAVING completed *Band On The Run*, McCartney started to look for replacements for drummer Denny Seiwell and guitarist Henry McCullough. Drummer Davy Lutton was employed as a temporary stand-in and, along with guitarist Jimmy McCulloch, he recorded with Wings at EMI Odeon Studios, Paris, in late 1973. McCulloch, who became a full-time member of the band, was best known for his work with Thunderclap Newman and had previously worked with John Mayall's band, which had also featured guitar legends Peter Green and Eric Clapton.

A guitarist with a stellar reputation, McCulloch was looking for something more stable, and Wings offered him that option. As he explained: "I'm sick and tired of being in and out of bands. I want to get something down on record that's going to be appreciated instead of always being in new bands that so few people hear."

McCartney held auditions for Seiwell's replacement at the Albery Theatre in London on April 26 1974. Competition for the job was fierce with around 50 drummers auditioning. Waiting in the wings that day was Geoff Britton. He was eager to play with his hero but left disappointed. Paul, Linda and Denny didn't play that day but sat out front while a surrogate band stood in for them.

Britton recalled: "I was a bit disappointed, actually, because I thought it would be a chance to play with McCartney, but they hired session men instead. I wasn't really nervous, although I might've been a bit apprehensive. We had to play about four numbers – some of it quite advanced stuff for an ordinary rock'n'roll drummer. Anyway, I got up there and did my stuff. A few days later I got this phone call and they said I was on the shortlist of five, and this time it would be Paul and the group playing. That time I had a 20 percent chance, yet I felt it was more hopeless than ever."

Despite his misgivings, Britton got the job and was whisked off to Nashville for rehearsals with Wings. In June and July 1974, during a six-week stay in Nashville, McCartney wrote some new songs, rehearsed the new line-up, and recorded 'Junior's Farm' and an instrumental, 'Walking In The Park with Eloise', written by his father. As Linda recalled, the recording came about almost by accident. "We were having dinner with Chet Atkins, the guitar player, one night in Nashville, and Paul had been playing a lot of his music for Chet, and he said: 'Here's one that my dad wrote a long time ago' – and he started playing it. Chet got talking to Paul, saying that the song should be recorded and that it would be nice for his dad. So we got Chet playing on it and Floyd Cramer, the piano player, and Chet got together a nice little band called The Country Hams with lots of other Nashville people."

McCartney said that his father was thrilled with his debut single. "He loved having a record out – but he's very shy ... and he didn't like all the publicity. I remember him being very emotional about it when I first played it to him. He said I really shouldn't have bothered, but I know he enjoyed it."

While McCartney was recording 'Country Dreamer' (B-side of 'Helen Wheels'; see October 1973) he improvised a melody that formed the basis of 'Bridge Over The River Suite'. Recorded with drummer Davy Lutton and guitarist Jimmy McCulloch at EMI's Paris studio in December 1973, it's untypical of Wings, although the introduction recalls 'Let Me Roll It' from the previous year. The brass section, scored by Paul and Tony Dorsey, was overdubbed in Nashville in July 1974.

'Walking In The Park With Eloise' data

The single was issued in Britain and the USA with generic EMI labels and picture sleeve. In America, EMI issued a mono/stereo demonstration single P-3997 (PRO-6993). In Britain, EMI issued demonstration copies with 'DEMO RECORD NOT FOR RESALE' on two lines below the spindle hole and an 'A' above the A-side label's spindle hole.

'JUNIOR'S FARM'

WHAT little Wings recorded in Nashville went relatively smoothly, but relations within the band remained tense. As early as August 1974, only weeks after the group's return to Britain, the *NME* carried the headline "Wings Upheaval". Speaking to *Sounds*, Denny Laine confirmed that all was not well. "It's not that these things hadn't been said before. Various things were said, like they're said in any group – you can't deny that. You know how it is. You say something, and if someone else doesn't respond to what you're saying then you're walking out, but the next minute you can be walking back. People have been thinking that finally I've said my piece, but that's not true – I've just said my piece about what's happening at this time."

Problems centred on money and contracts, as Laine explained. "We went to Nashville with the idea that we'd get this group together and we'd all sign contracts and be Wings, as a business thing. But then it seemed as if it was being a bit rushed. I thought, 'Hang on – let's make sure that this is the right group.' Then I started thinking about contracts, and I decided that I could be in any group without signing a contract. It just didn't seem necessary to me, and the minute I said this to Paul he said, 'Great, that's the way I want it too,' and then I realised that we were only going through this thing because we'd all been advised to do it. It wasn't what we wanted."

In an attempt to paper over the cracks, MPL issued a statement that only added to the confusion. (MPL is McCartney Productions Ltd, an umbrella company founded in 1971 by McCartney for his management and business interests.) Failing to confirm the band's status, the statement simply said: "Wings members are free to pursue their own musical careers. This will enable them to develop working relations free of contractual ties. In future Wings will have a fluid concept, which will be adapted to suit current and future projects."

Disputes over contracts and money had contributed to McCullough and Seiwell's departure and would beleaguer Wings throughout the 1970s. Consequently, the original concept of fluidity quickly became a reality, with various individuals joining and leaving the McCartney–Laine–McCartney core over the next few years.

'Junior's Farm' was recorded in Nashville and was partly inspired by Junior 'Curley' Putman, owner of the ranch near

'JUNIOR'S FARM' / 'SALLY G'
PAUL McCARTNEY AND WINGS
UK RELEASE October 25 1974; Apple R 5999; chart high No.16.
US RELEASE November 4 1974; Apple 1875; chart high No.3.

- **'Junior's Farm'** (McCartney)
Paul McCartney (bass, vocals), Linda McCartney (keyboards, vocals), Denny Laine (guitar, vocals), Jimmy McCulloch (guitar), Geoff Britton (drums).
- **'Sally G'** (McCartney)
Paul McCartney (bass, guitar, vocals), Linda McCartney (backing vocals), Denny Laine (guitar), Jimmy McCulloch (guitar), Geoff Britton (drums), Vassar Clements (fiddle), Buddy Emmons (pedal steel guitar), Johnny Gimble (fiddle).

Both recorded at Sound Shop Studios, Nashville, TN, USA.
Both mixed at Abbey Road Studios, London, England.
Both produced by Paul McCartney.

Lebanon, Nashville, where Wings were living and rehearsing. Bob Dylan's 'Maggie's Farm' provided further inspiration, as McCartney recalled. "To me, in a way, it was a bit reminiscent of Dylan's thing, 'ain't gonna work on Maggie's farm any more'. So the idea [was] we'll have another farm, rather than Maggie's farm. And so the idea was to just get a fantasy song about this person Junior – and we recorded it in Nashville with Jimmy McCulloch on guitar and Geoff Britton on drums. Jimmy played a really nice solo; we had a good session on that one." Thus Wings Mk.4 were born: Paul, Linda, and Laine plus McCulloch and Britton.

'Sally G' was also written and recorded during the Nashville sojourn. It's a country-flavoured ballad ,originally called 'Diane' after the singer Diane Gaffney. McCartney changed the title to 'Sally G' upon learning that Gaffney was suing a newspaper after her name had appeared in it without her permission. Explaining the song's genesis, he said: "When I'm in a place, it's not uncommon for me to want to write about where I am. Elton John did 'Philadelphia Freedom', you know? You see a lot of that: someone will turn up and write a song the next day."

While in Nashville, McCartney was taken to Printers Alley and spent some time in a bar called Skull's Rainbow Room. "There was a few people just playing country music," he said, "and we imagined a bit more than we had seen for 'Sally G'. I didn't see anyone named Sally G when I was in Printers Alley, nor did I see anyone who ran her eyes over me when she was singing 'a tangled mime'. That was my imagination adding something to it, the reality of it."

'Junior's Farm' data

This was the first Wings single in almost a year, their last issued by Apple, and the first by the Mk.4 line-up. In Britain, EMI subcontracted an unidentified manufacturer, possibly Decca, to press the single. The subcontracted pressings can be identified by their heavier weight, wider clearance between the push-out centre and the record, and the handwritten matrix number (7YCE21751 - 3). Both British and American pressings were issued with generic Apple labels and black paper sleeve.

Four label variants were issued in the USA. The first has a light green Apple label with 'STEREO' at 10 o'clock; Intro. and Total playing time at 3 o'clock; song title, writing credit, and band name bottom centre; 'Recorded in England' (although the single was, of course, recorded in America) at 11 o'clock. The second has identical text layout to the first but 'All rights reserved' etc. is on five lines below the catalogue number.

The third variant has a dark green Apple label with 'STEREO' at 10 o'clock; catalogue number at 9 o'clock; 'Recorded in England' at 8 o'clock; song title, writing credit, and band name bottom centre. The fourth US variant has a dark green Apple label with 'STEREO' at 10 o'clock; Intro. and Total playing time at 9 o'clock; song title, writing credit, band name, and 'Recorded in England' bottom centre.

In America, demonstration copies of both the A and B-side were issued with light green Apple labels with a black star at 7 o'clock. 'Junior's Farm' (P-1875 [PRO-6999]) was issued with a mono edit on the A-side and the full-length stereo version on the B-side. 'Sally G' (P-1875 [PRO-8000]) was presented in-full in mono on the A-side and stereo on the B-side. An alternative edit that removed the second verse was prepared for American radio stations and issued as a 7-inch single (SPRO-8003) with white labels.

In Britain, three different versions of the demonstration single were issued. The first had an edited version of 'Junior's Farm' on the A-side and a full-length version on the B-side. The second has a full-length version of 'Junior's Farm' on the A-side with a white A-side label with black text, while the B-side featured the commercial version of 'Sally G' and a sliced Apple B-side label. The third UK demostration single has reversed A and B-sides with the full-length version of 'Sally G' on the A-side.

The single was reissued in both Britain and the USA in the mid 1970s with black and silver Capitol 'dome' labels.

'#9 DREAM'

THIS was the second and last single issued from *Walls And Bridges*, and like Lennon's previous single it was a bigger hit in the USA than in Britain. Apple issued the single in America six weeks ahead of Britain. Neither American nor British pressings were issued in picture covers.

Promotional copies were issued in both countries. In America, Apple issued mono/stereo promotional singles of '#9 Dream' (P-1878), the stereo mix being a 2:55 edit. They also issued the B-side as a mono/stereo promotional single, 'What You Got' (P-1878) (PRO-8030).

Capitol reissued the single with orange Capitol labels in 1978 and again a few years later with purple Capitol labels.

In Britain, Apple issued two different versions of the promotional single, making '#9 Dream' available in edited and un-edited versions. Commercial copies of the single were also produced with minor label variations, some copies omitted the reference to the song being from the album *Walls And Bridges*.

'#9 DREAM' / 'WHAT YOU GOT'
JOHN LENNON
UK RELEASE January 24 1975; Apple R 5903; chart high No.23.
US RELEASE December 16 1974; Apple APPLE 1878; chart high No.9.

'SALLY G'

ISSUED as a demonstration single on both sides of the Atlantic, 'Sally G' was distributed to radio stations in an attempt to generate airplay and, it was hoped, to extend the single's chart run. Although Wings had recently recorded in Nashville and had commenced recording in New Orleans, there was little new material available to fill the gap between albums. Although the band had remained busy throughout 1974, much of what they recorded was either for other artists, such as McCartney's brother, or was not intended for commercial release.

So 'Junior's Farm' / 'Sally G' was flipped to exploit the lucrative country market. This worked in America, where country music was considerably more popular, and 'Sally G' reached Number 17 in the American charts in early 1975. However, in Britain this marketing ploy flopped.

American demonstration copies of the single were issued with a mono A-side and stereo B-side. British demonstration copies replicate the commercial single but with A- and B-sides flipped. Although 'Sally G' was promoted and a release date given for the British release, commercial copies of the single with A- and B-sides reversed have yet to surface.

'SALLY G' / 'JUNIOR'S FARM'
PAUL McCARTNEY AND WINGS
UK RELEASE February 7 1975; Apple R 5999; failed to re-enter chart.
US RELEASE December 24 1974; Apple 1875; chart high No.17

ROCK'N'ROLL

LIKE The Beatles' ill-fated *Get Back* project, which was recorded before but issued after *Abbey Road*, *Rock'N'Roll* spiralled out of control: production moved from one producer to another; an album of entirely new material (*Walls And Bridges*) was recorded and issued before it was completed; and Lennon returned to his roots.

With *Mind Games* yet to be released, Lennon began recording what he thought would be its follow-up. Holed up in Los Angeles, he decided the time was right to record an album of his favourite rock'n'roll oldies. Tired of having to write songs of his own, he wanted simply to be the singer. "I've had enough of this 'be deep and think'," he explained. "Why can't I have some fun?" However, he had another, more important reason for recording an album of oldies. He was contractually obliged to record three songs published by Big Seven Music.

As writer of 'Come Together', a track from The Beatles' *Abbey Road* album, Lennon was being sued for copyright infringement. Big Seven Music Corp., owned by Morris Levy (the man who had tried, unsuccessfully, to copyright the phrase 'rock'n'roll'), claimed that Lennon had appropriated lyrics from Chuck Berry's 'You Can't Catch Me'. Lennon's habit of borrowing from other songs to kick-start his writing had caught up with him. 'Come Together', originally intended as a campaign song for Timothy Leary, displayed more than a passing resemblance to Berry's primal rocker. Although Lennon's lawyers agreed that both songs shared similar lyrics, they argued that the meaning had been substantially changed and therefore there was no case to answer. The case dragged on for over two years, by which time Lennon was spending almost as much time in the courts as he was in the studio. Growing tired of Levy's litigation, Lennon instructed his lawyers to settle out of court. The agreement with Levy stipulated that "John Lennon agrees to record three songs by Big Seven publishers on his next album. The songs [he] intends to record at this time are 'You Can't Catch Me', 'Angel Baby', and 'Ya Ya', [and he] reserves the right to alter the last two songs to any other songs belonging to Big Seven."

Having reached an agreement with Big Seven and mapped out the record in his head, Lennon needed someone to produce it. Who better than rock's greatest producer, Phil Spector? It wasn't as if Lennon and Spector hadn't worked together before. However, Lennon had always controlled Spector's more eccentric tendencies. But this time, in order to get Spector to produce the album, Lennon gave him total control. Besides selecting some of the songs, Spector booked the studios and chose the musicians to record with. Slipping into megalomaniac mode, Spector called on a small army of top flight players to back Lennon. Spector believed that these sessions were going to be historic; consequently, everything had to be on a grand scale.

Sessions took place at A&M Studios in Los Angeles on the nights of October 17, 18, 20, 22, 24, 26, and 28 and November 28. They quickly descended into chaos. With upwards of 30 musicians at each session, set-up times were tedious affairs. To relieve the boredom of Spector's relentless recording technique, and with Lennon intent on having fun, the sessions took on a party atmosphere.

Drummer Jim Keltner recalled that a typical night at the studio would descend into disorder, with Lennon the lead hedonist. "He was drinking too much, and as the evening progressed John would get a little out of control – the whole thing would deteriorate." Spector attempted to maintain control by rehearsing the band for hours on end, but he was fighting a losing battle. For someone who had always insisted on professionalism in the studio, Lennon was now concerned with only thing: having a good time, at the expense of both his reputation and career.

Dr. John, who played on several of the Spector sessions, recalled how everyone was hell-bent on indulging Lennon's excesses. "Instead of sayin', 'Hey man, you're fuckin' up your own date,' they let it happen. It was the first time in my life that I ever felt sorry for the producer. There was nothin' that Spector could do. He would try and dole out the lush to John – and the cat would have it smuggled in. Next night, Phil would get somebody to make sure that John didn't drink more than a certain amount. The cat wouldn't cut 'til he had his taste. But when he had his taste, he *couldn't* cut!"

Several outtakes from the sessions reveal just how intoxicated Lennon became. Yet, despite this, he attempted to maintain some control over the sessions. During one exchange between singer and producer, Lennon pleaded: "Phil, it's our big chance at A&M, now let's not fuck it." Spector may not have been drinking, but he was no more stable than Lennon. He would arrive each night dressed in a different outfit and often carrying a handgun. One night, a minor incident between Spector and ex-Beatles road manager Mal Evans flew out of control. Spector pulled out his pistol and fired into the ceiling. Everyone, including Spector himself, was shocked into silence. The drunken chaos had been perfectly acceptable, all part of the hedonistic LA scene, but the gun incident was too much. Lennon and Spector had indeed fucked their chances at A&M. After a short break, recording resumed at Record Plant West. After three days (December 3, 11, and 14) everything came to an abrupt end. Spector had disappeared and the tapes with him.

Lennon didn't know it, but Spector had removed the tapes from the studio each night and taken them home with him. He then made a series of bizarre claims. First, he said that the studio had burned down. Next, he said that he had the John Dean Watergate tapes and that his house was surrounded. Finally, that he'd been involved in a serious car accident. The sessions were over and the project on hold until the tapes could be recovered. However, the chaos continued.

Looking for something to do, Lennon offered to produce an album for Harry Nilsson. The sessions for *Pussy Cats* were no less chaotic than they had been for *Rock'N'Roll*. The only way Lennon could finish his album was to move back to New York City. Convinced that he would never see the Spector tapes again, he began planning his next album, which he started to record in July 1974.

As fate would have it, the Spector tapes arrived out of the blue just days before Lennon entered the studio to begin work on *Walls And Bridges*. Capitol executive Al Coury had secured the tapes by paying Spector $90,000 and guaranteeing a three percent royalty on any of the tracks used. Lennon was hardly in the mood to start wading through hours of tape when he had a brand new album to record. Better to leave the Spector tapes until he'd finished work on his current project. This would have been fine, had he not agreed to include three Big Seven songs on his follow-up to *Mind Games*, which, it now turned out, would be *Walls And Bridges*. Lennon had no intention of including a batch of oldies on his new album; consequently, he was in breech of his agreement with Morris Levy, who expected to see three of his songs on John Lennon's next album.

No sooner had Lennon finished *Walls And Bridges* than he began work on completing his *Rock'N'Roll* album. His first task was to explain to Levy the reasons behind the delay. A meeting was arranged for October 8, at which Lennon and Levy discussed the project. Lennon recalled: "Harold Seider [Lennon's lawyer] told me that Morris wasn't too happy about the situation, about me not doing the songs or whatever I was supposed to do for that agreement we had made, and he wasn't too happy about 'Ya Ya' on *Walls And Bridges*. And it would be sort of cool if I came along and explained what happened to the Spector tapes ... explain what happened to the *Rock'N'Roll* album."

During the meeting, Levy mentioned that he was developing his empire to include mail-order albums advertised on television. A lucrative business, it removed the need for distributors and retailers. The idea also appealed to Lennon, who made enquiries about selling his album through mail-order. "I was thinking perhaps I could put it straight on TV and avoid the critics and avoid going through the usual channels. And Morris told me that is what he does. ... I said that's cool with me as long as it is all right with the record company." However, after he spoke to Capitol CEO Bhaskar Menon, Lennon abandoned the idea.

He decided to finish his rock'n'roll album with the band he'd used for *Walls And Bridges*, some of whom had played on the Spector sessions. To keep Lennon sweet and to ensure that the album didn't drag on any longer, Levy invited him and the band to rehearse at his farm in the Catskills (about 100 miles north of New York City). Ten days after his initial meeting with Levy, Lennon and band were busy rehearsing new material to complete the album. The band set up in a high-ceilinged room in Levy's farmhouse and ran through the songs Lennon intended to record to complete the album. They also rehearsed 'C'Mon Everybody', 'Thirty Days', and 'That'll Be The Day', and played a couple of impromptu jams. The weekend over, Lennon entered the Record Plant on October 21 and in just four days cut enough material to finish the record. The John Lennon of old had returned: the New York *Rock'N'Roll* sessions were the model of professionalism.

Jim Keltner said: "It was fantastic. ... He wasn't drinking – he was very controlled during those sessions and that made a huge difference." With the exception of 'Do You Want To Dance', Lennon insisted that the band stick as close as possible to the original arrangements. Keltner: "He liked that we played the songs as faithfully as we could to the original arrangement." This was fine, providing that the original songs featured similar instrumentation to the band Lennon was recording with. When it came to recording Buddy Holly's 'Peggy Sue', keyboards man Ken Ascher pointed out that the original recording didn't have a piano on it. Lennon was typically pragmatic, as Ascher recalled. "John said never mind, make it simple and play the changes."

With work on the basic tracks finished, Lennon concentrated on editing and mixing the tracks until mid November. On November 14 he had another meeting with Levy, at which he delivered rough mixes of the work-in-progress to the publisher. Levy now had the tapes, and later he would allege that a verbal agreement was made with Lennon to issue them on his Adam VIII mail order record label.

By January 1975, the Apple/Capitol version of *Rock'N'Roll* was nearing completion. The running order had been finalised and the artwork was well on the way to being completed. Lennon had chosen a stunning black-and-white photograph taken of him in Hamburg in 1960 by Jurgen Vollmer. Beside using Vollmer's photograph for the cover, Lennon invited him to design the album package, which was originally intended as an elaborate gatefold. However, Levy's Adam VIII version of the album, titled *John Lennon Sings The Great Rock'n'Roll Hits: Roots*, was issued on February 8, ahead of Apple/Capitol's release date. Consequently, the official version was brought forward and Vollmer's grand design scrapped.

The Adam VIII version was issued in a cheap yellow cover with a poorly cropped image of Lennon on the front and advertisements for another two Adam VIII albums on the rear. It included two tracks, 'Angel Baby' and 'Be My Baby', that were cut from Lennon's version of the album (both would later be issued, on *Menlove Ave.* and the *John Lennon Anthology* respectively).

Lennon immediately issued a cease and desist notice to Adam VIII, but not before the album had been advertised on television and a slow trickle of LPs shipped through the post. Lennon, an avid collector of his own bootlegs, ordered some copies for himself. "I've sent away for the other version of the album, but they haven't arrived yet," he told *Melody Maker*. "It's almost the same, with a couple of slight differences. It'll become a collectors item, I suppose, but it's nowhere near as good." *Roots* did become a collectors' item. Only 1,270 copies of the album and 175 copies of the 8-track were shipped by Adam VIII. Within days of Levy's version being made available, the official Apple/Capitol album had hit the shops, but this didn't sell particularly well either. Capitol's first pressing of *Rock'N'Roll* was of just 2,444 LPs and 500 8-track cartridges. Although *Rock'N'Roll* eventually sold in excess of 340,000 units, it shifted considerably fewer copies than either the previous *Walls And Bridges* or the *Shaved Fish* compilation issued eight months after *Rock'N'Roll*.

With both versions of the album available, each party sued the other. Levy sued Lennon for breach of a verbal agreement, claiming $42 million in damages. Lennon sued for unauthorised use of his recordings and image. He also sued for damages, claiming that his reputation had been marred by Levy's cheap packaging. Levy's case eventually came to court on January 12 1976, but failed as Levy's lawyer caused a mistrial when he began inspecting the cover of Lennon and Ono's *Two Virgins* in front of the jury. Levy vs Lennon round two began the following day, with the same judge who had presided over the original 1973 trial for copyright infringement. This new trial ended on February 5 and Judge Griesa gave his ruling 15 days later, in Lennon's favour. He said: "I conclude on the basis of the evidence about the October 8, 1974 meeting ... that no contract was entered into."

A month later, Lennon's counterclaim against Levy went to court. Lennon and his record company sued for lost income and Lennon for punitive damages for the harm that the unofficial *Roots* album had caused his reputation. Again, the case went in Lennon's favour. After Levy appealed, Lennon was eventually awarded $40,259 for lost sales, $14,567 for monies lost due to the reduced price of *Roots*, and $35,000 in punitive damages.

Rock'N'Roll songs

Lennon said: "'Be-Bop-A-Lula' was one of the first songs I ever learned, and I actually remember singing it the day I met Paul McCartney. I was singing at the church [fete] and McCartney was in the audience." Recorded by Gene Vincent in 1956, 'Be-Bop-A-Lula' became Vincent's biggest hit and signature tune. Issued by Capitol (F 3450) with 'Woman Love' in '56, it reached Number 7 in the charts. It was issued by Capitol in Britain, where it went to Number 17. The Beatles eventually met up with Vincent in Hamburg, where they performed the song regularly. A recording of the group performing the song at the Star-Club there, with Fred Fascher on vocals, was issued on *The Beatles Live At The Star-Club In Hamburg, Germany; 1962*.

(Lennon's new version was issued as a single in France, backed with 'Move Over Ms. L'. Sticking closely to Vincent's original arrangement but with additional piano, Lennon romps through this classic rocker with obvious delight. An alternative take was issued on the *John Lennon Anthology*.)

Lennon said that 'Stand By Me' was a favourite, "one of my big songs in the dance halls in Liverpool. That was a Ben E. King number. And the same goes for 'Be Bop A-Lula' in that I knew these songs as a child." Lennon would return to 'Stand By Me' again and again. He often jammed on the song, and he recorded an informal version during sessions for Harry Nilsson's *Pussy Cats* album with Paul McCartney, Stevie Wonder, Harry Nilsson, and Jesse Ed Davis, prior to cutting the track for *Rock'N'Roll*.

Issued as a single, Lennon's 'Stand By Me' was a Top 20 hit in America but fared less well in Britain, where it just managed a Top 30 placing. The song was remixed for the single release, with a string overdub that doubled the organ part. It was reissued by Capitol on its Starline imprint (6244) on April 4 1977, backed with 'Woman Is The Nigger Of The World', while the album version was issued in 1988 as a promotional 12-inch single with purple Capitol labels (SPRO-79453). Touted as the "new single from the album *Imagine: John Lennon*", it was never issued commercially.

Next on *Rock'N'Roll* comes a medley of two songs originally

ROCK'N'ROLL
JOHN LENNON
SIDE 1 'Be-Bop-A-Lula', 'Stand By Me', 'Rip It Up / Ready Teddy', 'You Can't Catch Me', 'Ain't That A Shame', 'Do You Want To Dance', 'Sweet Little Sixteen'.
SIDE 2 'Slippin' And Slidin'', 'Peggy Sue', 'Bring It On Home To Me / Send Me Some Lovin'', 'Bony Maronie', 'Ya Ya', 'Just Because'.
UK RELEASE February 21 1975; LP Apple PCS 7169; 8-track cartridge Apple 8X-PCS 7169; chart high No.6 (re-enters January 17 1981 chart high No.64).
US RELEASE February 17 1975; LP Apple SK 3419; 8-track cartridge Apple 8XK-3419; chart high No.6.

- **'Be-Bop-A-Lula'** (Davis, Vincent)
John Lennon (vocals, guitar), Jesse Ed Davis (guitar), Eddie Mottau (acoustic guitar), Ken Ascher (piano), Klaus Voormann (bass), Arthur Jenkins (percussion), Jim Keltner (drums).
- **'Stand By Me'** (King, Leiber, Stoller)
John Lennon (vocals, guitar), Jesse Ed Davis (guitar), Eddie Mottau (acoustic guitar), Peter Jameson (guitar), Ken Ascher (piano), Klaus Voormann (bass), Arthur Jenkins (percussion), Joseph Temperley (saxophone), Dennis Morouse (tenor saxophone), Frank Vicari (saxophone), Jim Keltner (drums).
- **'Rip It Up / Ready Teddy'** (Blackwell, Marascalco)
John Lennon (vocals, guitar), Jesse Ed Davis (guitar), Eddie Mottau (acoustic guitar), Ken Ascher (piano), Klaus Voormann (bass), Arthur Jenkins (percussion), Joseph Temperley (saxophone), Dennis Morouse (tenor saxophone), Frank Vicari (saxophone), Jim Keltner (drums).
- **'You Can't Catch Me'** (Berry)
John Lennon (guitar, vocals), Art Munson (guitar), Ray Neapolitan (bass), Michael Omartian (keyboards), William Perkins (woodwind), William Perry (guitar), Mac Rebennack (keyboards), Louie Shelton (guitar), Phil Spector (piano, guitar), Nino Tempo (saxophone, keyboards), Anthony Terran (trumpet), Andy Thomas (piano), Michael Wofford (piano), Jim Horn (saxophone), Plas Johnson (saxophone), Joseph Kelson (horn), Jim Keltner (drums), Bobby Keys (saxophone), Ronald Kossajda (instrument unknown), Michael Lang (piano), Ronald Langinger (saxophone), Barry Mann (piano), Julian Matlock (clarinet), Michael Melvoin (piano), Donald Menza (saxophone), Dale Anderson (guitar), Jeff Barry (piano), Hal Baine (drums), Jim Calvert (instrument unknown), Conte Candoli (trumpet), Frank Capp (drums), Larry Carlton (guitar), Gene Cipriano (saxophone), David Cohen (guitar), Gary Coleman (percussion), Steve Cropper (guitar), Jesse Ed Davis (guitar), Alan Estes (percussion), Chuck Findley (trumpet), Steven Forman (percussion), Terry Gibbs (piano or percussion), Bob Glaub (bass), Jim Gordon (drums), Robert Hardaway (woodwind), Leon Russell (keyboards), Jose Feliciano (guitar), Michael Hazelwood (instrument unknown), Thomas Hensley (bass), Dick Hieronymus (instrument unknown).
- **'Ain't That A Shame'** (Domino, Bartholomew)
Personnel as 'Rip It Up / Ready Teddy'.
- **'Do You Want To Dance'** (Freeman)
Personnel as 'Rip It Up / Ready Teddy'.
- **'Sweet Little Sixteen'** (Berry)
Personnel as 'You Can't Catch Me'.
- **'Slippin' And Slidin''** (Penniman, Bocage, Collins, Smith)
Personnel as 'Rip It Up / Ready Teddy'.
- **'Peggy Sue'** (Holly, Allison, Petty)
John Lennon (vocals, guitar), Jesse Ed Davis (guitar), Eddie Mottau (acoustic guitar), Ken Ascher (piano), Klaus Voormann (bass), Arthur Jenkins (percussion), Jim Keltner (drums).
- **'Bring It On Home To Me' (Cooke) / 'Send Me Some Lovin''** (Price, Marascalco)
Personnel as 'Rip It Up / Ready Teddy' except Klaus Voormann (bass and backing vocals).
- **'Bony Moronie'** (Williams)
Personnel as 'You Can't Catch Me'.
- **'Ya Ya'** (Robinson, Dorsey, Lewis)
Personnel as 'Bring It On Home To Me / Send Me Some Lovin''.
- **'Just Because'** (Price)
Personnel as 'You Can't Catch Me'.

All recorded at Record Plant East, New York City, NY, USA and produced by John Lennon, except 'You Can't Catch Me', 'Sweet Little Sixteen', 'Bony Moronie', 'Just Because' recorded at A&M Studios or Record Plant West, Los Angeles, CA, USA and produced by Phil Spector, arranged by John Lennon and Phil Spector.

recorded by Little Richard in 1956. Like Gene Vincent, Little Richard was a huge influence on The Beatles (and again, the band were personally introduced to him in Hamburg). Both songs were originally issued by Richard as a single, which gave him a Top 30 hit and million seller. Lennon recorded the song because "'Ready Teddy' was a sort of guitar-type song written by Little Richard and recorded by him". (An alternative take was issued on the *John Lennon Anthology*.)

Chuck Berry's 'You Can't Catch Me' was issued by Chess (1683) in the USA in 1957 and reached Number 2 in the charts. Issued in Britain by London (HLN 8575), the single failed to chart, and although The Beatles recorded several of Berry's songs for their albums and BBC radio performances, they never got around to tackling this classic rocker. Lennon was a huge fan of Berry and got to perform with him on TV on *The Mike Douglas Show* in 1972. Lennon introduced Berry to middle America with the words: "If you tried to give rock'n'roll another name, you might call it – Chuck Berry!" However, speaking just after the release of *Rock'N'Roll*, Lennon had little to say about the song that caused him so much trouble. "'You Can't Catch Me' was the Morris Levy song, but it was by Chuck Berry, so that was good enough reason to do it."

Fats Domino's classic 'Ain't That A Shame' was issued by Imperial (5348) in 1955. The song was a massive hit: while Fats' recording reached Number 10, Pat Boone's watered-down version hit the top spot in the USA. The song also did very good business in Britain, where it was issued by London (HLU 8173). It charted four times, once for Fats Domino, twice for Pat Boone, and once for The Four Seasons.

Lennon said: "'Ain't That a Shame' was the first rock'n'roll song I ever learned. My mother taught it to me on the banjo before I learned the guitar. Nobody else knows these reasons except me." Lennon's reading was scheduled to be issued as a single but was withdrawn at the last moment. Promotional copies of the single were issued to radio stations, and Apple issued the single in Mexico.

Originally a Number 5 US hit for Bobby Freeman, 'Do You Want To Dance' was issued on the Josie label in 1957, when Freeman was just 17 years old. It was better known in Britain through Cliff Richard's cover version, which he took to Number 2 in 1962. The song was another that Lennon often tried at jam sessions. "We [did it] at some jam sessions on the west coast," he said, "featuring numerous stars not worth mentioning the names of." He also admitted that he had tried, without much success, to get the *Rock'N'Roll* band to play a reggae version. "'Do You Want To Dance is the only one that I messed around with a bit more. I tried to make it reggae. ... This one makes you feel happy, but I don't know if it makes you want to dance, and that's the problem. It's definitely different from the original."

The second Chuck Berry song that Lennon attempted, 'Sweet Little Sixteen', was issued by Chess Records (1683) in 1957 and gave Berry his fifth million-selling single when it hit Number 2 in the charts. London issued it in Britain (HLM 8575), where it reached Number 11. The Beatles included the song in their stage repertoire, and a live recording by them appeared on *The Beatles Live At The Star-Club In Hamburg, Germany; 1962*. The group also recorded the song on July 10 1963 for the BBC, who broadcast the song on *Pop Goes The Beatles* 13 days later.

Issued in the USA on Specialty 572, Little Richard's second single was arguably his greatest and most successful. A million-seller, 'Long Tall Sally' / 'Slippin' And Slidin'' was a Number 1 single on the R&B charts and a Top 10 hit on the pop charts. 'Long Tall Sally' was equally successful in Britain, where, issued by London (HLO 8366), it reached Number 3. It was also a British hit for Pat Boone, who took it to Number 19 for two weeks, and it was covered by The Beatles and became a live favourite for them.

British pressings of the Little Richard single were backed with 'Tutti Frutti', so Lennon tracked down an import copy of the single. "The first time I heard this Little Richard track, a friend of mine imported it from Holland. It came out in Europe first," he recalled. "'Slippin' And Slidin' was the B-side of 'Long Tall Sally', which is the first Little Richard song I ever heard and was also recorded by Buddy Holly, so that covers a little of both. It was a song I knew. It was easier to do songs that I knew than trying to learn something from scratch, even if I was interested in the songs."

Another million-seller, 'Peggy Sue' was originally recorded by Buddy Holly & The Crickets and issued by Coral (60885) in America, where it went to Number 6. Issued by Coral (72293) in England, it was more successful, heading up to Number 4.

Holly's influence on The Beatles cannot be underestimated. Not only did the young Fabs spend their hard-earned cash recording one of his songs, 'That'll Be The Day' (later issued on The Beatles *Anthology 1*), Holly directly influenced their choice of band-name. Although The Beatles recorded several Holly songs during their career, they never got around to cutting 'Peggy Sue'.

It was another song etched into Lennon's consciousness, and he'd perform it for his own amusement. "I have been doing that since I started," he said. "Buddy Holly did it and, in fact, I used to sing every song that Buddy Holly put out." Paul McCartney was so impressed with Holly's songwriting that when his catalogue came up for sale, he bought it.

Next up on *Rock'N'Roll* is a medley of songs by Sam Cooke and Little Richard. 'Bring It On Home To Me' was issued by RCA (1296) in the USA in 1962 and peaked at Number 3. 'Send Me Some Lovin'' was issued by Specialty (588) in America in 1957 as a single coupled with 'Lucille', reaching Number 27. In Britain the single was issued by London (HLO 8446), where it went to Number 7 in the charts.

Lennon said: "'Bring It On Home To Me' is one of my all-time favourite songs and, in fact, I have been quoted as saying I wish I had written it. I love it that much, and I was glad to be able to do it. 'Send Me Some Lovin'' is a similar kind of song and it was done originally by Little Richard – again, one of my favourites – and also by Buddy Holly."

Not only did Klaus Voormann play bass on the album but also he got to sing backing vocals on 'Bring It On Home To Me'. Speaking in 2001, he confirmed that Lennon was recording at lightning speed and that he was slightly nonplussed when asked to sing backing vocals on the track. "John surprised me by asking me to sing the harmony on 'Bring It On Home'. One take, and John said, 'Thank you very much' – it was good enough. He was very quick with everything."

Not only did The Beatles cover Larry Williams songs, but both Lennon and McCartney recorded his work for solo albums. 'Bony Maronie' was originally issued by Specialty (605) in the USA in 1957. A million-seller, it reached Number 18 in the charts. Issued by London (HLN 8532) in Britain, it made Number 12. Speaking about his reasons for recording the song, Lennon said: "'Bony Maronie' was one of the very earliest songs [I learned] – along with 'Be-Bop-A-Lula' – and I remember singing it the only time my mother saw me perform before she died. So I was hot on 'Bony Maronie'. That is one of the reasons. Also, I liked Larry Williams, who recorded it."

Lee Dorsey's 'Ya Ya' was a Number 1 hit on the R&B charts

when issued by Fury (1053) in America in 1960. A year later, a version by Petula Clark, re-titled 'Ya Ya Twist', made the US Top 10 and went to Number 14 in Britain. The song was also a favourite with German audiences: Tony Sheridan recorded a version of the song, without The Beatles, for an EP (Polydor EPH 21485) and this Lennon reading was issued there as a single (1C 006-05 924) backed with 'Be-Bop-A-Lula'.

John had already recorded a spontaneous version of 'Ya Ya' with his son Julian and issued it on *Walls And Bridges*. As it was published by Big Seven, it was one of the songs he was obliged to record. "'Ya Ya' I did because it was Morris's and it was a good song," he explained.

Written by Lloyd Price, 'Just Because' was a truly independent record. Not only did Price write the song but also he played piano, produced the record, and issued it on his own label, Kent. Issued in early 1957, it was a sizeable regional hit before being picked up for national distribution by ABC-Paramount, who re-released the record, which climbed to Number 27 in the US charts. It was not issued in Britain.

Unlike the rest of the material recorded for *Rock'N'Roll*, Lennon was not familiar with the song. "'Just Because' I did because Phil Spector talked me into it," he said. The combination of unfamiliarity and alcohol meant that Lennon had to re-record his vocal in New York. Indeed, an outtake from the LA sessions, issued on the remastered *Rock'N'Roll* CD, reveals just how tired and emotional Lennon was when he recorded his vocal with Spector at the controls.

Towards the end of 'Just Because', Lennon signs off: "And so we say farewell from Record Plant East," a closing remark he later claimed was a conscious farewell to the business. Although he had plans to record a new album, it was scrapped when Ono became pregnant. In its place, Lennon issued a collection of hits and near misses. A summation of his career to that point, it was more of a semicolon than a full stop.

Rock'N'Roll data

The album was promoted with a radio spot issued to American radio stations and with trade advertisements placed in British music weeklies. Lennon also gave several interviews, played DJ at WNEW-FM in New York City, and filmed two promotional videos, of 'Stand By Me' and 'Slippin' And Slidin'', for BBC TV's *Old Grey Whistle Test*.

Apple issued promotional copies of 'Slippin' And Slidin'' (P-1883) to radio stations along with 'Ain't That A Shame' (P-1883). Although the American release of this coupling was cancelled, 'Slippin' And Slidin'' / 'Ain't That A Shame' was released in Mexico (Apple 7755). France issued 'Be-Bop-A-Lula' / 'Move Over Ms. L' (2C 004-05799), while 'Ya Ya' / 'Be-Bop-A-Lula' was issued in Germany (1C 006-05 924) and Japan (EAR-10827).

Apple issued *Rock'N'Roll* in the USA on February 17, although as the album was rush-released a few stores may have received copies earlier (and some sources suggest that the album was available as early as February 5). British pressings matched the American version of the album.

US copies were produced with two label variations. The first has a light green Apple label with a large '1' at 9 o'clock and the two song titles above the spindle hole; the second has a dark green Apple label with 'STEREO' and a small 'Side 1' below at 9 o'clock and three song titles above the spindle hole.

Capitol reissued the album in 1978 with purple Capitol labels and in October 1980 at budget price with green labels (SN-15969). The album was also issued at budget price in Britain by EMI subsidiary Music For Pleasure in November 1981 (MFP 50522). As with *Imagine*, *Rock'N'Roll* was reissued as part of EMI's centenary celebrations. Reissued in early 1997, the LP (LPCENT9) featured original packaging, 180 gram virgin vinyl, heavy quality cover, and analogue cutting from analogue tape.

The album was issued on 8-track cartridge in Britain (8X-PCS 7169) and the USA (8XK-3419).

EMI and Capitol both issued *Rock'N'Roll* on CD (CDP 7 46707 2) on May 18 1987. A remixed and remastered edition of the CD (542 4252) with four bonus tracks was issued on September 27 2004 (UK) and 2 November 2004 (USA).

'I SAW HER STANDING THERE'

LENNON'S first public appearance in three months was as a surprise guest at Elton John's sell-out concert at Madison Square Garden in New York City on November 28 that year. Elton had asked Lennon to appear with him if 'Whatever Gets You Thru The Night' reached Number 1 (Elton had played and sang on it). "I said sure," Lennon recalled, "not thinking in a million years it was gonna get to Number 1."

On November 24 1974, four days before the concert, the two Johns rehearsed with Elton's band at the Record Plant East in New York City. Lennon was to perform three songs, 'Lucy In The Sky With Diamonds', 'Whatever Gets You Thru The Night', and 'I Saw Her Standing There'. Elton originally suggested that Lennon perform 'Imagine', but Lennon rejected the idea, favouring 'I Saw Her Standing There', a song from The Beatles' debut album.

This may have been an attempt by Lennon to publicly re-establish his fractured relationship with Paul McCartney, whose song it was. Lennon intended to visit McCartney in early 1975 while McCartney was recording with Wings in New Orleans. Lennon never made the trip, but this gesture was the next best thing.

Come the day of the concert at Madison Square Garden, Lennon was a nervous wreck. Apple man Tony King recalled that Lennon was constantly running to the toilet because he was so nervous. He hadn't appeared on a concert stage for over two years, and this would be the first time without Ono at his side. Although he was on a roll, with a Number 1 album and single (*Walls And Bridges* and 'Whatever Gets You Thru The Night'), Lennon was unsure how the audience would react when he walked on stage. "I was quite astonished that the crowd was so nice to me," he said, "because I was only judging by what the papers said about me, and I thought I may as well not be around, you know? And the crowd was fantastic." Speaking after the show, Lennon said jokingly: "I had a great time, but I wouldn't want to do it for a living. Actually it was fantastic, so emotional. Everyone was crying and everything."

At the time, Lennon was still separated from Ono. Although he didn't know it, she was in the audience. He said later that if he'd known she was there, he wouldn't have been able to go on. Their meeting after the show was a turning point. Within a few months they were back together as if nothing had happened.

The Beatles originally recorded 'I Saw Her Standing There' at Abbey Road Studios on February 11 1963. Although Lennon later suggested that the song was entirely McCartney's work, it was an early collaboration, written some time in 1962. McCartney supplied the lyrics and initial musical theme; Lennon helped finish the song. Although Lennon said that he had never sung the song, what he meant was that he had not sung the lead vocal. Lennon is vocally present on The Beatles' original recording, providing harmonies to McCartney's lead.

Several live recordings by The Beatles have been issued. *The Beatles Live At the BBC* features a version recorded at the Playhouse Theatre on October 20 1963 and originally broadcast on *Easy Beat*. *Anthology 1* features a live recording made at Karlaplansstudion, Stockholm, Sweden on October 24 1963, and Paul McCartney included a performance on his 2003 live album *Back In The World*.

'PHILADELPHIA FREEDOM' / 'I SAW HER STANDING THERE'
THE ELTON JOHN BAND / THE ELTON JOHN BAND FEATURING JOHN LENNON WITH THE MUSCLE SHOALS HORNS
UK RELEASE February 28 1975; DJM DJS 354; chart high No.12.
US RELEASE February 24 1975; MCA MCA 40364; chart high No.1.

• **'I Saw Her Standing There'** (Lennon, McCartney)
John Lennon (vocals, guitar), Elton John (vocals, piano), Davey Johnstone (guitar), Dee Murray (bass), Nigel Olsson (drums), Ray Cooper (percussion), Muscle Shoals Horns (brass). Live recording at Madison Square Garden, New York City, NY, USA. Produced by Gus Dudgeon.

'I Saw Her Standing There' data

Lennon's version was first issued as the B-side of this Elton John single, 'Philadelphia Freedom'. All three songs performed by Lennon at Madison Square Garden on November 28 were issued as a 7-inch EP on March 13 1981. They were issued for the first time on CD on the *Lennon* boxed set, in 1990, and in a remixed form on Elton John's *Here And There* live album in 1996.

'STAND BY ME'

ORIGINALLY intended for *Walls And Bridges*, 'Move Over Ms. L' was an up-tempo rocker that saw Lennon poke fun at his estranged wife and several of life's institutions. He wrote the song and recorded home demos some time in 1974. Lennon then gave the song to his erstwhile drinking buddy and drummer with The Who, Keith Moon. He completed his album, *Both Sides Of The Moon*, just after Lennon finished recording *Walls And Bridges*. As Moon's arrangement is close to Lennon's, it's possible that Lennon sent him a rough mix of the track as a reference rather than one of his demos.

Moon's version beat Lennon's to the record stores, but only just. Lennon had planned to include 'Move Over Ms. L' on *Walls And Bridges* but removed it at the last minute. Moon's version hit the shops in April 1975 and was also issued as the B-side of his single 'Solid Gold' (the A-side of which featured another ex-Beatle, Ringo Starr).

An alternative version recorded by Lennon during the *Walls And Bridges* sessions was issued on the *John Lennon Anthology*.

'Stand By Me' data

Apple issued 'Stand By Me' with generic Apple labels in the USA and the British single was issued a little over a month later. American pressings were issued with two label variants. The first has a dark green Apple label; song title with composer credit and artist's name centre bottom; 'From the LP "ROCK 'N' ROLL" SK-3914' at 11 o'clock; 'STEREO' at 9 o'clock; catalogue number at eight o'clock; publisher, intro, and total playing time and producer credit on the right side of the label.

The second US label variant has a light green Apple label with the song title and composer credit centre bottom in bold; 'From the LP "ROCK 'N' ROLL" SK-3914' at 11 o'clock; 'STEREO' at 10 o'clock; the catalogue number at 9 o'clock; publisher, intro, and total playing time and producer credit on the right side of the label.

American promotional singles (P-1881) were issued with light green Apple labels with 'from the LP "ROCK 'N' ROLL" SK-3914' at 11 o'clock, 'MONO' at 10 o'clock, catalogue number at 9 o'clock, 'NOT FOR SALE' at 8 o'clock; publisher, introm and total playing time and producer credit on the right side of the label. The song title and composer credit appear centre bottom in bold

'STAND BY ME' / 'MOVE OVER MS. L'
JOHN LENNON
UK RELEASE April 18 1975; Apple R 5905; chart high No.30.
US RELEASE March 10 1975; Apple APPLE 1881; chart high No.20.

• **'Move Over Ms. L'** (Lennon)
John Lennon (vocals, guitar), Jesse Ed Davis (guitar), Eddie Mottau (acoustic guitar), Ken Ascher (piano), Klaus Voormann (bass), Arthur Jenkins (percussion), Little Big Horns: Bobby Keys, Steve Madaio, Howard Johnson, Ron Aprea, Frank Vicari (horns), Jim Keltner (drums).
Recorded at Record Plant East, New York City, NY, USA.
Produced by John Lennon.

with a black star placed just above and to the left of the song title.

First pressings of the British single credit the songwriters as King–Glick and the publisher as Trio Music Ltd. Later pressings have a light green label and credit the songwriters as King–Leiber–Stoller and the publisher as Carlin Mus. Corp. British promotional copies of the single replicate the commercial issue with the addition of a large 'A' at 11 o'clock, 'DEMO RECORD NOT FOR SALE' in the centre of the label, and '(18.4.75)' at 5 o'clock.

Capitol reissued 'Stand By Me' (6244) on its Starline label on April 4 1977, backed with 'Woman Is The Nigger Of The World'. Four variations of this single were issued: with tan Starline label, round Capitol 'C' logo, 'All Rights...' in white or black on label perimeter, publishing credit to 'Unichappel Music'; tan Starline label, round Capitol 'C' logo, 'All Rights...' in white or black on label perimeter, publishing credit to 'Belinda Music'; blue Starline label; black/colour band Starline label with perimeter print in colour band.

'LISTEN TO WHAT THE MAN SAID'

THE Beatles contract with EMI had come to an end and so Lennon, McCartney, Harrison, and Starr were free to do as they pleased. McCartney stayed with EMI, consolidated his solo career, recorded another Number 1 album, and planned a massive world tour.

Yet Wings were still far from stabilised; indeed, the band had begun to take on the appearance of a musicians' collective with Paul, Linda, and Denny Laine at its core. Arguments continued to undermine the new Mk.4 line-up before it had released a single note of music. That MPL didn't officially announce the arrival of Geoff Britton and Jimmy McCulloch until November 1974 suggests that Wings' future remained uncertain.

Speaking to the press about the delay, Britton said: "There was talk of contracts in the beginning, but we decided it was better if nothing was contracted. If you're a real pro and you've got a tour booked, you don't phone up and say, 'I'm not coming.' That's just not on." Despite Britton's apparent commitment, he quit the band just weeks into recording *Venus And Mars*. Once again a Wings album looked fated.

Contractual wranglings were not the only problem. Personality clashes that had plagued the band in the past re-emerged, this time between Britton and McCulloch. Britton had personal problems of his own. "I was in the States and we were starting work on *Venus And Mars*, and my wife started talking about separation and divorce. I came home to sort it out." Just weeks into their album, and Wings were without a drummer. Tony Dorsey, who was arranging the horn parts, recommended Joe English as a temporary stand-in, but McCartney was so impressed he asked the drummer to join the group full-time.

With or without a new drummer, attempts to record 'Listen To What The Man Said' were problematic, as McCartney recalled. "It was one of the songs we'd gone in with high hopes for. Whenever I would play it on the piano, people would say, 'Oh I like that one.' But when we did the backing track, we thought we really didn't get it together at all."

Dave Mason was asked to overdub some guitar parts, but the problem of what to do for a solo remained. As luck would have it, Tom Scott, a respected saxophonist, provided the solution. McCartney: "We said ... give him a ring, see if he turns up – and he turned up within half an hour. There he was, with his sax, and he sat down in the studio playing through." Improvising to the Wings backing track, Scott delivered an exceptional solo that transformed a good song into something extraordinary. His first take was the best, but as McCartney said: "No one could believe it, so we went out and tried a few more, but they weren't as good. I think what he plays on that song is lovely and that, overall, it worked."

A slice of radio-friendly pop, 'Listen To What The Man Said' was the ideal vehicle with which to introduce the new Wings line-up. It's a joyous celebration of love and life, buoyed by Linda's equally exuberant backing vocals, a sign of her growing confidence. Lifting the spirits like a glimpse of blue sky on a cloudy day, the song gave the band its first Top 10 single since 'Band On The Run'.

The B-side, 'Love In Song', was recorded at Abbey Road in late 1974 and offers yet another reworking of McCartney's favourite theme, love. He wrote the song on a 12-string acoustic guitar, and suggested that it just came to him. "I feel I don't have a lot of control over some songs, but some songs I do. But with this song I just started playing my guitar, singing those words, wrote them down, and I said to Linda, 'How do you like that?' And that was it." The measured arrangement and melancholic lyric suggest a slight distancing of its author from his subject, but the warmth of McCartney's vocal more than compensates for the song's guarded tone.

'LISTEN TO WHAT THE MAN SAID' / 'LOVE IN SONG'
WINGS
UK RELEASE May 16 1975; Capitol R 6006; chart high No.6.
US RELEASE May 26 1975; Capitol 4091; chart high No.1.

• **'Listen To What The Man Said'** (McCartney)
Paul McCartney (bass, piano, vocals), Linda McCartney (keyboards, backing vocals), Denny Laine (guitar, backing vocals), Jimmy McCulloch (guitar), Joe English (drums), Tom Scott (saxophone), Dave Mason (guitar). Recorded at Sea Saint Studios, New Orleans, LA, USA, and Wally Heider, Los Angeles, CA, USA.
• **'Love In Song'** (McCartney)
Paul McCartney (guitar, vocals), Linda McCartney (backing vocals), Denny Laine (guitar), Jimmy McCulloch (guitar), Geoff Britton (drums). Recorded at Abbey Road Studios, London, England.
Both produced by Paul McCartney.

'Listen To What The Man Said' data

This was Wings' first single for Capitol. Or was it? McCartney and the other ex-Beatles were still signed to EMI/Capitol but issued their solo releases with Apple labels, even though they were really EMI/Parlophone/Capitol releases. McCartney's contract did not expire until January 1976, but for some reason he seems to have chosen to release this record and the *Venus And Mars* album on Capitol, his US label. EMI/Apple issued 'Listen To What The Man Said' in Portugal (8E 006-96638), 'Letting Go' in Italy (3C 006 96940), and the *Venus And Mars* LP in Uruguay (SAPL 30.535) with Apple A and B-side labels. (Capitol issued mono/stereo edits to American radio stations of the 'Listen' A-side as a demonstration single (PRO-8183).)

VENUS AND MARS

ANOTHER album, another line-up. Despite personnel changes, Wings were on a roll and the Mk.5 line-up – Paul, Linda, Laine, and McCulloch with the addition of Joe English on drums – sounded confident and mature. Although the album benefited from an assured and sophisticated approach to record making, *Venus And Mars* was hampered by too many run-of-the-mill songs. More stylistically diverse than its predecessor, *Venus And Mars* reflects McCartney's musical tastes, his influences, and his delight in genre-hopping. However, his mix-and-match approach to compiling the album, which found roughhouse rockers juxtaposed with twee ballads, did little to bolster his standing with the critics.

Although the record was eagerly awaited, there had been a gap of some 18 months since *Band On The Run*, and *Venus And Mars* was considered a disappointing follow-up. But that didn't stop it topping the charts on both sides of the Atlantic.

Sessions for *Venus And Mars* began at Abbey Road in late 1974, with Geoff Britton occupying the drummer's stool. 'Love In Song', 'Letting Go' and 'Medicine Jar' were completed, along with an early attempt at 'Rock Show'. Then, in January 1975, Wings relocated to Sea Saint Studios in New Orleans. The band quickly fell into a routine that found them recording from late afternoon to early morning. The first song they recorded, 'Lunch Box/Odd Sox', failed to make the album (it was eventually issued in 1980 as the B-side to 'Coming Up').

Work continued in this fashion for several weeks before the band took a short break in early February to enjoy the Mardi Gras. After a five-day break, recording resumed on Ash Wednesday with 'My Carnival'. It was around this time that Geoff Britton quit the band and his replacement, Joe English, joined. With the basic tracks completed, Wings moved to Wally Heider Studios, Los Angeles, to add overdubs, backing vocals, and strings, the latter supervised by Sid Sharpe.

Their stay in Los Angeles coincided with the annual Grammy awards, at which Paul and Linda received an award for *Band On The Run*. The day after the ceremony, McCartney was driving Linda and the children back to their rented house in Malibu when he failed to stop at a red traffic light and was pulled over by a highway patrol man. On stopping the car, the officer claimed he smelt a strong aroma of marijuana; he later claimed to have found a lit joint on the floor of the car along with a quantity of the drug.

The McCartneys were arrested, but when Linda insisted that the marijuana belonged to her, Paul was allowed to drive the children home. Linda probably took the rap because she was an American citizen and Paul, already finding it hard to get work permits for the USA, would have found it even harder had he been found guilty of possession of an illegal substance. Had he been convicted, it's unlikely that the American authorities would have granted further work permits, and the proposed American tour would have been cancelled. Found guilty of possessing marijuana, Linda was offered psychiatric treatment and ordered to attend six sessions with a psychiatrist to overcome her problem. The charges were later dismissed as Linda had completed a six-month course in Britain on the dangers of drugs.

On their return to Britain, Wings undertook four months of rehearsals in preparation for what was to become their most technically complex and extensive tour – it covered ten countries during a 13-month period – and also the most successful. Wings Mk.5 gave their first official live performance in front of an invited audience at Studio 5, Elstree, to the north-west of London, on September 6 1975 (though they had earlier jammed with The Meters aboard a converted riverboat in the USA). The Elstree performance took place three days before the first date of their British tour, which commenced in Southampton. This concert, along with several others, notably Newcastle, Liverpool, and

Glasgow, were recorded and filmed for future use, but remain unseen (the footage was later superseded by film of the American tour, which was used for *Rock Show*).

Venus And Mars songs

At the time, many suspected that the Venus and Mars of the album's name and title track referred to Paul and Linda. But as McCartney explained, this couldn't have been further from the truth. "When we had a party in the States to celebrate having finished the album, someone came up to us and said, 'Hello Venus. Hello Mars.' I thought, 'Oh no.' When I write songs, I'm not necessarily talking about me, although a psychoanalyst would say, 'Yes you are mate.' But as far as I'm concerned, I'm not."

He was unaware that Venus and Mars held any symbolic meaning – in Greek mythology Venus is the god of love and Mars the god of war – or that the two planets are adjacent to one another. Those looking for any allegorical meaning in the title of the album and its opening track were disappointed. McCartney made it clear that the song had nothing to do with himself or Linda. "[It] is about an imaginary friend who's got a girlfriend who's the kind of person who asks you what your sign is before they say hello. That's it: 'a good friend of mine studies the stars.' In fact, in the first verse it's 'a good friend of mine *follows* the stars,' so it could be ambiguous: a groupie or an astrologer."

A lengthy coda segues 'Venus And Mars' with the best up-tempo song on the album, 'Rock Show'. It was written with the forthcoming world tour in mind, around references to venues that the band had played or which happened to provide a suitable rhyme. "I start off with an idea," explained McCartney. "Rock Show, boom! Concertgebouw came into my mind, because that's one of the places you play in Amsterdam. We played there, so I rhymed it with 'Rock Show' in an English pronunciation of gebouw. 'Long hair,' well, where else? Madison Square. 'Rock and Roll,' well, that rhymes with Hollywood Bowl. Often these things that turn out to be great afterwards are just searches for a rhyme. I could see how you may think, well, he's doing this, but for me it's just writing a song."

In fact, 'Rock Show' is a powerful no-frills rocker, with a pseudo-reggae middle eight, and does exactly what was asked of it – as Wings do a pretty good job of rockin' out.

McCartney wrote 'You Gave Me The Answer' as an affectionate homage to the golden age of the Hollywood musical, inspired by childhood memories of listening to the BBC Home Service and his father playing the piano. "When I started to listen to music, the kind of music was Fred Astaire and *The Billy Cotton Band Show*, Cole Porter's type of lyrics," he said. "I like the Fred Astaire films ... I think, wow, great, boy, can they dance! Boy, can they arrange tunes. They were only doing what we're doing now, but some of the time they were much better at it."

In an era of heavy metal and glam-rock, McCartney's decision

VENUS AND MARS
WINGS
SIDE 1 'Venus And Mars', 'Rock Show', 'Love In Song', 'You Gave Me The Answer', 'Magneto And Titanium Man', 'Letting Go'.
SIDE 2 'Venus And Mars (reprise)', 'Spirits Of Ancient Egypt', 'Medicine Jar', 'Call Me Back Again', 'Listen To What The Man Said', 'Treat Her Gently – Lonely Old People', 'Crossroads'.
UK RELEASE May 30 1975; LP Capitol PCTC 254; 8-track cartridge Capitol 8X-PCTC 254 released May 1975; chart high No.1.
US RELEASE May 27 1975; LP Capitol SMAS-11419; 8-track cartridge Capitol 8XT-11419; quadraphonic 8-track cartridge Capitol Q8W-11419; chart high No.1.

• **'Venus And Mars'** (McCartney)
Paul McCartney (bass, vocals), Linda McCartney (keyboards, backing vocals), Denny Laine (guitar, backing vocals), Jimmy McCulloch (guitar), Joe English (drums).
• **'Rock Show'** (McCartney)
Personnel as 'Venus And Mars' except add Allen Toussaint (piano).
• **'You Gave Me The Answer'** (McCartney)
Paul McCartney (piano, vocals), Linda McCartney (keyboards, backing vocals), Denny Laine (bass, backing vocals), Jimmy McCulloch (guitar), Joe English (drums).
• **'Magneto And Titanium Man'** (McCartney)
Personnel as 'Venus And Mars'.
• **'Letting Go'** (McCartney)
Personnel as 'Venus And Mars'.
• **'Spirits Of Ancient Egypt'** (McCartney)
Paul McCartney (bass, backing vocals), Linda McCartney (keyboards, backing vocals), Denny Laine (guitar, vocals), Jimmy McCulloch (guitar), Joe English (drums).
• **'Medicine Jar'** (McCulloch, Allen)
Paul McCartney (bass, backing vocals), Linda McCartney (keyboards, backing vocals), Denny Laine (guitar, backing vocals), Jimmy McCulloch (guitar, vocals), Joe English (drums).
• **'Call Me Back Again'** (McCartney)
Paul McCartney (bass, piano, vocals), Linda McCartney (keyboards, backing vocals), Denny Laine (guitar, backing vocals), Jimmy McCulloch (guitar), Joe English (drums).
• **'Treat Her Gently – Lonely Old People'** (McCartney)
Personnel as 'Call Me Back Again'.
• **'Crossroads'** (Hatch)
Paul McCartney (piano, bass), Linda McCartney (keyboards), Denny Laine (guitar), Jimmy McCulloch (guitar), Joe English (drums).
All recorded at Sea Saint Studios, New Orleans, LA, USA and Wally Heider, Los Angeles, CA, USA, except 'Letting Go' recorded at Abbey Road Studios, London, England, and Sea Saint Studios, New Orleans, LA, USA. All produced by Paul McCartney.

to rework a dead style seemed as anachronistic as the monochrome stock on which Astaire's movies were made. Nevertheless, 'You Gave Me The Answer' shouldn't have come as a surprise, for as George Martin noted: "Paul always had that sneaking regard for the old rooty-tooty music." Far from a radical departure, the piece continues where 'When I'm Sixty Four', 'Honey Pie', or 'Walking In The Park With Eloise' had left off.

McCartney wrote 'Magneto And Titanium Man' while on holiday in Jamaica. He remembered: "We'd go into the supermarket every Saturday, when they got a new stock of comics in. I didn't use to read comics from 11 onwards, I thought I'd grown out of them, but I came back to them a couple of years ago. I think it's very clever how they do it. I love the names; I love the whole comic book thing." Just as Lennon had taken the lyrics for 'Being For The Benefit Of Mr Kite' from a Victorian poster, so McCartney took his inspiration from a Marvel comic book. Apparently it's a song about heroes and villains; closer inspection reveals a subtext concerning a personal relationship, albeit a fictitious one.

He explores relationships of a more personal kind in 'Letting Go'. Like many of McCartney's songs, it's about Linda: her potential and inner strength. It also marks a moment of catharsis that sees McCartney symbolically offer Linda her independence. But this is limited autonomy and comes at a price. The cost? Celebrity, something Linda abhorred. McCartney's lyric implies that Linda's independence can only be assured by her participation in his world (showbusiness), which means she must distance herself from hers (home and family).

McCartney wanted to establish Wings as a band of equals and create the impression – for it was only that – of unity. From the outset, group members were encouraged to contribute ideas and songs of their own.

Inspired by a book about the Great Pyramids, McCartney wrote 'Spirits Of Ancient Egypt'. A pedestrian rocker, it was saved by a lyric as surreal as a Dali painting. McCartney let Denny Laine take the lead vocal, suggesting, perhaps, that he was not enamoured with the song. However, it was performed throughout Wings 1975/'76 world tour, and a live recording with an extended guitar solo was programmed for *Wings Over America*.

'Medicine Jar' dates from 1974, when Jimmy McCulloch introduced it to the band while they rehearsed in Nashville. McCartney liked the tune and suggested that Wings record it for their next album, but he obviously didn't pay much attention to the lyrics. A song about drug abuse, 'Medicine Jar' turned out to be sadly prophetic. McCulloch died of an overdose in late 1979.

Inspired by their surroundings, Paul and Linda both wrote songs about New Orleans, notably 'My Carnival' and 'New Orleans'. (Recorded during the *Venus And Mars* sessions, 'My Carnival' remained unreleased for ten years, eventually surfacing as the B-side to 'Spies Like Us' in 1985, and Linda's 'New Orleans' didn't appear until her posthumous solo album, *Wide Prairie*, in 1998.) While not referring specifically to the city, 'Call Me Back Again' was written during a stay at the Beverly Hills Hotel in 1974 and nevertheless bears traces of its influence.

Tight and sassy, it blends several influences into a musical cocktail that is as intoxicating as New Orleans itself. McCartney finished the lyrics while in the city and had Tony Dorsey write the brass arrangement. Influenced by some of New Orleans' finest soul singers, McCartney delivered a killer vocal that underlines a recording to relish. "I ended up just sort of ad libbing a bit," he said, "stretching out a bit. I like that myself. I had a chance to sing." Partly improvised, his vocal has a depth of emotion rarely equalled and reveals what a supreme vocalist he is.

'Treat Her Gently – Lonely Old People' was written in two parts, but unlike previous songs it wasn't completed by welding two unfinished fragments together. Rather, the second theme emerged from the first. McCartney: "I wrote the 'Treat Her Gently' bit as it fell into the key of D, and once I was in D I thought, 'Well, how do I get out of this?' And so I wrote the second half of the thing. It just fell together. They just fell into each other, and I wrote it as I was practising the other, almost."

Evoking what can be the melancholia of old age, McCartney's acute observation conveys the sense of alienation and loneliness many experience as they wait out their years in drab nursing homes in dull seaside towns. An essay in mental and physical disintegration, it's haunted by the ghost of Eleanor Rigby but sidesteps the finality of the former in favour of a secular purgatory, consisting of endless visits to the park and the monotony of daytime television. His lyric reveals what awaits us all, but, unlike the bleak 'Eleanor Rigby', which hints at the emptiness of old age, 'Treat Her Gently – Lonely Old People' has real compassion and points to the pleasures of companionship and love, even if it is set in a bleak urban landscape.

Venus And Mars closes with a version of 'Crossroads', the theme tune to a mundane British television soap opera. Outside of the UK, the tune meant little, as McCartney admitted when he was interviewed for the *NME*. "This fellow who was helping me [Tony Dorsey] thought it was a lovely tune. He thought I'd written it. He thought it was just a beautiful little tune, and it is."

He chose to close the album with *Crossroads* because "it's a bit of a British joke, but I'd still like to put it out. If you don't get the joke on it, it sounds like a closing theme. Sort of like, 'Ladies and gentlemen, Miss Diana Ross!' and Diana walks off with the orchestra going. But if you see the joke, it comes after 'Lonely Old People': nobody asked us to play, they're wondering what's going on, spending time, nobody gets involved with lonely old people. One of the big things for lonely old people in England is to watch *Crossroads*. That was it, just a joke at the end. Funnily enough, they're going to use it at the end of the [TV show] now, use our tune on it, which is great."

Indeed, Wings' version was used to close the television programme and thus, for a short while, it became one of the most played tracks from the album.

Venus And Mars data

The album was issued in a gatefold sleeve with cover photographs by Aubrey Powell (inner gatefold) and Linda (front cover). As the jacket did not feature the band's name, a circular sticker with 'WINGS' and red and yellow balls was adhered to the front cover. A printed inner sleeve, two posters, and two stickers completed the package.

The records were pressed with black and silver Capitol labels with red and yellow balls at 3 o'clock. American first pressings have 'manufactured by McCartney Music, Inc.' in the perimeter, while later editions have 'Manufactured by MPL Communications, Inc.' The LP was reissued by Columbia in 1980 (FC-36801 & JC-36801).

The album was issued on 8-track in Britain (8X-PCTC 2541) and the USA (8XW 11525). In America, Capitol issued a quadraphonic mix on 8-track (Q8W 11419). When Columbia acquired the rights to McCartney's back catalogue, they reissued *Venus And Mars* on 8-track (JCA 36801).

Venus And Mars was issued on CD by Columbia on February 29 1984 (CK 36801). Capitol reissued the CD in November 1988 (CDP 7 46984 2) and DCC Compact Classics issued a gold CD (GZS-1067) in 1994. EMI issued the CD (CD-FA 3213) in Britain on October 19 1987 and issued a remastered edition (CDPMCOL6) on July 7 1993.

'LETTING GO'

ALAN Parsons, an accomplished engineer who worked on The Beatles' *Abbey Road* and Pink Floyd's *Dark Side Of The Moon*, remixed 'Letting Go' at Abbey Road for release as the second single from *Venus And Mars*. His remix shortened the introduction and ending, placed the organ motif higher in the mix, and made McCartney's vocal much drier. Despite this, it did not perform particularly well in the UK or US charts. (The single was issued with customised Capitol 'dome' labels in a plain sleeve. In the USA, Capitol issued mono/stereo edits of the A-side as a demonstration single, on PRO-8225.)

'LETTING GO' / 'YOU GAVE ME THE ANSWER'
WINGS
UK RELEASE September 5 1975; Capitol R 6008; chart high No.41.
US RELEASE September 29 1975; Capitol 4145; chart high No.39.

'VENUS AND MARS'

THE THIRD and final single from *Venus And Mars* lifted three songs from Side 1 of the album. The A-side was an edit, which removed several seconds from 'Venus and Mars' and almost four minutes from 'Rock Show'. 'Magneto And Titanium Man' is the album version, complete.

Issued with customized Capitol 'dome' labels in a plain sleeve, 'Venus And Mars' failed to enter the British charts or stop the album's chart descent. It was, however, a hit in the USA.

'VENUS AND MARS', 'ROCK SHOW' / 'MAGNETO AND TITANIUM MAN'
WINGS
UK RELEASE November 28 1975; Capitol R 6010; failed to chart.
US RELEASE October 27 1975; Capitol 4175; chart high No.12.

Parlophone issued demonstration copies of the single with 'DEMO RECORD NOT FOR SALE' above the spindle hole and a large 'A' at 2 o'clock, with the date 21.11.75 below. Capitol issued mono/stereo edits of the A-side as a demonstration single (PRO-8261). The edit of 'Venus And Mars' / 'Rock Show' was later used for the *Wingspan – Hits And History* compilation, its first appearance on CD.

'IMAGINE'

'IMAGINE' was issued as a single in 1971 except in Britain. Bob Mercer, an EMI executive (and later a director), eventually suggested that Lennon issue the song as a single in his home country, primarily to promote his 'best of' album, *Shaved Fish*. A shrewd move, it gave Lennon a much needed hit and the attendant publicity helped push *Shaved Fish* into the Top 10.

The single, Lennon's last for Apple, was issued with generic Apple labels and picture sleeve. 'Imagine' became his most successful single ever. In the weeks following Lennon's death in 1980, demand for 'Imagine' was such that it reached Number 1. The song was reissued in 1999, when Lennon's lyric was voted Britain's favourite in a BBC poll as part of National Poetry Day.

'IMAGINE' / 'WORKING CLASS HERO'
JOHN LENNON
UK RELEASE October 24 1975; Apple R 5909; chart high No.6 (re-enters December 27 1980 chart high No.1; re-enters December 10 1988 chart high No.45; re-enters December 25 1999 chart high No.3).

SHAVED FISH

SHAVED *Fish* was Lennon's last public musical statement for five years. Speaking with Andy Peebles in 1980, he mused on whether or not *Shaved Fish* had been a farewell of sorts. "That was another thing – was it a subconscious move? Did I know I wasn't going to be on Capitol and EMI any more?' With The Beatles' contract with EMI about to expire, Lennon was free to sign with whoever he liked. However, EMI retained the right to issue compilation albums of their own design, which they did with undignified haste. Both group and solo compilations began to leak from EMI like secrets from a government department. Ringo Starr's *Blast From Your Past* followed *Shaved Fish* on December 12 and George Harrison's *The Best Of* was issued a little over a year later. *Wings Greatest* followed in December 1978.

Although Lennon had planned to record an album of new material to follow *Rock'N'Roll*, when Yoko Ono became pregnant he abandoned the idea and began work on this summation of his solo career. The task should have been easy, but when Lennon began putting the album together he discovered that several of his master tapes were missing. "What I found out was, when I went to look for the 'Cold Turkey' master tapes, nobody knew where they were. I had to use dubs of 'Power To The People' because the tapes were gone. Nobody could give a damn at the record companies because they weren't ... you know, that big. Big enough for them to be interested. ... I thought if I don't put this package together, some of the work is just going to go ... they will be lost forever." That several of the tracks were dubs, presumably from vinyl sources, didn't matter for the vinyl release, but it did when the album was mastered for CD (see below).

Shaved Fish data

Apple issued *Shaved Fish* with generic Apple labels and a cover designed by Roy Kohara with illustrations by Michael Bryan. An inner sleeve with lyrics to Lennon's songs was also included.

SHAVED FISH
JOHN LENNON/PLASTIC ONO BAND
SIDE 1 'Give Peace A Chance', 'Cold Turkey', 'Instant Karma!', 'Power To The People', 'Mother', 'Woman Is The Nigger Of The World'.
SIDE 2 'Imagine', 'Whatever Gets You Thru The Night', 'Mind Games', '#9 Dream', 'Happy Xmas (War Is Over)', 'Give Peace A Chance' (Reprise).
UK RELEASE October 24 1975; LP Apple PCS 7173; 8-track cartridge Apple 8X-PCS 7173; chart high No.8 (re-enters January 17 1981 chart high No.11).
US RELEASE October 24 1975; LP Apple SW 3421; 8-track cartridge Apple 8XW-3421; chart high No.12.

US copies of the LP were produced with three label variations. The first has a light green Apple label with 'STEREO' and a small 'Side 1' below at 9 o'clock, and one song title (Medley) above the spindle hole. The second is the same but with all song titles below the spindle hole, and the third has a large '1' at 9 o'clock and all song titles below the spindle hole.

Capitol reissued the album in 1978 with purple Capitol labels in covers with either an Apple or Capitol logo. The album was issued again by Capitol with black/colour band labels, also with covers with either an Apple or Capitol logo. The album was issued once more in 1983 with purple Capitol labels and covers with a Capitol logo. Greek pressings were issued with a gatefold sleeve. In Japan, *Shaved Fish* was reissued by Odeon (EAS-81457) on green vinyl.

The album was issued on 8-track by EMI (8X-PCS 7173) and Capitol (8XW-3421). *Shaved Fish* was the last Lennon album to be issued on 8-track in Britain.

When EMI began to issue The Beatles and related solo albums on CD, the company spent considerable time and effort on mastering The Beatles' CDs, even if it skimped on the packaging, but paid less attention to solo albums. Original copies of *Shaved Fish* were manufactured in Japan, a country known for its high standards, and shipped to Britain where they were married up with locally-printed inserts. *Shaved Fish* was issued on CD in Britain on May 25 1987. However, it was found to suffer from poor sound quality. Distribution was halted and the CD remastered. The new 'improved' version was issued in Britain on December 7 1987 and in the USA on May 17 1988.

WINGS AT THE SPEED OF SOUND

WINGS' fifth album again divided critics and fans. For some, including McCartney, the record presented Wings as originally envisaged: a democratic unit showcasing everyone's talents. Speaking at the time, he claimed he wanted to move away from centre stage, because taking 'star' billing had become "an embarrassment". He said: "It was never Paul McCartney & The Beatles, Paul McCartney & The Quarrymen, or Paul McCartney & The Moondogs. Wings is quicker and easier to say, and everybody knows I'm in the group anyway."

With this in mind, McCartney gave everyone in the band a vocal on this album. He also let the horn section write their own parts, as "they can really get behind it, because it's their bit," he explained. While some saw this revised group ethos as democracy, albeit on McCartney's terms, others criticised him for delegating responsibilities to less talented individuals.

An underrated gem of a record, *Wings At The Speed Of Sound* is

WINGS AT THE SPEED OF SOUND
WINGS
SIDE 1 'Let 'Em In', 'The Note You Never Wrote', 'She's My Baby', 'Beware My Love', 'Wino Junko'.
SIDE 2 'Silly Love Songs', 'Cook Of The House', 'Time To Hide', 'Must Do Something About It', 'San Ferry Anne', 'Warm And Beautiful'.
UK RELEASE March 26 1976; LP Parlophone PAS 10010; 8-track cartridge Parlophone 8X-PAS 10010; chart high No.2.
US RELEASE March 22 1976; LP Capitol SW-11525; 8-track cartridge Capitol 8XW-11525; chart high No.1.

• **Let 'Em In** (McCartney)
Paul McCartney (bass, piano, vocals), Linda McCartney (keyboards, backing vocals), Denny Laine (guitar, backing vocals), Jimmy McCulloch (guitar), Joe English (drums), Steve 'Tex' Howard (trumpet), Thaddeus Richard (saxophone), Howie Casey (saxophone), Tony Dorsey (trombone).
• **'The Note You Never Wrote'** (McCartney)
Paul McCartney (bass, backing vocals), Linda McCartney (keyboards, backing vocals), Denny Laine (guitar, vocals), Jimmy McCulloch (guitar), Joe English (drums).
• **'She's My Baby'** (McCartney)
Paul McCartney (bass, vocals), Linda McCartney (keyboards, backing vocals), Denny Laine (guitar, backing vocals), Jimmy McCulloch (guitar), Joe English (drums).
• **'Beware My Love'** (McCartney)
Personnel as 'She's My Baby'.
• **'Wino Junko'** (McCulloch, Allen)
Paul McCartney (bass, backing vocals), Linda McCartney (keyboards, backing vocals), Denny Laine (guitar, backing vocals), Jimmy McCulloch (guitar, vocals), Joe English (drums).
• **'Silly Love Songs'** (McCartney)
Personnel as 'Let 'Em In'.
• **'Cook Of The House'** (McCartney)
Paul McCartney (upright bass, backing vocals), Linda McCartney (keyboards, vocals), Denny Laine (guitar, backing vocals), Jimmy McCulloch (guitar), Joe English (drums), Thaddeus Richard or Howie Casey (saxophone).
• **'Time To Hide'** (Laine)
Paul McCartney (bass, backing vocals), Linda McCartney (keyboards, backing vocals), Denny Laine (guitar, vocals), Jimmy McCulloch (guitar), Joe English (drums), Steve 'Tex' Howard (trumpet), Thaddeus Richard (saxophone), Howie Casey (saxophone), Tony Dorsey (trombone).
• **'Must Do Something About It'** (McCartney)
Paul McCartney (bass, backing vocals), Linda McCartney (keyboards, backing vocals), Denny Laine (guitar, backing vocals), Jimmy McCulloch (guitar), Joe English (drums, vocals).
• **'San Ferry Anne'** (McCartney)
Personnel as 'Let 'Em In'.
• **'Warm And Beautiful'** (McCartney)
Paul McCartney (piano, vocals), Denny Laine (guitar), Jimmy McCulloch (guitar).
All recorded at Abbey Road Studios, London, England. All produced by Paul McCartney.

a near perfect pop LP. McCartney's most successful US chart album, it is Wings' finest moment and contains at least one post-Beatles classic in 'Warm And Beautiful'.

Wings At The Speed Of Sound songs

Let 'Em In was originally written for Ringo Starr, but McCartney decided to keep it for himself. He developed the song from a list of people he wanted to invite to a fantasy party. "That's what the song is about, it just sort of said there's someone knocking on the door, let 'em in. You know, let's have a party: why keep them outside? So in listing the kind of people who may be outside the door, I just naturally went to Auntie Gin, Brother Michael – Brother Michael being my own brother, Auntie Gin being my Auntie Gin – I mean, they all exist. Phil and Don being the Everly [Brothers]. I just wanted a parade of people that we could imagine outside the door, so I drew on the people I knew, really."

With its infectious chorus and disco thump, 'Let 'Em In' appeared to pay lip service to rock's deadly enemy, disco. For some this was axiomatic of McCartney's musical frivolity. Not for the first time was he condemned for taking a populist approach – but this didn't stop Let 'Em In becoming a massive hit when it was released a few months after the album.

'The Note You Never Wrote' was the first song recorded for the album, given to Denny Laine to sing. McCartney thought that Laine's recordings with the band had been lightweight and he wanted him to record something more substantial. While Laine did proffer a roughneck rocker of his own, 'Time To Hide', McCartney considered 'The Note You Never Wrote' as epic enough to provide Laine with the kind of vehicle that best suited his talents. McCartney recorded a lead vocal for his song, but Laine's replaced it on the finished master.

Next comes 'She's My Baby', a song of love inspired by and dedicated to Linda, and indebted to the emergent vogue for bass-heavy dance records. Adopting the same formula he'd employed here for 'Let 'Em In' and 'Silly Love Songs', McCartney placed the bottom end of Wings' rhythm section high in the mix. "That is the bass in your face. And that was really because we were making a dance record," he explained. A long time fan of R&B and soul, McCartney often fought to get more bass onto The Beatles' early records to make them 'dancer-friendly' and sound more American. A hybrid of genres, 'She's My Baby' reflects both the interests of its maker and the influence that American dance music was having on pop/rock music.

As if to dispel accusations that Wings were becoming a group of disco-loving softies, McCartney turned in 'Beware My Love', a mid-tempo rocker modelled on 'Soily' and 'Rock Show'. Replicating the band's live set-up in the studio, McCartney attempted to recreate the buzz of playing before an audience. "[We aimed to get all the] excitement in the backing track so it's human: you can hear we're all there," he explained. "Build on a great take and there's no problem. If it's a ropey take, which you're hoping to save further down the line – which I've also done – then it is a problem because it's like a rickety building that's going to fall down any minute. No foundations."

A lengthy preamble, featuring Linda's multi-tracked vocals, precedes an especially sensitive vocal from McCartney that evokes a feeling of emotional ambivalence, which his lyric suggests lies at the heart of any relationship.

Jimmy McCulloch co-wrote 'Wino Junko' with Stone The Crows drummer Colin Allen, and it was another song about alcohol and drug abuse. Less weighty than McCulloch's contribution to *Venus And Mars*, it nevertheless fits snugly alongside contributions from other members of the band. Its darker tone is masked by McCartney's airy production, which unfortunately tends to expose McCulloch's fragile vocal, a shortcoming that could have been disguised with a few deft production touches.

The conflicting tone of McCulloch's lyric and melody led some to suggest that a process of musical assimilation was taking place within the band. Individuals were apparently tailoring their material to fit McCartney's style, rather than their own. This seemingly revealed the extent to which McCartney continued to dominate the group. Despite this, band members were free to record outside of Wings. McCulloch did just that. Forming White Line for solo excursions, he released a single, 'Too Many Miles', through EMI. If there were any musical differences within Wings at this time, the escape route of solo projects appeared to dissipate any threat of a break-up. McCulloch appeared contented. "Wings are settled for years. It would be a shame if anything happened," he said. "I can't see anything cracking Wings in the foreseeable future."

McCartney wrote 'Silly Love Songs' at the piano while on holiday in Hawaii. He then transposed the melody to the bass, purposely making it the lead instrument. "We really pushed the bass and drums right out front," he said. "But it pushed the song along quite nicely. Pushed it hard. We wanted to make something you could dance to."

McCartney is often considered a sentimentalist, and the cosy interplay in 'Silly Love Songs' between husband and wife seemed to reinforce this view. However, McCartney said that the song was a deliberate response to these charges. "Originally, I wrote the song at about the time when the kind of material I did was a bit out of favour ... and you had Alice Cooper doing 'No More Mr Nice Guy' and that kind of hard parody. I rather picked up a feeling that ballads were being regarded as soppy and love songs as too sentimental."

For McCartney, 'Silly Love Songs' expressed sentiments that ran deeper than the song's seductive superficiality suggests. "You see, I'm looking at love not from the perspective of 'oh, boring old love,' I'm looking at it like when you get married and have a baby or something, that kind of love. I mean, that's pretty strong; it's not lurve, that stuff; it's something deeper."

McCartney's backhanded swipe at his critics was an attempt at ironic self-parody that many missed. The very title should have alerted the more astute to the fact that he was poking fun at his public image, as well as questioning those who criticised his values. McCartney wrote 'Silly Love Songs' in full knowledge of the criticism being levelled at him. As such, it's a knowing, ironic response to those who cast him as a sentimentalist and a self referential celebration of his own value system. (A reggae version was apparently attempted during the making of *Speed Of Sound*, but it remains unreleased. 'Silly Love Songs' would be re-recorded for *Give My Regards To Broad Street*, without improvement.)

In keeping with the spirit of *Speed Of Sound*, Linda was given a song written by her husband. 'Cook Of The House' is a 1950s-styled rocker, McCartney's tribute to his wife's culinary skills, written in November 1975 while Wings were touring Australia. "Late one night when we were on tour, renting a house in Australia, we were looking at one of those plaques found in many kitchens worldwide: 'Wherever I serve my guests, they like my kitchen best.' This led to a perusal of the contents of the shelves around us, which instantly became the lyric of the song," Paul said. A light-hearted rock'n'roll track, 'Cook Of The House' reveals Paul and Linda's love of the genre. "I was a rock'n'roll kid," recalled Linda. "My first greatest moment was going to an Alan Freed Rhythm & Blues Show at the Brooklyn Paramount in about 1957, when I was a junior in high school." It features McCartney on Presley sideman Bill Black's double bass, and the recording was mixed to mono to further enhance its claims for authenticity. Unfortunately, because of McCartney's desire to make the song appear out of fashion, 'Cook Of The House' sounds anachronistic, it being the one track on the album that ignored contemporary trends. It became the B-side of 'Silly Love Songs' and later surfaced on Linda's posthumous debut album, *Wide Prairie*.

Denny Laine's contribution, 'Time To Hide', was his first solo composition to feature on a Wings record since he joined the band in 1971. He released solo albums in 1973, 1976, and 1980, but has not been a prolific writer. Indeed, when he was a featured performer live with Wings, it was usually with material written or recorded in the 1960s, the exception being 'Time To Hide'. As competent as anything McCartney contributed to the album, it became a staple of the Wings live set during their 1975/'76 world tour.

There were some who complained that McCartney's allocation of songs to other members of the band was a waste. One critic suggested: "It's just about understandable letting your wife sing a track ... but to have drummer Joe English and [Denny] Laine have a go is simply not on when they're so obviously inferior singers to

Paul himself." But Joe English, given 'Must Do Something About It', provided the biggest surprise on the album. He has a remarkably expressive voice, which McCartney enthused about: "He can sing well ... but [that performance is] nothing to what he could do." Far from being 'inferior', English's performance is on a par with anything on the album, and it's debatable whether anyone could have improved on it. 'Must Do Something About It' was the ideal vehicle for his vocal mannerisms, which perfectly matched the blue-eyed-soul feel that McCartney was aiming for. Segued with Laine's 'Time To Hide', the song has a summery disposition and rolling cadence that offsets what in other hands could have become a morose lyric about loneliness.

'San Ferry Anne' is the antithesis of 'Must Do Something About It', as self-confident as the latter is self-effacing. This is pop, pure and simple, it demands little and, like the lifestyle to which it alludes, is a glamorous affirmation of the high-life.

If one song can be said to capture McCartney at his most idealistic, it's *Speed Of Sound*'s closing track, 'Warm And Beautiful'. A simple eight-bar phrase introduces the central motif, which, depending on one's point of view, is either compelling or tedious. McCartney's piano accompaniment supports a delicate interpretation of a lyric steeped in romantic idealism, which in the hands of others could have degenerated into mawkish pap. But his epistle to Linda is rescued by a typically mobile melody. Although the lyric is perhaps too idealised, the song's sweeping melody and McCartney's warm delivery largely dispose of any suggestions of mawkishness. A favourite of McCartney's, 'Warm And Beautiful' was at one point considered fit for release as a single but was overlooked in favour of more up-tempo material.

Wings At The Speed Of Sound data

Despite mixed reviews and the fact that Wings were competing with a renewed interest in The Beatles – EMI reissued all of The Beatles' singles, almost all of which found their way back into the charts – *Wings At The Speed Of Sound* fared remarkably well, spending 30 weeks in the British charts to become the forth bestselling British album of 1976 and 51 weeks on the US charts, including seven (non-consecutive) weeks at Number 1.

The album was issued with customised *'Speed Of Sound'* labels and printed inner sleeve. Linda took the cover photograph and Humphrey Ocean drew the picture for the inner sleeve, which depicts members of Kilburn & The Highroads (Ocean had played guitar in that band and was taught art at college by their singer, Ian Dury). Because the cover did not make it clear that this was Wings' new LP, Capitol manufactured a circular sticker with 'WINGS' in white text on a black background over a large 'W', which was adhered to the front cover. Columbia reissued the LP (FC-37409 & (PC 37409) with generic red labels on 13 July 1981.

The album was issued on 8-track in Britain (8X-PAS 10010) and the USA (8XW 11525). It was reissued by Columbia (JCA 37409) in the early 1980s.

EMI issued *Wings At The Speed Of Sound* on CD (CDP7481992) on July 10 1989 and issued a remastered edition (CDPMCOL7) on July 7 1993. Capitol issued the CD (CDP 7 48199 2) on June 20 1989.

'SILLY LOVE SONGS'

RELEASED in America at the height of Wingsmania, 'Silly Love Songs' became Wings' forth single to top the American charts. In the UK it stalled at number 2, kept from the top spot by 'Combine Harvester', a novelty hit by British west-country group The Wurzels.

In recent years, 'Silly Love Songs' has been remixed, sampled, and reissued on several promotional records. To promote *Wingspan – Hits And History*, McCartney commissioned three remixes, which were issued in Germany as a promotional CD (CDP 000587). These remixes were also issued in Italy by the Dance Factory label as a 12-inch single (7243 880073 6 8). In Britain, a 'Wings vs Loop Da Loop Mix' was issued as a promotional 12-inch single (12-WINDJ-002) backed with 'Coming Up' in a 'Linus Loves Mix'. According to the press release, only 50 copies of this record were pressed. In Holland, Lifted Records issued a house mix by Noir and Krusé as a CD single (334 50881). A sample from 'Silly Love Songs', licensed by MPL, was used for Jenn Cuneta's 'Come Rain Come Shine', a Top 5 single on the *Billboard* dance chart in 2005.

For its original release, Parlophone and Capitol issued 'Silly Love Songs' with customised *'Speed Of Sound'* labels in a paper sleeve. In America, the single was also issued with black and silver Capitol 'dome' labels.

Parlophone issued a demonstration 7-inch single with edited (A-side) and full length versions (B-side). The label has a large white 'A' above the spindle hole and (EDITED VERSION) below the song title. In the USA, Capitol issued a demonstration 7-inch single (P-4256) with white labels with black text and the Capitol logo top centre and 'NOT FOR SALE' bottom centre below 'WINGS'. The single featured edited and full-length versions of the A-side.

Columbia reissued the single (18-02171) in 1981 with generic orange and yellow labels that incorrectly give the A-side time as 5:52.

'SILLY LOVE SONGS' / 'COOK OF THE HOUSE'
WINGS
UK RELEASE April 30 1976; Parlophone R 6014; chart high No.2.
US RELEASE April 1 1976; Capitol 4256; chart high No.1.

'LET 'EM IN' / 'BEWARE MY LOVE'
WINGS
UK RELEASE July 23 1976; Parlophone R 6015; chart high No.2.
US RELEASE June 28 1976; Capitol 4293; chart high No.3.

'LET 'EM IN'

WITH *Wings At The Speed Of Sound* beginning its chart descent, a second hit from the album was required to boost album sales. Doubly successful, *Let 'Em In* reached the Top 5 in both Britain and the USA and pushed the album back into the Top 10. 'Let 'Em In' got an extra lease of chart life when Billy Paul hit with the song in the early months of 1977. Twenty-five years later, the song was remixed to promote *Wingspan – Hits And History*, and it was sampled and used to underpin 'Inside Thing', a duet between McCartney and Lulu that appeared on her 2002 album, *Together*.

As with the previous single, 'Let 'Em In' was issued with customised *'Speed Of Sound'* labels in a paper sleeve. In America, the single was also manufactured by Capitol with black and silver 'dome' labels. Capitol issued a 7-inch demonstration single (P-4293) with white labels with black text and the Capitol logo top centre and 'NOT FOR SALE' bottom centre, below 'WINGS'. The single featured a mono edit and the full-length stereo version of the A-side. In Britain, Parlophone issued a demonstration 7-inch single with a stereo edit on the A-side and the full-length version on the B-side. The label has a large white 'A' above the spindle hole, 'DEMO RECORD NOT FOR SALE' on three lines below the spindle hole, and (EDITED VERSION) below the song title. In France, the single was issued in a fake leopard-skin sleeve as a 12-inch single (2C 052 98062 Y), the first time one of McCartney's records had been released commercially on this format.

WINGS OVER AMERICA

WHILE John Lennon was preparing to take a break from the limelight, his former songwriting partner was readying himself for an extended period in its glare. McCartney was planning a world tour, something he had been building up to for years. He'd been honing his band and stage act for some time, and began with a short tour of English universities, followed six months later by a European tour. With Europe under his belt, McCartney toured larger venues in Britain in 1973, building his repertoire, reputation, and confidence.

The Wings world tour followed a similar pattern, growing in scale as it moved around the globe. Rehearsals were held at Elstree Studios, Borehamwood, north-west of London, where Wings gave a full dress performance to a specially invited audience of fans and record-company employees. The tour opened at the Southampton Gaumont before moving on to Australia, Europe, and North America.

Speaking to *Melody Maker* about his plans for the tour, McCartney said: "In England … the normal venues are like 3,000 [capacity], so very naturally we started off with 3,000 people, and then we went to 5,000, 6,000, 14,000 in Australia, and then we played some bigger halls in Europe, which were more like 15,000. … I like things like that. I like things step by step."

By the time Wings hit America, both band and tour machine were performing to perfection, and McCartney's confidence was justified. "We've spent months rehearsing Wings. And it's all been better than I thought it would be," he rejoiced. Linda shared his enthusiasm in the band, which she believed came across in his performances. "Paul didn't feel confidence in the band before," she said, "whereas this band, he really knows he can get up there and sing."

On his return to Britain, McCartney began listening to some 70 hours of live tapes of the tour, which had to be edited and mixed. The task was mammoth and he spent six weeks – reportedly working up to 14 hours a day – perfecting the album. *Wings Over America* represents a complete live show, capturing the band at its most dynamic and powerful. Wings' set drew on some of the strongest material from McCartney's back catalogue, with songs drawn from Wings' three most recent albums: five songs from *Band On The Run*, five from *Venus And Mars*, and four from *Speed Of Sound*. And for the first time, McCartney included songs associated with The Beatles, something he'd been unwilling to do previously.

Such a large tour inevitably created a number of associated projects. As well as recording many of the Wings concerts for release on record, the tour was filmed with a cinema release in mind. The resulting film, *Rock Show*, eventually premiered in New York City on November 26 1980 and received a limited cinema release before making it to video. To promote the movie, Miramax Films produced a one-sided 7-inch single (CPS-4202) that featured three 'radio spots'. (The single was manufactured with a white label with black text.)

In addition to the film, other mediums were used to make a visual record of the tour. Humphrey Ocean, who had drawn the inner sleeve for *Wings At The Speed Of Sound*, became artist in residence for the American leg of the tour. Commissioned to make paintings and drawings inspired by his travels with the band, Ocean eventually published his work as *Ocean Way*. A photo documentary, *Hands Across The Water – Wings Tour USA* was produced as a book by Hipgnosis.

Wings Over America songs

As with the rest of this book, live recordings already covered in their studio versions are not included in concert-record entries. So, for our purposes, the first 'new' track on *Over America* is 'Lady Madonna'. Borrowing the piano lick from 'Bad Penny Blues', a 1956 hit for Humphrey Lyttelton, McCartney wrote it in celebration of motherhood. In concert, Wings take the song at a slightly faster tempo than The Beatles' studio recording. Nevertheless, it's a faithful reading and comes complete with an accurate transcription of the original improvised saxophone arrangement.

'The Long And Winding Road' was released by The Beatles on their swansong album, *Let It Be*, but McCartney all but disowned the original version because of Phil Spector's heavy-handed production. He may have abhorred Spector's production, but the legendary producer had no choice other than to swamp the song with his 'wall of sound', as The Beatles' recording was little more than a rough sketch. The Beatles never returned to the song as by the time they completed the follow-up recording, *Abbey Road*, no one could face the job. Wings' reading has the advantage of a new synoptic introduction and fanfare-like horn arrangement, but Denny Laine's bass playing, albeit an improvement on Lennon's amateur attempt, is still far too plodding.

'Richard Cory', sung by Laine, was written by Paul Simon and originally recorded by Simon & Garfunkel for their album *Sound Of Silence*. Performed during Wings' acoustic set, a forerunner of the unplugged format, the song was programmed as a medley with 'Picasso's Last Words', also sung mainly by Laine. A piece of social commentary that no doubt went down well with student audiences in the mid 1960s, 'Richard Cory' is the tale of a capitalist who comes to a sticky end.

'I've Just Seen A Face' is another Beatles song, this time from *Help!*, and was originally an instrumental, 'Auntie Gin's Theme', until McCartney added the lyric. He would return to the song 25 years later when he performed it with Paul Simon at the Adopt-A-Minefield gala held at the Beverly Wilshire Hotel in Los Angeles.

Recorded for The Beatles' *White Album*, the acoustic ballad 'Blackbird' apparently came to McCartney with words and music complete. Inspired by a piece by Bach that he and George Harrison used to impress people with at parties, 'Blackbird' was a metaphor for Afro-American emancipation. As McCartney explained to Terry Gross: "'Blackbird' was something I wrote in the 1960s, and I used to play a kind of version of a Bach piece. I used to play a ... fingerpicking thing on that. [The] music was

WINGS OVER AMERICA
WINGS
SIDE 1 'Venus And Mars', 'Rock Show', 'Jet', 'Let Me Roll It', 'Spirits Of Ancient Egypt', 'Medicine Jar'.
SIDE 2 'Maybe I'm Amazed', 'Call Me Back Again', 'Lady Madonna', 'The Long And Winding Road', 'Live And Let Die'.
SIDE 3 'Picasso's Last Words', 'Richard Cory', 'Bluebird', 'I've Just Seen A Face', 'Blackbird', 'Yesterday'.
SIDE 4 'You Gave Me The Answer', 'Magneto And Titanium Man', 'Go Now', 'My Love', 'Listen To What The Man Said'.
SIDE 5 'Let 'Em In', 'Time To Hide', 'Silly Love Songs', 'Beware My Love'.
SIDE 6 'Letting Go', 'Band On The Run', 'Hi, Hi, Hi', 'Soily'.
UK release December 10 1976; LP Parlophone PCSP 720; 8-track cartridge Parlophone 8X-PCSP 720; chart high No.8.
US release December 10 1976; LP Capitol SWCO-11593; 8-track cartridge Capitol 8X3C-11593; chart high No.1.

• **'Lady Madonna'** (Lennon, McCartney)
Paul McCartney (piano, vocals), Linda McCartney (keyboards, backing vocals), Denny Laine (bass), Jimmy McCulloch (guitar), Joe English (drums), Steve 'Tex' Howard (trumpet), Thaddeus Richard (saxophone), Howie Casey (saxophone), Tony Dorsey (trombone). Live recording at Olympia Stadium, Detroit, MI, USA.
• **'The Long And Winding Road'** (Lennon, McCartney)
Personnel as 'Lady Madonna'. Live recording at Kemper Arena, Kansas City, KS, USA.
• **'Richard Cory'** (Simon)
Paul McCartney (guitar), Denny Laine (guitar, vocals), Jimmy McCulloch (guitar). Live recording at The Forum, Los Angeles, CA, USA.
• **'I've Just Seen A Face'** (Lennon, McCartney)
Paul McCartney (guitar, vocals), Linda McCartney (backing vocals), Denny Laine (guitar), Jimmy McCulloch (bass), Joe English (drums). Live recording at The Forum, Los Angeles, CA, USA.
• **'Blackbird'** (Lennon, McCartney)
Paul McCartney (guitar, vocals). Live recording at Boston Garden, Boston, MA, USA.
• **'Yesterday'** (Lennon, McCartney)
Paul McCartney (guitar, vocals), Steve 'Tex' Howard (trumpet), Thaddeus Richard (saxophone), Howie Casey (saxophone), Tony Dorsey (trombone).
Recording location unknown. Produced by Paul McCartney.
• **'Go Now'** (Banks, Bennett)
Paul McCartney (bass), Linda McCartney (keyboards, backing vocals), Denny Laine (piano, vocals), Jimmy McCulloch (guitar), Joe English (drums), Steve 'Tex' Howard (trumpet), Thaddeus Richard (saxophone), Howie Casey (saxophone), Tony Dorsey (trombone).
Live recording at The Forum, Los Angeles, CA, USA.
• **'Soily'** (McCartney)
Paul McCartney (bass, vocals), Linda McCartney (keyboards, backing vocals), Denny Laine (guitar), Jimmy McCulloch (guitar), J oe English (drums), Steve 'Tex' Howard (trumpet), Thaddeus Richard (saxophone), Howie Casey (saxophone), Tony Dorsey (trombone). Live recording at McNichols Sports Arena, Denver, CO, USA.
All produced by Paul McCartney.

inspired by that. And then the words were actually to do with the civil rights movement. I was imagining a Blackbird being symbolic for a young black woman living in America at the time, experiencing the injustices that were going on then, particularly. And this was hopefully to be an inspirational song where ... even though she was going through all these terrible times, she'll be able to look and listen to this song and be inspired by it to continue to fight against the injustices."

Evidence that this is what he intended and not historical revisionism can be found on a tape McCartney recorded with Donovan and Mary Hopkin while working on Hopkin's *Postcard* album. Having performed 'Blackbird', he jokes about playing the song to Diana Ross, who took offence (at being called a black bird). He then explains that "I'd read somewhere in the papers about riots and that". Whatever the inspiration, the clever use of slang combined with powerful imagery and a typically mobile McCartney melody created an enduring song of hope and aspiration.

McCartney claims he awoke one morning with the music for 'Yesterday' running through his head. At first he thought he must have heard the song elsewhere and played it to friends asking if they had ever heard it. He continued to work on the song throughout 1964, rewriting the lyrics and perfecting the melody, until confident enough to commit the song to tape. The group were unable to come up with an arrangement, and Lennon suggested that McCartney should record the song with just acoustic guitar. Thus armed, McCartney taped the song at Abbey Road on the evening of June 14 1965. Only two takes were recorded, the second being marked best (the first was later released on *Anthology 2*). At George Martin's suggestion, a string quartet was overdubbed three days later, but not without reservations from McCartney, who saw The Beatles as a rock band and thought strings unsuited to the band's image. Nevertheless, Martin persevered and persuaded him that a small string section would enhance the song.

Newly convinced, McCartney helped write the arrangement with the proviso that the players used no vibrato, lest they end up sounding like the records of easy-listening king Mantovani. The resulting song was a Number 1 single in America, but in Britain it remained buried on Side 2 of *Help!*, where there was less chance of it tarnishing the band's image. The song was eventually released as a single in Britain in 1976, when The Beatles' singles catalogue, along with two new couplings, 'Yesterday' / 'I Should Have Known Better' (R 6013) and 'Back In The USSR' / 'Twist And Shout' (R 6016), were issued by EMI. Despite its popularity, the song failed to make Number 1 in Britain, only managing Number 8. When released in 1965, it became something of an instant classic – in other words, it became a success for others. It eventually became one of the most covered songs in recording history, with some 2,000 versions to its credit, and went on to become the most played song on American radio with a total of seven million plays.

Bessie Banks recorded 'Go Now' in 1963, but The Moody Blues, with Denny Laine on vocals, had the hit the following year. Wings here reproduce the Moody Blues treatment, which they augment with a new horn arrangement and a restrained solo from Jimmy McCulloch. Whilst comparable to the Moody Blues reading, Wings' interpretation adds little to the original and was undoubtedly included to give Laine another vocal during the band's concerts.

Wings performed 'Soily' regularly during tours of Europe and Britain in 1972/'73. Originally shorter, slower, and less powerful than the version on *Wings Over America*, it was intended for the *Red Rose Speedway* album, initially planned as a double LP, but dropped at the last moment. By 1976, it had acquired a quasi-heavy metal arrangement and, thanks to some energetic drumming from Joe English, a tough dynamic. The addition of a horn arrangement helped transform 'Soily' into a piece of explosive rock hyperbole perfect for stadium performances and an ideal song with which to end *Wings Over America*.

Wings Over America data

Wings Over America was issued as a three-record set, and each LP had unique customised labels, with printed inner sleeves. Designed by the McCartneys and Hipgnosis, the package, which included a poster, was housed in a gatefold sleeve. Richard Manning provided the front cover painting, which symbolised Wings' arrival in America. A door in the side of an aircraft opens, revealing a shaft of bright white light which represents either a curtain being drawn back or music streaming from a stage. The theme is continued on the inner sleeves, the aperture becoming larger as it spreads across the three inner covers.

The album was issued on 8-track in Britain (8X-PCSP 720) and the USA (8X3C-11593). It was Wings' last album to be issued on 8-track in Britain. EMI issued the album as a two-CD set (CDP7481992) on May 25 1987; Columbia issued the CD (CK-37990/1) on February 29 1984; and Capitol reissued the CD (CDP 7 46715/6 2) on January 17 1988.

'MAYBE I'M AMAZED'

WHAT should have made a stunning debut solo single for McCartney was instead relegated years later to this, little more than a tool to promote *Wings Over America*. 'Maybe I'm Amazed' managed only two weeks in the UK Top 30 but was a Top 10 hit in the USA.

Parlophone and Capitol issued the single with customised labels in a paper sleeve. Parlophone issued a 7-inch demonstration single with a large grey 'A' above the spindle hole and 'DEMO RECORD NOT FOR SALE' on three lines below the spindle hole. In America, Capitol issued a 7-inch demonstration

'MAYBE I'M AMAZED' / 'SOILY'
WINGS
UK RELEASE February 4 1977; Parlophone R 6017; chart high No.28.
US RELEASE February 7 1977; Capitol 4385; chart high No.10.

single (PRO-8570) that featured mono/stereo versions of the A-side with black and sliver 'dome' labels. Capitol also issued a promotional 12-inch single ((S)PRO-8574) with mono/stereo edits of A-side. A mono edit and album version were issued on side one, a stereo edit and album version on side two. The 12-inch record was issued in a black sleeve with Wings' logo centre top and 'Maybe I'm Amazed from the album "Wings over America"' below. Capitol Records' logo appears bottom centre and 'NOT FOR SALE' in the bottom right corner of the sleeve.

'UNCLE ALBERT'

WHO IS Percy Thrillington? That was a question asked by many in early 1977. His name had appeared in several London newspapers, resulting in a small avalanche of media speculation that helped fuel interest in this unknown recording artist. The answer was, of course, Paul McCartney. (Issued by Regal Zonophone with generic red and silver labels, 'Uncle Albert/Admiral Halsey' / 'Eat At Home' failed to enter the charts and failed to inspire many to rush out and buy the album that followed.

UNCLE ALBERT/ADMIRAL HALSEY' / 'EAT AT HOME'
PERCY 'THRILLS' THRILLINGTON
UK RELEASE April 1977; Regal Zonophone EMI 2594; failed to chart.

- **'Uncle Albert/Admiral Halsey'** (Paul and Linda McCartney)
Vic Flick (guitar), Clem Cattini (drums), Herbie Flowers (bass, tuba solo), Steve Gray (piano), Jim Lawless (percussion), The Mike Sammes Singers (vocals), unknown (strings), unknown (brass, woodwind).
- **'Eat At Home'** (Paul and Linda McCartney)
Clem Cattini (drums), Herbie Flowers (bass), Roger Coulan (organ), Jim Lawless (percussion), The Mike Sammes Singers (vocals), unknown (brass, woodwind).

Both recorded at Abbey Road Studios, London, England.
Both produced by Paul McCartney.

RAM/THRILLINGTON

PERCY Thrillington was the first act signed to McCartney's MPL company. However, Mr Thrillington was a completely fictitious individual, as was the enigmatic Clint Harrigan who wrote the sleevenotes for this and Wings' debut album. Thrillington and Harrigan were pseudonyms used by McCartney, who went to considerable lengths to convince the public that they existed. Not only were business cards produced for Percy Thrillington, Paul and Linda even wrote his biography and took his photograph. "So we invented it all," admitted McCartney, "Linda and I, and we went around southern Ireland and found a guy in a field, a young farmer, and asked if he minded doing some photographic modelling for us. We wanted to find someone that no one could possibly trace, paid him the going rate, and photographed him in a field, wearing a sweater and then wearing an evening suit. But he never quite looked Percy Thrillington enough."

The *Thrillington* album was recorded over three days (June 15–17) in 1971 and resulted, among other things, from McCartney's desire to do something different with the songs he'd recorded for *Ram*. Explaining why he made the album, he said: "It all came about because I wanted someone to do a big-band version of *Ram* – but there were no takers, [so] I thought that I'd better be that someone."

McCartney's interest in the big-band era dates back to his childhood, when the sounds of bandleaders such as Glenn Miller and Ted Heath were practically all that was played on the conservative BBC. His fascination spread to writing convincing pastiches of old-time standards of the 1930s ('Honey Pie', 'You Gave Me The Answer') and employing big-band arrangements in songs such as 'You Want Her Too'.

To help him realise the project, McCartney called on the talents of Richard Hewson, who had orchestrated 'Those Were The Days', a song McCartney produced for the Apple recording artist Mary Hopkin, and had obviously gained his respect. McCartney gave Hewson the freedom to orchestrate the songs however he wanted; McCartney's only stipulation was that Hewson record with a relatively small 'pops' orchestra. Hewson was allowed to select the session musicians he wanted. "The musicians I chose were the small group of top players that I regularly used," he told Ian Peel. "Herbie Flowers on bass, Clem Cattini of The Tornados on drums, Vic Flick, a legendary guitarist, Roger Coulan on keyboards, the Dolmetsch family on recorders, The Mike Sammes Singers, and various top jazz players on saxes and brass, because I was and still am heavily into jazz. The strings and woodwind were all drawn from top session players of the day."

Although it was recorded in 1971, the *Thrillington* album was not issued until 1977. Released at the height of punk rock, its easy-listening style flew in the face of contemporary musical trends. It was, however, as radical as any punk record; perhaps more so. Rather than play the punk card – McCartney did consider releasing a punk song, 'Boil Crisis' – he issued an easy-listening version of an album that was the best part of six years old. *Thrillington* was a bold experiment that presented some of his most complex and melodic compositions in a new light. It may even have been a clever ironic statement that poked fun at critics who claimed that, post-Beatles, all he could produce was muzak.

To promote both single and album, MPL placed a number of cryptic advertisements in the personal columns of *The Evening Standard* and *The Times* newspapers. This low-cost, inventive advertising campaign eventually led to an article in the *Standard* that attempted to uncover the identity of the elusive Thrillington. As McCartney explained: "Then we started this whole business in *The Evening Standard* ad columns, which was the really fun thing, putting in things like 'Must get in touch with ... Thrillington', as a result of which the newspaper columns picked up on it – 'Has anyone seen this rubbish going on in *The Evening Standard* about Percy Thrillington?' – and it was good publicity. It was one of our madcap publicity schemes, as if we were managing this character called Percy Thrillington." For McCartney, at least, it did not really matter who controlled this project, as the whole Thrillington idea took on a conceptual feel. "You could say that Percy Thrillington was Richard Hewson, or just a fictitious leader of a band who never appeared anywhere," he explained.

Conceptual joke or serious project, Thrillington is one of the more intriguing of McCartney's albums. EMI also created an elaborate advertising campaign to promote the album. This included 5-inch-diameter 'thought bubble' stickers, publicity photographs, Percy Thrillington business cards and radio 'tease' advertisements.

Ram/Thrillington data

The album was issued in Britain by Regal Zonophone with generic red and silver labels. The cover painting, by Jeff Cummings, depicted a violinist with a ram's head. Cummings continued this theme on the rear cover and included McCartney's face, reflected in the window dividing the control room from the studio floor – a clue, if ever there was one, to McCartney's involvement. A thick black card inner sleeve completed the package. In the USA, Capitol issued the album

RAM
PERCY 'THRILLS' THRILLINGTON
SIDE 1 'Too Many People', '3 Legs', 'Ram On', 'Dear Boy', 'Uncle Albert/Admiral Halsey', 'Smile Away'.
SIDE 2 'Heart Of The Country', 'Monkberry Moon Delight', 'Eat At Home', 'Long Haired Lady', 'Ram On', 'The Back Seat Of My Car'.
UK RELEASE April 29 1977; Regal Zonophone EMC 3175; failed to chart.
US RELEASE May 16 1977; LP Capitol ST-11642; 8-track cartridge Capitol 8XT-11642; failed to chart.

- **'Too Many People'** (McCartney)
Clem Cattini (drums), Herbie Flowers (bass), Jim Lawless (percussion), The Mike Sammes Singers (vocals), unknown (brass).
- **'3 Legs'** (McCartney)
Vic Flick (guitar), Clem Cattini (drums), Herbie Flowers (bass), Jim Lawless (percussion), unknown (brass).
- **'Ram On'** (McCartney)
Vic Flick (guitar), Clem Cattini (drums), Herbie Flowers (bass), Jim Lawless (percussion), The Mike Sammes Singers (vocals), unknown (brass, woodwind), unknown (harp).
- **'Dear Boy'** (Paul and Linda McCartney)
Clem Cattini (drums), Herbie Flowers (bass), Jim Lawless (percussion), The Mike Sammes Singers (vocals).
- **'Uncle Albert/Admiral Halsey'** (Paul and Linda McCartney)
Vic Flick (guitar), Clem Cattini (drums), Herbie Flowers (bass, tuba solo), Steve Gray (piano), Jim Lawless (percussion), The Mike Sammes Singers (vocals), unknown (strings), unknown (brass, woodwind).
- **'Smile Away'** (McCartney)
Vic Flick (guitar), Clem Cattini (drums), Herbie Flowers (bass), Jim Lawless (percussion), Chris Karen (cuica drum), unknown (brass).
- **'Heart Of The Country'** (Paul and Linda McCartney)
Vic Flick (guitar), Clem Cattini (drums), Herbie Flowers (bass), Jim Lawless (percussion), The Mike Sammes Singers (vocals), unknown (woodwind).
- **'Monkberry Moon Delight'** (Paul and Linda McCartney)
Clem Cattini (drums), Herbie Flowers (bass), Jim Lawless (percussion), unknown (brass), unknown (strings).
- **'Eat At Home'** (Paul and Linda McCartney)
Clem Cattini (drums), Herbie Flowers (bass), Roger Coulan (organ), Jim Lawless (percussion), The Mike Sammes Singers (vocals), unknown (brass, woodwind).
- **'Long Haired Lady'** (McCartney)
Vic Flick (guitar), Clem Cattini (drums), Herbie Flowers (bass), Jim Lawless (percussion), The Mike Sammes Singers (vocals), unknown (brass, woodwind).
- **'The Back Seat Of My Car'** (McCartney)
Vic Flick (guitar), Clem Cattini (drums), Herbie Flowers (bass), Steve Gray (piano), Jim Lawless (percussion), Carl Dolmetsch Family (recorders), unknown (strings), unknown (brass).

All recorded at Abbey Road Studios, London, England.
All produced by Paul McCartney.

with purple Capitol labels. Capitol also issued the album on 8-track (8XT 11642).

Thrillington was released on CD on May 1 1995, which was a considerable achievement in itself. As McCartney noted: "What I didn't realise was that no one would want to release an album like that. Not even then. And no way would it get released now." The CD release received next to no publicity, few shops bothered to stock it, and it was deleted relatively quickly. Consequently, fans missed the opportunity to purchase a copy and it became a rarity itself. However, the CD was reissued on June 7 2004 with identical packaging and label artwork to the original, and the only difference being 'MADE IN EU' at bottom centre of the CD label, replacing 'MADE IN THE UNITED KINGDOM'.

'MULL OF KINTYRE' / 'GIRLS' SCHOOL'
WINGS
UK RELEASE November 11 1977; Capitol R 6018; chart high No.1.
US RELEASE November 14 1977; Capitol 4504; chart high No.33.

- **'Mull Of Kintyre'** (McCartney, Laine)
Paul McCartney (guitar, vocals), Linda McCartney (backing vocals), Denny Laine (guitar, backing vocals), Joe English (drums), The Campbelltown Pipe Band (pipes).
Recorded on RAK Mobile Studio at Spirit Of Ranachan Studio, High Park Farm, Scotland, and at AIR Studios and Abbey Road Studios, London, England.
- **'Girls' School'** (McCartney)
Paul McCartney (bass, backing vocals), Linda McCartney (keyboards, backing vocals), Denny Laine (guitar, backing vocals), Jimmy McCulloch (guitar), Joe English (drums).
Recorded at Abbey Road Studios, London.
Both produced by Paul McCartney.

'MULL OF KINTYRE'

LOVE it or loath it, 'Mull Of Kintyre' was Wings' bestselling single. It even outsold 'She Loves You', which had held the record as the bestselling single in Britain for 14 years.

Musically, the song is hardly typical of McCartney or Wings, but it does typify McCartney's fondness for romanticism. Using the drums and bagpipes of The Campbelltown Pipers, McCartney's Scottish ballad recalls the romantic idealism of Sir Edwin Landseer's *Monarch Of The Glen* or Burns' vernacular poetry.

Well aware that it would attract adverse criticism, McCartney at one point considered holding the single back. "I nearly didn't put it out – and that's a fact," he explained. "I knew old folks, Scottish people and The Campbelltown Pipers liked it ... but at that time it seemed that everything was punk. ... But you can't not release records because someone is gonna slag it ... you just go along with your instincts and hope that you're right." His gamble paid off: the record's anthemic qualities crossed boundaries of generation and taste. Punk may have given the finger to rock's elder statesmen, but the old-garde maintained its hegemony over the young pretenders, and sales of 'Mull Of Kintyre' were more than healthy.

A song about McCartney's fondness for the Scottish countryside, 'Mull Of Kintyre' was inspired by the rural setting he has enjoyed since buying a farm there in the mid 1960s. Speaking on Radio 1 to Mike Read, he said: "The thing about 'Mull Of Kintyre' was John had given me a sort of love of Scotland, and I'd eventually got a farm up there ... and I'd got to really like the place." Linda confirmed the McCartneys' love of the country. "Scotland was like nothing I'd ever lived in. It was the most beautiful land you have ever seen – it was way at the end of nowhere."

McCartney wanted to write about this part of Scotland, but also to write a song with a contemporary Scottish feel. "Being up there, I'd sort of heard some bagpipe music and stuff, it's very nice ... but it's all old," he said. "I couldn't relate to it and I thought, much as I like it, it would be nice if there was a sort of newer Scottish song. So I thought, 'Oh well, I'll try and write one.'" He began in 1974, completing it some time later with help from Denny Laine and Tony Wilson, Pipe Major with the Campbeltown Pipe Band, who instructed him about the keys in which bagpipes can play.

The finished song was recorded on the McCartneys' farm in the grandly named Spirit Of Ranachan Studios, a converted barn equipped with RAK's 24-track mobile studio. The backing track of guitars, snare drums, and bagpipes was recorded one August evening and remixed later in London. Jimmy McCulloch had by now quit the band and so doesn't feature, but Joe English does.

Although Wings had almost completed their forthcoming album, *London Town*, on return to Britain in the summer of 1977, McCulloch announced that he was leaving to join the reformed Small Faces (probably around early September). English left soon after that, joining Sea Level, a band fronted by piano player and session musician Chuck Leavell, and later putting together his own Christian rock group, The Joe English Band.

Although McCartney was reluctant to go into any great detail about the nature of Jimmy McCulloch's departure, it's obvious that relations between the two had become tense. "Jimmy leaving was a very complicated thing, but I think basically he didn't want to be committed to any group for too long a period when he joined," McCartney said. "Then he was offered the gig with The Small Faces, which he really fancied. We'd had what you might call one or two bad patches, and it seemed to make sense to call it quits."

The B-side, 'Girls' School', offered something a little less esoteric for those whose taste didn't run to bagpipes and Scottish ballads. McCartney chose it as the flip precisely because it represented the band's "more rocking side". He wrote it in the late summer of 1976, while on holiday in Hawaii, inspired by advertisements for pornographic films.

"I was looking through one of those American newspapers and the back page, at the end of the entertainment section, is always like the porno films," he said. "I rather liked the titles, so basically I took all the titles and made a song out of them. For example, there was a film called *School Mistress*, another called *Curly Haired*, one called *Kid Sister*, and another called *The Woman Trainer*, and I liked those titles so much I just wove them into a song."

'Girls' School' was recorded in February 1977 at Abbey Road and is a heads-down-no-nonsense-rocker; as such it was favoured by American DJs over the quaint 'Mull Of Kintyre'. Even so, 'Girls' School' was a relative flop there, managing only number 33 in the *Billboard* charts. (The edit of 'Girls' School', issued on demonstration copies of the single, later appeared as the bonus track on the first pressing of the *London Town* CD, and the remastered edition features the full-length version.)

'Mull Of Kintyre' data

Wings' most successful single, 'Mull Of Kintyre' / 'Girls' School' sold in millions around the world. It topped the charts in a number of countries, selling particularly well in Australia, where it became the country's biggest selling single, and Britain, where it sold over two and a half million copies. However, for some reason McCartney's Scottish-themed ballad didn't replicate its international success in the USA.

'Mull Of Kintyre' was issued with Capitol 'dome' labels and a picture sleeve. The single was issued with two label variations in America: black and silver Capitol 'dome' labels or 'purple' Capitol labels.

To promote the single, Capitol issued radio stations with edits of A and B-sides. American (SPRO-8746) and British (R 6018 [7YCE. 21798–DJ]) demonstration singles were issued with black and silver Capitol 'dome' labels.

The single was promoted with three different videos, each showing Paul, Linda, Denny, and The Campbelltown Pipers miming to the song, either in a studio or on location in and around the Mull of Kintyre. In addition, Wings appeared on *The Mike Yarwood Christmas Show* in a sketch with the comedian and miming to the song.

'WITH A LITTLE LUCK' / 'BACKWARDS TRAVELLER / CUFF LINK'
WINGS
UK RELEASE March 23 1978; Parlophone R 6019; chart high No.5.
US RELEASE March 20 1978; Capitol 4559; chart high No.1.

• **'With A Little Luck'** (McCartney)
Paul McCartney (bass, keyboards, vocals), Linda McCartney (keyboards, backing vocals), Denny Laine (guitar, backing vocal), Jimmy McCulloch (guitar, backing vocal), Joe English (drums). Mobile studio recording aboard motor-yacht Fair Carol.
• **'Backwards Traveller / Cuff Link'** (McCartney)
Paul McCartney (bass, guitar, keyboards, drums, vocals), Linda McCartney (backing vocals), Denny Laine (guitar, backing vocals).
Recorded at Abbey Road Studios and AIR Studios, London, England. Both produced by Paul McCartney.

'WITH A LITTLE LUCK'

McCARTNEY wrote 'With A Little Luck' on his farm in Scotland, and the song was recorded by Wings at Watermelon Bay in the Virgin Islands, aboard the yacht Fair Carol. The song remained unfinished until completed at Abbey Road in late autumn 1977, by which time Jimmy McCulloch and Joe English had left the group.

Relying on remarkably thin-sounding keyboards, the song's diluted, synthetic tone ironically echoes McCartney's equally weak lyric. McCartney's irritating optimism, both musically and lyrically, appears functional at best.

Regrettably, function over form summarises 'With A Little Luck', which lacks the unexpected melodic twists and turns that mark McCartney at his best. An over-reliance on synthetic instrumentation combined with a too-finely tuned sense of studio craftsmanship effectively negates any semblance of atmosphere or character.

Unfortunately, the more McCartney attempted to make his records sound effortless, the more they appeared suffused with artifice. Compounded by laborious overdubbing, which effectively distanced the band from any sense of performance and unity, 'With A Little Luck' is little more than writing by numbers and sadly predictable. It was a US Number 1.

'Backwards Traveller/Cuff Link' was recorded by Paul, Linda, and Denny Laine at Abbey Road in the last week of October 1977 and completed in January the following year. With McCulloch and English absent, McCartney played drums, bass, acoustic guitar, and keyboards. It's a medley of two songs: 'Backwards Traveller' is a typical McCartney pot-boiler and 'Cuff Link' an uninspired instrumental.

'With A Little Luck' data

The single was issued with customised 'London Town' labels, which were used for every release associated with the *London Town* album. To promote the single, an edit of the A-side – with the lengthy instrumental coda removed – was issued to radio stations. American copies of the demonstration single (PRO-8812) were issued with mono/stereo edits. British copies of the demonstration single were issued with the stereo edit on the A-side and the full-length version on the B-side (and the edit was later used for the *Wingspan* compilation album).

LONDON TOWN

AFTER the frenetic work schedule of the previous two years, McCartney decided to take a leisurely approach to recording Wings' next album, *London Town*. After completing their world tour in October 1976, the group took a three-month break; work on a new album beginning on February 7 1977 at Abbey Road. The sleevenotes suggest that sessions continued uninterrupted from early February until the end of March, but on February 20, Paul and Linda left Britain for Jamaica and a two-week holiday. Recording recommenced on their return before stopping again at the end of March. In early May, Wings moved to Watermelon Bay, Virgin Islands, where they recorded aboard the motor-yacht *Fair Carol*.

It was Denny Laine who hit on the idea of recording aboard a boat. He had lived on a houseboat, *Searchlight*, for a number of years, and a visit to a floating studio in Los Angeles confirmed the idea. Recording aboard a floating studio sounds idyllic, but the trip was not without incident. McCartney and Jimmy McCulloch suffered injuries to their knees, falling and cutting them badly, and sound engineer Geoff Emerick electrocuted his foot. McCulloch also managed to go deaf in one ear, which must have been something of a handicap when it came to recording.

If these minor irritations weren't enough, US Customs officials, searching for marijuana, raided the three yachts McCartney had hired for the trip. Although no action was taken against any member of Wings or the crew, they did receive an official warning.

During their four-week stay in the Virgin Islands, Wings recorded nine songs, seven of which found their way onto the finished album ('Waterspout' and Laine's 'Find A Way' did not make it). The group then returned to the UK, where, after another break, recording recommenced on October 25, probably to finish work on 'Mull Of Kintyre'. McCulloch and English had quit the band and Wings Mk.6 were now a three-piece comprising Paul, Linda, and Denny Laine. They spent five weeks at Abbey Road before switching to AIR, also in London, for 12 days in December, and then in January 1978 returned to Abbey Road for a further three weeks to finish the album.

LONDON TOWN
WINGS
SIDE 1 'London Town', 'Cafe On The Left Bank', 'I'm Carrying', 'Backwards Traveller', 'Cuff Link', 'Children Children', 'Girlfriend', 'I've Had Enough'.
SIDE 2 'With A Little Luck', 'Famous Groupies', 'Deliver Your Children', 'Name And Address', 'Don't Let It Bring You Down', 'Morse Moose And The Grey Goose'.
UK RELEASE March 31 1978; Parlophone PAS 10012; chart high No.4.
US RELEASE March 27 1978; LP Capitol SW-11777; 8-track cartridge Capitol 8XW-1177; chart high No.2.

• **'London Town'** (McCartney, Laine)
Paul McCartney (bass, keyboards, vocals), Linda McCartney (keyboards, backing vocals), Denny Laine (guitar, backing vocal), Jimmy McCulloch (guitar, backing vocal), Joe English (drums).
• **'Cafe On The Left Bank'** (McCartney)
Personnel as 'London Town'.
• **'I'm Carrying'** (McCartney)
Paul McCartney (guitar, Gizmo, vocals).
• **'Children Children'** (Laine, McCartney)
Paul McCartney (bass, guitar, keyboards, violin, autoharp, recorder, backing vocals), Linda McCartney (backing vocals), Denny Laine (guitar, recorder, vocals).
• **'Girlfriend'** (McCartney)
Paul McCartney (bass, guitar, keyboards, drums, vocals), Linda McCartney (backing vocals), Denny Laine (guitar, backing vocals).
• **'I've Had Enough'** (McCartney)
Personnel as 'London Town' except Jimmy McCulloch (guitar).
• **'Famous Groupies'** (McCartney)
Personnel as 'London Town' except Jimmy McCulloch (guitar).
• **'Deliver Your Children'** (Laine, McCartney)
Paul McCartney (bass, guitar, backing vocals), Linda McCartney (backing vocals), Denny Laine (guitar, vocals).
• **'Name And Address'** (McCartney)
Personnel as 'Deliver Your Children'.
• **'Don't Let It Bring You Down'** (McCartney, Laine)
Paul McCartney (bass, flageolet, vocals), Linda McCartney (backing vocals), Denny Laine (guitar, flageolet, backing vocal), Jimmy McCulloch (guitar), Joe English (drums).
• **Morse Moose And The Grey Goose** (McCartney, Laine)
Paul McCartney (bass, Mellotron, vocals), Linda McCartney (keyboards, backing vocals), Denny Laine (guitar, keyboards, backing vocal), Jimmy McCulloch (guitar), Joe English (drums).
All recorded on Mobile Studio aboard motor-yacht Fair Carol, Virgin Islands, and at AIR Studios, London, England, except: 'London Town' recorded at Abbey Road Studios, London; 'Children, Children', 'Girlfriend', 'Deliver Your Children, 'Name And Address' recorded at Abbey Road Studios and AIR Studios, London.
All produced by Paul McCartney.

London Town represents another defining moment – not because of musical excellence, but because during the 12 months in which the album was compiled, Wings returned once again to the McCartney–Laine–McCartney core. Although McCartney hoped that Wings would emulate the kind of democracy he'd experienced with The Beatles, the balancing act required to keep a group together became too much.

Speaking to the NME in 1978, he said: "From the very beginning, I never intended that Wings should be me, and [that] anyone would do to play back-up. But as to why there have been changes ... look, when you've been in bands, when you've been through all the hassles ... how can I put it? ... you reach a point where you realise you don't need a situation where, if someone is a brilliant player but just being around him gets to be obnoxious ... who needs it? I'm not saying that's the reason why we've had so many personnel changes in Wings, all I'm saying is that you've got to feel right together and enjoy one another's company."

Not for the first time, Wings were in trouble. When McCullough and Seiwell had left on the eve of recording a new album, Band On The Run, McCartney had appeared stoic at the loss of these musicians. This time, the guitarist and drummer left while recording was in progress, and the departure of McCulloch and English had a more profound effect. McCartney's dissatisfaction with the band was audible in the music he recorded.

London Town was a disappointment. Even McCartney recognised as much. Speaking immediately after its release, he said: "I'd like to make an adventurous album, and we're discussing the possibilities of doing just that, for the hell of it. No formula style ... I'd welcome the change ... [I] love having fun with the music instead of getting my head down and thinking along the lines of: I am Led Zeppelin and I've got to come out with something heavy because that's what they expect of me."

Despite his problems, McCartney still managed to record the band's most successful single ever, 'Mull Of Kintyre', and although London Town had its shortcomings, the album became Wings' most successful album since Band On The Run, with massive sales in Germany, Holland, Belgium, Italy, and Norway. An upfront hit single helped, as did an extensive promotional campaign.

'I'VE HAD ENOUGH' / 'DELIVER YOUR CHILDREN'
WINGS
UK RELEASE June 16 1978; Parlophone R 6020; chart high No.42.
US RELEASE June 5 1978; Capitol 4594; chart high No.25.

'I'VE HAD ENOUGH'
Parlophone issued 'I've Had Enough' with customised labels and a picture sleeve. Capitol issued the single with customised labels but without a picture sleeve, and issued a mono/stereo demonstration single (P-4595) with customised labels and a press release.

London Town songs

McCartney's jet-set lifestyle meant that many of the songs on *London Town* were written while he was on the road or on holiday. The album's opening track was written in November 1975 while Wings were in Perth, Australia completing the first leg of their world tour. Written with Denny Laine, 'London Town' was completed in Scotland between touring commitments. McCartney presents a romanticised view of London: part reportage and part fantasy, his description of the sprawling metropolis fuses idealisation with acute observations of everyday street life. Recorded with Wings Mk.5, it was one of the first songs completed for the album.

If 'London Town' was a well observed albeit idealised view of the nation's capital, 'Cafe On The Left Bank' was an equally pointed piece of observation about the English abroad. Recorded on the group's first day in Watermelon Bay, the song has more of a buzz to it than other songs recorded there, perhaps a consequence of it being recorded before the band slipped into holiday mode. One of the stronger tracks on the album, it's saved by McCulloch's robust playing.

'I'm Carrying' was recorded on May 5 aboard the *Fair Carol* and features McCartney playing acoustic guitar, double-tracked throughout. The string section was overdubbed in London, where McCartney also added an electric guitar part played with a Gizmo, a small handheld device for guitar that vibrates rather than plucks the strings, making for a sustained tone, which was combined with the orchestral strings. 'I'm Carrying' is a gentle ballad that restates much of what McCartney had expressed with 'Yesterday' – less adventurous melodically, but no less welcoming.

The first of two vocal contributions from Laine, 'Children Children' was inspired in part by a small waterfall in McCartney's garden. At the time of writing, Laine was missing his children and was "preoccupied by those kind of themes." Co-written with McCartney, 'Children Children' was originally titled 'Laine And Heidi' until McCartney suggested the new title, as he thought the original too sentimental. Recorded by the McCartney–Laine–McCartney line-up, it features McCartney and Laine on recorders and McCartney on violin.

'Girlfriend' is by far the most successful song on the album, thanks to Michael Jackson, and is an odd mix of soul ballad (chorus and verses) and pop song (middle eight and instrumental). Jackson would record the song for his multimillion selling *Off The Wall* album and suggested that it was written specifically for him. McCartney wrote 'Girlfriend' while on holiday in Switzerland and recorded a demo in November 1974, which would place it in circulation at the time the two stars met. But McCartney denies writing the song for Jackson. Nevertheless, on its release, McCartney wondered what the

'LONDON TOWN' / 'I'M CARRYING'
WINGS
UK release August 11 1978; Parlophone R 6021; chart high No.60.
US release August 14 1978; Capitol 4625; chart high No.39.

'LONDON TOWN'
Parlophone issued 'London Town' with customised labels and a plain sleeve. The Capitol issue matched the British release, but Capitol also issued a mono/stereo demonstration single (P-4625).

singer might make of it and made light-hearted references to it sounding like The Jackson Five, so the idea of having Jackson record it may have been on his mind for some time. However, it was only once Wings recorded 'Girlfriend' that Jackson, at the insistence of his producer, Quincy Jones, decided to attempt the song himself. One reason for it sounding like Jackson is McCartney's uncharacteristic falsetto, which is backed by equally high harmonies from Laine and Linda.

'I've Had Enough' was recorded by Wings Mk.5 in the Virgin Islands. Despite a half-decent riff and a snappy arrangement with dramatic stabs and accents, like much of the material on *London Town* it's not very effective. The song evolved from a jam session with McCartney improvising the chorus. "We recorded it on the boat ... but we still didn't have any words until we got back to London," he explained, "and then I wrote a few. I overdubbed the vocals in London, and it's just one of those 'fed-up' songs."

If Wings were recording in a holiday atmosphere, why was it that all McCartney could come up with was a chorus as negative as 'I've Had Enough'? Perhaps it reflects his attitude toward the band. Maybe relations within the group had already disintegrated, for it would appear that even when 'having fun' they were merely going through the motions.

'Famous Groupies' relates the tales of various fictitious musicians and roadies, not to mention groupies, and their exploits. McCartney wrote it in Scotland and recorded it in the Virgin Islands, and the song, originally an up-tempo rocker, was given a relaxed treatment that fits the album's generally pedestrian mood. McCartney could have drawn on a lifetime of experience to write this song and it could have been a real exposé of life on the road, yet he opted for a humorous fantasy narrative – perhaps to protect the innocent and his own squeaky-clean reputation. Another of McCartney's 'comedy' songs, 'Famous Groupies' fails to raise much of a laugh or to achieve much musically.

Denny Laine began writing 'Deliver Your Children' while Wings were recording *Venus And Mars*. McCartney helped complete the song, which was held over for *London Town*. Delivered up-tempo with a bright acoustic backing, its only weakness is a lyric that, although far from the worst on the album, tends to ramble from one theme to another.

'Name And Address' is a reworking of 1950s rock'n'roll and finds McCartney attempting to pay homage to the heroes of his youth. Like many musicians of his generation, he owed a huge debt to American rock'n'roll and Elvis Presley in particular. As he explained to Roy Carr, 'Name And Address' is "an Elvisy-type thing and not a screaming Little Richard-type track. It's held back". He wasn't wrong: 'Name And Address' is so held back it's almost comatose. This is rock'n'roll with its slippers on. It was recorded in London with McCartney on drums, bass, and lead guitar, and its only redeeming feature is its directness, which, in comparison with much of what appeared on the album, makes it sound surprisingly fresh.

McCartney's resolute optimism struck again in the form of 'Don't Let It Bring You Down', a mid-tempo ballad written over a two-year period. He started the song while on tour in Scotland in 1975. "I think we were in Aberdeen, sitting in our hotel bedroom, just before we were going to turn in for the night, and I had my 12-string guitar with me. I started plonking out a little tune and it became 'Don't Let It Bring You Down'."

The song's sanguine lyric is complimented by a pleasing see-saw melody that echoes the rise and fall of the fatalistic theme, which can be read as the musical equivalent of McCartney's apparent belief in eternal recurrence. McCartney and Laine added flageolets (Irish tin whistles), which alternate with McCulloch's warm fuzz-tone guitar. Combined, they suggest both a sense of place and an air of resigned fatalism.

While aboard the *Fair Carol*, McCartney and Laine began to experiment with an electric piano. McCartney played a series of unrelated notes that suggested Morse code while Laine occasionally gave the instrument a thump. This piece of atonal experimentation was recorded and formed the basis of 'Morse Moose And The Grey Goose'.

Using this as a 'bed', McCartney laid down a funky bass riff, while the rest of the band contributed a few dramatic stabs to add some much-needed verve. That's how the track remained until Wings returned to Britain. The song's countermelody, lyric, Mellotron, acoustic guitars, and vocals were added in London. 'Morse Moose And The Grey Goose' is a well developed jam that had a considerable amount of work done to it, nut it remains little more than a pot-boiler and is accordingly flimsy.

London Town data

The album was issued with customised labels, printed inner sleeve, and a large 33-inch by 23-inch double-sided poster – with Jimmy McCulloch and Joe English conspicuous by their absence. Capitol issued the album on 8-track (8XW 11777). EMI issued the album on CD (CD-FA 3223) on August 29 1989 and issued a remastered edition (CDPMCOL8) on July 7 1993. Capitol issued the CD (CDP 7 48198 2) on June 20 1989.

WINGS GREATEST
WINGS
SIDE 1 'Another Day', 'Silly Love Songs', 'Live And Let Die', 'Junior's Farm', 'With A Little Luck', 'Band On The Run'.
SIDE 2 'Uncle Albert/Admiral Halsey', 'Hi, Hi, Hi', 'Let 'Em In', 'My Love', 'Jet', 'Mull Of Kintyre'.
UK RELEASE December 1 1978; Parlophone PCTC 256; chart high No.3.
US RELEASE November 27 1978; LP Capitol SOO-11905; 8-track cartridge Capitol 8XOO-11905; chart high No.29.
For personnel, recording locations, and producer credits see original entries.

WINGS GREATEST

ALTHOUGH Wings had consistently fared better in America than in Britain, this first best-of sold better in the UK. Compiled with British and American markets in mind, *Wings Greatest* was little more than a pot-boiler that may have been produced to fulfil contractual agreements. McCartney had recently signed with Columbia in America and so may have owed EMI/Capitol an album before departing for his new label.

The sleeve was designed by Paul and Linda with assistance from Hipgnosis and was photographed at considerable expense by Angus Forbes. McCartney arranged for an art deco statuette to be flown to Switzerland and photographed on the Matterhorn – thus more money was spent on the cover of this record than some bands were spending on recording entire new albums.

The album was issued with customised labels (black, with the statuette top centre) and a 30-inch by 20-inch poster of Wings Mk.6. Capitol issued the album on 8-track cartridge (8XOO 11905). EMI issued the CD (CDP7460562) on February 4 1985 and Capitol on December 1 1986.

'GOODNIGHT TONIGHT'

McCARTNEY originally recorded 'Goodnight Tonight' as a solo project when sessions for *London Town* came to a close. It then sat on the shelf for almost a year, because he was unsure whether or not it would make a good single. Speaking to *Rolling Stone* just after its release, he said: "'Goodnight Tonight' was going to be the B-side and 'Daytime Nightime Suffering' was going to be the A-side. So we sat around for years – well, it seemed like years – discussing it, you know? The normal soul searching you go through. And we decided no, it isn't all right, we won't put it out. And about a week later, I played the record again. I thought, 'That's crazy, we've made it; it's stupid, why not put it out?' So we decided to do it."

Overdubbed during sessions for *Back To The Egg*, it was left off the album but became Wings' third bestselling single. A pop song pure and simple, 'Goodnight Tonight' had toes tapping, possessed an infectious chorus, and sounded great on the dance floor. Which is often all that's needed.

A favourite of McCartney's, 'Daytime Nightime Suffering' was recorded at Replica Studio, a copy of Abbey Road's Number Two studio situated in the basement of his MPL offices in Soho, London. The band were mixing *Back To The Egg* and due to finish for the week when McCartney challenged everyone to write a song over the weekend, the best to be recorded for possible inclusion on the album.

New drummer Steve Holly recalled: "So we all went off and we individually wrote songs. I can't remember quite what it was that I did. I did do a couple of tunes. And, of course, we played our songs, our best efforts from the weekend, one after the other. And then Paul said, 'Well, I wrote this,' and played 'Daytime Nightime Suffering'. Well, it's easy to see who won the competition."

The song features some sensational vocal harmonies and one of the best lead vocals that McCartney had delivered in some time. Its uncluttered arrangement and meticulous production (remixed 49 times before McCartney was satisfied) benefits one of his strongest B-sides.

Like Sandy Povey's 'Born A Woman', Helen Reddy's 'I Am Woman', or even John Lennon's 'Woman Is The Nigger Of The World', 'Daytime Nightime Suffering' was meant as a celebration

'GOODNIGHT TONIGHT' / 'DAYTIME NIGHTIME SUFFERING'
WINGS
UK RELEASE March 23 1979; Parlophone R 6023; 12-inch Parlophone 12Y R 6023; chart high No.5.
US RELEASE March 19 1979; Columbia 3-10939; 12-inch Columbia 23-10940; chart high No.5.

• **'Goodnight Tonight'** (McCartney)
Paul McCartney (bass, drums, keyboards, vocals), Linda McCartney (keyboards, backing vocals), Denny Laine (guitar, backing vocals), Laurence Juber (guitar, backing vocals), Steve Holly (percussion).
Recorded at Abbey Road Studios and Replica Studio, London, England. Produced by Paul McCartney.
• **'Daytime Nightime Suffering'** (McCartney)
Paul McCartney (bass, keyboards, vocals), Linda McCartney (keyboards, backing vocals), Denny Laine (guitar, backing vocals), Laurence Juber (guitar, backing vocals), Steve Holly (drums).
Recorded at Replica Studio and Abbey Road.
Produced by Paul McCartney and Chris Thomas.

of womanhood. "[That's] a pro-women song," McCartney recalled. "'What does she get for all of this?' Daytime nightime suffering. It's like the plight of women." Whatever its merits as a piece of pro-feminist dogma, it's a fine pop song, and sometimes that's all that matters.

Goodnight Tonight data

This was the first Wings single to be issued in Britain with generic Parlophone labels and was also their first UK 12-inch single. The 7-inch was issued with a plain sleeve; the 12-inch with a 1950s-style inner sleeve and laminated picture cover. In the USA, Columbia followed the British release, issuing both 7 and 12-inch singles with generic labels, the 12-inch with either a picture or generic sleeve. Columbia issued a mono demonstration 7-inch single (3-10939) with white labels with black text and the large Columbia logo in red, top centre. They also issued a demonstration 12-inch (23-10940) with white labels with black text, with the long and short stereo mixes on either side of the disc. In 1980, Columbia reissued 'Goodnight Tonight' (13-33405) with 'Getting Closer' on their Hall Of Fame imprint.

'OLD SIAM SIR' / 'SPIN IT ON'
WINGS
UK release June 1 1979; Parlophone R 6026; chart high No.35.

- **'Old Siam Sir'** (McCartney)
- **'Spin It On'** (McCartney)

Both with Paul McCartney (bass, keyboards, vocals), Linda McCartney (keyboards, backing vocals), Denny Laine (guitar, backing vocals), Laurence Juber (guitar), Steve Holly (drums). Both recorded on RAK Mobile Studio at Spirit of Ranachan Studio, Scotland.
Both produced by Paul McCartney and Chris Thomas.

'OLD SIAM SIR'

WHILE 'Goodnight Tonight' had explored the contemporary fascination with dance music, 'Old Siam Sir' / 'Spin It On' offered gritty slices of abrasive ROCK. With punk and new wave in ascendance, McCartney responded with some of the rawest material he'd recorded in years.

His musical tastes have always been eclectic, and as he told *Musician* magazine immediately after the release of *Back To The Egg*, it ranged from "Fred Astaire to The Sex Pistols". For McCartney, punk/new wave marked a return to the kind of musical primitivism expressed by rock'n'roll's originators. "The nice thing about new wave is that its got back to real music, rather than pop," he said.

McCartney had of course spent much of the 1970s exploring his pop sensibilities and distancing himself from 'real music'. One could argue that he'd been responsible for many of the worst excesses committed in the name of pop and epitomised many of the values that punk now railed against. But Wings' new sound wasn't a rejection of one style in favour of another, or a desperate attempt to appear to be in touch with the kids; rather, it combined pop sensibilities with a new-wave rush.

Linda developed the riff for 'Old Siam Sir' while rehearsing, and McCartney and Laine completed it later. McCartney added a lyric about a girl returning to Britain from Siam before recording a solo demo, titled 'Super Big Heatwave', at Rude Studio (a permanent well-appointed 4-track demo studio that McCartney installed at his Scottish farm in the early 1970s). Much of the lyric was improvised, but he decided to keep his nonsense verse for no other reason than because it "kinda stuck".

Never one to over-analyse his writing, McCartney often prefers to leave his original ideas virtually unchanged. It's not clear if this is due to laziness or superstition – he may be afraid of loosing the 'magic' that he believes is somehow bound to the songwriting process – but it too often leads to the release of substandard material. With a little more attention, 'Old Siam Sir' might have been saved. Yet despite Paul, Linda, and Denny having a hand in its writing, it remains little more than gritty but uninspired.

Another rocker, 'Spin It On' was recorded in one day, July 23 1978, and was the last song recorded during the *Back To The Egg* sessions held at McCartney's Scottish farm.

'Old Siam Sir' data

Parlophone issued 'Old Siam Sir' / 'Spin It On' with customised 'egg' labels and custom die-cut sleeve. Demo copies have 'DEMO RECORD NOT FOR SALE' on three lines above the spindle hole and a large 'A' below the spindle hole.

'GETTING CLOSER'

McCARTNEY began writing 'Getting Closer' in 1974 and recorded a piano-based demo with an unfinished middle-eight some time that year. Dropping the middle-eight and increasing the tempo, Wings transformed the song into an energetic rocker. The band recorded the basic track, with Laine and McCartney sharing lead vocals, at Abbey Road in October 1978. Influenced by the previous week's recording session with Rockestra, McCartney overdubbed numerous guitar parts to create a dense sonic aura. The song was completed at Replica Studio in March 1979 with keyboard overdubs and an edit.

'GETTING CLOSER' / 'SPIN IT ON'
WINGS
US RELEASE June 11 1979; Columbia 3-11020; chart high No.20.

- **'Getting Closer' (McCartney)**
Paul McCartney (bass, keyboards, vocals), Linda McCartney (keyboards, backing vocals), Denny Laine (guitar, backing vocals), Laurence Juber (guitar), Steve Holly (drums). Recorded at Abbey Road Studios, London, England. Produced by Paul McCartney and Chris Thomas.

'Getting Closer' data

Issued in the USA, Europe, and Japan in favour of 'Old Siam Sir', 'Getting Closer' performed better in America than its British counterpart. Issued with a die-cut sleeve and customised 'egg' labels similar to those used for the British release of 'Old Siam Sir', the single was also issued by Columbia with generic labels and black paper sleeve. Columbia issued a mono/stereo demonstration single with white labels with black text, and the large Columbia logo in red, top centre of the label. Columbia reissued 'Getting Closer' (13-33405) on their Hall Of Fame imprint, backed with 'Goodnight Tonight'.

BACK TO THE EGG

WINGS' seventh studio album was the first by the Mk.7 line-up (Paul, Linda, and Denny Laine, with the addition of Laurence Juber and Steve Holly). It would also turn out to be the last Wings album. With the departure of McCulloch and English in the summer of 1977, the group had again returned to its core line-up of McCartney–Laine–McCartney. Once *London Town* was completed, the search for a new drummer and guitarist began, but this time McCartney decided to recruit through friends of friends rather than advertise in the music press. Both of the new boys came through Denny Laine.

Laine met Steve Holly when he moved to the drummer's home village. Holly's audition took place in the basement of McCartney's London office, and he didn't have to wait long to discover if he had the job. "We played for about two or three hours," Holly recalled, "and Paul suddenly said, 'Fine. That's a good group: sounds great, let's go for it.'" His first job with Wings was filming the promotional video for 'With A Little Luck' on March 21 1978. Laurence Juber had previously appeared with Laine on *The David Essex Show* and had so impressed Laine with his playing that he got the job as Wings' lead guitarist.

With the new line-up assembled, rehearsals and recording sessions were arranged for the group's next album. As Linda had just given birth to the McCartneys' first son, exotic recording locations were rejected in favour of more modest surroundings nearer to home. Sessions began on the McCartneys' Scottish farm at the makeshift Spirit Of Ranachan studio on June 29 1978 and lasted for five weeks, until July 27. This remote location gave the album the working title *Wings In The Wild*, later dropped in favour of *We're Open Tonight*, before McCartney finally settled on *Back To The Egg*.

After a summer break, sessions resumed at Lympne (pronounced Lim) castle in Kent, from September 11–29 1978. Wings then moved to Abbey Road and the recently constructed Replica Studio to complete the album. The stereo master was finished on April 1 1979.

Speaking to the *NME* about the last record, *London Town*, McCartney had already hinted at a return to a harsher sound. "We didn't seem to be writing any real hard rockers," he explained. "Next time round well go for a bit more sweat." *Back To The Egg* was a lot more sweaty than its predecessor and found McCartney disavowing some of his more superficial pop sensibilities. But it also mirrored what he was listening to at the time. "The new wave thing was just happening," he recalled, "and I just realised that a lot of new wave was ... taking things at a faster tempo than we do. 'We' being what I call the Permanent Wave. So you get something like 'Spin It On' out of that."

Back To The Egg generated several related projects. As Wings were not planning to tour until the end of the year, and then only in Britain, McCartney commissioned Keff and Co to produce seven videos to promote the album. Filmed in and around Lympne Castle, they were designed to be shown individually or as a half-hour film (which was how they appeared when screened by the BBC). McCartney said that another major film project was in pre-production. MPL commissioned Willy Russell, author of the stage play *John, Paul, George, Ringo And Bert*, to write a film script for Wings. The film was tentatively titled *Band On The Run* and would have featured plenty of live footage as well as some form of narrative, but it never got past the planning stages.

As with previous albums, there were a number of outtakes. Superfluous songs by Laine and Juber eventually surfaced on solo albums, but most of McCartney's outtakes remain locked in the archives. While at Lympne, he wrote and recorded 'Robbers Ball', allegedly in one day, and completed another song, 'Cage'. Wings recorded an instrumental, 'Ranachan Rock', but this too failed to make the album. Many albums generate outtakes, but few recording projects generate a complete album of unreleased songs. That is, however, what happened with *Back To The Egg*. While recording at Spirit Of Ranachan, Wings recorded 12 songs in one day for a proposed Rupert The Bear film soundtrack. (They were 'Rupert Song 1', 'Tippi Tippi Toes', 'Flying Horses', 'When The Wind Is Blowing', 'The Castle Of The King Of The

Birds', 'Sunshine Sometime', 'Sea – Cornish Water', 'Storm', 'Nutwood Scene', 'Walking In The Meadow', 'Sea Melody', and 'Rupert Song 2'. 'Sunshine Sometime' and 'When The Wind Is Blowing' both date from late 1970. 'Sea Melody' was later adapted for *Standing Stone*. These demo recordings were scrapped when McCartney abandoned the idea of a feature-length film and began work on the less ambitious *Rupert And The Frog Song* animated short.)

After completing *Back To The Egg*, Wings took a summer break before returning to work in the autumn. Rehearsals were held for a short British tour, which took place during November and December 1979. The band were booked into small theatres rather than large stadiums – the largest date on the tour was the 10,000 capacity Wembley Arena. McCartney explained that he chose to play smaller venues to create a "feeling of togetherness as a group that you get from playing in front of an audience". The final night of the tour was officially Glasgow on December 17, but Wings made their last live appearance at the Hammersmith Odeon on December 29. UN Secretary General Waldheim approached McCartney and asked if Wings could give a charity concert for the war-ravaged people of Kampuchea (Cambodia). This developed into a series of concerts at the Hammersmith Odeon that included The Who, Queen, and The Clash as headliners. A great deal of speculation surrounded what turned out to be Wings' final concert: rumours circulated that McCartney might just be joined by the other ex-Beatles, but needless to say the proposed reunion didn't happen.

However, McCartney surprised the audience by performing an encore with most of the Rockestra line-up, which was augmented with several performers who'd supported Wings earlier that evening. Although history would record this as Wings' final live appearance, the band was far from finished. A concert tour of Japan was planned for January 1980, as well as proposed dates in China. However, a certain incident in Japan upset Wings' touring plans, and the band remained dormant during most of 1980. In October of that year, the group recorded more overdubs for McCartney's long-standing *Cold Cuts* album and commenced rehearsals for a proposed European tour and their next album, *Tug Of War*. (He began compiling *Hot Hits And Kold Kuts*, as it was originally titled, in the mid 1970s. Originally planned as a two-record set – hits on one disc, outtakes on the other – it was shelved in the early 1980s. Several songs intended for the *Cold Cuts* album were later issued as B-sides.)

Back To The Egg songs

'Reception' is the first of two short instrumentals recorded during Wings' residency at Lympne Castle. An early version of 2:32 duration had the main motif from *The Broadcast* superimposed over Wings' funky backing. Although McCartney probably intended to create a sense of incongruity, the result was ultimately messy.

Edited considerably for the album, 'Reception' remains little more than a doodle. McCartney's bass riff establishes a groove over which he places a random radio-scan and recitation by Mrs Margary (the early version had featured additional spoken passages from both Mr and Mrs Margary, owners of Lympne). The use of a radio as a chance generating mechanism was used by John Cage for his musique concrète experiments and appropriated by The Beatles for Lennon's 'I Am The Walrus', but here it's employed more for effect than for intellectual reasons.

McCartney had microphones set up on a spiral staircase at Lympne Castle for the recording of 'We're Open Tonight'. It's a simple ballad with a brittle acoustic guitar motif, and at one point its title was considered as a possible album title, but as with other ideas it was rejected.

Like many of the songs recorded at Spirit Of Ranachan, Laine's 'Again And Again And Again' was cut live, with guitar overdubs added later. Originally Laine had two separate songs, 'Little Woman' and 'Again And Again And Again' but combined them at McCartney's suggestion. It's a competent but uninspired Laine composition, and one of the weaker songs on the album.

'Arrow Through Me' finds McCartney bemoaning the pain of rejection and, uncharacteristically, casting himself as the loser. Even if his pessimistic lyric was autobiographical, his disappointment was masked by a buoyant melody. If this is a confession – and there's little to indicate a declaration of guilt and no attempt to match melody with narrative – then it's one scored through with ambivalence.

It's essentially a solo recording by McCartney with Holly on drums, and the basic track was recorded in Scotland, completed with overdubs at Replica Studios, London, in October 1978. At one point, it was given a saxophone solo, but this was deleted from the released version.

For 'Rockestra Theme', recorded at Abbey Road on October 3 1978, McCartney assembled some of Britain's finest musicians. Although almost everyone who'd been invited turned up, several of his musician friends failed to appear. Sadly, Keith Moon died the week before the session took place. Eric Clapton was invited but didn't arrive because, McCartney explained, "he didn't feel like it". Jeff Beck failed to show because he wanted to veto the track if he didn't like the way it turned out. Jimmy Page was also invited to the session, but he too failed to turn up. Laurence Juber recalled: "Jimmy Page never showed up. His amplifier was there but he never came. John Paul Jones is on the record and John Bonham. No Jimmy Page." However, it was Clapton and Beck's loss, and McCartney took the view that whoever showed up would be the Rockestra. The only musician to play on the session who wasn't part of the rock establishment was Bruce Thomas, bassist with Elvis Costello & The Attractions. McCartney admired the group: he invited them to support Wings at the Hammersmith Odeon in December 1979 and eventually co-wrote several songs with their vocalist and songwriter, Elvis Costello.

Before recording began, McCartney played the assembled musicians a demo of 'Rockestra Theme', recorded by Wings at Lympne Castle. He then spent about an hour rehearsing the group before tapes rolled at around 2 o'clock. When recording did begin, everything came together remarkably quickly. "It's amazing how tightly they all played together," McCartney said. "With people like Pete Townshend, Gary Brooker, Hank Marvin, Ronnie Lane, Ray Cooper, and Dave Gilmour, you would have expected a rougher, less controlled sound. But it didn't turn out that way. When you get 14 rock musicians together for the first time, they can be incredibly tight."

The secret to the piece's success was its simplicity. An over-elaborate arrangement would have detracted from the sheer power of the assembled group, whose sole purpose was to act as a whole rather than soloists. 'Rockestra Theme' was written as an ensemble piece, not to indulge the egos of those invited to take part. And this unity was reflected in the speed with which the ad-hoc group recorded the track. Only five takes were required before McCartney was satisfied that he had the track in the bag.

The event was filmed, which added to the technical problems involved in recording so many musicians at one time. In addition to a film crew and all of their equipment, which was hidden behind specially constructed false walls, the recording used 64 microphones and two synchronised tape recorders. McCartney got the Rockestra line-up to make one live appearance, too, which was also filmed and recorded as part of the Concerts For Kampuchea. (McCartney also produced a version of 'Rockestra Theme' for Duane Eddy's 1987 comeback album.)

With band, equipment, and the RAK mobile studio installed on McCartney's Scottish farm, recording commenced with an abrasive mid-tempo rocker, 'To You'. It was perhaps no surprise that McCartney, always perceptive to change, should react to current musical trends and produce a harsher, denser sound. When interviewed by Paul Gambaccini for *Rolling Stone* in 1979, he admitted to liking Supertramp's 'Logical Song' and Stevie Wonder, but also to liking "a few of the young bands ... I like Squeeze, Jam, and a few people. ... I like some of Elvis Costello's stuff. I like a lot of that stuff, anyway – the newer stuff."

The more musical of Britain's new wave groups shared with McCartney a common approach to melody, albeit one aligned with a rambunctious attitude to performance. While it's not surprising that he liked Squeeze or Costello, both of whom knew a good melody when they heard one, his admitting to liking Peter & The Test Tube Babies' 'Lord Lucan Is Missing' is more surprising. The corrosive bile that these fiercely independent bands spat into a jaded British music industry inevitably left its mark and affected McCartney's approach to *Back To The Egg*.

Recording 'To You' was a simple enough affair: the basic backing track was laid down on the first day's recording; vocal harmonies and Juber's guitar solo were overdubbed the following day.

'After The Ball' is downbeat and tentative, and finds McCartney contemplating the unknown and searching for security in the familiar – which means Linda. Firmly rooted in apprehension, its funereal cadence and sober melody offer little hope of redemption, particularly as the song remains unresolved; it segues with the equally thoughtful 'Million Miles'. Nevertheless, there is some light at the end of the tunnel – but is this an elegy for a loss of self-belief, or a paean to hope?

McCartney began 'Million Miles' in 1974 but was unable to complete it satisfactorily. To solve the problem, he made that segue with 'After The Ball', another incomplete song. It's essentially a solo track, and for the recording McCartney had a microphone set up on the roof of Lympne Castle and accompanied himself with some rudimentary concertina. 'Million Miles' consists of simple chords and a plaintive lyric; it hints at anticipation and attempts to conclude the questions raised in 'After The Ball', but McCartney's enquires into the human condition are eternal and as such unanswerable.

He wrote 'Winter Rose' in late 1976 or early 1977, recording it as a solo demo prior to completing *London Town* Wings then recorded the song, complete with an extended introduction, at Spirit of Ranachan, with McCartney on piano and harpsichord, and Laine and Juber on acoustic guitars. Its acoustic setting and sensitive arrangement evokes a dark, claustrophobic atmosphere that is contrasted with the optimistic lyric. The rose has often been employed as a metaphor for beauty and femininity; here it could symbolise Linda and the enchantment McCartney found in her radiant personality.

'Winter Rose' segues with 'Love Awake'. Wings recorded a version of it during sessions for *Back To The Egg* at the Scottish farm in July 1979. Described by Mark Vigars – the album's engineer – as a "rough guide version", it was little more than a rambling demo. Featuring a distinct harmonica part, this demo recording lasted 6:30. Re-recorded while Wings were encamped at Lympne Castle, the song's arrangement originally featured a slide guitar part, but this was scrapped when The Black Dyke Mills Band overdubbed a brass part at Abbey Road. Once the brass was in place, McCartney replaced his guide vocal to complete the recording.

'The Broadcast' was originally a brief acoustic-guitar instrumental, which McCartney recorded in 1977. Recorded at Lympne Castle by Wings, with McCartney on piano, it featured a vocal contribution from the castle's owner, Mr Margary. McCartney coaxed Mr Margary into reciting extracts from works by John Galsworthy and Ian Hay, while his wife appears on 'Reception', briefly reciting an extract from *The Poodle and the Pug* by A. P. Herbert. How these literary works were chosen, or whether they have any significance, has never been divulged. However, knowing McCartney's preoccupation

BACK TO THE EGG
WINGS
SIDE 1 'Reception', 'Getting Closer', 'We're Open Tonight', 'Spin It On', 'Again And Again And Again', 'Old Siam Sir', 'Arrow Through Me'.
SIDE 2 'Rockestra Theme', 'After The Ball', 'Million Miles', 'Winter Rose', 'Love Awake', 'The Broadcast', 'So Glad To See You Here', 'Baby's Request'.
UK RELEASE June 8 1979; Parlophone PCTC 257; chart high No.4.
US RELEASE June 11 1979; LP Columbia FC-36057; 8-track cartridge Columbia FCA-36057; chart high No.8.

• **'Reception'** (McCartney)
Paul McCartney (bass, keyboards), Linda McCartney (keyboards), Denny Laine (guitar), Laurence Juber (guitar), Steve Holly (drums), Mrs Margary (recitation).
Mobile Studio recording at Lympne Castle, Hythe, Kent, England.
• **'We're Open Tonight'** (McCartney)
Paul McCartney (guitar, vocals), Laurence Juber (12-string guitar).
Mobile Studio recording at Lympne Castle.
• **'Again And Again And Again'** (Laine)
Paul McCartney (bass, keyboards, backing vocals), Linda McCartney (keyboards, backing vocals), Denny Laine (guitar, vocals), Laurence Juber (guitar), Steve Holly (drums).
Recorded on RAK Mobile Studio at Spirit Of Ranachan Studio, Scotland.
• **'Arrow Through Me'** (McCartney)
Paul McCartney (bass, Moog, Fender Rhodes electric piano, Clavinet, vocals), Linda McCartney (backing vocals), Steve Holly (drums).
Recorded at Spirit Of Ranachan Studio, and at Replica Studio, London, England.
• **'Rockestra Theme'** (McCartney)
Paul McCartney (piano, keyboards), Denny Laine (guitar), Laurence Juber (guitar), Dave Gilmour (guitar), Hank Marvin (guitar), Pete Townshend (guitar), Steve Holly (drums), John Bonham (drums), Kenny Jones (drums), John Paul Jones (bass, piano), Ronnie Lane (bass), Bruce Thomas (bass), Gary Brooker (piano), John Paul Jones (piano), Linda McCartney (keyboards), Tony Ashton (keyboards), Speedy Acquaye, Tony Carr, Ray Cooper, Morris Pert (percussion), Howie Casey (saxophone), Tony Dorsey (trombone), Steve Howard (trumpet), Thaddeus Richard (saxophone).
Recorded at Abbey Road Studios, London, England.
• **'To You' (McCartney)**
Paul McCartney (bass, keyboards, vocals), Linda McCartney (keyboards, backing vocals), Denny Laine (guitar, backing vocals), Laurence Juber (guitar), Steve Holly (drums).
Recorded at Spirit Of Ranachan Studio.
• **'After The Ball'** (McCartney)
Paul McCartney (piano, vocals) Linda McCartney (keyboards, backing vocals), Denny Laine (guitar, backing vocals), Laurence Juber (guitar), Steve Holly (drums).
Mobile Studio recording at Lympne Castle.
• **'Million Miles'** (McCartney)
Paul McCartney (concertina, vocals).
Mobile Studio recording at Lympne Castle.
• **'Winter Rose'** (McCartney)
Paul McCartney (piano, harpsichord, bass, vocals), Linda McCartney (backing vocals), Denny Laine (guitar, backing vocals), Laurence Juber (guitar), Steve Holly (drums).
Recorded at Spirit Of Ranachan Studio.
• **'Love Awake'** (McCartney)
Paul McCartney (guitar, vocals), Linda McCartney (organ, backing vocals), Denny Laine (guitar, backing vocals), Laurence Juber (guitar), Steve Holly (drums), The Black Dyke Mills Band (horns).
Mobile Studio recording at Lympne Castle, and at Abbey Road.
• **'The Broadcast'** (McCartney)
Paul McCartney (piano), Mr Margary (recitation).
Mobile Studio recording at Lympne Castle.
• **'So Glad To See You Here'** (McCartney)
Personnel as 'Rockestra Theme'.
Recorded at Abbey Road.
• **'Baby's Request'** (McCartney)
Paul McCartney (bass, piano, vocals), Linda McCartney (keyboards, backing vocals), Denny Laine (guitar), Laurence Juber (guitar), Steve Holly (drums).
Recorded at Abbey Road.
All produced by Paul McCartney and Chris Thomas.

with chance, they were probably chosen at random from the castle's library, and any analysis of their content is most likely pointless.

'So Glad To See You Here' was recorded about an hour after completing 'Rockestra Theme'. Again, the backing track was recorded live, with McCartney supplying a rough guide vocal, which he replaced the following day. At the same overdub session, Linda and Laine added their harmonies. The reggae-influenced coda, which incorporates the opening line from 'We're Open Tonight', was added later by Wings.

McCartney wrote 'Baby's Request' in France, and it was originally intended as a demo for the old vocal group The Mills Brothers. At first, McCartney thought the song corny, but was swayed into recording it by his children. Considering that Wings had recorded the 'Rockestra Theme' the previous week, if nothing else 'Baby's Request' was a testament to the band's versatility. McCartney delivers a convincing vocal and Juber, who had been a member of the National Youth Jazz Orchestra, supplies some authentic jazz phrasing that captures a certain period feel. Although not intended for *Back To The Egg*, it replaced 'Cage', recorded at Lympne and originally destined for the album.

Back To The Egg data

Although sales of the album were initially strong, they were not sustained, and *Back To The Egg* spent only eight weeks in the British charts, the shortest chart run by any Wings album.

Publicity and promotion generated two very collectable items. A boxed-set was produced containing a copy of the album, a set of tea cards, an egg-shaped badge, key-ring, promotional photographs, and a T-shirt.

EMI also pressed 100 copies of a picture-disc version of *Back To The Egg* (PCTCP 257) that featured the front cover artwork on both sides. Other items, such as an egg-shaped jigsaw puzzle and lavish in-store displays, were employed to help promote the album.

'GETTING CLOSER'

PARLOPHONE issued Wings' final British single, 'Getting Closer' / 'Baby's Request', with customised 'egg' labels in a picture sleeve, bought off-the-shelf from Hipgnosis. Demo copies are identical to the commercial release except they have 'DEMO RECORD NOT FOR SALE' in black text printed above the spindle hole.

'ARROW THROUGH ME'

COLUMBIA issued 'Arrow Through Me' / 'Old Siam Sir' as Wings' final US single. It was issued with generic Columbia labels and paper sleeve. A Top 30 hit in America, it did even better in Canada where it peaked at Number 6.

Demonstration copies of the A-side were issued with white labels featuring black text and the large red Columbia logo positioned top centre of the label. The single was issued in Japan by Odeon (EPR-20657).

'GETTING CLOSER' / 'BABY'S REQUEST'
WINGS
UK RELEASE August 10 1979; Parlophone 6027; chart high No.60.

'ARROW THROUGH ME' / 'OLD SIAM SIR'
WINGS
US RELEASE August 13 1979; Columbia 3-11070; chart high No.29.

'SEASIDE WOMAN' / 'B SIDE TO SEASIDE'
SUZY AND THE RED STRIPES
UK RELEASE August 10 1979; A&M AMS 7461; 7-inch boxed set A&M AMSP 7461; failed to chart.
US RELEASE May 31 1977; Epic 8-50403; chart high No.59.

- **'Seaside Woman'** (Linda McCartney)
Linda McCartney (keyboards, vocals), Paul McCartney (bass), Denny Laine (guitar), Henry McCulloch (guitar), Denny Seiwell (drums).
Recorded at AIR Studios, London, England.
- **'B Side To Seaside'** (McCartney)
Linda McCartney (vocals), Paul McCartney (bass, drums, guitar, keyboards).
Recorded at Abbey Road Studios, London, England.
Both produced by Paul McCartney.

'SEASIDE WOMAN'

THIS single had been available in the UK as an American import for several years, but this was its first British release – and it wouldn't be the last. There are suggestions that it was recorded in demo form as early as 1970, but it's more likely that Linda wrote the song some time in 1971 in response to Sir Lew Grade's ATV lawsuit. Linda: "I did ... 'Seaside Woman' right after we'd been to Jamaica ... very reggae-inspired. That's when ATV was suing us, saying I was incapable of writing, so Paul said, 'Get out there and write a song.'" Although it was influenced by reggae, McCartney, like John Lennon, found it hard to get white musicians to play with any empathy for the music. One has only to compare Wings' attempt at reggae with the two songs cut by Lee 'Scratch' Perry for Linda in the summer of 1977 to realise that they were incapable of playing like their Jamaican contemporaries. (The Perry cuts were 'Mr Sandman' and 'Sugartime', later modified, and released on the posthumous Linda collection *Wide Prairie* in 1998).

Like previous side-projects, the 'Seaside Woman' single was issued using a pseudonym. Linda explained: "When we were in Jamaica, there had been a fantastic reggae version of 'Suzi Q', so they used to call me Suzi. And the beer in Jamaica is called Red Stripe, so that makes it Suzi and the Red Stripes." By the mid 1970s, McCartney had the idea of recording an album's worth of material in New York using the Suzy And The Red Stripes pseudonym. What exactly he had in mind is unclear, and the proposed project never materialised.

'Seaside Woman' was also used as the basis for an animated film, which Linda commissioned from Oscar Grillo. This was a tremendous success, playing in support of the Peter Sellers film *Being There*, and it won the Palme d'Or at Cannes.

McCartney wrote the aptly named 'B Side To Seaside' in Africa in 1973 but did not record it until March 1977. He played all the instruments and Linda sang lead and backing vocals.

'Seaside Woman' data

In Britain, A&M issued a yellow vinyl edition of the single with customised red and yellow labels in a glossy sleeve with red and white diagonal stripes, with the title top centre and the artist's name bottom right. The single was also released in a presentation 10-inch by 8-inch box that included 'saucy' seaside postcards and a badge. A&M issued a demonstration single on black vinyl with generic labels and paper sleeve.

In the USA, Epic issued a mono/stereo 7-inch demonstration single (8-50403) on red or black vinyl. They also issued a black vinyl 12-inch demonstration single (XSS 163108). Commercial copies of the Epic release were issued on 7-inch black vinyl with genetic Epic labels and paper sleeve.

'WONDERFUL CHRISTMASTIME' / 'RUDOLPH THE RED NOSE REGGAE'
PAUL McCARTNEY
UK RELEASE November 16 1979; Parlophone R 6029; chart high No.6.
US RELEASE November 26 1979; Columbia 3-11162; chart high No.8.

- **'Wonderful Christmastime'** (McCartney)
Paul McCartney (bass, guitar, keyboards, drums, percussion, vocals).
Recorded at home studio, Peasmarsh, Sussex or The Barn, High Park Farm, Scotland.
- **'Rudolph The Red Nose Reggae'** (Marks)
Paul McCartney (harpsichord, drums) Bob Loveday (violin).
Recorded at Abbey Road Studios, London, England.
Both produced by Paul McCartney

'WONDERFUL CHRISTMASTIME'

McCARTNEY'S attempt at a Christmas hit was, like most Christmas singles, recorded in the summer. It was made while he worked on *McCartney II* and became his first solo single since 'The Back Seat Of My Car', marking the beginning of the end for Wings.

'Wonderful Christmastime' may have had a seasonal theme but it lacks the joie de vivre of Slade's 'Merry Christmas Everybody' or the seasonal good cheer of Roy Wood's 'I Wish It Could Be Christmas Everyday', not to mention the universality of John Lennon's 'Happy Xmas (War Is Over)'.

McCartney's attempt at capturing the essence of Christmas is a letdown. Lightweight in the extreme, it's the kind of off-hand ditty that might have graced one of The Beatles' latter Christmas records. Despite this, it did rather well and sold better than any of the singles taken from *Back To The Egg*.

Released to coincide with Wings' British tour, which no doubt helped – it was performed nightly in front of packed houses – the single made its way deep into the Top 10 on both sides of the Atlantic. The song also became something of a favourite with compilers of Christmas albums, in particular EMI's perennial British *Now That's What I Call Christmas*, on which it appeared a number of times.

If the A-side was trite, the B-side was doubly so. The solo instrumental reading of 'Rudolph The Red Nosed Reindeer' was recorded in 1975 and dusted off for this B-side. Bob Loveday, who just happened to be delivering a violin to the studio, also plays. Even with a subtle change to the title, the arrangement is as far from reggae as you can get. This remains, perhaps, the nadir of McCartney's career.

'Wonderful Christmastime' data

Parlophone issued the single with generic labels and picture sleeve. Parlophone demonstration copies replicate the commercial pressing but with 'DEMO NOT FOR SALE' in three lines above the spindle hole.

The Columbia issue also came with generic labels, and picture sleeve identical to the British release. Columbia issued demonstration copies of the A-side with white labels with black text and the large Columbia logo in red, at top centre of the label. In 1983, Columbia reissued the single (38-040127) with a 'UPC' logo printed on the label and a stereo B-side (original pressings have the B-side in mono). In 1994, Capitol Records re-released the single on red vinyl (S7-17643-A).

1980-89

'COMING UP'

McCARTNEY recorded his song 'Coming Up' solo but also performed it with Wings during their 1979 British tour, so he released both solo/studio and band/live versions on either side of this single. His decision was a smart one. 'Coming Up' was a huge success on both sides of the Atlantic and helped sell the esoteric *McCartney II* to a less than enthusiastic audience.

Paul's solo reading was recorded during informal sessions held at his homes in Sussex and Scotland in the summer of 1979. Coming less than four months after he completed *Back To The Egg*, these sessions began as experiments and were not originally intended for commercial release or to re-launch McCartney as a solo artist. Wings were still very much a working band, but he wanted some time away from the group to record some songs "to play at parties". Fun meant one thing – improvisation. Almost all of the songs he wrote and recorded during these sessions were improvised, and as such they're too often directionless affairs. But 'Coming Up' was the exception.

As the summer progressed, McCartney drifted into an extended writing sojourn, during which he developed a compositional method that turned conventional writing techniques upside down. Working instinctively, he all but abandoned considered thought in favour of spontaneity and instant expression. He found this both inspirational and "magical", even if the results weren't.

"See, I find songwriting – writing new songs – to be a fascinating experience," he explained. "Some people have said to me, 'You actually believe in magic, don't you?' And I say, 'Yeah! Well, I saw my daughter born, and it seemed like magic, it seemed like a conjurer's trick to me. Like, how did we do that?' It's natural and it's magical, and in much the same way that's how I look at writing songs. It's like I don't know what it is, I don't know how it's done, but I know it's a part of nature too – human nature."

In that conversation, McCartney conveniently overlooks the fact that he has a vast knowledge of composition. This is either to elevate his songwriting to a spiritual or magical level, or to avoid having to analyse or discuss his work. George Martin maintained that McCartney took lessons in music theory during the 1960s but, finding it more difficult than he had expected and worried that it would inhibit the free flow of inspiration, he quickly gave up. Although he may not know how to write conventional musical notation, he certainly knows about the mechanics of composition. 'Coming Up', like many songs that "magically" emerged from the ether, is as much a product of his knowledge and experience as it is of improvisation and spontaneity. Originally five and a half minutes long, the song was edited and remixed for commercial release.

The live version of 'Coming Up' was recorded at the Glasgow Apollo on the last night of Wings' last British tour, December 17 1979. McCartney said he performed it because he "wanted to do something the audience hadn't heard before". Glasgow audiences are known to be demanding and notoriously hard to please, but it was during this performance that McCartney claimed he knew 'Coming Up' was a hit. "There was this one kid … bopping away, [and] I thought, 'Ah, this is a hit,' you know? You just get one of those feelings, just seeing him go, that's got to mean something, he's just into it." His intuition was right. The live recording outsold the studio version and topped the US singles charts.

'Lunch Box/Odd Sox' dates from 1975 when Wings Mk.4 were recording *Venus And Mars* at Sea Saint Studios in New Orleans. Speaking to Andy Peebles in 1980, McCartney said: "The B-side of 'Coming Up' was the first thing we recorded [then]. … Then we went ahead and did the rest of the album there." Wings manage to evoke something of the sassy character of New Orleans, and Linda's Mellotron riff gives the track its characteristic Wings 'sound', but unfortunately, other than that, it's uninspired and little more than hack work.

'COMING UP' / 'COMING UP' (LIVE), 'LUNCH BOX / ODD SOX'

PAUL McCARTNEY / PAUL MCCARTNEY AND WINGS

UK RELEASE April 11 1980; Parlophone R 6035; chart high No.2.

US RELEASE April 14 1980; Columbia 1-11263; chart high No.1.

- **'Coming Up'** (McCartney)
Paul McCartney (bass, guitar, keyboards, drums, vocals).
Recorded at home studio, Peasmarsh, Sussex or The Barn, High Park Farm, Scotland.
- **'Coming Up' (Live)** (McCartney)
Paul McCartney (bass, vocals), Linda McCartney (keyboards, vocals), Denny Laine (guitar, vocals), Laurence Juber (guitar), Steve Holly (drums), Steve 'Tex' Howard (trumpet), Thaddeus Richard (saxophone), Howie Casey (saxophone), Tony Dorsey (trombone).
Live recording at Glasgow Apollo, Glasgow, Scotland.
- **'Lunch Box'/'Odd Sox'** (McCartney)
Paul McCartney (bass, piano, vocals), Linda McCartney (keyboards, vocals), Denny Laine (guitar, vocals), Jimmy McCulloch (guitar), Geoff Britton (drums).
Recorded at Sea Saint Studios, New Orleans, LA, USA.

All produced by Paul McCartney.

'Coming Up' data

Parlophone issued *Coming Up* with generic labels and a monochrome picture sleeve. Demonstration copies replicate the commercial release but with 'DEMO RECORD NOT FOR SALE' printed on three lines above the spindle hole.

In the USA, Columbia issued the single with generic labels

and picture sleeve identical to the British release. It also issued 7-inch (1-11263) and 12-inch (AS 775) demonstration singles. The 7-inch has white labels with black text and the large Columbia logo in red top centre of the label. The 12-inch single has white labels with black text. Columbia also issued a one-sided 33⅓ rpm promo single (AE7 1204) of the live recording of 'Coming Up'. These were issued with initial pressings of *McCartney II*. It was also issued as a free one-sided single (AE7 1204) with Canadian pressings of *McCartney II*.

Twenty-one years after its original release, 'Coming Up' was remixed to promote the 2001 *Wingspan – Hits And History* album. Two new mixes were produced: the first, 'Song For Stella' (Linus Loves Mix), extended the song to 5:20; the second, 'Zak's Mix', edited the song to 3:05. Parlophone issued the 'Song For Stella' (Linus Loves Mix) on the B-side of the 'Silly Love Songs' promotional 12-inch single (WINDJ 002).

McCARTNEY II

AS WITH his first solo album, McCartney recorded this record at home. Although he had a 4-track studio on his Scottish farm, he didn't use that. Instead he went to work in makeshift studios using a 16-track tape machine hired from EMI, rigged so that microphones could be plugged straight in without a mixing board. Most of the songs were recorded in what McCartney referred to as the barn, possibly the same one once named Spirit Of Ranachan Studio.

McCartney II was intended as an experiment. He improvised almost all of it using avant-garde techniques that encourage exploration and unorthodox creativity. But he relies too much on rudimentary forms and structures that betray a musical conservatism. While Lennon let his hair down, completely abandoning his pop sensibility, McCartney seemed unable to escape his talent as a melodist, which ostensibly effaced any avant-garde ambitions. Consequently, too much of *McCartney II* sits uncomfortably between the unconventional and the commonplace.

The album was issued in the wake of considerable publicity. A month after Wings completed their British tour, they were scheduled to visit Japan and were due to play China, although dates for this leg of the tour were unconfirmed. However, when the band arrived in Japan on January 16 1980, customs officers suspected that Linda was in possession of marijuana. This time it was Paul's turn to take the rap.

He was arrested for attempting to carry 219 grams (7.72 ounces) of marijuana into Japan, which carried a potential mandatory sentence of five years. McCartney spent eight days and nine nights in a detention centre before being deported back to Britain. He concluded that it was a stupid thing to do; others saw it as typically arrogant. Either way, he should have known better: he had been denied entry to Japan in 1975 because of his convictions for possessing the drug. With the tour cancelled, the remaining members of Wings dispersed to various parts of the globe. Laurence Juber and Steve Holly headed for New York; Denny Laine went to the south of France and wrote his 'Japanese Tears' single, Linda remained in Japan with the children until Paul was released.

Despite much media attention, the bust did him little real harm and may have even raised his credibility. Only months after the incident, he was made 'Personality of the Year' at the British Rock and Pop Awards, sponsored by the BBC and *The Daily Mirror* newspaper. In May, he was presented with an Ivor Novello award in recognition for his "international achievements", no less.

However, the incident signalled the beginning of the end for Wings. McCartney was growing tired of the group and his run-in with the law exacerbated tensions. During 1980, Paul, Linda,

MCCARTNEY II
PAUL McCARTNEY
SIDE 1 'Coming Up', 'Temporary Secretary', 'On The Way', 'Waterfalls', 'Nobody Knows'.
SIDE 2 'Front Parlour', 'Summer's Day Song', 'Frozen Jap', 'Bogey Music', 'Darkroom', 'One Of These Days'.
UK RELEASE May 16 1980; Parlophone PCTC 258; chart high No.1.
US RELEASE May 26 1980; LP Columbia FC-36511 (initial copies included a one sided single, 'Coming Up' (Live), AE7 1204); 8-track cartridge FCA 36511; chart high No.3.

• **'Temporary Secretary'** (McCartney)
Paul McCartney (bass, guitar, keyboards, drums, vocals).
• **'On The Way'** (McCartney)
Paul McCartney (bass, guitar, drums, vocals).
• **'Waterfalls'** (McCartney)
Paul McCartney (electric piano, keyboards, vocals).
• **'Nobody Knows'** (McCartney)
Paul McCartney (bass, guitar, drums, vocals).
• **'Front Parlour'** (McCartney)
Paul McCartney (keyboards, drums).
• **'Summer's Day Song'** (McCartney)
Paul McCartney (keyboards, vocals).
• **'Frozen Jap'** (Paul McCartney)
Paul McCartney (keyboards, drums).
• **'Bogey Music'** (Paul McCartney)
Paul McCartney (bass, guitar, keyboards, drums, vocals).
• **'Darkroom'** (McCartney)
Paul McCartney (keyboards, drums, percussion, vocals).
• **'One Of These Days'** (McCartney)
Paul McCartney (guitar, vocals).
All recorded at home studio, Peasmarsh, Sussex or The Barn, High Park Farm, Scotland.
All produced by Paul McCartney.

Laine, Juber and Holly all worked on solo projects. In November 1980, they began rehearsals began for Wings' follow-up to *Back To The Egg*. Although they rehearsed several songs that appeared on *Tug Of War* and *Pipes Of Peace*, professional recordings were probably not made, despite press reports top the contrary (and despite rehearsal takes turning up on bootlegs).

McCartney II was originally meant to be a double album but was whittled down to a single disc for commercial, if not artistic, reasons. Two songs removed from the original running order, 'Secret Friend' and 'Check My Machine', appeared in extended and edited forms as B-sides, while another five tracks remain unreleased ('All You Horse Riders', 'Blue Sway', 'Mr H Atom', 'You Know I'll Get you Baby', and 'Bogey Wobble').

McCartney II songs

McCartney's experiments with synthesisers and varispeed recording were fused on the opening track, 'Temporary Secretary', his ode to the girl from the temp agency or bureau. Combining randomly generated synthetic sounds with drum and guitar parts, he constructs a rich textural soundscape, out of which an uneasy tension emerges. The random rhythmic effects suggested a kind of "space typewriter", which determined his lyric about an agency typist.

McCartney explained that the song was "written from the point of view of a fella who just wants a disposable secretary, and he's writing to a bureau to try and get one". The middle section was apparently influenced by something Paul heard by Ian Dury & The Blockheads. Dury hit his stride as a recording artist in the late 1970s with a string of hit singles, and 'Reasons To Be Cheerful (PT.3)' was high in the charts while Paul was recording, so it may be that record he was referring to. At one point, a British recruitment company, the Alfred Marks Agency, wanted to use the song in an advertising campaign, but McCartn rejected the idea.

Next comes 'On The Way'. McCartney left its backing track lying dormant for almost a month before he wrote its lyric, influenced by a television programme about the blues presented by British blues maverick Alexis Korner. A blues song in the broadest sense of the term, 'On The Way' features some of the sloppiest bass playing McCartney has ever committed to record. Instead of reworking his improvised bass lines, he left his stumbling passages and bum notes intact. His belief in revealing the moment of conception ultimately spoiled what is otherwise one of the album's better tracks.

One of the few songs he wrote in advance of recording, 'Waterfalls' benefits from a considered approach and restrained production. He had been recording for a number of weeks, but having grown tired of improvisation, returned to a song he'd already completed. Accompanying himself on an electric piano and scoring the string parts with synthesisers, McCartney created a simple ballad about emotional frailties, contemplating the passage of time and the realisation that it's one of our most precious commodities.

'Waterfalls', he said, "is basically saying don't go doing a load of dangerous stuff, cos I need you. And that's a kind of more mature thought for me than I would have been able to have done 20 years ago, cos I just didn't realise that it's not all gonna be here forever. That's the kind of thing you realise when you pass 30."

The minimal arrangement suits the song, but McCartney said later that he felt it is under-produced and that he could have made a better record of it. However, the limitations forced upon him gave it a fragility that unnecessary production would have stifled. Two alternative versions of 'Waterfalls' appeared with its release as a single. An edit was produced for radio stations, while the video soundtrack featured a longer introduction played on electric piano.

Another song inspired by Alexis Korner's television programme about the blues was the up-tempo rocker 'Nobody Knows', and like its laidback brother, it is less experimental than most of the album. Coasting along on autopilot, McCartney relies on tried and tested rock'n'roll clichés with little attempt at stretching himself. Again, his playing is amateurish, although he maintained that this was intended to mirror the imperfections of the early blues innovators. "On many blues records," he said, "they're never very exact, so on this track I do the same thing."

As its title suggests, 'Front Parlour' was recorded in a "little front parlour, which has still got the old wallpaper on it and a little fireplace," said McCartney, "[that] was where the main track was recorded". Initially the piece was untitled. "So I called it Front Parlour'."

McCartney improvised both the writing and recording of 'Front Parlour', and as such it encapsulates his entire approach to the *McCartney II* album. Advances in technology and multi-track recording gave him the freedom to experiment. "Instead of spending hours scoring string sections, you can just sit down at this machine and get a very similar sound immediately," he said. "It's a bit more spacey than a real string section, but you can do your own writing as you go and experiment more easily." Working spontaneously, he often kept the first idea that came to mind. While this creative free play afforded him greater room for experimentation, the results weren't always revolutionary or aesthetically pleasing. Despite the experimental nature of its genesis, 'Front Parlour' remains little more than an inchoate doodle.

For 'Summer's Day Song' McCartney was inspired by an unspecified "classical sounding" piece and originally conceived it as an instrumental piece. His vocals were only added after he'd done a rough mix and selected it for the original double album. What the song does, extremely well, is to evoke the feeling of a sultry summer's day. McCartney's rhythmic delivery, combined with dreamy textures and soporific melody, capture perfectly an atmosphere of stillness and drowsy relaxation.

Experimenting with the sounds on his synthesisers, McCartney happened to stumble on "something which sounded very oriental". This moment of serendipity led him to write 'Frozen Jap', a vaguely oriental sounding but pedestrian instrumental. Written some months before "the Japanese incident", 'Frozen Jap' was a working title that somehow stuck. Consequently, when it was released in Japan it was titled 'Frozen Japanese' because, he said, "we did not want to offend anyone there".

He was commissioned to write some music for a proposed film of the Raymond Briggs book *Fungus The Bogeyman*, and wrote 'Bogey Music' and the unreleased 'Bogey Wobble'. Using Briggs's narrative, he improvised some lyrics over a simple 12-bar backing track. "I had the book in the studio one day and opened it to a page where the young people in Bogeyland rebel against the old people who hate music," he explained. "They all start to get dressed in warm clothes – kind of Teds' outfits. So I took that page, looked at it a bit, and just thought: 'Well, it looks a bit like rock'n'roll.' So I made up the track and called it 'Bogey Music'." His children liked the song, but whether it should have ever seen the light of day is questionable. Needless to say, the proposed McCartney–Briggs collaboration never materialised.

While recording the album, McCartney developed a practice of recording a drum track and improvising over it. 'Darkroom' was one of the results. It's essentially an instrumental with one line of lyric, and the song is built on a groove. "That's one you can really tell I made up as I went along," he admitted. At first it was destined to remain an outtake. "The original version is a very long track and goes on through all sorts of crazy little noises. But I edited it down because I like it." The commercial version was remixed and edited – an electric guitar part was removed and the final mix tightened up. Some thought it referred to Linda – perhaps a reference to her photography. However, this wasn't the author's intention; for him the word simply "had lots of connotations. It could be a darkroom, a photographic darkroom, or a room which is dark. And you know, a fellow saying to a girl 'Come to my darkroom' is a bit like 'Let me take you to the Casbah' kind of thing."

While he was recording the album, McCartney was visited by a Hare Krishna devotee. "He was a nice fellow, very sort of gentle," he recalled. Inspired by his visitor's serenity, he wrote the reflective 'One Of These Days'. "The song seemed very right as a very simple thing," McCartney continued, "and it basically just says: 'One of these days I'll do what I've been meaning to do the rest of my life.'" Sounding relaxed and reflective, 'One Of These Days' offers stark contrast to the frantic, mechanical clatter or pseudo-funk grooves of the album's improvised songs and better captures McCartney than the electronic onslaught of 'Check My Machine' or 'Temporary Secretary'. It seems more like an outtake from *The White Album*, and this understated ballad is worth the price of admission on its own.

McCartney II data

Issued with generic Parlophone labels, *McCartney II* reached number 1 in Britain, but strong initial sales were not sustained. A press pack issued to the media included a T-shirt, poster, four black-and-white photographs, and an interview with DJ Paul Gambaccini. Copies were later made available through Wings Fun Club for £4.99, a fraction of its current value.

In the USA, Columbia issued the LP with generic red labels and a one-sided 7-inch single of the live recording of 'Coming Up' (AE7 1204). Some examples of the LP featured a burgundy rectangular sticker that stated it came with a bonus single. Later pressings were issued with a red rectangular sticker that stated that the album "Features the Hits 'COMING UP' & 'WATERFALLS'".

Promotional copies of the Columbia pressing were issued with black-and-white Columbia labels and 'FOR PROMOTION ONLY OWNERSHIP RESERVED BY CBS SALE UNLAWFUL' stamped in gold leaf in the top left corner of the rear cover.

'CHECK MY MACHINE'

THIS B-side is often cited as the first song that McCartney recorded in the summer of 1979, but he maintains that 'Front Parlour' has this distinction. Based on a simple keyboard riff, 'Check My Machine' is little more than a groove over which he repeats the title. The song was edited for commercial release from its original 8:39 to a slightly less rambling 5:51 seconds, but this did little to make it any more enjoyable.

'Waterfalls' / 'Check My Machine' data

The single was released in Britain with generic Parlophone labels and a picture sleeve and sold well enough to place it in the Top 10. Parlophone issued a 3:22 edit of the A-side as a demonstration single (R 6037A-DJ). Issued with generic black and silver labels, it has 'DEMO RECORD NOT FOR SALE' on three lines about the spindle hole and '(3,22)' below the title.

Columbia released the single in the USA with generic labels and picture sleeve. They also issued demonstration copies with the full-length version on the A-side and an edit on the B-side. These were issued with white labels with black text and the large Columbia logo in red, top centre.

'WATERFALLS' / 'CHECK MY MACHINE'
PAUL McCARTNEY
UK RELEASE June 13 1980; Parlophone R 6037; chart high No.9.
US RELEASE July 22 1980; Columbia 11335; chart high No.83.

• **Check My Machine** (McCartney)
Paul McCartney (bass, keyboards, banjo, drums, vocals).
Recorded at home studio, Peasmarsh, Sussex or The Barn, High Park Farm, Scotland.
Produced by Paul McCartney.

'SEASIDE WOMAN'

THIS was re-released to coincide with the appearance of Oscar Grillo's animated film based on the song. Grillo's short was supporting the Peter Sellers movie *Being There* in Britain. This time, Linda received full credit for the song in the vain hope that it might generate extra sales. It didn't. The single appeared on both 7-inch and 12-inch formats, althuogh the musical content of both is identical. A new picture sleeve, which featured stills from the film, was produced to accompany the re-release. Despite the attendant publicity, the single still failed to chart and probably sold fewer copies than it had the previous year. However, the saga of 'Seaside Woman' was far from over.

'SEASIDE WOMAN' / 'B SIDE TO SEASIDE'
LINDA McCARTNEY ALIAS SUZY AND THE RED STRIPES
UK RELEASE July 18 1980; A&M AMS 7548; 12-inch A&M AMSP 7548; failed to chart.

'TEMPORARY SECRETARY' / 'SECRET FRIEND'
PAUL McCARTNEY
UK release September 15 1980; 12-inch Parlophone 12 R 6039; failed to chart.

• **Secret Friend** (McCartney)
Paul McCartney (bass, keyboards, guitar, drums, percussion, vocals).
Recorded at home studio, Peasmarsh, Sussex or The Barn, High Park Farm, Scotland.
Produced by Paul McCartney

'SECRET FRIEND'

'TEMPORARY Secretary' was the third and final single from *McCartney II*, issued as a 12-inch in a limited edition of 15,000. The A-side was identical to the album version, but the flip featured an outtake from *McCartney II*, 'Secret Friend' – all 10:30 of it. It's an atmospheric epic inspired by a family saying, an early divergence for McCartney into minimalist dance music that can now be seen as a precursor to his later excursions into the world of ambient dance material.

'Temporary Secretary' / 'Secret Friend' data

Released as a 12-inch single and only in Britain, limited quantities were exported to other territories. The sleeve featured a drawing by Jeff Cummin that had additional splashes of colour added by McCartney. Parlophone issued a one-sided 7-inch demonstration single (R 6039) with generic labels and 'DEMO RECORD NOT FOR SALE' on three lines above the spindle hole.

'(JUST LIKE) STARTING OVER'

LENNON'S first single in five years and the first new, original material in almost six was much anticipated. News of Lennon's return to the recording studio made headlines around the world. Music papers were buzzing with speculation. What would he and Yoko Ono have to say? More importantly, how would they say it? The answer came in the form of '(Just Like) Starting Over', a retro-tinged rocker that, after Lennon's five-year silence, was a slight disappointment.

Many expected him to return with an album of blistering rockers. He'd been working with producer Jack Douglas, known for records with Cheap Trick and Aerosmith, but Lennon was playing it safe. This was, after all, his big comeback, and he wasn't going to blow it. Furthermore, Lennon was creeping into middle age and had mellowed considerably. But then so had his fellow ex-Beatles. Compare Lennon's slick craftsmanship with that of McCartney's or Harrison's and one finds Lennon more in step with his ex-bandmates than ever. He may have enjoyed listening to punk rock, but he sure as hell wasn't going to record any.

The Lennons signed with Geffen Records on September 22 1980, and the single was issued a little over four weeks later. There was no promotional video to accompany the release, although John and Yoko were filmed walking through Central Park and pretending to make love. They were also filmed in the studio, but Lennon was apparently unhappy with the footage and had it destroyed. US record stores received cardboard countertop browser boxes to display the single; British shops were issued with a colourful but plain 21-inch by 8-inch poster.

'(Just Like) Starting Over' was initially more successful in America than in Britain. In the week beginning December 5, the single sat at Number 7 in the US *Cash Box* charts but had started to make its way down the British charts. There it peaked at Number 9, dropping to 11 in the first week of December. However, after Lennon's death on December 8, demand for the single pushed it to the top of the charts on both sides of the Atlantic. By Friday 12, EMI had received orders of 200,000 for both 'Imagine' and 'Happy Xmas (War Is Over)'. Although no figures were given by Warner Bros, they too must have received similar orders for '(Just Like) Starting Over'. The single spent one week at Number 1 on the British charts, being replaced by 'Imagine', and five weeks at the top of the US charts.

Lennon suggested that all the songs on *Double Fantasy* came to him in a rush of inspiration, but he'd laboured over '(Just Like)

Starting Over' for weeks or maybe months. He developed it from several unfinished fragments that he brought together to form the finished song. This was nothing new, of course: Lennon and McCartney often combined uncompleted bits and pieces to finish a composition. Lennon had reworked several solo songs, but rarely to this extent.

It began as 'My Life', which shared melodic elements with the slow introduction used for the finished item. Over the following weeks, he worked several melodic fragments into new compositions that, when combined, would constitute '(Just Like) Starting Over'. Playing with the melody of Buddy Holly's 'Raining In My Heart', he reworked 'My Life' into another uncompleted song, 'I Watch Your Face'; like 'My Life', this had a melancholic tone.

Lennon then worked on a song called 'Don't Be Crazy', which, with a little revision, would become the verse of '(Just Like) Starting Over'. Finally, he started on 'The Worst Is Over', which would form the chorus. All that remained was for him to combine the various elements into one song, which he did once he'd returned from a holiday in Bermuda. Back home at the Dakota in New York City, he recorded demos of the completed song just days before returning to the studio.

The theme was emotional, spiritual, and creative rebirth. His first solo album had been introduced with the tolling of funeral bells; now, to symbolise this new beginning, he used four rings from a small Japanese wishing bell. However, Lennon's rebirth was firmly rooted in the past. Five years earlier he'd said goodbye with an album of rock'n'roll standards. His return was marked by another dose of rock'n'roll, this time of his own making. Influenced in part by Roy Orbison's 'Only The Lonely', Lennon shaped a comeback single that was as much about his past as it was about the present.

He talked to Andy Peebles about the song's origins. "It was really called 'Starting Over' but, while we're making it, people kept putting things out with the same title. You know, there was a country and western hit called 'Starting Over', so I added 'Just Like' at the last minute. And to me it was like going back to 15 and singing à la Presley. All the time I was referring to John [Smith], the engineer, here in the room I was referring to Elvis Orbison. It's kinda like ... 'Only The Lonely', you know ... a kind of parody but not really parody." Not only was this rock'n'roll tempered by parody, but also by age.

Ono's 'Kiss Kiss Kiss' is more musically and lyrically adventurous than Lennon's A-side. Although it's more adult-orientated rock than avant-garde, it combined elements from both genres. Ono suggested that the song was about liberation and having the courage to express vulnerability rather than mask it. However, when it came to recording her vocal, she was more than a little embarrassed by her display of openness. The song ends with her double-tracked, recorded at the Hit Factory on September 19, simulating an orgasm, which she found embarrassing to perform in front of a group of men. "I started to do it," she recalled, "and then I suddenly looked and all these engineers were all looking, and I thought, I can't do that, you know? So I said, well, turn off all the lights and put the screen around me, and I did it that way."

'(Just Like) Starting Over' data

The single was issued on both sides of the Atlantic with generic Geffen labels and a black-and-white picture sleeve. Promotional copies featuring mono/stereo mixes of the A-side were issued in America. Canadian promotional copies of the single featured the commercial A and B-sides but had 'PROMOTIONAL COPY' printed on the label at 2 o'clock. The single was also issued as a 12-inch promotional record (PRO-A-919) featuring an extended coda.

'(Just Like) Starting Over' was reissued in the USA on June 5 1981 backed with 'Woman' (GGEF 0408). Warner Bros, distributors of Geffen Records, had a policy of combining hit singles to create double A-side oldies. They issued this pressing with six label variants. Three had a cream label: the first with a thin Geffen Records logo and small perimeter print; the second with bold logo and small print; and the third with bold logo without perimeter print. The others have a black label: the first with silver and white print, issued as part of the Back To Back *Hits* series; the second with the same print but a one-inch by half-inch white box on the label that has no UPC symbol; and the third is the same as this but the box has a UPC symbol.

In 1994, Capitol's Special Markets Division issued '(Just Like) Starting Over' (72438-57894-7) as a jukebox single. Pressed on blue vinyl, it was backed with 'Watching The Wheels'. In 2000, '(Just Like) Starting Over' was issued as part of a CD sampler (DPRO 7087) to promote the remastered versions of *John Lennon/Plastic Ono Band* and *Double Fantasy*.

'(JUST LIKE) STARTING OVER' / 'KISS KISS KISS'
JOHN LENNON / YOKO ONO
UK RELEASE October 24 1980; Geffen K 79186; chart high No.1.
US RELEASE October 20 1980; Geffen GEF 49594; chart high No.1.

- **'(Just Like) Starting Over'** (Lennon)
John Lennon (vocals, guitar), Earl Slick (guitar), Hugh McCracken (guitar), Tony Levin (bass), George Small (keyboards), Arthur Jenkins (percussion), Michelle Simpson, Cassandra Wooten, Cheryl Mason Jacks, Eric Troyer (backing vocals), Andy Newmark (drums).
- **'Kiss Kiss Kiss'** (Ono)
Yoko Ono (vocals), Earl Slick (guitar), Hugh McCracken (guitar), Tony Levin (bass), George Small (keyboards), Arthur Jenkins (percussion), Andy Newmark (drums).

Both recorded at Hit Factory, New York City, NY, USA, and mixed at Record Plant, New York City. Both produced by John Lennon, Yoko Ono, and Jack Douglas.

DOUBLE FANTASY

WITH the birth of Sean Taro Ono Lennon in 1975, John Lennon abandoned record making. Rather than release an album of new material, he put out *Shaved Fish* as a symbolic summation of his career to date. Besides announcing Sean's birth and John's retirement, it drew a line under his career. The dream was well and truly over, but the myth persisted. If anything, Lennon's withdrawal from music making created more column inches than if he'd remained active. Nevertheless, the birth of his second son gave him the chance to distance himself from the rock'n'roll lifestyle he'd helped define and to consider his future.

Lennon was determined to devote the next five years of his life to bringing up Sean. However, like anyone who finds themselves suddenly removed from the things that give their life meaning, he quickly grew bored. Fatherhood was great for a few months, but he soon became listless. The urge to create continued to gnaw away at him and, although he abandoned the recording studio, he continued to write. However, with no specific project in mind, the best he could come up with was a number of half-finished sketches. Far from feeling contented, Lennon sank into a deep depression that manifested itself in his songs as a sense of aimless drifting.

In the summer of 1976, Lennon revived a song he'd started six years earlier. 'Sally And Billy', the story of a couple unable to decide what to do with their lives, mirrored his own sense of purposelessness. Speaking in 1980, he confirmed that he found it hard to cope with his self-imposed silence. "The first half year or year I had this sort of feeling in the back of my mind that I ought to [write] and I'd go through periods of panic ... I mean, you know, I just didn't exist any more."

Lennon's early house-husband period saw him returning to the kind of introspective probing that he'd engaged in immediately after The Beatles stopped touring. The only difference was that in 1966 he'd set out on a psychedelic voyage of discovery. What he discovered now was gloomy indeed, and things weren't about to get any better. John and Yoko took an extended holiday to Japan, to meet Yoko's relatives. Feeling increasingly alienated, Lennon allegedly told John Green: "I'm dead. Yoko killed me; this placed killed me." While in Tokyo, he wrote 'Mirror Mirror', a searching piece of self-analysis that alluded to the emptiness he was experiencing. Although he recognised the problem, any solution seemed out of reach.

From the same period came 'I Don't Want To Face It', a song that with a little revision would appear on the posthumous *Milk And Honey*. Like 'Mirror Mirror', it reveals his troubled mind, unable to decide which path to take. Life at the Dakota was proving to be less emotionally and creatively satisfying than Lennon had hoped for. Nevertheless, he continued to amass demos of new songs, many of which formed the basis of *Double Fantasy* and its follow-up, *Milk And Honey*.

In an attempt to ease her husband out of his depression, Ono sent Lennon on a series of holidays. These trips took him on another voyage of self-discovery. For the first time in years, he had to fend for himself. A trip to Hong Kong was a revelation. Lennon found that he was free to walk the streets and enjoyed the experience of being one of the masses. "I wandered around Hong Kong at dawn, alone, and it was a thrill," he said. "It was rediscovering a feeling that I once had as a youngster walking the mountains of Scotland with my auntie. This is the feeling that makes you write or paint."

Further trips followed: South Africa; Egypt. But the turning point came with a holiday to Bermuda. By the time Lennon visited the island in June 1980 his depression had cleared and his thoughts turned to recording again. Further into that summer, Lennon had accumulated a number of incomplete songs, all of which needed a great deal of work before they could be recorded. With his five-year sabbatical drawing to a close, he set about reworking what songs he had, writing new ones, and planning his next album.

A visit to a nightclub, his first in years, exposed Lennon to contemporary pop music. Citing the B-52s' 'Rock Lobster' as a minor epiphany, Lennon convinced himself that the time was right to make his return. "It's time to get out the old axe and wake the wife up!" he told *Rolling Stone*. However, Lennon was keeping his plans close to his chest. When a *New Musical Express* reporter spotted him at Disco 40 and asked if he was planning to make a comeback, Lennon said: "You can't do it if it's not there." In fact it was there, if not in a usable form.

Now that he had an objective in mind, Lennon set about finishing the songs he'd accumulated with an energy he hadn't possessed in years. He cut a number of demos in Bermuda, laying the foundation for *Double Fantasy*, intending them to be a reference source for both the producer and musicians. The producer would be issued with a set prior to entering the studio and Lennon often referred back to them while recording. It was also while he was in Bermuda that Lennon found the title of the new album. While visiting a garden, he came across a variety of freesia. The plant in question was called Double Fantasy, a name that neatly summed up the album's theme of "sexual fantasies between men and women". The fact that the album was almost devoid of songs relating to this theme made no odds. It was a good title and that's what mattered.

While Lennon was putting the finishing touches to his songs, Ono contacted Jack Douglas, who had previously worked for the Lennons as an engineer, to ask if he would like to co-produce the album. Initially, Douglas wanted sole production rights, but consented to a co-production role when Ono agreed to increase his fee. Douglas claims that he assembled the band within days of signing with John and Yoko but was sworn to secrecy and unable to tell anyone who their employers were. Speaking on WMFU in December 2003, he claimed to have rehearsed the band for some weeks before they entered the studio and that it was only when rehearsals moved to the 'white room' at John and Yoko's Dakota apartment that Lennon revealed himself.

However, Lennon maintained that it was he and Ono who picked the musicians, using numerology. The only concession was guitarist Hugh McCracken, whom Lennon insisted on hiring as he wanted to work with at least one musician he had worked with before. Lennon also revealed that he had originally wanted Willie Weeks to play bass, but he was booked for a George Harrison session and unavailable. Nevertheless, Lennon was delighted with Weeks's replacement, Tony Levin, whom he considered the best musician in the group. The band – at this stage Lennon, Ono, McCracken, and keyboardist George Small, plus 'musical associate' Tony Davilio and producer Jack Douglas – began rehearsing at the Dakota on Friday August 1, resuming again on the 4th. Recording proper began three days later on Thursday 7th at New York City's Hit Factory studio.

Once Lennon walked into the studio it was business as usual. He quickly established the ground rules: simplicity was the key, there would be no slacking, and there was no room for prima donnas. Just as with *Imagine*, his goal was to record two songs a day, a target they achieved with relative ease. In the first three days, the band cut six songs and completed a total of 22 basic tracks in a little under two weeks. Fourteen songs were selected for *Double Fantasy*; the remainder were earmarked for *Milk And Honey*. 'Walking On Thin Ice' had been programmed for *Double Fantasy* but was put aside for a solo Ono EP, *Yoko Only*. But the EP, which was to have included 'Open Your Box', was scrapped, and instead 'Thin Ice' was issued as a standalone single early in 1981.

The Lennons' recording sessions were models of efficiency and pragmatism. John and Yoko quickly adopted a routine where Ono worked during the day and Lennon in the late evening. This was not simply an effective use of expensive studio time, but, if Douglas is to be believed, it was the only way Lennon and Ono could work without constantly arguing. Although *Double Fantasy* was a collaborative project, Douglas maintains that the pair did not work well together in the studio. His solution was to think of the record as two solo projects.

"Those two could not work at the same time." he recalled. "If she were there, it would have been impossible. It was just impossible. I had to treat that album as two separate albums. I know that they're both artists on the record, but I had to treat it as a John album and as a Yoko album. My routine was like this. 9:00am, breakfast with John. Yoko from 11:00am, and then John would go home. Yoko from 11 o'clock until about 6:30pm. And

DOUBLE FANTASY
JOHN LENNON AND YOKO ONO
SIDE 1 '(Just Like) Starting Over', 'Kiss Kiss Kiss', 'Cleanup Time', 'Give Me Something', 'I'm Losing You', 'I'm Moving On', 'Beautiful Boy (Darling Boy)'.
SIDE 2 'Watching The Wheels', 'Yes, I'm Your Angel', 'Woman', 'Beautiful Boys', 'Dear Yoko', 'Every Man Has A Woman Who Loves Him', 'Hard Times Are Over'.
UK RELEASE November 17 1980; Geffen K 99131; chart high No.1.
US RELEASE November 17 1980; LP Geffen GHS 2001; 8-track cartridge Geffen GEF-W8-2001; chart high No.1.

- **'Cleanup Time'** (Lennon)
Personnel as 'I'm Losing You' plus Howard Johnson, Grant Hunderford, John Parran, Seldon Powell, George 'Young' Opalisky, Roger Rosenberg, David Tofani, Ronald Tooley (horns).
- **'Give Me Something'** (Ono)
Personnel as 'I'm Moving On' plus Michelle Simpson, Cassandra Wooten, Cheryl Mason Jacks, Eric Troyer (backing vocals).
- **'I'm Losing You'** (Lennon)
John Lennon (vocals, guitar), Earl Slick (guitar), Hugh McCracken (guitar), Tony Levin (bass), George Small (keyboards), Arthur Jenkins (percussion), Andy Newmark (drums).
- **'I'm Moving On'** (Ono)
Yoko Ono (vocals), Earl Slick (guitar), Hugh McCracken (guitar), Tony Levin (bass), George Small (keyboards), Arthur Jenkins (percussion), Andy Newmark (drums).
- **'Beautiful Boy (Darling Boy)'** (Lennon)
Personnel as 'I'm Losing You' plus Robert Greenridge (steel drum).
- **'Watching The Wheels'** (Lennon)
Personnel as 'I'm Losing You' except Lennon (vocals, keyboards) plus Matthew Cunningham (hammer dulcimer), Michelle Simpson, Cassandra Wooten, Cheryl Mason Jacks, Eric Troyer (backing vocals).
- **'Yes, I'm Your Angel'** (Ono)
Personnel as 'I'm Moving On'.
- **'Woman'** (Lennon)
Personnel as 'I'm Losing You' plus Michelle Simpson, Cassandra Wooten, Cheryl Mason Jacks, Eric Troyer (backing vocals).
- **'Beautiful Boys'** (Ono)
Personnel as 'I'm Moving On'.
- **'Dear Yoko'** (Lennon)
Personnel as 'I'm Losing You' plus Michelle Simpson, Cassandra Wooten, Cheryl Mason Jacks, Eric Troyer (backing vocals).
- **'Every Man Has A Woman Who Loves Him'** (Ono)
Personnel as 'I'm Moving On' plus Lennon (vocals).
- **'Hard Times Are Over'** (Ono)
Personnel as 'I'm Moving On' plus Lennon (vocals), Benny Cummings Singer – Kings Temple Choir (choir).

All recorded at Hit Factory, New York City, NY, USA, plus 'Give Me Something' and 'Watching The Wheels' mixed at Record Plant, New York City.
All produced by John Lennon, Yoko Ono, and Jack Douglas.

then she would go home. John would come in at 7:00pm and would work until about one or two in the morning. I never worked with both of them at the same time. It was impossible. Because she drove John crazy." There are, however, a number of photographs that show the couple working together in the studio, so it couldn't have been all bad. But there is also evidence that Lennon was quick to lose his temper with Ono.

Lennon always recorded quickly, and this time was no exception. He and Ono drove themselves and the band hard, and it's to everyone's credit that they maintained such high standards. However, on this occasion Lennon had an ulterior motive: he was picking up the bill. They had decided to self-finance the album and then offer the finished item to record companies. Lennon didn't want to get himself in the kind of contractual tangle that had beset his earlier career; by financing the project themselves, the Lennons remained in control. Several major labels approached them, but it was the newly formed Geffen Records who won the contract.

David Geffen was making a comeback of his own. Returning to the music business after a cancer scare, he was in the process of setting up his label just as the Lennons were recording their album. He sent them a telegram, with little hope of a response, asking if they would be interested in working with him. Geffen's luck was in, and within weeks of his making contact, he had a contract drawn up and signed by the Lennons. One reason Lennon and Ono signed with Geffen was that, unlike the majors, who were put off by Ono's involvement, Geffen didn't ask to hear the album in advance. Geffen also had the advantage of being an independent, albeit with backing from the massive Warner Bros corporation, who would deal with the Lennons face to face.

The basic tracks were completed by August 19, and by the 25th a provisional track listing had been compiled. Overdub sessions were booked for September, with mixing commencing later in the month at New York's Record Plant. Lennon and Ono then returned to the Hit Factory in October for more mixing, which was completed on the 13th, and the final master was compiled seven days later.

The pair's first album together for eight years marked the end of a self-imposed five-year silence. Their return to public discourse would be made through a series of musical dialogues, of which *Double Fantasy* was the first. Just as their first collaboration, *Two Virgins*, had marked an emblematic beginning, *Double Fantasy* signified rebirth. Lennon was obviously energised by his return and gave several comprehensive interviews to promote the album.

Interviewed by RKO Radio, he said he felt that *Double Fantasy* was "just the start and this was our first album. I know we have worked together before, and we've even made albums before, but we feel like this is the first album". Fuelled by a burst of creative energy, he had high hopes for the album. They both thought the album a Number 1 record – but although it sold well, it looked doubtful that *Double Fantasy* would top the charts. As most of their promotional activities were concentrated on the US market, the album at first performed better there than in Britain.

The record did not go down well with British critics. *Melody Maker* described it as "a god awful yawn! The whole thing positively reeks of an indulgent sterility". *NME* described it thus: '*Double Fantasy* is right: a fantasy made for two … . It sounds like a great life. But unfortunately it makes a lousy record." Lennon was particularly keen for the album to succeed in Britain, but within weeks of its release it was slipping down the charts. By the second week of December, *Double Fantasy* had dropped to number 46 in the British charts. Unbelievably, acts like Barry Manilow and Ken Dodd (a Liverpudlian comedian) were outperforming John and Yoko. The success that Lennon hoped for in Britain was only achieved posthumously. The week after his death, *Double Fantasy* climbed to Number 2; the following week it was Number 1.

Double Fantasy songs

As with '(Just Like) Starting Over', 'Cleanup Time' explored the notion of rebirth. This opening song on the album was inspired by a phone conversation Lennon had with producer Jack Douglas before the two had properly met. "I was in Bermuda," Lennon recalled, "and we were talking about the 1970s and that. We were talking about cleanin' up and gettin' out of drugs and alcohol and those kind of things – not me personally, but people in general. He said, 'Well, it's cleanup time, right?' I said, 'It sure is,' and that was the end of the conversation. I went straight to the piano and started boogieing, and 'Cleanup Time' came out."

Although it took on a universal tone, 'Cleanup Time' reveals how Lennon and Ono set about cleansing themselves of the troubles that beset them. With their trials behind them, all was contentment. They had survived. By following a strict macrobiotic diet and adopting positive thinking, they emerged from the 1970s as well-rounded individuals. At least that's how Lennon chose to present it.

Constructing a picture of comfortable domesticity, as sentimental as any Victorian painting, Lennon's mythologising was, nevertheless, rooted in reality. The pair had cleaned up their act in more ways than one. Thanks to Ono's investment sense and economic acumen, they were financially secure. Lennon had brought up their son and taken on the role of homemaker. Both had kicked debilitating drug habits. They had wiped the slate clean and begun afresh. They were now ready to show the world how it too could clean up, and they offered their relationship as a model of perfect heterosexual harmony. Work to record the basic track began on August 13 at the Hit Factory. The horn section was overdubbed on September 5, and Lennon recorded his vocal on September 17.

Recording for the next track, 'Give Me Something', began on August 18 and was completed on September 23, when Ono cut her vocal. Her blend of hard rock and avant-garde vocalising mirror an equally taught lyric, which with a surgeon's precision cut through Lennon's mawkish efforts. Rather than paint a picture of romantic bliss, Ono alludes to the realities of their relationship.

The two were communication junkies. They loved the telephone and used it incessantly, often preferring to call one another rather than talk face to face. Ono often used the phone to play mind games with Lennon. Her calls were the equivalent of the cryptic messages she sent him when they first met. During his 'lost weekend' – an 18-month alcohol-fuelled Ono-sanctioned separation – she would call him as many as 20 times a day, often with infuriating results.

Lennon, of course, also loved to call Ono, and 'I'm Losing You' stems from his frustration at being unable to contact her while he was on holiday in Bermuda. However, the song had existed in a previous form for some time before he channelled his frustration into finishing it. It was originally titled 'Stranger's Room', which Lennon recorded as a slow, brooding ballad prior to his visit to Bermuda. Speaking later to the BBC, he stressed that he was on the island when inspiration struck. "[I] was actually in Bermuda. I called [Ono] and I couldn't get through. I got really mad, and I wrote this song in the heat of passion, as it were."

In reality, all he did was rework 'Stranger's Room', which already had the verse, chorus, and theme that formed the basis of 'I'm Losing You'. Its lyric even contained a reference to the telephone, although in this instance it was Lennon who wasn't answering. His lyric also included a reference to bleeding, which, in light of the shocking events of December 8, became even more unnerving and seemingly prophetic. But Lennon probably intended it as a metaphor for the emotional pain he was experiencing at being separated from Ono. During this period he may have felt as if his emotional and creative energies were draining from him, as he explained. He said the song "is expressing the losing you, of the 18 months lost … it was everything … losing one's mother, losing one's everything – everything, losing everything you've ever lost is in that song."

'I'm Losing You' was, then, as angst-ridden as anything on *John Lennon/Plastic Ono Band*, and Lennon intended to give it an abrasive reading. To reinforce his sense of loss and perhaps in an attempt to reconnect with the pain he experienced while recording that earlier album, he cites 'Long Lost John', a song he'd improvised with Ringo Starr and Klaus Voormann during those sessions.

Unlike most of what appeared on *Double Fantasy*, 'I'm Losing You' was somewhat difficult to capture successfully. The first attempt at recording the song took place on August 12 1980 at the Hit Factory. Jack Douglas called on the talents of guitarist Rick Nielsen and drummer Bun E. Carlos from Cheap Trick to bring an edge to the proceedings. With Lennon providing second guitar and Tony Levin bass, the quartet recorded two tracks, 'I'm Losing You' and Ono's 'I'm Moving On'. Lennon was unhappy with the results, reasoning that they were too gritty and too close to his early *Plastic Ono Band*/'Cold Turkey' period. He decided to scrap these tracks and start again. (That first version of 'I'm Losing You' would eventually be issued on the *John Lennon Anthology*, albeit in an edited form and without Nielsen's guitar overdub. The edit also appeared on the 1998 collection *Wonsaponatime* and the British two-track promotional CD 'I'm Losing You' / 'Only You' [LENNON 001]. The unedited version appeared on *Howtis* [DPRO-13515], a CD issued to promote the *John Lennon Anthology* boxed set.)

Work on the remake of 'I'm Losing You' began on August 18, with Lennon playing the band his earlier attempt and giving them instructions as to how he wanted it played. However, this session did not go well either, and a third and final attempt at recording the song was booked for August 26. Satisfied that he had at last captured the definitive version, Lennon overdubbed a horn arrangement on September 5 and added his vocal to the track on the 22nd. The horns were then removed at Lennon's insistence because of a large bill he received from the musicians for their services, but artistic reasons must have also played a part when he decided to delete this part of the arrangement.

Ono had rejected the first version of 'I'm Moving On', also recorded with Nielsen and Carlos from Cheap Trick, and re-recorded the song on August 26. She completed it on September 19, adding her vocals to the backing track. It establishes a musical dialogue between husband and wife, and indeed this song and 'I'm Losing You' both speak of loss but from different perspectives. If Lennon felt traumatised at the thought of losing his partner, the same cannot be said for Ono. Her sense of independence is writ large in this song, which she told David Sheff of *Playboy* magazine is about "the sense of 'Well, I've had enough. I'm moving on.' But it's not about any specific incident. It's just the feeling: 'I don't want to play the games. I like everything straight.' That's a feeling I have had. I'm proud of the song."

Next on *Double Fantasy* is 'Beautiful Boy (Darling Boy)', a lullaby for Lennon's son, Sean, that reveals the extent of his feelings for his second-born. To say that he doted on Sean would be an understatement. Sean was the apple of his eye, but to begin with he found it difficult to write a song that described how he felt. It was only when he gave up thinking about the idea that the song took shape. He appears to have finished 'Beautiful Boy (Darling Boy)' in Bermuda, where he recorded several takes of the song with help from his assistant, Fred Seaman. Back in New York City, Lennon recorded the basic track on August 12 and added his vocal on September 17. (An alternative take, without the numerous overdubs that were applied to the master version, was issued on the *John Lennon Anthology*.)

Many found Lennon's five-year silence unfathomable. Why would someone make a conscious decision to squander their talent and distance themselves from friends and the razzmatazz of showbiz? Extended career breaks were almost unheard of in the late 1970s. Artists were expected to remain on the album-tour-album treadmill to satisfy both record company and public. But Lennon had long since stopped playing that game. The Beatles broke with tradition in 1966 by demanding a cessation of their hectic touring schedule, and by his own admission Lennon had grown tired of having to produce an album every year.

'Watching The Wheels' was an attempt to answer his critics

while promoting the myth that all was light and happiness during his five-year break. "It's a song version of the love letter from John and Yoko," he told David Sheff. "It's an answer to: 'What have you been doing?' 'Well, I've been doing this – watchin' the wheels.'" But Lennon had been contemplating more than the fast-turning wheels of showbiz. Religion and spirituality had influenced him. Where previously he'd tried to imagine a world without religion, he now found himself drawn to it. The Bahá'í Faith may have affected Lennon: its central belief, that humanity is one single race and that the day has come for its unification in one global society, was condensed into a pithy aphorism, "One World, One People", and inscribed into the dead wax of the '(Just Like) Starting Over' single. The wheels Lennon found himself contemplating were, more often than not, those governing destiny: the karmic wheels that influence the spiritual evolution of humanity as a whole.

Lennon developed 'Watching The Wheels' from a song he'd written in 1975. 'Tennessee', inspired by his fondness for the writer Tennessee Williams, was intended for the follow-up to *Walls And Bridges*. It then formed part of a new song, 'Memories', written some time in 1977 or '78. This developed into 'Watching The Wheels', although it too was reworked and revised on several occasions before Lennon was satisfied. He made several demo recordings of the song but appears to have made the definitive demo while in Bermuda. The song was finally committed to tape at the Hit Factory on August 18: nine takes of the basic track were recorded, number eight being marked best. Lennon added his vocal on September 20 and mixed the track at the Record Plant nine days later.

'Yes, I'm Your Angel' was intended as a joke, a pastiche of the kind of show tunes that populated Hollywood films from the 1930s. In fact, Ono's pastiche was so successful that the publishers of Gus Kahn's 'Makin' Whoopee' sued. While Ono's blend of avant-gardism and hard rock placed her at the centre of New York City's post-punk scene, 'Yes, I'm Your Angel' must have sent all but the most hardened fans reaching for the fast-forward button.

Songs asking for forgiveness are scattered throughout Lennon's oeuvre. Writing in the 1960s, he tended to view women as mere objects of desire. Ono opened his eyes to feminism, and by the early 1970s he'd began a slow transition from chauvinist to pseudo-feminist. Women, or more specifically Ono, were more likely to be referred to as equals and occasionally as enlightened goddesses. He began to express his feelings of regret as apologies, developing the theme with a string of songs that found their way onto his later albums.

Written for Ono, 'Woman' states, very simply and precisely, how Lennon was still struggling to come to terms with his actions. He explained: "['Woman'], that's to Yoko and to all women in a way. My history of relationships with women is very poor – very macho, very stupid, but pretty typical of a certain type of man, which I was, I suppose: a very insecure, sensitive person acting out very aggressive and macho. Trying to cover up the feminine side, which I still have a tendency to do, but I'm learning. I'm learning that it's all right to be soft and allow that side of me out."

A combination of 'Jealous Guy' and 'Aisumassen (I'm Sorry)', 'Woman' extends Lennon's self-criticism and takes the art of apologising to new highs. Exquisitely constructed, if a little sentimental, it has the melodic edge over anything Lennon wrote for this album, reflecting the depth of emotion that he felt for Ono. An extremely personal song, it was given universal appeal by extending the concept to embrace all women.

Lennon knew he'd written something special and constantly referred to the song as the album's Motown/Beatles track. Its melodic simplicity and rich arrangement lent it a sophisticated tone that echoed The Beatles at their best. It is the equivalent of George Harrison's 'Something' or Paul McCartney's 'Here There And Everywhere': a classic love song. It may not be the greatest song John Lennon ever wrote, but it reaffirmed his talent and established a benchmark for others to match.

Before he recorded the song at the Hit Factory, Lennon made several demo recordings, perfecting the melody, lyrics, and phrasing each time. Recording proper began on August 8. With the basic tracks recorded, the process of sweetening began with a number of overdubs. He re-recorded his acoustic guitar part and went to considerable lengths to refine his vocal, double-tracking it and dropping in certain key words to create the perfect take. To complete the track, an overdub session was booked for September 15, during which the backing vocal arrangement was refined to Lennon's satisfaction.

'Beautiful Boys' was Ono's answer to Lennon's 'Beautiful Boy (Darling Boy)', inspired by her husband and their son but also addressing a wider audience. "It's a message to men," she explained. "John and Sean inspired me, but the third verse is about all the beautiful boys of the world. That's sort of like the extension of the idea. I had relationships with men, but it was always: 'You know where the door is.' I didn't really trouble to find out what their needs were, what their pains were. With John, that changed. He found out my pain, and I had to find out his pain." Ono's analysis of her relationship with Lennon was insightful and honest. It flattered and encouraged, expressing everything that a loving wife would wish for her husband. It was also a pretty good description of men in general that neatly companioned Lennon's 'Woman'.

Just as Lennon signed off his *Imagine* album with a song inspired by his wife, he chose to conclude his contribution to *Double Fantasy* in similar style. 'Dear Yoko', referred to by Lennon as 'Oh Yoko!' part two, reaffirms his love for Ono but also reveals that its author craved reassurance at times of self-doubt. Every bit as jubilant and celebratory as 'Oh Yoko!', it lacks the poetic allusions that lifted that song from a work of craft to something approaching art.

He made demo recordings of 'Dear Yoko' at his Cold Spring Harbour home on Long Island in the spring of 1980, unusually performing directly to a video camera, and again while on holiday in Bermuda. The studio recording took place on August 14 and was completed in six takes. One of these, possibly take 1, was issued on the *John Lennon Anthology*. Instrumental overdubs were recorded in late August before John added his vocal on September 22.

Ono's 'Every Man Has A Woman Who Loves Him' restates much of what had already been said with 'Beautiful Boys'. All that she had to say about the song was "it's about love". The track features a harmony vocal by Lennon that was later presented as a bona fide lead vocal, which it is not. (Remixed in 1984, it was issued with Lennon's vocal on the Ono tribute album *Every Man Has A Woman Who Loves Him* [823 490-1 Y-1]. Polydor also issued it as a single [881 378-7 US and POSP 712 UK]. Lennon's version was included on the four-CD boxed set *Lennon* [CDS 79 5220 2], issued by EMI on October 30 1990. Both versions of the song were issued as a promotional single by Capitol [7PRO 6 15898 7] in 2001 to promote the remastered *Double Fantasy* and *Milk And Honey* CDs.)

Just as Lennon revived old songs, so did Ono. 'Hard Times Are Over' was the oldest song on the album. Dating from 1973, it was destined for the follow-up to *Feeling The Space, A Story*, which remained unreleased until 1997. It was inspired by a cross-country car journey that the pair took while attempting to kick their drug habit. Speaking with Gillian Gaar in 1997, Ono confirmed that the hard times referred to in the song were the result of drug use. "We were going to withdraw. And we were withdrawing while we were going cross-country. Can you imagine that? It was a station-wagon [that] Peter Bentley, our assistant was driving, and we were trying to get off drugs. And it was really frightening! So we're standing on a corner looking at each other and saying, 'OK, we're going to get off drugs,' it's great." The basic track was recorded on August 19 with overdubs added on September 11 (choir), 19th (Ono's vocals) and 23rd (Lennon's vocals).

Double Fantasy data

Geffen Records issued *Double Fantasy* with generic Geffen labels, inner sleeve with lyrics, and black-and-white cover. Initial copies of the LP were issued with an incorrect track listing on the rear cover, an indication of the speed with which the album was completed.

Double Fantasy was mastered by George Marino at Sterling Sound, New York City, and British pressings were produced from lacquers cut in the USA. Several sets were cut for each country that issued the record. British first pressings were manufactured from UK set 1 (side 2) and UK set 2 (side 1). As demand for the album skyrocketed, the LP was repressed with UK set 3 (side 2) with side 1 being produced from a new lacquer. When the LP was repressed in America, the label had no perimeter text and a slightly larger logo.

Double Fantasy was issued as a Columbia Record Club edition with the track listing corrected on the rear cover. Three editions were manufactured with and without 'CH' on the cover. A black-label edition without 'CH' on the cover was also issued. RCA Music Service also issued the LP (R 104689). In November 1982, the LP was issued by Nautilus Recordings (NR-47) as a half-speed master edition, with a sepia-tone cover, corrected track listing, and a full-colour poster.

The album was reissued in 1989 by Capitol/Columbia House with black/colour band labels (C-1-581425, USA, and EST 2083 UK). In Mexico, it was issued by Warner Bros Records (LWB 5443) on green vinyl.

Although by the late 1970s British record companies had dropped the 8-track cartridge format, *Double Fantasy* was issued in the USA in this form. Three variants were issued. The first by Geffen (GEF-W8-2001), the second by Columbia Record Club (W8-2001), and the third by RCA Record Club in 1981 (S-104689).

Double Fantasy was issued on CD in the USA on September 15 1987 and came in three variations. Most of the CDs were manufactured in Germany and have 'Made in West Germany' printed on the disc. A very small number of the first pressing were manufactured in America and have 'Made in USA' printed on the disc. The CD was also issued by Columbia Record Club (M2G-2001). This version has 'Manufactured by Columbia House under license' added to the backing-tray card. *Double Fantasy* was issued on CD (299131-2) in Britain on October 13 1986, with the first pressing manufactured in Britain. In 1989, EMI/Capitol obtained the rights to issue *Double Fantasy* and released the album on LP, cassette, and CD (CDP 7 91425 2). Next to issue the CD were MFSL Original Master Recordings (UDCD-1-590), in 1994. The album was remastered and reissued by EMI/Capitol on October 9 2000 with three bonus tracks ('Help Me To Help Myself', 'Walking On Thin Ice', and 'Central Park Stroll').

'WOMAN'

SELECTED by Lennon as the follow-up to '(Just Like) Starting Over', 'Woman' was the first posthumous release taken from *Double Fantasy* and a massive hit. Number 1 on both sides of the Atlantic, it spent 11 weeks in the British charts and 17 weeks in the US.

It was issued in the UK and USA with generic Geffen labels and a black-and-white picture sleeve. The single was released in Britain as a cassette single, a format then in its infancy and being heavily promoted as a possible replacement for the vinyl single. 'Woman' was reissued in America on June 5 1981 backed with '(Just Like) Starting Over' (GGEF 0408) as part of Geffen's Back To Back hits series.

'WOMAN' / 'BEAUTIFUL BOYS'
JOHN LENNON / YOKO ONO
UK RELEASE January 16 1981; LP Geffen K 79195; cassette Geffen K 79195M; chart high No.1.
US RELEASE January 12 1981; Geffen GEF 49644; chart high No.2.

THE McCARTNEY INTERVIEW

THIS McCartney interview was given to *Musician* magazine and originally intended to promote *McCartney II*. At first distributed to American radio stations, the two-record set was issued with black-and-white Columbia labels (A2S 821). Disc 1 featured the complete interview, Disc 2 banded excerpts. Some copies of the album included a copy of the *Musician* magazine carrying the original print interview.

The McCartney Interview was then issued commercially, "due to high public demand". Columbia issued the album at budget price with generic red and yellow labels in a limited edition of 57,000. EMI issued the album at a reduced price with black and silver Parlophone labels and deleted it the same day.

THE McCARTNEY INTERVIEW
PAUL McCARTNEY
SIDE 1 'McCartney II', 'Negative criticism of Beatles & Wings', 'His influences', 'Venus And Mars', 'Wild Life, Band On The Run, Musical direction', 'Ringo', 'George', 'Hey Jude, The White Album', 'Tension? Helter Skelter', 'Abbey Road', 'Musical background', 'Trumpet, guitar, piano', 'Learning bass in Hamburg', 'Early Beatles mixes', 'Motown & Stax influences', 'The Sgt Pepper story', 'The Beach Boys' Pet Sounds', 'Rubber Soul', 'Revolver', 'Fame and success', 'Paul's and John's reactions', 'Stage fright during The Beatles & Wings', 'How Wings started', 'New Wave', 'Early Beatles, Creating The Beatles' sound', 'Love Me Do & early songs'.
SIDE 2 'The Beatles' conquest of America', 'Beatles' haircuts and image', 'Paying dues in Hamburg & Liverpool', 'Early tours', 'Weathering pressures', 'The break-up', 'Video of Coming Up', 'Reliving the Beatle image', 'Playing bass', 'Lennon & McCartney songwriting', 'Dislike of formulas', 'Beatles imitators', 'I Am The Walrus', 'The Black Carnation', 'Sgt Pepper LP cover', 'New Wave', 'Bowie, Ferry, Elvis, Pop music & radio', 'Getting married', 'Changing perspective', 'Waterfalls', 'Give Ireland Back To The Irish', 'Hi, Hi, Hi', 'Banned songs', 'Mary Had A Little Lamb'.
UK RELEASE February 23 1981; Parlophone Chat 1; chart high No.34.
US RELEASE December 8 1980; Columbia PC-36987; chart high No.158.

- **'Interview'**

Paul McCartney (speech). Recorded at MPL, London, England.

'WALKING IN THE PARK WITH ELOISE'

WHEN McCartney appeared on the long-running BBC Radio Four programme *Desert Island Discs* on January 30 1982, one of the records he chose was 'Walking In The Park With Eloise', the instrumental written by his father, and EMI reissued the record to coincide with the broadcast.

The reissue is similar to the original, the only difference being a new label: EMI's red and brown design is replaced with a cream label with black text and the EMI box logo in red, bottom centre. Like the original release, it sold in minuscule quantities and became instantly collectable, so much so that a counterfeit picture-disc was produced for those unable to find an official copy.

'WALKING IN THE PARK WITH ELOISE' / 'BRIDGE OVER THE RIVER SUITE'
THE COUNTRY HAMS
UK RELEASE March 1 1982; EMI EMI 2220; failed to chart.

'LUCY IN THE SKY WITH DIAMONDS'

ALTHOUGH EMI suggested that it had no plans to exploit Lennon's back catalogue, the fact that its pressing plant was working overtime to fulfil demand for his records and that a boxed set was planned obviously didn't count as exploitation. Other record companies were quick to issue archive material. DJM Records issued three songs Lennon performed with Elton John on November 28 1974 at Madison Square Garden. This turned out to be his last concert performance (although his last public appearance was on June 13 1975 at a Lew Grade tribute, where he sang a live vocal over pre-recorded backing tracks).

The A-side of this three-track EP had previously been issued as the B-side of Elton John's 'Philadelphia Freedom', but the remaining two live recordings were unreleased. Lennon had of course written 'Lucy In The Sky With Diamonds' in 1967 for The Beatles' groundbreaking *Sgt. Pepper's Lonely Heart's Club Band* album. He was inspired by a painting that his son, Julian, brought home from school. Lennon's dreamy melody and shimmering vocal made it a psychedelic classic, and many assumed that it was influenced by LSD. Its powerful hallucinogenic imagery seemed to confirm as much, but Lennon was adamant that it was not.

Elton John had started performing 'Lucy' in concert in 1974. The song went down remarkably well with British audiences, but

'I SAW HER STANDING THERE' / 'WHATEVER GETS YOU THRU THE NIGHT', 'LUCY IN THE SKY WITH DIAMONDS'
THE ELTON JOHN BAND FEATURING JOHN LENNON WITH THE MUSCLE SHOALS HORNS
UK RELEASE March 13 1981; DJM DJS 10965; chart high No.40.

• **'Lucy In The Sky With Diamonds'** (Lennon, McCartney)
John Lennon (vocals, guitar), Elton John (vocals, piano), Davey Johnstone (guitar), Dee Murray (bass), Nigel Olsson (drums), Ray Cooper (percussion), Muscle Shoals Horns (brass). Live recording at Madison Square Garden, New York City, NY, USA. Produced by Gus Dudgeon.

John discovered that many Americans were unfamiliar with the song. He decided to record his version while in the USA and asked Lennon to play on it. Gus Dudgeon, who produced the record, recalled that Lennon contributed the reggae middle-eight and played guitar on the track, although Gudgeon was only able to use Lennon's guitar part for the middle-eight because the rest was too ragged. Lennon also contributed backing vocals. Elton's reading was issued as a single in 1974, reaching Number 1 in the US charts. The live recording faithfully reproduces the studio arrangement, with Lennon taking lead vocals during the extended chorus.

'Lucy In The Sky With Diamonds' data

DJM prepared white-label test pressings of this 'Saw Her Standing There' EP with the A-side cut at 45 rpm and the B-side at 33 rpm. Commercial pressings of the EP were issued with both sides of the record cut at 33 rpm. DJM placed full-page advertisements in a number of British music weeklies and issued a poster to shops that ordered 25 or more copies. Twelve-inch pressings of the record were issued in Germany and Mexico, where it was pressed on green vinyl.

'WATCHING THE WHEELS'

THE THIRD and final single lifted from *Double Fantasy*, 'Watching The Wheels' was issued on both sides of the Atlantic with generic Geffen labels and a full-colour picture cover. As with the previous Geffen single, it was issued in Britain as a cassette single. It was reissued by Geffen backed with 'Beautiful Boy (Darling Boy)' in 1982 (GGEF 0415) and again in 1986 with black Geffen labels with silver and white print but without the 'Back To Back Hits' logo.

CONCERTS FOR THE PEOPLE OF KAMPUCHEA

THE KHMER Rouge, a Maoist-extremist organisation, ruled Kampuchea (Cambodia) with a brutal grip. Millions were either starved or murdered by the regime before it was removed from power in 1979. Kampuchea was in crisis. In an attempt to raise funds for the stricken country, UN Secretary-General Kurt Waldheim asked Paul McCartney if he would play a one-off benefit concert in aid of the people of the country.

This developed into a series of concerts at the Hammersmith Odeon, London, that featured some of Britain's leading groups. Queen headlined on the first night, The Clash topped the bill on the second, and The Who brought things to a close on the third. Wings closed the short run of concerts on December 29 1979.

A very good audience recording of the Wings/Rockestra set was bootlegged as a double album, *Cold Turkey For Kampuchea*. The band's set for that night reproduced their standard 1979 repertoire, but moved 'Let It Be' to the encore. Wings' set that night was: 'Got To Get You Into My Life', 'Getting Closer', 'Every Night', 'Again And Again And Again', 'I've Had Enough', 'No Words', 'Cook Of The House', 'Old Siam Sir', 'Maybe I'm Amazed', F'ool On The Hill', 'Hot As Sun', 'Spin It On', 'Twenty Flight Rock', 'Go Now', 'Arrow Through Me', 'Coming Up', 'Goodnight Tonight', 'Yesterday', 'Mull Of Kintyre', 'Band On The Run', 'Rockestra Theme', 'Lucille', 'Let It Be', and 'Rockestra Theme'.

All four nights were recorded and filmed, and the money raised from ticket, record, and film sales was donated to UNICEF in aid of the people of Kampuchea.

'Got To Get You Into My Life' was McCartney's attempt as a Beatle at writing a contemporary R&B hit. Influenced by Tamla Motown, he augmented The Beatles' sound with a brass section that included members of Georgie Fame's band – then a hot attraction on the club scene. The other big influence was marijuana. The Beatles had been experimenting with the drug for some time and found it an enlightening experience. McCartney said later: "'Got to Get You Into My Life' was one I wrote when I had first been introduced to pot. I'd been a rather straight working-class lad, but

'WATCHING THE WHEELS' / 'YES, I'M YOUR ANGEL'
JOHN LENNON / YOKO ONO
UK RELEASE March 27 1981; LP Geffen K 79207; cassette Geffen K 79207M; chart high No.30.
US RELEASE March 13 1981; Geffen GEF 49695; chart high No.10.

when we started to get into pot it seemed to me to be quite uplifting. It didn't seem to have too many side-effects like alcohol or some of the other stuff, like pills, which I pretty much kept off. I kind of liked marijuana. I didn't have a hard time with it and to me it was mind-expanding, literally mind-expanding. So 'Got To Get You Into My Life' is really a song about that, it's not to a person, it's actually about pot. It's saying, 'I'm going to do this. This is not a bad idea.' So it's actually an ode to pot, like someone else might write an ode to chocolate or a good claret."

When Wings performed the song, the brass arrangement was restructured to include an introductory fanfare, which allowed the band to open with a few bars of music before McCartney made his big entrance. However, the fanfare was edited out when issued on record.

Because of the special nature of the concerts, there was much talk of a Beatles reunion. Although McCartney had something special planned, neither Lennon, Harrison, nor Starr appeared. Instead, an all-star Rockestra line-up, augmented by several musicians not on the studio recording, made its live debut. Introduced by comedian Billy Connolly, the band played a four-song set, playing 'Rockestra Theme' twice, to close the Wings performance and the concert.

McCartney performed 'Lucille' regularly with The Beatles, eventually recording a version for the BBC in September 1963. The Rockestra version is slightly marred by McCartney forgetting two of the song's three verses. Nevertheless, he gave a solid performance, delivered with gusto. (To promote the album in America, Atlantic issued a promotional 12-inch single on PR 388 that coupled 'Every Night' and 'Lucille' with 'Sister Disco' by The Who And 'Little Sister' by Rockpile and Robert Plant.)

McCartney wrote 'Let It Be' as The Beatles were breaking up, as an attempt to deal with the tensions he experienced at the band's gradual disintegration. Many thought the reference to Mother Mary a religious reference, and the song's spiritual tone apparently confirmed as much. However, its author explained that it was a reference to his mother, who came to him in a dream and told him to "let things be". Performed with Rockestra at the Kampuchea concert, the song builds slowly to take in the full dynamic of the band. Reworking Phil Spector's wall of sound, but with considerably more clout, Rockestra's reading is a little ragged – but all the better for that.

JOHN LENNON
JOHN LENNON
Boxed set, includes seven albums: Plastic Ono Band – Live Peace In Toronto 1969; John Lennon/Plastic Ono Band; Imagine; Some Time In New York City; Mind Games; Walls And Bridges; Rock'N'Roll; Shaved Fish.
UK RELEASE June 15 1981; EMI JLB8; failed to chart.

CONCERTS FOR THE PEOPLE OF KAMPUCHEA
VARIOUS ARTISTS
WINGS 'Got To Get You Into My Life', 'Every Night', 'Coming Up', 'Lucille', 'Let It Be', 'Rockestra Theme'.
UK RELEASE April 3 1981; Atlantic K 60153; chart high No.39.
US RELEASE March 30 1981; Atlantic SD 2-7005; chart high No.36.

- **'Got To Get You Into My Life'** (Lennon, McCartney)
Paul McCartney (bass, vocals), Linda McCartney (keyboards, vocals), Denny Laine (guitar, vocals), Laurence Juber (guitar), Steve Holly (drums), Steve 'Tex' Howard (trumpet), Thaddeus Richard (saxophone), Howie Casey (saxophone), Tony Dorsey (trombone).
- **'Lucille'** (Collins, Penniman)
Personnel as 'Got To Get You Into My Life' plus John Bonham (drums), Billy Bremner (guitar), Gary Booker (keyboards), Dave Edmunds (guitar), James Honeyman-Scott (guitar), Kenny Jones (drums), Ronnie Lane (bass), Robert Plant (bass), Bruce Thomas (bass), Pete Townshend (guitar).
- **'Let It Be'** (Lennon, McCartney)
Personnel as 'Lucille'.

All recorded live on RAK Mobile at Hammersmith Odeon, London, England, and at Island Studios, London, England. Produced by Chris Thomas.

JOHN LENNON

DESPITE EMI's statement that it had no plans to issue any posthumous material, temptation was too great and this monumental but disappointing boxed set was issued in the summer of 1981. Impressive as it is, it contains eight of Lennon's solo albums. His avant-garde output is conspicuous by its absence, and the set contained no new material. The only incentive was a glossy 20-page magazine produced by *The Liverpool Echo* newspaper. All the albums came with their original covers and inserts, except for *Plastic Ono Band – Live Peace In Toronto 1969*, which did not include the calendar, and *John Lennon/Plastic Ono Band* and *Imagine*, which did not have printed inner sleeves.

'EBONY AND IVORY'

'EBONY And Ivory' and 'Rainclouds' were intended for Wings' follow-up to *Back To The Egg*, but events beyond McCartney's control radically altered his plans. Pre-production for the eighth Wings album began in late summer 1980 with rehearsals at various locations in southern England. McCartney asked George

Martin to produce the album and began work with him in October. They began, without Wings, by recording 'We All Stand Together' for the *Rupert And The Frog Song* soundtrack. By the time Wings were due to enter the studio, McCartney and Martin had abandoned the idea of using the group, and instead planned a more flexible approach to recording.

McCartney began writing 'Ebony And Ivory', he said, "after a little marital tiff with Linda. It was like: Why can't we get together? Our piano can." He developed the metaphor to encompass racial concordance, and later recalled some inspiration. "[It was] an idea of Spike Milligan's. I'd read somewhere that he said on a keyboard you need black and white notes to make harmony, and I thought it was a great analogy."

'Ebony And Ivory' reveals how similar Lennon and McCartney were. Like *Imagine*, it asks the listener to envision a world without prejudice. McCartney piled on the sugar-coating to reach as wide an audience as possible, for some its pure pop aesthetic was just too lightweight to convey the complexities of global harmony. McCartney, however, thought otherwise. "When I did 'Ebony And Ivory' with Stevie Wonder – which was a perfectly harmless attempt at promoting racial harmony – some people said, 'Oh, it's just pap.' Well – says you, you know? I mean, tough. The point is, there is some kind of black-and-white problem. ... You can't deny that. I just wanted to do something good, to do a song that I thought might take a little tension out of the situation."

He demoed the song in the summer of 1980 and rehearsed it with Wings at Finchden Manor, Kent, later the same year. But he was unable to take the song any further than the first verse and chorus. "I was thinking it would be a good idea to write a second verse and continue the thought," he explained. "I tried a couple of things, but I just couldn't say anything beyond the bold statement of just the piano analogy." However, by the end of October's rehearsals the song and arrangement were essentially complete. McCartney then made another demo recording at AIR Studios, London, with George Martin, in December 1980.

With the song at last completed, McCartney decided the best way to interpret his new composition would be to work with someone like Stevie Wonder. "I thought, well, it would be really good to do it with a black guy and a white guy and really literally ... show the feeling that you are trying to get over anyway." On February 1 1981, Paul, Linda, and Denny Laine flew to Montserrat to continue work with George Martin on the album they had started in London. Stevie Wonder arrived on the 25th and recording began the next day. McCartney and Wonder warmed up with some jamming, during which Stevie improvised the song's instrumental solo, before beginning work on the basic track. McCartney overdubbed more synthesiser and vocoder parts when he returned to Britain.

As with 'Mull Of Kintyre', you either love or loathe 'Ebony And Ivory'. Both songs have deceptively simple melodies and are sentimental to the point of mawkishness. Nonetheless, this pair of schmaltzy ballads were two of McCartney's biggest hits. 'Ebony And Ivory' is far from the best song he has released, but it's also far from the worst.

McCartney's solo reading of the song, issued on the B-side of the 12-inch, is essentially identical to the A but without Wonder's vocals. There's some speculation that this was McCartney's guide vocal, but it's more likely that he recorded this as a new vocal without Wonder when he resumed recording at AIR London in early 1981.

The other B-side track is 'Rainclouds', a McCartney–Laine composition originally rehearsed with Wings in October-November 1980. In rehearsal it had a country feel, which McCartney rejected in favour of a vigorous 'folk' treatment when he recorded it without Wings. Paddy Maloney, the first of several guests asked to contribute to the project, overdubbed a Celtic-flavoured uilleann pipes solo to complete the song.

'Ebony And Ivory' data

Parlophone issued the single with generic labels and picture sleeve. An alternative version of the 7-inch picture sleeve was produced with a photograph of McCartney and Wonder taken by Linda while recording in Montserrat. However, it was quickly withdrawn, if indeed copies ever reached the stores.

EBONY AND IVORY' / 'RAINCLOUDS'
PAUL McCARTNEY WITH STEVIE WONDER
UK RELEASE March 29 1982; Parlophone R 6054; 12-inch Parlophone 12 R 6054 'Ebony And Ivory' / 'Rainclouds', 'Ebony And Ivory' (Solo Version); chart high No.1.
US RELEASE March 29 1982; Columbia 18-02860; 12-inch 44-02878, released 12 April 1982, 'Ebony And Ivory' / 'Rainclouds', 'Ebony And Ivory (solo version)'; chart high No.1.

• **'Ebony And Ivory'** (McCartney)
Paul McCartney (bass, guitar, synthesisers, vocoder, piano, percussion, vocals), Stevie Wonder (electric piano, synthesisers, drums, percussion, vocals).
Recorded at AIR Studios, London, England, AIR studios, Montserrat, and Strawberry Studios, Dorking, England.
• **'Rainclouds'** (McCartney, Laine)
Paul McCartney (guitar, vocals), Linda McCartney (backing vocals), Denny Laine (guitar, backing vocals), Paddy Maloney (uilleann pipes).
Recorded at AIR Studios, London.
• **'Ebony And Ivory' (Solo Version)** (McCartney)
Paul McCartney (bass, guitar, synthesisers, vocoder, piano, percussion, vocals), Stevie Wonder (electric piano, synthesisers, drums, percussion).
Recorded at AIR Studios, London, England, AIR studios, Montserrat, and Strawberry Studios, Dorking, England.
All produced by George Martin.

Early pressings of the 12-inch erroneously credit McCartney as the sole composer of 'Rainclouds'; it was, of course, co-written with Laine.

Columbia in the USA issued the single on 7- and 12-inch vinyl in both commercial and demonstration variants. They also issued a white vinyl 12-inch single (*A Sample From 'Tug Of War' April 1982* on AS 1444) that featured 'Ebony And Ivory', 'Ballroom Dancing', and 'The Pound Is Sinking'.

TUG OF WAR

ORIGINALLY conceived as Wings' eighth studio album, and a double at that, *Tug Of War* marked the renaissance of McCartney as a solo artist. However, before work commenced, he had several projects to complete. In the summer of 1980, Paul, Linda, and Laurence Juber spent ten days recording with Ringo Starr at Super Bear Studios in the small French village of Bear Les Alpes. McCartney produced five songs, including four for Ringo: 'Private Property' and 'Attention', both McCartney compositions, Carl Perkins's 'Sure To Fall', and 'You Can't Fight Lightning', a song ad-libbed by Ringo. He also produced the first version of Linda's 'Love's Full Glory', which remains unreleased (a re-recorded version would appear on Linda's *Wide Prairie* album).

After a summer break, Wings returned to work and began rehearsing in England at Finchden Manor near Tenterden, Kent, where they worked on versions of 'Ballroom Dancing', 'Rainclouds', 'Average Person', 'Keep Under Cover', and 'Ebony And Ivory'. The band then spent a brief spell in Eastbourne before moving to Reading – possibly to Martin Rushent's Genetic Studios in Goring – where they recorded overdubs for the ongoing *Cold Cuts* album. This was the last time that Wings recorded as a group, for when McCartney and George Martin began pre-production work on *Tug Of War* they decided to drop the group. When recording began in late 1980, Denny Laine was the only survivor from Wings involved with the project.

There were many reasons for McCartney abandoning Wings, not least of which was his disappointment with the group's progress. Interviewed by *Playboy* in 1983, Linda said: "I think Paul was very frustrated. He wanted it to work with Wings, but he just picked the wrong people. He needed the best to work with, but he had to carry all of the weight." His increased interest in bona fide solo projects and a growing frustration with the group format distanced McCartney from Wings.

Listening to the band's final rehearsals, one can't help but be reminded of the lethargy and tension that surrounded The Beatles' *Get Back/Let It Be* project. By 1980, Wings had come to the end of its serviceable life. The band could have continued as a three-piece, as it had before, but declining sales, indifferent reviews, and frustrations with a continuously changing line-up must have influenced McCartney's decision to start afresh.

After eight years, Wings had become an anathema. Discussing the matter with George Martin, McCartney decided to 'cast' the new album like a play or film and recruit the best players available for each song. "We decided not to be as restricted, and just write anything and then get in anyone we thought could play it," said McCartney. "So we started a new era, working with whoever we thought was most suitable for the tune. If it was a thing that needed [drummer] Steve Gadd's particular kind of thing, we decided we'd get him, rather than just asking someone to be *like* Steve Gadd."

By April 1981, with much of *Tug Of War* recorded, Denny Laine announced that he was leaving and returning to live performance, something McCartney was then unwilling to contemplate. Effectively forcing McCartney's hand, Laine's departure meant that on April 27 1981 Wings were officially disbanded.

Although McCartney had amassed a large backlog of songs, which he hoped to record for his new album, George Martin dismissed several as substandard and told him to rethink, rework, or rewrite much of what he'd submitted. Martin laid down some strict ground rules. He told McCartney: "If it's really going to work out, you're going to have to accept some stick from me, and you may not like it, because you've been your own boss for so long."

As producer, Martin did what he had always done: he weeded out the bad songs from the good and brought some discipline to the project. What McCartney missed most as a solo artist was a first-rate collaborator, someone he could respect and who would tell him if something was second-rate. While *McCartney II* was a Number 1 album, its sales tailed off quickly, and many considered McCartney capable of better things. He needed to produce something special or watch his career nosedive, and Martin was the producer he needed to bring out the best in him.

Recording began in December 1980 with 'Keep Under Cover', 'Ballroom Dancing', 'Rainclouds', 'Ode To A Koala Bear', and an inevitably unreleased McCartney composition, 'All The Love Is There'. After a Christmas break, recording recommenced at Martin's AIR Studios on the island of Montserrat, where McCartney recorded most of his guests' contributions. In March, McCartney returned to England and recorded the inevitably unreleased 'Stop You Don't Know Where She Came From', a song written and demoed in 1980. After another short break, overdubbing and mixing took place at various studios before work on the title track commenced in London and Hastings.

Considerable care was taken over every aspect of *Tug Of War*, so much so that the album was rescheduled no fewer than five times before it was eventually released on April 26 1982. McCartney and Martin's perfectionism was rewarded with an Ampex Golden Reel Award, presented when albums professionally

TUG OF WAR
PAUL McCARTNEY
SIDE 1 'Tug Of War', 'Take It Away', 'Somebody Who Cares', 'What's That You're Doing', 'Here Today'.
SIDE 2 'Ballroom Dancing', 'Wanderlust', 'Get It', 'Be What You See' (Link), 'Dress Me Up As A Robber', 'Ebony And Ivory'.
UK RELEASE April 26 1982; Parlophone PCTC 259; chart high No.1.
US RELEASE April 26 1982; LP Columbia TC-37462; 8-track cartridge Columbia TCA-37462; chart high No.1.

• **'Tug Of War'** (McCartney)
Paul McCartney (bass, guitar, synthesisers, drums, vocals), Campbell Maloney (military snares), Denny Laine (guitar), Eric Stewart (guitar, backing vocals), Linda McCartney (backing vocals), orchestra led by Kenneth Silito.
• **'Take It Away'** (McCartney)
Paul McCartney (bass, guitar, piano, vocals), Ringo Starr (drums), Steve Gadd (drums), Linda McCartney (backing vocals), George Martin (electric piano), Eric Stewart (backing vocals).
• **'Somebody Who Cares'** (McCartney)
Paul McCartney (guitar, vocals), Stanley Clarke (bass), Steve Gadd (drums, percussion), Denny Laine (guitar synthesister), Adrian Brett (pan pipes), Linda McCartney (backing vocals), Eric Stewart (backing vocals).
• **'What's That You're Doing'** (McCartney, Wonder)
Paul McCartney (bass, guitar, drums, vocals), Stevie Wonder (synthesisers, vocals), Andy Mackay (Lyricon), Linda McCartney (backing vocals), Eric Stewart (backing vocals).
• **'Here Today'** (McCartney)
Paul McCartney (guitar, vocals), Jack Rothstein (violin), Bernard Partridge (violin), Ian Jewel (viola), Keith Harvey (cello).
• **Ballroom Dancing** (McCartney)
Paul McCartney (bass, piano, guitar, drums, percussion, vocals) Denny Laine (guitar), Jack Brymer (clarinet), Linda McCartney (backing vocals), Eric Stewart (backing vocals), Peter Marshall (narration).
• **'The Pound Is Sinking'** (McCartney)
Paul McCartney (guitar, synthesisers, vocals), Stanley Clarke (bass), Denny Laine (guitar), Linda McCartney (backing vocals), Eric Stewart (backing vocals).
• **'Wanderlust'** (Paul McCartney)
Paul McCartney (bass, guitar, piano, vocals), Adrian Sheppard (drums, percussion), Denny Laine (bass), Linda McCartney (backing vocals), Eric Stewart (backing vocals), The Philip Jones Brass Ensemble (horns).
• **'Get It'** (McCartney)
Paul McCartney (bass, guitar, synthesisers, percussion, vocals), Carl Perkins (guitar, vocals).
• **'Be What You See' (Link)** (McCartney)
Paul McCartney (guitar, vocoder).
• **'Dress Me Up As A Robber'** (McCartney)
Paul McCartney (bass, guitar, vocals), Dave Mattacks (drums, percussion), Denny Laine (synthesiser, guitar), George Martin (electric piano), Linda McCartney (backing vocals).
All recorded at AIR Studios, Montserrat and AIR studios, London, England, except: 'Take It Away' at Montserrat only; 'Here Today', 'Ballroom Dancing', 'Wanderlust', 'Be What You See' at London only; 'Tug Of War' at London plus Genetic Studios, Goring, England, Strawberry Studios, Dorking, England, and unknown studio, Hastings, Kent, England.
All produced by George Martin.

mastered entirely on Ampex tape reached gold record status. When issued in Japan, *Tug Of War* became the first number 1 and biggest selling album there by a European artist since 1977: proof, if any where needed, that the 'Japanese incident' had done little damage to McCartney's career.

Tug Of War songs

If the album had a theme, then its title track expressed it as well as any other song on the record. Introduced with the sounds of a tug of war, its intimate acoustic setting conveys a sense of brooding resignation. A sublime orchestral statement introduces an air of emotional tension, before it is shattered by crashing, overdriven electric guitars in the middle eight, and then the orchestra returns to signify contemplation of the ultimate question – the meaning of life.

As McCartney explained, 'Tug Of War' is "a song about life really being a tug of war. I think when I was younger, I had always thought that life was a pretty groovy affair and that tragedies happened to other people, not really to me, [which I think] is one of the things of youth. I wouldn't say … my personal relationships, but just generally you have to admit [that] it is a bit up and down at some point. And this is really my song admitting that there's a lot of up and down." Although McCartney had explored this theme before, this time he more successfully matched lyric and melody, and the simple but effective metaphor conveys better than previous attempts the uncertainties and tensions he'd hoped to express.

Ringo Starr's arrival in Montserrat fuelled press speculation about an imminent Beatles reunion or a tribute to the murdered John Lennon. Although *Tug Of War* featured McCartney's tribute to Lennon, it didn't involve Starr. Rather, the drummer had arrived to help record 'Take It Away', a song McCartney originally wrote with him in mind. However, as McCartney explained, "I thought it would suit me better the way it went into the chorus and stuff; I didn't think it was very Ringo."

He recorded a solo demo before attempting the song properly with Starr. But before he did that he altered the last verse: the flowers waiting in the jar had originally been a couple waiting for the band. To assist the other musicians, George Martin recorded a guide piano part. Normally this wouldn't have made the final mix, but McCartney decided to keep it, because "I thought he did some really good stuff. I said, 'Come on George, get in there.' He doesn't normally play the part of a musician, he's normally the producer or arranger." Back in London, McCartney worked on the song with Eric Stewart, who did much to develop its stunning vocal harmonies. Stewart had been guitarist and singer with The Mindbenders, and later 10CC.

Leading bass player Stanley Clarke and session veteran Steve Gadd joined McCartney during his second week in Montserrat. Again, several tracks were recorded, although only 'Somebody Who Cares' and 'The Pound Is Sinking' made it onto *Tug Of War*. McCartney wrote 'Somebody Who Cares' while in Montserrat. "I wrote it out one Sunday afternoon ... and this Sunday afternoon I was anticipating Steve Gadd's arrival and [Stanley Clarke's], and I liked the idea of writing something for them coming. You know, so it would be fresh for everyone." Made with Clarke, Gadd, and Laine, the recording underlined the value of McCartney and Martin's ethos of quality over quantity, and the song's sense of melancholy, cogitation, and revelation was captured perfectly by this select group of musicians.

Stevie Wonder arrived in Montserrat to record 'Ebony And Ivory', but like many of the other guests he ended up writing and recording another song with his host. After recording the basic tracks for 'Ebony And Ivory', McCartney and Wonder got together for an impromptu jam, which became 'What's That You're Doing'. Wonder improvised a keyboard riff that influenced the entire feel of the song, while McCartney added drums, which, at Wonder's suggestion, he re-recorded. Despite it being little more than an extended jam, the recording took them all night, with the backing track and vocal overdubs finished early on the morning of Wonder's departure. Back in London, Paul, Linda, and Eric Stewart added backing vocals, and Andy Mackay of Roxy Music overdubbed a solo on Lyricon, a wind-instrument synthesiser.

Immediately after Lennon's murder, McCartney and George Harrison felt compelled to express their feelings about the loss of a close and dear friend. Writing about their loss, each gave vent to emotions that neither had expressed while Lennon was alive and which, perhaps, they now wished they had.

Harrison and Starr recorded the basic track for Harrison's 'All Those Years Ago' in the last week of November 1980, and Paul, Linda, and Denny Laine added their backing vocals to the recording early in 1981. This marked the first time the surviving ex-Beatles appeared together on the same record, even if they had recorded their parts at different times.

Explaining the need to voice his feelings, McCartney talked about 'Here Today'. "I was just sitting down trying to write a song; I just felt like writing something. I got the opening chords, and I was just thinking about him and stuff, and I'd had these thoughts in my mind – it was round about the time just after John's thing – and I'd sort of wanted to do something. But the worst thing would have been to do something a bit corny cos I know he would have just parted the clouds and blown a raspberry at me. ... So I tried to put into words what my thoughts were, which was if you were here today, what would you say when someone says, 'What was John like, then?' I'd start saying, 'Oh he was like this, and he was like that,' and I can imagine him blowing the raspberries. This is what the song is, you know: I'm sort of saying even though you blow that raspberry, I really did actually know you, and you were a great guy."

Both McCartney and George Martin believed that a string quartet was the best way to treat this emotional ballad. But having previously shied away from references to The Beatles, McCartney didn't want to commit himself to anything too self-referential. However, neither did he want to dismiss a musical idiom out of hand just because it was associated with a particular song. "I thought, well, this is stupid, it's like saying because you've used a guitar once in 1980 you should never use a guitar again. It's silly condemning this format of a string quartet just cos we'd used it once on a famous record – you know, 'Yesterday'. So I then said to George look, let's just try a string quartet, let's get it all worked up, let's do it. There's no reason why we shouldn't keep using string quartets till we drop."

Years later, McCartney revealed how personal his lyric was. During an interview for *Good Morning America* in May 2001 he said: "The night we cried was a real night when [Lennon and I had] been diverted from Jacksonville down South. We stayed up all night and we got drunk and we talked a lot. And we got way too deep and got into each other's characters. We never had enough time to do that with The Beatles, so this was probably a good thing. And we ended up crying. I'm just reminding myself that we got that intimate. That's why we loved each other so much in The Beatles." Like 'Yesterday', which looks backwards to a simpler and better time, 'Here Today' makes similar allusions to a past that appeared infinitely preferable to the present.

Next on *Tug Of War* comes a rocker dressed in taffeta and sequins. 'Ballroom Dancing' combines the sophistication of Geraldo's Cunard Yanks with the laddish bravado of a Liverpool youth on the pull. Mixing rock'n'roll with the big-band sounds of his youth, McCartney found that it evoked memories of his youth. He said: "Basically, it's all my childhood memories distilled into one song, which develops into memories of being a teenager and going to dance halls and ballrooms – only they're called discos now." The arrangement also makes reference to the popular British television programme *Come Dancing*. Peter Marshall, who provides the narration, was a commentator on the show, which televised ballroom-dancing competitions.

McCartney recorded a demo of 'Ballroom Dancing' in the summer of 1980 and rehearsed the song later that year with Wings. He recorded the basic tracks at AIR London on December 7 1980. Overdubs of Jack Brymer's clarinet and Denny Laine and Eric Stewart's guitars were added on March 17 1981. (McCartney re-recorded the song with a line-up that included Ringo Starr and guitarist Dave Edmunds for the 1984 album *Give My Regards To Broad Street*.)

McCartney had been working on 'The Pound Is Sinking' since 1977. He completed it in the summer of 1980 by incorporating another unfinished song, 'Hear Me Lover'. He explained that the song was influenced by "the apparent ridiculousness of the money market – the ups and downs and the indexes and stuff. ... For me it's just a funny thing about the pundits day-to-day giving us an update so that all the people who've got money can gauge it all, like the weather. It's a funny idea; I like the idea of all the ants doing what the lead ant tells them. You know: the oracle." Whether the changes in tempo were intended to mirror the ups and downs of the stock market or not, when combined with Martin's slick production, they effectively mask the fact that the bridge in 'Hear Me Lover' bears little relation to the main body of the song.

'Wanderlust' was influenced by an incident that occurred while Wings were recording aboard a flotilla of motor-yachts moored off the Virgin Islands. US Customs officials searched the yachts for marijuana, which upset the captain of the yacht on which McCartney and his family were staying. "[He] was a little sort of heavier than the other captains," said McCartney, "he sort of took it a little more seriously. And at some stage we had an argument with him, and I said, 'You know, we don't need all this aggro stuff,' and we wanted to get off onto this other boat that happened to be in the harbour. These people had said we could come on this boat, and this boat happened to be called *Wanderlust*, so it became a symbol of freedom to me, this catamaran called *Wanderlust*."

Documenting yet another run-in with the authorities, McCartney concocted a deliberately ambiguous lyric that makes implicit reference to his views on soft drugs. "What petty crime was I found guilty of?" he asks, knowingly. Hiding behind a smokescreen of pseudo-religiosity, McCartney's lyric could easily be read as referring to any number of things other than the rights and wrongs of smoking pot. A sublime brass arrangement played by The Philip Jones Brass Ensemble combined with Martin's understated production gives further credence to the theme of deliverance and freedom that McCartney's uplifting melody evokes. Few would suspect that the song concerns the impending threat of another high-profile drugs bust rather than personal redemption.

Carl Perkins arrived in Montserrat on February 21 to record 'Get It'. Perkins was a true rock'n'roll pioneer: he wrote 'Blue Suede Shoes', toured with Johnny Cash, and influenced The Beatles, who recorded several of his songs. Before he and McCartney began the serious task of recording, they engaged in some nostalgic jamming. To warm up, they ran through casual versions of 'Honey Don't', 'Boppin' The Blues', and 'Lend Me Your Comb'. They also attempted 'Red Sails In The Sunset', 'Cut Across Shorty', 'When The Saints Go Marching In', 'Please Please Me', and 'Love Me Do'. None of these recordings was released, but when McCartney met up with Perkins backstage in Memphis on April 27 1993 they ran through similar material, some of which found its way onto Perkins's *Go Cat Go!* video.

A cute song, 'Get It' benefits from Perkins's rockabilly licks and the intimacy of its recording. Coupled with Perkins's infectious laugh, these elements make 'Get It' as pleasant a song as anything on the album. His laughter resulted from McCartney's use of an expression he had heard his visitor use earlier in the week. While attending a party aboard an expensive yacht, Perkins had remarked that back home he would have referred to his lavish surroundings as "shitting in high cotton". McCartney's use of the phrase to refer to a particularly good take caused Perkins's outburst, which was left in place, minus McCartney's comment,.

Perkins was so taken with his host's hospitality that the night after recording 'Get It' he wrote 'My Old Friend', which he recorded the following day. McCartney completed the song at his Hog-Hill studio by overdubbing bass, piano, harmonies, and drums onto the multi-track tape. Scheduled for release as a Carl Perkins single in 1983, it remained in the can until released on Perkins's *Go Cat Go!* album.

McCartney recorded 'Be What You See' (Link) solo to link 'Get It' and 'Dress Me Up As A Robber', and it's nothing more than a musical fragment. While it's more considered than those used as links on *Wild Life*, it's still a fragment. How it links these two disparate songs thematically is anyone's guess.

He wrote 'Dress Me Up As A Robber' in 1977 and recorded a solo demo in the summer of 1980. When George Martin heard the song in its rough state he was unsure of its potential and prompted McCartney to finish it. He recorded a second demo, which did pass Martin's quality control. The song completed, it was recorded with Laine, drummer Dave Mattacks, and Martin in Montserrat on February 3 1981.

Despite the work he'd put into completing the song, McCartney suggested that, like many of his songs, 'Dress Me Up As A Robber' had just come to him. Typically dismissive of his lyrics, he implied that it could be about being true to yourself. "You can do whatever you like to me, you can tell me what you like, but I'll still be what I am; you can dress me up as a sailor, a robber, a soldier, but it won't really matter, I will still be me."

Tug Of War data

Parlophone issued *Tug Of War* in the UK with customised labels and printed inner sleeve. The cover featured artwork by Brian Clarke, who, with this album, began a lengthy partnership with the McCartneys. Test pressings were manufactured with plain green labels for use by EMI's sales reps. Promotional copies of the LP were issued with three A4 sheets of press information housed in an outer sleeve based on Clarke's red and blue abstract motif.

Columbia issued the album in the USA on vinyl and 8-track cartridge (TCA-37462). 8-tracks were produced with either black, grey, or blue shells.

'I'LL GIVE YOU A RING'

'TAKE It Away' was remixed and the cross-fade from *Tug Of War* removed for its release as a single. McCartney wrote the B-side, *I'll Give You A Ring*, in 1974, and the recording features him playing all of the instruments with the exception of clarinet, which was played by Tony Coe. A skilful arrangement and solid production mask the song's more obvious shortcomings.

Issued by Parlophone in Britain with generic labels and a picture sleeve designed by Hipgnosis, both 7- and 12-inch versions featured identical artwork. Columbia issued the single in the USA with generic labels and picture sleeve identical to the British release. Promotional copies of the Columbia 7-inch single have white labels with black print and MPL's 'juggler' logo on the left side of the label.

'TUG OF WAR'

THE A-SIDE was remixed for release as a single, removing the audio-vérité and creating a clean fade, while 'Get It' had the cross-fade from 'Be What You See' (Link) removed. Both Parlophone and Columbia issued the single with generic labels. Parlophone issued the record with a picture sleeve; Columbia with a generic paper sleeve.

'TAKE IT AWAY' / 'I'LL GIVE YOU A RING'
PAUL McCARTNEY
UK RELEASE June 21 1982; Parlophone R 6056; 12-inch Parlophone 12 R 6056 'Take It Away' / 'I'll Give You A Ring', 'Dress Me Up As A Robber'; chart high No.15.
US RELEASE June 21 1982; Columbia 18-03018; 12-inch Columbia 44-03019 'Take It Away' / 'I'll Give You A Ring', 'Dress Me Up As A Robber; chart high No.10.

• **'I'll Give You A Ring'** (McCartney)
Paul McCartney (bass, piano, guitar, drums, percussion, vocals), Linda McCartney (backing vocals), Eric Stewart (backing vocals), Tony Coe (clarinet).
Recording location unknown. Produced by George Martin.

'TUG OF WAR' / 'GET IT'
PAUL McCARTNEY
UK RELEASE September 20 1982; Parlophone R 6057; chart high No.53.
US RELEASE September 13 1982; Columbia 38-03235; failed to chart.

'THE GIRL IS MINE' / 'CAN'T GET OUTTA THE RAIN'
MICHAEL JACKSON & PAUL McCARTNEY
UK RELEASE October 29 1982; Epic EPC A2729; picture disc Epic EPC A 11-2729; red vinyl 7-inch Epic MJ 1-5 released November 25 1983; chart high No.8 (re-enters January 1983, chart high No.75).
US RELEASE October 25 1982; Epic 34-03288; one-sided edition Epic ENR-03372; chart high No.2.

• **'The Girl Is Mine'** (Jackson)
Michael Jackson (vocals), Paul McCartney (vocals), Greg Phillinganes (keyboards), David Paich (keyboards), David Foster (keyboards), Steve Porcaro (keyboards), Dean Parks (guitar), Steve Lukather (guitar), Louis Johnson (bass), Jeff Porcaro (drums).
Recorded at Cherokee Studios, Ocean Way Studios, and Westlake Audio, Los Angeles, CA, USA.
Produced by Quincy Jones.

'THE GIRL IS MINE'

RUMOURS of a McCartney–Jackson collaboration had been circulating since April 1980. Press speculation suggested that Jackson was to contribute to *Tug Of War*, but 'The Girl Is Mine', from Jackson's *Thriller* album, was the first real evidence of a collaboration between the two.

McCartney met Jackson for the first time in New Orleans in early 1975, but there was little real contact between the two until Jackson had his manager present McCartney with a gold disc of *Off The Wall* (which featured a cover of McCartney's 'Girlfriend'). Then, in early 1980, Jackson phoned McCartney, suggesting they get together to write some 'hits'. The pair eventually met in May 1981 and worked on two songs, 'Say Say Say' and 'The Man', both destined for *Pipes Of Peace* and recorded before McCartney worked with Jackson on 'The Girl Is Mine' in April 1982.

When he came to record Jackson's song, McCartney voiced concerns about the lyrics. "I didn't like 'the dog-gone girl is mine'." He asked Jackson if he was sure about the line. "Michael said, 'Yeah it's great.' I said, 'Well, if you're into it, I haven't got a problem with it.'"

McCartney also felt troubled by the spoken middle section, which he found a little too Barry White. Yet he was loath to challenge either Jackson or Quincy Jones because of their reputations. "I'm working with Michael and I'm working with Quincy Jones, don't forget, who's one dude, you know. He's something else, Quincy, and he's a massive talent right there. So, if Quincy thinks it's good, I'm not going to argue with someone like him. I mean I could have, in fact I did. I said, 'Wait a minute, this is a bit [puts on Barry White voice] 'hello girl'. But he said, 'No, do it, it'll be great.'" If only McCartney had persisted, we might have been spared one of the more embarrassing moments in his career.

'The Girl Is Mine' data

In Britain, Epic issued the single with generic blue labels and picture sleeve. In an attempt to boost the single's chart position, the company also issued a limited-edition picture disc (EPC A 11-2729). The single was later issued on red vinyl (MJ 1-5) as part of a nine-single pack that brought together most of Jackson's Epic singles.

In the USA, Epic issued two versions of the commercial 7-inch single. Besides the standard two-song edition, Epic issued a one-sided pressing (ENR-03372) as part of a marketing campaign that sold one-track singles at about half the price of a standard two-sided version. Promotional copies of the single issued to American radio stations were issued without the McCartney–Jackson dialogue.

THE JOHN LENNON COLLECTION
JOHN LENNON
SIDE 1 'Give Peace A Chance', 'Instant Karma!', 'Power To The People', 'Whatever Gets You Thru The Night', '#9 Dream', 'Mind Games', 'Love', 'Happy Xmas (War Is Over)'.
SIDE 2 'Imagine', 'Jealous Guy', 'Stand By Me', '(Just Like) Starting Over', 'Woman', 'I'm Losing You', 'Beautiful Boy (Darling Boy)', 'Watching The Wheels', 'Dear Yoko'.
The US release does not include 'Happy Xmas' or 'Stand By Me', and 'Dear Yoko' precedes 'Watching The Wheels'.
UK RELEASE November 1 1982; LP Parlophone EMTV 37; CD Parlophone CDEMTV 37 released October 23 1989; chart high No.1.
US RELEASE November 8 1982; LP Geffen GHSP 2023; 8-track cartridge Geffen GEF-L8-2023; chart high No.33.

'LOVE' / 'GIVE ME SOME TRUTH'
JOHN LENNON
UK RELEASE November 15 1982; Parlophone R 5958; chart high No.41.

THE JOHN LENNON COLLECTION

THE SECOND overview of Lennon's career, this album updated the previous compilation, *Shaved Fish*, with the addition of songs from his last album, *Double Fantasy*. Because it included material issued by Geffen Records, the album was delayed by almost a year – it had been planned for late 1981. The problem was solved by EMI/Parlophone issuing the album in Britain and Geffen in the USA. Perhaps because Geffen had fewer tracks to licence, the American release did not include 'Happy Xmas (War Is Over)' or 'Stand By Me'. However, Geffen did issue 'Happy Xmas' as a single (7-29855) to promote the album. In Britain, *The John Lennon Collection* was promoted with the single release of 'Love' (R 5958).

Geffen also issued Quiex II audiophile pressings to promote the album. These promotional records have a Quiex II sticker, track list sticker, and gold embossed text 'Lent For Promotional Use Only' on the front cover.

In Britain, EMI promoted the album with television advertising and in-store displays that featured 12-inch-square cover flats, 20-inch by 30-inch full-colour posters, and life-size cut-outs of Lennon. The campaign was a huge success. *The John Lennon Collection* sold 300,000 copies in its first week and a million by its third.

EMI issued the LP with generic Parlophone labels and full-colour inner sleeve with lyrics. Geffen issued the LP with generic Geffen labels and cover and inner sleeves identical to the British release. EMI issued the CD (CD EMTV 37) on October 23 1989 with two extra songs, 'Move Over Ms. L' and 'Cold Turkey'. Geffen did not have the rights to issue the album on CD, and instead it was issued by Capitol (CDP 7 91516 2) on January 29 1990.

'LOVE'

ISSUED to promote *The John Lennon Collection*, 'Love' was released by Parlophone with generic labels and a full-colour picture cover. It was remixed for single release, with the quiet piano intro and fade-out placed much higher in the mix in an attempt to make it radio-friendly.

'SAY SAY SAY'

McCARTNEY co-wrote 'Say Say Say' with Michael Jackson in London early in 1981. He already had the bare bones of the song and used the same tried-and-trusted technique he'd employed when writing with John Lennon to finish it with Jackson. He talked about the mechanics of the process. "I could see when [Jackson] liked something, and I could see when I was getting somewhere, and he started to throw little ideas in and stuff. … Then he came back the next day and he had done a lot of the words to it, so it was just a to and fro thing."

Although the song was written quickly, its recording stretched over several months and spanned two continents. Basic tracks were recorded in May 1982 at AIR London before the horn section was overdubbed at Cherokee in Los Angeles. Final overdubbing was completed when Jackson returned to stay with the McCartneys in February 1983.

Although it features Michael Jackson, who unlike Stevie Wonder got equal billing, 'Say Say Say' made erratic progress in the British singles charts. It entered at Number 25, rising the following week to 10, which ensured an airing of the video on the key TV chart show, *Top Of The Pops*. However, McCartney or someone at his record company decided to delay showing the expensive promotional video as the soundtrack wasn't quite right. No doubt everyone assumed that the single would continue its steady climb to the top of the charts. After all, Michael Jackson was hot property. But the following week the single dropped and the *Top Of The Pops* policy was only to feature artists whose records were ascending the charts.

With the McCartney camp unable to get the most prestigious music programme on British television to change its criteria, hurried negotiations took place between EMI and the BBC. The video was eventually premiered on Noel Edmonds's *Late Late Breakfast Show* on October 29 1983, but only on the proviso that McCartney participated in a live interview, which to his obvious discomfort he did. The ploy worked, and the following week 'Say Say Say' rose to Number 4 and eventually Number 2. The single fared even better in the USA, where it went to Number 1, staying there for a total of five weeks over the Christmas period.

The B-side, 'Ode To A Koala Bear', was recorded at AIR Studios in late 1980 and, like the animal to which it refers, is too cute for its own good. Once again, McCartney employs a cuddly animal as a metaphor for love. The result is unconvincing: the image is too sugary and ineffective, and merely confirms McCartney's predilection for sentimentality and that he was running out of ideas.

'SAY SAY SAY' / 'ODE TO A KOALA BEAR'
PAUL McCARTNEY & MICHAEL JACKSON
UK RELEASE October 3 1983; Parlophone R 6062; 12-inch Parlophone 12 R 6062 'Say Say Say (Remix)' / 'Say Say Say (Instrumental)', 'Ode To A Koala Bear'; chart high No.2.
US RELEASE October 3 1983; Columbia 38-04 168; 12-inch Columbia 44-04 169 'Say Say Say (Remix)' / 'Say Say Say (Instrumental)', 'Ode To A Koala Bear'; chart high No.1.

• **'Say Say Say'** (McCartney, Jackson)
Paul McCartney (keyboards, guitar, vocals), Michael Jackson (vocals), Bill Wolfer (keyboards), Nathan Watts (bass), Hughie Burns (guitar), Jerry Hey (horns), Gary E Grant (trumpet), Ernie Watts (saxophone), Chris Smith (harmonica), Ricky Lawson (drums).
Recorded at AIR Studios, London, England, and Cherokee Studios, Los Angeles, CA, USA.
• **'Ode To A Koala Bear'** (McCartney)
Paul McCartney (bass, piano, guitar, drums, vocals), Linda McCartney (backing vocals), Eric Stewart (backing vocals).
Recorded at AIR Studios, London, England.
Both produced by George Martin.

'Say Say Say' data

Parlophone issued 'Say Say Say' on 7 and 12-inch formats with generic labels and picture sleeve. The 7-inch single featured a 3:51 mix by George Martin. The 12-inch offered a John 'Jellybean' Benitez remix and a seven-minute instrumental mix (essentially the backing track without vocals). Columbia issued the record on 7 and 12-inch formats with generic labels and picture sleeve identical to the British release. Demonstration copies of the Columbia 7-inch single had the stereo version of the A-side on each side of the disc and white labels with black text. Demonstration copies of the 12-inch had generic red Columbia labels with the addition of 'DEMONSTRATION NOT FOR SALE' top centre.

PIPES OF PEACE

TUG OF *War* had received generally favourable reviews, with Nick Kent of the *NME* suggesting that it was "arguably as fine a piece of work as McCartney has ever put his name to". But *Pipes Of Peace* was savaged. Despite reports concerning the quantity and quality of songs McCartney and Martin were producing, this new album was generally recognised as being little more than a collection of mediocre outtakes.

McCartney had too much material to choose from when compiling *Tug Of War*, but the same cannot be said for *Pipes Of Peace*, which was assembled from the leftovers that didn't make the previous album. This time the *NME* considered it "a dull, tired and empty collection of quasi-funk and gooey rock arrangements ... with McCartney cooing platitudinous sentiments on a set of lyrics seemingly made up on the spur of the moment."

The paper's pejorative use of "quasi-funk" to describe the album neatly described the direction in which George Martin wanted to take McCartney's songs. Martin said: "Way back when we started *Tug Of War*, my thoughts to Paul were, 'Let's make a slightly harder, a more funky album than perhaps you have done in the past.' ... In fact, the *Pipes Of Peace* album became more what we were looking for in *Tug Of War*." Thankfully, *Tug Of War* didn't turn out as Martin intended. Unfortunately, *Pipes Of Peace* did.

As with the previous album, McCartney–Martin 'cast' the album, but took their idea a step further by considering each song as part of a spectacular stage production. McCartney had the idea of using sound effects and other gimmicks to create 'visual vignettes' – perhaps an attempt to distract the listener from the insipid nature of his songs. Sadly, the idea backfired. Where *Tug Of War* engaged, *Pipes Of Peace* merely palled. Where the previous album appeared to indicate something of a renaissance, *Pipes Of Peace* marked the beginning of a creative rut for McCartney that lasted throughout the 1980s. It was also, relatively, a commercial disappointment. Despite its two Number

PIPES OF PEACE
PAUL McCARTNEY
SIDE 1 'Pipes Of Peace', 'Say Say Say', 'The Other Me', 'Keep Under Cover', 'So Bad'.
SIDE 2 'The Man', 'Sweetest Little Show', 'Average Person', 'Hey Hey', 'Tug Of Peace', 'Through Our Love'.
UK RELEASE October 31 1983; LP Parlophone PCTC 1652301; CD Parlophone CDP 7460182 released February 29 1984; chart high No.4.
US RELEASE October 31 1983; LP Columbia QC-39419; CD Columbia CDP 7460182 released February 29 1984; chart high No.15.

• **'Pipes Of Peace'** (McCartney)
Paul McCartney (piano, bass drums, percussion, vocals), Linda McCartney (backing vocals), Eric Stewart (backing vocals), James Kippen (tabla), Pestalozzi Children's Choir (backing vocals).
• **'The Other Me'** (McCartney)
Paul McCartney (vocals, bass, keyboards, guitar, percussion, drums).
• **Keep Under Cover** (McCartney)
Paul McCartney (vocals, piano), Denny Laine (guitar), Linda McCartney (backing vocals), Stanley Clarke (bass), Gavin Wright (violin), Steve Gadd (drums).
• **'So Bad'** (McCartney)
Paul McCartney (bass, keyboards, vocals), Linda McCartney (backing vocals), Eric Stewart (backing vocals), Ringo Starr (drums).
• **The Man** (McCartney, Jackson)
Paul McCartney (bass, keyboards, vocals), Michael Jackson (vocals), Bill Wolfer (keyboards), Hughie Burns (guitar), Nathan Watts (bass), Jerry Hey (horns), Gary Herbig (flute), Ricky Lawson (drums).
• **'Sweetest Little Show'** (McCartney)
Paul McCartney (bass, guitar, piano, drums, vocals), Linda McCartney (backing vocals), Eric Stewart (backing vocals).
• **'Average Person'** (McCartney)
Paul McCartney (bass, keyboards, vocals), Linda McCartney (backing vocals), Eric Stewart (backing vocals), Ringo Starr (drums).
• **'Hey Hey'** (McCartney, Clarke)
Paul McCartney (guitar, keyboards), Denny Laine (guitar), Stanley Clarke (bass), Steve Gadd (drums).
• **'Tug Of Peace'** (McCartney)
Paul McCartney (bass, guitar, percussion, vocals), Linda McCartney (backing vocals), Eric Stewart (backing vocals), George Martin (percussion).
• **'Through Our Love'** (McCartney)
Paul McCartney (bass, vocals), Linda McCartney (backing vocals), Eric Stewart (backing vocals), Geoff Whitehorn (guitar), George Martin (piano), Dave Mattacks (drums).
All recorded at AIR Studios, London, England, except: 'Keep Under Cover', 'Average Person', 'Hey Hey', 'Tug Of Peace' also at AIR Studios, Montserrat; 'The Man' also at Cherokee Studios, Los Angeles, CA, USA.
All produced by George Martin.

1 singles – 'Pipes Of Peace' and 'Say Say Say' – the album failed to reach Number 1 in either Britain or America. Indeed, US sales were so disappointing that it didn't even crack the Top 10, McCartney's first such failure.

Pipes Of Peace songs

McCartney wrote the opening title track in response to a request from a jazz musician. As he recalled: "George Melly wrote to me and said, 'There's this children's organisation and they want a sort of peaceful song for children, a hopeful song for the future. Would you be interested?' So I set about trying to do it. Then it became a song for me."

McCartney wanted to write a song that answered some of the points raised by 'Tug Of War'. He thought that song had been about opposites, duality, and the impossibility of balancing conflicting forces. 'Pipes Of Peace' was his metaphor for the coming together of individuals, countries, and races. "I didn't want to leave the question posing, 'How do you ever get the dualities together?' And on 'Pipes Of Peace' there's a little quote from Rabindranath Tagore … would you believe, Indian lovers? He was an Indian poet, and he just had a little thing about 'In love, life's contradictions dissolve and disappear'. … There is this big paradox and duality. But in love, somehow, it mystically goes away. Somehow there aren't any problems with black and white if they … love each other. So in trying to find an answer, this one is a bit more towards: 'The answer is love.'" He reinforced the theme of reconciliation by insisting that the song also contained an anti-war statement: "This is the song you should use if you're an anti-war person, as I am," he remarked.

A solo recording, 'The Other Me' was McCartney's attempt to explore facets of his identity. "This one is actually just a song about the other man in me, the new man in me, the other side of me that's lurking and waiting to get out. For me, there's a side of me I don't like so much; there's a side of me that I prefer. I suppose the thing is to try and get a little more contact with the side of myself that I prefer, and control myself, instead of just flying off the handle."

But 'The Other Me' tells us little, if anything, that we didn't already know: Linda was the realist and Paul the romantic. Melodically, he reveals little of his other self, and if he was trying to explore another side of his musical personality, then he failed. Neither did he do his reputation as a wordsmith any favours. Rhyming "For treating you the way I did" with "And I acted like a dustbin lid" was either an act of laziness or an example of his misplaced belief in the 'magical' qualities of stream-of-consciousness composition. Either way, the result was indeed wince-inducing.

McCartney had recorded a demo of 'Keep Under Cover' before rehearsing it with Wings in 1980. Like several compositions intended for *Tug Of War*, it was discarded in favour of stronger material before finding its way onto *Pipes Of Peace*. Recorded in early December 1980 at AIR London, it received a bass overdub by Stanley Clarke at AIR Montserrat, in 1981. 'Keep Under Cover' sounds as if it were constructed from two incomplete song fragments, as the slow introduction has little in common with the main body of the song. If this is the case, McCartney brought the two halves together before he made his demo or rehearsed it with Wings. The completed master has an additional instrumental bridge, absent from the home demo, and a proper ending, which was missing from earlier versions of the song.

Next up is 'So Bad', a typical McCartney ballad, written while he was extemporising at the family piano. Surrounded by his children, including the infant James, dad felt obliged to include a reference to his son in what became an otherwise schmaltzy love song. "I started singing it at home with the kids and Linda," said McCartney. "and 'Girl I love you so bad' was fine for everyone except James, who would have been about four and a half, and I felt I was leaving him out. So just for him I sang: 'Boy I love you so bad,' and he would go all shy and it was lovely. Then I worked it into a song as 'And she said Boy I love you so bad.'" Admitting that the song had little more to say then "I love you", he continued: "It was a little melody I had, and I started writing words. They seemed to be very simple and very corny, but they seemed to fit. There was no way I could make them more grammatical. Girl I love you so bad-ly... it had to be Girl I love you so bad."

Michael Jackson approached McCartney early in 1980 and asked if he'd like to write some 'hits' with him. Having just worked with Carl Perkins and Stevie Wonder, McCartney was in a particularly receptive mood and agreed to the collaboration. The result was 'Say Say Say' and 'The Man'. McCartney had already written the music for 'The Man' and asked Jackson to help finish the lyrics. They made a demo recording, but as Jackson continued to work on the lyrics it became redundant. Once Jackson had finished the lyric, they made a second demo before recording the song properly at Cherokee in Los Angeles.

When asked about the song, McCartney claimed that 'the man' in question held no special significance for him, but he thought Jackson may have been referring to God, as at the time he was a practising Christian. 'The Man' was scheduled for release as a single (R 6066) on February 12 1984 but before it was issued the McCartneys were again arrested for possession of cannabis, and the single was shelved.

McCartney wrote 'Sweetest Little Show' in stages, constructing it from several unfinished song fragments. "That just came out of a jam, just a little chord sequence that was lying around for a while," he said. "It nearly got into a medley with two other pieces, and we suddenly didn't like the two other pieces, but we liked the 'Sweetest Little Show' bit. So then I added the guitar show – I fancied playing a bit of guitar – so I played a little bit of acoustic in the middle of it. And that got a little bit of applause, and that became the Little Show."

He made a demo recording in 1980, which reveals that he ditched the offending melodic sketches before entering the studio. The finished master was taken at a faster tempo than the demo and, because of its extended guitar solo, is somewhat longer. George Martin's deft production touches deserted him on this occasion. His everything-but-the-kitchen-sink approach only managed to smother the song, demolishing the simple charm that McCartney captured with his home demo.

McCartney recorded a demo of 'Average Person' in the summer of 1980 and rehearsed it with Wings in October the same year. Then in early 1981 he recorded a version at AIR Montserrat with Dave Mattacks on drums. He was obviously unhappy with this version as he re-recorded the song with Ringo Starr for *Pipes Of Peace*.

McCartney's narrative recounts the desires and aspirations of a number of imaginary 'average people' whom one might meet anywhere – but these characters are so dull that one wonders why he bothered to invent them at all. Overproduced and uninspired, 'Average Person' is as unadventurous as it is pedestrian. It does, however, contain a moment of delicious irony. McCartney and Martin created a bridging section, to link the waitress and boxer verses, which is so overblown and humourless that it can only be considered as self-mockery. At least one hopes so.

The day after bassist Stanley Clarke arrived in Montserrat, he and McCartney spent the day jamming. 'Hey Hey', recorded on February 2 1981, was the result. Although it features two of the world's finest bass players, it's little more than an improvised, directionless doodle. Why McCartney–Martin selected it for the album is unclear. Surely there was stronger material available than this?

McCartney chose to follow 'Hey Hey' with the drear 'Tug Of Peace'. Another quasi-instrumental, it was obviously meant to establish some kind of theme by extending the metaphor of 'Tug Of War' and providing continuity to the project. But its odd mixture of textures – which range from left-field vocal arrangements to pseudo-ethnic percussion effects created by McCartney and Martin banging bunches of garden canes on the studio floor – only acted to highlight the album's weaknesses and inconsistencies.

'Through Our Love' epitomises the desire of McCartney–Martin to 'cast' the album and create a kind of staged musical on record. However, there is too much style and not enough content. Geoff Whitehorn, who played acoustic guitar on the track, recalled that the song was recorded at lightning speed. "Paul was actually playing bass, George Martin was playing electric piano, and Dave Mattacks played drums, and we knocked this song off in about ... an hour. It was a nice session. ... Linda McCartney was charming." Despite being efficiently and effectively recorded, the song is failed by Martin's arrangement. On this occasion, the producer's skills as an arranger appeared to have deserted him. It's overblown, full of its own importance, and no more than expensive muzak.

Pipes Of Peace data

Issued in Britain by Parlophone, the LP featured a gatefold sleeve with a cover photograph by Linda, printed inner sleeve with lyrics, and customised labels. The A-side label reproduced an old-style blue and gold Parlophone design, while a detail of Van Gogh's chair by Clive Barker was used for the B-side. The CD was delayed by about four months as EMI were still manufacturing CDs in Japan and importing them into Britain.

Columbia issued the album in the USA with identical artwork to the British edition but with generic labels. Some copies of the LP were issued with a sticker that proclaimed '11 New McCartney Classics Including The Hits Say Say Say, The Man, So Bad'.

'PIPES OF PEACE'

RELEASED while 'Say Say Say' remained in the singles charts, 'Pipes Of Peace' became McCartney's third Number 1 single in Britain but his first as a solo artist. With this release, he became one of a select handful of artists to have simultaneous Number 1 singles on either side of the Atlantic, but with different songs: 'Say Say Say' remained at Number 1 in the USA throughout the Christmas period.

'Pipes Of Peace' / 'So Bad' was probably released to boost album sales; by its fourth week of release, the album had dropped to Number 30 in the British charts. The single had the desired effect, with the album climbing back up to Number 8. In America, this single had its A and B-sides flipped, and reached number 23 in the charts.

'Pipes Of Peace' was nominated for an Ivor Novello Award for Best Song Musically And Lyrically, but lost out to 'Every Breath You Take' by The Police.

'Pipes Of Peace' was remixed for single release and given a clean introduction, but the B-side is identical to the album version.

Issued with a picture sleeve, the single featured generic Parlophone (UK) or Columbia (US) labels with MPL logos. The Columbia demonstration 7-inch single has a white label with black text and MPL's 'juggler' logo.

'PIPES OF PEACE' / 'SO BAD'
PAUL McCARTNEY
UK RELEASE December 5 1983; Parlophone R 6064; chart high No.1.

'SO BAD' / 'PIPES OF PEACE'
PAUL McCARTNEY
US RELEASE December 5 1983; Columbia 38-0429; chart high No.23.

'PAUL McCARTNEY'S THEME FROM THE HONORARY CONSUL' / 'CLARA'S THEME'
JOHN WILLIAMS
UK RELEASE December 19 1983; Island IS 155; failed to chart.

• **'Theme From The Honorary Consul'** (McCartney)
John Williams (guitar). Recording location unknown. Produced by Stanley Myers and Richard Harvey.

'THEME FROM THE HONORARY CONSUL'

WHILE this is not strictly a McCartney release, he did write the A-side, and while he did not play on the recording, he nevertheless got star billing. So it's included here. John McKenzie, director of *The Honorary Consul*, commissioned the theme, which McCartney probably wrote as a favour – McKenzie had directed his 'Take It Away' video. McCartney recorded a demo with classical guitarist John Williams, possibly at AIR Studios, but the melody was re-recorded as a solo piece by Williams for single release.

Originally scheduled for release on December 19 1983, the single did not appear in stores until the end of January or the beginning of February 1984. When it was issued, few bothered to buy it, and it sank without trace. The single was issued with the Island Records 'palm tree' label in a picture sleeve.

HEART PLAY

YOKO Ono's first record for Polydor was a solo album, *It's Alright*. It was followed by a series of archive releases, beginning with this John and Yoko interview recorded with David Sheff for *Playboy* magazine. Sheff's interview with the Lennons took place over several days, and he recorded over 22 hours of conversation during September 1980, 42 minutes of which were

HEART PLAY – UNFINISHED DIALOGUE
JOHN LENNON AND YOKO ONO
SIDE 1 'Section One', 'Section Two', 'Section Three'.
SIDE 2 'Section Four', 'Section Five', 'Section Six', 'Section Seven'.
UK RELEASE December 16 1983; Parlophone 817 238-1; failed to chart.
US RELEASE December 5 1983; Geffen 817 238-1 Y-1; chart high No.95.

selected for the album. Parts of the interview had been published in the January 1981 issue of *Playboy*, and a longer version appeared in the book *The Playboy Interviews With John Lennon And Yoko Ono*. As much of the interview had already been published, there was little of revelation on the album.

Polydor issued *Heart Play – Unfinished Dialogue* in the USA with generic red Polydor labels and a four-inch by two-and-a-quarter-inch rectangular black sticker with white text 'SPECIAL LOW PRICE 1980 Conversations With John Lennon & Yoko Ono' adhered to the front cover. An insert in the form of a letter from Yoko explaining each section was included with the LP.

Polydor issued the album in Britain with labels and sleeve identical to the American release. To promote the album, half-page advertisements appeared in British music weeklies, and although it failed to chart, *Heart Play – Unfinished Dialogue* generated advance publicity for the much anticipated *Milk And Honey*.

'NOBODY TOLD ME' / 'O' SANITY'
JOHN LENNON / YOKO ONO
UK RELEASE January 9 1984; Polydor POSP 700; chart high No.6.
US RELEASE January 9 1984; Polydor 817 254-7; chart high No.5.

- **'Nobody Told Me'** (Lennon)
John Lennon (vocals, guitar), Earl Slick (guitar), Hugh McCracken (guitar), Tony Levin (bass), George Small (keyboards), Arthur Jenkins (percussion), Andy Newmark (drums).
Recorded at Hit Factory, New York City, NY, USA. Produced by John Lennon and Yoko Ono.
- **'O' Sanity'** (Ono)
Yoko Ono (vocals), John Tropes (guitars), Steve Love (guitars), Elliot Randall (guitars), Paul Griffin (piano), Neil Jason or Wayne Pedziwiatr (bass guitar), Yogi Horton or Allan Schwartzberg (drums).
Recorded at A&R Studios or Sterling Sound, New York City, NY, USA, or The Automat, San Francisco, CA.
Produced by Yoko Ono.

'NOBODY TOLD ME'

AS WITH '(Just Like) Starting Over', 'Nobody Told Me' was greeted with considerable anticipation. Everyone knew that there were unreleased songs from the *Double Fantasy* sessions ready to be issued and it was only a matter of time before they would appear. News that Ono was preparing material for record began to appear in the press in mid 1983. By early autumn that year, it had been confirmed that mixing was almost complete and that *Milk And Honey*, the follow-up to *Double Fantasy* that Lennon and Ono had discussed prior to Lennon's death, would be issued early in 1984.

'Nobody Told Me' was another song that Lennon had hanging about and revived for the *Double Fantasy* sessions. He had begun to write it in 1976 and may have intended it for the aborted album he planned to follow *Walls And Bridges*. Originally titled 'Everybody', it underwent considerable revision. The song remained unfinished until 1980, when he began to rework it.

To begin with, Lennon simply overdubbed a new vocal and guitar onto the existing piano demo of 'Everybody' and sang new lyrics over the chorus. Next he reworked the verses and recorded a new demo, this time backing himself on acoustic guitar and rhythm box. The reworked verses offer the listener a number of conflicting images and paradoxes to contemplate. They are a mixture of the banal and the bizarre, evoking a sense of discontinuity that the revised chorus summarised and reinforced. To complete the song, Lennon fashioned a jumpy riff to link the verse and chorus, which provides the song with its melodic hook and matches the sense of suspension established in the verses.

Before deciding to keep 'Nobody Told Me' for himself, Lennon considered offering the song to Ringo Starr, who was in the process of recording his *Stop And Smell The Roses* album. But he kept it – and recorded the song at the Hit Factory on the second day of the *Double Fantasy* sessions. As usual, Lennon recorded a live vocal with every take, and that's what appeared on the record. (An alternative take was issued on the *John Lennon Anthology*.)

Ono's 'O' Sanity' was recorded some time after the *Double Fantasy* sessions, as were all her songs on the *Milk And Honey* album. Lacking a memorable melody or lyric, 'O' Sanity' is little more than an adumbrated sketch. It appears even less finished than many of Lennon's songs on the album.

'Nobody Told Me' data

Polydor issued the single in Britain and America. British pressings were manufactured with blue die-cut Polydor labels and full-colour picture sleeve. The company also issued a one-sided white label 7-inch single to radio stations and the media. In the USA the record came with red Polydor labels and a picture sleeve identical to the British release.

Commercial copies of the US single were manufactured with several label variations. The first label has 'Manufactured by Polydor Incorporated...' perimeter print, and 'stereo' on the label. The second has the same perimeter print, without 'stereo' on the label.

The third US label variant has 'Manufactured and Marketed by Polygram...' perimeter print, with 'stereo', '45 RPM', and a small '19' to the left of the Ono Music logo. The other four variants are similar to the third, except that one has 'stereo', '45 RPM', and '26' above the Ono Music logo; the next has 'stereo', '45 RPM', and '49'; another has 'stereo', '45 RPM', and '54' left of the Ono Music logo; and the last has 'stereo', '45 RPM', and '72'.

To promote the single in the USA, Polydor issued a

promotional 12-inch (PRO 250-1). The single was also promoted with an extensive poster campaign and a specially commissioned video that consisted of clips from the Lennons' personal archive. 'Nobody Told Me' achieved considerable success on both sides of the Atlantic.

Like Geffen, Polydor coupled hit singles and issued them as double A-sides, on its Timepieces imprint. 'Nobody Told Me', backed with 'I'm Stepping Out', was reissued on this imprint in America on April 30 1990 (883927-7). This coupling was reissued in 1992 on the Collectibles label (COL-4307), the B-side incorrectly listing the song title as 'Steppin' Out'.

MILK AND HONEY – A HEART PLAY

THIS WAS the long awaited follow-up to *Double Fantasy*, issued by Polydor in January 1984. Lennon had recorded his songs while making *Double Fantasy* and had planned to return to them early in 1981. He'd spoken about the album in interviews just before his death, and rumours about its imminent release began to circulate as early as 1981. However, Ono found the task of compiling the album too distressing. Instead, she set about recording her solo album, *Season Of Glass*, and put *Milk And Honey* on hold. Had it appeared so soon after Lennon's death it would have smacked of cash-in, and Ono was careful to avoid such allegations.

When the album was issued, Lennon's songs were presented as he had left them, without the layers of sonic dressing he'd applied to *Double Fantasy*. Because his songs are presented 'naked', *Milk And Honey* has a vitality, freshness, and wit that would have been lost had he ever returned to it. Although the songs required a little fixing, they remained as works-in-progress (apart from adding echo to Lennon's vocal to give the impression of double-tracking). Although Jack Douglas was responsible for producing the basic tracks, he was not involved in mixing or sequencing *Milk And Honey*. Nor did he receive a production credit. Having fallen out with Ono over money, he was suing for unpaid royalties. Consequently, production credits went to John Lennon and Yoko Ono.

Milk And Honey songs

While on holiday in Bermuda, Lennon visited a nightclub with his personal assistant, Fred Seaman. He hadn't been to a disco in years but returned from his night out enthused, a little hung over, and inspired. Determined to document his adventures in clubland, he set about writing 'I'm Stepping Out'. The experience obviously had a marked effect on him. It's obvious that he yearned to escape the stultifying self-imposed lifestyle he had grown into.

A good time rock'n'roll song, 'I'm Stepping Out' crackles with pent-up excitement and anticipation. Besides dispelling the myth that Lennon spent all his time as a househusband locked away in the Dakota, it reveals that he'd lost none of his sense of humour, hedonism, or joie de vivre.

MILK AND HONEY – A HEART PLAY
JOHN LENNON AND YOKO ONO
SIDE 1 'I'm Stepping Out', 'Sleepless Night', 'I Don't Wanna Face It', 'Don't Be Scared', 'Nobody Told Me', 'O' Sanity'.
SIDE 2 'Borrowed Time', 'Your Hands', '(Forgive Me) My Little Flower Princess', 'Let Me Count The Ways', 'Grow Old With Me', 'You're The One'.
UK RELEASE January 23 1984; LP Polydor POLH 5; picture disc Polydor POLHP5 released March 26 1984; CD Polydor 817 159-2; chart high No.3.
US RELEASE January 23 1984; LP Polydor 817 159-1 Y-1; CD Polydor 817 159-2; chart high No.11.

- **'I'm Stepping Out'** (Lennon)
John Lennon (vocals, guitar), Earl Slick (guitar), Hugh McCracken (guitar), Tony Levin (bass), George Small (keyboards), Arthur Jenkins (percussion), Andy Newmark (drums). Recorded at Hit Factory, New York City, NY, USA. Produced by John Lennon and Yoko Ono.
- **'Sleepless Night'** (Ono)
Yoko Ono (vocals), John Tropes (guitars), Steve Love (guitars), Elliot Randall (guitars), Ed Walsh (synthesisers), Pete Cannarozzi (synthesisers), Paul Griffin (piano), Neil Jason (bass), Wayne Pedziwiatr (bass), Howard Johnson (baritone sax), Billy Alessi, Bob Alessi, Carlos Alomar, Gordon Grody, Kurt Yahijan, Pete Thom (backing vocals), Jimmy Maelen (percussion), Yogi Horton (drums), Allan Schwartzberg (drums). Recorded at A&R Studios or Sterling Sound, New York City, NY, USA or The Automat, San Francisco, CA, USA. Produced by Yoko Ono.
- **'I Don't Wanna Face It'** (Lennon)
Personnel, location, and production as 'I'm Stepping Out'.
- **'Don't Be Scared'** (Ono)
Personnel, location, and production as 'Sleepless Night'.
- **'Borrowed Time'** (Lennon)
Personnel, location, and production as 'I'm Stepping Out'.
- **'Your Hands'** (Ono)
Personnel, location, and production as 'Sleepless Night'.
- **'(Forgive Me) My Little Flower Princess'** (Lennon)
Personnel, location, and production as 'I'm Stepping Out'.
- **'Let Me Count The Ways'** (Ono)
Yoko Ono (vocals, piano). Recorded at The Dakota, New York City, NY, USA. Produced by Yoko Ono.
- **'Grow Old With Me'** (Lennon)
John Lennon (vocals, piano). Recorded at The Dakota. Produced by John Lennon and Yoko Ono.
- **'You're The One'** (Ono)
Personnel, location, and production as 'Sleepless Night'.

He'd made several demo recordings of the song while in Bermuda, one of which was used as a reference source on the first day of recording at the Hit Factory, August 6 1980. 'I'm Stepping Out' was the first song Lennon recorded with his new band. Despite it being the first day, his confidence was high and, leading the musicians through the song, he coaxed a tight performance from them (take 2 was strong enough to be issued later on the *John Lennon Anthology*). The only problem they encountered was a tendency to speed up when coming out of the verses. The original recording featured an additional verse, which was edited from the commercial release. It is unclear if Lennon decided to remove the offending verse at an early stage in the recording or if it was removed when the song was mixed in 1983.

Ono had been honing her skills as a writer of pop songs since the early 1970s. The avant-garde compositions and free-form music that had her labelled as a musical weirdo were replaced by a slick pop voice that was obviously intended to elevate her from experimental ghetto land into the pop mainstream. She embraced pop music, and the technology that drove it, to ever greater heights of sophistication, and her albums had grown increasingly accomplished. Yet despite the sophisticated production of 'Sleepless Night', when one compares it to the two Lennon songs that sit either side of it, it sounds downright amateurish and prosaic.

'I Don't Want To Face It' took Lennon full circle. *John Lennon/Plastic Ono Band* found him exploring a side of his personality that he preferred to hide behind a mask. 'I Don't Want To Face It' explored similar ground and was no less honest or revealing. However, the post-primal angst that informed Lennon's songwriting in 1970 had been replaced by a more relaxed attitude.

The song had its roots in a much earlier composition, 'Mirror Mirror (On The Wall)', written in 1977 after a less than enjoyable holiday in Japan. This study in melancholia remained unfinished, but provided the kernel of an idea that became 'I Don't Want To Face It'. Lennon began work on the song before his visit to Bermuda but continued to tinker with it while there.

As with 'Nobody Told Me', Lennon presents the listener with a series of paradoxes, but here they summarise his butterfly personality. Lampooning his foibles, he seems better to understand the contradictions that fame had brought him. Like George Harrison, he had learnt to deal with life's contradictions, balancing emotional, physical, and mental desires that had previously disturbed him. Yet while Harrison used his knowledge to guide himself spiritually, here Lennon used his to psychologically unburden himself.

Recorded with much exuberance, 'I Don't Want To Face It' developed into a spiky, hard-nosed rocker that rivalled anything in Lennon's oeuvre. He was still fine tuning the song while recording; an alternative version issued on the *John Lennon Anthology* has an extended introduction and coda.

Double Fantasy found the Lennons reassuring themselves and imagining a future together. In the weeks and months after John's death, Ono had to reassure both herself and their son Sean and imagine a future without her husband. Naturally, she wrote a number of songs that expressed her deepest feelings. 'Don't Be Scared' was not only a paean of reassurance, it advocated positive personal projection, a credo that lay at the heart of John and Yoko's philosophy.

Lennon never did get any of New York's session musicians to play reggae convincingly, but that didn't stop him from trying. Jamaican music had a strong and early influence on Lennon and The Beatles. The middle eight in 'I Call Your Name' was directly influenced by ska, a predecessor of reggae. Lennon experimented with dub when producing Ono's 'Paper Shoes' from her *Yoko Ono/Plastic Ono Band* album, and attempted reggae with another of her songs, 'Sisters, O Sisters'. He tried to assimilate the style into several of his own songs, but no matter how hard he tried he couldn't get NYC's white rockers to understand the genre. His attempts at recording reggae were always hampered by the musicians he worked with, and 'Borrowed Time' suffered a similar fate.

He wrote the song while in Bermuda and had been influenced by Bob Marley. Inspired by a line from Marley's 'Hallelujah Time', which contained the phrase "We got to keep on living / Living on borrowed time", Lennon began work on his own song. Recording at the Hit Factory, he guided the musicians through the arrangement by referring them to The Isley Brothers' 'Twist And Shout' and 'Spanish Twist'. Those two songs were also his reference points for a horn arrangement he planned to add to the song. Several takes were recorded, with take 3 being marked best and given a guitar overdub by Lennon.

'Borrowed Time' was a song that celebrated life; the fact that Lennon's would be taken from him so senselessly only added poignancy to the song. He depicts himself as contented, more relaxed, and accepting of his past. Where previously he may have turned to outsiders for help, here he looks inwards. Reflecting on his life, he concludes that it's good to be older. The future looked bright, everything was clear, and now was the time to act. He was not yet 40 when he wrote the song, but he was obviously thinking of the future and growing older. In the interviews he gave in the weeks before he died, Lennon spoke longingly of growing old with Yoko. Sadly, this wasn't to be.

Ono sings 'Your Hands' in Japanese and English, mourning her late husband. Focusing on parts of his body – hands, skin, mouth, arms, and eyes – to represent the whole, she reflects that losing him was not made any easier by the time they spent together. At least, that's how one reads it in this context. But as *Milk And Honey* was intended to develop the theme of "sexual fantasies between men and women" begun with *Double Fantasy*, it could be read entirely differently.

Lennon's oeuvre is scattered with songs asking Ono for

forgiveness. It's a theme that appears to have haunted him, as he returned to it again and again. '(Forgive Me) My Little Flower Princess' revisits this theme but adds little. The song was never completed satisfactorily. Lennon made demo recordings while in Bermuda but had still to finalise the lyrics by the time he entered the Hit Factory to record the song. Although he was only interested in recording the backing track, he seemed indifferent to the task and allowed the band to wander through the song without any real enthusiasm. The least distinguished recording to emerge from the *Double Fantasy/Milk And Honey* sessions, it would have been better left in the archives.

The album ends with a pair of demo recordings made by Lennon and Ono that are central to the record's theme. The couple liked to imagine themselves as reincarnations of Robert and Elizabeth Barrett Browning. The Brownings expressed their love for one another as publicly as the Lennons. Each published volumes of poetry that expressed how they had been affected by the other's love. Inspired by the Brownings' romantic relationship and poetry, the Lennons wrote a song each based on poems by the Brownings. Ono's borrowed from Elizabeth Barrett Browning's Sonnet 43 *How Do I Love Thee? Let Me Count The Ways* from *Sonnets From The Portuguese* (1850). As with Lennon's *Grow Old With Me*, Ono here evokes a number of adolescent metaphors to describe how she feels about her husband. Perhaps both of them would have been better advised to set the Brownings' poems to music rather than attempt their own.

Lennon based 'Grow Old With Me' on a line from Robert Browning's poem *Rabbi Ben Ezra*. Like Ono's Browning-influenced song, it's romantic and personal; it also restates much of what he'd said previously. Ono suggested that Lennon continued to work on the song while recording *Double Fantasy* but that he never completed a satisfactory arrangement. She alleged that he had planned a rich orchestral arrangement for the song, which it eventually received when she asked George Martin to write a suiutable orchestral setting. 'Grow Old With Me' would duly appear with Martin's orchestral backing on 1998's *John Lennon Anthology*. However, it is Lennon's original piano demo that has the charm and pathos. One suspects that, had he survived, Lennon would have rejected Martin's overblown arrangement.

Ono's 'You're The One', a love song with a contemporary pop feel, brought *Milk And Honey* to a close. Like the songs Lennon wrote for her, it reinforces the myth that they were just like everyone else, a boy and girl in love. By her own admission, Ono knew this to be a fiction. As if to reinforce the strength and pre-eminence of their relationship, she juxtaposes the media perspective of John and Yoko with how they saw themselves, as romantic, magical, and quixotic. The fight to prove that their love was true had been long and hard, but for Ono they had prevailed. The world may have lost a Beatle, but Ono had lost the very person who gave her life meaning.

Milk And Honey data

Polydor issued the album with generic red Polydor labels, an inner sleeve with lyrics, a poster, and a gatefold cover. The original concept for the cover was to have 200 heart-shaped photographs of Lennon and Ono. This idea was dropped and an outtake from the *Double Fantasy* photo session used instead.

The album was issued in Britain as a picture disc (POLHP 5) in an edition of 2,000, and a second pressing of 1,000 was produced as demand quickly outstripped supply. Coloured vinyl pressings of the album also appeared, although these were unauthorised editions probably made by an employee at Polydor's pressing plant during downtime. The record was pressed on yellow, green and gold vinyl.

Milk And Honey was the first album by any of The Beatles to be issued on CD. First pressings of the CD (817 159-2) were manufactured in Germany and came with a full-colour four-page booklet. EMI issued a remastered version of the CD (535 9582) with four bonus tracks on September 27 2001.

'BORROWED TIME'

POLYDOR issued this single in Britain as the follow-up to 'Nobody Told Me' in several variants. The 7-inch single was issued with silver die-cut labels and a picture sleeve. An edition of 10,000 came with a poster sleeve (POSPG 701). Promotional copies (PODJ 701) were issued with an edit of the A-side in stock copies of the picture sleeve. 'Borrowed Time' was also issued as a 12-inch (POSPX 701) with a 15-inch by 11-inch full-colour poster and Ono's 'Never Say Goodbye' (not on *Milk And Honey*) included as a bonus track on the B-side.

In the USA, Polydor issued 'Borrowed Time' with generic red Polydor labels and a picture sleeve that was later used for the British release of 'I'm Stepping Out'. There were two variants, the first with a small number '19' printed above the Ono Music logo and '45 RPM' printed on the label, and the second with a small number '26' printed on the label, without '45 RPM'.

A promotional video was made for this and the two other singles taken from *Milk And Honey* consisting of footage taken from the Lennons' archives, and it received considerable television exposure. This did little to help the single on its chart journey.

'BORROWED TIME' / 'YOUR HANDS'
JOHN LENNON / YOKO ONO
UK RELEASE March 9 1984; Polydor POSP 701; 12-inch Polydor POSPX 701; 7-inch with poster Polydor POSPG 701 released March 16; chart high No.32.
US RELEASE May 14 1984; Polydor 821-204-7; chart high No.108.

'GIVE PEACE A CHANCE'

AS PART of a shortlived golden-oldies reissue campaign, EMI released two early Lennon solo A-sides as a double A-side 7-inch single. Although put out by EMI, the picture-sleeved single was manufactured with Apple labels.

'I'M STEPPING OUT'

POLYDOR issued this single in Britain as the third and final one from *Milk And Honey*. British 7-inch pressings were issued with silver die-cut labels and a picture sleeve based on the American sleeve for 'Borrowed Time'. As with the previous single, it was issued as a 12-inch with the added 'bonus' of Yoko's 'Loneliness', taken from her *It's Alright* album.

Polydor issued the single in the USA with a picture sleeve and generic red Polydor labels, with or without '45 RPM' and with the numbers '19', '26', or '54' printed on the label. Polydor also issued a demonstration 7-inch single (821 107-7-DJ) with album and edited versions of the song. Issued with the commercial picture sleeve, the demonstration record was manufactured with a small number '26' on the label.

EVERY MAN HAS A WOMAN
VARIOUS ARTISTS
JOHN LENNON 'Every Man Has A Woman Who Loves Him'; Spirit Choir 'Now Or Never'.
UK RELEASE September 21 1984; LP Polydor POLH 13; CD Polydor 823 490-2 released November 16; failed to chart.
US RELEASE September 17 1984; LP Polydor 422-823 490-1 Y-1; CD Polydor 823 490-2 released November 19; failed to chart.

- **'Every Man Has A Woman Who Loves Him'** (Ono)
John Lennon (vocals, guitar), Earl Slick (guitar), Hugh McCracken (guitar), Tony Levin (bass), George Small (keyboards), Arthur Jenkins (percussion), Andy Newmark (drums).
Recorded at Hit Factory, New York City, NY, USA.
Produced by John Lennon.
- **'Now Or Never'** (Ono)
John Lennon (guitar), Stan Bronstein (saxophone), George Young (saxophone), Gary Van Scyoc (bass), Adam Ippolito (piano, organ), Wayne 'Tex' Gabriel (guitar), Richard Frank Jr. (drums, percussion).
Recorded at The Record Plant East, New York City.
Produced by John & Yoko Plastic Ono Band with Elephant's Memory.

'GIVE PEACE A CHANCE' / 'COLD TURKEY'
PLASTIC ONO BAND
UK RELEASE March 12 1984; Apple G45 2; failed to chart.

'I'M STEPPING OUT' / 'SLEEPLESS NIGHT'
JOHN LENNON / YOKO ONO
UK RELEASE July 15 1984; Polydor POSP 702; 12-inch Polydor POSPX 702; failed to chart.
US RELEASE March 19 1984; Polydor 821-107-7; chart high No.55.

EVERY MAN HAS A WOMAN

ISSUED to mark Ono 50th birthday (actually it was a little late), *Every Man Has A Woman* was conceived as a tribute album featuring both new and archive recordings from an eclectic group of musicians.

Despite record company hype, Lennon's reading of his 'Every Man Has A Woman Who Loves Him', did not feature a lead vocal. Rather, his harmony to Ono's lead vocal was remixed at Sigma Sound in July 1984 with the intention of presenting it as a genuine lead vocal. At around the same time, Ono revealed that there was a version of 'Hard Times Are Over' with Lennon taking the lead vocal; this remains unreleased. Whether or not it is a genuine lead vocal or another harmony vocal remixed and presented as the real thing is not clear.

Lennon's other contribution to the album was his guitar-playing on a middle-of-the-road version of Ono's 'Now Or Never'. Recorded in February and March 1972 while the Lennons were in full-on political mode, it was, perhaps, an attempt to engage with middle America. The pair had already appeared on *The Mike Douglas Show* in an effort to reach the masses, so this may have been intended to spread the message beyond the small circle of Lennon fans and counterculture rebels who were their main audience in 1972.

The album was issued with generic red Polydor labels and lyric sheet, as well as on CD.

'EVERY MAN HAS A WOMAN WHO LOVES HIM'

POLYDOR issued this as a single in Britain with silver die-cut labels and picture sleeve. Some copies were also put out with a poster similar to that issued with the 12-inch pressing of 'Borrowed Time'.

'EVERY MAN HAS A WOMAN WHO LOVES HIM' / 'IT'S ALRIGHT'
JOHN LENNON / SEAN ONO LENNON
UK RELEASE November 16 1984; Polydor POSP 712; failed to chart.
US RELEASE October 8 1984; Polydor 881 387-7; failed to chart.

The single was issued by Polydor in the USA with red Polydor labels and picture sleeve identical to the British release. Commercial pressings were manufactured with minor typographical differences: stock copies can be found with the numbers '19', '22', or '172' printed on the label. Polydor also issued a demonstration 7-inch single (881 378-7-DJ) with the stereo version on both sides of the disc. A small number '22' was printed on the label.

'NO MORE LONELY NIGHTS'

McCARTNEY wrote 'No More Lonely Nights' for a scene in the film *Give My Regards To Broad Street* that he and the film's director thought required a piece of music. He got the bare bones of the melody while jamming at AIR Studios. "I'd been messing about with a bass and I was just jamming one day when I had nothing to do. I'd come in and just have a bit of fun on some of the equipment, and this was a bass I had with an echo device on it ... and it made this tune and it was a riff. ... I asked them to tape it just in case, cos I thought it was a good little idea for something, somewhere. I thought it might be good for a chase scene or something in the film." The bass riff that he improvised was arranged to provide incidental music for the film.

Although he had the tune, writing a song based on the film's title proved more problematic. McCartney said: "I couldn't for the life of me think how I was going to write a song ... unless it was 'I'm off on holiday, love, and I'm missing Leicester Square, so give my regards to Broad Street.' It didn't work. Approaching the task from a different angle, he wrote a ballad that had little to do with the film's narrative but that matched the mood of the scene for which it was required.

The song was recorded early in November 1982 in one very productive session. Pink Floyd's David Gilmour was particularly impressed with the way the song was recorded. "I found it quite amazing doing 'No More Lonely Nights' with Paul McCartney," he marvelled. "In one three-hour session with a band we learnt it and put it down, and Paul played piano and sang the lead vocal live, and I put the guitar solo down, bang."

The 'Playout' version was produced at the request of 20th Century Fox as they wanted something upbeat playing as audiences left the cinema. This version was given a number of remixes and edits: George Martin produced an 8:10 remix, and Arthur Baker a 6:55 remix and 3:56 edit.

Re-recorded for the *Broad Street* film, 'Silly Love Songs' features members of American rock band and FM-radio favourites Toto. It is essentially the same arrangement as the original and so adds little to Wings' original.

'NO MORE LONELY NIGHTS' (BALLAD) / 'NO MORE LONELY NIGHTS' (PLAYOUT VERSION)
PAUL McCARTNEY
UK RELEASE September 24 1984; Parlophone R 6080; second 7-inch Parlophone R 6080 'No More Lonely Nights' (Ballad) / 'No More Lonely Nights' (Special Dance Mix) released October 8 1984; 12-inch Parlophone 12 R 6080 'No More Lonely Nights' (Extended Version) / 'Silly Love Songs', 'No More Lonely Nights' (Ballad); 12-inch picture disc Parlophone 12 RP 6080 'No More Lonely Nights' (Extended Version) / 'Silly Love Songs', 'No More Lonely Nights' (Ballad) released October 8 1984; 12-inch Parlophone 12 RA 6080 'No More Lonely Nights' (Extended Playout Version) / 'Silly Love Songs', 'No More Lonely Nights' (Ballad) released October 29 1984; chart high No.2.
US RELEASE October 8 1984; Columbia 38-04581; 12-inch Columbia 44-05077 'No More Lonely Nights' (Extended Version) / 'Silly Love Songs', 'No More Lonely Nights' (Ballad); 12-inch picture disc Columbia 8C8 39927-S1 'No More Lonely Nights' (Extended Version) / 'Silly Love Songs', 'No More Lonely Nights' (Ballad); second 12-inch Columbia 44-05077 'No More Lonely Nights' (Special Dance Mix) / 'Silly Love Songs', 'No More Lonely Nights' (Ballad) released January 1985; chart high No.6.

• **'No More Lonely Nights'** (Ballad) (McCartney)
Paul McCartney (piano, vocals), Linda McCartney (backing vocals), Eric Stewart (backing vocals), Herbie Flowers (bass), Stewart Elliot (drums), Ann Dudley (synthesiser), David Gilmour (guitar).
• **'No More Lonely Nights' (Playout Version)** (McCartney)
Paul McCartney (bass, keyboards, drums, vocals), Linda McCartney (backing vocals), Eric Stewart (backing vocals), Derek Watkins (horns), John Barclay (horns), Chris Pyne (horns), Stan Sulzmann (horns), Dan Wallis (horns).
• **'Silly Love Songs'** (McCartney)
Paul McCartney (electric harpsichord, vocals), Linda McCartney (keyboards, backing vocals), Eric Stewart (backing vocals), Steve Lukather (guitar), Jeff Porcaro (drums), Louis Johnson (bass), Laurence Williams (horns), Thomas Fergerson (horns), Charles Loper (horns), Jerry Hey (horns).
All recorded at AIR Studios, Abbey Road Studios, and CTS Studios, London, England.
All produced by George Martin.

'No More Lonely Nights' data

This was McCartney's first single issued on multiple formats. In Britain, five different editions were issued (two 7-inch singles, with identical catalogue numbers, and three 12-inch singles). Only two versions of the song were recorded: all variants are either remixes or edits that originate from the George Martin-produced master.

To ensure a high chart placing, Parlophone/EMI issued different editions of the single over a four-week period. Initially, 'No More Lonely Nights' was made available on 7-inch and 12-inch singles. A week later, EMI issued a limited-edition picture disc that featured material identical to the first 12-inch. These were superseded by new editions released in October.

The second 7-inch was distinguished by '(ballad) B-side special dance mix remixed by Arthur Baker' added to the sleeve in pink type. Both 7-inch singles have identical catalogue and matrix numbers, the only difference being the number '5' which was added to the B-side matrix number of the second edition. The second 12-inch is easier to distinguish as it has an 'A' added to the catalogue number. Both sets of records were issued with similar artwork and featured generic Parlophone labels. Additionally, 300 copies of Arthur Baker's 'Mole Mix' were pressed as one-sided 12-inch singles, offering a unique mix unavailable elsewhere.

In the USA, Columbia followed EMI's lead and issued both versions of the 7- and 12-inch singles and the 12-inch picture disc. In addition, the company issued three demonstration singles: a 7-inch single with white labels and black text; a 12-inch single with the 'Ballad' version of *No More Lonely Nights* on both sides of the disc (AS 1940); and a 12-inch single with the 'Special Dance Mix' on both sides (AS 1990).

GIVE MY REGARDS TO BROAD STREET

THE ORIGINS of this project stretched back to late 1979. McCartney commissioned playwright Willy Russell to write a film script that would exploit his music. Unsatisfied with Russell's script, and apparently several others that were offered, he set about writing his own. His original idea was to produce a television programme featuring some of his songs, but this grew into a feature-length film that he wrote and (initially) financed. His plot, what there is of it, revolved around a missing master tape that had to be found before midnight to stop an unscrupulous businessman claiming the McCartney millions.

The film is essentially an excuse to incorporate a number of expensive music videos into the most flimsy of narratives, and would have been better served had McCartney employed a professional scriptwriter like Russell.

One thing that McCartney hoped to achieve while filming was to record all of the performances live. For the first time in cinema history, recording and playback took place using 24-track machines synchronised to cameras, making for a complex technical problem that was nevertheless successfully overcome. While McCartney wanted to record only the performances he gave on the film set, George Martin suggested that they should hedge their bets and pre-record all of the music. So although the soundtrack was pre-recorded, the musicians played live to a backing track. This meant that some of the songs on the album are probably composites of recordings made in the studio and those recorded on the film set.

Several wholly live recordings were made by McCartney, guitarists Dave Edmunds and Chris Spedding, and Ringo Starr, who jammed on some old rock'n'roll tunes in London's East End some time in early 1983. Although they were recorded for posterity, these recordings were never intended to feature in the film and remain in McCartney's archives. The album is rumoured to have generated several outtakes, including 'Hey Jude', 'The Fool On The Hill', and 'Band On The Run'. However, if new recordings of these songs were made, they have yet to surface.

Give My Regards To Broad Street songs

The opening song on the album was 'Good Day Sunshine', a Beatles song that McCartney composed during one of his many writing sessions at Lennon's Weybridge home. It was inspired by The Lovin' Spoonful's 'Daydream' and the glorious summer weather. He remembered: "I was upstairs there one very nice day. It was a warm breezy summer and we seemed to be getting a little time off, and I used to go out to John's house to write. It was just a happy-go-lucky summer song." McCartney's remake for *Broad Street*, recorded with George Martin on piano, failed to match the original *Revolver* recording.

'Corridor Music', one of several pieces of incidental music, was included on the album, but 'Glorina', featured in the *Broad Street* documentary, was omitted.

With McCartney re-recording solo and Beatles material, inevitably 'Yesterday' found its way onto the soundtrack. Rearranged for brass and taken at a slightly slower tempo, his remake should have sounded more mature and reflective, but if anything it's the opposite.

McCartney also wrote 'Here There And Everywhere', another favourite from *Revolver*, at Lennon's home. He appears to have been inspired by an interest in the songwriters of the past. "I wanted the beginning of it to be like an old-fashioned love song, with the verse as an introduction," he explained. "John and I were both very interested in that feature of songs, because they were no longer written like that, and we related to our parents and their music." Brian Wilson's innovative work with The Beach Boys also influenced the Beatle arrangement. For the *Broad Street* remake, a brass arrangement, played by The Philip Jones Brass Ensemble, replaces The Beatles' three-part harmonies, giving the song a crisp, bright feel.

'Here There And Everywhere' segues into a new version of 'Wanderlust'. Almost identical to the version McCartney recorded two years previously, it was scheduled for release as the second single (R 6089) from the album, possibly backed with the new recording of 'Ballroom Dancing', but did not appear.

An extended Edmunds–Spedding line-up provided the backing for the remake of 'Ballroom Dancing'. Since McCartney was playing keyboards, ex-Led Zeppelin man John Paul Jones was recruited to play bass. As the 'Ballroom Dancing' scene included a fight, a few guitar stabs were added to give the piece some dramatic tension. A longer guitar solo was also added, which extended the song by about 50 seconds.

The song was probably mixed using both live and studio takes, as at one point in the *Broad Street* documentary McCartney and George Martin are shown attempting to mix the song using McCartney's pre-recorded vocal and another recorded live on the film set. Apart from the problem of being unable to locate McCartney's original vocal, mixing was made all the more complicated by an improvised edit.

One of two new songs written for the film, 'Not Such A Bad Boy' was influenced by its author's personal experiences, which he claimed were "slightly inflated" for creative purposes. The last verse probably refers to a recent run-in with the law, and although McCartney claimed the chorus was influenced by something said by one of the film's characters, it may also be self-referential. The song's untidy ending was probably intended to give it a 'live' feel.

McCartney claims to have dreamt 'No Values' with the music and lyric for the chorus complete. As he recounted: "I was on holiday, and just as I was waking up I was in a dream and I was watching The Rolling Stones. I couldn't quite hear all the lyrics but I heard all the chorus, and I woke up and thought: I really like that song they do. Then I thought, wait a minute – there is no song called 'No Values'. They don't do that song: my brain had just created it – or however it happens."

GIVE MY REGARDS TO BROAD STREET
PAUL McCARTNEY
SIDE 1 'No More Lonely Nights', 'Good Day Sunshine', 'Corridor Music', 'Yesterday', 'Here There And Everywhere', 'Wanderlust', 'Ballroom Dancing', 'Silly Love Songs'.
SIDE 2 'Silly Love Songs' (Reprise), 'Not Such A Bad Boy', 'No Values', 'No More Lonely Nights' (Ballad Reprise), 'For No One', 'Eleanor Rigby', 'Eleanor's Dream', 'Long And Winding Road', 'No More Lonely Nights' (Playout Version), 'Good Night Princess'*.
Track marked * appears only on the CD.
UK RELEASE October 22 1984; LP Parlophone PCTC 2; CD Parlophone CDP 7 460432 released 22 October 1984; chart high No.1.
US RELEASE October 22 1984; LP Columbia SC-39613; CD Columbia CK 39613; chart high No.21.

• **'Good Day Sunshine'** (Lennon, McCartney)
Paul McCartney (bass, drums, vocals), George Martin (piano).
• **'Corridor Music' (McCartney)**
Paul McCartney (guitar, drums).
• **'Yesterday'** (Lennon, McCartney)
Paul McCartney (guitar, vocals), The Philip Jones Brass Ensemble (horns).
• **'Here There And Everywhere'** (Lennon, McCartney)
Paul McCartney (guitar, vocals), Ringo Starr (drums), The Philip Jones Brass Ensemble (horns).
• **'Wanderlust'** (McCartney)
Paul McCartney (piano, vocals), Ringo Starr (drums), The Philip Jones Brass Ensemble (horns).
• **'Ballroom Dancing'** (McCartney)
Paul McCartney (piano, vocals), Ringo Starr (drums), John Paul Jones (bass), Dave Edmunds (guitar), Chris Spedding (guitar), Linda McCartney (piano, backing vocals), Jack Armstrong (horns), John Barclay (horns), Alan Donney (horns), Henry MacKenzie (horns), Dougie Robinson (horns), Tommy Whittle (horns), Ray Swinfield (horns), David Willis (horns).
• **'Not Such A Bad Boy'** (McCartney)
Paul McCartney (bass, vocals), Dave Edmunds (guitar), Chris Spedding (guitar), Linda McCartney (keyboards, backing vocals), Jody Linscott (percussion), Ringo Starr (drums).
• **'No Values'** (McCartney)
Personnel as 'Not Such A Bad Boy'.
• **'For No One'** (Lennon, McCartney)
Paul McCartney (guitar, vocals), Gabrielli String Quartet (strings), Jeff Bryant (French horn).
• **'Eleanor Rigby'** (Lennon, McCartney)
Personnel as 'For No One'.
• **'Eleanor's Dream'** (Paul McCartney)
Orchestra led by Kenneth Sillito.
• **'The Long And Winding Road'** (Lennon, McCartney)
Paul McCartney (piano, vocals), Dick Morrisey (saxophone), Dave Mattacks (drums), Trevor Barstow (keyboards), Herbie Flowers (bass).
• **'Good Night Princess'** (McCartney)
Paul McCartney (spoken words), Ronnie Hughes (trumpet), Bobby Haughey (trumpet), Chris Smith (trombone), Derek Grossmith (alto saxophone), Eddie Mordue (tenor saxophone, clarinet), Vic Ash (tenor saxophone), Pat Hulling (violin), Laurie Lewis (violin), Raymond Kennlyside (violin), Tony Gilbert (violin), John Dean (drums, percussion), Russ Stableforth (bass), Eric Ford (guitar), Gerry Butler (piano).
All recorded at AIR Studios, Abbey Road Studios, and CTS Studios, London, England. All produced by George Martin.

McCartney attempted to record 'No Values' in Montserrat while working on *Tug Of War* but reworked it for *Broad Street*. Featuring Edmunds and Spedding again, it was bound to sound a little tougher than recent recordings. But it sounds nothing like The Rolling Stones.

McCartney wrote *For No One* as his relationship with Jane Asher came to an end, and it too was recorded by The Beatles for *Revolver*. Here, his timeless melody is enhanced by a complementary French horn part, on this occasion played by Jeff Bryant.

'Eleanor Rigby' was another *Revolver* song resurrected for the film. Largely written by McCartney, it was finished at Lennon's Weybridge home with all four Beatles contributing to the final lyric. The name of the central character went through a number of changes before McCartney settled on Eleanor Rigby. Daisy Hawkins was his first choice, and, according to Lionel Bart, at one point he'd settled on Eleanor Bygraves. Likewise, Father MacKenzie was originally Father McCartney, but McCartney changed it, thinking "it would be too much, as if I was trying to involve my dad in some way". Recreated for the film, the remake does not improve on the original.

'Eleanor's Dream' is an instrumental based on themes and motifs from 'Eleanor Rigby', recalling McCartney–Martin's earlier film score, *The Family Way*. McCartney's melody is developed and arranged to provide musical settings for several short scenes that comprise the film's dream sequence. The seven-minute composition was edited down to three for the LP, but was made available in full on the CD.

'The Long And Winding Road' was never recorded properly by The Beatles; instead, Phil Spector added copious strings and backing vocals to a basic track recorded at Apple Studios in January 1969. McCartney was furious at the way Spector smothered the song with strings and a choir, which were added without his knowledge. The string arrangement was by Richard Hewison, and although McCartney lambasted both Hewison and the arrangement, which was too much like Mantovani for his taste, he nevertheless employed Hewison to orchestrate the instrumental version of *Ram*, recorded only 18 months after the *Let It Be* fiasco.

Strange too that for this remake McCartney should opt for a schmaltzy, middle-of-the-road arrangement that echoes Spector's overblown production. Perhaps he envisioned the song this way from the beginning? He did, however, alter the song's structure. A lengthy saxophone solo introduces it, and a solo replaces an omitted second verse. 'The long And Winding Road' also got a decent bass part, played by Herbie Flowers, which Lennon was unable, or unwilling, to provide for the original.

Recalling the big-band sounds of the 1930s and '40s, 'Good Night Princess' was issued as a bonus track on the CD version of *Broad Street*. But it isn't much of a bonus – and it's probably fair to say that McCartney had more fun recording it than most of us had listening to it. In fact, his only contribution was to say, "Thank you for joining us. We hope you've had as much pleasure listening as we've had making it for you," and to encourage the band to "lay it on 'em".

Give My Regards To Broad Street data

The album was issued with a gatefold sleeve, printed inner sleeve, and customised labels. Columbia prepared a black rectangular sticker that alerted people to the fact that the album featured the new single 'No More Lonely Nights' and re-recorded Beatles and Wings classics.

The CD and cassette included several extra minutes of music and dialogue, the first time a McCartney release had been marketed in this way. This was both a result of the extended playing time the new format offered and an incentive to get people to invest in CD hardware, which at the time was still relatively expensive. The album was promoted with radio and press interviews, a one-hour television special on the film and soundtrack, a poster campaign, and television advertisements.

'WE ALL STAND TOGETHER'

McCARTNEY'S second soundtrack single in as many months came from another new film project, *Rupert And The Frog Song*. This was originally conceived as a full-length animated feature, but costs and time restraints reduced the film to an eight-minute animated featurette – though even this took upwards of four years to complete.

His idea of producing a British animated feature, with Rupert as the main character, had been in pre-production for some time. During sessions for *Back To The Egg*, Wings recorded an entire album's-worth of material intended for a proposed soundtrack. But McCartney didn't write 'We All Stand Together' until 1980, when he recorded a demo at Park Gate Studio in Battle, East Sussex, England.

'We All Stand Together' was recorded at AIR London between October 31 and November 3 1980. George Martin wrote the orchestral arrangement and St Paul's Boys Choir contributed backing vocals. The vocal arrangement also features The King's Singers (who, several years later, performed a number of Lennon and McCartney songs at London's Albert Hall as part of the Proms season).

A huge hit with children of all ages, 'We All Stand Together' won an Ivor Novello Award for Best Film Theme of the year.

Some readers may remember novelty records from their childhood, such as 'The Laughing Policeman', 'Sparky's Magic Piano'. 'We All Stand Together' is cut from the same cloth, but unlike earlier records made for children, it sparkles with McCartney's melodic inventiveness. Forget the fact that it was

'WE ALL STAND TOGETHER' / 'WE ALL STAND TOGETHER' (HUMMING VERSION)
PAUL McCARTNEY AND THE FROG CHORUS
UK RELEASE November 12 1984; Parlophone R 6086; shaped picture disc Parlophone RP 6086 released 3 December 1984; chart high No.3.

- **'We All Stand Together'** (McCartney)
- **'We All Stand Together' (Humming Version)** (McCartney)

Both with Paul McCartney (keyboards, vocals), The King's Singers (backing vocals), St Paul's Boys Choir (backing vocals). Both recorded at AIR Studios, London, England and produced by George Martin.

written for children: sit back and revel in his sweeping melody and George Martin's rich production.

Like McCartney's previous single, the B-side to this one featured an alternative version of the A-side. The 'Humming Version', credited to Paul McCartney And The Finchley Frogettes, also featured in the film. It is mostly instrumental.

Parlophone issued the single in the UK with generic labels and picture sleeve. It was also issued as a 7-inch shaped picture. It was not issued in the USA.

'SPIES LIKE US'

COMMISSIONED to write the theme song for a 'comedy' movie by John Landis, McCartney came up with 'Spies Like Us', his third consecutive single from a film soundtrack. Written midway through recording the new *Press To Play* album, 'Spies' was a rushed job recorded over four nights in September 1985. The film studio "wanted it yesterday", McCartney recalled. Although he was no stranger to working quickly, this apparently represented a dramatic change in working practices. "I generally don't like to go crazy, [I like] to take things pretty easy," he said. "But sometimes ... you need the challenge, to sharpen you up a bit." Whether or not the project sharpened him up is questionable – the *Press To Play* album suggests not.

McCartney co-produced the song with Phil Ramone, a producer who has worked with everyone from Frank Sinatra to Madonna. Ramone considerably influenced the way the song sounded. McCartney said that Ramone's approach was to "whack that on, louder, [a] bigger type of sound, with me playing rock'n'roll, gritty guitar up front, drums and stuff – and I kinda think, well, I do that all the time, don't I? I forget that that isn't my image, people would expect a sort of ballad for 'Spies'."

The final master was produced at McCartney's new 48-track studio, Hog-Hill, which he'd installed in a restored windmill near the village of Icklesham, East Sussex. Part of this master used the drum track from his demo, simply because he'd managed to capture a good drum sound. He played all the instruments except for keyboards, which were supplied by Eddie Rayner of Split Enz. He recruited his cousin, Kate Robins, to sing backing vocals.

As with previous singles, several edits and remixes were issued. The DJ version simply fades the song one minute earlier than the commercial version. A seven-minute 'Party Mix' by John Potoker only managed to make the song tedious, as most of its best moments were removed in favour of dialogue from the film. The Art Of Noise's 'Alternative Mix Known To His Friends As Tom' gives the song some extra clout, without deconstructing it beyond the point of recognition, but fails to improve on the single mix.

When Wings visited New Orleans in early 1975 to record *Venus And Mars* they did so at the height of Mardi Gras. McCartney wrote 'My Carnival' immediately after his experience of the event, recording it with Wings Mk.5 at Sea Saint Studios (and dedicating it to the legendary New Orleans musician Professor Longhair). The recording featured two of New Orleans' finest musicians –

'SPIES LIKE US' / 'MY CARNIVAL'
PAUL McCARTNEY / PAUL McCARTNEY AND WINGS
UK RELEASE November 18 1985; Parlophone R 6118; 12-inch Parlophone 12 R 6118 'Spies Like Us' (Party Mix)', 'Spies Like Us' (Alternative Mix Known To His Friends As Tom) / 'Spies Like Us' (DJ Version), 'My Carnival' (Party Mix); 12-inch picture disc Parlophone 12 RP 6118 'Spies Like Us' (Party Mix), 'Spies Like Us' (Alternative Mix Known To His Friends As Tom) / 'Spies Like Us' (DJ Version), 'My Carnival' (Party Mix) released December 2 1985; shaped picture disc RP 6118 released 9 December 1985; chart high No.13.
US RELEASE November 18 1985; Capitol B-5537; 12-inch Capitol V-15212 'Spies Like Us' (Party Mix), 'Spies Like Us' (Alternative Mix Known To His Friends As Tom) / 'Spies Like Us' (DJ Version), 'My Carnival' (Party Mix); chart high No.7.

- **'Spies Like Us' (McCartney)**

Paul McCartney (bass, keyboards, drums, vocals), Eric Stewart (guitar, backing vocals), Eddie Rayner (keyboards), Ruby James (backing vocals), Kate Robins (backing vocals).
Recorded at Hog-Hill Studio, East Sussex, England.
Produced by Paul McCartney, Phil Ramone, and Hugh Padgham.

- **'My Carnival' (McCartney)**

Paul McCartney (bass, piano, vocals), Linda McCartney (keyboards, backing vocals), Denny Laine (guitar, backing vocals), Jimmy McCulloch (guitar, backing vocals), Joe English (drums), George Porter (trombone), Benny Spellman (vocals).
Recorded at Sea Saint Studios, New Orleans, LA, USA.
Produced by Paul McCartney.

R&B singer Benny Spellman, who provides the baritone vocal parts, and trombonist George Porter. Intended for *Venus And Mars*, it was withdrawn from the running order at the last minute and remained in the can until issued here as the B-side of 'Spies Like Us'. Remixed by Gary Langan for the 12-inch single, 'My Carnival' was butchered merely to follow the vogue for dance mixes.

'Spies Like Us' data

Parlophone issued *Spies Like Us* in Britain on four formats: 7-inch and 12-inch black vinyl with generic labels and picture sleeve; 7-inch shaped picture disc (RP 6118); and 12-inch picture disc (12 RP 6118). Seven-inch demonstration copies featured an edit of the A-side and were issued with generic labels and a unique paper sleeve with the title printed in black, top centre.

Capitol in the USA issued 7-inch (B-5537) and 12-inch (V-15212) editions with black/rainbow labels and picture sleeve. They also issued 7 and 12-inch demonstration singles. The 7-inch had a white label with black text and a black keyhole in the top right corner. The 12-inch (SPRO-9556) featured a 4:40 version on one side and a 3:46 edit on the other.

'JEALOUS GUY'

'JEALOUS GUY' / 'GOING DOWN ON LOVE'
JOHN LENNON
UK RELEASE November 18 1985; Parlophone R 6117; 12-inch Parlophone 12 R 6117 'Jealous Guy' / 'Going Down', 'Oh Yoko!'; chart high No.65.

ISSUED in the UK to promote the release on home video of *Imagine – The Film*, 'Jealous Guy' had already hit the Number 1 spot in Britain when covered by Roxy Music. This time, however, the song barely scraped into the lower end of the charts. Issued by Parlophone with generic labels as 7 and 12-inch singles, it was released in a picture sleeve designed by Shoot That Tiger!. A video compiled from footage from the *Imagine* film was used to promote the single. EMI provided stores with a 20-inch by 30-inch full-colour poster that advertised the *Imagine* video, the 'Jealous Guy' single, the *John Lennon Collection*, and the *Imagine* album.

LIVE IN NEW YORK CITY

HER CONTRACT with Polydor having expired, Ono re-signed with EMI and began work on releasing more Lennon material from the archives. *Live In New York City* was the first of two albums consisting of archive material that she issued in 1986. The recording here was taken from the Lennons' One To One concert, which took place at Madison Square Garden on August 30 1972. It was now made available on LP and CD, and the concert was also issued on video with extra material, including Ono's 'Sisters, O Sisters' and 'Born In A Prison'.

The One To One concert took place on the cusp of the Lennons' retreat from radical left-wing politics. Lennon was under FBI surveillance and was being threatened with deportation. Although they had plans to tour and continue with their political activities, John and Yoko were desperate to remain in America, and the only way they could achieve this was to appear less threatening and more like caring members of society. By the time President Nixon was re-elected, Lennon's commitment to the radical left was all but extinguished. However, before Nixon made it into the White House for a second term, the Lennons gave their final full-length concert together.

Lennon and Ono were approached by Geraldo Rivera, who invited them to participate in a charity event he was organising to benefit the Willowbrook Hospital. Rivera had discovered the terrible conditions in which mentally handicapped children were living and wanted to do something about it. As the Lennons had already appeared at several charity concerts, and were desperate to do whatever it took to stay in the USA, Rivera had few problems in securing their services for the event.

The concert was arranged at short notice. Rivera made contact with the pair in late July, which left less than four weeks to arrange everything. Rehearsals with Elephant's Memory were held at Butterfly Studios and the Fillmore East concert hall in New York City. As usual, Lennon taped everything. The rehearsals at Butterfly Studios were recorded and those at the Fillmore East filmed. During the rehearsal period, Lennon, Ono, Elephant's Memory, and Rivera recorded radio spots for broadcast, informing the public that a second matinee performance had been added due to the huge demand for tickets.

On the afternoon of August 30, hundreds of mentally handicapped children enjoyed the One To One festival in Central Park. At 2 o'clock, the matinee performance at Madison Square Garden kicked off with Sha Na Na, Roberta Flack, and Stevie Wonder; John and Yoko topped the bill. That evening, the entire concert was repeated. The Lennons also donated $59,000 to the charity because Rivera felt that not enough money was being raised by the event. He really needn't have worried: Lennon and Ono's generosity helped raise over $1,500,000. Besides giving their time and the money from ticket sales, the Lennons arranged for both matinee and evening shows to be filmed and recorded. The rights to broadcast the concert film were sold to ABC Television for $350,000, which also went to the charity.

Compared with his previous appearances, Lennon's performance at the One To One concert was stunning. He was in fine voice and was particularly animated. Dressed in army fatigues, he looked every bit the king of the counterculture. The rehearsals had paid off. Nothing had been left to chance. The stage set was minimal but beautifully lit, and the sound in the concert hall was spectacular. Although it is generally accepted that the evening performance was the superior of the two, with Lennon referring to the matinee performance as "the rehearsal", it was that matinee show that was used for this album. Tapes of the evening concert proved to have unacceptable levels of tape hiss, which is why they were not used. Later, with the advance of digital technology, the tapes were digitally enhanced, and three songs from the evening concert were included on 1998's *John Lennon Anthology*.

Prior to the release of *Live In New York City*, only a brief extract of 'Give Peace A Chance', performed at the evening concert only, had been made commercially available, cross-faded with 'Happy Xmas (War Is Over)' on the *Shaved Fish* compilation. Part of the Lennons' performance was broadcast by the ABC network as one of their *In Concert* series on December 14 1972. The show was also broadcast by the *King Biscuit Flower Hour*, which provided bootleggers with a good audio source. An edited version of the original ABC Television broadcast, which drew on the evening rather than the matinee concert, was issued by BMG on laserdisc in 1992.

Live In New York City songs

Issued in 1969 by Apple as the B-side to 'Something', 'Come Together' was a swampy, blues-based rocker recorded as The Beatles spiralled out of control. Lennon had been inspired by Dr. Timothy Leary's political campaign slogan, fashioning a potent brew of sexual innuendo and political rhetoric. The lyric echoed Lennon's previous psychedelic utterances, which no doubt delighted Leary, for whom the song was originally intended. There was, however, a more symbolic meaning to Lennon's nonsense verse. The coming together he envisioned was, perhaps, the coming together of the counterculture tribes. Woodstock was just around the corner and the Establishment was looking unstable. In light of the Lennons' peace campaign, it may also have been a plea for global harmony.

That it was the only song from The Beatles' repertoire that Lennon chose to perform during the One To One concert suggests that he intended it as a rallying call of some kind. Performed while he was still committed to radical change, it retained its political impact. But within the context of the concert, it could have also been an appeal for a socially equal society, where those with handicaps are no different from those without them.

Musically, Lennon borrowed from Chuck Berry's 'You Can't Catch Me' as a way into his song. He did this all the time and wasn't alone in doing so. George Harrison borrowed from The Edwin Hawkins Singers' 'Oh Happy Day' when writing 'My Sweet Lord', for which he was sued; not because it resembled 'Oh Happy Day' but because, it was claimed, of similarities with The Chiffons' 'He's So Fine'. Usually, Lennon had the sense to disguise his borrowings. This time, however, he retained a line from Berry's original and was sued for breach of copyright. The case dragged on for years and Lennon ended up in court – although he eventually came out the winner.

A massive hit for Elvis Presley, 'Hound Dog' was originally recorded by Big Mama Thornton in 1953. Elvis heard a reworked version by Freddie Bell & The Bellboys and decided to have a go at recording the song himself. The result was a defining moment in rock'n'roll history. Like Presley, Lennon loved the song, which is why he decided to perform it at the One To One concert. If not the best version ever captured on tape, it is one of the most committed and spirited. Lennon was having fun, and that's what comes across.

The other songs Lennon performed at the One To One concerts don't improve on the original studio versions, but they are among the best live recordings he made. Performing material from his *Plastic Ono Band*, *Imagine*, and *Some Time In New York City* albums, Lennon, backed by Elephant's Memory, was on top form. Previous live shows had been ragged affairs, but the One To One concerts were models of professionalism. He delivered a virtuoso performance that matched the equally stunning performance that George Harrison gave at the Concert For Bangla Desh at the same venue the previous year.

Live In New York City data

Parlophone issued the album in the UK with generic labels and full-colour inner sleeve. The CD, issued two months after the vinyl, was manufactured by Nimbus and issued with a four-page booklet.

LIVE IN NEW YORK CITY
JOHN LENNON
SIDE 1 'New York City', 'It's So Hard', 'Woman Is The Nigger Of The World', 'Well Well Well', 'Instant Karma! (We All Shine On)'.
SIDE 2 'Mother', 'Come Together', 'Imagine', 'Cold Turkey', 'Hound Dog', 'Give Peace A Chance'.
UK RELEASE February 24 1986; LP Parlophone PCS 7301; CD Parlophone CDP 7 46096 2 released April 28 1986; chart high No.55.
US RELEASE January 24 1986; LP Capitol SV-12451; CD Capitol CDP 7 46096 2 released May 26 1986; chart high No.41.

- **'Come Together'** (Lennon, McCartney)
- **'Hound Dog'** (Leiber, Stoller)

Both with John Lennon (vocal, guitar), Yoko Ono (piano), Stan Bronstein (saxophone), Gary Van Scyoc (bass), John Ward (bass), Adam Ippolito (piano), Richard Frank Jr. (drums and percussion), Jim Keltner (drums).
Both recorded live at Madison Square Garden, New York City, NY, USA.
Both produced by Yoko Ono; original recordings supervised by Phil Spector.

In the USA, Capitol issued the LP with black/colour band labels and full-colour inner sleeve. The LP was also issued as a Columbia House edition (SV-512451) and as a RCA Music Service edition (R-144497). RCA Music Service also issued a white-shell 8-track cartridge (S-144497).

Although no singles were pulled from the album for commercial release, Capitol issued a 12-inch promotional single to radio stations. 'Imagine', backed with 'Come Together', was issued in a plain white card sleeve with a three-and-a-quarter-inch by seven-inch sticker attached to the top left corner. The 33 rpm record (SPRO-9575 / 9576) was issued with black/colour band labels. 'Imagine' / 'Come Together' was also issued as a promotional 7-inch single (PRP-1163) in Japan. In-store displays and promotional posters advertising both the record and video were issued to record stores.

'SEASIDE WOMAN'

THIRD time round for Linda's reggae song, but the first time on EMI/Capitol. Both sides underwent substantial remixing by Alvin Clark, who added a new keyboard part and drums. Both A and B-sides were given extended mixes. Although Paul McCartney was originally credited as producer, this time Super Weed got the credit – an ironic nod towards the McCartneys' taste in certain illegal substances, perhaps.

EMI issued 7 and 12-inch singles with black and silver labels and a new picture sleeve. In America, Capitol issued 7-inch and 12-inch singles with black/colour band labels. The 7-inch single was issued with a picture sleeve, the 12-inch with a generic grey sleeve with a rectangular sticker with red stripes, a grey palm tree, diving female figure, artist, and title adhered to the front cover. Capitol issued a 7-inch demonstration single (P-B-5608) with white labels with black text and the Capitol logo top centre, in a grey paper sleeve.

'PRESS'

McCARTNEY chose 'Press', a lacklustre song with a seemingly incomprehensible lyric, to preview his first collection of new material since *Pipes Of Peace* in 1983. Recorded at his new studio in Sussex, he produced 'Press' and the album *Press To Play* in tandem with Hugh Padgham. He was still searching for new sounds, and Padgham's production style differed considerably from George Martin's, who had produced his three previous albums with varying degrees of success.

Where Martin would have used technological innovations, such as synthesisers and drum machines, with a degree of subtlety, Padgham, as was the practice at the time, piles on the effects. Technology, of course, is no bad thing; it's down to the way it's used. The Beatles had always experimented with new recording techniques and technology: they embraced multi-track recording, used the Mellotron, and were one of the first groups in Britain to use a Moog synthesiser. But listening back today, there is something about 1980s technology and the way it was used that sounds very sterile. The digitisation of the studio may have banished tape hiss and other problems associated with analogue recording. It may have simplified editing and made sampling quick and easy. But it did the music no favours. The apparent perfection it produced did not create character, it destroyed character. McCartney, like many in the 1980s who came under the spell of digital technology, fell into its glittering trap. Ever the perfectionist, he thought he had found it in the silicon chip. But the machine aesthetic of *Press To Play* only succeeded in producing a processed blandness, which McCartney was ultimately to reject in favour of more organic modes of recording.

'SEASIDE WOMAN' / 'B SIDE TO SEASIDE'
SUZY AND THE RED STRIPES
UK RELEASE July 7 1986; EMI EMI 5572; 12-inch EMI 12 EMI 5572 'Seaside Woman' / 'B Side To Seaside'; failed to chart.
US RELEASE August 11 1986; Capitol B-5608; 12-inch Capitol V-15244 'Seaside Woman' / 'B Side To Seaside'; failed to chart.

Despite its glossy perfection, the 'Press' single failed to hit with the public. This was perhaps down to the song's obtuse lyric, which came in for much discussion at the time. McCartney explained that the words had simply flowed from his subconscious. "'Oklahoma was never like this.' That can mean whatever you want it to mean. To me, when you're writing songs, you often get a line you assume you're going to edit later: you're going to knock it out and put something sensible in. But every time I came to that line I couldn't sing anything but [that; it was] just the scanning, the way it sang." As usual the 'magic' was left unchanged and a more considered lyric was never written.

Of course, McCartney may have been referring to the Rodgers & Hammerstein musical, possibly with a touch of post-modern irony. But as he explained, "Oklahoma" simply represented a distant, perhaps imagined place. "People would have understood it if it was 'Liverpool was never like this,' but it wouldn't have sung the same. It's a symbol for the provinces, the sticks, the out-of-the-way places. The line just wouldn't change, and when you meet such resistance from the lyrics themselves you have to give in." Although the reference to Oklahoma was chosen for no other reason than because it sounded good – another example of

McCartney's love of scansion – his lyric did include an implicit reference to a hit from the 1970s, "Right there, that's it, yes", from Gary Glitter's 'Do You Wanna Touch Me'. It was perhaps the most suggestive lyric McCartney had used since 'Hi, Hi, Hi', but this piece of sexual innuendo went completely unnoticed.

McCartney attacks his critics with the impeccably produced ballad 'It's Not True'. Yet, despite his best intentions, he fails to fully address the problem; denial doesn't achieve anything. His attempts to express his feelings for Linda also fall short of the mark. We all know how Paul and Linda felt about one another, but your impressions might be different if this was all you had to go on. At best this is adolescent, at worst poorly conceived. Thankfully, McCartney has expressed his thoughts more forcefully and convincingly elsewhere. (An alternative Julian Mendelsohn mix, which appears as a bonus track on the CD of *Press To Play,* removed Carlos Alomar's guitar and added a saxophone solo.)

'PRESS' / 'IT'S NOT TRUE'
PAUL McCARTNEY
UK RELEASE July 14 1986; Parlophone R 6133; 10-inch Parlophone 10 R 6133 'Press' / 'It's Not True' (Remixed By Julian Mendelsohn), 'Press' (Bevans–Forward Video Edit) released 18 August 1986; 12 inch Parlophone 12 R 6133 'Press' (Remixed By Bevans–Forward), 'It's Not True' (Remixed by Julian Mendelsohn) / 'Hanglide', 'Press' (Bevans–Forward Dubmix); second 7-inch Parlophone R 6133 'Press' (Video Edit) / 'It's Not True'; second 12-inch Parlophone 12 R 6133 'Press' (Video Edit), 'It's Not True' (Remixed By Julian Mendelsohn) / 'Hanglide', 'Press' (Bevans–Forward Dubmix); chart high No.25.
US RELEASE July 14 1986; Capitol B-5597; 12-inch Capitol V-15212 'Press', 'It's Not True' / 'Hanglide', 'Press' (Dubmix); chart high No.21.

• **'Press'** (McCartney)
Paul McCartney (bass, keyboards, guitar, vocals), Eric Stewart (guitar, backing vocals), Carlos Alomar (guitar), Eddie Rayner (keyboards, synth bass), Jerry Marotta (drums), Linda McCartney (backing vocals), Ruby James (backing vocals), Kate Robins (backing vocals).
• **'It's Not True'** (McCartney)
Paul McCartney (bass, keyboards, vocals), Eric Stewart (guitar, backing vocals), Carlos Alomar (guitar), Eddie Rayner (keyboards), Jerry Marotta (drums), Dick Morrisey (saxophone), Linda McCartney (backing vocals), Ruby James, (backing vocals), Kate Robins (backing vocals).
• **'Hanglide'** (McCartney, Stewart)
Paul McCartney (bass, guitar, keyboards), Eric Stewart (guitar, keyboards).
All recorded at Recorded at Hog-Hill Studio, East Sussex, England. All produced by Paul McCartney and Hugh Padgham.

The 12-inch single featured 'Hanglide', a McCartney–Stewart instrumental based on a simple bass guitar riff, keyboard swells, and extensive backwards guitar. Little more than a throwaway, the track is merely an excuse in studio doodling – the co-author credit is probably a result of jamming – and it may well have been recorded for no other reason than to test the new studio.

'Press' data

In America, Capitol issued both 7 and 12-inch singles with black/colour band labels and a picture sleeve. Demonstration copies were also issued as 7 and 12-inch records. The 7-inch (P-B-5597) has white labels with black text with the Capitol 'dome' logo top centre. The 12-inch (SPRO-9763) has black/colour band labels and the 'Video Edit' version of the song on both sides of the disc.

Parlophone issued 'Press' as 7, 10 and 12-inch singles in the UK. However, like 'No More Lonely Nights', initial pressings were quickly replaced with new mixes. While 'Lonely Nights' had been available for some weeks before new editions were released, initial pressings of 'Press' were replaced within one week. All versions of the single came with generic labels and picture sleeves. The second 7 and 12-inch editions had 'Video Edit' or 'Video Soundtrack' added to the label credits, although only the 7-inch featured a new edit of the Bevans–Forward video mix. The second 12-inch pressing claimed to feature a new mix but did not. Another mix of 'Press' by Hugh Padgham was made available on a 10-inch single, issued in a edition of 6,000 with a circular sleeve. It also included a 5:50 mix of 'It's Not True'.

PRESS TO PLAY

McCARTNEY'S first album of new material in over two and a half years, *Press To Play* was a bold departure. He had opened the decade by reuniting with Beatles producer George Martin. Although the partnership began successfully, it soon became apparent that they were finding it difficult to replicate previous successes. Searching for a new direction, McCartney teamed up with producer of the moment Hugh Padgham to record what he considered an adventurous and experimental advance on previous albums. Padgham certainly pushed him into exploring new avenues, both technically and creatively. It was McCartney's most contemporary sounding album for some time. Its rich, dense, electronically-processed sound placed it firmly in the mid 1980s. But the final result was a disappointing mishmash of quasi-psychedelia and silicon slick pop, and the public all but ignored it.

McCartney wrote many of the songs on *Press To Play* with his new songwriting collaborator, Eric Stewart. Six McCartney–Stewart compositions appeared on the album and another three as B-sides. The pair also wrote several songs that didn't feature on the album. 'Don't Break The Promises' appeared on the 10CC album *Meanwhile*, albeit slightly rewritten by Graham Gouldman. McCartney eventually released his version in 1997 as a bonus track on the CD single of 'The World Tonight' (CDR 6472). 'Code Of Silence' appeared on another 10CC album, *Mirror Mirror.* Eric Stewart recalled that it was written "after a very heavy lunch with Paul. He felt like doing some recording at my home studio and we ended up with the backing track to 'Code Of Silence' that is pure McCartney. He played some cricket sounds and things like that; it was all MIDI [electronic] instruments. I was really excited about the song. In March of 1989, I was living in a house in Bethersden, Kent, and Paul dropped in and sang lead vocals on a version of the song." That same 10CC album featured another McCartney–Stewart composition, 'Yvonne's The One'. McCartney recorded a demo of the song, but his version remains unreleased. Bert Bevans is supposed to have mixed another McCartney–Stewart song, 'Right Of Way', but it too remains unreleased.

On completing *Press To Play*, McCartney began work on another project with producer Phil Ramone. Recording began at Power Station Studios in New York City during August 1986 with members of Billy Joel's band. Two tracks were recorded before McCartney moved to Audio International Studios in London in the first week of February 1987. Recording then shifted to Hog-Hill in Sussex. Further sessions took place at Abbey Road on July 1 1987, where George Martin overdubbed orchestral arrangements onto three of McCartney's songs. The next day, Julian Mendelsohn remixed some of the Phil Ramone tracks at Sarm West Studios. Whether this session was to mix the songs overdubbed the previous day is not clear. McCartney worked for a 12-month period with Ramone, who produced the following songs: 'Beautiful Night', 'The Loveliest Thing', 'Once Upon A Long Ago', 'Back On My Feet', 'P.S. Love Me Do', 'Love Come Tumbling Down', 'Return To Pepperland', 'Love Mix', 'Atlantic Ocean', 'This One', 'Big Day', 'Christian Bop', and 'Peacocks'. But with the exception of 'Once Upon A Long Ago' and 'P.S. Love Me Do', of which more later, most of this material remained unreleased until issued as bonus tracks for the three singles taken from 1997's *Flaming Pie*.

Press To Play songs

Side one kicks off with 'Stranglehold', a mid-tempo rocker chosen as an American single. McCartney and Stewart vamp away on acoustic guitars evoking a down-home feel, but when the high-tech production kicks in, any notion of bluesy authenticity is forsaken for a typically bland, silicon-slick mid-1980s workout.

'Stranglehold' was the first song that McCartney and Stewart wrote together and was essentially an exercise in rhythm rather than melody – the lyrics were added mainly to enhance the groove. As with previous examples, such as 'Bip Bop' or 'Big Barn Bed', words are used for the sound they make rather than their meaning. McCartney said: "We started off 'Stranglehold' putting rhythmic words in, using lyrics like a bongo, accenting the words."

Unfortunately, McCartney's fondness for scansion too often fails to convince, and Stewart simply doesn't have Lennon's flair with words. Nevertheless, McCartney thought that working with Stewart rekindled memories of writing with Lennon. "I remembered the old way I'd written with John, the two acoustic guitars facing each other – like a mirror, but better! Like an objective mirror: you're looking at the person playing chords, but you're not."

While too many of the songs on *Press To Play* fail to satisfy, McCartney combined two compositions, 'Good Times Coming' and 'Feel The Sun', to create one of its highlights. An evocation of idyllic summers both real and imagined, the piece captures perfectly the carefree atmosphere of long, hot childhood summers. A breezy, sun-soaked pop song, it nevertheless has its darker moments, which find its author questioning former successes. "To me, the song is three summers," McCartney revealed. "One when I was a kid going to Butlin's in my short trousers, feeling embarrassed because I wanted to be in long trousers. … Then the second verse is a bit more grown up. … I associate that second verse with The Beatles – 'It was a silly season, was it the best? / We didn't need a reason, just a rest!' That's one of my favourite lines on the album. … Then the third line is kind of ominous, talking about a great summer before the war. … That's the twist in the tail of the song."

'Feel The Sun' was originally several verses longer before McCartney decided to link it with 'Good Times Coming'. Edited from its original 3:30 seconds to 1:25, all that remained was one verse and a chorus motif that acts as the coda.

McCartney wrote and recorded the basic track for 'Talk More Talk' in one day, and the lyric, he explained, was derived from an interview with Tom Waits. "Lyrically, I was picking out quotes that I liked from, I think, a Tom Waits interview. 'I don't like sitting-down music,' great things like that, random cut-outs." Alluding to the 'random' nature of his lyric, McCartney employed a babble of voices to introduce and close the song. This nod to avant-gardism was unfortunately moderated by the requirement to produce commercial pop product. "I eventually always come back to having to get sensible, so that's why there is the bit in between. In another world, they'd be the album." No matter what McCartney may have wanted for the song, there is little that he could have done to save it. He may have employed avant-garde techniques to kick-start it, but 'Talk More Talk' is little more than run-of-the-mill pop that should have been resigned to the outtakes box.

McCartney was inspired to write 'Footprints' in the winter of 1984/'85 after watching a magpie search for food in the snow. "It just seemed like a romantic idea for a song, really," he recalled.

PRESS TO PLAY
PAUL McCARTNEY
SIDE 1 'Stranglehold', 'Good Times Coming', 'Feel The Sun', 'Talk More Talk', 'Footprints', 'Only Love Remains'.
SIDE 2 'Press', 'Pretty Little Head', 'Move Over Busker', 'Angry', 'However Absurd', 'Write Away'*, 'It's Not True*', 'Tough On A Tightrope'*.
Tracks marked * appear only on the CD.
UK RELEASE September 1 1986; LP Parlophone PCSD 103; CD Parlophone CDP 7 46269 2; chart high No.8.
US RELEASE August 25 1986; LP Capitol PJAS-12475; CD Capitol 46269; chart high No.30.

• **'Stranglehold'** (McCartney, Stewart)
Paul McCartney (bass, guitar, vocals), Eric Stewart (guitar, vocals), Jerry Morotta (drums), Nick Glennie-Smith (keyboards), Gary Barnacle (saxophone), Gavin Wright (violin), John Bradbury (saxophone), Dick Morrisey (saxophone), Lennie Pickett (saxophone).
• **'Good Times Coming / Feel The Sun'** (McCartney)
Paul McCartney (bass, piano, guitar, vocals), Eric Stewart (guitar, vocals), Carlos Alomar (guitar), Jerry Marotta (drums), Eddie Rayner (guitar, keyboards), Dick Morrisey (flute), Linda McCartney (backing vocals), Ruby James, (backing vocals), Kate Robins (backing vocals).
• **'Talk More Talk'** (McCartney)
Paul McCartney (bass, keyboards, vocals), Eric Stewart (guitar, backing vocals), Jerry Marotta (drums, percussion), James McCartney (spoken words), Linda McCartney (spoken words).
• **'Footprints'** (McCartney, Stewart)
Paul McCartney (bass, guitar, spinet, vocals), Eric Stewart (guitar, backing vocals), Jerry Marotta (drums, percussion).
• **'Only Love Remains'** (McCartney)
Paul McCartney (piano, synth bass, wine glass, vocals), Eric Stewart (guitar, harpsichord, backing vocals), Jerry Marotta (marimbas, drums), Dick Morrisey (saxophone), Linda McCartney (backing vocals), Ruby James (backing vocals), Kate Robins (backing vocals).
• **'Pretty Little Head'** (McCartney, Stewart)
Paul McCartney (bass, guitar, drums, vocals), Eric Stewart (keyboards, guitar, backing vocals), Jerry Marotta (vibraphone), Linda McCartney (backing vocals), Ruby James (backing vocals), Kate Robins (backing vocals).
• **'Move Over Busker'** (McCartney, Stewart)
Paul McCartney (bass, piano, vocals), Eric Stewart (guitar, backing vocals), Carlos Alomar (guitar), Jerry Marotta (drums), Ruby James (backing vocals), Kate Robins (backing vocals).
• **'Angry'** (McCartney, Stewart)
Paul McCartney (bass, vocals), Pete Townshend (guitar), Phil Collins (drums), Linda McCartney (backing vocals), Ruby James (backing vocals), Kate Robins (backing vocals), Dick Morrisey (saxophone), Lennie Pickett (saxophone).
• **'However Absurd'** (McCartney, Stewart)
Paul McCartney (bass, piano, vocals), Eric Stewart (guitar, backing vocals), Jerry Marotta (drums), Eddie Rayner (keyboards), Nick Glennie-Smith (keyboards), Dick Morrisey (saxophone), Lennie Pickett (saxophone).
• **'Write Away'** (McCartney)
Paul McCartney (bass, piano, vocals), Eric Stewart (keyboards, backing vocals), Carlos Alomar (guitar), Jerry Marotta (drums), Lennie Pickett (saxophone), Linda McCartney (backing vocals), Ruby James (backing vocals), Kate Robins (backing vocals).
• **'Tough On A Tightrope'** (McCartney, Stewart)
Paul McCartney (bass, guitar, vocals), Eric Stewart (guitar, backing vocals), Carlos Alomar (guitar), Eddie Rayner (keyboards), Jerry Marotta (drums), Linda McCartney (backing vocals), Ruby James (backing vocals), Kate Robins (backing vocals).
All recorded at Hog-Hill Studio, East Sussex, England, except 'Only Love Remains' recording location unknown.
All produced by Paul McCartney and Hugh Padgham.

Rather than employ another animal metaphor, McCartney and Stewart took a more literal approach. "We started off with the magpie looking for food, but then it seemed like a nature programme ... you know? All about this magpie. So it became a person who was actually looking around for logs, just a lonely fella, a bit like the character in 'Eleanor Rigby'." But where the characters in 'Eleanor Rigby' are developed through a series of ambiguous, unsettling images, 'Footprints' merely describes a particular scenario, leaving little to the imagination. A relationship between the listener and Eleanor Rigby is established almost instantaneously, but the same cannot be said for the lonely figure in 'Footprints'. He simply passes by without affecting the listener on any emotional level.

The big production number on *Press To Play* was 'Only Love Remains', a solo McCartney composition. He described it as "a straightforward love song about: if you buzz off, I'm not going to like it". Typical of his considered balladeering, the song has a classic McCartney melody and a lush orchestral arrangement by Tony Visconti. The orchestra was recorded live with the band, suggesting that it was recorded in a studio other than McCartney's. The only song from the album that McCartney played live, 'Only Love Remains' was performed on just two occasions: first, at the *Royal Variety Show* on November 24 1986, where it was performed with a band but without orchestra; second, on December 11 on the television music show *The Tube*, where it was performed with just piano, saxophone, and two backing singers. In that naked form, 'Only Love Remains' revealed McCartney's innate ability to write timeless melodies, even when exploring a much-visited subject.

A Bevans–Forward remix of 'Press' opens side two of the album, and allegedly two different versions were used for initial and subsequent British pressings: a 4:37 mix for the first pressing (matrix number PCSD 103 B-7-1-1), of which EMI pressed about 45,000 copies, replaced with a 4:17 mix when the album was re-pressed (matrix number PCSD 103 B-3U-1-2-1).

McCartney wrote and recorded 'Pretty Little Head' at Hog-Hill, partly to explore the new studio's technical capabilities and partly to test the abilities of the musicians he was working with. The basic track featured McCartney on drums, Eric Stewart on keyboards, and Jerry Marotta on vibes. Built on a groove supplied by Marotta's percussion, 'Pretty Little Head' suffers from the absence of a decent melody and an over-reliance on studio trickery.

The song remained an instrumental for some time before McCartney added another oblique lyric. His fantasy narrative alluded, once again, to the family. Attempting to explain his words, he said: "I see it as a tribe who live in the hills, who descend from their caves once every blue moon to bring silks and precious stones, so that their princess doesn't have to worry her pretty little head. What's nice is that it can also be an ordinary family, and the pretty little head is the kid." For some reason this eccentric McCartney–Stewart composition was chosen as the second single from the album (America went with 'Stranglehold'). Needless to say, it failed to chart and probably did little to encourage the public to rush out and buy *Press To Play*.

'Move Over Busker' sounds like the bastard offspring of 'Not Such A Bad Boy'. A typical mid-tempo rocker, it has a riff-heavy intro that gives way to the kind of pub-rock predictability that McCartney is capable of knocking off in his sleep. He thought it had "a good American rock'n'roll feel" but, ironically, it is too melodic for its own good. Great rock'n'roll is never over-reliant on melody, and McCartney's attempts to combine the two often efface both, especially when a simple 12-bar would have sufficed.

His throwaway lyric was changed from the laddish "move over buster", which he thought "a bit ordinary", to the less rock'n'roll "move over busker". He claimed that the change opened up more possibilities from a writer's perspective, as it allowed him to develop both the characters and the narrative. Loaded with double entendres and innuendo, the lyric drew on his sense of the absurd as a way into the song rather than as an attempt at writing a joke – the lyric really isn't very funny.

In a self-referential move, McCartney included an obscure reference to his old band's often quirky sense of humour. He explained: "Mae West's 'sweaty vest' – that's an old Beatles joke." It may have raised a wry smile with his former bandmates, but to outsiders this is nonsense – and appears to confirm accusations that McCartney all too often pays scant attention to his lyrics.

Next up on *Press To Play* is 'Angry', based on a chord riff that McCartney had been working on for some time and which he'd intended to use for another song. It was recorded in a little over two hours by McCartney, Pete Townshend, and Phil Collins. McCartney invited The Who's energetic guitarist to play on the song because "every time I played it I felt like Pete Townshend. There was plenty of those windmill arms when I played it, and I'd always imagined him doing it". Recorded live in the studio in an attempt to capture the adrenaline rush of live performance, 'Angry' is too paced and workmanlike, a result of all three musicians creeping into middle age.

'Angry' finds its author on his high horse giving vent to his feelings, in particular those concerning the abuse of power. With a few notable exceptions, McCartney never appeared as politically committed as Lennon, but by the mid 1980s even he felt compelled to comment on political issues. "What makes me angry are things like [British prime minister] Thatcher's attitude to the blacks in South Africa, and [US president] Reagan calling it South America," he said. "People who burn children with cigarettes. That sort of thing makes me angry."

'Angry' was remixed by Larry Alexander, who managed to improve on McCartney and Padgham's flat mix, and pencilled in as an American single, but instead the new mix appeared as the B-side of the US single 'Stranglehold' and on the British 12-inch pressing of 'Pretty Little Head'.

Revisiting his past for inspiration, McCartney came up with 'However Absurd', an affectionate pastiche of the kind of psychedelic nonsense that was once peddled as subversive. At first he was unsure of the track, because it sounded too much like The Beatles, but eventually decided that the self-referencing was no reason to discard it.

Aware that any reference to The Beatles would be analysed to the point of excess, McCartney had long steered clear of attempting to recreate "the Beatles sound". In the previous 15 years he had tried his hardest to escape his past rather than identify himself with it.

"I resisted it for a little while," he said, "but I kept coming back to 'Why?' Tell me one good reason why you're resisting this Beatles influence? Because if anyone's got the right to do it, there's three guys alive who've got the right to do it."

The song's lyric is a hotchpotch of unrelated images meant to recreate an atmosphere of hallucinogenic unease. That the words and images they chose were "a bit bizarre" was intended to complete the effect.

On the surface, they appear almost meaningless but, like 'I Am The Walrus', McCartney's lyric was an attempt at unravelling the epistemology of language. "I find that things in life don't always conveniently come wrapped up with a little sticker that says, 'This is very sensible!'" he said. "Sometimes they are completely absurd, which is what the song is about." McCartney's lyrics are, then, a playful attempt at examining the limitation of language to express meaning, emotion, and knowledge. As he explained, the song's middle eight was an attempt to break through the barrier of language. "In the middle, it explains itself a little bit, less surrealist:

'Something special between us ... Words wouldn't get my feeling through ... However absurd it may seem.' That's taken off *The Prophet* by Kahlil Gibran – there's a line of his that always used to attract me and John, which was, 'Half of what I say is meaningless, but I say it just to reach you.' So it's that kind of meaning to However Absurd.'" Lennon included the line in 'Julia', a song about his mother and Yoko Ono, on The Beatles' *White Album*.

'Write Away' is a McCartney–Stewart composition recorded at Hog-Hill and recalls Lennon and McCartney's early attempts at writing pop songs. Like 'P.S. I Love You', McCartney's starting point was the expressive and emotional release of writing to a loved one. It's also a rare example of him employing homophones in a lyric. It was usually Lennon who delighted in using wordplay to evoke childlike qualities and develop layers of intricate meaning. McCartney, however, is equally capable of using language in creative and playful ways.

The album closes with 'Tough On A Tightrope', which is pleasant enough, but the obvious metaphor isn't helped by an over-simplistic lyric, which only convinces in the middle eight when tension arises between lyric and melody. The song may reveal some of McCartney's concerns and anxieties, but he has expressed them more convincingly and imaginatively when he has some real worries to contemplate.

Press To Play data

Parlophone and Capitol issued *Press To Play* with customised labels, a gatefold sleeve (the inside of which featured drawings that McCartney made to aid the mixing process), and a printed inner sleeve with lyrics. George Hurrell, a veteran of the Hollywood motion picture industry, took the cover photograph. Capitol prepared a circular red sticker that lists four song titles – 'Press', 'Only Love Remains', 'Stranglehold', 'Angry' – and this was adhered to the front cover.

'LINDA'

TO CELEBRATE Linda's 44th birthday, McCartney recorded Jack Lawrence and Ann Robell's 'Linda'. Her father, Lee Eastman, a successful lawyer, commissioned the song from Lawrence and Robell because, while there were plenty of songs that used girls names in their titles, there was none called 'Linda'. As a bonus, Eastman had Linda's photograph used for the cover of the sheet music. The song became reasonably popular, with cover versions by surf duo Jan & Dean and Dick James, The Beatles' music publisher.

McCartney recorded two versions of 'Linda', big-band and Latin style, with a group of session players who were sworn to secrecy. Little is known about either the recording session or the record – only one was pressed. McCartney eventually acquired the publishing rights to the song, thus completing the circle. It was performed at Linda's memorial service on June 8 1998., but the likelihood of McCartney's version ever entering the public domain is remote.

'LINDA' (LATIN VERSION) / 'LINDA' (BIG BAND VERSION)
PAUL McCARTNEY
One-off pressing; no commercial release.

• **'Linda'** (Lawrence, Robell)
Paul McCartney plus unknown session musicians.
Recording location unknown.
Produced by Paul McCartney.

'PRETTY LITTLE HEAD' (LARRY ALEXANDER REMIX) / 'WRITE AWAY'
PAUL McCARTNEY
UK RELEASE October 27 1986; Parlophone R 6145; 12-inch Parlophone 12 R 6145 'Pretty Little Head' (John 'Tokes' Potoker Remix) / 'Angry' (Larry Alexander Remix), 'Write Away'; cassette single Parlophone TCR 6145 'Pretty Little Head' (John 'Tokes' Potoker remix), 'Angry' (Larry Alexander Remix), 'Write Away'; failed to chart.

'PRETTY LITTLE HEAD'

ALTHOUGH McCartney was working hard to promote his new *Press To Play* album, sales remained sluggish. What he needed was a hit single, but no one could decide which track to release. 'Talk More Talk' was a strong contender and new mixes were prepared, but it was held over for the B-side of 'Only Love Remains'. America went with 'Stranglehold', but after much procrastination 'Pretty Little Head' was finally selected.

Larry Alexander produced a new 'radio-friendly' mix for the 7-inch, which omits the lengthy introduction, and John 'Tokes' Potoker remixed the song for the 12-inch. Although Potoker extended the song by almost two minutes, his bass-heavy mix does little to enhance the original and merely reduced what there was of a song to a lengthy piece of run-of-the-mill twaddle.

Parlophone issued 'Pretty Little Head' as 7 and 12-inch singles with generic labels and picture sleeves. The single was also issued as a limited-edition cassette (2,000 copies) with the same content as the 12-inch single. But the song failed to chart; McCartney's hoped-for hit never materialised; and *Press To Play* continued on its way down the charts.

'STRANGLEHOLD'

'STRANGLEHOLD' / 'ANGRY'
PAUL McCARTNEY
US RELEASE November 3 1986; Capitol B-5636; chart high No.81.

CAPITOL issued this as a 7-inch single with black/colour band labels and picture sleeve. Seven-inch demonstration copies with white labels and black text were manufactured and distributed to radio stations. Two 12-inch singles were produced for promotional use: 'Stranglehold' (SPRO-9861) and 'Angry' (SPRO-9797), both with black/colour band labels.

MENLOVE AVE.

THIS album drew on outtakes from two albums that bookend a turbulent period in Lennon's solo career. *Rock'N'Roll* and *Walls And Bridges* each had their own unique atmosphere influenced by events in Lennon's life. He rode an emotional roller-coaster during the nine months in which these recordings were made, and the emotions he experienced and expressed then appear all the more concentrated here.

The *Rock'N'Roll* outtakes reveal Phil Spector's chaos-and-control production technique and dispel Lennon's assertions that they were unusable. Lennon may have described these outtakes as unworkable, but the sense of relief and joy he found while recording a soundtrack to his youth leaps from the speakers. They may not be the greatest songs either Lennon or Spector made, but they reveal that not all was doom and gloom during Lennon's LA sojourn.

The recordings that followed his return to New York City reveal just how down Lennon was in the wake of his 'lost weekend'. Recorded during rehearsals for *Walls And Bridges*, they are suffused with a depth of loneliness and pain that is almost palpable. Lacking the sophisticated production of the finished masters, these rehearsal takes are stripped-to-the-bone renditions that expose Lennon's inner darkness. When issued on *Walls And Bridges* they lost some of the psychological gloom audible on these early cuts, but still revealed a troubled mind. That doesn't mean that there is no light to illuminate the proceedings here: Lennon improvised several lyrics, often with hilarious results.

Unlike *Live In New York City*, the *Menlove Ave.* album was a relative flop. It failed to enter the top 100 in either Britain or America and received minimal to no publicity.

Menlove Ave. songs

'Here We Go Again' is the only Lennon–Spector song to emerge from their four-year partnership. What or how much Spector contributed to the song is difficult to confirm. A solo Lennon demo, recorded before he entered the studio with Spector, reveals little of the producer's influence. Recorded during the infamous *Rock'N'Roll* sessions, 'Here We Go Again' bears no resemblance to anything else recorded at these sessions. Obviously, it was not intended for Lennon's proposed album of rock'n'roll standards, and its monumental wall-of-sound production excluded it from *Walls And Bridges*. The reason for its recording, like Spector's co-author credit, remains a mystery.

From its serpentine introductory notes that seem to spiral into eternity, to its swirling brass arrangement, 'Here We Go Again' finds Lennon contemplating the meaning of life. It is both a personal and philosophical examination of the eternal question, and it also echoes George Harrison's meditations on the theme of eternal return. However, unlike Harrison, Lennon sounds resigned to the fact that we are bound by karmic laws and unable to transcend them. The song seems to undermine what he'd proposed only three years earlier with 'Instant Karma!'. The egalitarianism of that song is replaced by a vision of disparate also-rans. Lennon's dream of global harmony through positive projection appears tarnished by a realisation, perhaps brought about by the efforts of the American authorities to deport him, that far from reaching a state of enlightenment, mankind is doomed to repeat its mistakes, forever.

Lennon had been attempting to perfect his 'Rock And Roll People', an outtake from the *Mind Games* album, for some time. He began work on the song in late 1970, when he made a demo recording at his Tittenhurst home. It remained dormant for almost three years before he attempted another demo recording.

With the song foremost in this mind, Lennon tried to record it with the band of session players he was using to record *Mind Games*. It both celebrates and belittles rock musicians, and it never really caught fire. As with McCartney's account of life in a rock'n'roll band, 'Famous Groupies', Lennon's attempts at humour and wordplay for once eluded him. Several takes were attempted, but even Lennon grew tired of the band's inability to *rock* and gave up on the track. Obviously, the band were having an off day. The predictable arrangement verges on third-rate pub-rock, and Jim Keltner's drum fills verge on the amateur.

For some reason, 'Rock And Roll People' was issued as a promotional single for the *Menlove Ave.* album and must have done more harm than good. Almost any other track from side one would have made a better advertisement than this. ('Rock And Roll People' had first appeared commercially on Johnny Winter's 1974 album *John Dawson Winter*. Shelly Yakus, who engineered several of Lennon's albums including *Mind Games*, produced Winter's album and suggested that he might record the song. Lennon agreed, but did not contribute to Winter's recording.)

'Angel Baby' had been intended for *Rock'N' Roll* and was issued on the *Roots* version but pulled from the official release at the last moment. Originally recorded by Rosie & The Originals in 1959, it was written by Rosie Hamlin at the age of 14. The song started life as a poem about a boyfriend before she added the melody. The original was recorded on a 2-track tape machine in an aircraft hangar and by necessity was a model of simplicity. Issued by the independent Highland Records (H-5001), 'Angel Baby' became a huge hit, reaching Number 5 on the *Billboard* charts. Issued in Britain by London Records (HL-U 9266) it did not make an impact on the British charts but become a classic must-have among rock'n'roll aficionados.

Although Lennon decided against including 'Angel Baby' on his *Rock'N'Roll* album, it would not have sounded out of place. A typical Phil Spector production transforms the original teen ballad into a monolithic slab of rock'n'roll.

Elvis Presley recorded 'Since My Baby Left Me' in 1956 as an act of recognition and rebellion. Already tiring of the Tin Pan Alley material his record company were suggesting he record, Presley turned to Arthur Crudup's rustic blues in an attempt to distance himself from the mainstream he was slowly drifting toward. It was also an act of solidarity with the blues singer. Presley had already cut Crudup's 'That's Alright Mama', and by recording 'Since My Baby Left Me' he consolidated his allegiance with Crudup and pushed up a notch his claim for authenticity. The song was issued in Britain by HMV as the B-side of Presley's 'I Want You, I Need You, I Love You' (POP 235), which reached Number 9 in the UK charts. Issued in America by RCA, it was a Number 1. Spector transformed Presley's slice of rockabilly for Lennon: slashing the tempo, he created a call-and-response party record that might have been difficult to dance to but which sounded monumental.

'To Know Him Is To Love Him' was a 1957 hit for Phil Spector's first group, The Teddy Bears, for whom he played guitar and wrote their sole hit in tribute to his late father. It was issued by Dore Records (45-503) and became Spector's first American Number 1. Issued in Britain by London Records (HL 8733), the song reached Number 2.

It was another long-standing favourite of Lennon's, and featured in The Beatles' pre-fame repertoire. When the group auditioned for Decca at the company's London studio it was a nervous John Lennon who sang lead on this Spector ballad. The Beatles' recording, with Pete Best on drums, was briefly issued by AFE Records (AFELP 1047) in 1982. A few years earlier, a live recording, this time with Ringo Starr on drums, was issued by Lingasong Records on the two-LP set *Live! At The Star-Club In Hamburg, Germany: 1962* (LNL1). The Beatles also taped the song for the BBC, recording a version at the Corporation's Paris

MENLOVE AVE.
JOHN LENNON

SIDE 1 'Here We Go Again', 'Rock And Roll People', 'Angel Baby', 'Since My Baby Left Me', 'To Know Her Is To Love Her'.
SIDE 2 'Steel And Glass', 'Scared', 'Old Dirt Road', 'Nobody Loves You (When You're Down And Out)', 'Bless You'.
UK RELEASE November 3 1986; LP Parlophone PCS 7308; CD Parlophone CDP 7 46576 2 released April 13 1987; chart high No.119.
US RELEASE October 27 1986; LP Capitol SJ-12533; CD Capitol CDP 7 46576 2 released April 7 1987; chart high No.127.

• **'Here We Go Again'** (Lennon, Spector)
John Lennon (vocals), Art Munson (guitar), Ray Neapolitan (bass), Michael Omartian (keyboards), William Perkins (woodwind), William Perry (guitar), Mac Rebennack (keyboards), Louie Shelton (guitar), Phil Spector (piano, guitar), Nino Tempo (saxophone, keyboards), Anthony Terran (trumpet), Andy Thomas (piano), Michael Wofford (piano), Jim Horn (saxophone), Plas Johnson (saxophone), Joseph Kelson (horn), Jim Keltner (drums), Bobby Keys (saxophone), Ronald Kossajda (instrument unknown), Michael Lang (piano), Ronald Langinger (saxophone), Barry Mann (piano), Julian Matlock (clarinet), Michael Melvoin (piano), Donald Menza (saxophone), Dale Anderson (guitar), Jeff Barry (piano), Hal Baine (drums), Jim Calvert (instrument unknown), Conte Candoli (trumpet), Frank Capp (drums), Larry Carlton (guitar), Gene Cipriano (saxophone), David Cohen (guitar), Gary Coleman (percussion), Steve Cropper (guitar), Jesse Ed Davis (guitar), Alan Estes (percussion), Chuck Findley (trumpet), Steven Forman (percussion), Terry Gibbs (piano or percussion), Bob Glaub (bass), Jim Gordon (drums), Robert Hardaway (woodwind), Leon Russell (keyboards), Jose Feliciano (guitar), Michael Hazelwood (instrument unknown), Thomas Hensley (bass), Dick Hieronymus (instrument unknown).
• **'Rock And Roll People'** (Lennon)
John Lennon (vocals and guitar), Ken Ascher (keyboards), David Spinozza (guitar), Gordon Edwards (bass), Jim Keltner (drums).
• **'Angel Baby'** (Hamlin)
Personnel as 'Here We Go Again'.
• **'Since My Baby Left Me'** (Crudup)
Personnel as 'Here We Go Again'.
• **'To Know Her Is To Love Her'** (Spector)
Personnel as 'Here We Go Again'.
All recorded at A&M Studios or Record Plant West, Los Angeles, CA, USA and produced by Phil Spector/arranged by John Lennon and Phil Spector, except 'Rock And Roll People' recorded at Record Plant East, New York City, NY, USA and produced by John Lennon.

Theatre (in London) on July 16 1963. This recording was issued by Apple on *Live At The BBC* (PCSP 726) in 1994.

As with 'Since My Baby Left Me', Spector slowed the tempo, turning 'To Know Him Is To Love Him' into a pop requiem for his father. Lennon adds to the sense of loss with a vocal loaded with vulnerability. Set against Spector's echoing volley of drums and trademark wall-of-sound, he presents a masterclass in how to deliver a song and manipulate the listener's emotions.

Menlove Ave. data

Capitol issued a promotional 12-inch single of 'Rock And Roll People' (SPRO-9917) to American radio stations, but no commercial singles were pulled from the album. *Menlove Ave.* seems to have been assembled in something of a hurry. Ono's sleevenotes are minimal, and the American LP cover credits the author of 'Since My Baby Left Me' as "unknown". It was of course written by Arthur Crudup. This error appeared on cover proofs printed in Britain but was corrected for commercial copies of the LP (and these early proofs also have the EMI box logo in the bottom right corner of the rear cover, rather than the Parlophone logo that appeared on finished copies). British pressings of the LP were issued with generic black labels; American pressings with Capitol's black/colour band labels. The album was issued on CD in Britain on April 13 1987 and in America on April 7 1987.

THE ANTI-HEROIN PROJECT – IT'S A LIVE IN WORLD
VARIOUS ARTISTS
PAUL McCARTNEY 'Simple As That'.
UK RELEASE November 24 1986; EMI AHP LP 1; failed to chart.

'SIMPLE AS THAT' (McCARTNEY)
PERSONNEL Paul McCartney (bass, guitar, piano, keyboards, drums, percussion), Stella McCartney, Mary McCartney, James McCartney (backing vocals).
Recorded at Hog-Hill Studio, East Sussex, England.
Produced by Paul McCartney.

'ONLY LOVE REMAINS' (TOM BOYER REMIX) / 'TOUGH ON A TIGHTROPE'
PAUL McCARTNEY
UK RELEASE December 1 1986; Parlophone R 6148; 12-inch Parlophone 12 R 6148 'Only Love Remains' (Tom Boyer Remix)' / 'Tough On A Tight Rope' (Julian Mendelsohn Remix), 'Talk More Talk' (Paul McCartney And Jon Jacobs Remix); chart high No.34.
US RELEASE January 19 1987; Capitol B-5672; failed to chart.

'SIMPLE AS THAT'

EMI ISSUED The Anti–Heroin Project in Britain as a two-record set to raise money for Phoenix House, a charity providing specialist treatment services for drug and alcohol users. An esoteric collection of pop stars including Ringo Starr, Elvis Costello, Wham!, and Eurythmics wrote, performed, and donated songs for the album. But as is the way with such compilations, it sold in small numbers and probably did little to raise either cash or awareness about the dangers of drug abuse.

McCartney's appearance on an anti drugs album may seem ironic, but while he took a liberal stance on soft drugs – he believes they should be decriminalised – hard drugs were always a no-go area. He had, after all, seen the effects hard drugs had on Lennon and several of his close friends. With a grown-up family to think about, the message he now proffered was of abstinence. McCartney declared in 1986: "I must say – and at the risk of sounding goody-goody again – that I personally feel, from this perspective, today, that my favourite thing is to be clean and straight. I think you can enjoy your life better that way."

With the anti-drugs message in mind, he wrote 'Simple As That' specifically for the charity and recorded it in 1986 with three of his children on backing vocals. Although the message is blunt – do hard drugs and you're likely to wind up dead – it's perhaps typical of McCartney that the song is presented in a breezy, upbeat manner. For the real message is a positive one: make the right choice and live life to the full. 'Simple As That' was later included as a bonus track on the mid-price reissue of the *Pipes Of Peace* CD.

'ONLY LOVE REMAINS'

WITH *Press To Play* plummeting down the album charts – its decline was rapid, falling from 37 to 70 to 94 – drastic measures were required to restore it to the upper reaches. Consequently, 'Only Love Remains' was rush-released in the hope that a hit would boost album sales. While the single, which featured a new Jim Boyer remix, gave McCartney another Top 40 hit in the UK, it didn't generate album sales. By December, *Press To Play* was no longer in the Top 200 album charts.

Parlophone issued the single with generic labels and a picture sleeve. Capitol issued the single with black/colour band labels and picture sleeve identical to the British release. Capitol also issued demonstration copies of the single with white labels and black text.

PRINCE'S TRUST 10TH ANNIVERSARY

McCARTNEY'S first live performance since Wings' brief jaunt around Britain in 1979 had been as the closing act at the Live Aid concert in July 1985. Although his performance was marred thanks to an inept roadie unplugging his microphone, McCartney found that playing in front of an audience whetted his appetite for more live shows. When he got a call from the Prince's Trust asking if he would be interested in closing their 10th anniversary show, he jumped at the chance. Initially he agreed to perform two songs, but at the last m inute added a third, 'Get Back', to his short set.

Rehearsals took place on the morning of June 20 1986 with McCartney already having committed himself to playing in specific keys. However, not having played either of the two songs in almost a quarter of a century, he discovered that he was having trouble reaching some of the high notes. "[The Prince's Trust] called me up and … I said yeah, you know, sounds good to me, I'll do that," he recalled. "The day before it, I was in the studio, and I picked up my guitar – I thought I'd better practice. It is 20 years, after all, since I'd done 'Long Tall Sally'. So I picked up the guitar, thought all right, 'Long Tall Sally', [it's in] G. So it went G, F-sharp, F, E. I sounded like Pat Boone! So I thought, 'Oh no,' … because he did some pretty rough versions of Little Richard's stuff. … So I thought it's gonna have to be in E. But when I got to the rehearsal, I'd told them that it was gonna be in G, and I didn't dare tell them I was gonna switch it to E. So [with] just the adrenalin … I thought right, I'll have a go."

The three songs he performed were issued here out of sequence. In fact he opened the show with 'I Saw Her Standing There', followed by 'Long Tall Sally' and 'Get Back'. In addition, he played acoustic guitar with Mick Jagger and David Bowie on their version of 'Dancing In The Street'. Jagger and Bowie performed unannounced, and their duet on The Marvelettes' 'mod' anthem was not included on the album, probably due to contractual difficulties.

THE PRINCE'S TRUST 10TH ANNIVERSARY BIRTHDAY PARTY
VARIOUS ARTISTS
PAUL McCARTNEY 'Get Back', 'Long Tall Sally', 'I Saw Her Standing There' (not all on each format).
UK RELEASE April 24 1987; LP Prince's Trust/A&M AMA 3906; bonus single Free 21 'Long Tall Sally' / 'I Saw Her Standing There' included with vinyl pressings; CD Prince's Trust/A&M CDA 3906 (omits 'I Saw Her Standing There'); failed to chart.
US RELEASE May 11 1987; Prince's Trust/A&M SP 3906; failed to chart.

- **'Get Back'** (Lennon, McCartney)
Personnel as 'Long Tall Sally' plus Tina Turner (vocals), Paul Young (vocals).
- **'Long Tall Sally'** (Johnson, Penniman, Blackwell)
Paul McCartney (guitar, vocals), Phil Collins (drums), Ray Cooper (percussion), Mark King (bass), John Illsley (bass), Elton John (piano), Howard Jones (keyboards), Eric Clapton (guitar), Midge Ure (guitar), Bryan Adams (guitar), Mark Knopfler (guitar), Rick Parfitt (guitar), Francis Rossi (guitar).
- **'I Saw Her Standing There'** (Lennon, McCartney)
Personnel as 'Long Tall Sally'.
Recorded on Advision Mobile at Wembley Arena, London, England.
Produced by Andrew Sheehan.

Prince's Trust songs

Elton John and Tina Turner persuaded McCartney to add 'Get Back' to his short set. Turner had featured the song as part of her stage act for some time, and so the two ended up performing the song with assistance from Paul Young.

'Get Back' had developed from a lose jam performed while The Beatles were making *Let It Be*. As the song progressed, its improvised lyrics moved from a tongue-in-cheek dig at politician Enoch Powell, to a German-language rant, to including sly references about transvestism and soft drugs. 'Get Back' was originally issued by Apple in April 1969 and reached Number 1 in Britain and America. It was performed by The Beatles in public three times during their short roof-top set at Apple's headquarters in Savile Row, London.

A lifelong fan of Little Richard, McCartney performed a number of his songs with The Beatles and often sang 'Long Tall Sally' during early Wings concert tours. The Beatles cut their version in 1964, in one take, with McCartney making 'Long Tall Sally' his in the same way that Lennon had with 'Twist And Shout'. McCartney takes the Prince's Trust concert version at a slightly slower tempo than the original but nevertheless kicks up a storm.

On the evening of the concert, McCartney took to the stage armed with an acoustic guitar and immediately launched into 'I Saw Her Standing There'. Written by Lennon–McCartney, it was one of their earliest songs incorporated into The Beatles' repertoire. They performed it regularly at the Cavern Club, and the song quickly became a live favourite. When it was included as the first track on their debut album, it introduced The Beatles to the world. The group rarely performed the song after 1963, but Lennon played it when he appeared with Elton John at Madison Square Garden in 1974. 'I Saw Her Standing There' obviously meant a lot to both writers, and in choosing it that night, Lennon may have been attempting to close the gap between himself and his former songwriting partner. McCartney may have been backed by an impressive line-up of Britain's rock elite, but his live recording here still fails to match The Beatles' original studio recording. He would return to the song for his 1989/'90 world tour and in 2000 when he made a triumphant return to the Cavern Club to promote his *Run Devil Run* album.

Prince's Trust data

Released on the Prince's Trust's label, distributed by A&M, the album was issued in Britain with a limited, bonus 7-inch single, 'Long Tall Sally' / 'I Saw Her Standing There' (FREE 21). All three songs were later included on the 1990 double CD *Royal Concert*, which included highlights from both the 1986 and '87 Trust gigs.

Promotional copies of the LP issued by A&M in America were pressed on Quiex vinyl and had a gold 'PROMO' stamp on the back cover.

ALL THE BEST

THIS compilation was released in favour of a new Phil Ramone-produced album that McCartney had spent the best part of a year recording, and was issued just in time to catch the lucrative Christmas market. The title was suggested by manager Richard Ogden, as McCartney often wrote "all the best" when signing autographs and the phrase summed up both the album's content and McCartney's positive attitude. During the record's chart run, staff at McCartney's MPL company were requested to sign their correspondence with "all the best".

Replacing the now obsolete *Wings Greatest,* which remained on catalogue, *All The Best* included some of McCartney's biggest hits. For the first time, EMI tailored a marketing campaign for Britain and the USA with the sole aim of ensuring a Number 1 chart placing. To this end, the company compiled two different versions of the album to include the biggest hits in each country.

The British album was to have included two new recordings. Besides the soon-to-be hit 'Once Upon A Long Ago', it was to have featured 'Waterspout', an outtake from *London Town*. However, 'Waterspout' was removed because *All The Best* was intended as a 'hits' package rather than a collection of unreleased material. But hits, new or old, weren't enough: an extensive three-phase media campaign supported the release.

To publicise the album, EMI issued to radio stations a boxed set of nine 7-inch singles one week ahead of the album's release. A £500,000 television and radio advertising campaign and the release of 'Once Upon A Long Ago' helped push the album to Number 1 in the British charts (and two weeks after its release, *All The Best* was declared double-platinum with sales in Britain of 600,000). Due to the majority of publicity and promotion being focused on the British release, *All The Best* was not as successful in the USA, where it peaked at Number 62.

'Once Upon A Long Ago' was the first song to emerge from McCartney's collaboration with producer Phil Ramone. However, this was no precursor to the expected Ramone-produced album, which for some reason McCartney decided to scrap. Instead, it was used to promote the new compilation.

McCartney had been recording with Ramone in various studios with different musicians for some time and had recorded 'Long Ago' at Abbey Road with a group of session musicians, featuring a violin solo by Nigel Kennedy. Speaking about the session, Kennedy marvelled at the contrast between classical and pop recording work. "We recorded at Abbey Road, and I'd just been in there the day before doing some concerto with André Previn. With Previn, we already knew what we were going to do when we went in there. But with McCartney, he just said, 'Play,' and it was up to me to lock into his personality and what he was saying."

Parlophone and Capitol issued *All The Best* as a two-record set

ALL THE BEST
PAUL McCARTNEY
UK VERSION: SIDE 1 'Jet', 'Band On The Run', 'Ebony And Ivory', 'Listen To What The Man Said'.
SIDE 2 'No More Lonely Nights', 'Silly Love Songs', 'Let 'Em In', 'C Moon', 'Pipes Of Peace'.
SIDE 3 'Live And Let Die', 'Another Day', 'Maybe I'm Amazed', 'Goodnight Tonight', 'Once Upon A Long Ago'.
SIDE 4 'Say Say Say', 'With A Little Luck', 'My Love', 'We All Stand Together', 'Mull Of Kintyre'.
UK RELEASE November 2 1987; LP Parlophone Records PMTV 1; CD Parlophone CDPMTV 1 (omits 'Maybe I'm Amazed', 'Goodnight Tonight', 'With A Little Luck'); chart high No.2.

US VERSION: SIDE 1 'Band On The Run', 'Jet', 'Ebony And Ivory', 'Listen To What The Man Said'.
SIDE 2 'Live And Let Die', 'Another Day', 'C Moon', 'Junior's Farm', 'Uncle Albert / Admiral Halsey'.
SIDE 3 'No More Lonely Nights', 'Silly Love Songs', 'Let 'Em In', 'Say Say Say'.
SIDE 4 'Coming Up' (Live), 'Goodnight Tonight', 'With A Little Luck', 'My Love'.
US release December 1 1987; LP Capitol CLW-48287; CD Capitol 48287; chart high No.62 .

• **'Once Upon A Long Ago'** (McCartney)
Paul McCartney (bass, guitar, vocals), Nigel Kennedy (violin), Stan Sulzmann (saxophone), Nick Glennie-Smith (keyboards), Tim Renwick (guitar), Henry Spinetti (drums).
Recorded at Abbey Road Studios, London, England.
Produced by Phil Ramone, mixed by George Martin.

with custom labels, gatefold sleeve, and printed inner sleeves with lyrics. The inner sleeve of the British edition incorrectly identifies 'Maybe I'm Amazed' as the live single version. However, early proofs correctly identify it as the studio version from *McCartney*.

'ONCE UPON A LONG AGO'/ 'BACK ON MY FEET'

'ONCE UPON A LONG AGO' / 'BACK ON MY FEET'
PAUL McCARTNEY1
UK RELEASE November 16 1987; Parlophone R 6170; 12-inch Parlophone 12 R 6170 'Once Upon A Long Ago' (Long Version), 'Back On My Feet' / 'Midnight Special', 'Don't Get Around Much Anymore'; 12-inch 12 RX 6170 'Once Upon A Long Ago' (Extended Version), 'Back On My Feet' / 'Lawdy Miss Clawdy', 'Kansas City' released November 30 1987; CD single Parlophone CDR 6170 'Once Upon A Long Ago', 'Back On My Feet', 'Kansas City', 'Midnight Special'; chart high No.10.

- **'Back On My Feet'** (McCartney, Costello)
Paul McCartney (bass, vocals), Tim Renwick (guitar), Nick Glennie-Smith (keyboards), Charlie Morgan (drums), Louis Jardim (percussion).
- **'Midnight Special'** (trad arr McCartney)
Paul McCartney (bass, vocals), Mick Green (guitar), Micky Gallagher (keyboards), Chris Whitten (drums).
- **'Don't Get Around Much Anymore'** (Ellington, Russell)
Paul McCartney (guitar, vocals), Micky Gallagher (keyboards), Nick Garvey (bass), Henry Spinetti (drums).
- **'Kansas City'** (Leiber, Stoller)
Personnel as 'Midnight Special'.
- **'Lawdy Miss Clawdy'** (Price)
Personnel as 'Midnight Special'.

All recorded at Hog-Hill Studio, East Sussex, England and produced by Paul McCartney, except 'Back On My Feet' recorded at Abbey Road Studios, London, England and produced by Phil Ramone.

McCARTNEY met Elvis Costello in early 1982 at AIR Studios, London, where they were both recording new albums: McCartney *Tug Of War* and Costello *Imperial Bedroom*. (Geoff Emerick was working on both albums simultaneously, producing Costello's while engineering McCartney's on the days he wasn't working for Costello.)

Five years and several albums later McCartney and Costello met again, this time to write songs. As they hadn't worked together before, neither was sure of how things would work out, so each brought along unfinished songs for the other to help complete.

To break the ice, McCartney brought along 'Back On My Feet', a song he had recorded in early 1987 but which he thought needed a better lyric. Costello refashioned the lyric and the partnership flourished into the most prolific and creative for McCartney since working with John Lennon. Costello's talent as a songwriter, his ear for melody and a willingness to push back boundaries impelled McCartney to reconsider both the content and style of his songs. Costello's cynicism, like Lennon's, proffered an alternative to McCartney's zealous optimism, and it runs through the 'Feet' lyric like Blackpool runs through rock.

In the early summer of 1987, McCartney invited a number of musicians to informal Friday-night jam sessions at a secret studio in London. "Just to kick around some songs and keep in practice, you know?" he said. "Each week we'd change who the people were, it was like Henry Spinetti on drums one week, the other Chris Whitten … all sorts of people. I mean, Trevor Horn came down one day on bass, because he's an ex-bass player as well as being a producer.' Other attendees at the Friday-night sessions included drummer Terry Williams from Rockpile and Dire Straits and guitarist Johnny Marr of The Smiths.

Inevitably, they played songs from McCartney's youth, and that meant one thing: rock'n'roll. For a generation brought up in post-war Britain, whose only entertainment was BBC radio's Light Programme, American culture in the form of Elvis Presley and his contemporaries signified glamour, rebellion, and the promise of an alternative lifestyle. Rock'n'roll offered freedom from the values and attitudes of a stifling, conservative, class-obsessed post-war Britain.

It's not surprising, then, that the songs McCartney jammed on at the Friday-night bashes were mainly American and from the 1940s and 1950s. This was more than a nostalgic trip down memory lane; these were the songs that shaped a generation. They were a Rosetta Stone from which Lennon and McCartney learnt the rudiments of composition and built their own lexicon of style. McCartney was so pleased with the informal rehearsals that he decided to record many of the songs they performed.

But before rock'n'roll made itself felt in Britain, there was skiffle. Skiffle's reliance on simple chords and do-it-yourself instruments meant that it could be mastered by even the most musically inept. The result was that skiffle became remarkably popular among British youths; more than a cult, it became a boom industry that influenced thousands of young British males to pick up guitars, washboards, and banjos and make music. Because of its simple musical structure, 'Midnight Special' was a favourite with skiffle groups, and a regular feature in The Beatles' early stage act. This traditional blues song made popular by Leadbelly reached a wider audience courtesy of Lonnie Donagan and his Skiffle Group, who recorded a version in 1956. Recalling the country-folk roots feel of both the Leadbelly original and the British skiffle imitators, McCartney's reading of 'Midnight Special', while not essential, is nevertheless enjoyable.

Recorded by McCartney on July 21 1987, 'Don't Get Around Much Anymore' had been a favourite with American soldiers stationed in Europe during World War II. Written by Duke Ellington, it captured the sense of loss that many GIs must have experienced while stationed in Britain. A little too jazzy to be part of The Beatles' early repertoire, the song nevertheless remained in circulation long after the GIs had packed their bags and returned home. Reworked here into a bluesy rumba, the song is an unexpected highlight from the informal sessions.

'Kansas City' was written by Jerry Leiber and Mike Stoller. It was first recorded in 1952 by Little Willie Littlefield as 'KC Loving' but reached Number 1 in the US charts in 1959 when cut by Wilbert Harrison. McCartney first recorded 'Kansas City' in 1964 with The Beatles for their album *Beatles For Sale*. Twenty-two years later, he cut a live version at the Prince's Trust concert, followed a year later by this studio version. He continued to perform the song regularly, and another live version was programmed for 1993's *Paul Is Live*.

'Lawdy Miss Clawdy' was a Number 1 hit for its author, Lloyd Price, in 1952. On crossing the Atlantic, it became an essential part of any self-respecting British rock'n'roll band's repertoire. McCartney and co give a gritty reading here but never really catch fire, and nor do they escape the clutches of pub-rock predicability.

'Once Upon A Long Ago' data

Parlophone issued the single on 7-inch and two 12-inch singles with generic labels and picture sleeves. The company also issued a four-song CD single (McCartney's first CD single). As with previous singles, a number of different mixes of the A-side were produced. The 7-inch featured a 4:12 mix and the first 12-inch single (12 R 6170) a 4:34 mix. McCartney remixed 'Once Upon A Long Ago' for the second 12-inch single (12 RX 6170), extending the song to 6:06.

IMAGINE: JOHN LENNON, MUSIC FROM THE MOTION PICTURE
JOHN LENNON
SIDE 1 'Real Love', 'Twist And Shout', 'Help!', 'In My Life', 'Strawberry Fields Forever', 'A Day In The Life'.
SIDE 2 'Revolution', 'The Ballad Of John And Yoko', 'Julia', 'Don't Let Me Down', 'Give Peace A Chance'.
SIDE 3 'How?', 'Imagine' (Rehearsal) / 'God', 'Mother', 'Stand By Me'.
SIDE 4 'Jealous Guy', 'Woman', 'Beautiful Boy (Darling Boy)', '(Just Like) Starting Over', 'Imagine'.
UK release October 10 1988; LP Parlophone PCSP 722; CD Parlophone CD PCSP 722; chart high No.64.
US release October 4 1988; LP Capitol C1-90803; CD Capitol CDP 7 9080302; chart high No.31.

• **'Real Love'** (Lennon)
Personnel: John Lennon (vocals and guitar).
Recorded at The Dakota, New York. Produced by John Lennon.

IMAGINE: JOHN LENNON

THIS was a career overview that doubled as the soundtrack to the Lennon biopic, *Imagine: John Lennon*. Work on the Ono-sanctioned documentary began in 1988 when David Wolper and Andrew Solt were given unrestricted access to the Lennons' extensive film archive. A forerunner to The Beatles' *Anthology* project, the film featured much rare footage, and old interviews with Lennon were used to provide a narrative. As with The Beatles' *Anthology*, the film was marketed with a home video release, a soundtrack album, and a large, glossy book. Although intended as such, the album did not qualify as a soundtrack, because the musical performances in the film differed from those issued on the record. Furthermore, the album presented the songs in a different sequence to the film. EMI insisted on this to make the listening experience as enjoyable as possible.

For the first time, songs from The Beatles' catalogue appeared on a John Lennon album, but it was not the first time that group and solo material had been mixed on an album. *The Best Of George Harrison* (PAS 10011), issued by Parlophone in 1976, featured one side of songs performed by The Beatles and another of solo compositions.

Even before it was transformed into a new Beatles single, 'Real Love' had a remarkable history. The song was, in fact, a composite of two pieces that eventually metamorphosed into a charming Lennon ballad. Lennon began by combining elements of ' The Way The World Is' and 'Baby Make Love To You'. Once he had glued the various melodic fragments together, he wrote a lyric that recounted his day-to-day routine.

Lennon's early attempts at the lyric reflected his desire to chronicle his activities with a chorus of "it's real life", which he later changed to "it's real love". He made more changes to the lyrics as work on the song progressed. Once he'd rewritten the verses and changed the chorus, Lennon began to make more demo recordings. The version used for the later Beatles recording was piano-based, but the version presented here was performed on guitar. Despite some interesting chord changes and an intimate atmosphere, 'Real Love' has nothing new or significant to say. Having run out of things to say about himself, Lennon seemed to have had little to say on other matters either. As compelling as it is, 'Real Love' is craftsman-like but uninspired.

***Imagine: John Lennon* data**

Parlophone issued the album as a two-record set with generic black labels, printed inner sleeves, and gatefold cover. The Capitol issue featured purple Capitol labels. To promote the album, Capitol issued 'Stand By Me' as a promotional 12-inch single (SPRO-79453) with a rectangular white sticker that proclaimed "'Stand By Me' The new single from the album Imagine John Lennon Music From The Original Motion Picture". The single was not issued commercially.

'JEALOUS GUY'

CAPITOL released 'Jealous Guy' / 'Give Peace A Chance' to promote the *Imagine: John Lennon* album, issued as a 7-inch single with generic purple labels and a picture sleeve. Demonstration copies of the A-side were issued as a 7-inch single (B-44230) and a one-track CD single (DPRO-79417).

'IMAGINE'

PARLOPHONE issued a three-track 7-inch single, 'Imagine' / 'Jealous Guy', 'Happy Xmas (War Is Over)' with generic black labels and a picture sleeve. They also issued it as a 7-inch picture disc, 12-inch, and a CD single. The CD featured a bonus track, 'Give Peace A Chance'. However, this was merely the live version from the One To One concert cross-faded with 'Happy Xmas (War Is Over)', as on the *Shaved Fish* album. Parlophone had planned to issue a 12-inch picture disc but did not. Due to consumer demand for Lennon product on the tenth anniversary of his death, EMI reissued the CD single in Europe on November 19 1990. Although identical to the original issue, it was given a new catalogue number, 20415242.

'JEALOUS GUY' / 'GIVE PEACE A CHANCE'
JOHN LENNON
US RELEASE September 19 1988; Capitol B-44230; chart high No.91.

'IMAGINE' / 'JEALOUS GUY', 'HAPPY XMAS (WAR IS OVER)'
JOHN LENNON
UK RELEASE November 28 1988; Parlophone R 6199; picture disc Parlophone RP 6199 released December 5; 12-inch Parlophone 12 R 6099; CD single CDR 6099; chart high No.45.

'FERRY 'CROSS THE MERSEY' / 'ABIDE WITH ME'
VARIOUS ARTISTS
UK RELEASE May 2 1989; PWL PWL 41; chart high No.1.

- **'Ferry 'Cross The Mersey'** (Marsden)
Paul McCartney (guitar, vocals), The Christians (vocals), Holly Johnson (vocals), Gerry Marsden (guitar, vocals), Mike Stock (keyboards), Matt Aitken (keyboards), Pete Waterman (keyboards).
Recorded at PWL Studios, London, England. Produced by Stock, Aitken and Waterman.

'FERRY 'CROSS THE MERSEY'

THIS was conceived as a charity record to raise funds for the families of 95 Liverpool Football Club supporters who lost their lives at the Hillsborough stadium on April 15 1989. Besides a guitar and vocal contribution from McCartney, the record featured vocals from the song's author, Gerry Marsden, plus Holly Johnson (Frankie Goes To Hollywood) and Russell and Gary Christian (The Christians). It was not a bona fide Paul McCartney release but is included here because of his significant contribution to the record. Stock, Aitken and Waterman produced the song at their PWL Studios on April 20 1989 and released it on PWL Records with generic labels and a picture sleeve.

'MY BRAVE FACE'

THE A-SIDE is an infectious blast of retro pop that McCartney wrote with Elvis Costello, who brought a new dimension to his writing. For much of the 1980s, McCartney had been trying unsuccessfully to find a place for himself in an increasingly fickle marketplace. Searching for a musical identity, he'd hidden behind a thumbs-up, mop-top facade that was wearing as thin as the vinyl his records were pressed on. Costello made him shed his mask and return to what mattered – the song.

Speaking to *Musician*, Costello said: "There's no denying that [McCartney] has a way of sort of defending himself by being charming and smiling and thumbs-up and all the bit. I said once that I thought he should try and step from behind that, at least insofar as the music was concerned." Freed from the media image of himself, which he'd previously been unable or unwilling to shake off, McCartney discovered that at last he could be true to himself.

He and Costello quickly discovered that they could reproduce the creative spark that had made McCartney's earlier partnership with Lennon so rewarding. Costello again: "What I thought I could add – it's not as if he needs a lot of help to write songs – was the friction that is creative, and get him to refer to a musical vocabulary that is second nature to me from Beatle music."

Indeed, many of the Beatlesesque qualities in 'My Brave Face', such as the bridge and descending harmonies, which many thought originated from McCartney, were Costello's. Costello also suggested that McCartney add a melodic bass part to the song, referring him to 'Taxman' and 'Paperback Writer'. And it was Costello who suggested that he dig out his old Hofner bass to record with – he liked its warm analogue sound.

Having written several songs together, the pair decided to record them together. Initially, they co-produced five of the songs, but McCartney was dissatisfied with the backing tracks, so he scrapped them. Guitarist Hamish Stuart, who worked on these sessions, suggested that Costello's ideas didn't always run parallel with McCartney's. "Elvis's thinking may have been just a little too radical," he suggested. "Once, Elvis said, 'Let's double-track this backing vocal, then we'll bounce it down a couple of times to lose some quality.' And he was serious."

Finding the sound too raw, McCartney began afresh and re-recorded 'My Brave Face' with producers Mitchell Froom and Neil Dorfsman at Olympic studio.

'My Brave Face' formed the first wave of a massive promotional campaign that would re-launch its author onto the world's stage. Yet despite it being one of the strongest singles he had issued for some time, it only managed to scrape its way into the bottom of the Top 20 in Britain and Top 30 in the USA.

'Flying To My Home' was recorded largely by McCartney, who plays most of the instruments, with a few more added by Hamish Stuart and drummer Chris Whitten (and the vocal harmonies that introduce the song deliberately reference the complex vocal structures employed by Brian Wilson). Returning to a favourite theme of love, McCartney elevates the subject of his song, probably Linda, with references to royalty. While not as strong as anything that would appear on *Flowers In The Dirt*, 'Flying To My Home' was nevertheless a high-quality B-side.

'I'm Gonna Be A Wheel Someday' was from the sessions that produced *Choba B CCCP*. (Originally issued exclusively in the Soviet Union on vinyl in 1988, *Choba B CCCP* was issued in Britain and America on CD in 1991: see the entry there for more details.) However, before McCartney made *Choba* available on CD, he issued several songs as B-sides, like 'Wheel' (recorded July 20 1987). The original had appeared as the B-side of Fats Domino's 1959 hit 'I Want To Walk You Home', issued by Imperial (5606) in July that year and reaching number 17 in the US charts. McCartney's version is an up-tempo rocker performed with utter joy and verve: it crackles like lightning in a summer storm.

'Ain't That A Shame' is another Fats Domino song and was Domino's first pop hit. Issued by Imperial (5348) in 1955, it reached Number 10 in the USA, although a cover version by Pat Boone reached Number 1. When Lennon recorded the song for his *Rock'N'Roll* album in 1975, little did he know it would make his former songwriting partner envious. After hearing about Lennon's project, McCartney considered recording an album of similar material, but rejected the idea. "[It would] just look like John does a rock'n'roll album, I've got to do one," he explained. "It's like I'm competing with him, you know? So I never really wanted to do it after that." Putting the idea on hold for over a decade, when Paul did begin his own album of rock'n'roll covers, he didn't even realise that Lennon had beaten him to the song. He needn't have worried: the two versions are as alike as chalk and cheese. McCartney replicates Domino's original arrangement, even at times sounding like the Fat Man, while Lennon throws some horns into the mix and takes a few more liberties with his vocal.

'MY BRAVE FACE' / 'FLYING TO MY HOME'
PAUL McCARTNEY
UK RELEASE May 8 1989; Parlophone R 6213; 12-inch Parlophone 12 R 6213 'My Brave Face', 'Flying To My Home' / 'I'm Gonna Be A Wheel Someday', 'Ain't That A Shame'; CD single Parlophone CDR 6213 'My Brave Face', 'Flying To My Home', 'I'm Gonna Be A Wheel Someday', 'Ain't That A Shame'; cassette single Parlophone TCR 6213 'My Brave Face', 'Flying To My Home' same both sides; chart high No.18.
US RELEASE May 8 1989; Capitol B-44367; CD single Capitol CDP 7154682 'My Brave Face', 'Flying To My Home', 'I'm Gonna Be A Wheel Someday', 'Ain't That A Shame'; chart high No.25.

• **'My Brave Face'** (McCartney, MacManus)
Paul McCartney (bass, guitar, percussion, vocals), Hamish Stuart (guitar), Chris Whitten (drums), Robbie McIntosh (guitar), Mitchell Froom (keyboards), David Rhodes (Ebow guitar), Chris Davis (saxophone), Chris White (saxophone), Dave Bishop (saxophone).
Recorded at Olympic Sound Studios, Barnes, England.
Produced by Paul McCartney, Mitchell Froom, and Neil Dorfsman
• **'Flying To My Home'** (McCartney)
Paul McCartney (bass, autoharp, drums, keyboard, organ, percussion, guitars, vocals), Hamish Stuart (guitar, backing vocals), Chris Whitten (drums).
Recorded at Hog-Hill Studio, East Sussex, England.
Produced by Paul McCartney.
• **'I'm Gonna Be A Wheel Someday'** (Bartholomew, Hayes, Domino)
Paul McCartney (bass, vocals), Mick Green (guitar), Micky Gallagher (keyboards), Chris Whitten (drums).
Recorded at Hog-Hill Studio, Sussex. Produced by Paul McCartney.
• **'Ain't That A Shame'** (Domino, Bartholomew)
Paul McCartney (guitar, vocals) Micky Gallagher (keyboards), Nick Garvey (bass), Henry Spinetti (drums).
Recorded at Hog-Hill Studio, Sussex.
Produced by Paul McCartney.

My Brave Face data

Parlophone issued the single in 7 and 12-inch formats with newly designed generic labels and picture sleeve. It was also issued on CD and cassette. Demonstration copies of the 7-inch single were issued with green and white 'A' labels and generic green paper sleeve.

Capitol issued the single with generic purple labels and a picture sleeve. Demonstration copies were manufactured with white labels with black text. A promotional one-track CD single (DPRO-79590) with black screen-printed label with white text was distributed to American radio stations.

FLOWERS IN THE DIRT

McCARTNEY ended the 1980s on a creative and commercial high with *Flowers In The Dirt,* his most successful album since *Tug Of War*. Although his release schedule had slowed, his recording calendar remained busy, and *Flowers* drew on material stockpiled over the previous five years. During this time he'd worked with several producers, and the album boasted no fewer than six production teams – but despite this, it has consistency.

McCartney had planned to co-produce the album with Elvis Costello and recorded several tracks with him, but dropped the idea because he thought there was "too much of Elvis" coming through. Costello's style proved too extreme for McCartney, who found some of his colleague's production ideas a little too avant-garde. McCartney wanted to made a sophisticated pop record, but Costello had other ideas. Things came to a head one day when Costello pushed McCartney's patience to breaking point. McCartney recalled the altercation: "I said to Elvis, 'Look. man, we're trying to make records, scintillating fab hit records that are gonna make people go WOW!' I kept bringing in all these happening hits, and Elvis was bringing in Eskimo drum music and the Bulgarian All Stars." Although a McCartney–Costello produced album would have made interesting listening, McCartney was probably right to go the way he did and work with a number of different producers, tailoring their skills to his needs.

He knew he had to get a grip on his career and start producing music of quality rather than music in quantity. He hadn't taken an extended career break, as Lennon had in the mid 1970s, but *Flowers In The Dirt* was McCartney's comeback album.

Sales of his records had declined, and his desire to resume large-scale touring made him realise that he would have to reconsider his entire method of operation. Recording with George Martin hadn't worked, nor had the attempt to reinvent himself with *Press To Play*. Simply churning out another album wasn't enough, and he didn't have the luxury of starting again and rebuilding his career step by step, as he had with Wings. It was time to deliver. "I really wanted an album I could go out on tour with, an album people could relate to," said McCartney. "I just didn't want some crummy album dogging the tour."

Flowers In The Dirt became his biggest record in years. It went to Number 1 in Britain, sold over a million copies in Europe, and hit the Top 10 in Japan. However, despite an American tour to promote the album, it didn't do as well as expected in the USA. Airplay, essential for any artist, wasn't particularly forthcoming, but it still sold 600,000 copies there in its first six months and stayed in the charts for a year before being certified a gold record.

Flowers In The Dirt songs

The album opens with 'My Brave Face'. Then comes 'Rough Ride', which was recorded with Trevor Horn on keyboards and Steve Lipson playing guitar and programming the drum machine. During the 1980s Horn was considered as Britain's best producer. McCartney began the session by playing Horn a number of new songs, but it was an unfinished fragment that caught the producer's ear. Inspired by a television programme about the blues, 'Rough Ride' was originally little more than a simple guitar riff with a minimalist lyric. Recalling the song's origins, McCartney said: "It was like a 12-bar; me trying to be Big Bill Broonzy."

Trevor Horn's reputation was as an innovative perfectionist who took his time in the studio, and this proved to be a blessing and a curse. McCartney loved his ideas but didn't want to spend months perfecting a backing track. To get the best from Horn, he insisted that they spend no longer than two days recording each song. McCartney: "It seemed to me that it might be a good idea if we could try and limit him to a short period and see what we could get done." The ploy worked. Under Horn's direction, McCartney's original blues-influenced fragment developed into a funky, quasi-reggae arrangement and acquired a fresh live sound.

'You Want Her Too' recalls the interplay that Lennon and McCartney enjoyed as singers and songsmiths, with McCartney and Costello slipping into well-defined roles. Having got McCartney to refer to an earlier musical vocabulary, Costello upped the ante and deliberately assumed Lennon's musical personality. Speaking about an earlier composition, Costello recalled: "I started writing the bridge of 'My Brave Face', that Beatle-y descending 'Ever since you've been away...'. We were doing a vocal rehearsal in the kitchen and he sang the line 'Take me to that place.' I hit the low harmony on 'place' and he went, 'Oh no, no. This is getting to be too much. That's exactly like 'There's A Place' or 'I'll Get You'." Despite reservations, McCartney conceded that if anyone had the right to sound like The Beatles, he did. He found himself in the unusual position of consciously adopting his own persona. "I said to Elvis, 'Look, this is really getting a bit me and John, I'm being Paul and you're really being John.'"

However, McCartney wasn't entirely happy, and at one point

attempted a solo reading of 'You Want Her Too'. Realising that this only made it sound "really corny", he re-recorded the song and reinstated Costello's vocals. The brass motif that closes the song wasn't added until Hamish Stuart contributed a guitar figure during an overdub session. Delighted with the phrase, McCartney used it as "the ultimate tease, because they play, and as soon as you're into them – they fade".

'Distractions' is a typical McCartney ballad and finds him contemplating the problem of balancing a private life with a career. "It's a question for me," he explained. "Some people ask me this, 'Why do you do it, man? Why bother with the distractions? You're rich.' Because I think everyone's little dream, certainly mine when I was at school, was [that] what you'll do is get a lot of money and then you'll go on holiday forever. But when you grow up, you realise it doesn't work. A year of that, maybe, is dead funny and a great groove. But after a year you think, 'What do I do in life again?'." Although 'Distractions' addresses the universal struggle for inner harmony, it's essentially a love song that comments on the depth of his love for Linda.

Featuring new recruits Stuart and Whitten, the song was produced by McCartney and engineered by longtime stalwart Geoff Emerick. McCartney commissioned Clare Fisher, an American who worked out of Los Angeles, to create an arrangement he described as "very Hollywood, [and the] nearest time frame I could associate it with is Doris Day movies". The orchestral elements were recorded at Mad Hatter Studios in Los Angeles with Fisher conducting.

McCartney wrote 'We Got Married' after talking to Paul Simon and Lorne Michaels (creator of the TV show *Saturday Night Live*). Simon was suffering from writer's block, so Michaels suggested that he write about his personal experiences. The idea appealed to McCartney and he wrote 'We Got Married'. Speaking to Paul Du Noyer, he said: "I took the idea of celebrating marriage, because I don't want to shy away from it. I think there's millions of people who are well into it, and if you're lucky its something that should be celebrated, but also there's a slightly cynical edge to it because it isn't all that sweet."

'We Got Married' was one of three songs that McCartney recorded with American producer David Foster in October 1984, considered to be for an EP release, but it remained unfinished until he completed it for *Flowers In The Dirt*. McCartney recalled the song's long gestation. "You could say that was written over a period of six years. It was actually in two bursts. It was just a nice song and I [had] just never got round to finishing it." (In America, Capitol issued a four-minute edit of 'We Got Married' as a one-track promotional CD single [DPRO-79979] with screen-printed labels with blue text and a white wedding-ring motif.)

'Put It There' was a song inspired by McCartney's father. "It's something my dad used to say, 'Put it there if it weighs a ton,' a Liverpool expression." Family sayings tend to cross generations, and as McCartney noted, the sentiment is "the kind of thing you'd say to your own son". For McCartney, this simple phrase meant a great deal. Not only was it a link with the past and his father, but also it was a way of forging a relationship with his own son. "I mean, it's fairly simple, 'while you and I are here, put it there,' but ... you can either say that's really simplistic, but to me that's really deep. But it is ... something that's a bit of a choker for me, that line."

The song became very popular with live audiences, and this may have prompted its release as the forth single from the album. When McCartney performed it live, he tagged the coda from 'Hello Goodbye' onto the end, for no other reason than that it has a similar bouncy cadence.

McCartney was attracted to producer Trevor Horn's perfectionism, but he also wanted to coarsen the edges a little. To achieve this, he decided to record the bass, vocals, and drums for 'Figure Of Eight' live in the studio before he let Horn start work with the computers. The combination of performance and technology was exactly what McCartney was looking for. "To me, that's what's interesting about now and this album – working with people who are used to being very finished and accurate. I'm not really a great admirer of that, so what I'm trying to do is force them to come a little bit towards what I like, which is loose ends and roughness." Although Horn appeared to capture what he wanted, McCartney remade 'Figure Of Eight' with his touring band, playing live in the studio.

McCartney developed the lyric for 'This One' from "the words 'this one' [which] kept coming back to me as 'this swan', and I got off on that". The image of a swan led him to make associations with Indian imagery and brightly-coloured illustrations of Krishna, which influenced the rest of the lyric. "You have this idyllic picture and this little blue God with flowers all over him, and that's Krishna riding on this swan floating over this beautiful clear pond with lovely pink lilies on it."

McCartney also claimed that 'This One' was about the sense of regret we experience at loosing the moment. "You have an argument, for instance, ... you think, if I'd only been smart I could just have said ... 'you're right,' for instance, would be a real cool thing to say – which I'm not always the one to say." He went on to suggest that too many people neglect the present while dreaming of the past or imagining the future. "It's about that kind of thing, you know ... this moment, this *now*. If you could just appreciate it all the time, you'd do better. But you're always off on some other moment, either the past or dreaming of the future. Now is never really important to most people, but it's really all you've got. It's really all we live in."

As with the other songs written and initially produced by McCartney–Costello, McCartney and Mitchell Froom reworked 'Don't Be Careless Love'. All that remains of the original backing track are McCartney's vocal and Costello and Hamish Stuart's harmonies, which recall the kind of gospel arrangement that feature on 'That Day Is Done'.

Once again, Costello's influence made itself felt: his references

FLOWERS IN THE DIRT

PAUL McCARTNEY

SIDE 1 'My Brave Face', 'Rough Ride', 'You Want Her Too', 'Distractions', 'We Got Married', 'Put It There'.
SIDE 2 'Figure Of Eight', 'This One', 'Don't Be Careless Love', 'That Day Is Done', 'How Many People', 'Motor Of Love', 'Ou Est Le Soleil?'*.
The track marked * appears only on the CD (UK and USA).
UK RELEASE June 5 1989; LP Parlophone PCSD 106; CD Parlophone CDP 7 91653 2; chart high No.1.
US RELEASE June 6 1989; LP Capitol C1-91653; CD Capitol 91653; chart high No.21.

• **'Rough Ride'** (McCartney)
Paul McCartney (synthesiser, guitar, drum overdub, percussion, vocals), Steve Lipson (bass, computer, drum programming, guitar), Trevor Horn (keyboards), Linda McCartney (backing vocals).
Recording location unknown. Produced by Trevor Horn, Paul McCartney, and Steve Lipson.

• **'You Want Her Too'** (McCartney, MacManus)
Paul McCartney (bass, guitars, percussion, vocals), Elvis Costello (keyboards, vocals), Hamish Stuart (guitar, backing vocals), Chris Whitten (drums, percussion), Robbie McIntosh (guitar), Mitchell Froom (keyboards).
Recorded at Olympic Sound Studios, Barnes, England.
Produced by Paul McCartney, Neil Dorfsman, Mitchell Froom, and Elvis Costello.

• **'Distractions'** (McCartney)
Paul McCartney (bass, guitar, percussion, vocals), Hamish Stuart (guitar, backing vocals), Chris Whitten (drums, percussion), Linda McCartney (backing vocals).
Recorded at Hog-Hill Studio, East Sussex, England and Mad Hatter Studios, Los Angeles, CA, USA.
Produced by Paul McCartney.

• **'We Got Married'** (McCartney)
Paul McCartney (bass, Mexican guitar, tom-tom, vocals), Dave Gilmour (guitar), Robbie McIntosh (guitar), David Foster (keyboards), Dave Mattacks (drums), Hamish Stuart (backing vocals), Guy Barker (trumpet), Chris Whitten (percussion).
Recorded at Hog-Hill Studio, Sussex, Olympic Sound Studios, Barnes, and AIR Studios, London.
Produced by Paul McCartney and David Foster.

• **'Put It There'** (McCartney)
Paul McCartney (guitar, percussion, vocals), Hamish Stuart (bass, percussion), Chris Whitten (hi-hat, percussion), Peter Henderson (computer programming).
Recorded at Hog-Hill Studio, Sussex.
Produced by Paul McCartney.

• **'Figure Of Eight'** (McCartney)
Paul McCartney (bass, celeste, guitar, percussion, handclaps, vocals), Steve Lipson (guitar, computer programming), Trevor Horn (keyboards, handclaps), Chris Whitten (drums, handclaps), Linda McCartney (Minimoog, handclaps).
Recording location unknown. Produced by Trevor Horn, Paul McCartney and Steve Lipson.

• **'This One'** (McCartney)
Paul McCartney (bass, guitar, keyboards, sitar, wine glasses, harmonium, percussion, vocals), Hamish Stuart (guitar, backing vocals), Chris Whitten (drums, percussion), Robbie McIntosh (guitar), Linda McCartney (backing vocals), Judd Lander (harmonica).
Recorded at Hog-Hill Studio, Sussex.
Produced by Paul McCartney.

• **'Don't Be Careless Love'** (McCartney, MacManus)
Paul McCartney (bass, guitar, percussion, finger snaps, vocals), Hamish Stuart (guitar, percussion, backing vocals), Chris Whitten (drums, backing vocals), Mitchell Froom (keyboards), Elvis Costello (keyboards, backing vocals).
Recorded at Olympic Sound Studios, Barnes and Sunset Sound Factory, Los Angeles, CA, USA.
Produced by Paul McCartney, Elvis Costello, and Mitchell Froom.

• **'That Day Is Done'** (McCartney, MacManus)
Paul McCartney (bass, vocals), Hamish Stuart (guitar, backing vocals), Robbie McIntosh (guitar), Chris Whitten (drums, percussion), Elvis Costello (backing vocals), Nicky Hopkins (piano), Mitchell Froom (keyboards), John Taylor (cornet), Tony Goddard (cornet), Ian Peters (euphonium), Ian Harper (tenor horn).
Recorded at Olympic Sound Studios, Barnes.
Produced by Paul McCartney, Elvis Costello, Neil Dorfsman, and Mitchell Froom.

• **'How Many People'** (McCartney)
Paul McCartney (bass, guitar, Mellotron, piano, flugelhorn, percussion, vocals), Steve Lipson (computer, drum programming, guitar), Trevor Horn (keyboards, backing vocals), Hamish Stuart (second vocal), Chris Whitten (synth drums, cymbals, backing vocals), Linda McCartney (backing vocals), Jah Bunny (tongue styley).
Recorded at AIR Studios, London.
Produced by Paul McCartney, Trevor Horn, and Steve Lipson.

• **'Motor Of Love'** (McCartney)
Paul McCartney (bass, guitar, piano, vocals), Greg Hawkes (keyboards), Hamish Stuart (guitar, backing vocals), Chris Hughes (computer, drum programming).
Recorded at Hog-Hill Studio, Sussex.
Produced by Chris Hughes, Paul McCartney, and Ross Cullum.

• **'Ou Est Le Soleil?'** (McCartney)
Paul McCartney (guitar, violin, keyboard, saw, drum overdubs, bongos, vocals), Steve Lipson (bass, keyboards, computer, drum programming), Trevor Horn (computer drums, keyboards), Hamish Stuart (guitar), Chris Whitten (tom-toms), Eddie Klein (computer programming).
Recorded at Hog-Hill Studio, Sussex.
Produced by Trevor Horn, Paul McCartney, and Steve Lipson.

to dismembered bodies and horrible goings on in the shadows are particularly dark. But despite its film noir narrative, the song's weightless melody negates any notion of menace that the macabre lyric may evoke. The dark, brooding 'That Day Is done' is about death and loss, reflecting the depression Costello felt at the death of his grandmother. "[It] was quite a personal story to me," he said. "I think that was a real test of whether we could really write together." Costello may have had reservations about asking McCartney to help with the song, but it was McCartney who provided the melodic potency that made it so memorable. Costello again: "I was quite happy for it to have the detail of the verses and pay it off with just the title line, but he said, 'No, you've got to develop that title and repeat it musically. Then you end up with a song with more substance.' He would start with that and then add a melodic invention on top of it. Which is the chorus of 'That Day Is Done'."

McCartney and Costello began by producing the song together, but only parts of their original backing track were retained for the final master. The piano and vocal were kept, and perhaps Costello's harmony vocal, but the rest of the instrumentation was scrapped and replaced by Stuart, McIntosh, Whitten, and Froom. In addition, a brass section was overdubbed to evoke the feel of a New Orleans marching band, which Costello had been aiming at with his original treatment. The song was such a departure from McCartney's usual style that when he first played it at home, his housekeeper found it hard to believe that it was him. McCartney: "She said to Linda, 'Is that him, Lin? No! Is that him?' She was totally into it. For hours she wouldn't believe it was me."

McCartney wrote 'How Many People' while on holiday in Jamaica. Initially, he thought the song too simple and considered reworking it into something more complex. Recorded by the same team who worked on 'Rough Ride', with the addition of Stuart and Whitten, the track also features Jah Bunny on percussion. Influenced by the death of Chico Mendes, McCartney dedicated the song to his memory as a mark of solidarity with the ecological campaigner.

'Motor Of Love' is the album's power ballad, a song McCartney recorded twice before he was satisfied with the results. Written and recorded in the early autumn of 1988, it was destined to remain unfinished until he decided to invest some more time on it. Although he liked the song, he didn't like his original recording. Re-recorded with producers Chris Hughes and Ross Cullum, the new version evokes notions of spirituality – which can be read as either deeply personal or universal. Referring to a trick he had previously used in 'Let It Be', McCartney noted: "Heavenly Father is an old trick for me, it's like Mother Mary. I have a father who is no longer with us, so you could say that's 'Heavenly Father' looking down from above."

'Ou Est Le Soleil?' was originally available only on the CD and cassette versions of the album, but eventually was released as the B-side of 'Figure Of Eight' and later as a single in its own right in Europe and the USA. McCartney suggested that it developed during a spontaneous studio jam. "[It was] a very wacky thing where we decided to make something up. This is always a fatal idea because you're off in no-no-land from the word go, which is generally what you don't want to be doing in the studio." But he had recorded a home demo of the song in 1975, so when it came to record it with Trevor Horn he had a good idea of what he wanted. It borrows the guitar riff from Ian Dury's 'Sex And Drugs And Rock And Roll'.

McCartney had planned to improvise a lyric, but scrapped the idea and replaced it with a minimalist French verse that is little more than a joke. For what is basically a throwaway, 'Ou Est Le Soleil?' was lavished with considerable time and effort. Shep Pettibone produced several remixes, issued on the commercial 12-inch single (V-15499), the B-sides of the 'Figure Of Eight' 7 and a 12-inch singles, and a British promotional single (12 SOL 1).

Flowers In The Dirt data

Parlophone and Capitol issued the album with customised labels, a printed inner sleeve, and lyric sheet. Linda and artist Brian Clarke, who produced the stage backdrops for the 1989/'90 world tour, created the cover artwork. In Britain, Parlophone issued promotional copies of the CD in a 10-inch gatefold sleeve with a brief biography, black-and-white photographs, and a print interview. Parlophone also promoted the album with an impressive marketing campaign. The album was advertised on television, full-colour press advertisements were placed in daily newspapers and magazines, four-sheet street posters were placed in 250 sites throughout Britain, and a 50-minute documentary about the making of the album was broadcast on BBC-1 on June 10. To promote the album in the USA, Capitol issued a promotional CD, *Paul McCartney Rocks* (DPRO-79743), which featured songs from *Flowers In The Dirt*, B-sides, and classic McCartney oldies.

'THIS ONE' / 'THE FIRST STONE'

'THIS One' was selected as the second A-side to be lifted from *Flowers In The Dirt,* and the single was issued in Britain in six different editions, which between them featured four new McCartney songs, an outtake from the *Choba B CCCP* sessions, and a new recording of 'The Long And Winding Road'.

'The First Stone', a McCartney–Stuart song about the nefarious activities of a television evangelist, ought to have been strong enough to appear on the album. According to Hamish Stuart, it was one of the first things he recorded with McCartney. "In December 1987, I went to the studio in Sussex. There was Paul, Nicky Hopkins on keyboards, and [drummer Chris Whitten]. Paul and I half-wrote [this] song and worked on it a little bit."

A new version of 'The Long And Winding Road' appeared on

'THIS ONE' / 'THE FIRST STONE'
PAUL McCARTNEY
UK RELEASE July 17 1989; Parlophone R 6223; second 7-inch (postcard pack) Parlophone RX 6223 'This One' / 'The Long And Winding Road' released July 24 1989; 12-inch Parlophone 12 R 6223 'This One', 'The First Stone' / 'I Wanna Cry', 'I'm In Love Again' released July 31 1989; second 12-inch Parlophone 12 RX 6223 'This One', 'The First Stone' / 'Good Sign' released July 31 1989; CD single Parlophone CDR 6223 'This One', 'The First Stone', 'I Wanna Cry', 'I'm In Love Again'; cassette single Parlophone TCR 6223 'This One', 'The First Stone'; chart high No.18.
US RELEASE August 1 1989; cassette single Capitol 4JM44438; chart high No.94.

• **'The First Stone'** (McCartney, Stuart)
Paul McCartney (bass, keyboards, vocals), Hamish Stuart (guitar, backing vocals), Chris Whitten (drums), Nicky Hopkins (piano).
• **'The Long And Winding Road'** (Lennon, McCartney)
Paul McCartney (piano, vocals), Linda McCartney (keyboards, backing vocals), Hamish Stuart (bass, backing vocals), Robbie McIntosh (guitar, backing vocals), Paul 'Wix' Wickens (keyboards, backing vocals), Chris Whitten (drums).
• **'I Wanna Cry'** (McCartney)
Paul McCartney (guitar, vocals), Micky Gallagher (keyboards), Nick Garvey (bass), Henry Spinetti (drums).
• **'I'm In Love Again'** (Domino, Bartholomew)
Paul McCartney (bass, vocals), Mick Green (guitar), Micky Gallagher (keyboards), Chris Whitten (drums).
• **'Good Sign'** (McCartney)
Paul McCartney (bass, piano, drums, vocals), Robbie McIntosh (guitar), Hamish Stuart (guitar, backing vocals).
All recorded at Hog-Hill Studio, East Sussex, England, except 'Good Sign' also at Mad Hatter Studios, Los Angeles, CA, USA. All produced by Paul McCartney except 'Good Sign' with additional production by Neil Dorfsman.

the postcard-pack version of the single, recorded at Hog-Hill in April 1988 for the *Put It There* television programme. This was McCartney's third attempt at recording the song outside of The Beatles – earlier solo readings appear on *Wings Over America* and *Give My Regards To Broad Street*.

'I Wanna Cry' was the only McCartney original recorded during the *Choba B CCCP* sessions. An unremarkable 12-bar, lacking invention or character, it's little more than an uninspired throwaway, and if nothing else it proves that white men can't sing the blues.

'I'm In Love Again' was originally recorded by Fats Domino and issued by Imperial (5386), reaching Number 3 in the US in 1956. It was the third Fats Domino song that McCartney recorded for *Choba B CCCP*, cut at Hog-Hill on July 20 1987 with Mick Green, Chris Whitten, and Micky Gallagher. It wasn't included on original Russian LP but was later issued on the 1991 CD (CDPCSD-117).

'Good Sign' had been intended for *Flowers In The Dirt* but was removed at the last minute. Originally, it had a brass arrangement by Clare Fisher, recorded at Mad Hatter Studios, which was removed during mixing. Duncan Bridgeman and Joe Dworniak produced a 'Groove Mix', extending the song to 7:22, issued as a 12-inch promotional single (GOOD 1) limited to 200 copies. As the title of the remix suggests, 'Good Sign' was based on a groove with some breakbeats thrown in for good measure. This is goodtime dance music and has little to say other than "Let's party".

'This One' data

To promote the single, Matt Butler produced a remix, 'The Club Lovejoys Mix', issued as a one-sided 12-inch single (12 R LOVE 6223) and limited to 500 copies. Butler's remix was later issued as a bonus track on the 'Figure Of Eight' 12-inch single (12 R 6235).

Parlophone issued 'This One' on 7 and 12-inch with pink and white generic labels and a picture sleeve. A second 7-inch (RX 6223) was issued with a white outer envelope that contained the single and a set of six postcards. The single was also issued on CD and cassette.

In the USA, Capitol issued 'This One' as a cassette single. A 7-inch demonstration single (7PRO-79700) was issued with white labels and black text in a generic sliver and black paper sleeve.

'OU EST LE SOLEIL?'

CAPITOL released this 12-inch with purple labels and a full-colour picture sleeve. To promote the single, the company issued a one-track CD of the 'Shep Pettibone Edit' (DPRO-79836) with a blue screen-printed label with grey text.

Parlophone issued the single in Europe with generic black labels and a picture sleeve identical to the US issue. In Britain, Parlophone issued 'Ou Est Le Soleil?' as a promotional only 12-inch single (12 SOL 1), reserving the new mixes for the B-side of 'Figure Of Eight'.

'OU EST LE SOLEIL?' / 'OU EST LE SOLEIL?' (TUB DUB MIX), 'OU EST LE SOLEIL?' (INSTRUMENTAL MIX)
PAUL McCARTNEY
US RELEASE July 25 1989; 12-inch Capitol V-15499; failed to chart.

'FIGURE OF EIGHT'

TO PROMOTE the *Flowers In The Dirt* album and his upcoming world tour, McCartney and band recorded new versions of 'Figure Of Eight' and 'Rough Ride'. EMI's marketing department worked overtime and issued the new recordings in eight format variations. New material, however, was thin on the ground: only one new song, the Phil Ramone-produced 'The Loveliest Thing', was issued; the rest had already been released on previous singles.

'FIGURE OF EIGHT' / 'OU EST LE SOLEIL?'
PAUL McCARTNEY
UK RELEASE November 13 1989; Parlophone R 6235; 12-inch Parlophone 12 R 6235 'Figure Of Eight' / 'This One' (The Club Lovejoys Mix); 12-inch Parlophone 12 RS 6235 'Figure Of Eight', 'Ou Est Le Soleil?' / etched B-side, released 20 November 1989; 12-inch Parlophone 12 RX 6235 'Figure Of Eight' / 'Ou Est Le Soleil?', 'Ou Est Le Soleil? (Tub Dub Mix) released November 27 1989; 3-inch CD single Parlophone CD3R 6235 'Figure Of Eight', 'Rough Ride', 'Ou Est Le Soleil?' released December 3 1989; 5-inch CD single gatefold sleeve Parlophone CDRS 6235 'Figure Of Eight', 'The Long And Winding Road', 'The Loveliest Thing'; 5-inch CD single with standard jewel case Parlophone CDR 6235 'Figure Of Eight', 'The Long And Winding Road', 'The Loveliest Thing'; cassette single Parlophone TCR 6223 'Figure Of Eight' / 'Ou Est Le Soleil?'; chart high No.42.
US RELEASE November 14 1989; cassette single Capitol 4JM44489; chart high No.92.

- **'Figure Of Eight'** (McCartney)
Paul McCartney (bass, vocals), Hamish Stuart (guitar, backing vocals), Chris Whitten (drums), Robbie McIntosh (guitar, backing vocals), Paul 'Wix' Wickens (keyboards, backing vocals), Linda McCartney (keyboards, backing vocals).
Recorded at Hog-Hill Studio, East Sussex, England.
Produced by Chris Hughes, Paul McCartney and Ross Cullum.
- **'The Loveliest Thing'** (McCartney)
Paul McCartney (piano, vocals), Neil Jason (bass), David Brown (guitar), David Lebolt (keyboards), Liberty Devitto (drums).
Recorded at The Power Station, New York City, NY, USA.
Produced by Phil Ramone.
- **'Rough Ride'** (McCartney)
Paul McCartney (bass, vocals), Linda McCartney (keyboards, backing vocals), Hamish Stuart (guitar, backing vocals), Robbie McIntosh (guitar, backing vocals), Paul 'Wix' Wickens (keyboards, backing vocals), Chris Whitten (drums).
Recorded at Hog-Hill Studio, Sussex.
Produced by Trevor Horn, Paul McCartney, and Steve Lipson.

The new version of 'Figure Of Eight' was recorded at Hog-Hill with producers Chris Hughes and Ross Cullum while the band rehearsed for McCartney's 1989-'90 world tour. It sounds too busy and fails to match the studio recording. Hughes attempted a mix, but Bob Clearmountain completed the final mix on September 12 1989. Two versions of his mix were issued: a 5:16 mix appeared on the 7-inch and 12-inch pressings, the cassette, and the 3-inch CD single; and a 4:03 edit was issued on promo copies of the single (RDJ 6235) and the 5-inch CD single.

Shep Pettibone produced several mixes of 'Ou Est Le Soleil?' for its release as a single: a 4:50 mix issued on the 7-inch single and 3-inch CD single; a 7:10 mix and a 4:30 'Tub Dub Mix' issued on 12 RX 6235; a 4:50 mix issued on 12 RS 6235; and a 3:57 mix issued on the B-side of the promotional 7-inch single (RDJ 6235).

Issued on the 5-inch CD single (CDRS 6235), 'The Loveliest Thing' was recorded with producer Phil Ramone in 1986. It's one of two songs recorded with Billy Joel's band, a charming McCartney ballad that could quite easily have been released as a successful standalone single. Unfortunately, McCartney's piano-based ballad was destined to reach only a fraction of the audience it deserved.

The new version of 'Rough Ride' was recorded at Hog-Hill during the same session that produced the new recording of 'The Long And Winding Road'. Unlike later versions, this recording reveals the band's lack of confidence. Compared with the cut made in Paris ten months later, this rehearsal take never takes off. Available on CD in Britain for the first time, it had previously been issued on the Japanese limited-edition double CD of *Flowers In The Dirt* (TOCP-6118-19).

'Figure Of Eight' data

The various configurations of 'Figure Of Eight' can appear confusing. However, the 7- and 12-inch (12 RS 6235) both feature identical material – all of the 12-inch releases feature the same 5:16 version of 'Figure'.

Both sides of the 7-inch were placed on the A-side of 12 RS 6235, which had a laser-etched B-side. The B-side of 12 R 6235 featured the 'Club Lovejoys' mix of 'This One', which had previously been made available as a one-sided 12-inch white label (12 R LOVE 6223). The cassette featured the same material as the 7-inch on both sides of the tape.

The 5-inch CD single (CDRS 6235) featured a 4:03 edit of 'Figure Of Eight', 'The Long And Winding Road', and 'The Loveliest Thing'. The 3-inch CD single (CD3R 6235) featured the 5:16 version of 'Figure', 'Rough Ride', and a 4:50 mix of 'Ou Est Le Soleil'?

All vinyl pressings were issued with generic labels, except for the 7-inch, which had a silver die-cut label.

Capitol released 'Figure Of Eight' as a cassette single. To promote it, the company issued 7-inch white-label singles

(7PRO-79889) with 'Mastered by Capitol' and 'SRC' factory-stamped in the dead wax. They also issued a two-track promotional CD single (DPRO-79871) with a yellow screen-printed label and red text, which featured a 7-inch version and 12-inch version of the A-side.

'PARTY PARTY'

A NEW package of the *Flowers In The Dirt* album was released to coincide with McCartney's world tour, and it included a Pete Frame family tree, a large colour poster, a bumper sticker, a tour itinerary, six colour postcards, and either a 7-inch single or 3-inch CD single of a new song, 'Party Party'.

The first song credited as a band composition, 'Party Party' was improvised during rehearsals for the tour, a piece used to encourage the band to let off steam and relax at the end of a hard day's rehearsal. It's a dance track with minimal lyrics and little in the way of melody. However, it's a fun track and probably deserved a wider audience.

The one-sided 7-inch single was issued with a generic label (A-side), a back label (B-side), and McCartney's drawing of some flowers etched onto the B-side, in a picture sleeve. The 3-inch CD was issued with a multicoloured screen-printed label and a picture sleeve. To fill the demand for an American release, British pressings were exported and distributed by Capitol.

Bruce Forest remixed 'Party Party' at Sarm Studios in London on October 15 1989 and this version was issued as a promotional 12-inch single (12 RDJ 6238) limited to 500 copies. Two batches were produced – and each was flawed in some way. The first had A-side labels on both sides of the record; the second had A- and B-side labels reversed. A 3:40 edit of 'Party Party' was issued on the US promo CD *Rocks* (DPRO-79987).

FLOWERS IN THE DIRT
PAUL McCARTNEY
SIDE 1 'My Brave Face', 'Rough Ride', 'You Want Her Too', 'Distractions', 'We Got Married', 'Put It There'.
SIDE 2 'Figure Of Eight', 'This One', 'Don't Be Careless Love', 'That Day Is Done', 'How Many People', 'Motor Of Love', 'Ou Est Le Soleil?'*.
The track marked * appears only on the CD.
UK RELEASE November 27 1989; LP Parlophone PCSDX 106; CD Parlophone CDPCSX 106; bonus vinyl 7-inch single Parlophone R 6238 or CD single CD3R 6238 'Party Party'; chart high No.1.

• **'Party Party'** (McCartney, Stuart, Whitten, McIntosh, Wickens, McCartney)
Paul McCartney (bass, vocals), Linda McCartney (keyboards, backing vocals), Hamish Stuart (guitar, backing vocals), Robbie McIntosh (guitar, backing vocals), Paul 'Wix' Wickens (keyboards, backing vocals), Chris Whitten (drums).
Recorded at Hog-Hill Studio, East Sussex, England.
Produced by Trevor Horn, Paul McCartney, and Steve Lipson.

1990-99

'PUT IT THERE' / 'MAMA'S LITTLE GIRL'

WINGS Mk.2 recorded 'Mama's Little Girl' at Olympic during sessions for *Red Rose Speedway* in 1972. McCartney's deceptively simple song, a bouncy ballad with chiming acoustic guitars and close harmony vocals, neatly evokes notions of childhood, and the use of a woodwind section completes the allusion. Inspired by Paul and Linda's two young daughters, like many songs written in the early 1970s, it reflects the McCartneys' interests and combines themes that lay at the heart of their lives.

'Same Time Next Year' was recorded in May 1978 as the proposed theme-song for the Alan Alda film of the same name. This lush piano ballad has a nostalgic tone, with McCartney's romantic melody and sensitive lyric yearning for a more innocent past or perfect moment. The basic track was recorded at RAK with Wings Mk.7 and then overdubbed with a 68-piece orchestra at Abbey Road.

'Put It There' data

In Britain, Parlophone issued the single on three formats, all of which featureda identical material. Two versions of the 12-inch were produced, one with and one without a 'limited edition' print of McCartney's cover drawing. The 7-inch single was issued with silver die-cut labels. Capitol released the recordings as a cassette single, although they issued a 7-inch demonstration single (7PRO-79074) with white labels and black text to radio stations.

'PUT IT THERE', 'MAMA'S LITTLE GIRL'
PAUL McCARTNEY
UK RELEASE January 29 1990; Parlophone R 6246; 12-inch Parlophone 12 R 6246 'Put It There', 'Mama's Little Girl' / 'Same Time Next Year'; CD Single Parlophone CDR 6246 'Put It There', 'Mama's Little Girl', 'Same Time Next Year'; cassette single Parlophone TCR 6246 'Put It There', 'Mama's Little Girl'; chart high No.32.
US RELEASE May 1 1990; cassette single Capitol 4JM44570; failed to chart.

• **'Mama's Little Girl'** (McCartney)
Paul McCartney (bass, vocals), Linda McCartney (backing vocals), Denny Laine (guitar, backing vocals), Henry McCullough (guitar), Denny Seiwell (drums). Recorded at Olympic Sound Studios, Barnes, England.
• **'Same Time Next Year'** (McCartney)
Paul McCartney (piano, vocals), Linda McCartney (backing vocals), Denny Laine (bass), Laurence Juber (guitar), Steve Holly (drums).
Recorded at RAK Studios and Abbey Road Studios, London, England.
Both produced by Paul McCartney and Chris Thomas.

'IT'S NOW OR NEVER'

THE LAST *Temptation Of Elvis* was conceived by *NME* journalist Roy Carr to raise money for the Nordoff-Robbins Music Therapy Centre. McCartney had been involved with this charity for some time – he appeared in a British television programme about the centre on October 26 1988 – so it's not surprising that he should donate a song to the project. He was the first artist Carr approached, and it was his commitment to the project that encouraged others to provide specially recorded versions of Presley songs for the album.

Presley hit big with 'It's Now Or Never' in 1960, and as big fans The Beatles included it in their stage act that same year. The group never recorded any of Presley's songs for EMI, but they did cut several for the BBC (and their version of 'That's Alright Mama' was eventually released on *The Beatles At The BBC*).

Recalling Presley's influence, McCartney said: "I started to see pictures of Elvis, and that started to pull me away from the academic path. 'You should see these great photos...' Then you'd hear the records – 'But wait a minute, this is very good!' – and then the tingles started going up and down your spine, 'Oh this is something altogether different.'"

Despite McCartney's enthusiasm for the song, 'It's Now Or Never', an outtake from the *Choba B CCCP* sessions, he gave it an unadventurous pub-rock reading. But even if some of Presley's magic is missing, it would appear that those involved enjoyed revisiting the past once again: listen for McCartney's giggle at the song's end.

THE LAST TEMPTATION OF ELVIS
VARIOUS ARTISTS
PAUL McCARTNEY 'It's Now Or Never'.
UK RELEASE March 24 1990; LP NME NME 038/039; CD NME CD 038/039; failed to chart.

• **'It's Now Or Never'** (Schroeder, Gold)
Paul McCartney (bass, vocals), Mick Green (guitar), Micky Gallagher (keyboards), Chris Whitten (drums). Recorded at Hog-Hill Studio, East Sussex, England. Produced by Paul McCartney.

The Last Temptation Of Elvis data

Released on the *NME* label, the album was originally available only through mail order but was later sold in high-street shops. In addition to the commercial album, the *NME* pressed a limited edition of 500 copies of a promotional 10-inch single (NMEPRO10-1990) that coupled McCartney's 'It's Now Or

Never' with Bruce Springsteen's 'Viva Las Vegas'. It was issued with custom labels and plain white sleeve. A promotional CD single (NMECDPRO1990) was also issued, in a black and grey card sleeve.

KNEBWORTH / 'HEY JUDE'

THE FIRST live tracks to emanate from McCartney's 1989/'90 comeback world tour were issued on another charity album in support of Nordoff-Robbins Music Therapy and the BRIT School Of Performing Arts & Technology. On June 30 1990, McCartney (and band) performed at Knebworth Park to his largest British audience ever – around 120,000 people turned up for the concert, which was headlined by Pink Floyd.

He appeared as the penultimate act and performed an abbreviated 11-song set that focused on his past rather than current solo material. The set-list was: 'Coming Up', 'Back In The USSR', 'I Saw Her Standing There', 'We Got Married', 'Birthday', 'Let It Be', 'Live And Let Die', 'Hey Jude', and a medley of 'Strawberry Fields Forever', 'Help!', 'Give Peace A Chance', 'Yesterday', and 'Can't Buy Me Love'.

Four songs from the mini-set – 'Coming Up', 'Birthday', 'Hey Jude', and 'Can't Buy Me Love' – were issued on the video *Knebworth – The Event Vol.1* and in Germany on a CD video single. BBC Radio One broadcast almost all of his set along with a brief backstage interview; thus most of the performance was made available for public consumption. You might have thought that McCartney and band, having played over 90 concerts in just over a year, would have been suffering from severe road fatigue. But at Knebworth they sounded as fresh and vital as when they started.

McCartney had begun to write 'Hey Jude' while driving to see Julian Lennon. His father had just moved in with Yoko Ono, so McCartney began composing a lyric to hearten Julian's spirits. Like several of his songs, it's the sound of the words that is important, not their meaning. Although he intended to change several improvised lines, Lennon insisted that they remain untouched, as he knew exactly what they meant.

He performed 'Hey Jude' throughout the '89/'90 world tour, and it had become a highlight of McCartney's concerts, not least because of its sing-along coda, which was perfect for audience participation.

LENNON

ISSUED to celebrate what would have been Lennon's 50th birthday, this was a 73-track, four-CD set that covered his solo career from 1969 to 1980. The compilation, which takes tracks from every Lennon album from *Live Peace In Toronto – 1969* to

KNEBWORTH: THE ALBUM
VARIOUS ARTISTS
PAUL McCARTNEY 'Coming Up', 'Hey Jude'.
UK RELEASE August 6 1990; LP Polydor 843 921 1; CD Polydor 843 921 2; chart high No.1 (Compilation and CD chart).
US RELEASE August 7 1990; LP Polydor 847 042-1; failed to chart.

• **'Hey Jude'** (Lennon, McCartney)
Paul McCartney (piano, vocals), Linda McCartney (keyboards, backing vocals), Hamish Stuart (bass, backing vocals), Robbie McIntosh (guitar, backing vocals), Paul 'Wix' Wickens (keyboards, backing vocals), Chris Whitten (drums).
Recorded live at Knebworth Festival, Knebworth, Herts, England.
Produced by Paul McCartney, mixed by Chris Kimsey.

LENNON
JOHN LENNON
DISC 1 'Give Peace A Chance', 'Blue Suede Shoes', 'Money (That's What I Want)', 'Dizzy Miss Lizzy', 'Yer Blues', 'Cold Turkey', 'Instant Karma! (We All Shine On)', 'Mother', 'Hold On', 'I Found Out', 'Working Class Hero', 'Isolation', 'Remember', 'Love', 'Well, Well, Well', 'Look At Me', 'God', 'My Mummy's Dead', 'Power To The People', 'Well (Baby Please Don't Go)'.
DISC 2 'Imagine', 'Crippled Inside', 'Jealous Guy', 'It's So Hard', 'Give Me Some Truth', 'Oh My Love', 'How Do You Sleep?', 'How?', 'Oh Yoko!', 'Happy Xmas (War Is Over)', 'Woman Is The Nigger Of The World', 'New York City', 'John Sinclair', 'Come Together', 'Hound Dog', 'Mind Games', 'Aisumasen (I'm Sorry)', 'One Day (At A Time)', 'Intuition', 'Out The Blue'.
DISC 3 'Whatever Gets You Thru The Night', 'Going Down On Love', 'Old Dirt Road', 'Bless You', 'Scared', '#9 Dream', 'Surprise, Surprise (Sweet Bird Of Paradox)', 'Steel And Glass', 'Nobody Loves You (When You're Down And Out)', 'Stand By Me', 'Ain't That A Shame', 'Do You Want To Dance', 'Sweet Little Sixteen', 'Slippin' And Slidin'', 'Angel Baby', 'Just Because', 'Whatever Gets You Thru The Night' (Live Version), 'Lucy In The Sky With Diamonds' (Live Version), 'I Saw Her Standing There' (Live Version).
DISC 4 '(Just Like) Starting Over', 'Cleanup Time', 'I'm Losing You', 'Beautiful Boy (Darling Boy)', 'Watching The Wheels', 'Woman', 'Dear Yoko', 'I'm Stepping Out', 'I Don't Wanna Face It', 'Nobody Told Me', 'Borrowed Time', '(Forgive Me) My Little Flower Princess', 'Every Man Has A Woman Who Loves Him', 'Grow Old With Me'.
UK RELEASE October 1 1990; Parlophone CDS 7 95220 2; failed to chart.
US RELEASE July 1991; Capitol CDS 7 95220 2; failed to chart.

Menlove Ave., was compiled by Beatles expert Mark Lewisohn and approved by Yoko Ono.

It contained seven tracks issued on CD for the first time, four from *Live Peace In Toronto – 1969* and three from Lennon's performance with Elton John at Madison Square Garden in 1974. All of the tracks were digitally remastered, with several treated with a 'No Noise' system to eliminate tape hiss.

The four CDs were issued in a substantial card case with a booklet featuring lyrics and photographs. Although the set was issued worldwide on October 1 1990, large numbers manufactured by EMI in Britain were exported. Capitol, for example, imported the set from Britain and didn't get around to officially issuing it until July 1991. Capitol considered issuing the set on cassette, but did not.

'BIRTHDAY'

ANOTHER track from the live recording made at Knebworth on June 30 1990, 'Birthday' was released to coincide with John Lennon's 50th birthday and marked an exceptional about-face in McCartney's attitude to performing Beatles songs.

Speaking in December 1990, he said: "I'd shied away from The Beatles stuff with Wings – it was a bit near to the break-up of The Beatles and it was a painful break-up – a bit like, I hear, a divorce. And the idea was that you don't want to sing any of the ex-wives' songs. And all of us had that feeling independently, [that we] wanted to establish a new life after The Beatles. Now, I thought, I don't have to do that any more, I don't have to deny The Beatles' songs. ... So that was a great unblocking."

He had performed some Beatles songs when Wings toured in 1976, but this time he dug deep into the group's back catalogue. He originally wrote and recorded 'Birthday' on September 18 1968 for the *White Album*. McCartney started the song at the piano, although the final arrangement, replicated note for note in this live version, was guitar-based.

'P.S. Love Me Do' was recorded during McCartney's record-breaking concert at the Maracana Stadium in Brazil on the world tour, and the song had been available before as a studio recording on the Japanese *Flowers In The Dirt* special edition. He rarely performed it in concert, but did perform it at every show he gave while in Japan. But a bad idea is a bad idea. Conceived by Phil Ramone, who should have known better, 'P.S. Love Me Do' is a sorry excuse for a song, a medley based on two early Lennon–McCartney compositions, 'P.S. I Love You' and 'Love Me Do'.

'BIRTHDAY', 'GOOD DAY SUNSHINE'
PAUL McCARTNEY
UK RELEASE October 8 1990; Parlophone R 6271; 12-inch Parlophone 12 R 6271 'Birthday', 'Good Day Sunshine' / 'P.S. Love Me Do', 'Let 'Em In'; CD single Parlophone CDR 6271 'Birthday', 'Good Day Sunshine', 'P.S. Love Me Do', 'Let 'Em In'; cassette single Parlophone TCR 6271 'Birthday', 'Good Day Sunshine'; chart high No.29.
US RELEASE October 16 1990; cassette single Capitol 4JM44645; failed to chart.

- **'Birthday'** (Lennon, McCartney)
Paul McCartney (bass, vocals), Linda McCartney (keyboards, backing vocals), Hamish Stuart (guitar, backing vocals), Robbie McIntosh (guitar, backing vocals), Paul 'Wix' Wickens (keyboards, backing vocals), Chris Whitten (drums).
Recorded live at Knebworth Festival, Knebworth, Herts, England.
- **'P.S. Love Me Do'** (Lennon, McCartney)
Paul McCartney (bass, vocals), Linda McCartney (keyboards, backing vocals), Hamish Stuart (guitar, backing vocals), Robbie McIntosh (guitar, backing vocals), Paul 'Wix' Wickens (keyboards, backing vocals), Chris Whitten (drums).
Recorded live at Maracana Stadium, Rio, Brazil.
Both produced by Paul McCartney, Bob Clearmountain, and Peter Henderson.

'Birthday' data

In Britain, Parlophone issued 'Birthday' as 7-inch, 12-inch, CD, and cassette singles with picture sleeves. The 7 and 12-inch singles were issued with generic labels. They issued a 7-inch demonstration single with a 1960s-style white and red 'A' label and paper sleeve. In the USA, Capitol issued it as a cassette single. The A-side was issued as a one-track promotional CD single (DPRO-79392) in a jewel case with full-colour rear inlay card.

TRIPPING THE LIVE FANTASTIC

JUST as McCartney issued a triple live album after Wings' 1975/'76 tour, this further mammoth three-record set was issued after the 1989/'90 tour. Of the 102 gigs the band played, 83 were recorded, using a 36-track digital mobile studio. This ensured that at least one recording from every major sales territory could be included on the album. While this may have been a shrewd marketing ploy, it was also a way of allowing fans from around the world to re-live a moment that many had waited a long time for.

"What we tried to do with the album," said McCartney, "was to give people a chance to take home with them a souvenir of the show; a better quality bootleg of what we hoped was just a good, fun, party night out." Of course this didn't stop the bootleggers: several illegal records emerged as the tour made its way around the globe.

As well as recording his concert performances, McCartney also recorded soundchecks. For some bands, working up new material

TRIPPING THE LIVE FANTASTIC
PAUL McCARTNEY
SIDE 1 'Showtime', 'Figure Of Eight', 'Jet', 'Rough Ride', 'Got To Get You Into My Life', 'Band On The Run', 'Birthday'.
SIDE 2 'Ebony And Ivory', 'We Got Married', 'Inner City Madness', 'Maybe I'm Amazed', 'The Long And Winding Road', 'Crackin' Up'.
SIDE 3 'The Fool On The Hill', 'Sgt. Pepper's Lonely Hearts Club Band', 'Can't Buy Me Love', 'Matchbox', 'Put It There', 'Together'.
SIDE 4 'Things We Said Today', 'Eleanor Rigby', 'This One', 'My Brave Face', 'Back In The USSR', 'I Saw Her Standing There'.
SIDE 5 'Twenty Flight Rock', 'Coming Up', 'Sally', 'Let It Be', 'Ain't That A Shame', 'Live And Let Die', 'If I Were Not Upon The Stage', 'Hey Jude'.
SIDE 6 'Yesterday', 'Get Back', 'Golden Slumbers', 'Carry That Weight', 'The End', 'Don't Let The Sun Catch You Crying'.
UK RELEASED November 5 1990; LP Parlophone PCST 7346; CD Parlophone CDS 7 947782; chart high No.17.
US RELEASED November 6 1990; LP Capitol C1-94778; CD Parlohpne 94778; chart high No.26.

• **'Inner City Madness'** (McCartney, McCartney, Stuart, Whitten, Wickens, McIntosh)
Recorded live at NEC, Birmingham, England.
• **'Crackin' Up'** (McDaniel)
Recorded live at The Forum, Los Angeles, CA, USA.
• **'The Fool On The Hill'** (Lennon, McCartney)
Recorded live at Wembley Arena, London, England.
• **'Sgt. Pepper's Lonely Hearts Club Band'** (Lennon, McCartney)
Recorded live at The Forum, Los Angeles, America.
• **'Can't Buy Me Love'** (Lennon, McCartney)
Recorded live at Olympiahalle, Munich, Germany.
• **'Matchbox'** (Perkins)
Recorded live at Wembley Arena, London, England.
• **'Together'** (McCartney, McCartney, Stuart, Whitten, Wickens, McIntosh)
Recorded live at The Horizon, Chicago, IL, USA.
• **'Things We Said Today'** (Lennon, McCartney)
Recorded live at Palicio des Sportes, Madrid, Spain.
• **'Back In The USSR'** (Lennon, McCartney)
Recorded live at Tokyo Dome, Tokyo, Japan.
• **'Twenty Flight Rock'** (Fairchild, Cochran)
Recorded live at Wembley Arena, London, England.
• **'Sally'** (Haines, Leon, Towers)
Recorded live at Wembley Arena, London, England.
• **'If I Were Not Upon The Stage'** (Sutton, Turner, Bowsher)
Recorded live at Riverfront Coliseum, Cincinnati, OH, USA.
• **'Golden Slumbers / Carry That Weight / The End'** (Lennon, McCartney)
Recorded live at Skydome, Toronto, Canada.
• **'Don't Let The Sun Catch You Crying'** (Greene)
Recorded live at The Forum, Montreal, Canada.
All with Paul McCartney (guitar, vocals), Linda McCartney (keyboards, backing vocals), Hamish Stuart (bass, backing vocals), Robbie McIntosh (guitar, backing vocals), Paul 'Wix' Wickens (keyboards, backing vocals), Chris Whitten (drums), except: 'The Fool On The Hill', 'Sally', 'If I Were Not Upon The Stage', 'Don't Let The Sun Catch You Crying' substitute Paul McCartney (piano, vocals); and 'Inner City Madness', 'Can't Buy Me Love', 'Together', 'Things We Said Today', 'Back In The USSR' substitute Paul McCartney (bass, vocals), Hamish Stuart (guitar, backing vocals). All produced by Paul McCartney, Bob Clearmountain and Peter Henderson.

at soundchecks is standard practice; releasing the results on record was an innovation.

To put the tour in perspective, McCartney and his band played to approximately 2,843,297 people in 13 countries. The tour outsold Madonna, The Grateful Dead, and Janet Jackson (all of whom were on the road at the same time) and broke new attendance records at several US stadiums. All of the American concerts sold out, and it was voted International Tour Of The Year by *Performance* magazine.

As with previous tours, a concert film was made. This one was *Get Back*, by Richard Lester, director of *A Hard Days Night* and *Help!*. Like many of McCartney's film projects, it was delayed, but eventually it gained a very limited cinema release before being released on video.

McCartney used the tour to promote green issues. Friends Of The Earth were present at most shows, and part of the free tour programme included information about environmental issues, vegetarianism, and relevant support groups.

Tripping The Live Fantastic songs

As with the rest of this book, live recordings of songs already covered in their studio versions are not included in concert-record entries. So, for our purposes, the first 'new' track on *Tripping* is 'Inner City Madness'. The pressures of touring can make people do strange things. To pass away the hours, some of rock's more exuberant performers have wrecked hotel rooms or done unspeakable things with fish. McCartney and his band jammed to relieve their ennui. 'Inner City Madness' may have sounded great on a leftfield jazz album, but as an exercise in freeform noisemaking it was probably more fun to play than listen to.

Bo Diddley's influence on early beat groups was substantial: his primitive rhythms and simple chord changes were distinctive yet easy to learn. With its hypnotic beat and insistent riff, 'Crackin' Up' was perfect for improvisation. The version here was recorded at a soundcheck, and the band's tight, concise reading stays close to the original.

Unlike other Lennon–McCartney songs that McCartney performed during this tour, 'The Fool On The Hill' was subtly reworked for live performance. He had written it as The Beatles reached the peak of their hippie period, at a time when anything seemed possible. It's a song about hope and social change, capturing perfectly the childlike disposition of the beautiful people while at the same time commenting on the realities of an increasingly troubled society.

The live recording here features an extended section with extracts from speeches given by Dr Martin Luther King. As a signifier of social change, King was perhaps more relevant and emotive for American audiences; nevertheless, it was a neat trick that brought the song's theme of peaceful change to the fore.

The live recording of 'Birthday', issued as a single in October 1990, had already confirmed that McCartney was more than capable of writing and performing blistering rock'n'roll. By including toughened versions of 'Back In The USSR' and an extended 'Sgt. Pepper's Lonely Hearts Club Band', he effectively staked a claim as a rocker par excellence. From its conception, 'Pepper' was planned as a heavy track, its crashing drums and screeching guitars prefiguring the proto-metal of 'Helter Skelter'. Performed now in concert, the song was transformed into a powerhouse guitar extravaganza that swaggered from beat-group stomper to psychedelic freak-out. Complete with introductory sound effects, it appears a little sluggish to begin with, but explodes with a shift in tempo that signalled the guitar duel between McCartney and Robbie McIntosh.

For many, the sight of McCartney singing classics from his Beatle past came close to an epiphany. Unlike the previous tour, which had showcased a mere handful of Beatles songs, this time relatively obscure album tracks nestled alongside hit singles. The Beatles recorded 'Can't Buy Me Love' at EMI's Pathé Marconi studio in Paris, France in January 1964. This simple blues-based song with a country influenced solo and sprightly singalong chorus remained a stage favourite 25 years after its first release. Although McCartney discreetly rearranged some Beatles songs for concerts, 'Can't Buy Me Love' remained unchanged because, as McIntosh explained, "I think the guitar solos in [that song] and 'Back In The USSR' are integral parts of the songs. They're sort of sacred. You've got to do the song justice and treat it with a bit of respect."

Touring can be a dispiriting experience, even for superstars. However, with this one, McCartney was intent on having fun, as McIntosh recalled. "You'd think this is his first band, the way he goes on. You see him at soundchecks, going around in circles and doing these silly little jumps. It's a real novelty to him to have a band again – and he treats it like that."

Having fun meant one of two things: improvising or performing rip-roaring rock'n'roll. 'Matchbox', a song The Beatles recorded but not sung by McCartney (Ringo at EMI; Lennon at the BBC), was a favourite warm-up item for Paul and band, and the version here is from a Wembley soundcheck. An alternative version, also recorded at a soundcheck, was later broadcast on McCartney's *Oobu Joobu* radio series (and McCartney performed the song with its author, Carl Perkins, backstage at the Liberty Bowl Memorial Stadium in Memphis on June 27 1993).

'Together' was improvised at a soundcheck and is little more than a doodle. Had it been developed it might have been quite pleasing. Despite its obvious shortcomings, it is one of the better throwaways on the album.

McCartney wrote 'Things We Said Today' in The Bahamas in early 1964, and it first appeared on The Beatles' *A Hard Days Night* album. Reflecting his frustration at being parted from his girlfriend of the time, Jane Asher, the song finds him in an uncharacteristically dark mood. It quickly became a live favourite, which was why McCartney chose to perform the song on this tour. He sticks to The Beatles' arrangement and gives a strong reading, but like every remake or live performance given by an ex-Beatle, it simply isn't comparable with the original. That's not negative criticism: it's just that The Beatles were an extraordinary band, and the parts could never be as good as the whole.

McCartney wrote 'Back In The USSR' while studying meditation with the Maharishi Mahesh Yogi in India, and this rocker did for Soviet Russia what Brian Wilson and Chuck Berry had done for America. Issued at the height of America's ideological war with Russia and its real war with Vietnam, his tongue-in-cheek rocker seemed to some Americans like an anti-USA tirade. But how wrong they were: like The Beach Boys' records that influenced it, 'Back In The USSR' was meant as nothing more than a piece of inoffensive fun. Here, McCartney and his band rip into it with obvious affection and delight. Close your eyes and you could almost be listening to a beefed-up Beatles. It's all here: note-perfect guitar solos and backing vocals, and McCartney singing his heart out.

McCartney performed 'Twenty Flight Rock' when he first met Lennon at Woolton Parish Church garden fate on July 6 1957, a performance he has since cited as the defining moment of his career. Lennon and the other Quarry Men were so impressed by his knowledge of Eddie Cochran's rocker that they offered him a place in the group. 'Twenty Flight Rock' remained in The Beatles' repertoire until they tidied up their act and started to perform truncated 30-minute sets. McCartney continued to play the song at rehearsals and soundchecks, and performed it with Wings during their 1979 British tour, but its appearance on *Tripping* marked its first appearance on a McCartney album. It's obvious that he loves this kind of music; you can hear it in his voice. He's having fun and it's infectious. If you're looking for an example of McCartney the rocker, it doesn't get much better than this.

Delving even further into his cultural past, McCartney performed 'Sally', a song made famous by Gracie Fields. Ms Fields was a famous north-country actress and singer, and 'Sally' had long been her theme song. It evokes memories of her working-class roots and the industrial atmosphere of her hometown. For

McCartney, it was little more than a novelty song performed tongue-in-cheek. He even went as far as to affect Gracie's characteristic warble.

For someone who enjoys the spontaneity of improvisation, it's odd that McCartney should choreograph his live performances so rigidly. Even his ad libs are rehearsed, and this fragment of an old music hall standard was performed as a joke – night after night after night.

'Golden Slumbers / Carry That Weight / The End', with its electrifying shifts in mood and dynamics, was the ideal way to end the world-tour performances. McCartney wrote 'Carry That Weight' as The Beatles spun out of control, and it alludes to the group's legacy, the inescapable 'ex-Beatle' tag that group members would carry with them for eternity. Unable now to ignore his past, McCartney was trapped: his Beatle-heavy set exposed the erratic nature of his solo career, but to ignore his past would have been folly. The lyric, which in 1969 appeared mildly prophetic, now seemed sadly inescapable. The spectacle of watching McCartney performing some of the songs that defined an epoch could be an exceptional, if occasionally paradoxical experience.

Ray Charles's 'Don't Let The Sun Catch You Crying' closes *Tripping*. The Beatles had included it in their early stage repertoire; this version was recorded at the Montreal soundcheck. McCartney gives a confident reading and the band are remarkably tight, which suggests they performed the song a number of times before committing it to tape. Only the weedy, synthetic horn sound spoils an otherwise enjoyable track.

Tripping The Live Fantastic data

Parlophone and Capitol issued this live album as a three-LP set with customised labels and specially designed inner sleeves. A 12-inch square 28-page booklet completed the package, which came in a single sleeve with a sticker adhered to the front cover. The CD was issued as a two-disc set with two booklets, one for each disc.

TRIPPING THE LIVE FANTASTIC – HIGHLIGHTS

RELEASED in Britain on the same day as the 'All My Trials' single, this *Highlights* collection was just that: an edited version of the sprawling triple-LP/double CD set. It contained only two solo songs and instead focused on McCartney's career with The Beatles, perhaps in an attempt to coerce the casual buyer who didn't want to splash out on the expensive full set.

'All My Trials' was the only song here that was not on the complete live album, and was also McCartney's surprise Christmas single for 1990. He only performed it once during his 102-date world tour, in Milan on October 27 1989. 'All My Trials' was originally part of the traditional *An American Trilogy*, a medley of three 19th-century songs made popular by Elvis Presley when he began performing it in concert in the early 1970s. 'Trials', a protest song with an established heritage, neatly summarises many of McCartney's beliefs and values, and was the perfect song with which to round off the year and consolidate the message he had spent so much time disseminating.

TRIPPING THE LIVE FANTASTIC – HIGHLIGHTS
PAUL McCARTNEY
CD 'Got To Get You Into My Life', 'Birthday', 'We Got Married', 'The Long And Winding Road', 'Sgt. Peppers Lonely Hearts Club Band', 'Can't Buy Me Love', 'All My Trials', 'Things We Said Today', 'Eleanor Rigby', 'My Brave Face', 'Back In The USSR', 'I Saw Her Standing There', 'Coming Up', 'Let It Be', 'Hey Jude', 'Get Back', 'Golden Slumbers / Carry That Weight / The End'.
LP omits 'Got to Get you Into My Life', 'We Got Married', 'Things We Said Today', 'Back In The USSR', 'Golden Slumbers / Carry That Weight / The End'.
UK RELEASED November 26 1990; CD Parlophone CDPCSD 114; cassette TCPCSD 114; failed to chart.
US RELEASED November 20 1990; CD Capitol CDP 7 95379 2; LP Columbia House edition C1-595379; chart high No.141.

• **'All My Trials'** **(trad arr McCartney)**
Paul McCartney (guitar, vocals), Linda McCartney (keyboards, backing vocals), Hamish Stuart (bass, backing vocals), Robbie McIntosh (guitar, backing vocals), Paul 'Wix' Wickens (keyboards, backing vocals), Chris Whitten (drums).
Live recording at Polatrussardi, Milan, Italy.
Produced by Paul McCartney, Bob Clearmountain, and Peter Henderson.

Highlights data

In Britain, *Highlights* was only issued on CD and cassette. An LP (PCSD 114) had been scheduled, but was not issued. The album was issued on LP in America, but only through Columbia House mail-order, who issued two versions, with American or Canadian addresses. The LP was also issued in countries where vinyl still outweighed CD sales. Czech pressings (21 0079-1 311), with sleeves manufactured in Britain, were pressed on red or green vinyl.

'STRAWBERRY FIELDS' MEDLEY

AT THE tour's Liverpool show (and later at Knebworth) McCartney had performed a medley of three songs written by John Lennon. He had been planning a tribute to his partner for some time. At first, he thought it might take the form of intimate renditions of 'Imagine' and 'Here Today', and then considered an elaborate affair with large-scale pictures of Lennon, but rejected this as too showbiz.

Instead, what emerged was this brief medley. "I thought it would be nice to just do a little something," he recalled. "I didn't want to go crazy with it. I didn't want any, 'Oh sacred memory of the great loved one.' I didn't want to get too precious with it. But I did feel good about popping a little medley together like that: they're nice songs to sing, and given the emotion of me singing John's songs, for the first time in my life, it had to be Liverpool. So I finally got to sing John's part on 'Help!' and 'Strawberry Fields', which was always one of my favourite John tracks."

'Strawberry Fields Forever' was always going to be difficult to recreate on stage, even with advances in technology. Rather than attempt to recreate the original arrangement note-for-note, McCartney attempted to capture the atmosphere of the original. Yet his version is too slick and lacks the unsettling, other-worldly atmosphere that made the original a classic of British psychedelia. But that's to miss the point. This was meant as a tribute to a close friend, not an exercise in recreating the authentic analogue textures of 1960s pop records.

The medley also included the first verse and chorus of 'Help!', taken at a slower pace than the original. (McCartney's reworking is remarkably similar to a demo Lennon made when he returned to the song in November 1970 and made a brooding home demo at the piano. Lennon was perhaps considering a remake of the song, as he always thought that the original recording was rushed.) The medley was rounded off with the chorus from 'Give Peace A Chance', which McCartney was forced to reprise because the audience wouldn't stop singing it.

Whether Lennon would have loved or loathed the medley is debatable. He would, however, have appreciated the sentiment, even though he would have shrugged it off with a typically flippant remark.

'ALL MY TRIALS', 'C MOON'
PAUL McCARTNEY
UK RELEASE November 26 1990; Parlophone R 6278; 12-inch Parlophone 12 R 6278 'All My Trials', 'C Moon' / 'Mull Of Kintyre', 'Put It There'; CD single Parlophone CDR 6278 'All My Trials', 'C Moon', 'Mull Of Kintyre', 'Put It There'; CD single Parlophone CDRX 6278 'All My Trials', 'C Moon', 'Strawberry Fields Forever / Help! / Give Peace A Chance' released 3 December 1990; cassette single Parlophone TCR 6278 'All My Trials', 'C Moon'; chart high No.35.

• **'Strawberry Fields Forever / Help! / Give Peace A Chance'** (Lennon, McCartney)
Paul McCartney (piano, vocals), Linda McCartney (keyboards, backing vocals), Hamish Stuart (bass, backing vocals), Robbie McIntosh (guitar, backing vocals), Paul 'Wix' Wickens (keyboards, backing vocals), Chris Whitten (drums).
Live recording at Kings Docks, Liverpool, England.
Produced by Paul McCartney, Bob Clearmountain, and Peter Henderson.

'All My Trials' data

Parlophone issued 'All My Trials' with generic labels and a picture sleeve. A demonstration 7-inch was issued with black and purple 'A' labels and generic 'harlequin' sleeve. Parlophone also issued a 12-inch single, two CD singles, and a cassette single.

UNPLUGGED – THE OFFICIAL BOOTLEG

MTV'S *Unplugged* series originated with a concert by Chris Difford and Glenn Tilbrook, who were asked to give a low-key performance with Syd Straw. Difford and Tilbrook arrived at the television studio with acoustic guitars – and the format, which forbade musicians from using amplification, was born (and remained unchanged until Bruce Springsteen appeared on the show and insisted on playing with amplification). Before long, some of the world's biggest players were queuing up to appear on the show. McCartney was one of the first big names to embrace the format and his appearance in 1991, along with the release of this album, helped popularise the programme.

Playing with acoustic instruments led the musicians to interesting performances, particularly as amplification had come to play such an important role in making rock music. "It made us realise how much there is to hide behind with electric music," Hamish Stuart explained. "Acoustically, as soon as you play a note, it's right there, very naked." When considering what to perform on the show, musicians had to more carefully consider the song, which was laid bare before the audience.

For his performance, McCartney opted for a mixture of melodic pop and stripped-down rock'n'roll. Explaining how he made his selection, he said: "Whenever I pick up an acoustic at home I always go way, way back to when I was a teenager – and that's way back, believe me. I remember 'Cut Across Shorty', 'Be-Bop-A-Lula', the first record I ever bought, all the Elvis stuff like 'That's Alright Mama', 'Good Rockin' Tonight', and 'Love Me Tender'. ... We tried all those songs simply because those are the first songs I ever tried to learn on an acoustic, and those are the ones that have stuck."

Although the performance appeared spontaneous, McCartney rehearsed the band for two weeks at his Hog-Hill studio to ensure perfection. They performed 22 songs on the show, and all but five were included on the album. 'Mean Woman Blues', 'Matchbox', 'The Fool', 'Midnight Special', and 'Things We Said Today' remained in the can, although two were eventually issued – 'Things We Said Today' as the B-side of the 1993 US single 'Biker Like An Icon' and 'Midnight Special' on the European double-CD *Off The Ground*, also issued in '93.

The band's opener, 'Mean Woman Blues', would retain its position in the set for several of their 'secret' gigs but remained commercially unavailable on record (although it did appear on the promotional CD of the 'Biker Like An Icon' single). Of the remaining material, only three songs had previously been performed live. McCartney played 'Blackbird' and 'I've Just Seen A Face' during Wings' 1976 world tour and had aired 'Blue Moon Of Kentucky' on Wings' 1972 European tour.

McCartney's MTV show was recorded on January 25 1991 at Limehouse Television Studios in Wembley, north-west London, and the *Unplugged – The Official Bootleg* album was the first MTV *Unplugged* show to gain a commercial release. This was partly to deter bootleggers – the programme was broadcast on American radio on April 3 1991, so it would have been easy to obtain high quality recordings of the show – and partly because McCartney was so impressed by the performance that he considered releasing it as his next record. As he explained: "We decided to bootleg the show ourselves. ... By the time we got home, we'd decided we'd got an album – albeit one of the fastest I've ever made."

Unplugged songs

According to Beatles author Mark Lewisohn, 'Be-Bop-A-Lula' was one of the songs that McCartney performed when he first met John Lennon and his group The Quarry Men at the Woolton Parish Church garden fate. And when the song's author, American rocker Gene Vincent, played Liverpool in 1960, The Quarry Men were there taking notes.

Vincent continued to influence the group, and by the time they hit Hamburg as The Beatles, they looked like black-leather clad Vincent clones. Neither McCartney nor Lennon (who covered the song for his *Rock'N'Roll* album) managed to capture the spirit of Vincent's original. Where the original appeared lascivious, McCartney's version merely confirms how far the spirit of rock'n'roll has been diluted by mainstream culture.

Written in the same year as Vincent's seminal song, 'I Lost My Little Girl 'was McCartney's first attempt at songwriting. Rejected by The Quarry Men because of its twee lyric, it took the passing of 35 years before McCartney had the courage to perform it in concert. Despite the song's naiveté, he obviously felt some pride in his first attempt at songwriting, as he noted that even at this early stage the simple musical structure had something to offer. He said it was "a very innocent little song – C, G7, C – but quite interesting, because the chords go down as the melody goes up; it's a clear musical trick, but it's also interesting to see such ideas around in my first song."

UNPLUGGED – THE OFFICIAL BOOTLEG
PAUL McCARTNEY
SIDE 1 'Be-Bop-A-Lula', 'I Lost My Little Girl', 'Here There And Everywhere', 'Blue Moon Of Kentucky', 'We Can Work It Out', 'San Francisco Bay Blues', 'I've Just Seen A Face', 'Every Night', 'She's A Woman'.
SIDE 2 'Hi-Heel Sneakers', 'And I Love Her', 'That Would Be Something', 'Blackbird', 'Ain't No Sunshine', 'Good Rockin' Tonight', 'Singing The Blues', 'Junk'.
UK RELEASE May 13 1991; LP Parlophone/Hispavox PCSD 116; CD Parlophone CDPCSD 116; chart high No.7.
US RELEASE June 4 1991; LP Parlophone/Hispavox PCSD 116; CD Parlophone 7964131; chart high No.14.

- **'Be-Bop-A-Lula'** (Vincent, Davis)
- **'I Lost My Little Girl'** (McCartney)
- **'Blue Moon Of Kentucky'** (Monroe)
- **'We Can Work It Out'** (Lennon, McCartney)
- **'San Francisco Bay Blues'** (Fuller)
- **'She's A Woman'** (Lennon, McCartney)
- **'Hi-Heel Sneakers'** (Higgenbottom)
- **'And I Love Her'** (Lennon, McCartney)
- **'Ain't No Sunshine'** (Withers)
- **'Good Rockin' Tonight'** (Brown)
- **'Singing The Blues'** (Endsley)

All with Paul McCartney (guitar, vocals), Linda McCartney (harmonium, percussion, backing vocals), Hamish Stuart (bass, backing vocals), Robbie McIntosh (guitar, backing vocals), Paul 'Wix' Wickens (piano accordion, shaker, backing vocals), Blair Cunningham (drums), except: 'Ain't No Sunshine' Paul McCartney (drums), Linda McCartney (harmonium, percussion, backing vocals), Hamish Stuart (guitar, backing vocals), Robbie McIntosh (piano, backing vocals), Paul 'Wix' Wickens (guitar, shaker, backing vocals), Blair Cunningham (percussion).
All recorded live at Limehouse Television Studios, Wembley, London, England; live recording and mixing by Geoff Emerick.

McCartney performed 'Blue Moon Of Kentucky' with Wings as early as 1972 but dropped it from their repertoire soon after the first European tour. The song was first recorded in 1946 by bluegrass legend Bill Monroe but reworked by Elvis Presley into an up-tempo rockabilly rave-up for his second Sun single in 1954. McCartney chose the song simply because he had confidence in singing it. "It's funny," he recalled, "I never meant to record it, but I did it on the early Wings tours, which we recorded, and now [*Unplugged*], and it's become a bit more than I intended it, really. But that's OK.'

'We Can Work It Out' was originally issued by The Beatles as a standalone single after McCartney had written it in response to his failing relationship with Jane Asher. Eternally optimistic, his response was to suggest that they should work out their differences rather than go their separate ways. The song's downbeat middle eight was added by Lennon and is typical of his pessimistic responses to McCartney's optimism. In front of the TV studio audience, McCartney couldn't remember his words, and the song broke down three times before a satisfactory take was captured on tape.

'San Francisco Bay Blues' was written by Jesse Fuller but a hit for Ramblin' Jack Elliott. It had all the right characteristics to become popular with folk and skiffle groups alike, and a measure of its popularity is the number of artists who have covered it and the number of Beatles who attempted the song. Besides his own reading, McCartney suggested that George Harrison may have dabbled with it, and John Lennon busked a version while making *Imagine*.

McCartney wrote 'She's A Woman', apparently in the studio, because The Beatles needed a new rocker with which to close their live shows. It contains one of the earliest references to the group's marijuana intake: the line "turns me on when I get lonely" was supposedly suggested by Lennon as a reference to their recent meeting with Bob Dylan, who allegedly introduced them to the drug.

Carl Perkins had been inspired by a pair of blue suede shoes, but Robert Higgenbottom was obviously infatuated with another kind of footwear. His 'Hi Heel Sneakers' was a hit for Tommy Tucker in 1964 – and McCartney's choice of the song for this set was unusual in that it wasn't a hit during his youth but during the height of Beatlemaina. Covers of the song had been made by artists as diverse as Stevie Wonder and Jerry Lee Lewis, who gave one of the definitive readings. Where Lewis imbued the song with raw sexual energy, McCartney's take is less an invitation to party than to gently amble through the park.

'And I Love Her' featured in The Beatles' first film, *A Hard Days Night*, and became an instant classic: in other words, it was covered by others who saw its hit potential. The group's first attempt at the song, which makes them sound like any run-of-the-mill Merseybeat combo, was released on *Anthology 1*. Re-recorded with acoustic instruments, the Fabs gave McCartney's starry-eyed lyric a more suitable setting. For this *Unplugged* performance, McCartney slows the tempo and subtly alters the vocal melody, giving the song a smokey, late-night feel.

Although the band's set focused on early rock'n'roll and McCartney originals, they also performed a version of Bill Withers' 'Ain't No Sunshine'. They switched instruments: McCartney plays drums, Wickens bass, Macintosh piano, and Stuart lead vocals. McCartney said: "I wanted Hamish to do something, and during a break in jams we often swap around instruments – I get on drums and Hamish might start doing 'Ain't No Sunshine'. It was good fun doing it [here]." 'Ain't No Sunshine' was reprised for the New World Tour (February to December 1993) with McCartney once again taking his place on drums.

'Good Rockin' Tonight' was a hit in the late 1940s for Wynonie Harris but became a standard when recorded by Elvis Presley, Scotty Moore, and Bill Black for Sun records in 1954. McCartney's version is based on Presley's rockabilly take rather than its earlier R&B incarnation.

Presley's influence is again evident in 'Singing The Blues'. Taken to the top of the American hit parade by Guy Mitchell, it's best known in Britain thanks to Tommy Steele. In the late 1950s, British recording artists like Steele tended to follow American trends rather than set their own. A string of home-grown stars were promoted as Britain's answer to Elvis Presley, and these watered-down clones were all that many had as their point of reference. However, for the die-hard music fan such as McCartney, authentic versions had to be hunted down, which only made the music on the shiny black discs all the more exciting. Combining melodic pop with roughhouse rock, 'Singing The Blues' was catchy enough to be hummed by parents and radical enough to appeal to teenagers.

Fifty years later, it's hard to image how important this type of material was in defining attitudes and identities within British youth cultures. However, it does reveal the effect McCartney's music had on British musicians. With the release of 'Love Me Do' in 1962, British music would never be the same again – and pale imitations of American hits would be consigned to the bargain bin of history.

Unplugged data

Unplugged – The Official Bootleg was released on LP, CD, and cassette, all of them limited editions. At McCartney's request, vinyl copies were made to resemble EMI's Spanish imprint, Hispavox (and to maintain authenticity, the sleevenotes were written in Spanish). The CD was issued with a ten-page booklet, which included photos taken during the performance and brief notes about each song. A total of 500,000 copies of all three variants were manufactured for global distribution: the largest number was for the CD, and the vinyl edition was rapidly depleted. The CD and cassette formats were available for many years after the initial 'limited' release. Despite being issued as a 'limited edition', the album managed a Top 10 placing in Britain, although it quickly dropped out of the charts because dealers were unable to reorder stock from EMI after initial orders had been dispatched.

CHOBA B CCCP: THE RUSSIAN ALBUM

IN 1987, McCartney held a number of informal Friday night jam sessions where he indulged his passion for rock'n'roll. Inspired by these sessions, he decided to record much of what he'd rehearsed. Recording over two days, he and a band of veteran pub rockers knocked out 22 songs, 14 of which would appear on the

Choba B CCCP CD. But the tapes then sat around for almost a year before it was decided that something should be done with them.

Richard Ogden, McCartney's manager, had the idea for the album. The two had discussed issuing the record in the Soviet Union, so Ogden had 50 LPs made to resemble Russian bootlegs as a Christmas present for McCartney.

McCartney was so impressed with Ogden's gesture that he instructed him to contact the Soviet Union's only record label, Melodiya, to discuss the possibility of having the album released there. Negotiations were successful and Melodiya were granted permission to press 400,000 copies of *Choba B CCCP*. Unused to dealing with artists who had complete control over their records, the label made an initial batch of 50,000 LPs with 12 song titles and incorrect sleeve notes. McCartney insisted the error be corrected, and MPL authorised an LP with 13 titles, made available on October 31 1988. The 14-song CD appeared in 1991.

Choba songs

Presley and his contemporaries may have exerted a considerable influence on the fledgling Beatles, but the soul and R&B that came out of New York, Detroit, and Memphis proved to be no less an influence. Many black performers influenced Lennon and McCartney, who eagerly consumed as much R&B as they could find. Elvis may have sparked their desire to become performers, but the music of black America – largely underrated in the USA at the time – influenced their songwriting as much as the likes of Buddy Holly or Gene Vincent. Cover versions of songs by then obscure black American artists litter the group's early records, but one name was conspicuous by its absence: Sam Cooke. Although it appears that The Beatles overlooked Cooke in favour of Arthur Alexander or Smokey Robinson, he obviously remained a favourite of Lennon and McCartney, as both decided to cover 'Bring It On Home To Me' for their respective rock'n'roll albums. McCartney delivers a strong vocal but is let down by his band, who walk rather than swing their way through the song. Lennon managed to get his band to swing a little more, but neither managed to capture the feel of the original.

Little Richard recorded 'Lucille' in 1957 and it reached Number 21 in the US charts and 10 in the UK. Wings Mk.2 performed 'Lucille' in their stage act (and were filmed playing the song at the ICA in early 1972). McCartney returned to the song when he performed it with Rockestra at the Hammersmith Odeon in London on New Year's Eve 1979. This solo rendition is tighter than Rockestra's spontaneous reading and may just outdo The Beatles' 1963 BBC recording.

Both Presley songs that McCartney chose to record for *Choba* were originally made in the summer of 1954 at Sun Studios, Memphis. These early Sun recordings, raw, energetic and innovative, represent for many the apogee of Presley's career. They had a huge influence on Lennon and McCartney, both of whom certainly considered this period of Presley's career his best.

CHOBA B CCCP: THE RUSSIAN ALBUM
PAUL McCARTNEY
CD 'Kansas City', 'Twenty Flight Rock', 'Lawdy Miss Clawdy', 'I'm In Love Again', 'Bring It On Home To Me', 'Lucille', 'Don't Get Around Much Anymore', 'I'm Gonna Be A Wheel Someday', 'That's Alright Mama', 'Summertime', 'Ain't That A Shame', 'Crackin' Up', 'Just Because', 'Midnight Special'.
UK RELEASED September 30 1991; CD Parlophone CDPCSD 117; chart high No.63.
US RELEASED October 29 1991; CD Capitol CDP 7 97615; failed to chart.

- **'Bring It On Home To Me'** (Cooke)
- **'Lucille'** (Collins, Penniman)
- **'That's Alright Mama'** (Crudup)
- **'Summertime'** (Gershwin)
- **'Just Because'** (Shelton, Shelton, Robin)

All with Paul McCartney (bass, vocals), Mick Green (guitar), Micky Gallagher (keyboards), Chris Whitten (drums).
All recorded at Hog-Hill Studio, East Sussex, England.
All produced by Paul McCartney.

Speaking to *Q* magazine in 1999, McCartney said: "We were mad Elvis fans before he went into the Army. We thought the Army made him a little too grown up, but he was fantastic."

Rather than replicate Presley's classic Sun sound, McCartney gives 'That's Alright Mama' a rough country treatment, complete with honky tonk piano, that differs dramatically from Presley's minimal interpretation.

The Beatles included 'Summertime' in their concert repertoire until about 1960. Typical of the melodic ballads the group chose to perform, this George Gershwin tune had also been covered by Gene Vincent, which may have influenced their reading. While Vincent gave the song kudos – and it's difficult to imagine Lennon being enamoured with this type of material without Vincent's name being associated with it – Gershwin's tune suited McCartney to a tee. This type of well-crafted song, as much as rock'n'roll, was the model upon which McCartney based his craft. Eager to be the best, he often worked with this type of song at the back of his mind. 'Summertime' remains in his musical vocabulary and he often revisits it at rehearsals and soundchecks. Here he delivers a strong, bluesy vocal, and while his band provide competent support, they sound a little stiff and find it hard to capture the feel of a humid summer day. But these songs were recorded in a hurry, so that's a minor criticism – and McCartney more than makes up for their deficiencies.

Presley recorded 'Just Because' in September 1954, and RCA released it in the same month. McCartney's version here is tough, rough, and ready, and the ghost of Elvis haunts his delivery, which recalls many of the King's idiosyncratic vocal mannerisms.

Choba data

Although it was not intended for release in the West, copies of *Choba* quickly found their way into shops in Britain and the USA, where it sold at highly inflated prices.

For those unable to obtain the new album, or unwilling to pay the high prices it was fetching, several songs were made available as B-sides. ('Midnight Special', 'Don't Get Around Much Anymore', 'Lawdy Miss Clawdy', and 'Kansas City' were issued as the B-sides of the two 1987 'Once Upon A Long Ago' 12-inch singles; 'I'm Gonna Be A Wheel Someday' and 'Ain't That A Shame' were released as the B-side of the 1989 'My Brave Face' 12-inch single; and 'I Wanna Cry' and 'I'm In Love Again' appeared on the B-side of the 1989 'This One' 12-inch single). An outtake, 'It's Now Or Never', was issued on the 1990 *NME* charity album *The Last Temptation of Elvis*.

MPL also imported copies of the LP into Britain and sold them through McCartney's fan club, first as issue 51 of the *Club Sandwich* magazine, and then through the club, which was the only official outlet in the West.

When it was released in 1991 in the West, the CD featured a bonus track, 'I'm In Love Again'. EMI made provisions for a vinyl edition of the album but there was not sufficient demand for one. Vinyl editions of the album (A60 00415 006) were only produced in the Soviet Union, where two variants were made. The first pressing (50,000 copies) was issued with a yellow rear cover, sleeve notes by Andrei Gavrilov and red Melodiya labels. Some sources (MPL) suggest that this pressing was also issued with a laminated cover, although unlaminated copies have also surfaced. In addition, first pressings featured twelve songs, rather than MPL's suggested thirteen. Melodiya thought it technically unrealistic to press an album with more than six songs on each side, so *Summertime* was omitted from side two. Second pressings (approximately 350,000 copies) have white Melodiya labels and MPL logos, which were omitted from the first pressing. This version came with a white rear sleeve and sleeve notes by Paul and Roy Carr – these were used for the CD and cassette version of the album produced in the West.

'THE WORLD YOU'RE COMING INTO'

EMI'S marketing department must have found itself in a dilemma. How could they promote a major new classical work by a pop artist to antithetical markets? It's unlikely that many classical music buffs, or admirers of Kiri Te Kanawa, rushed out to buy the single; they much prefer albums. It's similarly unlikely that it influenced many pop fans to buy the forthcoming album. Nevertheless, the project had to be promoted, and a release of this sort, although unsatisfactory in that it appealed to neither pop nor classical audiences, was probably the best option.

Taken from 'Movement VII – Crises' of McCartney's *Liverpool Oratorio*, 'The World You're Coming Into' was not a Paul McCartney single as such – he did not appear on the recording, and Kiri Te Kanawa's name received top billing – but is included here because it formed part of his oratorio project and its subsequent promotion. While it was promoted as Dame Kiri's new single, as was the second single from the album, it was nevertheless inextricably linked to one of the biggest projects that McCartney had committed himself to for some time.

'THE WORLD YOU'RE COMING INTO' / 'TRES CONEJOS'
KIRI TE KANAWA
UK RELEASE September 30 1991; EMI Classics KIRIS 1; CD single EMI Classics KIRICD 1 'Introduction To Movement VII', 'The World You're Coming Into', 'Tres Conejos'; cassette single EMI Classics KIRITC 1 'The World You're Coming Into', 'Tres Conejos'; failed to chart.

• **'The World You're Coming Into'** (McCartney, Davis)
Dame Kiri Te Kanawa (vocals), Royal Liverpool Philharmonic Orchestra & Choir, Choristers of Liverpool Cathedral, Carl Davis (conductor), Malcolm Stewart (solo violin), Ian Balmain (solo trumpet), Timothy Walden (solo cello), Anna Cooper (cor anglais).
• **'Tres Conejos'** (McCartney, Davis)
Dame Kiri Te Kanawa, Sally Burgess, Jerry Hadley, Willard White, (vocals), Royal Liverpool Philharmonic Orchestra & Choir, Choristers of Liverpool Cathedral, Carl Davis (conductor), Malcolm Stewart (solo violin), Ian Balmain (solo trumpet), Timothy Walden (solo cello), Anna Cooper (cor anglais).
Both recorded at Liverpool Anglican Cathedral, Liverpool, England.
Both produced by John Fraser and exclusively produced by Paul McCartney.

'The World You're Coming Into' data

Released by EMI Classics, the single was issued on 7-inch, CD, and cassette. The 7-inch was issued with silver die-cut labels, the CD in a slimline case, and the cassette in a card sleeve.

LIVERPOOL ORATORIO

McCARTNEY'S first major classical composition was nothing if not impressive. Lasting one-and-a-half hours, the *Liverpool Oratorio* is a semi-autobiographical work that focuses on his early childhood in Liverpool. Three years in the making, during which time McCartney toured the world and recorded one of his better solo pop albums, the *Oratorio* was commissioned by the Royal Liverpool Philharmonic Orchestra, who wanted something to celebrate their 150th anniversary.

The commission came about through a series of chance meetings that began in 1988 when the McCartneys made a guest appearance in the BBC sitcom *Bread* – written by their friend and fellow animal rights campaigner, Carla Lane. While filming their appearance, Paul and Linda struck up a friendship with actress Jean Boht, the wife of conductor Carl Davis. It was about this time that the Liverpool Philharmonic suggested that he might like to write something for them. At this point the 'something' was unspecified, and McCartney could have written a short orchestral work if he'd wanted to. But something considerably more substantial was forthcoming. What emerged was a full-scale oratorio in the English tradition.

The English oratorio developed during the 18th century. Unstaged musical settings, usually of biblical narratives, were performed in response to censorship from powerful religious figures, who considered the staging of biblical subjects profane and immoral. As provincial theatres and amateur choral groups developed during the next century, composers were encouraged to write for the form, and oratorios became increasingly popular. The composers also started to explore secular subjects, which previously had been frowned upon. Working within this tradition, McCartney's oratorio fuses religious and secular themes with autobiography.

To prepare for this project, McCartney attended operas and other classical concerts as well as performances by the Royal Liverpool Philharmonic Orchestra. While he had never attempted anything in this genre or on this scale, he was already well versed in the classical tradition. His childhood home was filled with music, both the home-made and professional variety. And when he moved into the house Jane Asher shared with her parents, he was exposed to classical music (Asher's mother was an oboist with various orchestras and a music teacher). Living in London, McCartney attended performances by many of the world's leading orchestras, and by the mid 1960s he had become an active participant in a multi-faceted culture that for some saw Stockhausen consumed as enthusiastically as The Yardbirds.

McCartney's hunger for new musical experiences was matched by his attitude to seemingly disparate cultural and musical sources. Rather than reject musical ideas from previous eras, he incorporated them into his musical vocabulary. George Martin was another important figure, introducing The Beatles to a wide range of classical music. Never one to reject a good idea, Martin encouraged The Beatles to experiment with textures not normally associated with pop music. When McCartney heard Bach's Second Brandenburg Concerto on television he immediately thought of incorporating the high piccolo trumpet into 'Penny Lane'. Speaking to the *New Statesman* in 1997, McCartney noted that his songwriting "developed when George Martin suggested putting a string quartet on 'Yesterday'. I helped him orchestrate it and realised I was getting into a different type of music".

McCartney had worked with a number of collaborators but he had never worked with anyone whose musical background differed so radically from his own. The union between pop and classical music often produces crass or embarrassing anomalies, but there are always exceptions. McCartney and Carl Davis were the exception. Together they produced an enjoyable, lively, and exquisitely crafted oratorio that followed classical conventions but also featured moments that were pure McCartney.

His choice of collaborator seems inspired. Davis had the knowledge that McCartney lacked – he could physically write the score and suggest musical forms and alternative voicings. Like McCartney, he'd worked in a number of genres and wasn't threatened by the pop conventions McCartney brought with him. McCartney was unable to write down the notation, but using a second party to transcribe notation was hardly new: Irving Berlin and Frederick Delius both used assistants to put their music onto paper. But this didn't mean that Davis played a secondary role. Indeed, he led from the start.

Although McCartney and Davis were constrained by the conventions placed on them by their chosen form, each was able to develop ideas that a classically trained practitioner may have

PAUL McCARTNEY'S LIVERPOOL ORATORIO

PAUL McCARTNEY AND CARL DAVIS

SIDE 1 'Movement I – War', 'Movement II – School'.
SIDE 2 'Movement III – Crypt', 'Movement IV – Father'.
SIDE 3 'Movement V – Wedding', 'Movement VI – Work'.
SIDE 4 'Movement VII – Crises', 'Movement VIII – Peace'.
UK RELEASE October 7 1991; LP EMI Classics PAUL 1; CD EMI Classics CDPAUL 1; chart high No.36.
US RELEASE October 22 1991; CD EMI Classics CDS 7 54371 2; chart high No.177.

- **'Movement I – War'** (McCartney, Davis)
- **'Movement II – School'** (McCartney, Davis)
- **'Movement III – Crypt'** (McCartney, Davis)
- **'Movement IV – Father'** (McCartney, Davis)
- **'Movement V – Wedding'** (McCartney, Davis)
- **'Movement VI – Work'** (McCartney, Davis)
- **'Movement VII – Crises'** (McCartney, Davis)
- **'Movement VIII – Peace'** (McCartney, Davis)

With Dame Kiri Te Kanawa, Sally Burgess, Jerry Hadley, Willard White (vocals), Royal Liverpool Philharmonic Orchestra & Choir, Choristers of Liverpool Cathedral, Carl Davis (conductor), Malcolm Stewart (solo violin), Ian Balmain (solo trumpet), Timothy Walden (solo cello), Anna Cooper (cor anglais). Recorded at Liverpool Anglican Cathedral, Liverpool, England. Produced by John Fraser and exclusively produced by Paul McCartney.

rejected. Indeed, their different musical backgrounds were beneficial, as McCartney explained. "I prefer to think of myself as a primitive, rather like the primitive cave artists who drew without training. Hopefully, the combination of Carl's classical training and my primitivism will result in a beautiful piece of music. That was always my intention."

Although he had written a few extended pieces for film scores, the *Liverpool Oratorio* was the first time McCartney had attempted anything on a large scale. For him, songwriting was a quick, sometimes spontaneous process that often appeared magical; it was not comparable to composing a big classical work. However, the scale and complexity of the project didn't deter him. Rather, his experience of working in a popular genre proved a distinct asset. Speaking about a later classical piece in 1997, he noted: "John (Lennon) and I just knew the form: a couple of verses, a chorus, middle eight, a new verse, chorus. Now, instead of the short story, this is the novel." More accustomed to writing 'short stories' than 'novels', McCartney had to learn a new musical syntax.

McCartney was always one to push back musical boundaries, and his whole musical philosophy was grounded in a cultural synthesis that ensured a healthy appetite for knowledge. McCartney and Davis were open to one another's views, ideas, and working practices. For McCartney, the writing process was as much about learning as it was about making music.

Talking to *Musician* magazine he recalled: "Carl would occasionally say: 'Let me give you a little lesson,' and, depending on what mood I was in, sometimes I would say, 'No Carl, we won't do that,' because I felt too much like a student. But occasionally if I was in a receptive mood I'd say: 'Go on.' And he'd say: 'This movement is based on the rondo form.' So I'd say: 'What's a rondo?' And Carl would explain. If I was interested in it and thought it would be a good idea for us, then we would use it, which we did in the last movement: 'Peace' is roughly based on the rondo form. But he tried to sit me down one day with Benjamin Britten's *Young Person's Guide To The Orchestra* and I wouldn't do it. I refused and said, 'No, Carl, it's too late for that, luv.'"

Having completed the first draft, the two honed the piece to perfection. A trial recording of the oratorio was made at Liverpool Anglican Cathedral on March 27 1991 to test the building's acoustics and to enable McCartney to check for any flaws in the piece – as he was unable to read music, this was the only way he could analyse the final work. Minor refinements were required, but rather than leave the alterations to Davis, McCartney continued to collaborate, and it was he who insisted that the central violin solo was rewritten to maintain the highest concert standards.

For the world premiere and recording, the 90-strong Royal Liverpool Philharmonic Orchestra was joined by 160 choristers from the Royal Liverpool Philharmonic Choir, 40 Choristers Of Liverpool Cathedral, and four of the world's leading classical singers. The most famous of the four, Dame Kiri Te Kanawa, was no stranger to the Top 10 herself. A popular figure in both classical and popular realms, her status as one of the world's leading female singers was assured when she was invited to sing at the wedding of Prince Charles and Lady Diana Spencer. Dame Kiri's presence gave the *Liverpool Oratorio* project credibility and helped sell the recording to a sceptical classical audience.

As with almost everything McCartney has released as a solo artist, reviews for the oratorio were mixed. Many in the classical world were unprepared to admit that a 'pop' musician was capable of writing a large-scale classical piece. *The Guardian* was scathing in its attack, but Howard Reich's review of the oratorio's New York premiere was fulsome in its praise. Writing in the *Chicago Tribune*, Reich described the oratorio as "a first-class work that speaks in distinctly humble tones".

In the years after its premieres (there were three, in Liverpool, London, and New York City), the *Liverpool Oratorio* became a regular on the classical circuit, with performances taking place around the world. The Liverpool premiere was filmed and released on video and laser disc, and a documentary about the making of the oratorio (*Ghost Of The Past*) was released on video after it had been broadcast by the BBC.

Depending on which UK chart you consult, the album reached either Number 36 or Number 1. *Music Week*, the official British music industry magazine, placed the album at 36 in its pop charts, but after several weeks it reached Number 1 in its classical charts. The album gained a high place in the classical charts because sales were compiled only from specialist classical retailers and consequently was only measured against other classical albums. A better indicator of its overall success is probably shown by its placing at 36 in the pop charts, where it did remarkably well competing with a much wider range of recording artists – few classical albums cross over into the pop charts. But while it dropped out of the pop charts fairly quickly, it remained in the classical charts for almost a year, eventually leaving the Top 40 in October 1992.

Liverpool Oratorio data

EMI Classics issued *Liverpool Oratorio* as a two-LP set with generic labels in a boxed set. A double CD and tape were also issued. The CD came with a 40-page booklet that was also issued with the vinyl edition.

'SAVE THE CHILD'

THE SECOND single lifted from the *Liverpool Oratorio* featured Dame Kiri Te Kanawa and Jerry Hadley. As with the previous single, McCartney did not feature on the recording. Whether this release did much to promote the album is doubtful, as practically everyone who wanted a copy had bought one by the time it was

'SAVE THE CHILD' / 'THE DRINKING SONG'
KIRI TE KANAWA AND JERRY HADLEY
UK RELEASE November 25 1991; EMI Classics KIRIS 2; CD single EMI Classics KIRICD 2 'Save The Child', 'The Drinking Song'; CD single EMI Classics CDKIRIS 2 'Save The Child', 'The Drinking Song', 'The World You're Coming Into' released 2 December 1991; cassette single EMI Classics KIRITC 2 'Save The Child', 'The Drinking Song'; failed to chart.

issued. The single may have generated some extra airplay on a few specialist radio stations, but exposure on the all-important pop stations was probably nil. As with the previous single, it was issued with generic EMI Classics labels and a picture sleeve.

LIVERPOOL ORATORIO – HIGHLIGHTS

PAUL McCARTNEY'S LIVERPOOL ORATORIO – HIGHLIGHTS
PAUL McCARTNEY AND CARL DAVIS
CD 'War', 'School', 'Crypt', 'Father', 'Wedding', 'Work', 'Crises', 'Peace'.
UK RELEASE October 5 1992; CD EMI Classics 7 54642 2; failed to chart.
For recording, personnel, conductor, and producer credits see Paul McCartney's Liverpool Oratorio.

THIS was a CD-only release of edited highlights from the *Liverpool Oratorio*, strictly for those with a short attention span.

'HOPE OF DELIVERANCE'

A SLICE of lightweight pop, 'Hope Of Deliverance' marked the first new studio material from McCartney in two years, and was unrepresentative of the tougher rock approach found on the new album, *Off The Ground*.

McCartney wrote the song using a 12-string acoustic guitar with a particularly jangly timbre. This, he said, suggested "cathedrals and Christmas", which "led me to the field of hope, of deliverance, and then I added about the darkness that surrounds us."

The song encompasses a broad spectrum of human suffering and, like 'Let It Be', is a consideration of faith. And like 'Let It Be', the deliberately ambiguous lyric can be read as either secular or religious in tone. McCartney certainly thought that the song had a spiritual theme. "It says 'you', whoever you is, [and] you can read that different ways; 'you will always understand', there is some sort of spirit that will make it all right."

Steve Anderson was commissioned to remix 'Hope', but McCartney didn't want it swamped with samples from obscure soul records. Anderson's task was to remix the track using only samples from *Off The Ground* and, thereby, retain some of its original character. However, when Anderson's remix was issued as a promotional record, McCartney's identity was not revealed. The artist obscured his involvement by circulating a rumour that the record was by a house group called Big Mac from Brixton in south London.

Even after the truth emerged, reactions to Anderson's remix were more than favourable. Pete Tong, BBC Radio One's foremost dance DJ, claimed the record was "a housed-up monster of a groove, ... absolutely huge, regardless of who is behind it". Although McCartney's part in producing the mix was probably minimal, it fuelled his interest in contemporary dance music and led to a number of other songs getting the remix treatment. Promotional copies were very limited – between 500 and 1,000 – but demand for the track was such that both of Anderson's mixes were made available as a limited commercial 12-inch on January 15 1993.

Although its success in America was limited, 'Hope Of Deliverance' was a sizeable hit in Britain and a massive hit in Europe. It was so popular in Germany that it became the most played record on German radio, ever. Its success in Europe ensured that it went on to become one of McCartney's bestselling singles, with worldwide sales of over four million.

'Long Leather Coat' was recorded along with 22 other songs for *Off The Ground* and finds McCartney engaged with animal rights. When he was writing for the new album he decided to include personal views on topics beyond those he'd previously explored. Speaking just after the release of *Off The Ground*, he said: "I thought, I'm coming up to 50, not much point in trying to be cutesy. So what do I really think about, what do I do, what do I spend my time on? Well, Friends Of The Earth, PETA, vegetarianism – how the world would be a much better place and be able to feed itself a lot better if we stopped eating meat. [They're] very practical, the arguments, you know. It's not all tofu pie in the sky."

'Long Leather Coat' was his attempt to express those beliefs through the medium he knew best. It may have eased his conscience, but whether it did much for the animal rights movement is debatable.

He wrote 'Big Boys Bickering' in Japan in 1990, and in it he rails against the lack of concern politicians have for environmental issues. "I think it was [my] first protest song since 'Give Ireland Back To The Irish'," he said. "I've avoided them, thinking 'this is for the politicians' or something; I can say it in interviews. You have to be very incensed to find the inspiration to do it right."

He was so outraged by their intransigence that, uniquely, he resorted to strong language to get his point across. "I wrote 'Big Boys Bickering' and, for the first time in a song, I used the word fucking – which I knew would upset some people," he said. For McCartney, at least, using the word was important in that it expressed his feelings. A spokesperson for MPL said that McCartney had considered changing the lyric to "muckin' it up", or "cockin' it up", but felt that these words simply weren't powerful enough.

His lyric may have been hardnosed, but the musical setting did nothing to convey his sense of anger. Little more than a pleasant singalong, McCartney's setting fails to match the anger that boiled over in his lyric. Although some criticised him for using the f-word, EMI didn't insist on any changes to the lyric – a sign of changing attitudes – and didn't even insist on a parental warning sticker. Nevertheless, the BBC and MTV banned the song, although a version recorded for MTV's *Up Close* was broadcast on the British ITV network complete with offending lyric.

'Kicked Around No More' is a typical McCartney ballad, and one that deserved better than to be hidden away at the end of a CD single. Featuring all the classic McCartney trademarks – lush harmonies, strong melody and lyric – the song would have made a fine album track. However, an abundance of material meant that something had to go, and so one of McCartney's better compositions was resigned to relative obscurity.

'HOPE OF DELIVERANCE' / 'LONG LEATHER COAT'
PAUL McCARTNEY
UK RELEASE December 28 1992; Parlophone R 6330; 12-inch Parlophone 12 R 6330 'Deliverance' / 'Deliverance Dub', 'Hope Of Deliverance' released 15 January 1993; CD single Parlophone CDRS 6330 'Hope Of Deliverance', 'Long Leather Coat', 'Big Boys Bickering', 'Kicked Around No More'; cassette single Parlophone TCR 6330 'Hope Of Deliverance', 'Long Leather Coat'; chart high No.18.
US RELEASE January 12 1993; CEMA Special Markets Division 7-inch Capitol S7-56946; cassette single Capitol 4KM07777 'Hope Of Deliverance', 'Long Leather Coat'; CD single Capitol C2 7 15950 2 'Hope Of Deliverance', 'Long Leather Coat', 'Big Boys Bickering', 'Kicked Around No More'; chart high No.83.

- **'Hope Of Deliverance'** (McCartney)
Paul McCartney (bass, guitar, vocals), Linda McCartney (autoharp, backing vocals), Hamish Stuart (backing vocals), Robbie McIntosh (guitar), Blair Cunningham (backing vocals, percussion), Paul 'Wix' Wickens (piano, Linndrum, drum programming, percussion, backing vocals), David Giovannini (percussion), Dave Pattman (percussion), Maurizio Ravalico (percussion).
- **'Long Leather Coat'** (Paul and Linda McCartney)
Paul McCartney (bass, vocals), Linda McCartney (backing vocals), Hamish Stuart (guitar, backing vocals), Robbie McIntosh (guitar), Blair Cunningham (drums, percussion), Paul 'Wix' Wickens (keyboards).
- **'Big Boys Bickering'** (McCartney)
Paul McCartney (guitar, vocals), Linda McCartney (backing vocals), Hamish Stuart (bass, backing vocals), Robbie McIntosh (dobro), Blair Cunningham (drums, percussion), Paul 'Wix' Wickens (accordion, backing vocals).
- **'Kicked Around No More'** (McCartney)
Paul McCartney (piano, vocals), Linda McCartney (backing vocals, percussion), Hamish Stuart (guitar, backing vocals), Robbie McIntosh (guitar), Blair Cunningham (drums, percussion), Paul 'Wix' Wickens (synth bass, drum programming, keyboards, backing vocals).

All recorded at Hog-Hill Studio, East Sussex, England.
All produced by Paul McCartney and Julian Mendelsohn.

'Hope Of Deliverance' data

Parlophone issued the single in the UK on 7-inch, CD, and cassette formats. The 7-inch was issued with die-cut Parlophone labels, the 12-inch with a unique white Parlophone label and white sleeve with a 2-inch-square sticker. Parlophone issued a promotional 12-inch single (12 DELIVDJ 1) with two remixes of 'Hope Of Deliverance'. The records were issued with green labels with 'DELIVERANCE' in red text and black sleeves. Parlophone also issued a four-track promotional CD single (PMINT 1) in a jewel case without artwork.

Capitol issued the single in the USA on 7-inch, cassette, and CD formats. The 7-inch single (S7-56946) was issued with generic purple labels through Capitol's CEMA *Special Markets Division*. A one-track promotional CD single (DPRO 776579) was issued in a jewel case with artwork similar to the commercial release.

OFF THE GROUND

COMING off the back of a world tour, this album found McCartney returning to a tougher live sound and recording with a band for the first time since *Back To The Egg*. "The nice thing about this band," he said, "is they're all good players, so we can make a good little noise just with the six of us. That was the idea: to do a simple little band album rather than anything very produced or complicated."

Off The Ground began to take shape in late 1991 when McCartney completed a number of unfinished songs, which he made into rough demos, recorded directly onto a Sony Walkman cassette machine. His usual method had been to work up fairly sophisticated demos, fleshing out ideas and completing arrangements before handing them over to the musicians, who simply reproduced the parts he'd committed to tape. This time he deliberately left the arrangements open, to encourage input from the band. He also took greater care with his lyrics, something he has admitted to overlooking. Yet, despite poet Adrian Mitchell's intervention, the occasional asinine couplet slipped through.

Work on the album began in the last week of November 1991. Two weeks were spent rehearsing with co-producer Julian Mendelsohn at Hog-Hill before recording proper began in December. Returning to the type of strict studio practices that were common in the early 1960s – the band worked from noon to 8:00pm, five days a week – everything was recorded live in the studio, with McCartney delivering a vocal with each take.

Comparisons with The Beatles' early studio practices were inevitable. McCartney said: "We worked the way The Beatles did. Come in, look at the song, which we knew a bit from the rehearsal, and do a really good live take of the song."

Rather than piece each song together over a number of takes, McCartney preferred strong performances that captured feel over perfection. Overdubs were kept to a minimum, and many of the vocals were live takes. A total of 23 songs were recorded, 22 of which would be made commercially available (the McCartney–Stuart composition 'Is It Raining In London?' remains unreleased). The track listing was selected through a democratic process. Each member of the group voted for their favourite songs, and the 13 with the highest score were put on the album.

Off The Ground songs

The title track was recorded as sessions for the album came to a close. Having recorded for several months in a very natural way, McCartney and keyboard player Wix Wickens decided to return to a more technically-oriented way of recording. The idea was to drop the band format and go into the studio and write a song from scratch. However, rather than approach the project completely unprepared, McCartney took an unfinished song with him, just in case inspiration wasn't forthcoming.

'Off The Ground' started as a fragment, which, he explained, "at that time was a little folk song". He added electric guitar, programmed bass, and percussion, and by the end of the day the song was all but finished. Robbie McIntosh added backing vocals and a guitar solo to complete it. It's a gritty, mid-tempo rocker with plenty of hooks to engage the listener, but you can't help thinking that McCartney knocks off this kind of song in his sleep.

He recorded several 'protest' songs during this period, but only 'Looking For Changes' made it onto the album. Paul and Linda had been vegetarians for a considerable time and were increasingly involved with green politics in the 1990s. They became good friends with writer Carla Lane, who is active within the animal rights movement and received both moral and financial support from Linda. Both Paul and Linda supported various green organisations, and Linda successfully launched a line of ready-made vegetarian meals. The couple raised animal rights and green issues through McCartney's *Club Sandwich* fan magazine, which had a regular 'Green Corner' that covered topics as diverse as antivivisection and vegetarian recipes. To promote the Australian leg of his New World Tour in March 1993, McCartney stressed environmental issues rather than promote the tour (which had probably sold out anyway). In June 1993 at the first Annual Earth Day Awards he was given an award for his work in raising public awareness of environmental issues. And in July 1993, Paul and Linda issued a statement calling on the International Whaling Commission to continue its ban on whaling.

Although McCartney's feelings on vegetarianism were strong, he nevertheless thought it easier to write a love song than something like 'Looking For Changes'. Influenced by antivivisectionist magazines *The Animal's Voice* and *Animal Agenda* and incensed by a photograph of a cat with a machine in its brain, he felt obliged to say something that might highlight this abhorrent kind of scientific experimentation. Performed throughout the New World Tour, 'Looking For Changes' became a live favourite and was included on 1993's *Paul Is Live*.

'Mistress And Maid' is by McCartney–MacManus, the latter the real surname of McCartney's some-time collaborator Elvis Costello. The song was inspired by a painting by Vermeer. McCartney somehow got the idea that the song was "gonna be a little bit sexy ... all a little bit ... kinky gear, French maid, mistress, and I was seeing it in that way, you know? Sort of how you might think Madonna would interpret it." Thankfully, he dropped his sexist theme and, with Costello's assistance, wrote the song from a woman's perspective. To complete this one, he called on Carl Davis to write the horn arrangement, which he based on McIntosh and Stuart's guitar parts. You can hear Costello in the song, the ying to McCartney's yang; Costello's dark tale of a dying relationship is balanced by a charming waltz-time melody from McCartney. It's a pity they didn't continue the partnership, as it produced some very compelling songs, including this one. (On March 23 1995 the two would perform an acoustic arrangement of it with the Brodsky Quartet at a charity concert to raise money for the Royal College of Music.)

McCartney wrote 'I Owe It All To You' while on holiday in France, inspired by a trip he made to the Cathedrale d'Images. "They have dozens of projectors and ... throw these images on the walls. Suddenly the whole place lights up and it's an Egyptian temple; next thing, it's all stained glass." More than an account of a holiday experience, like many of McCartney's songs it's about Linda. A typically melodic ballad with McCartney's dreamy Mellotron motif, it recalls the kind of textures The Beatles were using while recording *Sgt. Pepper* and *Magical Mystery Tour*.

During the November rehearsals, Mendelsohn set up a few microphones in the studio to get a feel for the room's acoustics and to provide the band with a rough idea of what they were sounding like. Although these recordings were never intended as anything other than demos, when the band re-entered the studio in early February 1992, Mendelsohn suggested that November's rehearsal recordings were good enough to release as they stood.

Robbie McIntosh recalled: "'Biker Like An Icon' was the first thing we recorded after Paul first played us the songs. All we were doing was getting sounds. We took about 15 minutes to learn the shape of it, then we just did it." McCartney often likes to record quickly, and this kind of spontaneity neatly dovetailed with his simplified recording ethos. As he said: "'Biker' [is] such a simple little song that you can ruin it if you go over it 50 times. ... We just did it and got lucky."

Unfortunately, the song suffers from a weak lyric, arrived at through wordplay. Linda had been talking about her preference for Leica and Nikon cameras, and somehow the words "I like a Nikon" became "biker like an icon". The narrative developed from there.

'Peace In The Neighbourhood' was recorded at November's rehearsals and remade later, but McCartney decided to use the rehearsal take, because it had "such a good feel that we couldn't improve on it, a beautiful slappin' sound on the drums, real R&B". Alluding to McCartney's immediate family and the wider community, this is a song about aspiration, racial harmony, and people's ability to rise above the struggles of day-to-day existence. Uniting the personal with the universal, McCartney created a utopian vision that echoes Lennon's earlier pleas for global harmony.

'Golden Earth Girl' was inspired by Linda. McCartney originally intended to give the song a lush orchestral arrangement but decided on a sparse band performance instead. The only concession to his intended orchestration was the addition of oboe and flute embellishments, scored by Carl Davis and played by Gordon Hunt and Susan Milan (an arrangement for string quartet would appear on 1999's *Working Classical*).

Explaining what inspired him, McCartney said: "This was very much composed as a vision of Linda: a gently tanned, blonde nature girl. I had this vision of someone living in a giant mossy nest – a really comfortable, snug environment. I could really imagine her living just like that, out in the open and enjoying the sights and sounds and smells of nature."

A tender ballad, 'Golden Earth Girl' combines his love for Linda with a love of nature. Echoing earlier songs that play with notions of oneness with nature to romanticise the couple's relationship, it's a visionary reworking of the classical myth of the birth of Venus, with Linda's metaphorical rebirth symbolic of beauty's emergence into the world. Unfortunately, McCartney's graceful melody is not matched by the lyric, an unexceptional piece of work that fails to match the passion of his emotions.

'The Lovers That Never Where' was apparently the first song McCartney and Elvis Costello completed from scratch. Unsure of how they should tackle their first joint composition, McCartney suggested they write something with Smokey Robinson in mind. This was the result. The duo recorded a demo at McCartney's London offices and then co-produced a version early in the *Flowers In The Dirt* sessions, which Paul rejected.

Wickens confirmed that the song had been recorded prior to the *Off The Ground* sessions. "'Lovers That Never Were' is a great song, I think. It was written by Paul and Elvis Costello before *Flowers In The Dirt* and there is a version recorded, but we re-cut it and it turned out great." The new version may have sounded great, but the original acoustic demo (since bootlegged), as ragged as it is, still has a certain unsophisticated charm that the final version lacks. In particular, McCartney's vocal has a raw, emotive quality that is absent from the completed master.

As work on the song progressed, the arrangement developed to include synthesisers and a heavy drum sound, which dominate the song. Blair Cunningham, however, found it difficult to meet McCartney's exacting standards. "It was a waltz and not working until Paul said, 'How about putting a 4/4 on top of this thing.' And that was so complicated, waltz and 4/4 at the same time. ... A real head twister, but it was such a groove. Made the song happen."

'Get Out Of My Way' was recorded live in the studio and features McIntosh's first attempt at his guitar solo. McCartney's only concession to studio artifice was to overdub a five-piece horn section. But attempting to create rock'n'roll in a sterile studio atmosphere isn't easy. To get rock'n'roll songs sounding authentic is, McCartney admitted, "difficult". But with its simple structure, minimal instrumentation, and driving bassline, 'Get Out Of My Way' successfully reworks rock'n'roll's fascination with girls and cars.

Simple and understated, 'Winedark Open Sea' covers similar ground to 'Golden Earth Girl', although its references to nature can be read as metaphors for timelessness and spirituality rather than rebirth. McCartney's audible direction to the band to "finish it now" confirms that, like the rest of the material recorded for *Off The Ground*, 'Winedark Open Sea' was recorded live in the studio and its lengthy coda probably the result of jamming.

If there's one thing McCartney is constantly criticised for, it's his lyrics. Conscious that the lyrics for 'C'Mon People' might be wanting, he enlisted poet Adrian Mitchell to come up with a few improvements. Mitchell's suggestion was to change "coming in" to "rushing in", which he thought better expressed the author's intentions.

An attempt to raise political awareness among his audience, 'C'Mon People' rails – in the nicest possible way – against the Thatcher–Reagan right-wing anti-society politics of the 1980s. Like 'Hope Of Deliverance', its theme is salvation – only this time it's gained through political rather than spiritual means. "If enough people get together and tell the politicians how we want the world to progress – and I think it is beginning to happen, by the way – then we can make a difference," said McCartney. 'C'Mon People' calls for positive individual activism to change the system,

OFF THE GROUND
PAUL McCARTNEY
SIDE 1 'Off The Ground', 'Looking For Changes', 'Hope Of Deliverance', 'Mistress And Maid', 'I Owe It All To You', 'Biker Like An Icon'.
SIDE 2 'Peace In The Neighbourhood', 'Golden Earth Girl', 'The Lovers That Never Where', 'Get Out Of My Way', 'Wine Dark Open Sea', 'C'Mon People', 'Cosmically Conscious'.
UK RELEASE February 2 1993; LP Parlophone PCSD 125; CD Parlophone CDPCSD 125; chart high No.5.
US RELEASE February 9 1993; CD Capitol CDP 7 80362 2; chart high No.17.

• **'Off The Ground'** (McCartney)
Paul McCartney (drums, percussion, vocals), Linda McCartney (backing vocals), Hamish Stuart (percussion, backing vocals), Robbie McIntosh (guitar, percussion), Paul 'Wix' Wickens (drum programming, backing vocals, synth bass, piano).
• **'Looking For Changes'** (McCartney)
Paul McCartney (bass, guitar, vocals), Linda McCartney (backing vocals), Hamish Stuart (guitar, backing vocals), Robbie McIntosh (guitar, backing vocals), Blair Cunningham (drums, backing vocals), Paul 'Wix' Wickens (clavinet, backing vocals).
• **'Mistress And Maid'** (McCartney, MacManus)
Paul McCartney (bass, guitar, percussion, vocals), Linda McCartney (percussion), Hamish Stuart (guitar, backing vocals), Robbie McIntosh (guitar), Blair Cunningham (drums), Paul 'Wix' Wickens (keyboards), Gordon Hunt (oboe), Susan Milan (flute), Frank Lloyd (horn), Colin Sheen (trombone), Paul Archibald (trumpet), Richard Martin (trumpet), Stephen Wick (tuba), Belinda Bunt (violin), Jonathan Evans-Jones (violin), Roger Garland (violin), Roy Gillard (violin), David Juntz (violin), Pauline Lowbury (violin), Brendan O'Reilly (violin), Maciej Rakowski (violin).
• **'I Owe It All To You'** (McCartney)
Paul McCartney (guitar, Mellotron, percussion, mouth percussion), Linda McCartney (celeste, clavinet, backing vocals), Hamish Stuart (bass, backing vocals), Robbie McIntosh (slide guitar), Blair Cunningham (drums, percussion), Paul 'Wix' Wickens (piano, percussion).
• **'Biker Like An Icon'** (McCartney)
Paul McCartney (guitar, percussion, vocals), Linda McCartney (keyboards), Hamish Stuart (bass, backing vocals), Robbie McIntosh (slide guitar), Blair Cunningham (drums), Paul 'Wix' Wickens (keyboards).
• **'Peace In The Neighbourhood'** (McCartney)
Paul McCartney (guitar, congas, vocals), Linda McCartney (percussion, backing vocals), Hamish Stuart (bass, backing vocals), Robbie McIntosh (guitar, backing vocals), Blair Cunningham (drums, percussion), Paul 'Wix' Wickens (piano, backing vocals), Keith Smith (concluding conversation), Eddie Klein (concluding conversation).
• **'Golden Earth Girl'** (McCartney)
Paul McCartney (piano, vocals), Linda McCartney (harmonium, backing vocals), Hamish Stuart (bass, backing vocals), Robbie McIntosh (guitar), Blair Cunningham (drums), Paul 'Wix' Wickens (keyboards, percussion), Gordon Hunt (oboe), Susan Milan (flute).
• **'The Lovers That Never Where'** (McCartney, MacManus)
Paul McCartney (bass, percussion, vocals), Linda McCartney (percussion, backing vocals), Hamish Stuart (guitar, percussion, vocals), Robbie McIntosh (guitar, mandolin, percussion), Blair Cunningham (drums, percussion), Paul 'Wix' Wickens (piano, Hammond organ, percussion).
• **'Get Out Of My Way'** (McCartney)
Paul McCartney ((bass, vocals), Linda McCartney (harmonium, train whistle, percussion), Hamish Stuart (guitar), Robbie McIntosh (guitar), Blair Cunningham (drums), Paul 'Wix' Wickens (piano), Frank Mead (alto saxophone), Nick Payne (baritone saxophone), Andy Hamilton (tenor saxophone), Nick Pentelow (tenor saxophone), Martin Drover (trumpet).
• **'Winedark Open Sea'** (McCartney)
Paul McCartney (Wurlitzer electric piano), Linda McCartney (harmonium), Hamish Stuart (guitar, backing vocals), Robbie McIntosh (guitar), Blair Cunningham (drums), Paul 'Wix' Wickens (synth bass, percussion).
• **'C'Mon People'** (McCartney)
Paul McCartney (guitar, piano, celeste, whistling, vocals), Linda McCartney (Moog), Hamish Stuart (bass, backing vocals), Robbie McIntosh (guitar), Blair Cunningham (drums, congas), Paul 'Wix' Wickens (synth strings, synth orchestra, congas), Irvine Arditti (violin), Alan Brind (violin), Benedict Cruft (violin), Miranda Fulleylove (violin), Roger Garland (violin), Roy Gillard (violin), Pauline Lowbury (violin), Rita Manning (violin), David Ogden (violin), Bernard Partridge (violin), Jonathan Rees (violin), Michael Rennie (violin), Celia Sheen (violin), Galina Solodchin (violin), Barry Wilde (violin), Donald Weekes (violin), Jeremy Wlliams (violin), David Woodcock (violin), Roger Chase (violin), Ken Essex (violin), Andrew Parker (violin), George Robertson (viola), Graeme Scott (viola), John Underwood (viola), Robert Bailey (viola), Paul Kegg (cello), Ben Kennard (cello), Anthony Pleeth (cello), Roger Smith (cello), Jonathan Williams (cello), Paul Cullington (bass), Chris Laurence (double-bass), Skaila Kanga (harp), Nicholas Busch (horn), Frank Lloyd (horn), Josephine Lively (oboe), Richard Morgan (oboe), Martin Parry (flute), Jane Pickles (flute), Guy Barker (trumpet), Derek Watkins (trumpet), Terence Emery (percussion), Tristan Fry (percussion).
• **'Cosmically Conscious'** (McCartney)
Paul McCartney (guitar, sitar, ocarina, vocals), Linda McCartney (harmonium), Hamish Stuart (bass, backing vocals), Robbie McIntosh (mandolin), Blair Cunningham (drums), Paul 'Wix' Wickens (piano).
All recorded at Hog-Hill Studio, East Sussex, England, except 'C/Mon People' also recorded at Abbey Road Studios, London, England. All produced by Paul McCartney and Julian Mendelsohn.

and it did so with cunning subversion. Who would suspect such an unassuming song of promulgating counterculture values?

The basic track was captured in one take at the end of a session called to an early close because of a broken tape machine. McCartney's intention was to return to the song at a later date, but as with many of the tracks on *Off The Ground*, the first take turned out to be the best. He thought that 'C'Mon People' had a distinct Beatle-like feel but felt it needed something to make it more of an anthem. George Martin wrote the orchestral arrangement and conducted the 43-piece orchestra at Abbey Road.

McCartney wrote 'Cosmically Conscious' in early 1968 in Rishikesh, India. While The Beatles recorded a large number of songs written during that Indian sojourn, most of which found their way onto the *White Album*, a number remained unreleased or unrecorded. This was one, and while it was written in the 1960s, its idealistic theme wasn't as out of place in the consumer-led 1990s as it may at first seem. The rejection of modernity, which appeared idealistic in the 1960s, was by the 1990s almost a necessity. Never had green issues been so strongly debated, and 'Cosmically Conscious' prefigured the green aphorism "act locally, think globally" by some 20 years.

McCartney's simple song of cosmic oneness neatly summarised his global mission and encapsulated the album's message in one short musical statement. A longer version of the song (4:40) was released on *Off The Ground The Complete Works* (see data below).

'C'MON PEOPLE' / 'I CAN'T IMAGINE'
PAUL McCARTNEY
UK RELEASE February 22 1993; Parlophone R 6338; CD single Parlophone CDR 6338 'C'Mon People', 'I Can't Imagine', 'Keep Coming Back To Love', 'Down To The River'; CD single Parlophone CDRS 6338 'C'Mon People', 'Deliverance', 'Deliverance' (Dub Mix); cassette single Parlophone TCR 6338 'C'Mon People', 'I Can't Imagine'; chart high No.41.
US RELEASE July 20 1993; Capitol S7-17489; CD single Capitol C2 7 15988 2 'C'Mon People', 'I Can't Imagine', 'Keep Coming Back To Love', 'Down To The River'; failed to chart.

• **'I Can't Imagine'** (McCartney)
Paul McCartney (bass, vocals), Linda McCartney (backing vocals), Hamish Stuart (guitar, backing vocals), Robbie McIntosh (guitar), Blair Cunningham (drums, percussion), Paul 'Wix' Wickens (keyboards).
• **'Keep Coming Back To Love'** (McCartney, Stuart)
Paul McCartney (piano, guitar, vocals), Linda McCartney (backing vocals), Hamish Stuart (bass, backing vocals), Robbie McIntosh (guitar), Blair Cunningham (drums, percussion), Paul 'Wix' Wickens (keyboards).
• **'Down To The River'** (McCartney)
Paul McCartney (guitar, harmonica, vocals), Linda McCartney (backing vocals), Hamish Stuart (bass, backing vocals), Robbie McIntosh (guitar), Blair Cunningham (drums, percussion), Paul 'Wix' Wickens (accordion).
All recorded at Hog-Hill Studio, East Sussex, England.
All produced by Paul McCartney and Julian Mendelsohn.

Off The Ground data

Packaged in a gatefold sleeve with a cover photograph by Clive Arrowsmith and collages by Eduardo Paolozzi, the vinyl edition of the album was issued with customised labels and an inner lyric sleeve. The CD was issued with a full-colour screen-printed label and 28-page booklet. To promote the album, Parlophone issued a boxed set of the CD and cassette.

Although McCartney's world tour was not designed to promote the album, coming in the wake of so much publicity, its mediocre chart success must have come as a disappointment.

Perhaps because sales were less than elephantine, various territories released limited variants of the album to boost sales. In Japan, Toshiba EMI included a bonus 3-inch CD, which included 'Kicked Around No More' and 'Long Leather Coat', while EMI in Germany released a double 24-track CD, *Off The Ground The Complete Works* (7243 8 28227 21).

As part of their promotional activities, Capitol pressed up limited-edition white vinyl 7-inch singles of 'Biker Like An Icon' (17,000), 'Off The Ground' (17,000), and 'Hope Of Deliverance' (22,000). 'Biker Like An Icon' was also scheduled to be issued in Britain as the third single from the album, but MPL decided against a commercial release as McCartney was out of the country and unable to promote the record.

Nevertheless, 300 copies of a promotional CD single (CDRDJ 6347) were pressed and distributed to radio stations to prolong the album's shelf-life.

'C'MON PEOPLE'

THE A-SIDE of this single had appeared on *Off The Ground*, but 'I Can't Imagine' finds McCartney returning to a favourite subject, love – or the prospect of a world without it. The song is a reaffirmation of his love for Linda, but is surprisingly uninspired. Perhaps if he had imagined what a world without love would really be like it would have turned out differently.

'Keep Coming Back To Love' suggests that there is little else other than love worth living for. All too often, McCartney appears transfixed by the subject, and this could easily qualify as his theme song. This time, however, the title came from Hamish Stuart, who co-wrote the song.

'Down To The River' first appeared in 1991 when McCartney performed it during his short European tour. Transferred to the studio, the song lost none of its charm, but although its naiveté recalls the kind of material he was writing in the early 1970s, it's little more than a cute, well-developed throwaway.

'C'Mon People' data

In Britain, Parlophone issued the single as a 7-inch, with generic die-cut labels, and as two CD singles: CDR 6338 in a Compac Plus sleeve and CDRS 6338 in a jewel case. A promotional CD single (CDRDJ 6338) featured the album version and a four-minute radio edit of the A-side.

In the USA, Capitol issued a four-track CD single and a limited edition white vinyl 7-inch (S7-17489). They also issued a two-track promotional CD single (DPRO-79743) with the same content as the British promo.

'BIKER LIKE AN ICON'

THIS was due to be the third single from Off The Ground but was not released. A promo single did appear. As well as the A-side, there were three outtakes from *Unplugged*.

'Things We Said Today' had previously appeared live on *Tripping The Live Fantastic*, but this stripped-down reading adds little to either the original or that concert version. Midnight Special had also been treated to a live version before, on *Off The Ground The Complete Works*, but it too is far from essential.

'Mean Woman Blues' was originally recorded by Elvis Presley for the soundtrack for his 1957 film, *Loving You*. It was later issued along with 'Blue Bayou' as a single by Roy Orbison and went to Number 5 in the US *Billboard* charts. McCartney opened his Unplugged set at Limehouse with 'Mean Woman Blues' and continued to open with it for several low-key shows he gave early in 1991.

'BIKER LIKE AN ICON', 'THINGS WE SAID TODAY', 'MIDNIGHT SPECIAL', 'MEAN WOMAN BLUES'
PAUL McCARTNEY
UNRELEASED promotional-only CD single Parlophone CDRDJ 6347.

- **'Things We Said Today'** (Lennon, McCartney)
- **'Midnight Special'** (trad arr McCartney)
- **'Mean Woman Blues'** (Demetrius)

All with Paul McCartney (guitar, vocals), Linda McCartney (keyboards, percussion, backing vocals), Hamish Stuart (bass, backing vocals), Robbie McIntosh (guitar, backing vocals), Paul 'Wix' Wickens (piano, accordion, shaker, backing vocals), Blair Cunningham (drums).
All recorded live at Limehouse Television Studios, Wembley, London, England; live recording and mixing by Geoff Emerick.

'OFF THE GROUND' / 'COSMICALLY CONSCIOUS'
PAUL McCARTNEY
US RELEASE April 6 1993; Capitol S7-17318; CD single Capitol 2 7 15966 2 'Off The Ground', 'Cosmically Conscious', 'Style Style', 'Sweet Sweet Memories', 'Soggy Noodle' released April 27 1993; cassette single Capitol 4KM-44924 'Off The Ground', 'Cosmically Conscious' released April 27 1993; failed to chart.

- **'Sweet Sweet Memories'** (McCartney)
Paul McCartney (bass, guitar, vocals), Linda McCartney (backing vocals), Hamish Stuart (guitar, backing vocals), Robbie McIntosh (guitar), Blair Cunningham (drums, percussion), Paul 'Wix' Wickens (keyboards).
- **'Style Style'** (McCartney)
Paul McCartney (bass, vocals), Linda McCartney (backing vocals), Hamish Stuart (guitar, backing vocals), Robbie McIntosh (guitar), Blair Cunningham (drums, percussion), Paul 'Wix' Wickens (keyboards).
- **'Soggy Noodle'** (McCartney)
Paul McCartney (guitar).

All recorded at Hog-Hill Studio, East Sussex, England.
All produced by Paul McCartney and Julian Mendelsohn.

'OFF THE GROUND'

A FURTHER single from the album, this offered the uncluttered, live sound of 'Sweet Sweet Memories', typical of the material recorded for *Off The Ground*. It's a mid-tempo rocker with a catchy chorus and rich vocal harmonies, but was nevertheless destined to remain a B-side.

Clocking in at six minutes, 'Style Style' is a song about a woman who relies on her style to make her way in the world. A perfunctory McCartney composition that suffers from a unresolved lyric and would have benefited from some judicious editing. 'Soggy Noodle' is a brief guitar doodle recorded by McCartney to introduce the *Off The Ground* video. At 28 seconds it's one of the shortest instrumentals he has issued – and one wonders why he bothered.

'Off The Ground' data

Capitol issued the isngle in the USA as a limited-edition white vinyl 7-inch and a five-track CD single. To promote it, they issued three one-track promotional CD singles that featured new mixes of 'Off The Ground'. The promotional CD singles were issued with identical covers but with stickers detailing which version of the song the disc featured. DPRO-79670 2 was issued with a 3:40 Bob Clearmountain Mix, DPRO-79783-2 with a 3:42 Keith Cohen Remix, and DPRO-79792-2 with a 3:35 AC Edit; Keith Cohen Remix. (A 5-inch CD single was issued in Japan, on ODEON TOCP-7942, with a 3:52 Keith Cohen Remix.)

PAUL IS LIVE

ANOTHER world tour, another live album. Hot on the heels of McCartney's 1989/'90 comeback tour, the '93 New World Tour took in Australia, New Zealand, the USA, Europe, and Britain. Having toured just three years earlier, McCartney changed large parts of his repertoire so as not to duplicate previous concert performances. Once again, he dug deep into The Beatles' oeuvre, with the result that his concerts and the live album included Beatles standards alongside more recent songs from *Off The Ground*.

The tour also saw the reinstatement of an acoustic segment, which was used to highlight old and new acoustic-based songs. (Although not included on this album, 'I Lost My Little Girl', which made its first appearance on *Unplugged*, was featured during the acoustic section at many concerts.)

Most of the album was recorded during the US leg of the tour, the bulk selected from recordings made in Boulder, Charlotte, and Kansas City. The mixing and selection process began in mid June 1993 when McCartney, along with his regular engineer Geoff Emerick, began to compile the album at Hog-Hill. With more concerts in the pipeline, work on the album was put on hold until October. Speaking in the October 1993 issue of *Q* magazine, he said he had listened to "ten shows, that's 320 songs. [I've] got to have it ready by the end of the week: EMI want it before Christmas". Although this gave the impression that the album was finished in a hurry, most of the work was completed long before October, probably sometime in mid to late summer 1993.

The album's title referred to the 'Paul is dead' rumours that circulated in the late 1960s suggesting that McCartney had died and been replaced by a mysterious doppelganger. Several clues that 'verified' the fact are supposed to appear in certain Beatles songs and album covers. Playing along with this fiction, McCartney decided to include some clues of his own that refuted the myth. On July 22 1993 he returned to Abbey Road with photographer Iain Macmillan. The idea was to photograph him on the now famous zebra crossing and, with the aid of technology, to drop in various elements from the original 1969 photograph. This turned out to be a little more difficult than originally planned, so instead, McCartney, his son's pet dog, and several new clues were dropped in to one of Macmillan's original photographs. The result was used for the album cover (and the unedited version of McCartney and dog on the crossing for the sampler promo CD).

Paul Is Live songs

McCartney conceived and completed 'Drive My Car' at John Lennon's house in Weybridge. His original lyric had the chorus: "I can give you golden rings, I can give you anything, baby I love you." Aware that the idea had been used twice before, he took the song to Lennon. Speaking to Matt Lauer on the *Today Show*, McCartney recalled how he and Lennon worked on the song. "It was kind of my song. But it was supposed to be something about golden rings, ... and things were just getting nowhere, you know? I can't remember what happened. But I somehow ... I got into this idea of a car. And it all got very tongue-in-cheek. It was sort of an LA actress starlet saying, 'You know, baby, you can drive my car.' So once that fun lyric kicked in, we were away."

In 1965, McCartney suggested that he and Lennon had been writing some 'comedy' songs, which they considered would be "the next thing after protest songs". 'Drive My Car' fell into this category: its ironic twist, which saw traditional gender roles reversed, provided the punch line. It was inspired, in part, by Otis Redding's reading of 'Respect', and the song's central motif, played in unison by bass and lead guitar, certainly gave the song an American soul feel, which McCartney termed 'plastic soul'. This aphorism, subtly altered, became the title of The Beatles' sixth album, and 'Drive My Car' appeared as its opening track. As with many other songs he drew from the Beatle catalogue, McCartney here reproduces the original arrangement note for note.

McCartney wrote 'All My Loving' as a piece of poetry, marking the first time he had written a complete lyric before putting it to music, and the group recorded it for *With The Beatles*. Inspired by his then girlfriend, Jane Asher, the song deals with their enforced separation due to a hectic tour schedule. Written while touring with Roy Orbison, the lyric came to McCartney while on the bus between gigs. The music was added when the touring entourage arrived at that night's venue. It's a light-hearted pop song that received so much airplay it became the lead song on their fourth EP. It was also chosen by the group to open their debut appearance on the US *Ed Sullivan Show*. Watched by an estimated audience of 73 million, the band's performance formed a seminal moment for millions of Americans – many of whom relived the moment when McCartney performed the song in concert some 29 years later.

'Robbie's Bit' was of course performed by Robbie McIntosh, a Chet Atkins-style instrumental played while the stage was being re-set for the acoustic segment of the concert.

The Beatles recorded 'Michelle' for their *Rubber Soul* LP. The song was originally little more than a fragment that sounded vaguely French and which McCartney used to busk at parties in the hope of appearing sophisticated. As with 'Drive My Car', 'Michelle' began life as a 'comedy' song that developed into something more serious. McCartney decided to include some French words in his lyric and had Jan Vaughan, a French teacher and wife of his school-friend Ivan, translate his lines "these are things that go together well". Vaughan has also suggested that it was she who came up with the couplet "Michelle, ma belle", which then encouraged McCartney to complete his lyric. The middle eight was suggested by Lennon. He was inspired by Nina Simone's 'I Put A Spell On You', which also used the phrase "I love you", and recommended that the emphasis should be placed on the word love. For the New World Tour, Paul 'Wix' Wickens added accordion to spice up the song's quasi-French feel.

McCartney had the idea for *Magical Mystery Tour* as a follow-up to *Sgt. Pepper's Lonely Hearts Club Band*, inspired by Ken Kesey's Marry Pranksters – a group of acid-heads who toured America in a psychedelic bus holding 'acid tests' and generally acting like counterculture rebels.

Made in the wake of Brian Epstein's death, *Magical Mystery Tour* took The Beatles' impromptu approach to songwriting, record-making, and film-making to new extremes. They made up much of the story as they went along, touring the country in a bus full of eccentrics and circus performers, searching for suitable locations that they hoped would fit their loose plot and fuel their imaginations. Shown in black-and-white on BBC television on December 26 1967 – and in colour on BBC-2 a few weeks later – the film was slated by the press and marked the group's first artistic failure.

Like the film, McCartney's theme song began life as little more than a fragment of an idea. Armed with the opening three chords and the first line of a lyric, he entered Abbey Road on April 25 1967 and attempted to wrap up the song with help from the other Beatles. A few key phrases emerged, but there was not enough to finish the words, which McCartney completed at a later date. For the New World Tour live performances, he rearranged the song and gave it an extended instrumental section.

McCartney mixed Beach Boys-like vocal harmonies with a distinctive bass riff for 'Paperback Writer', his attempt to reference the swinging sixties milieu of British writers, musicians, and artists who emerged from the regions and made their names in the capital. The song's genesis has since been disputed: one theory has McCartney inspired by helping John Dunbar catalogue the stock for his Indica bookshop, while others suggest that McCartney had been asked by one of his aunts if he could write a song that wasn't about love, and that the subject came to him after receiving a letter from an aspiring author. Either way, the song was

PAUL IS LIVE
PAUL McCARTNEY
SIDE 1 'Drive My Car', 'Let Me Roll It', 'Looking For Changes', 'Peace In The Neighbourhood', 'All My Loving', 'Robbie's Bit (Thanks Chet)'.
SIDE 2 'Good Rockin' Tonight', 'We Can Work It Out', 'Hope Of Deliverance', 'Michelle', 'Biker Like An Icon', 'Here There And Everywhere'.
SIDE 3 'Magical Mystery Tour', 'C'Mon People', 'Lady Madonna', 'Paperback Writer', 'Penny Lane', 'Live And Let Die'.
SIDE 4 'Kansas City', 'Welcome To The Soundcheck', 'Hotel In Benidorm', 'I Wanna Be Your Man', 'A Fine Day'.
UK RELEASE November 8 1993; LP Parlophone PCSD 147; CD Parlophone CDPCSD 147; chart high No.34.
US RELEASE November 16 1993; CD Parlophone CDP 8 27704 2; chart high No.78.

• **'Drive My Car'** (Lennon, McCartney)
Paul McCartney (bass, vocals), Linda McCartney (keyboards, backing vocals), Hamish Stuart (guitar, backing vocals), Robbie McIntosh (guitar, backing vocals), Blair Cunningham (drums), Paul 'Wix' Wickens (keyboards, backing vocals). Live recording at Arrowhead Stadium, Kansas City, KS, USA.
• **'All My Loving'** (Lennon, McCartney)
Paul McCartney (bass, vocals), Linda McCartney (backing vocals), Hamish Stuart (guitar, backing vocals), Robbie McIntosh (guitar, backing vocals), Blair Cunningham (drums), Paul 'Wix' Wickens (guitar, backing vocals).
Live recording at Giants Stadium, New York, NY, USA.
• **'Robbie's Bit (Thanks Chet)'** (McIntosh)
Robbie McIntosh (guitar). Live recording at Blockbuster Pavilion, Charlotte, VA, USA.
• **'Michelle'** (Lennon, McCartney)
Paul McCartney (guitar, vocals), Linda McCartney (percussion, backing vocals), Hamish Stuart (bass, backing vocals), Robbie McIntosh (guitar, backing vocals), Blair Cunningham (drums), Paul 'Wix' Wickens (accordion, backing vocals).
Live recording at Folsom Stadium, Boulder, CO, USA.
• **'Magical Mystery Tour'** (Lennon, McCartney)
Paul McCartney (piano, vocals), Linda McCartney (keyboards, backing vocals), Hamish Stuart (bass, backing vocals), Robbie McIntosh (guitar, backing vocals), Blair Cunningham (drums), Paul 'Wix' Wickens (keyboards, backing vocals).
Live recording at Paramatta Stadium, Sydney, Australia.
• **'Paperback Writer'** (Lennon, McCartney)
Personnel as 'Drive My Car'.
Live recording at Blockbuster Pavilion, Charlotte, VA, USA.
• **'Penny Lane'** (Lennon, McCartney)
Personnel as 'Drive My Car'.
Live recording at Folsom Stadium, Boulder, CO, USA.
• **'Welcome To The Soundcheck'** (McCartney)
Paul McCartney (vocals).
Recording location unknown.
• **'Hotel In Benidorm'** (McCartney)
Paul McCartney (bass, vocals), Linda McCartney (keyboards), Hamish Stuart (guitar), Robbie McIntosh (guitar), Blair Cunningham (drums), Paul 'Wix' Wickens (accordion).
Live recording at Folsom Stadium, Boulder, CO, USA.
• **'I Wanna Be Your Man'** (Lennon, McCartney)
Paul McCartney (guitar, vocals), Linda McCartney (keyboards, backing vocals), Hamish Stuart (bass, backing vocals), Robbie McIntosh (guitar, backing vocals), Blair Cunningham (drums), Paul 'Wix' Wickens (keyboards, backing vocals).
Live recording at Paramatta Stadium, Sydney, Australia.
• **'A Fine Day'** (McCartney)
Paul McCartney (bass, vocals), Linda McCartney (keyboards), Hamish Stuart (guitar, backing vocals), Robbie McIntosh (guitar), Blair Cunningham (drums), Paul 'Wix' Wickens (keyboards).
Live recording at Giants Stadium, New York, NY, USA.
All produced by Paul McCartney.

conceived while he was on the way to Lennon's house for one of their songwriting sessions. McCartney apparently liked the words "paperback writer" and weaved them into a song. Performing it on the 1993 tour, McCartney stuck with the original arrangement, complete with the less than serious "frère Jacques" backing vocals.

One of the finest songs Paul wrote while with The Beatles, 'Penny Lane' was also one of the highlights of the New World Tour. He wrote it late in 1966, although the song's theme emerged while Lennon and McCartney were writing material for *Rubber Soul*. Besides turning their hands to writing 'comedy' songs, they also considered writing about their childhood. Lennon's 'In My Life' was the first such song the group recorded, and it was he who suggested using Penny Lane, a street in Liverpool, as the subject for a song, although it was McCartney who used the idea. Lennon went on to write 'Strawberry Fields Forever' while filming *How I Won The War* in Spain, and this, coupled with 'Penny Lane', formed The Beatles' finest single.

The Beatles' backing track for 'Penny Lane' was constructed over several sessions and used numerous studio gimmicks. The distinctive piano sound consisted of approximately five different piano parts combined to create one super-piano. Although the song was not as problematic to record as Lennon's 'Strawberry Fields', it was certainly complex – and this caused a number of problems for McCartney during these later concert performances. While technology could replicate what had taken The Beatles and George Martin hours to create in a studio, it was the lyrics that caused him most trouble. During his appearance at the Palais Omnisports in Paris, he completely forgot the words and had to start the song from scratch.

On 'Welcome To The Soundcheck', crickets chirrup, helicopters buzz, and McCartney announces the 'Soundcheck' title. Presumably it had to be copyrighted for legal reasons, but musical content is nil. Next is 'Hotel In Benidorm', improvised at a soundcheck. Those performing it probably had more fun than those listening to it.

'I Wanna Be Your Man' is an early Lennon–McCartney composition that originally featured a vocal from Ringo Starr when it made its debut on *With The Beatles* in November 1963. The song was written while they toured Britain in 1963 and the pair finished it at a meeting with The Rolling Stones. Andrew Loog Oldham, the Stones' manager, had asked them if they had anything suitable for his new charges. 'I Wanna Be Your Man' was offered, accepted, and recorded by the Stones as their second single.

McCartney's 1993 version slows the tempo to give the song a bluesy feel, reminiscent of the Stones and Bo Diddley. The version on the album was recorded at a soundcheck in Sydney, Australia, but the song was also performed when the band appeared on MTV's *Up Close* programme and featured in some but not all shows on the tour.

'A Fine Day' is another improvised song: the band had to play something so the crew could check sound levels. A note on the sleeve warned that these improvised 'songs' "may not be suitable for people of a critical disposition". So why bother to include them?

Paul Is Live data

Parlophone issued the album as a two-record set with customised labels and printed inner sleeves. Parlophone and Capitol issued the CD with a miniature poster featuring a collage of photographs taken while on tour. To promote the album, Parlophone issued a five-song CD (PMLIVE 1), with 'Magical Mystery Tour', 'Biker Like An Icon', 'My Love', 'Paperback Writer', and 'Live And Let Die'.

STRAWBERRIES OCEANS SHIPS FOREST

THIS was conceived by McCartney as a remix project, realised by the producer Youth. To what extent McCartney was involved in making the album remains unclear. Although he provided new sounds and attended part of the remix session, the main work in constructing the tracks was undertaken by Youth and his team.

As McCartney explained: "I originally got in touch with Youth [to] ask him to do a couple of dance mixes from the *Off The Ground* project. The brief from me was that he should only use stuff from our recordings, because dance mixes often feature a kick-drum sample or a James Brown snare sound and, as a consequence, the record ends up sounding a bit like someone else's. So I told Youth that I'd prefer any sound he might select to come off our recordings, mainly using *Off The Ground*."

Youth, however, thought it inappropriate to remix any of the material in the way he had been briefed. Rather, he suggested sampling specific sounds from the multi-track tape, which would then be used to create a 'new' piece of music that, while consisting of elements from *Off The Ground*, would have little in common with the original album.

Before the remix was attempted, various tapes were reviewed at Hog-Hill and McCartney was asked to whisper a few phrases and to play some banjo, flute, and upright bass, which were sampled and incorporated into the new track. Samples were taken from vocal sections of 'Cosmically Conscious', a bass riff from one of the *Off The Ground* album tracks, and spoken passages from *Back To The Egg*. Then, over a four-day period, Youth brought the various elements together to create the final piece of music. The titles were arrived at on impulse, as Youth explained. "I wasn't really thinking too much about them. They came spontaneously – it was a full moon that night, so I was getting quite esoteric – 'Transpiritual Stomp' had a kind of pagan feel, I could imagine a caveman kicking up the dust to it, and 'Sunrise Mix' was the last one of the night, done as the sun came up over the horizon." Youth completed nine mixes, which he planned to edit down for a one-off 12-inch single. McCartney, however, was so impressed by the body of work that he decided to release all nine tracks as an album.

Strawberries Oceans Ships Forest was perhaps the album McCartney had long wanted to make. Spontaneous and conceptual, it combines elements that had intrigued him since the mid 1960s. An inveterate experimentalist, he had been producing tape loops – an early form of sampling – at the same time as his interest in avant-garde music-making developed. He attended avant-garde concerts and events in London and was influenced by Cornelius Cardew of AMM, by John Cage, and by Stockhausen. As his interest in the avant-garde grew, The Beatles were transformed from a rock'n'roll band into a complex experimental laboratory, where free play became the order of the day.

Interviewed by Classic *FM* magazine more recently, McCartney recalled his early experiments. "I was doing lots of these little crazy loops – I did a loop symphony – and then the loops would find their way onto 'Tomorrow Never Knows'. But the symphony was just for me and my mates getting stoned around the corner. I said to John, 'I've got all this stuff, and I'm thinking of putting it out as an album called *Paul McCartney Goes Too Far.*'"

Youth, however, had his doubts about releasing the material as an album. "I had slight reservations," he said, "because if I had known it was going to be an album I would have done them slightly differently. As a bunch of 12-inch mixes they're excellent, very spontaneous and, though I don't want to get bogged down in the dogma of conceptual music, they have a charming naiveté. But, to be honest, as an album it may fall a little short."

Youth was right. Any attempt to listen to the album in one sitting would be a mistake. Perhaps a better way to engage with the music is to select one or two tracks at random.

Despite Youth's reservations, McCartney was obviously pleased with the album, as he included extracts from it in the pre-concert tape played during his 1993 world tour. He was, nevertheless, pragmatic, and recognised that some might find the album difficult. Speaking in his *Club Sandwich* magazine, he said: "Not everyone will enjoy it, and I admit that your taste has to be in that direction for you to enjoy it, but I really like it as a record. I think it's a very interesting album."

He chose to release the album using a pseudonym, although careful inspection of the publisher credits and the fact that the album was issued by Parlophone gave some clues to the identity of the mysterious artist. The music is published by Juggler Music; the logo for Paul's company is a juggler; Juggler Music and Juggler Films are subdivisions of MPL; and Juggler Films released Linda's photo-film of The Grateful Dead.

Strawberries Oceans Ships Forest data

Parlophone issued the album in the UK as a two-record set on clear vinyl with customised 'Fireman' labels and white paper inner sleeves. Promotional copies of the LP (FIRE 1) were also pressed on clear vinyl with similar labels (red and green A-sides with white 'Fireman' logos and white B-sides with red or green text). Five-hundred promotional copies were made of the LP, with reversed covers with red text (front) and green text (back) on a white background. Each album was individually machine numbered on the back cover. Parlophone and Capitol (USA) issued the CD with the Fireman logo screen-printed in red on the disc and with a four-page booklet.

STRAWBERRIES OCEANS SHIPS FOREST
THE FIREMAN
SIDE 1 'Transpiritual Stomp', 'Trans Lunar Rising'.
SIDE 2 'Transcrystaline', 'Pure Trance'.
SIDE 3 'Arizona Light', 'Celtic Stomp'.
SIDE 4 'Strawberries Oceans Ships Forest', '4 4 4', 'Sunrise Mix'.
UK RELEASE November 15 1993; LP Parlophone PCSD 145; CD Parlophone CDPCSD 145; failed to chart.
US RELEASE February 22 1994; CD Capitol CDP 8 271672; failed to chart.

- **'Transpiritual Stomp'** (The Fireman)
- **'Trans Lunar Rising'** (The Fireman)
- **'Transcrystaline'** (The Fireman)
- **'Pure Trance'** (The Fireman)
- **'Arizona Light'** (The Fireman)
- **'Celtic Stomp'** (The Fireman)

All with Paul McCartney (whispering, banjo, flute, upright bass, vocals) Mrs Margary (recitation), Hamish Stuart (backing vocals), Paul 'Wix' Wickens (synth bass), Matt Austin (programming).
All produced by Youth.

'A LEAF'

ON COMPLETING the *Liverpool Oratorio*, McCartney said that his next classical project would take the form of solo piano pieces. He wrote the first of these, 'A Leaf', "in an attempt to write something that was as far away as possible from a large-scale choral work".

'A Leaf' was debuted at St James's Palace in London on March 23 1995. Anya Alexeyev, a Russian pianist who at the time of recording was a student at the Royal College Of Music, was chosen to perform it. She said of the piece: "It is lyrical and pensive, sometimes a bit sad and quite. As with any piece of music, you can interpret it differently." Indeed, 'A Leaf' later appeared with an orchestral setting on 1999's *Working Classical*. McCartney chose Alexeyev to play the piece as it was too complicated for him to perform in concert; proficient as he is, the piece was considered "technically tricky" and to require the skills of a concert pianist to bring out its subtle nuances.

'A LEAF'
ANYA ALEXEYEV
UK RELEASE April 24 1995; CD EMI Classics LEAF 1; cassette single EMI Classics TC LEAF 1; failed to chart.

- **'A Leaf'** (McCartney)
Anya Alexeyev (piano).
Recorded at St James's Palace, London, England.
Produced by John Fraser.

The version released on CD was recorded live at a charity concert, *An Evening With Paul McCartney And Friends*, held in aid of the Royal College Of Music and featuring McCartney, Elvis Costello, The Brodsky Quartet, singers Sally Burgess and Willard White, and Alexeyev. At the end of the concert, McCartney was awarded an honorary fellowship by the Royal College Of Music – their highest award – in "recognition of his remarkable talents".

Beatles Monthly reported that McCartney had a grand piano installed at his Hog-Hill studio and was considering recording the piece there with Alexeyev. If a studio recording exists, it has yet to surface.

ROCK AND ROLL CIRCUS

BACK in 1968, The Rolling Stones were looking for a way to promote their soon-to-be-released album *Beggar's Banquet*, and they hired Michael Lindsey-Hogg to make a one-hour television special to feature them and their friends. Lindsey-Hogg suggested that the film take the form of a travelling circus, but with pop stars in place of lion-tamers. Established acts and newcomers mixed with circus performers and a one-off supergroup fronted by John Lennon.

Rehearsals began on Tuesday December 10 at Stonebridge House, Wembley, north-west London before filming began the next day. The audience was admitted to the studio from the early afternoon, but Lennon didn't take to the stage until late in the evening. Speaking to John Peel on the night of December 11, Lennon suggested that he'd agreed to appear at the last moment. Stevie Winwood had cancelled abruptly and Jagger asked Lennon if he could fill the gap.

Forming The Dirty Mac, Lennon was backed by Eric Clapton on guitar, Keith Richards on bass, and Mitch Mitchell on drums, and they took to the stage at around 10:00pm, performing a blistering version of 'Yer Blues', not dissimilar to Lennon's version on Live Peace In Toronto, except it is a little tighter. Several takes later, it was Yoko Ono's turn. Backed by The Dirty Mac, she was joined by Ivry Gitlis on violin, and they jammed on a simple blues riff for 'Whole Lotta Yoko'. Ono gives her usual vocalisations and Gitlis scrapes away in the vain hope of keeping up with the band. While this kind of jamming could occasionally produce spectacular results, as on *Yoko Ono/Plastic Ono Band*, here it fails to impress.

The Stones eventually performed in the early hours of the morning of December 12, and although their performance was said to be one of their best, the film was scrapped. It's been suggested that they were unhappy with their performance and felt up-staged by The Who, who delivered a powerful reading of 'A Quick One (While He's Away)'.

Rock And Roll Circus data

Scheduled for release in 1995, the CD and video of the performances were put on hold until 1996. Issued by Mercury Records, the CDs were manufactured in America and imported into Britain. The album was not issued on vinyl. A DVD of the film was issued on October 12 2004 and featured bonus previously-unseen footage of the backstage meeting between Jagger and Lennon plus an alternative take of Lennon performing 'Yer Blues'.

'YOUNG BOY'

McCARTNEY spent much of 1994/'95 immersed in The Beatles' *Anthology* project. Reviewing tapes of his old band, he was surprised at how quickly and simply they recorded, and decided that his next album would be made in the same unfussy manner.

Intrigued by the renewed interest in his father's early work, McCartney's son James engaged in some archaeological digging himself, and while rifling through his parents' record collection

ROCK AND ROLL CIRCUS
VARIOUS ARTISTS
THE DIRTY MAC 'Yer Blues'; **YOKO ONO, IVY GITLIS & THE DIRTY MAC** 'Whole Lotta Yoko'.
UK RELEASE October 14 1996; CD Mercury 526 771-2; failed to chart.
US RELEASE October 15 1996; CD Mercury 8 21954 2; chart high No.92.

- **'Yer Blues'** (Lennon, McCartney)
John Lennon (vocals, guitar), Eric Clapton (guitar), Keith Richards (bass), Mitch Mitchell (drums). Recorded on Olympic Mobile Recording Truck at InterTel Television, London, England.
Produced by Jimmy Miller, Jody Klein, and Lenne Alink.
- **'Whole Lotta Yoko'** (Ono)
John Lennon (vocals, guitar), Yoko Ono (vocals), Ivy Gitlis (violin), Eric Clapton (guitar), Keith Richards (bass), Mitch Mitchell (drums).
Recorded on Olympic Mobile Recording Truck at InterTel Television, London, England.
Produced by Jimmy Miller, Jody Klein, and Lenne Alink.

discovered an album by Steve Miller, which his dad had contributed to. James's chance discovery led to McCartney re-establishing contact with Miller with the intention that he might play on "a few tunes". Miller obliged by inviting the McCartneys to his Idaho studio, where he and Paul recorded a number of songs, some of which would find their way onto 1997's *Flaming Pie*.

McCartney and Miller first met on May 9 1969 when both happened to be working at Olympic Studios in London. The Beatles were due to record there that night, but an argument about Allen Klein and Apple business matters erupted and the session broke up. Miller, who was recording in one of the adjacent rooms, got chatting to McCartney, who in an attempt to cheer himself up asked Miller if they could record something together.

That night, McCartney added drums, bass, guitar, and backing vocals to 'My Dark Hour'. The song appeared on Steve Miller's 1969 album *Brave New World* with McCartney credited as Paul Ramone – a name he'd first used when touring Scotland with The Beatles in support of Johnny Gentle. The two appeared to have little contact in the years that followed, but when they started recording again it was as if they had never been apart. To kick-start the partnership, McCartney and Miller played a number of standards before proper recording began.

McCartney wrote 'Young Boy' on August 18 1994 to a self-imposed deadline. It came to him while he was on Long Island, waiting for Linda to finish a cookery assignment with *The New York Times*. As he recalled: "I had taken my guitar and was sitting around in a nearby room when a song came up. I was thinking about all the young people I know, and remembering my early days." Originally titled 'Poor Boy', which he thought too derivative of early rock'n'roll, the title was changed to 'Young Boy', as he claimed this gave more scope to explore the song's theme, which centred around the "great questions" of life. It's an upbeat pop song with some decent playing from Steve Miller, amounting to a pleasant but unremarkable piece.

Miller was determined to get McCartney singing some Texas blues and arrived at the studio "with millions of little blues riffs". Working instinctively, the pair recorded 'Broomstick' at Hog-Hill on May 4 1995. Yet despite Miller's influence, this sounds like it was recorded on the banks of the Mersey rather than the Red River. And at just over five minutes, it would have benefited from an edit.

'Looking For You' was recorded at Hog-Hill in May 1995. Featuring Ringo Starr on drums and congas, it was recorded the same day they made 'Really Love You'. While working on The Beatles' *Anthology*, McCartney remembered how much fun he'd had recording with Ringo and asked the drummer if he'd like to play on his forthcoming album, which would become *Flaming Pie*. Starr contributed to three songs, 'Beautiful Night', 'Really Love You', and 'Looking For You'. Slightly more structured than 'Really Love You', 'Looking For You' is a very simple song with an instinctive arrangement and some fine dynamic interplay between McCartney and Starr.

'YOUNG BOY', 'LOOKING FOR YOU'
PAUL McCARTNEY
UK RELEASE April 28 1997; Parlophone RP 6462; CD single Parlophone CDRS 6462 'Young Boy', 'Looking For You', 'Oobu Joobu – Part 1' ('I Love This House'); CD single Parlophone CDR 6462 'Young Boy', 'Broomstick', 'Oobu Joobu – Part 2' ('Atlantic Ocean'); chart high No.19.

- **'Young Boy'** (McCartney)
Paul McCartney (bass, guitar, Hammond organ, drums, vocals), Steve Miller (guitar, backing vocals).
Recorded at Steve Miller's Studio, Sun Valley, ID, USA.
Produced by Paul McCartney.
- **'Broomstick'** (McCartney)
Paul McCartney (bass, guitar, organ, piano, drums, percussion, sound effects, vocals), Steve Miller (guitar).
Recorded at Hog-Hill Studio, East Sussex, England.
Produced by Paul McCartney.
- **'Looking For You'** (McCartney)
Paul McCartney (bass, organ, vocals), Ringo Starr (drums, congas), Jeff Lynne (guitars, backing vocals).
Recorded at Hog-Hill Studio, East Sussex, England.
Produced by Paul McCartney and Jeff Lynne.
- **'Oobu Joobu Theme'** (McCartney)
Paul McCartney (vocals, bass, guitar, drums), Linda McCartney (backing vocals).
Recorded at Hog-Hill Studio, East Sussex, England.
Produced by Paul McCartney.
- **'I Love This House'** (McCartney)
Paul McCartney (bass, guitar, vocals), David Foster (keyboards), Dave Mattacks (drums), Dave Gilmour guitar).
Recording location unknown.
Produced by David Foster.
- **'Atlantic Ocean'** (McCartney)
Paul McCartney (bass, guitar, keyboards, vocals), Phil Picket (keyboards), Louis Jarmin (percussion), Stuart Elliott (drums), Martin Barre (guitar).
Recorded at Hog-Hill Studio, East Sussex, England.
Produced by Phil Ramone.

A feature of all of the CD singles lifted from *Flaming Pie* was the specially recorded 'Oobu Joobu' segments. *Oobu Joobu*, a 15-part radio series consisting of one-hour programmes hosted by McCartney, was syndicated by the American Westwood One network. The shows featured unreleased McCartney material, some of his favourite records, a cookery corner featuring Linda, and occasional special guests. McCartney had been working on the idea since 1973, but nothing happened until 1981, when he met the show's producer, Eddy Pumer.

The *Oobu Joobu* title was inspired by French surrealist and playwright Alfred Jarry. One play in particular, *Ubu Cocu*, broadcast by the BBC in the mid 1960s, inspired McCartney to include Jarry's invented word 'pataphysical' in 'Maxwell's Silver

Hammer'. In 1973, McCartney recorded a six-minute version of the 'Oobu Joobu' theme, the first of many versions he attempted over the years.

Like all good radio programmes, the show had its own theme song. Forty-eight different versions of 'Oobu Joobu' were featured on the US radio series, but one particular version, recorded at Hog-Hill in February 1989, was used for all of the CD singles. It's a brief jingle, similar to 'Now Hear This Song Of Mine', the 'song' that Paul and Linda recorded to promote their *Ram* album.

As well as the theme, each CD single featured a different piece of unreleased music as part of the 'Oobu Joobu' segment. The first here was 'I Love This House', produced by David Foster in September 1984. Typical of mid 1980s pop, it has a big drum sound and lots of sequencers. A slightly different mix was featured in episode three of the *Oobu Joobu* radio series.

The second 'Oobu Joobu' segment here features 'Atlantic Ocean', recorded in March 1987 and broadcast in an edited form (1:35) in episode one of *Oobu Joobu*. Having little in the way of melody, the piece does little to engage the listener, but probably sounded fantastic played over a loud sound system. Before he issued the song, McCartney replaced his original vocal, which meant he had to remix the track. Various parts of the original instrumentation were removed for the released version, which was slightly shorter than the original 'rough mix'.

'Young Boy' data

Parlophone issued the single in Britain as a 7-inch picture disc, a first for McCartney, with a wraparound card sleeve and PVC cover (RP 6462). They also issued two CD singles: part one (CDRS 6462) was issued in a 'digipak' case with room for the second CD (CDR 6462), issued in a standard jewel case. Promotional copies of the single were issued in two formats: a one-track CD single (CDRDJ 6462) with a custom label featuring McCartney's flaming pie logo, and a limited 'Juke Box' single (RLH 6462) with black die-cut labels in a plain white sleeve.

FLAMING PIE

McCARTNEY released few records between the end of 1993 and early 1997, but he had been working on a number of long-term projects, which all came to fruition in the late 1990s. The Liverpool Institute for the Performing Arts was opened; he completed his *Oobu Joobu* series, which was broadcast on US radio; he completed work on his second large-scale classical piece, *Standing Stone*; and The Beatles' *Anthology* film and audio project was released to wide acclaim.

In the three years between *Off The Ground* and *Flaming Pie*, it had been the *Anthology* project that most preoccupied McCartney. Besides recording with the remaining Beatles, he spent many hours listening to tapes of stripped-down performances by the group, which influenced his approach to *Flaming Pie*.

"In looking at *Anthology*, I saw the standards that The Beatles had reached," he said. "Looking back at The Beatles' early material ... sort of surprised me. ... It's a long time ago – so it surprised me how simple and direct it was."

Although McCartney wasn't planning a new album – indeed he was informed by EMI that they didn't want a solo album from him for another two years – it was with this attitude in mind that his recordings took shape. At first, he felt slightly insulted by EMI's remark, but conceded that "it would be silly to [compete] against yourself in the form of The Beatles. So I fell in with the idea and thought, 'Great, I don't have to think about an album.'" In spite of this, he continued to write songs "just for the fun of it" and stockpiled recordings without a definite album in mind.

With no deadline to meet, McCartney was free to choose when and with whom he recorded. With no regular group – The Paul McCartney Band had by this time gone their separate ways – most of the recordings were solo affairs augmented with guest appearances. McCartney's son James made his recording début; Ringo Starr likewise made his first appearance on one of McCartney's solo records; and Steve Miller joined forces with McCartney for the first time in 26 years. Although the album had several producers, including George Martin, who was working with McCartney for the first time since 1984, it was Jeff Lynne, the ex-ELO frontman and part-time Traveling Wilbury, who co-produced eight of the album's 14 songs.

Lynne is a huge fan of The Beatles, and he made no attempt to hide the influence they had on his band, The Electric Light Orchestra, which was an attempt to carry on where The Beatles had left off. Unfortunately, Lynne tends to impose his musical traits on almost everyone he produces, with the consequence that everything ends up sounding like a second-rate ELO.

Lynne had become friends with George Harrison through Dave Edmunds, which led him to co-produce Harrison's *Cloud Nine* album and both Traveling Wilburys records. And it was Harrison who suggested Lynne as producer for The Beatles' 1995 reunion single, 'Free As A Bird', something that at first made McCartney apprehensive. "I had been a bit worried about working with him. As I said to him, 'A lot of people are wary of your sound.' George Martin remarked that 'Free As A Bird' was very Jeff Lynne."

McCartney was right to be wary, but once he overcame his initial reservations he found working with Lynne an enjoyable experience. Nevertheless, while Lynne helped co-produce the majority of *Flaming Pie*, McCartney decided to produce some of the songs himself, as he thought an album's worth of songs produced solely by Lynne would be "boring". Harrison later terminated his partnership with Lynne, stating: "I have stopped working with Jeff Lynne because I did not want him to make ELO albums out of my songs."

Like most of McCartney's solo work, *Flaming Pie* received

FLAMING PIE
PAUL McCARTNEY
SIDE 1 'The Song We Were Singing', 'The World Tonight', 'If You Wanna', 'Somedays', 'Young Boy', 'Calico Skies', 'Flaming Pie'.
SIDE 2 'Heaven On A Sunday', 'Used To Be Bad', 'Souvenir', 'Little Willow', 'Really Love You', 'Beautiful Night', 'Great Day'.
UK RELEASE May 5 1997; LP Parlophone PCSD 171; CD Parlophone CDPCSD 171; chart high No.1.
US RELEASE May 27 1997; LP Capitol C1 8 56500 1; CD Capitol 7243 8 56500 2 4; chart high No.2.

• **'The Song We Were Singing'** (McCartney)
Paul McCartney (bass, double bass, guitar, harmonium, drums, vocals), Jeff Lynne (guitar, keyboards, backing vocals).
• **'The World Tonight'** (McCartney)
Paul McCartney (bass, guitar, piano, drums, percussion, vocals), Jeff Lynne (guitar, keyboards, backing vocals).
• **'If You Wanna'** (McCartney)
Paul McCartney (bass, guitar, drums, vocals), Steve Miller (guitar, backing vocals).
• **'Somedays'** (McCartney)
Paul McCartney (bass, guitar, vocals), Keith Pascoe (violin), J ackie Hartley (violin), Rita Manning (violin), Peter Manning (violin), Christian Kampen (cello), Martin Loveday (cello), Peter Lale (violia), Levine Andrade (viola), Andy Findon (alto flute), Martin Parry (flute), Michael Cox (flute), Gary Kettel (percussion), Skaila Konga ((harp), Roy Carter (oboe, cor anglais), David Snell (conductor).
• **'Calico Skies'** (McCartney)
Paul McCartney (guitar, knee slap, percussion, vocals).
• **'Flaming Pie'** (McCartney)
Paul McCartney (bass, piano, guitar, drums, vocals), Jeff Lynne (guitar, backing vocals).
• **'Heaven On A Sunday'** (McCartney)
Paul McCartney (bass, guitar, Fender Rhodes electric piano, vibraphone, harpsichord, drums, percussion, vocals), Jeff Lynne (guitar, backing vocals), James McCartney (guitar), Linda McCartney (backing vocals), Michael Thompson (French horn), Richard Bissill (French horn), Richard Watkins (French horn), John Pigneguy (French horn).
• **'Used To Be Bad'** (McCartney)
Paul McCartney (bass, guitar, drums, vocals), Steve Miller (guitar, vocals).
• **'Souvenir'** (McCartney)
Paul McCartney (bass, guitar, piano, harpsichord, drums, vocals), Jeff Lynne (guitar, keyboards, vocals), Kevin Robinson (trumpet), Chris 'Snake' Davis (saxophone), Dave Bishop (baritone saxophone).
• **'Little Willow'** (McCartney)
Paul McCartney (bass, guitar, piano, harpsichord, Mellotron, percussion, vocals), Jeff Lynne (electric spinet, harpsichord, backing vocals).
• **'Really Love You'** (McCartney, Starkey)
Paul McCartney (bass, guitar, Wurlitzer electric piano, vocals), Jeff Lynne (guitar, backing vocals), Ringo Starr (drums).
• **'Beautiful Night'** (McCartney)
Paul McCartney (bass, guitar, piano, Wurlitzer electric piano, Hammond organ, percussion, vocals), Jeff Lynne (guitar, backing vocals), Ringo Starr (drums, percussion, backing vocals), Linda McCartney (backing vocals), John Barclay (trumpet), Andrew Crawley (trumpet), Mark Bennett (trumpet), Richard Edwards (trombone), Andy Fawbert (trombone), Michael Thompson (horn), Richard Watkins (horn), Nigel Black (horn), Marcia Crayford (violin), Adrian Levine (violin), Belinda Bunt (violin), Bernard Partridge (violin), Jackie Hartley (violin), Keith Pascoe (violin), David Woodcock (violin), Roger Garland (violin), Julian Tear (violin), Briony Shaw (violin), Rita Manning (violin), Jeremy Williams (violin), David Ogden (violin), Bogustav Kostecki (violin), Macej Rakowski (violin), Jonathan Rees (violin), Robert Smissen (viola), Stephen Tees (viola), Levine Andrade (viola), Philip Dukes (viola), Ivo Van Der Werff (viola), Graeme Scott (viola), Anthony Pleeth (cello), Stephen Orton (cello), Martin Loveday (cello), Robert Bailey (cello), Chris Laurance (double bass), Robin McGee (double bass), Susan Milan (flute), David Theodre (oboe).
• **'Great Day'** (McCartney)
Paul McCartney (guitar, leg slap, percussion, vocals), Linda McCartney (backing vocals).
All recorded at Hog-Hill Studio, East Sussex, England. except: 'Somedays' also at AIR Lyndhurst, London, England; 'Beautiful Night' also at Abbey Road Studios, London, England.
All produced by Jeff Lynne and Paul McCartney, except: 'If You Wanna', 'Somedays', 'Used to Be Bad' McCartney only; 'Calico Skies', 'Great Day' by McCartney and George Martin.

mixed reviews. Some thought it mediocre but an improvement on previous attempts. Others hated it (the London *Times* said it was "the sound of rock'n'roll with its teeth in a glass of water by the bedside") or loved it (*Q* said it was "the sound of a pop genius remembering that his primal gift is that of instinctive simplicity"). Despite all that, it became McCartney's most successful album for some time. It reached Number 1 in Britain and 2 in the USA, where it sold half a million copies in its first three days and became McCartney's 81st gold disc.

Flaming Pie is a strong, consistent album let down by the material that McCartney improvised with Ringo Starr. Its mix of charming ballads and rough-and-tumble rockers is the perfect antidote to a grey winter's day.

Flaming Pie songs

For McCartney, 'The Song We Were Singing' was an evocation of times spent in the 1960s relaxing with friends. A nostalgic view of that swinging decade, when anything seemed possible, his lyric suggests that there was a longing for something more lasting than fame and wealth. To help realise the song, he called on Jeff Lynne, who had just produced 'Free As A Bird', and fashioned the song around a demo he had made while on holiday in Jamaica.

An atmospheric ballad with good dynamics, 'The Song We Were Singing' is redolent of the acoustic work McCartney produced with Wings for *Back To The Egg*. He employs a simple but catchy chorus to counterpoint a wordy but melodically dry verse, and it's this clever juxtaposition that gives the song its appeal.

According to McCartney, 'The World Tonight', written while he was in America in August 1995, "started out folky". But Linda insisted that he play more electric guitar on the album, and the song developed a harder rock feel. Recording began on November 13 1995. McCartney provided the rhythm section, onto which he overdubbed his guitar parts and Lynne added keyboards, acoustic guitar – probably played in unison with McCartney – and harmony vocals. The result is a mid-tempo rocker with a tough guitar riff, and it has enough melodic twists to engage the listener.

McCartney was inspired by Prince to write 'If You Wanna' when he was in Minneapolis, and his ode to the road was an attempt at writing a simple pop song. He admitted that writing this kind of song could be difficult, and 'If You Wanna' proves his point: it's far too pedestrian. The song should have been driven hard, yet neither McCartney nor Steve Miller were in the mood to take it to the limit. As it is, it comes over as the musical equivalent of a Chinese meal, temporarily satisfying but ultimately lacking substance.

Another song written to an arbitrary deadline, 'Somedays' was written by McCartney on March 18 1994 while he accompanied Linda on a cookery assignment. Removed to the bedroom of his host's son, he was surrounded by football memorabilia, which influenced at least one line in the song. Nevertheless, he did admit that 'Somedays' was written with Linda in mind.

McCartney taped his guitar, bass, and vocal parts at Hog-Hill on November 1 1995, but 'Somedays' remained untouched until he asked George Martin if he could orchestrate the song. Martin considered it "a classic song. I think it's one of those simple ones, deceptively simple, that's so difficult to write". Enthused by the song, Martin wrote a string arrangement, conducted by David Snell at AIR Lyndhurst on June 10 1996.

Although most of *Flaming Pie* was recorded during 1995/'96, two songs, 'Calico Skies' and 'Great Day', had been recorded on February 22 1992 at Hog-Hill. He wrote 'Calico Skies' while stranded on Long Island and described it as "a love song that became a 1960s protest song, recorded in the vein of 'Blackbird', without drums or an arrangement". Reminiscent of both 'Mother Nature's Son' and 'Blackbird', 'Calico Skies' combines the optimism of the former with the fingerpicking folk stylings of the latter. Rejecting even a sympathetic string arrangement, McCartney's acoustic setting complements perfectly the song's aching beauty.

While the surviving Beatles were making the *Anthology* series, a dispute arose as to who actually gave the group its name. While he was out horse-riding, McCartney remembered a piece that John Lennon had written for *Mersey Beat* in 1961 on the origins of The Beatles. With Lennon's story in mind, McCartney responded by writing a series of apparently meaningless lines to a melody he had improvised the previous week with Jeff Lynne. As he explained: "I was … searching for a rhyme with 'sky': 'bye', 'cry', 'pie'. The story came back and I thought, 'Ooo, flaming pie.'" With his lyric in place, McCartney completed 'Flaming Pie' on February 27 1996. Keen to re-establish the kind of working practices adopted by The Beatles before they developed their mid-1960s studio tan, McCartney insisted that the song be recorded at breakneck speed and set a four-hour deadline for himself and Lynne to complete the task.

The last song written and recorded for the album was composed by McCartney while he was on holiday in America. 'Heaven On A Sunday' came to him while out sailing, something he'd taken up in recent years. The first line led to the idea that heaven, like the secular world, might be busy during the week but peaceful on a Sunday. Recording began on September 16 1996, again with Lynne co-producing, and the production turned out to be a real family affair. Linda made a rare appearance – she had been absent from Paul's records for some time – and added backing vocals, while son James made his debut, playing call-and-response guitar licks to his father's more mature phrases.

When McCartney visited Steve Miller's studio in Idaho he recorded several songs, but only 'Young Boy' made it onto the album. After the American meeting, he asked Miller over to his studio in Sussex, where they recorded several more songs in May 1995. One of the first they cut at Hog-Hill was the blues-influenced 'Broomstick', and it was one of two songs recorded the following day that made it onto the album. Recorded on May 5, 'I Used To Be Bad' evolved from a jam based on one of Miller's guitar riffs. Guitar and drums were recorded live before bass and guitar overdubs were added to the basic track.

The lyric was influenced by Miller who, McCartney recalled, "came up with some words, suggesting we use old blues lines like: 'I used to be bad but I don't have to be bad no more'". With the lyric complete, McCartney suggested they sing alternate lines, and to make the recording slightly more intimate share the same microphone. Maintaining this spirit of spontaneity, McCartney and Miller recorded their vocals in one take. Likewise, guitar overdubs were recorded quickly, something McCartney suggested Miller was not used to. "His roadie, Dallas Shue, said, 'Steve's very fussy about what guitar he uses – because he's got a huge collection of guitars – and it'd take a long time.'" Nevertheless, Miller was coerced into working quickly, and the duo recorded a second unreleased duet the same day.

'Souvenir' was recorded in the same way as 'Somedays'. In an attempt to recapture the atmosphere of his original demo – he'd written and demoed the song while on holiday in Jamaica – McCartney suggested to Lynne: "Let's take this demo but, instead of what we normally do, take all the information off and renew it and wreck it. Let's make sure that everything that's going on is at least as good and has the flavour of the demo."

McCartney's arrangement attempted to recreate the feel of 1960s soul records, with the intention of selling the song to a contemporary soul singer. "I'm looking forward, I hope, to an R&B singer doing it," he said. While it may have made a suitable vehicle for Otis Redding, it's hard to imagine many contemporary soul singers queuing up to interpret the song, and so far few have tried.

The scratchy effects and distorted vocal were achieved by recording McCartney's vocal onto a key-fob with a tiny sampler inside. It is perhaps the most elaborate production piece on the album, and McCartney even considered it possible single material – but changed his mind as he reckoned that "no one on earth would ever have chosen it as a single".

At one point, he decided he wanted to add some "heavy-ish guitars" to the track: "We had the amps belting in the studio," he recalled, "playing the guitars in the control room with long leads, and while the engineers were getting the sound we started vamping and found a few chords and some funky riffs. I started shouting a bit of a melody and so I asked the engineer to stick it on a DAT tape. We just jammed, but then I suggested we turn it into a song." The resulting melody became *Flaming Pie*.

Speaking to the London *Times* in April 1997, McCartney said: "Music has always been a consolation for me. When you get the teenage blues, the great remedy is to write a song." Immersing himself in songwriting had often provided catharsis: 'Let It Be', 'Too Many People', and 'Here Today' all acted as a release for emotions of one kind or another. "I do it all the time," he said. "Half of my songs are very much me doing therapy with myself, and half of them I'm just writing about Desmond and Molly." When Ringo Starr's first wife died, a close friend of the McCartneys, Paul turned to music once again.

'Little Willow' finds him attempting to express his feelings of loss, while writing with Maureen and Ringo's children in mind. "The morning I heard the news I couldn't think of anything else, so I wrote this to convey how much I thought of her. It's certainly heartfelt and I hope it'll help the kids. Instead of writing a letter, I wrote a song," he explained. the result is a sensitive ballad with a sympathetic arrangement, with McCartney playing most of the instruments himself, although Lynne added some keyboards and harmony vocals. McCartney took a break after recording 'Little Willow', recommencing work on the album in February 1996.

Coming off the back of recording new songs for The Beatles' *Anthology* project, McCartney was keen to do some more work with Ringo Starr. Recalling the reunion sessions, he said: "It was just such a laugh, that I said I was doing a new album and I'd love for him to drum on a couple of tracks." When Starr arrived at Hog-Hill on May 13 1996 to help record 'Beautiful Night', it marked his debut appearance on a solo McCartney album.

Having completed 'Beautiful Night', McCartney recorded another two songs with Starr. 'Looking For You' appeared on the B-side of 'Young Boy' while an impromptu jam, 'Really Love You', made it onto the album. "Once me and Ringo had done 'Beautiful Night', it wasn't enough. I'd had too much fun and I didn't want to stop," he explained. "So as he was here in the studio, playing great, I suggested that we did a jam together – and that became 'Really Love You'." Although McCartney's three-note bass riff appeared spontaneous, Starr recalled that before McCartney entered the studio, "he had a few ideas for a jam". Nevertheless, attempting to write something spontaneous and meaningful proved problematic. Although McCartney had established a practice of setting self-imposed deadlines in which to write songs, he hadn't attempted anything like his. "I had to fulfil the actor's worst dream, of being on stage but not knowing what play he's in – my version of this is that I have to sing words to a song that is being made up on the spot."

McCartney attempted 'Beautiful Night' with producer Phil Ramone in 1986, but while he liked the song he was unhappy with the recording. McCartney said he'd always liked the song. "People who heard an early recording that I made in New York, with some of Billy Joel's players, have said that they liked it too. But I always felt we hadn't quite pulled it off."

Before working on the song with Starr, he reworked it, adding a new coda and revising the lyrics. The pair recorded the basic track, Starr on drums and McCartney on piano and vocal, on their first day together. Backing vocals and Lynne's guitar and keyboard parts were added later. 'Beautiful Night' then remained untouched for nine months before George Martin orchestrated the song. The addition of a 38-piece orchestra, conducted by David Snell on February 14 1997, was the final piece of work done for the album before mixing and sequencing.

The oldest song on the album, 'Great Day' was written in early 1970. McCartney 'rediscovered' the song during a power cut that disrupted a family holiday on Long Island. With no power, the McCartneys were forced into making their own entertainment. Digging deep into his memory, McCartney pulled out a ballad that he and Linda used to perform "sitting around the table or when the kids were dancing". A song of hope that may have been sung as a simple act of celebration, 'Great Day' undoubtedly brought some light into the too-often dark days of the early 1970s.

Flaming Pie data

Despite CDs having eclipsed vinyl sales, McCartney insisted that the album be issued on vinyl. Parlophone and Capitol issued *Flaming Pie* with customised labels, printed inner sleeve, and gatefold cover. McCartney also had 200 white-label LPs pressed for distribution to business friends and celebrities. Manufactured by Masterdisc (032 597), these were issued with a signed letter and a custom sleeve featuring Paul's flaming pie logo. The CD was issued with a custom screen-printed label and 24-page booklet. In the USA, Capitol issued a promotional CD (CDP 8 56500 2) with a white label with 'Paul McCartney Flaming Pie Advance CD' printed top centre in black. The CD came in a white cardboard sleeve with a sticker detailing the track listing adhered to the front.

'THE WORLD TONIGHT'

'SQUID' was first broadcast in episode 13 of McCartney's *Oobu Joobu* radio series. A striking instrumental that mixes acoustic guitars, keyboards, and some snappy lead guitar work, it was edited for the radio and featured McCartney's statement, "Be a vegetarian," which was removed from this commercial release. It's a solo McCartney recording dating from December 1986.

McCartney wrote 'Don't Break The Promises' with Eric Stewart while working on 1986's *Press To Play*, but it remained unreleased until reworked by Graham Gouldman for 10CC's 1992 album, *Meanwhile*. McCartney's version was recorded at Hog-Hill in June 1988.

'The World Tonight' data

In Britain, Parlophone issued the single as a 7-inch picture disc with a wraparound card sleeve and PVC cover (RP 6472). Part one of the CD set (CDRS 6472) was issued in a digipak case with room for the second CD, which was issued in a standard jewel case. Both CD singles featured newly recorded 'Oobu Joobu' segments and previously unavailable songs. 'Oobu Joobu – Part 3' featured McCartney explaining how he wrote 'The World Tonight', while 'Part 4' found him speaking about his interest in reggae.

A one-track promotional CD single (CDRDJ 6472) was issued in a slim line jewel case with an orange flaming pie logo screen printed onto the front of the case.

In the USA, Capitol issued 'The World Tonight' as a two-track cassette single and three-track CD single.

'THE WORLD TONIGHT' / 'USED TO BE BAD'
PAUL McCARTNEY
UK RELEASE July 7 1997; Parlophone RP 6472; CD single Parlophone CDRS 6472 'The World Tonight', 'Used To Be Bad', 'Oobu Joobu – Part 3' ('Squid'); CD single Parlophone CDR 6472 'The World Tonight', 'Really Love You', 'Oobu Joobu – Part 4' ('Don't Break The Promise' [Solo Version]); chart high No.23.

'THE WORLD TONIGHT', 'LOOKING FOR YOU'
PAUL McCARTNEY
US RELEASE May 6 1997; cassette single Capitol 4KM-8 58650; CD single Capitol C2 8 58650 2 'The World Tonight', 'Looking For You', 'Oobu Joobu – Part 1'; chart high No.64.

- **'Squid'** (McCartney)

Personnel: Paul McCartney (keyboards, guitars, drum machine).

- **'Don't Break The Promises' (Solo Version)** (McCartney, Stewart)

Paul McCartney (bass, guitar, harmonium, vocals), Hamish Stuart (guitar, backing vocals).
Both recorded at Hog-Hill Studio, East Sussex, England.
Both produced by Paul McCartney.

STANDING STONE

RICHARD Lyttleton, president of EMI Classics, commissioned *Standing Stone* to help celebrate EMI's 100th year and its close ties with McCartney.

Having completed the *Liverpool Oratorio*, McCartney began thinking about his next large-scale classical project. Although he wrote it without a full-time collaborator, he employed a number of musicians to help him with the project. Initially, he began to compose themes on the piano, producing rough demo recordings that were then transcribed by Steve Lodder. He then used an Apple computer to transcribe his musical ideas onto paper. Although the computer helped, it also produced a few anomalies, some of which he explored and some of which he corrected.

"I was making a lot of very modern-sounding music," said McCartney. "But I started to enjoy some of the 'mistakes', realising that if I had thought them up then I would have rejected them. Since they happened by accident and sounded strong, I thought it would be an interesting way to write. I put in anything that was atonal, anything that was disturbing, but my natural inclination made sure that I underpinned it all with a melody."

McCartney's lack of experience in voicing instruments and the computer-generated aberrant notation was corrected with assistance from David Matthews, who worked on the first draft of his manuscript. Recalling his first impressions of the score, Matthews said: "I was impressed with his instinctive orchestral ability, his imagination; it wasn't an orchestral imagination, it wasn't rock music which was translated to orchestra, it was real orchestral music."

One thing that critics picked up on when reviewing the finished item was McCartney's primitivism – something the rock press had continuously chastised him for. However, on this occasion his ability to convey meaning succinctly was considered a positive attribute. It was only when the presence of his assistants became too obtrusive that critics felt the work "depersonalised" and disappointing.

While others may have found the transition from pop to classical daunting, McCartney refused to see barriers. "There is a thread going through it all," he said. "My interest began with the rock'n'roll people: Elvis, Little Richard, Buddy Holly, Chuck Berry. We moved on to composing our own songs with The Beatles, which developed when George Martin suggested putting a string quartet on 'Yesterday'. I helped him orchestrate it and realised I was getting into a different type of music. We put a French Horn solo on 'For No One' and a string arrangement for 'Eleanor Rigby', with no backing at all."

For McCartney, *Standing Stone* formed part of a musical evolution that began with 'Love Me Do'. "It's all an ongoing education for me, and it's fascinating," he said. "But I do have what I consider to be this primitive approach, to all my work. It's primitive because I don't quite know how it's done. Sure I know how to write a song, but I don't understand – and I don't want to understand – the process of magic that goes on; how it is that this song or this melody that previously wasn't in your head can suddenly come into your head."

He also called on the skills of saxophonist John Harle to help with the project. Harle advised him on a number of matters and suggested that certain motifs, which he thought had been disposed of too quickly, might be more fully developed. "John advised me on the structure of the piece," McCartney confirmed, "helping me shape the sketches I'd made. He also made sense out of the second movement's 'Lost at sea' section, translating what was on the computer into recognisable notation, and worked on the 'Trance' section in the third movement."

In addition, he called on the expertise of Richard Rodney Bennett, who oversaw the orchestration and highlighted certain weak areas which he felt could be improved. While McCartney had 35 years experience as a writer and performer of popular music, he nevertheless acknowledged that when it came to classical music he was a novice. However, Bennett's criticism still came as a shock. "I would often fax a section of music from my computer to [him]," McCartney recalled. "I'd send him one, thinking it was pretty good. A few minutes later I got a fax back with the word FEEBLE scribbled across it. I phoned him straight back and said, 'Richard, that's what my teacher wrote on essays.' You're a sensitive artist. If you don't like something, could you please write: 'That's a little below par.'"

McCartney was partly motivated to write *Standing Stone* by the death of his friend, Ivan Vaughan. Vaughan's death from Parkinson's disease moved him to express his feelings through poetry, which formed part of the narrative upon which *Standing Stone* was constructed (McCartney's poem is published in the booklet that accompanies both the CD and vinyl pressings).

To help structure the piece, he also tried to imagine how his distant ancestors might have experienced the world. Extending his narrative to take in Celtic myths and legends, he made paintings to help him visualise and structure the piece. Celtic myths and surrealism may sound like an odd combination, and *Standing Stone* is neither surrealistic in structure or Celtic in feel. Nevertheless, McCartney found inspiration there and transformed these influences into musical themes and motifs.

In parts, the narrative echoes that of the biblical creation, and McCartney's first movement, representative of the primeval chaos from which life first crawled, echoes Haydn's introduction for his oratorio, *The Creation*. Both composers create what amounts to a musical maelstrom that evokes the formlessness of the origins of life. Haydn created his soundscape by using shifting harmonies and tonal modulations; McCartney created his by divesting the orchestra of its artifice.

"So we've this void and this ball of fire, and we know nothing – we don't even know what fire is," McCartney explained. "I needed to find a sound for that. Something primitive. I needed to rob the players of all their expensive tuition. So for the first three minutes or so, we only hear open notes. No fingering. So we've got these open strings in divided cellos and basses, kind of rubbing up against each other, creating this really earthy rhythmic friction."

The emergence of man in the second movement recalls the creation of Adam, and it's at this point that McCartney asks the big question: what is the meaning of life? Although the eternal question is posed, no answer is given. Rather, the solitary figure begins a voyage of self-exploration that leads him to discover other people, the forces of evil, and to marvel at the wonders of nature – which provides salvation from foreign invaders – before the narrative leads to an optimistic climax.

McCartney had written *Standing Stone*'s climatic finale some years before began work on the piece. Representative of him at his most melodic, 'Celebration' exhibits his talent for melodic composition that works equally effectively in both pop and classical genres. The closing melody could quite easily have formed part of a 'classic' McCartney ballad, and yet it functions perfectly as a piece of contemporary classical music.

'Celebration' finds McCartney returning to favoured subject

STANDING STONE
PAUL McCARTNEY
SIDE 1 'Movement I: After heavy light years'.
SIDE 2 'Movement II: He awoke startled'.
SIDE 3 'Movement III: Subtle colours merged soft contours'.
SIDE 4 'Movement IV: Strings pluck, horns blow, drums beat'.
UK RELEASE October 6 1997; CD EMI Classics CDC 5564842; LP EMI Classics EL 5564841 released 1 December 1997; classical chart high No.1.
US RELEASE September 23 1997; CD EMI Classics 5564842; classical chart high No.1.

- **'Movement I: After heavy light years'** (McCartney)
- **'Movement II: He awoke startled'** (McCartney)
- **'Movement III: Subtle colours merged soft contours'** (McCartney)
- **'Movement IV: Strings pluck, horns blow, drums beat'** (McCartney)

All with London Symphony Orchestra and London Symphony Chorus, Janice Graham (leader), Stephen Westrop (chorus master), Lawrence Foster (conductor).
Recorded at Abbey Road Studios, London, England.
Produced by John Fraser, exclusively produced by Paul McCartney.

matter when it reveals that the central character's journey was a quest for love. Indeed, the elemental force of nature and a universalising theme, which McCartney constantly revisits, runs throughout *Standing Stone.*

As with the *Liverpool Oratorio*, test recordings were made for *Standing Stone*, this time at Abbey Road Studios, so McCartney could hear the completed work with a full orchestra. Until this point he had only the computer simulation as a reference. It also gave his assistants the opportunity to iron out any last-minute kinks, such as the problem John Fraser encountered when recording began at Abbey Road's Studio 1.

Working next door were Oasis, whose volume was so excessive that any recording soon became impossible. Fraser asked the band if the volume could be kept down, but Oasis were unrepentant and their reply was apparently, if unsurprisingly, not polite. Furious at being asked to turn down their amplifiers, the band stormed out of the studio, to much publicity and some considerable cost to EMI in lost studio fees.

Standing Stone is a very accessible work, full of melodic invention and strong ideas. However, it lacks the stylistic unity of *Liverpool Oratorio*, and McCartney tends to repeat ideas rather than develop them. *Standing Stone* isn't a classical masterpiece, but it's a powerful and at times moving piece of music.

Standing Stone data

Issued by EMI Classics, *Standing Stone* was lavishly packaged. The CD came with a custom label, based on Linda's cover photograph, a 48-page booklet (also used for the vinyl edition), and outer card cover. The two-record set was limited to 2,500 copies and issued as a deluxe boxed set with customised labels and printed inner sleeves. Although no singles were taken from the album, 'Celebration' was issued as a promotional single (PMC 2) to accompany the press pack for the album.

LENNON LEGEND – THE VERY BEST OF JOHN LENNON
JOHN LENNON
SIDE 1 'Imagine', 'Instant Karma!', 'Mother', 'Jealous Guy', 'Power To The People'.
SIDE 2 'Cold Turkey', 'Love', 'Mind Games', 'Whatever Gets You Through The Night', '#9 Dream'.
SIDE 3 'Stand By Me', '(Just Like) Starting Over', 'Woman', 'Beautiful Boy (Darling Boy)', 'Watching The Wheels'.
SIDE 4 'Nobody Told Me', 'Borrowed Time', 'Working Class Hero', 'Happy Xmas (War Is Over)', 'Give Peace A Chance'.
UK RELEASE October 27 1997; LP Parlophone 8 21954 1; CD Parlophone 8 21954 2; chart high No.4.
US RELEASE February 24 1998; CD Capitol 8 21954 2; LP Capitol 8 21954 1 released March 10 1988; chart high No.65.

LENNON LEGEND

THIS was a remastered and revamped version of 1982's *The John Lennon Collection*. As with that previous best-of, this overview of his solo career sold extremely well, due in part to a massive advertising campaign and careful remastering, which made this the best-sounding Lennon album issued so far.

Parlophone issued it as a two-record set in a gatefold cover with printed inner sleeves and black labels. The LP set was also issued in America by Parlophone with 'Made in U.S.A.' printed on the back cover.

The CD, manufactured by EMI, was issued with a ten-page booklet that included rare photographs taken during the recording of *Imagine*. 'Advance Listening' copies of the CD (CDPP 037) were issued prior to the official release date. The CD was re-promoted in 2003 with a new colourised outer sleeve and catalogue number (595 0672).

In Britain, the album was promoted with TV advertising, in-store displays, and billboard-size posters in major British cities and on the London Underground.

Parlophone issued two one-track promotional CD singles; 'Imagine' (IMAGINE 001), limited to 2,000 copies, and 'Happy Xmas (War Is Over)' (IMAGINE 002), issued in the run-up to Christmas. In Spain, the album was promoted with a one-track promo CD single of *God* (PE 98030).

'BEAUTIFUL NIGHT'

CUT FROM the same cloth as 'Only Love Remains', 'Same Love' was recorded at Hog-Hill with Hamish Stuart and Nicky Hopkins. When Stuart was interviewed for McCartney's *Club Sandwich* magazine in late 1988, he said that some 20 songs had been recorded for *Flowers In The Dirt*. Although 'Same Love' wasn't programmed for that album, it's a considered piece of writing too good to be hidden away as a bonus track on a CD single.

Love Come Tumbling Down was produced by Phil Ramone at Hog-Hill in March 1987 and featured some of the players who recorded 'Once Upon A Long Ago'. Coming off the back of *Press To Play*, another album of slick mid-tempo material may have seemed like the wrong kind of follow-up. Thus the proposed album was scrapped and this pleasant but uninspired McCartney ballad was resigned to the archive shelf.

'Love Mix' was issued as the main musical element of 'Oobu Joobu – Part 6', produced by Phil Ramone. Originally a solo Paul McCartney track, it was given a guitar overdub by Robbie McIntosh in April 1987.

An up-tempo track built around a simple keyboard motif, it had previously appeared in episode four of McCartney's US radio series, albeit in an edited form.

'BEAUTIFUL NIGHT' / 'SAME LOVE'
PAUL McCARTNEY
UK RELEASE December 15 1997; Parlophone RP 6489; CD single Parlophone CDRS 6489 'Beautiful Night', 'Love Come Tumbling Down', 'Oobu Joobu – Part 5' ('Beautiful Night' [Original Version]); CD single Parlophone CDR 6489 'Beautiful Night', 'Same Love', 'Oobu Joobu – Part 6' ('Love Mix'); chart high No.25.

• **'Same Love'** (McCartney)
Paul McCartney (vocals), Hamish Stuart (guitar), Nicky Hopkins (piano).
Recorded at Hog-Hill Studio, East Sussex, England.
Produced by Paul McCartney.
• **'Love Come Tumbling Down'** (McCartney)
Paul McCartney (vocals), Tim Renwick (guitar), Nick Glennie-Smith (keyboards), Charlie Morgan (drums).
Recorded at Hog-Hill Studio, East Sussex, England.
Produced by Paul McCartney and Phil Ramone.
• **'Love Mix'** (McCartney)
Paul McCartney (Yamaha DX7 bass, other keyboards, vocals), Robbie McIntosh (guitar).
Recorded at Hog-Hill Studio, East Sussex, England.
Produced by Paul McCartney and Phil Ramone.

Beautiful Night data

Parlophone issued the single as a 7-inch picture disc with a wraparound card sleeve and PVC cover (RP 6489) and two picture CD singles. Part one of the CD set (CDRS 6489) was issued in a 'digipak' case with room for the second CD, which was issued in a standard jewel case. Both CD singles featured newly recorded 'Oobu Joobu' segments and previously unavailable songs. A one-track promotional CD single (CDRDJ 6489) was issued in a slimline jewel case with the yellow flaming pie logo screen printed on the front of the case.

'A ROOM WITH A VIEW'

FOR HIS reading of Noël Coward's *A Room With A View*, McCartney went for authentic period feel rather than contemporary revision. He manages to capture the style and feel of Coward's original with the minimum of musical backing and without falling into ridiculous parody. Rather, he replicates Coward's unique, clipped vocal delivery with ironic, affectionate pleasure. McCartney's backing band, Ron & His Mood Men, is nothing more than a Mellotron, the same one used to record 'Strawberry Fields Forever', an instrument that McCartney appears to find both sleazy and hilarious. He also plays the stylistically authentic guitar solo.

RUSHES

THE SECOND low-key release by McCartney and Martin Glover (aka Youth) offered an equally opaque but more diverse musical experience than their first collaboration. Like the previous Fireman album, *Rushes* features over 70 minutes of ambient music. However, unlike its predecessor, which offered little more than a number of different mixes of the one basic track, this collection featured eight new McCartney compositions.

With Youth's assistance, he created a series of rich, sensual, hypnotic epics that far excel those on their previous album. Some of the compositions suggest a return to improvisation, and at least one track, 'Bison', sounds like it may have been assembled using the same 'subconscious' layering technique that produced some of the more ambient music that featured on *McCartney II*. His fondness for exploring the accident is evident throughout the album, and if nothing else this alone forms a nexus with earlier works, even the carefully structured *Standing Stone*.

The album was promoted with some bizarre press statements and events. A press release, of sorts, was issued to the media, but this consisted of little more than bizarre aphorisms. "The Fireman likes the sound of mud," read one part. *Club Sandwich* reported that McCartney had been recording mud at his Hog-Hill studio for the album, but this may have been more nonsense designed to intrigue. However, knowing McCartney's experimental nature, it might also be true. The most telling phrase in the release seemed to confirm that McCartney was responsible for playing everything on the album. "The Fireman plays it all; bass, water-colour, guitar, keyboards, cymbals."

McCartney gave an equally bizarre live webcast. Unrecognisable beneath a black ski mask, dark glasses, and floppy yellow rain-hat, he played live guitar and keyboards over pre-recorded backing tracks, which were remixed during the webcast by Youth. McCartney answered questions emailed in from fans – but he remained silent and had his oblique answers read by a

TWENTIETH CENTURY BLUES: THE SONGS OF NOËL COWARD
VARIOUS ARTISTS
Paul McCartney 'A Room With A View'.
UK RELEASED April 13 1998; CD EMI 494 6312; failed to chart.
US RELEASED November 16 1999; CD Ichiban KALA 6401; failed to chart.

• **'A Room With A View'** (Coward)
Paul McCartney (guitar, Mellotron, vocals). Recorded at Hog-Hill Studio, East Sussex, England.
Produced by Paul McCartney.

young girl. The album had its own website, which was as impenetrable as the press release and the webcast.

Rushes data

To publicise *Rushes*, two versions of a promotional single were manufactured. Three tracks, 'Fluid', Appletree Cinnabar Amber', and 'Bison', were chosen to represent the album and issued on both 12-inch and CD formats. 'Bison', which lasts a mere 2:40 on the album, was presented in its unedited glory at 7:55 on the CD single. The version issued on the 12-inch single is a 5:50 edit.

Two versions of the 12-inch single were issued in very limited numbers. Initial copies featured a special 3D label based on the Fireman logo and were issued with a giant poster featuring the same photograph of the naked girl that appeared on the album's inner sleeve. A second pressing was issued with blank white labels and a plain white paper sleeve. The promotional CD was issued with a bright yellow screen-printed label in a card sleeve featuring the naked-girl photograph.

Parlophone issued *Rushes* as a two-record set with customised labels and printed inner sleeves. The CD was issued with a bright red screen-printed label and a fold-out inner sleeve featuring a series of seemingly unrelated images.

RUSHES
THE FIREMAN
SIDE 1 'Watercolour Guitars', 'Palo Verde'.
SIDE 2 'Auraveda'.
SIDE 3 'Fluid', 'Appletree Cinnabar Amber'.
SIDE 4 'Bison', '7 am', 'Watercolour Rush'.
UK RELEASE September 21 1998; LP Parlophone/Hydra 4970551; CD Parlophone/Hydra 4970552; failed to chart.
US RELEASE October 20 1998; CD Hydra 4970552; failed to chart.

- **'Watercolour Guitars'** (The Fireman)
- **'Palo Verde'** (The Fireman)
- **'Auraveda'** (The Fireman)
- **'Fluid' (The Fireman)**
- **'Appletree Cinnabar Amber'** (The Fireman)
- **'Bison'** (The Fireman)
- **'7 am'** (The Fireman)
- **'Watercolour Rush'** (The Fireman)

All with Paul McCartney (bass, guitar, keyboards, Mellotron, cymbals), Linda McCartney (spoken word).
Recorded at Hog-Hill Studio, East Sussex, England.
Produced by Paul McCartney and Youth.

JOHN LENNON ANTHOLOGY

THE VOGUE for retrospective multi-disc boxed sets, often with unreleased material, hit its peak in the late 1990s. Some of the world's greatest musicians, as well as many minor players, had their careers reviewed and neatly packaged in well designed boxes, often with generous booklets stuffed with scholarly essays about the artist. John Lennon was the first and so far only ex-Beatle to have his entire solo career condensed and issued in a boxed set.

(George Harrison's later solo work would be reissued as a boxed set after his death, but, unlike the *Lennon Anthology*, *George Harrison: The Dark Horse Years* consisted of remastered solo albums with little in the way of unreleased material. The only real bonus was the inclusion of a DVD featuring rare footage.)

The *John Lennon Anthology* was issued in November 1998, but the idea had been around for almost a decade. The project began to take form when EMI acquired the master tapes that Lennon recorded in America while contracted to them. Although EMI had paid for Lennon's sessions, their London archives only held the stereo masters, not the multi-track tapes. However, in the late 1980s, EMI had 477 reels of Lennon studio outtakes shipped to Abbey Road for safekeeping.

At around the same time, Yoko Ono sanctioned what would become a long-running weekly radio programme, *The Lost Lennon Tapes*, syndicated by Westwood One, which featured unheard material from the Lennon archives. Perhaps aware that the programmes would be bootlegged, EMI and Ono agreed to produce a Lennon boxed set that would draw on the best material from *The Lost Lennon Tapes* and the recently acquired studio outtakes.

EMI's next move was to employ Beatles expert Mark Lewisohn to listen to everything that had been shipped from the USA and compile a proposed track listing for a CD boxed set. Between 1991 and 1993, Lewisohn set about compiling what he considered to be the best of the studio outtakes and demo recordings from Lennon's personal tape archive. Lewisohn completed his task in 1994, and then, for some unknown reason, the project ground to a halt.

Enter Rob Stevens, a New Yorker, who had worked on several projects with Ono. It was now Stevens' turn to trawl through the Lennon archive and compile his version of the boxed set. Having listened to everything, he selected about 50 hours of recordings, which he then began to present to Ono so that she could make the final selection. Stevens had one advantage over Lewisohn; he was a studio engineer. Unlike Lewisohn, whose job it was to compile the set, Stevens was also charged with restoring and mixing the tapes. Some of the recordings were cleaned using the Cedar system to remove tape hiss, while the multi-track tapes were mixed at Quad Recording Studios using a variety of vintage consoles.

Besides selecting which songs and takes to include in the boxed set, Ono sequenced the CDs. Stevens maintains that she put a lot of work into this part of the project, sequencing the discs many times until she was completely happy with them. Yet despite her hard work, several discs have anomalies. Disc 2, for example, which focuses on the 1971–73 period, features 'Real Love', recorded around 1979/'80, spoiling the continuity and narrative of the set.

The Stevens/Ono set differed from that complied by Lewisohn. Several songs, including outtakes of 'Cold Turkey', the home demo of 'Give Me Some Truth', 'Just Because' with Lennon greeting his old friends, Paul, George, and Ringo, and an early version of 'The Luck Of The Irish', all failed to make the set. Despite this, the *John Lennon Anthology* was packed with great performances and oodles of unreleased material. Ono noted that there was a lot of good material left off the set that may be issued in the future. "I found that there were many more takes and stuff that really were very presentable," she told *Beatles Monthly*. "In the beginning, I was thinking that this was going to be the ultimate John Lennon box. And I thought, no, we shouldn't call it the ultimate, because there's so much more there. There are still more beautiful songs, but I couldn't fit them all in there. It's possible that this is not the last presentation of John's work."

John Lennon Anthology songs

Much of the best-of material on this set has been dealt with elsewhere in this book, of course, and here we concentrate on the unreleased material it collected. First of these is 'Maggie Mae', famously ad-libbed during The Beatles' *Get Back* sessions. But it was a warm-up favourite that Lennon returned to while taping a batch of home demos for what would become *Double Fantasy*, and the song was obviously haunting him as he attempted this further casual reading.

While Lennon often found it difficult to remember his own lyrics, he had no trouble recalling those of other artists that he'd performed as a youth in Liverpool. 'Long Lost John', a traditional folk song given an up-tempo treatment by Lonnie Donegan, was probably based on the story of Long John Green, a convict with an amazing ability to outrun his pursuers. The version here was recorded during the *Plastic Ono Band* sessions, with Lennon, Starr, and Voormann giving a convincing, spontaneous performance that suggests they were all well acquainted with it. Lennon returned to the song while recording his vocal for 'I'm Losing You', ad-libbing it as the song fades.

Before he donated 'I'm The Greatest' to Ringo Starr, Lennon may have considered recording it himself. He began the song in late 1970. Having just finished his *Plastic Ono Band* album, Lennon recorded a brace of piano demos at his Tittenhurst home along with several new compositions destined for what would become his *Imagine* album. During sessions for that record, he attempted a studio demo of 'I'm The Greatest', the lyrics to which he either hadn't finished or couldn't remember. Once completed, 'I'm The Greatest' was both autobiographical and a statement of self-assurance. Knowing that if he issued the song himself it might be read as merely arrogant, Lennon offered it to Starr.

Starr was in Los Angeles working on his third and arguably best album, *Ringo*. It featured contributions from a raft of great musicians, including Lennon, McCartney, and George Harrison. By the time John and Yoko arrived to record 'I'm The Greatest', Harrison had already contributed to the *Ringo* sessions. Harrison happened to call the studio, to see how things were going, on the evening that Lennon and Starr were scheduled to record 'I'm The Greatest'. Lennon seized the opportunity to involve Harrison and told him to hightail it down to the studio to help finish the song. For the first time in three years, three of The Beatles found themselves in the same studio and recording together. Starr's reading of 'I'm The Greatest' was a tour de force and set the trend for future collaborations. Lennon's guide vocal was never intended to be released, but issued on this *Anthology* it reveals that he never gave less than 100 percent – even when he knew that his vocal would not be used.

The follow-up to Starr's *Ringo* album took its title from another Lennon composition written especially for the drummer. Lennon wrote 'Goodnight Vienna' (a Liverpudlian expression meaning "let's get out of here") and recorded this studio demo while producing Harry Nilsson's *Pussy Cats* album. Starr took the song away with him and recorded his version at Sunset Sound on August 6 1974, with Lennon adding piano. Issued as a single (Apple 1882) in the USA only it reached Number 29, becoming Starr's penultimate Top 30 *Billboard* hit.

'Yesterday' offers a brief parody of Paul McCartney's most successful song. Although it was of course written by and will forever be associated with McCartney, Lennon grew to accept the fact that, despite having nothing to do with its creation, he would also be associated with it. He often quipped that he'd be serenaded with 'Yesterday' when he entered restaurants or bars. Here it's performed just for laughs.

A favourite of Lennon's, 'Ain't She Sweet' was his first professionally recorded lead vocal. The Beatles' version was recorded in Hamburg, Germany, in June 1962. Issued at the height of Beatlemania, it made Number 29 in Britain and 19 on the US charts. At the time, The Beatles were none to happy at having something as old as 'Ain't She Sweet' issued as a single. But that's not to say that it didn't remain a favourite. While recording *Abbey Road*, The Beatles returned to the song, performing a ragged but authentic reading that paid homage to Gene Vincent's 1956 version, which had inspired them in the first place. Fast-forward five years, and Lennon returned to the song once again, this time with Nicky Hopkins on piano. Rough, ready, and played for laughs, the song sees Lennon hamming it up for the guys in the studio.

'Be My Baby' was written by Phil Spector with Jeff Barry and Ellie Greenwich as a showcase for Ronnie Bennett. Recorded by The Ronettes for Spector's Philles label, the majestic song screamed pop classic. From the moment the needle hit the vinyl, the much imitated drum intro and rich, echo-laden production ensured its greatness. A Top 5 hit in America and Britain, it marked the high point in The Ronettes' career. Although they would have several other hit singles, they would never again equal the success of 'Be My Baby'.

Spector's reworking of The Ronettes' greatest moment for Lennon's *Rock'N'Roll* sessions was every bit as grandiose as the original. Outtakes from the sessions reveal just how unfocused Lennon could be at that time. That Spector managed to coax acceptable vocals from him is a testament to his skill as a producer and of Lennon's ability to perform even when severely relaxed. The scale of wantonness during those sessions did little to ground Lennon and in all probability pushed him close to the edge.

His reading of 'Be My Baby' reveals just how alienated he'd become. Unlike the original, Lennon's version is a primal plea for forgiveness and redemption. It should come as no surprise that he decided to leave this track out from his *Rock'N'Roll* album – not because of any musical deficiencies, but because it exposes a fragile and fracturing psyche that he would rather forget. Lennon, however, had the strength of will to overcome his demons and Spector's eccentricities to emerge from the sessions a wiser and more sober person.

Inspired by Bob Dylan's conversion to Christianity, Lennon composed 'Serve Yourself'. It's a stinging parody that set out to answer Dylan's 'Gotta Serve Somebody', the sharpest and funniest song Lennon had written for years. He obviously enjoyed the song, as can be heard by the giggles from him and Ono at the end of the recording. Indeed, he had so much fun that he made several more demo recordings, but none caught the spirit and vitriol of this spontaneous take.

Lennon wrote 'Life Begins At 40' speculatively for Ringo Starr, who like Lennon was facing 40, but he never got further than the simple sketch presented here. But it's little more than a throwaway, and even Starr would have been hard pushed to make it sound convincing.

Although Lennon spent a good deal of his househusband period travelling, very few of the places he visited seem to have impressed him enough to write about them. Instead, he decided to compose a song inspired by a visit he made to India 12 years previously. The Beatles' visit to India, to study with the Maharishi, inspired many of the songs they recorded for the *White Album*. In fact, Lennon, McCartney, and Harrison wrote so many songs while in India that they were unable to include them all on that mammoth double album.

After the group split up, songs from that trip continued to turn up on solo albums by McCartney and Harrison, but Lennon appeared content to keep them private. What he intended to do with 'The Rishi Kesh Song' is unclear. There was no obvious place for it on *Double Fantasy* or *Milk and Honey*. However, he certainly seemed preoccupied with India. Besides writing the still unreleased 'India', a song that fused the melodies of 'Memories' and 'Serve Yourself' with a new set of lyrics, he also wrote 'The Maharishi Song' and made passing references to the country in 'The Great Wok', also included on this *Anthology*.

On 'Sean's Loud', Sean Lennon plays guitar, very badly and loudly. An intimate moment between father and son, it's charming but far from essential. 'Mr. Hyde's Gone (Don't Be Afraid)' is a home demo from 1980 that finds Lennon once again contemplating his self-image and relationship with Ono. However, this tired pastiche suggests that his talent for probing self-analysis had temporarily deserted him. Perhaps it was intended to answer Ono's equally tired 'Yes, I'm Your Angel'. Both songs share a similar musical style – and Mr. Hyde was a

JOHN LENNON ANTHOLOGY

JOHN LENNON

DISC 1 (Ascot) 'Working Class Hero', 'God', 'I Found Out', 'Hold On', 'Isolation', 'Love', 'Mother', 'Remember', 'Imagine' (Take 1), 'Fortunately', 'Well (Baby Please Don't Go)', 'Oh My Love', 'Jealous Guy', 'Maggie Mae', 'How Do You Sleep?', 'God Save Oz', 'Do The Oz', 'I Don't Want To Be A Soldier', 'Give Peace A Chance', 'Look At Me', 'Long Lost John'.

DISC 2 (New York City) 'New York City', 'Attica State' (Live), 'Imagine' (Live), 'Bring On The Lucie (Freda Peeple)', 'Woman Is The Nigger Of The World', 'Geraldo Rivera – One to One Concert', 'Woman Is The Nigger of The World' (Live), 'It's So Hard' (Live), 'Come Together' (Live), 'Happy Xmas (War Is Over)', 'Luck of the Irish' (Live), 'John Sinclair' (Live), 'The David Frost Show', 'Mind Games (I Promise)', 'Mind Games (Make Love, Not War)', 'One Day At A Time', 'I Know', 'I'm The Greatest', 'Goodnight Vienna', 'Jerry Lewis Telethon', 'A Kiss Is Just A Kiss', 'Real Love', 'You Are Here'.

DISC 3 (The Lost Weekend) 'What You Got', 'Nobody Loves You When You're Down And Out', 'Whatever Gets You Thru the Night' (Home), 'Whatever Gets You Thru the Night' (Studio), 'Yesterday (Parody)', 'Be-Bop-A-Lula', 'Rip It Up', 'Ready Teddy', 'Scared', 'Steel And Glass', 'Surprise, Surprise (Sweet Bird of Paradox)', 'Bless You', 'Going Down On Love', 'Move Over Ms. L', 'Ain't She Sweet', 'Slippin' And Slidin'', 'Peggy Sue', 'Bring It On Home To Me', 'Send Me Some Lovin'', 'Phil And John 1', 'Phil And John 2', 'Phil And John 3', 'When In Doubt, Fuck It', 'Be My Baby', 'Stranger's Room',

DISC 4 (Dakota) 'I'm Losing You', 'Sean's Little Help', 'Serve Yourself', 'My Life', 'Nobody Told Me', 'Life Begins At 40', 'I Don't Wanna Face It', 'Woman', 'Dear Yoko', 'Watching The Wheels', 'I'm Stepping Out', 'Borrowed Time', 'The Rishi Kesh Song', 'Sean's Loud', 'Beautiful Boy', 'Mr. Hyde's Gone (Don't Be Afraid)', 'Only You', 'Grow Old With Me', 'Dear John', 'The Great Wok', 'Mucho Mungo', 'Satire 1', 'Satire 2', 'Satire 3', 'Sean's In The Sky', 'It's Real'.

UK RELEASE November 2 1998; CD Capitol 830 6042; chart high No.62.

US RELEASE November 3 1998; CD Capitol C2 830 6042; chart high No.99.

fitting metaphor for Lennon's own split personality. Certainly, Lennon's self view could be read as opposing Ono's vision of herself as an angel. If Lennon did intend this as a companion to her song, even he had to laugh at his hackneyed, improvised clichés, which suggests that he was being less than serious when he committed this rough draft to tape. If it was intended to answer Ono, the picture it paints is too simplistic. Thankfully, Lennon had the good sense to drop the idea and leave the song in his personal tape archive.

Having written the title song for Starr's *Goodnight Vienna* album, Lennon suggested he record The Platters' 'Only You', and to help, he recorded a guide vocal. However, 'Only You', with Lennon's vocal in place of Starr's, almost didn't make it onto the *John Lennon Anthology*. The multi-track tape only came to light two days before the album was due to be mastered, which accounts, perhaps, for it being placed out of sequence on disc 4. The track was mixed, authorised by Ono, and minor adjustments made just hours before the mastering deadline.

Starr's version was issued by Apple as a single in 1974. A hit on both sides of the Atlantic, it reached Number 6 in the US charts but only 28 in his home country.

'Dear John' is an unfinished song that Lennon recorded at

- **'Maggie Mae'** (trad arr Lennon)
John Lennon (vocals, guitar). Recorded at The Dakota, New York City, NY, USA.
- **'Long Lost John'** (trad arr Lennon)
John Lennon (vocals, guitar), Klaus Voormann (bass), Ringo Starr (drums).
Recorded at Abbey Road Studios, London, England.
- **'I'm The Greatest'** (Lennon)
John Lennon (vocals, piano), George Harrison (guitar), Klaus Voormann (bass), Ringo Starr (drums).
Recorded at Sunset Sound, Los Angeles, CA, USA
- **'Goodnight Vienna'** (Lennon)
John Lennon (vocals, piano), Lon Van Eton (guitar), Jesse Ed Davis (guitar), Ringo Starr (drums).
Recorded at Record Plant West, Los Angeles, CA, USA.
- **'Yesterday'** (Lennon, McCartney)
John Lennon (vocals, guitar).
Recorded at Record Plant East, New York City, NY, USA.
- **'Ain't She Sweet'** (Yellen, Ager)
John Lennon (vocals, guitar), Nicky Hopkins (piano).
Recorded at Record Plant East, New York City.
- **'Be My Baby'** (Spector, Greenwich, Barry)
John Lennon (vocals), Art Munson (guitar), Ray Neapolitan (bass), Michael Omartian (keyboards), William Perkins (woodwind), William Perry (guitar), Mac Rebennack (keyboards), Louie Shelton (guitar), Phil Spector (piano, guitar), Nino Tempo (saxophone, keyboards), Anthony Terran (trumpet), Andy Thomas (piano), Michael Wofford (piano), Jim Horn (saxophone), Plas Johnson (saxophone), Joseph Kelson (horn), Jim Keltner (drums), Bobby Keys (saxophone), Ronald Kossajda (instrument unknown), Michael Lang (piano), Ronald Langinger (saxophone), Barry Mann (piano), Julian Matlock (clarinet), Michael Melvoin (piano), Donald Menza (saxophone), Dale Anderson (guitar), Jeff Barry (piano), Hal Baine (drums), Jim Calvert (instrument unknown), Conte Candoli (trumpet), Frank Capp (drums), Larry Carlton (guitar), Gene Cipriano (saxophone), David Cohen (guitar), Gary Coleman (percussion), Steve Cropper (guitar), Jesse Ed Davis (guitar), Alan Estes (percussion), Chuck Findley (trumpet), Steven Forman (percussion), Terry Gibbs (piano or percussion), Bob Glaub (bass), Jim Gordon (drums), Robert Hardaway (woodwind), Leon Russell (keyboards), Jose Feliciano (guitar), Michael Hazelwood (instrument unknown), Thomas Hensley (bass), Dick Hieronymus (instrument unknown).
Recorded at A&M Studios or Record Plant West, Los Angeles, CA, USA.
- **'Serve Yourself'** (Lennon)
John Lennon (vocals, guitar). Recorded at The Dakota.
- **'Life Begins At 40'** (Lennon)
John Lennon (vocals, guitar). Recorded at The Dakota.
- **'The Rishi Kesh Song'** (Lennon)
John Lennon (vocals, guitar). Recorded at The Dakota.
- **'Sean's Loud'**
John Lennon (spoken word), Sean Lennon (guitar).
Recorded at The Dakota.
- **'Mr. Hyde's Gone (Don't Be Afraid)'** (Lennon)
Personnel: John Lennon (vocals, piano). Recorded at The Dakota.
- **'Only You'** (Ram, Rand)
John Lennon (vocals, guitar), Steve Cropper (guitar), Jesse Ed Davis (guitar), Billy Preston (electric piano), Harry Nilsson (backing vocals), Ringo Starr (drums).
Recorded at Sunset Sound, Los Angeles, CA, USA.
- **'Dear John'** (Lennon)
John Lennon (vocals, guitar).
Recorded at The Dakota.
- **'Mucho Mungo'** (Lennon)
John Lennon (vocals, guitar).
Recorded at The Dakota.
- **'Satire 1/2/3'** (Lennon)
John Lennon (vocals, guitar).
Recorded at The Dakota.
- **'Sean's In The Sky'**
John Lennon, Yoko Ono, Sean Lennon (spoken word).
Recorded at The Dakota.
- **'It's Real'** (Lennon)
John Lennon (vocals, guitar). Recorded at The Dakota.

All produced by John Lennon, except: 'Long Lost John' produced by John & Yoko and Phil Spector; 'I'm The Greatest', 'Only You' produced by Richard Perry; 'Be My Baby' produced by Phil Spector/arranged by John Lennon and Phil Spector.

home some time in 1980, in effect a lazy rewrite of 'Hold On', which he'd written some ten years earlier. Like its predecessor, it finds Lennon reassuring himself. However, here he sounds tired and world-weary. Lacking either a chorus or middle eight, this is the most synoptic of sketches, and Lennon never returned to it.

Lennon wrote 'Mucho Mungo' with guitarist Jesse Ed Davis in mind but eventually gave it to Harry Nilsson, who, with the help of both Davis and Lennon, recorded it for his *Pussy Cats* album. A pleasant song, typical of the kind Lennon donated to his friends, it formed the first half of a medley with 'Mt. Elga', a Nilsson composition. Lennon had already made demo recordings of the song in 1973, so why he decided to make further home recordings three years after the event is unclear. Perhaps, like the 'satires' that follow, it was just for fun.

On the three 'Satire' pieces, Lennon pokes fun at his old pal, Bob Dylan. They're hardly essential listening and not even very funny, and so it's hard to imagine why these recordings were issued, or, indeed, what Dylan thought of them. On 'Sean's In The Sky' Lennon and Ono share the facts of life with an inquisitive Sean, while 'It's Real' has Lennon playing the guitar and whistling. That's all.

John Lennon Anthology data

The boxed set was promoted with a media blitz that included specially prepared videos, electronic press kits (EPKs), and a dedicated *Anthology* website. Launched on what would have been Lennon's 50th birthday, the site featured press releases, excerpts from Anthony DeCurtis's liner notes, audio and video clips, and photographs.

A lavish *Lennon Anthology* press pack was issued to the media. It consisted of a gatefold A4 presenter, two-track promo CD of I'm Losing You / Only You' (LENNON 001) in a slim-line jewel case, seven assorted colour and black-and-white 5-inch by 7-inch lustre-finish photographs (all printed on Kodak paper), two A4 pages of immediate release information (dated September 11 1998), one A4 page of immediate release information with more details on the boxed set (dated September 3 1998), ten A4 pages of introduction to the *Lennon Anthology* by Yoko Ono, seven A4 pages of a John Lennon mini biography by DeCurtis, and two A4 pages of immediate release information on the *Wonsaponatime* album (dated October 13 1998).

Ono recorded an interview that was issued as *Howtis* (DPRO-13515), a promotional CD that included an unedited version of 'I'm Losing You'. The interview was also filmed for use as an EPK. A second promotional CD, *Excerpts From John Lennon Anthology* (DPRO-13507), issued in early October 1998, featured 'I'm Losing You', 'Working Class Hero', 'God', 'How Do You Sleep', 'Imagine', 'Only You', and 'Sean's In The Sky'.

Finally, 'Happy Xmas (War Is Over)' and 'Be-Bop-A-Lula were issued as a promotional CD single (LENNON 002) to promote both the *John Lennon Anthology* and the *Wonsaponatime* album.

To promote the boxed set on television, Capitol produced a video of 'I'm Losing You' that featured Rick Nielson, Bun E. Carlos, and Tony Levin. Lennon was represented by his animated drawings that float through the video and interact with the musicians.

This onslaught of promotional activity had the desired effect. The *John Lennon Anthology* was certified gold in December 1998, having sold 125,000 copies in the USA (each set counted as four CDs making a total of 500,000 units). It also received critical acclaim: *Rolling Stone* voted it Boxed Set Of The Year. In Britain, sales were also strong, with the boxed set climbing to Number 62 in the charts, a remarkable feat for an expensive four-CD set. Originally issued in a 'cube' with the four CDs and booklet in digi-pack sleeves, the boxed set was repackaged in October 2004 in the more conventional 'long box' format.

WONSAPONATIME
JOHN LENNON
SIDE 1 'I'm Losing You', 'Working Class Hero', 'God', 'How Do You Sleep?'.
SIDE 2 'Imagine' (Take 1), 'Baby Please Don't Go', 'Oh My Love', 'God Save Oz', 'I Found Out'.
SIDE 3 'Woman Is The Nigger Of The World' (Live), 'A Kiss Is Just A Kiss (As Time Goes By)', 'Be-Bop-A-Lula', 'Rip It Up', 'Ready Teddy', 'What You Got', 'Nobody Loves You When You're Down And Out'.
SIDE 4 'I Don't Wanna Face It', 'Real Love', 'Only You', 'Grow Old With Me', 'Sean's In The Sky', 'Serve Yourself'.
UK RELEASE November 2 1998; CD Capitol CDP 4 97639 2; LP Capitol 497 6391 released January 18 1999; chart high No.76.
US RELEASE November 3 1998; CD Capitol CDP 4 97639 2; failed to chart.

WONSAPONATIME

A BEST-of of the *John Lennon Anthology*, this was issued for the casual listener rather than the committed fan. It was released as a two-record set and a single CD. The LP was issued with customised labels, printed inner sleeves, and gatefold cover. The CD came in a card digi-pack.

BAND ON THE RUN

THE 25TH anniversary of *Band On The Run* was marked by the release of a special edition double album, which consisted of the American version of the album (in other words, including 'Helen

Wheels') and a documentary disc that included both new and archive recordings.

Rarities, however, were few; only a remix of 'Helen Wheels' originated from 1973. Most of the new material originates from rehearsals for McCartney's world tours of 1989/'90 and 1993. Although they give a rare insight into what are normally closed sessions, they don't shed any new light on the original recording sessions.

When McCartney was refused entry into Japan in 1975, Wings had to cancel the Japanese leg of their world tour. He recorded an apology and performed a version of 'Bluebird' with Wings. The extract presented here is incomplete, but a slightly longer version, complete with apology, would be featured in the 2001 *Wingspan* documentary.

Band On The Run data

Parlophone issued *Band On The Run 25th Anniversary Edition* as a two-record set with customised labels, printed inner sleeves, and a gatefold cover. Parlophone and Capitol issued the CD with a mini version of the original poster and a 24-page booklet. In America, Capitol issued the documentary disc as a promotional CD (DPRO 7087 6 13558 2 6) with bonus tracks that have the between-song dialogue removed.

'FEEDBACK'
PAUL McCARTNEY
Unreleased heard only at video installation at Seigen, Germany in May 1999. Six monitor screens mounted in dark grey steel columns, each 174cm by 53cm by 39cm; video tape; blue light focussed on loudspeaker openings.

• **'Feedback'** (McCartney)
Recorded at Hog-Hill Studio, East Sussex, England.
Produced by Paul McCartney.

'FEEDBACK'

TO ACCOMPANY the exhibition of his paintings in Seigen, Germany, McCartney created a video installation specifically for the gallery environment. The result was 'Feedback', an audio-visual piece that linked his music and his fine art.

According to McCartney, the project began in the mid 1990s, when he recorded some guitar feedback purely for his own amusement. To this he decided to add the sound of a chainsaw. As

BAND ON THE RUN 25TH ANNIVERSARY EDITION
PAUL McCARTNEY AND WINGS
SIDE 1 'Band On The Run', 'Jet', 'Bluebird', 'Mrs Vandebilt', 'Let Me Roll It'.
SIDE 2 'Mamunia', 'No Words', 'Helen Wheels', 'Picasso's Last Words (Drink To Me)', 'Nineteen Hundred And Eighty Five'.
SIDE 3 'Paul McCartney' (Dialogue Intro), 'Band On The Run' (Nicely Toasted Mix), 'Band On The Run' (Original), 'Paul McCartney' (Dialogue Link 1), 'Band On The Run' (Barn Rehearsal, July 21 1989), 'Paul McCartney' (Dialogue Link 2), 'Mamunia' (Original, background), 'Denny Laine' (Dialogue), 'Mamunia' (Original, background), 'Linda McCartney' (Dialogue), 'Paul McCartney' (Dialogue Link 3), 'Bluebird' (Live Version, Australia 1975), 'Bluebird' (Original, background), 'Paul McCartney' (Dialogue Link 4), 'Paul McCartney' (Dialogue Link 5), 'No Words' (Original, background), 'Geoff Emerick' (Dialogue), 'Paul McCartney' (Dialogue Link 6), 'Tony Visconti' (Dialogue), 'Band On The Run' (Original, Illustration), 'Tony Visconti' (Dialogue), 'Jet' (Original from Picasso's Last Words, background)', 'Paul McCartney' (Dialogue Link 7), 'Jet' (Original from Picasso's Last Words, background)', 'Al Coury' (Dialogue), 'Jet' (Berlin Soundcheck, September 3 1993).
SIDE 4 'Paul McCartney' (Dialogue Link 8), 'Clive Arrowsmith' (Dialogue), 'Nineteen Hundred And Eighty Five' (Original, background), 'Paul McCartney' (Dialogue Link 9), 'James Coburn' (Dialogue), 'Paul McCartney' (Dialogue Link 10), 'John Conteh' (Dialogue), 'Mrs Vandebilt' (Original, background), 'Paul McCartney' (Dialogue Link 11), 'Kenny Lynch' (Dialogue), 'Let Me Roll It' (Cardington Rehearsal, February 5 1993), 'Paul McCartney' (Dialogue Link 12)', 'Paul McCartney (Dialogue Link 13)', 'Mrs Vandebilt' (background), 'Michael Parkinson' (Dialogue), 'Linda McCartney' (Band On The Run Photo Shoot, Dialogue), 'Michael Parkinson' (Dialogue), 'Helen Wheels' (Crazed), 'Paul McCartney' (Dialogue Link 14), 'Christopher Lee' (Dialogue), 'Band On The Run' (Strum Bit), 'Paul McCartney' (Dialogue Link 15), 'Clement Freud' (Dialogue), 'Picasso's Last Words' (Original, background), 'Paul McCartney' (Dialogue Link 16), 'Dustin Hoffman' (Dialogue), 'Picasso's Last Words' (Drink To Me, Acoustic Version), 'Band On The Run' (Nicely Toasted Mix), 'Paul McCartney' (Dialogue Link 17), 'Band On The Run' (Northern Comic Version).
UK RELEASE March 15 1999; CD Parlophone 4991762; LP Parlophone 4991761 released March 22 1999; chart high No.69.
US RELEASE March 15 1999; CD Capitol 4991762; LP Capitol 4991761; Billboard reissue chart high No.1.

• **'Bluebird' (Australia 1975)** (McCartney)
Paul McCartney (vocals), Linda McCartney (backing vocals), Denny Laine (guitar, backing vocals), Jimmy McCulloch (guitar), Joe English (backing vocals).
Recorded at unknown hotel room, Australia.
Produced by Paul McCartney.

he explained: "That was a coincidence … . Some days I would just go out into the studio and make music, and it would turn out according to my mood. It was like a journey in sound. On one of those days I'd been in the woods, cutting back the undergrowth to clear paths. I was using the chainsaw for this, and I thought it would be a good idea to record the noise it made, because it had a certain similarity with the music."

'Feedback' consisted of six similar but not identical sequences, and was never performed the same way twice, because the video monitors were started at random intervals. "These random events are like nature," he said, "where, for instance, there is never the same rainstorm twice." 'Feedback' wasn't a radical departure for McCartney, but did provide for an extension of his interest in avant-garde music, film, and performance.

CLEAN MACHINE

IN 1998, Linda sponsored the world's first vegetarian professional cycling team. When the team launched its own website, McCartney provided two versions of 'Clean Machine' exclusively for their home page. His dance track was an attempt to convey the team's green credentials in a concise musical statement. The combination of vegetarianism and an environmentally friendly mode of transport had, McCartney reasoned, produced a clean machine.

Typical of McCartney's remix projects, 'Clean Machine' owes more to house music than to the ambient trance of his Fireman project. Featuring a brief sample of The Beatles' 'Penny Lane', 'Clean Machine' was only the second time a sample of The Beatles' music had been sanctioned by Apple for use on another artist's recording; the first was for the Ferry Aid single. It was also the first time McCartney had made his music available on the internet.

'CLEAN MACHINE'
PAUL McCARTNEY
UNRELEASED web post only, on Linda McCartney Pro Cycling Team Home Page www.lindamccartney-pct.co.uk

• **'Clean Machine'** (McCartney)
Produced by Paul McCartney.

'FLUID'

McCARTNEY commissioned Nitin Sawhney to remix two songs from *Rushes* and again insisted that only musical elements he'd recorded should be used for the remix. At the time, Sawhney was living in a bedsit in London and working with a small computer to produce his music. Having received the material that he'd been asked to remix, he got a phone call saying that McCartney would like to visit and see how things were going. While at Sawhney's flat, McCartney recorded a new guitar part. As Sawhney recalled: "OK, I've got to record Paul McCartney in my room in my piddly little studio that doesn't really work that well. It was kind of set up for me, and that was it." Besides recording a new guitar part, McCartney also offered to play some sitar, which he recorded at Hog-Hill and sent to Sawhney a few days later.

'FLUID' (OUT OF BODY AND MIND MIX), 'FLUID' (OUT OF BODY MIX)' / 'FLUID (OUT OF BODY WITH SITAR MIX)', 'BISON'
THE FIREMAN
UK RELEASED September 6 1999; 12-inch Parlophone/Hydra HYDRA 12008; failed to chart.

• **'Fluid'** (The Fireman)
Paul McCartney (bass, guitar, sitar, keyboards, Mellotron, cymbals). Recorded at Hog-Hill Studio, Sussex.
Produced by Paul McCartney and Youth.

McCartney kept in touch with Sawhney and continues to mention him in interviews. "He's stayed quite a good friend, which is nice," said Sawhney. "He said some really nice stuff about me the other day, someone told me, on the Howard Stern show in America. He's been really supportive. He even came to my gig at the Royal Albert Hall four days after George Harrison died, which I was amazed by. He's a lovely bloke and he's always been really supportive."

'Fluid' data

Parlophone issued the 12-inch single with customised labels in a fold-out sleeve. They also issued a clear vinyl promotional CD single (HYPROCD008) in a slim-line jewel case.

RUN DEVIL RUN

McCARTNEY'S first proper album since Linda's death found him returning to his roots, again. Working with a select group of dyed-in-the-wool rockers, he created what many agreed was his most consistent and potent album for some time. Although he had recorded an album of similar material 12 years previously, *Run Devil Run* proved to be superior to its 1987 predecessor, *Choba B CCCP*, in almost every respect. Positive, touching, expressive, electrifying, motivated, and raw, *Run Devil Run* is the apogee of McCartney the rocker, and makes *Choba* sound lacklustre in comparison.

McCartney wanted to record the album to fulfil a project he had discussed with Linda and to complete it before the close of the 20th century. "This rock'n'roll album is something Linda wanted to do, wanted me to do," he recalled. Sadly, Linda wouldn't live to see the album completed.

After Linda's death in April 1998, McCartney understandably took some time out from the music business. "I had a year of doing nothing," he said. "Everyone said to me, 'You must keep busy.' I said, 'No, that's like denial.' I refused to get busy. I had a whole year of letting any emotion come sweeping over me. And it did."

Although he wrote a number of songs during this time, rather than record an album of grief-stricken ballads, McCartney revived this rock'n'roll project and returned to the songs of his youth. As well as recalling vivid memories of his adolescence, recording raucous rock'n'roll was a form of catharsis. Freed from the demands of being Paul McCartney, he indulged in raw music to escape the realities and traumas of his recent past.

Two concepts, spontaneity and authenticity, ensured that the album didn't get bogged down in detail and over-fussy production. To capture the primitive atmosphere of his favourite rock'n'roll recordings, McCartney returned to Abbey Road Studio 2, The Beatles' home from home, with a band of seasoned professionals. To ensure the songs sounded as fresh as the originals, he decided to record three or four songs a day. He said: "When I was thinking about how to record *Run Devil Run*, I was looking back over past recording sessions, and I think the sweetest and most productive [were from] the period when we didn't have the clout to be indulgent."

Forced to think on his feet, he gave himself over to instinct. "You had to just get in, and you had to do four songs a day. Right there, that's a panic, but it's a kind of good panic. It just focuses your mind right up, and there's like no way out, there's no escape." To avoid over-preparation, which would have stifled spontaneity, no one involved was given prior knowledge of what they were to record.

McCartney called on a number of musicians: some he knew (Dave Mattacks, David Gilmour, Mick Green); others he didn't (Geraint Watkins, Ian Paice). Gilmour and Green, two guitarists he much admired, were particularly apt choices, as their contrasting styles complemented one another perfectly. McCartney had approached Ringo Starr for the project, but he was unavailable due to touring commitments. Co-producer Chris Thomas recommended Paice, drummer with Deep Purple, and it's Paice who features on most of the album. Although the group was semi-fluid, a nucleus formed around McCartney, Gilmour, Green, Paice, and Pete Wingfield, a line-up that performed live regularly in support of the album both on television and at special one-off concerts, such as McCartney's memorable return to the rebuilt Cavern Club in Liverpool.

When it came to selecting material for the album, McCartney chose songs that meant something to him. Musical quality was only a secondary consideration. Armed with a cassette of his favourite rock'n'roll songs, he set about transcribing the lyrics, just as he had as a youngster. Even at this early stage, he found himself enthused by the songs. "I sat at home exactly as I had done when I was a teenager, listening to a new 45 I wanted to learn up," he said. "The only difference was that back then I'd be playing these records on a Dansette [vinyl disc player]; now I was playing them on a cassette. ... I thought, 'Wow, I love this! I haven't done this since I was 15.'" His enthusiasm continued when he moved to the studio, as Mick Green noted. "Paul was singing his bollocks off and playing bass as well. He sounds 18 years old."

Rather than over-familiarise himself with the original recordings, McCartney relied on decades-old memories to formulate the arrangements. And to ensure that the band worked spontaneously to their own 'head' arrangements, he kept rehearsals to a minimum. McCartney: "I'd pull out a song and say, 'Anybody know 'No Other Baby'?' ... 'No.' So I'd say, 'It goes like this,' and play it to the band for 15 minutes on an acoustic to show them the song. Then we'd split to our various instruments and would just do it." The sessions continued in this way, with McCartney pulling songs out of an envelope, playing them to the band, and recording them. Within a week, almost all of the songs that made it onto the album had been recorded.

Having not sung in over a year, and unfamiliar with the bass parts, McCartney entered Abbey Road Studio 2 on March 1 1999 in trepidation. Despite his nerves, he consoled himself with the fact that everyone else was in a similar situation. Mick Green confirmed that the first day's recording was a little stressful, but "from Tuesday afternoon it really started rockin'". Two songs recorded on day one, 'Coquette' and 'I Got Stung', made it on to the album. The first song they attempted, Charlie Gracie's 'Fabulous', failed to make *Run Devil Run* but turned up as a bonus track on the 'No Other Baby' single. Despite being the first song the band attempted, it has a suave confidence that hides any tensions that must have been in play while it was being cut.

Run Devil Run was considered a return to form that re-established McCartney's rock credentials. Always considered the balladeer, a stereotypical image he has both fostered and attempted to negate, in truth McCartney has never strayed far from his roots. On this occasion, the project was tinged with a sense of loss and melancholy but mixed with exuberance and joie de vivre. McCartney fused these emotional opposites to create a poignant roller-coaster ride that focuses on pleasure but never forgets the pain. Working with Chris Thomas for the first time since *Back To The Egg*, he created an authentic-sounding fireball of an album that managed to replicate the feel of 1950s rock'n'roll while sounding fresh and contemporary.

Run Devil Run songs

McCartney approached the album with the intention of making

the songs his own rather than faithfully replicating the originals. 'Blue Jean Bop', however, was the exception to the rule. "There were a couple of songs [where] I just wanted to stay faithful to the originals," he said, "because my memory of them was so clear and I loved them so much." Gene Vincent's 'Blue Jean Bop' was one such song where he chose to pay homage by faithfully reproducing Vincent's arrangement. He said the song and Vincent had always been favourites. "The first record I ever bought was 'Be-Bop-A-Lula'. We loved Gene."

The Beatles certainly were fans of Vincent's sweet, southern drawl and leather-clad image, and they met the American rocker while in Hamburg, Germany, and mimicked his visual style prior to their grooming by Brian Epstein. For four teenagers from Liverpool, meeting a 'star' of Vincent's standing was a magical moment that would stay with them for the rest of their lives.

Like any other teenagers obsessed with America, Lennon, McCartney, Harrison, and Best were as awed by their heroes as a later generation of teenagers would be by them. However, their encounter with Vincent and other stars quickly led to the realisation that these heroes were ordinary people just like them. But while they were closer to their heroes than others, as McCartney explained, "it [was] the magic drama they created in the music that was important, not the person".

Out of necessity, McCartney's new reading was even more skeletal than the original. "When we had two guitars in, it was too jangly and it didn't swing, so I was talking to Ian [Paice] and singing it to him with the echo on, just me on bass and him on drums." On to this minimal structure, Gilmour and Green suspended alternating solos; any less, and McCartney would have been performing the song a cappella.

"The last track we did was 'She Said Yeah'," recalled Green, "and I thought I knew that one too, but I didn't. So I was making mistakes, and the drummer started making mistakes as well. And as it was all live, we just had to keep doing take after take. But Paul was good: he just stopped everything and said, 'Look, guys, we can do this; we're all grown men and we will get it.' And we did."

Originally recorded by Larry Williams, 'She Said Yeah' was a song McCartney had intended to record for some time but had never got around to. The Beatles recorded several songs by Williams, including 'Slow Down' and 'Bad Boy', both featuring Lennon on lead vocals, but not 'She Said Yeah'.

Sounding nothing like The Beatles, but maintaining all the energy and drive that his former group had invested in their versions of Williams's pile-driving anthems, McCartney and band delivered a heavy-duty, overdriven reading of the seminal rocker. Precise and to the point, this is rock'n'roll with attitude.

Despite suggestions that *Run Devil Run* was recorded in one Monday-through-Friday period, further work took place at Abbey Road several weeks after the initial five-day session. Unable to attend these sessions, Paice and Wingfield were replaced by drummer Dave Mattacks and Welsh keyboard wizard Geraint Watkins. On May 4 they committed Presley's 'All Shook Up' to tape. Imbued with all the swagger of the original – and then some – plus a new riff, a pounding backbeat, and a powerful vocal, 'All Shook Up' was transformed into a quasi-heavy-metal monster. Imagine Led Zeppelin crossed with Rockpile.

As well as recording some of his favourite rock'n'roll songs, McCartney also recorded three of his own recent compositions. On day three, the band tackled 'Run Devil Run', a song inspired by a brand of bath salts that claimed to ward off evil. "I was looking in the shop window," recalled McCartney, "and I saw this bottle of bath salts called Run Devil Run. I thought that was a good title for a song."

Like many of his songs, McCartney wrote 'Run Devil Run' while on holiday. "I was actually out sailing when I did the verses," he explained. Combining the poetics of Chuck Berry with the voodooism of Screaming Jay Hawkins, he fashioned a blistering rocker, the likes of which he hadn't recorded since the 1960s. Rarely has he sounded so aggressive on record; all to often he appears unwilling to expose this side of his persona, deferring instead to a polished, lightweight substitute. When asked by Jim Irvin of *Mojo* if he channelled any anger into these recordings, McCartney replied: "That's just me singing. I don't know if I was angry or not, can't remember. ... It was just the spirit of the week."

Dickie Bishop & The Sidekicks originally recorded No Other Baby in the late 1950s. Written by Bishop, it was one of the earliest, if not *the* first rock'n'roll' song written by a British recording artist to be covered by an American: Bobby Helms. Previously, British rockers had produced inferior versions of American rock'n'roll. However, Bishop's song began a trend that would later reach it's peak with The Beatles. However, McCartney was inspired by an early cover version of the song by The Vipers, a group recording for Parlophone and produced by George Martin.

A fairly obscure British rockabilly record, it took on a deeper significance for McCartney in the shadow of Linda's death. Although he maintains that he never owned the record, nor could he remember who originally recorded the song or fathom how it got so deeply embedded in his memory, 'No Other Baby' had haunted him for some time. One of a number of songs he would call upon when indulging in his favourite musical pastime – jamming – this was not the first time he had attempted the song. He'd recorded a version for *Choba B CCCP*, but it was not issued, and had regularly performed the song at soundchecks during his 1993 New World Tour.

When McCartney came to record it for *Run Devil Run*, no one in the band had heard of it. McCartney's dark, broody handling of Bishop's original transforms it from a country-tinged ballad into a bleak requiem for his late wife. Evoking a sense of longing and loss, the relentless funereal backing produces a dark dynamic that oscillates between the two emotions that reflect McCartney's emotional frame of mind.

RUN DEVIL RUN
PAUL McCARTNEY
SIDE 1 'Blue Jean Bop', 'She Said Yeah', 'All Shock Up', 'Run Devil Run', 'No Other Baby', 'Lonesome Town', 'Try Not To Cry', 'Movie Magg'.
SIDE 2 'Brown Eyed Handsome Man', 'What It Is', 'Cocquette', 'I Got Stung', 'Honey Hush', 'Shake A Hand', 'Party'.
UK RELEASE October 4 1999; CD Parlophone 5223512; limited edition CD with bonus interview CD Parlophone 5233042; LP Parlophone 5223511 released October 10 1999; minidisc Parlophone 5223518 released December 6 1999; interview CD RDRINT 005; chart high No.12.
US RELEASE October 5 1999; CD Parlophone CDP 5223512; chart high No.27.

• **'Blue Jean Bop'** (Vincent, Levy)
Paul McCartney (bass, vocals), Mick Green (guitar), Dave Gilmour (guitar), Ian Paice (drums).
• **'She Said Yeah'** (Williams)
Paul McCartney (bass, vocals), Mick Green (guitar), Dave Gilmour (guitar) Pete Wingfield (piano), Ian Paice (drums).
• **'All Shook Up'** (Blackwell, Presley)
Paul McCartney (bass, vocals), Mick Green (guitar), Dave Gilmour (guitar, backing vocals), Geraint Watkins (piano), Dave Mattacks (drums).
• **'Run Devil Run'** (McCartney)
Paul McCartney (bass, vocals), Mick Green (guitar), Dave Gilmour (guitar, lap steel guitar), Pete Wingfield (piano), Ian Paice (drums).
• **'No Other Baby'** (Bishop, Watson)
Paul McCartney (bass, vocals), Mick Green (guitar), Dave Gilmour (guitar, backing vocals), Pete Wingfield (Hammond organ), Ian Paice (drums).
• **'Lonesome Town'** (Knight)
Paul McCartney (bass, vocals), Mick Green (guitar), Dave Gilmour (guitar, backing vocals), Pete Wingfield (piano), Geraint Watkins (piano), Ian Paice (drums), Dave Mattacks (percussion).
• **'Try Not To Cry'** (McCartney)
Paul McCartney (bass, vocals, percussion), Mick Green (guitar), Dave Gilmour (guitar), Geraint Watkins (piano), Dave Mattacks (drums, percussion).
• **'Movie Magg'** (Perkins)
Paul McCartney (bass, guitar, vocals), Mick Green (guitar), Dave Gilmour (guitar), Ian Paice (drums, percussion).
• **'Brown Eyed Handsome Man'** (Berry)
Paul McCartney (bass, guitar, percussion, vocals), Mick Green (guitar), Dave Gilmour (guitar), Pete Wingfield (piano), Chris Hall (accordion), Ian Paice (drums, percussion).
• **'What It Is'** (McCartney)
Paul McCartney (bass, guitar, vocals), Mick Green (guitar), Dave Gilmour (guitar), Pete Wingfield (piano), Ian Paice (drums).
• **'Cocquette'** (Green, Kahn, Lombardo)
Paul McCartney (bass, guitar, vocals), Mick Green (guitar), Dave Gilmour (guitar), Pete Wingfield (piano), Ian Paice (drums).
• **'I Got Stung'** (Schroeder, Hill)
Paul McCartney (bass, vocals), Mick Green (guitar), Dave Gilmour (guitar), Pete Wingfield (piano), Ian Paice (drums).
• **'Honey Hush'** (Turner)
Paul McCartney (bass, guitar, vocals), Mick Green (guitar), Dave Gilmour (guitar), Pete Wingfield (Wurlitzer electric piano), Ian Paice (drums).
• **'Shake A Hand'** (Morris)
Paul McCartney (bass, guitar, vocals), Mick Green (guitar), Dave Gilmour (guitar), Pete Wingfield (piano, Hammond organ), Ian Paice (drums).
• **'Party'** (Robinson)
Paul McCartney (bass, vocals), Mick Green (guitar), Dave Gilmour (guitar), Pete Wingfield (piano), Ian Paice (drums).
All recorded at Abbey Road Studios, London, England.
All produced by Chris Thomas and Paul McCartney.

On April 10 1999 the star-studded Concert For Linda took place at the Albert Hall in London. Throughout the evening, artists as diverse as Elvis Costello and George Michael performed songs written by McCartney, many of which had been inspired by Linda. For many in the audience this was an emotional event. Even more so for McCartney, of course, who originally declined to appear. But to the surprise of many, McCartney did take to the stage, to deliver three songs. Backed by The Pretenders and Elvis Costello, he performed 'All My Loving', 'Let It Be', and for the first time on stage 'Lonesome Town'. ('All My Loving' and 'Lonesome Town' where broadcast by BBC radio and television, who presented edited highlights from the concert.)

Ricky Nelson might not spring to mind when considering who or what influenced The Beatles. But Lennon, McCartney, and Harrison had eclectic tastes which took in country and western, rock'n'roll, and ballads from popular musicals of the day. One thing that distinguished them from other beat groups was a willingness to accommodate the kind of material that might appeal to the parents of their teenage audience, as well as to teenagers themselves. Nelson was a performer who, like Elvis Presley and Buddy Holly, blurred the boundaries between rock and pop. The clean-cut all-American boy was the antithesis of the leather-clad, hard rocking image The Beatles gravitated towards while in Hamburg.

But as McCartney explained: "I liked Ricky Nelson … 'Stood Up', 'Believe What You Say' … but I loved 'Lonesome Town'. It's like 'Heartbreak Hotel', it's a place we all know." Nelson recorded some fine rockabilly-influenced records, thanks to his guitarist, James Burton, who later played in Elvis Presley's band. Although he was no Pat Boone, Nelson had a teen/heartthrob image that often obscured his fondness for rock. Consequently, he tended to issue ballads as A-sides, while rockers were hidden away on the flips. 'Lonesome Town' was issued as an A-side in the USA by Imperial (5545) in September 1958.

Recording at Abbey Road a month prior to performing the song at the Albert Hall, McCartney had intended to base his interpretation on Nelson's original, as he thought he wouldn't be able to better it. He wanted to evoke a sense of loss and agony that Nelson's original only hints at. However, at the last moment he decided to move the vocal up an octave. This was fine until he hit the chorus, where he was forced to sing so high that it "sounded like Mickey Mouse".

To solve the problem, he called on Dave Gilmour to sing the melody, while he sang the harmony above it. "That was good, and that was exactly how we would work with The Beatles," said McCartney. "Someone would come up with a good idea, and you didn't take two weeks to go through the bureaucracy of whether it was a good idea. You just did it, and I like that." A favourite of both Paul and Linda's, Nelson's bittersweet ballad assumed even greater significance for McCartney in the wake of Linda's death. "For me," he said, "now it is more meaningful. It means more now than it ever meant before ... just because it does."

With hindsight, 'Try Not To Cry' appears as bittersweet as 'Lonesome Town' or 'No Other Baby'. However, McCartney maintained that "in writing and recording 'Try Not To Cry', it hadn't occurred to me that it actually is quite poignant". He wrote it as an exercise to see if he could write around the snare drum, and his simple autobiographical lyric was written without much concern for meaning while he searched for interesting sounds. As he explained: "Sounds like 'eee' aren't as good to sing as 'ahhhh', when you sing them. So words like 'night' are great to sing and 'me...ee' aren't. I was just going, 'try, try, cry, cry, high, high' when I was writing it, not so much looking for meaning of the words as their sound." Although the two other McCartney compositions had managed to capture something of the project's spirit, 'Try Not To Cry' sounds too contemporary and too much like a cast-off.

'Movie Magg' was apparently one of the first songs that Carl Perkins wrote, predating by some considerable time his most famous composition, 'Blue Suede Shoes'. A simple song about taking his girlfriend to the movies on the back of his mule, Becky, 'Movie Magg' recalls an era of innocent, simple pleasures, the antithesis of the urban American myth that rock'n'roll propagated. McCartney had fond memories of Perkins explaining the song to him, and so decided to record it as an homage. Despite the song's apparent simplicity, McCartney said that it was probably the most worked-on on the album.

Chuck Berry's 'Brown Eyed Handsome Man' had been covered by another of McCartney's heroes, Buddy Holly, and it was his version that he'd first encountered. However, McCartney's interpretation here owes more to Johnny Allen's cajun reworking of another of Berry's songs, 'Promised Land', than it does to either Holly's version or Berry's original. Rather than giving Berry's poetic narrative a sound thrashing, McCartney applies a swinging, accordion-led treatment to 'Brown Eyed Handsome Man' that is irresistibly self-assured.

McCartney wrote 'What It Is' while Linda was still alive, "with half an idea in the back of my mind that I might do this rock'n'roll album," he said. "I was playing bluesy riffs on the piano, and this song started to come out." Sounding less generic although no less 'authentic' than 'Run Devil Run', 'What It Is' is a love song inspired by a relationship so intense and secure that it fired McCartney for over 30 years and would continue to do so long after Linda's death. Moving from desire to loss, 'What It Is' sees him longing to express his feelings for Linda at a time when their future together was uncertain. If the song lacks romanticism and subtlety, its vigour more than compensates for any shortcomings.

For 'Cocquette', McCartney delivered a vocal rich with Fats Domino's vocal inflections. However, he felt it a little too close to parody for comfort. "We tried fixing little bits of it because I thought, 'God, this is too much like a pub singer,' but we ended up going back to the earliest mix. I just said, 'Oh sod it, we don't want to fix this, it just has a feeling.' That's the pub song – the Glasgow Saturday-night one! ... It's just me doing Fats, and I love it so much that I could not do it any other way."

If as Mick Green suggests things only started to jell on the second day, one only has to listen to 'I Got Stung' to realise how quickly and effectively things coalesced. For an ad-hoc, unrehearsed band they produced the kind of self-assuredness that normally only comes with years of interaction. Oozing with confidence, McCartney and co give Presley's 'I Got Stung' a rambunctious reading. Stripping the song of its inoffensive light-heartedness, they transform it into an unabashed angst-driven powerhouse. Compared with his previous attempts at transcribing Presley's material, this reading crackles with energy. Post-Army Presley had never fired The Beatles in the way his earlier material had. Nevertheless, inspired by the song's intro, McCartney decided the time was right to pay it a visit.

Fuelled by his new-found enthusiasm and recalling the curative effects of Presley's primitive rock'n'roll, McCartney combined subtle elements of Presley's much-parodied vocal style with that of his hero Little Richard. Driven by Ian Paice's thunderous drumming and Green and Gilmour's chain-saw guitars, this band of middle-aged men sound like a group of teenagers. Presley rarely packed so much energy into a performance, and McCartney has only occasionally sounded so unrestrained.

In keeping with the spirit that infused the album, McCartney recorded an electrifying version of Big Joe Turner's 'Honey Hush'. "When we were making this album, I came in one morning a little tired and confused," he confessed, "and did this one just to blow all the cobwebs away."

Mick Green was assigned the role of lead guitarist, as he had recorded the song with his band The Pirates for their album *A Fist*

Full Of Doubloons. Yet because of the speed with which they were working, he had problems recalling the song's more intricate nuances. "Well, you think you know, don't you?" he said. "Until you suddenly remember there's a middle eight and its got a different verse there and another bit here."

'Honey Hush' was written by Turner but radically rearranged by Johnny Burnette for his debut album. Although McCartney was familiar with both recordings, he opted for Burnette's arrangement, which was ideally suited to Green's distinctive rhythm-and-lead style. But McCartney had trouble transcribing the lyric through Burnette's distinctive rockabilly 'hiccup'.

"It was one of those songs that I hadn't been able to get all the lines down when I was writing out the lyrics at home, I just couldn't figure out the lyric on one line," he explained. "So I thought I'd just write it down phonetically and find a lyric sheet later, when we went to record. But I never got the lyric sheet, I never found out the real words. So when we were recording it, I thought I'd sing it phonetically. The real lyrics are nothing like what I sing, but it was the spirit of the album not to even care what the lyric was."

McCartney's delight in performing the politically-incorrect lyric was unabashed, as he recalled. "It's my favourite on the whole album to sing. For some reason, it's just lovely to sing that song." Similarly, the band's enthusiasm is obvious, and the song quickly became a staple of their brief and rare live performances.

'Shake A Hand' was an obscure B-side recorded by Little Richard, but it had made such an impression on McCartney that even 30 years after having heard the original he felt compelled to record it. He said: "I have this image of being in Hamburg, and there was one bar we used to go to. ... And that was the only place I ever heard 'Shake A Hand'."

That he should want to revisit this obscure flip-side makes perfect sense. The Beatles learnt and perfected their trade in Hamburg, and without the long hours spent finding out how to 'mach schau', it's probably fair to say that they wouldn't have matured as musicians as quickly or in the way they did. Performing in Hamburg was a pivotal moment in their career, and despite the deprivations they experienced there, the city obviously fostered powerful memories. That both McCartney and Lennon should choose to revisit the scene of their coming of age through the songs they learnt there demonstrates how important the period was for them. Returning to 'Shake A Hand' all these years later, McCartney delivers a gritty vocal and Gilmour and Green trade blistering solos that highlight their contrasting styles. For Green, 'Shake A Hand' was "a good example of two live solos showing our opposing styles: I'm rough and ready, and Dave's smooth and tasteful". McCartney experienced a problem with the song at the Cavern show, and although it didn't break down, it was obvious he was pushing his voice to the limit of his range.

Originally recorded by Elvis Presley for his film *Loving You*, 'Party' is simply a goodtime rock'n'roll song with no pretensions other than to entertain. Intrigued by the song's lyric, which he had never been able to fully translate, McCartney recorded the song with all the impetuosity that fuelled his youth. His enthusiasm for the song is obvious. While the rest of the band attempt to bring it to a close, he drives the song on, exclaiming: "I'm not giving up, man!" It was a statement of intent addressed as much to himself as to the band.

Run Devil Run data

Maintaining the project's period feel, McCartney elected to reinstate a 1950s-style label for both vinyl and CD formats. In Britain, Parlophone issued the LP with a purple label with gold text, and a printed inner sleeve. The album cover had a yellow sticker with 'Paul McCartney' in black text adhered to the front. The rear listed the songs from 1 to 15, with track 9 starting side two. Beside the standard CD, Parlophone issued a limited-edition double set that included a 40-minute interview produced by Eddy Pumer. The album was also issued on minidisc, McCartney's first to be issued on this shortlived format.

To promote the album, Parlophone issued several special CDs. An 'advance listening' CD of the full album (CDLRL019) was issued, with black labels with blue text, and a blue sleeve. Three CD singles issued in full-colour card sleeves and purple Parlophone labels were distributed to radio stations and the media. RDR 001 consisted of 'No Other Baby', 'Brown Eyed Handsome Man', 'Blue Jean Bop', 'Run Devil Run', and 'Party'. RDR 002 featured 'Run Devil Run' and 'Blue Jean Bop'. RDR 004 had 'No Other Baby' and 'Brown Eyed Handsome Man'. RDR 003, a 7-inch single, was issued with 'Run Devil Run' and 'Blue Jean Bop'.

In the USA, Capitol issued the commercial CD with a purple 'dome' label. It also issued two limited-edition 'value-added' CDs through the Best Buy and Musicland/Sam Goody stores. CDs issued to these stores had rectangular green stickers adhered to the front cover advertising each bonus CD. CDs available through Best Buy were issued with the interview disc in a card sleeve. CDs available through Musicland/Sam Goody were issued with a four-track CD that featured original recordings of the songs McCartney covered for *Run Devil Run*. Capitol issued two one-track promotional CD singles, both with purple 'dome' labels: 'Try Not To Cry' (DPRO 7087) and 'No Other Bab'y (DPRO13851).

Further promotion came in the form of press kits. Parlophone produced a kit consisting of a copy of the CD, a one-page press release, a six-page interview transcript, and two ten-by-eight colour publicity photos housed in an A4 custom picture folder.

Capitol produced a press pack with a two-page press release with full album track-listing, an 11-page interview, a colour 35mm slide featuring a photo taken by Richard Haughton from the *Run Devil Run* photo session, and a ten-by-eight black-and-white publicity photograph taken in 1993 on The New World Tour by Kevin Winter, all housed in a generic black card folder.

WORKING CLASSICAL

THIS WAS an introspective re-examination of some of the best songs McCartney wrote for Linda, and as such is inevitably tinged with sadness. But this was no bible-black sepulchre in which McCartney wallowed in grief; rather, *Working Classical* is a graceful consideration of Linda's life-force and influence. Where *Run Devil Run* had seen McCartney attempting to deal with his grief by revisiting escapist teenage fantasies, this album found him firmly rooted in the shadow of Linda's death.

The album is dominated by a theme that runs throughout McCartney's work: love, that is, and in particular his love for Linda. While planning her memorial service, he began thinking about the kind of music she might have chosen herself. "It might have been some loud rock'n'roll, or perhaps something of mine," he explained. "So I made a list of songs I had written specifically with Linda in mind."

The songs performed at her memorial service formed the basis of *Working Classical*. New arrangements were written for string quartet and premiered in Britain by the Brodsky Quartet. They were later performed at Linda's memorial service in New York City by the Loma Mar Quartet, who recorded them for *Working Classical*.

In some cases, the purity of the form highlights McCartney's talent as a melodist, which at its best transcends musical boundaries. 'Warm And Beautiful', a song described by Elvis Costello as "one of the most beautiful songs that Paul ever wrote for Linda", exemplifies this aspect of McCartney's work.

But not everything translates successfully. Few of McCartney's pop songs were improved by their new settings, and several highlight the fact that one setting was simply exchanged for another. A quick listen to 'My Love', for example, reveals that a great pop song doesn't become classical music merely by being performed by a string quartet, no matter how skilfully it's executed.

Had *Working Classical* consisted of nothing but classical interpretations of McCartney's pop songs, it would be easy to dismiss it as little more than a high-class easy listening album. However, it's saved by the inclusion of weightier themes, which prove that McCartney is more than capable of working with skill and confidence in classical idioms. Despite the apparent disparities, *Working Classical* mixes McCartney's pop and classical aspirations with surprising ease.

WORKING CLASSICAL
PAUL McCARTNEY
SIDE 1 'Junk', 'A Leaf'.
SIDE 2 'Haymakers', 'Midwife', 'Spiral'.
SIDE 3 'Warm And Beautiful', 'My Love', 'Maybe I'm Amazed', 'Calico Skies', 'Golden Earth Girl', 'Somedays'.
SIDE 4 'Tuesday', 'She's My Baby', 'The Lovely Linda'.
UK RELEASE October 18 1999; CD EMI Classics 5568972; LP EMI Classics 5568971 released December 13 1999; minidisc EMI Classics 5568978; classical chart high No.2.
US RELEASE October 19 1999; CD EMI Classics CDQ 5 56897 2; classical chart high No.1.

- **'A Leaf'** (McCartney)
London Symphony Orchestra, Lawrence Foster (conductor). Recorded at Abbey Road Studios, London, England. Produced by John Fraser.
- **'Spiral'** (McCartney)
Personnel, location, production as 'A Leaf'.
- **'Tuesday'** (McCartney)
London Symphony Orchestra, Andrea Quinn (conductor). Recorded at AIR Studios, London, England. Produced by John Fraser.

Working Classical songs

As with the rest of this book, we do not deal here with 'new' versions of songs already recorded and considered earlier. So the first of the truly new pieces here is 'A Leaf', arranged for orchestra by Jonathan Tunick and recorded at AIR London with The London Philharmonic Orchestra on July 23 1996. Described by *Billboard* magazine as redolent of Vaughan Williams, 'A Leaf' opens with a waltz theme that is developed to take in synoptic themes and broad sweeps of the orchestral palette before returning to the opening motif.

'Spiral' was conceived as a solo piano piece, which was then orchestrated by Richard Rodney Bennett. No less descriptive than 'A Leaf', its compelling shifts in timbre evoke impressions of timeless, natural beauty. Yet somehow McCartney elicits a sense of unease from his melody that undermines the sense of rootedness suggested by the introductory theme. This is counterbalanced by the emergence of a second theme, introduced by the high clear tones of the strings and woodwind, which relieves this sense of menacing ambiguity.

The last of the three new orchestral pieces is 'Tuesday', which originated as the theme for an animated film. McCartney extended the central motif by "work[ing] in a number of new themes" to give the piece a more episodic structure. The film was premiered at the Venice film festival in September 2001.

Working Classical data

Although the classical world had all but abandoned vinyl, EMI Classics issued *Working Classical* as a two-record set with a gatefold sleeve and four-page booklet. The CD was issued with a custom screen-printed label and 16-page booklet. In Britain, EMI Classics issued the album on minidisc, the second and last of McCartney's albums available on this format. A four-track promo CD (PROMOWC), consisting of 'A Leaf', 'Warm And Beautiful',

'NO OTHER BABY' / 'BROWN EYED HANDSOME MAN', 'FABULOUS'
PAUL McCARTNEY
UK RELEASE November 25 1999; Parlophone R 6527; CD single Parlophone CDR 6527 'No Other Baby', 'Brown Eyed Handsome Man', 'Fabulous'; CD single (mono) Parlophone CDRS 6527 'No Other Baby', 'Brown Eyed Handsome Man', 'Fabulous'; chart high No.42.

'NO OTHER BABY' / 'TRY NOT TO CRY'
PAUL McCARTNEY
US RELEASE November 23 1999; Capitol 72438-58823-7-1; failed to chart.

- **'Fabulous'** (Land, Sheldon)

Paul McCartney (bass, guitar, vocals), Mick Green (guitar), Dave Gilmour (guitar), Pete Wingfield (piano), Ian Paice (drums).
Recorded at Abbey Road Studios, London, England.
Produced by Chris Thomas and Paul McCartney.

'Midwife', and 'My Love', was made available to radio stations and as part of the press pack. EMI Classics also issued *Working Classical – Interview*, a five-minute question-and-answer CDR (with 'McCartney' in large text top centre, 'Working Classical Interview' bottom centre, and the EMI Classics logo at 3 o'clock). The disc had no catalogue number and came in a card sleeve with the interviewer's questions printed on the front.

'NO OTHER BABY'

THIS single included 'Fabulous', an outtake from the *Run Devil Run* sessions. Performed with all the lustful energy of an expectant teenager on his first date, it evokes the sights, sounds, and smells of a late-1950s fairground and is the sonic equivalent of teen rebellion – even if it is played by a group of 50-year-olds.

'No Other Baby' data

In Britain, Parlophone issued the single as a 7-inch with vintage Parlophone labels and generic sleeve. Two CD singles were issued in mono and stereo. The mono edition was issued with a gatefold sleeve, a hand-tinted poster and was pressed on clear vinyl, while the stereo was issued with a screen-printed label in a slimline case.

In the USA, Capitol issued 'No Other Baby' / 'Try Not To Cry' as a 7-inch 'jukebox' single with generic purple labels. They also issued 'No Other Baby' as a one-track promotional CD single (7087 6 13851 2 0) with a purple Capitol 'dome' label, and issued the US B-side, 'Try Not To Cry', as a one-track promotional CD single (7087 6 13852 2 9) with a purple Capitol 'dome' label.

RUN DEVIL RUN LIMITED EDITION

PARLOPHONE issued the *Run Devil Run* album as this boxed set of eight 7-inch singles, limited to an edition of 7,000. Released in a retro-style carrying case with a redesigned booklet, it did little to abate the album's chart descent, but at least provided fans with an instant, if expensive, collector's item.

'IMAGINE'

REISSUED in the UK "due to massive public demand", 'Imagine' once again found its way into the higher reaches of the British charts. It was issued as an enhanced CD single, including the original video for 'Imagine'. A promotional CD single (CDRDJ 6534) was issued in a card sleeve with the classic photograph of Lennon at his white baby-grand piano.

RUN DEVIL RUN LIMITED EDITION 7-INCH SINGLES BOX
PAUL McCARTNEY
'Blue Jean Bop' / 'She Said Yeah' 5232301
'All Shock Up' / 'Run Devil Run' 5232311
'No Other Baby' / 'Lonesome Town' 523231
'Try Not To Cry' / 'Movie Magg' 5232331
'Brown Eyed Handsome Man' / 'What It Is' 5232341
'Coquette' / 'I Got Stung' 5232351
'Honey Hush' / 'Shake A Hand' 5232361
'Party' / 'Fabulous' 5232371
UK RELEASE December 6 1999; Parlophone 5322291; failed to chart.
For recording location, personnel, and producer credits see Run Devil Run.

'IMAGINE', 'HAPPY XMAS (WAR IS OVER)', 'GIVE PEACE A CHANCE', 'IMAGINE' (VIDEO)
JOHN LENNON
UK RELEASE December 13 1999; CD single Parlophone CDR 6534; chart high No.3.

together alone

2000-07

GARLAND FOR LINDA

THIS album brought together nine contemporary composers to celebrate the life of Linda McCartney. Stephen Connock, a businessman who also suffered from cancer, came up with the idea for the Garland Appeal to establish a major fundraising project in aid of cancer research and to support the "life enhancing power of music".

Connock asked McCartney for his consent to use Linda's name in conjunction with the project; not only did McCartney comply with his request but also he agreed to contribute a new composition. "I always jump at a project if I like the sound of it, and I jumped right at this one," he said. "I thought, I'll write something, and if it's no good I'll just say sorry. But I didn't want to deliberate. I just wanted to write whatever that little inspiration was."

McCartney's piece, 'Nova', was premiered in England on July 18 1999 at the Memorial Chapel of Charterhouse School in Godalming, Surrey at a charity concert that launched the Garland Appeal as well as new works by some of the country's leading composers. Also performed at the event was a song cycle, arranged for chorus by Stephen Jackson, which included 'Here There And Everywhere', 'Lady Madonna', and 'Let It Be'.

Despite McCartney having several classical albums under his belt, the prospect of working alongside several leading classical composers remained a daunting prospect. He was unaware of the conventions demanded by a song cycle, that the composer is required to set a text by another author to a musical setting of their own. McCartney: "John Tavener said to me, 'Where is your text from,'" he recalled. "I said, 'I wrote it myself, John.' And he said, 'Oh.' 'I don't know better, John,' I told him. 'I don't know your not supposed to write it yourself.'"

McCartney's prose conveys a profound sense of loss and uncertainty. Addressing the audience, he asks the question, "God, where are you?" For McCartney, this expressed real doubts, but it also allowed him to develop the narrative. Instead of accepting God's presence, he introduces a sense of doubt that is quashed by God's reply. McCartney explained: "I like the idea of starting off with a doubt, and then pay off, you know?"

Writing for Linda had always fired his imagination, often driving him to create some of his most sensitive and moving music. He wrote 'Nova' between November 1998 and May 1999, and the piece is typically melodic, with an interplay of harmonies and textures that effortlessly match the emotional tension he intended to convey. Speaking to *Classic FM* magazine about 'Nova', he said: "Tunes have always fascinated me and I've always loved them ... but [this is] more personal and loving. It's to do with emotion."

Like the *Run Devil Run* rock'n'roll project that ran concurrently with writing this, 'Nova' enabled McCartney to reflect on Linda's absence and to reconsider their relationship. He acknowledged that the projects he engaged in after her death were part of the grieving process, but more importantly that they allowed him to consider what he wanted and who he was, even if what he found was disturbing. As he recalled: "After about a year and two months, I found that I'd found something out. I still don't know what it is. But I'm another person."

The London Symphony Orchestra later recorded 'Nova' at Abbey Road for the American Cancer Society, issued on *Music Of Hope* on February 13 2001 by Tim Janis Ensemble Records.

GARLAND FOR LINDA
VARIOUS ARTISTS
PAUL McCARTNEY 'Nova' (arranged by John Harle).
UK RELEASE February 7 2000; CD EMI Classics CDC 5569612; classical chart high No.9.
US RELEASE April 26 2000; CD EMI Classics CDC 5 569621 2; failed to chart.

- **'Nova'** (McCartney)

The Joyful Company of Singers: Patricia Bentley, Hilary Brennan, Polly Carnegie, Cathryn Caunt, Bridget Corderoy, Sally Donegani, Harriet Fraser, Armanda Gibbs, Claire Hills, Victoria Kendall, Rachel King, Felice Kum, Helen Morton, Clare Porter, Katherine Wills (sopranos), Debbie Bright, Kathryn Cook, Rosemary Day, Denise Fabb, Henrietta Hillman, Yvette Miller, Rachel Reeves, Fiona Robinson, Lorna Young (altos), Simon Colston, Colin Fleming, Alex Hates, Andrew Shepstone, Paul Zimmerman (tenors), Tim Bull, Tim Colborn, Peter Da Costa, Michael King, Andy Mackinder, Greg Masters, David Rees-Jones, Stephen Garrod, Chris Williams (basses), Peter Broadbent (conductor).
Recorded at All Saints Church, Tooting, London.
Produced by John Fraser.

Garland For Linda data

EMI Classics issued a three-track promotional CD single (GARLAND 1) in a card sleeve. *Highlights From a Garland For Linda* featured John Tavener's 'Prayer For The Healing Of The Sick', John Rutter's 'Musica Dei Donum', and McCartney's 'Nova'.

MAYBE BABY

McCARTNEY was invited by comedian and author Ben Elton to contribute a song to the film *Maybe Baby*, and he obliged with a cover of the title song made famous almost half a century earlier by Buddy Holly. Recorded in Los Angeles – McCartney was there to promote *Run Devil Run* with a charity concert for PETA – 'Maybe Baby' promised more than it delivered. Despite a red-hot

MAYBE BABY ORIGINAL SOUNDTRACK
VARIOUS ARTISTS
PAUL MCCARTNEY 'Maybe Baby'.
UK RELEASE June 5 2000; CD Virgin CDV 2916; failed to chart.

• **'Maybe Baby'** (Holly)
Paul McCartney (bass, guitar, vocals), Mick Green (guitar), Dave Gilmour (guitar), Ian Paice (drums).
Recorded at Capitol Studio, Los Angeles, CA, USA.
Produced by Paul McCartney and Jeff Lynne.

band and the inspirational surroundings of the legendary Capitol studio on Vine Street, the cut is a dud. Partly the problem is the song – it was lightweight pop even when recorded by Holly – and partly the choice of Jeff Lynne as producer, who makes it sound like a Traveling Wilburys outtake.

LIVERPOOL SOUND COLLAGE

IF YOU thought The Fireman albums radical and seek nice pop songs, then look elsewhere. McCartney had long talked about making an album called *Paul McCartney Goes Too Far*, and *Liverpool Sound Collage* goes some way to fulfilling his ambition. There are no 'songs' on this album; rather, he pushes experimentation to the limit. The album contains exactly what it says on the label: sound collages.

Artist Peter Blake was curating an exhibition, *About Collage*, for the Tate Gallery in Liverpool and asked McCartney if he would like to contribute to the show. He agreed and delivered two pieces, *The World* (a work on paper) and a companion sound collage, which was broadcast in the gallery alongside his visual artwork.

To construct *Liverpool Sound Collage*, he recorded students from the Liverpool Institute For Performing Arts, shoppers, and street sounds. He also used snippets from his *Liverpool Oratorio* and Beatles recordings (studio chat from sessions for 'Think For Yourself', 'I Call Your Name', 'I'll Be Back', 'This Boy', 'Good Night', 'Mr Moonlight', and 'Your Mother Should Know'). But although he described *Liverpool Sound Collage* as "a new little piece of Beatles", and 'Free Now' as "a manic Beatles single", actual Beatles content is minimal, and musically the album has more in common with 'Revolution 9' than 'She Loves You'.

What he does it to use the fragments as 'found' sounds, in much the same way as avant-garde artists such as Marcel Duchamp and Kurt Schwitters used 'found' objects to create works of art. Influenced by Cage, Stockhausen, and Berio, *Liverpool Sound Collage* espouses avant-garde theories and practices that first came to light in the 1950s and 1960s. McCartney's references to musique concrète, a compositional technique that manipulates taped sounds by speeding up, reversing, or distorting them, was an attempt to evoke brutal urban imagery through the use of sound.

This kind of music may have appeared avant-garde in the 1960s, but its main principles were quickly absorbed into pop music. The Beatles were among the first to realise the benefit of editing together sounds recorded at different times and in different places to manufacture a performance – 'Tomorrow Never Knows' and 'I Am The Walrus', for example.

By the 1980s, dance music took the process a step further. By sampling and looping sounds from other records, DJs and recording artists could evoke notions of cultural disparity, history, and authenticity. New records could be created with multifocal points of reference, often with a critical or celebratory agenda. These kinds of collages have become so common that we now barely notice their jarring juxtapositions and cross-referencing. Quoting sounds, rather than images, McCartney calls on a shared cultural repertoire to evoke the feel of life in late 20th century Britain. Interweaving newly recorded sounds with moments from his past, the result is a temporal whirlpool of random simultaneity and cross-cultural encounters.

He enlisted Youth and the Welsh band Super Furry Animals to remix various elements of his collage. He had met Cian Ciaran of

LIVERPOOL SOUND COLLAGE
PAUL McCARTNEY
'Plastic Beetle' (Paul McCartney, The Beatles), 'Peter Blake 2000' (Super Furry Animals, The Beatles), 'Real Gone Dub Made In Manifest In The Vortex Of The Eternal Now' (Youth), 'Made Up' (Paul McCartney, The Beatles), 'Free Now' (Paul McCartney, The Beatles, Super Furry Animals).
UK RELEASE August 21 2000; CD Hydra LSC01; failed to chart.
US RELEASE September 26 2000; CD Hydra 7243 528817 2 7; failed to chart.

• **'Plastic Beetle'**
• **'Peter Blake 2000'**
• **'Real Gone Dub Made In Manifest In The Vortex Of The Eternal Now'**
• **'Made Up'**
• **'Free Now'**
All with Paul McCartney (vocals), John Lennon (vocals), George Harrison (vocals), Ringo Starr (vocals).
All recorded at Abbey Road Studios, London, at Hog-Hill, Sussex, field-recordings made in Liverpool, England, and at unknown studio.
Produced by Paul McCartney.

Super Furry Animals when he attended the *NME* Awards in 1999, and Ciaran offered the services of his band should McCartney ever want anything remixing. McCartney duly obliged, but stipulated that they were not to add any of their own sounds to those he had already collected. Gruff Rhys from Super Furry Animals explained: "Next thing, a box of tapes turned up from Apple Corps. The letter said, 'This contains unreleased Beatles material. Do not copy, use, broadcast, or sell down the market.' It was quite heavy."

The mix by Super Furry Animals, 'Peter Blake 2000', is introduced by a random radio scan, loops, backwards sounds, and fragmented conversations, and it owes something to 'Revolution 9', musique concrete, and contemporary dance music. "Our bit was to make a 20-minute sound piece," said Rhys, "using only the stuff that was posted down. There's George on guitars, Ringo on drums, with vocals taken from conversations between John and Paul in the studio. I think the only people to remix them before were Phil Spector and Jeff Lynne." But this was more than a remix: it was a radical deconstruction/reconstruction of McCartney's found sounds. And although he had the final say, responsibility for the way the sounds were arranged was deferred to the Super Furry Animals.

Liverpool Sound Collage data

The album was issued by Hydra in a gatefold digi-pack. To promote the album, Hydra issued a promotional single, 'Free Now', as a one-sided 7-inch single (FREE002) and one-track CD single (FREECD002).

'HELP ME TO HELP MYSELF'

ISSUED as a bonus track on the remastered *Double Fantasy*, 'Help Me To Help Myself' had previously been broadcast on the *Lost Lennon Tapes* and issued on bootlegs. One of the better unissued songs Lennon wrote and recorded while preparing the album, this is a gospel-style ballad that finds him contemplating his acquisitiveness and self-destructive nature.

Reviewing his life, Lennon avows that now is the time to accept some divine intervention. While his relationship with God and organised religion was ambivalent at best, this was no radical U-turn. 'Help Me To Help Myself' was more than a plea for redemption, it was a pragmatic statement of protestant self-help that restates the maxim "heaven helps those who help themselves".

Seen in this light, the song extends the theme of personal projection and individual development that had occupied Lennon from the outset. Stripping away the lyrical ambivalence that made *Imagine* so appealing, he offers his own experiences as a paradigm for others to employ as they journey through life.

DOUBLE FANTASY
JOHN LENNON
UK/US RELEASE October 9 2000; remastered edition Capitol 528 7392.

• **'Help Me To Help Myself'** (Lennon)
John Lennon (vocals, piano).
Recorded at The Dakota, New York City, NY, USA.
Producer: John Lennon

BRAND NEW BOOTS AND PANTIES

IAN DURY was a veteran pub rocker, an artist, a playwright, a pop star, an actor, a teacher, and a songwriter – but this brief listing of his achievements doesn't do justice to his talents. He trod the boards of London's pubs and clubs for much of the early 1970s with his band Kilburn & The High Roads. But although they released a few records and gained some notoriety, commercial success was not forthcoming. Dury then signed with Stiff Records in 1977 and released *New Boots And Panties*, which received the attention he had long deserved.

Despite a slow start, the album eventually reached Number 5 in Britain, thanks to the non-album hit single 'Hit Me With Your Rhythm Stick', and stayed in the charts for 104 weeks. Christening his band The Blockheads, Dury hit his peak in the late 1970s with a string of hit singles and concert tours. For a while Blockheadmania burned bright but was shortlived. Splitting from The Blockheads, Dury pursued a solo career until, some 18 years later, he returned with The Blockheads and a comeback album, *Mr Love Pants*. Although he was diagnosed with cancer in 1997, he continued to tour with the Blockheads and took up a new challenge as an official envoy for UNICEF, until his death in 2000.

McCartney's friendship with Dury was brief, but when asked if he would contribute to a new version of the classic *New Boots And Panties*, he agreed readily. Called on to supply a vocal for the album, McCartney chose 'I'm Partial To Your Abracadabra', a song about human sexuality. Dury apparently thought he had "fucked that one up", as the song failed to express his original intentions. As he explained: "I wanted to make that hermaphrodite. No – hermaphrodite implies something sexy or some duality. It just seems to me that, inevitably, the human race will evolve eventually into one sex. Women will have their babies in a nice box, and we'll all fancy each other for what we are instead of what we're supposed to be, or tits, or all of that bollocks."

Given a new interpretation by The Blockheads, who recorded their backing before McCartney was called on to interpret Dury's

BRAND NEW BOOTS AND PANTIES
VARIOUS ARTISTS
PAUL McCARTNEY & THE BLOCKHEADS 'I'm Partial To Your Abracadabra'.
UK RELEASE April 9 2001; CD East Central One NEWBOOTSCD2; LP East Central One NEWBOOTS2LP released May 12 2001; chart high No.44.

• **'I'm Partial To Your Abracadabra'** (Dury)
Paul McCartney (vocals), Chaz Jankel (guitar, keyboards), Mickey Gallagher (keyboards), Davey Payne (saxophone), John Turnbull (guitar), Norman Watt-Roy (bass), Jools Holland (piano), Steve Sidwell (drums).
Recorded at Helicon Mountain, London, England.
Produced by Laurie Latham.

freethinking lyric, 'I'm Partial To Your Abracadabra' remains as evocative now as when it was first recorded in 1977. Three takes were all that were needed to secure McCartney's vocal, which producer Laurie Latham combined for the master. As his jubilant vocal demonstrates, McCartney obviously relished singing about kinky boots and panties. If only he'd do it more often.

Brand New Boots And Panties data

East Central One Records issued the album on CD and as a gold vinyl LP in a limited edition of 1,000 copies. 'I'm Partial To Your Abracadabra' was issued as a one-track promotional CD single (NEWBOOTS 2 PRO).

WINGSPAN – HITS AND HISTORY

RELEASED to coincide with a Wings *Anthology*-style TV documentary, this compilation was an eclectic mix of hits and misses that gave a better idea of what McCartney and the band were about than previous collections. That said, it's neither a Wings album nor a Paul McCartney album. It's a compromise, and we all know were they lead. Too many songs from the periods either side of McCartney's career with Wings are included at the expense of album tracks, B-sides, and rarities from Wings.

Wingspan – Hits and History was little more than an excuse to exploit McCartney's back catalogue and fill the extra demand for product that the television documentary would inevitably create. It was a victim of product placement and mass marketing. McCartney targeted *Wingspan – Hits and History* at a mass audience, and to ensure its success he decided to "expand the envelope", as he put it, by including non-Wings material. He said: "It's a shame not to have songs like 'Pipes Of Peace' and 'No More Lonely Nights', which were big hits and from the period but were recorded solo. So the categories became Paul McCartney, and Wings – and [we included] any song that fitted into either of those categories."

But as anyone who saw the documentary will know, it focused on the years 1970 to 1980. 'Pipes Of Peace' and 'No More Lonely Nights' were recorded long after Wings had ceased to exist. Including them didn't do Wings any favours and only confused matters. One could argue that the album would have been better served had it not featured songs like 'Pipes Of Peace', even if it was a hit – but McCartney's ploy appeared to work, as the album went straight into the Top 5, something he hadn't achieved for some time. Although the track selection tends to paint a too cosy picture of Wings, McCartney had intended to include 'Give Ireland Back To The Irish', but record company nervousness about renewed terrorist activity meant that it was pulled.

While it offers little for the committed fan, *Wingspan – Hits And History* did feature previously unavailable edits, which were used to free up space for extra songs, and as the two-CD set sold for the price of a single CD, it did offer value for money. As most of the material had already featured on previous albums, an unreleased acoustic reading of 'Bip Bop/Hey Diddle' was included to entice those who already owned everything McCartney had committed to record.

WINGSPAN – HITS AND HISTORY
PAUL McCARTNEY
CD 1 'Listen To What The Man Said', 'Band On The Run', 'Another Day', 'Live And Let Die', 'Jet', 'My Love', 'Silly Love Songs', 'Pipes Of Peace', 'C Moon', 'Hi, Hi, Hi', 'Let 'Em In', 'Goodnight Tonight', 'Junior's Farm', 'Mull Of Kintyre', 'Uncle Albert/Admiral Halsey', 'Coming Up', 'No More Lonely Nights'.
CD 2 'Let Me Roll It', 'The Lovely Linda', 'Daytime Nightime Suffering', 'Maybe I'm Amazed', 'Helen Wheels', 'Bluebird', 'Heart Of The Country', 'Every Night', 'Take It Away', 'Junk', 'Man We Was Lonely', 'Venus And Mars', 'Rock Show', 'The Back Seat Of My Car', 'Rockestra Theme', 'Girlfriend', 'Waterfalls', 'Tomorrow', 'Too Many People', 'Call Me Back Again', 'Tug Of War', 'Bip Bop/Hey Diddle', 'No More Lonely Nights' (Playout Version).
UK RELEASE May 7 2001; CD Parlophone 532 8676 2; LP Parlophone 532 850 1; chart high No.5.
US RELEASE May 7 2001; CD Capitol CDP 5 32943 2; chart high No.2.

• **'Bip Bop/Hey Diddle'** (McCartney)
Paul McCartney (guitar, vocals), Linda McCartney (backing vocals).
Recorded at High Park Farm, Scotland.
Produced by Paul McCartney.

Performed au naturel by Paul and Linda with giggling children, 'Bip Bop/Hey Diddle' was recorded by a film crew and captures the McCartneys at play. McCartney has long considered 'Bip Bop' one of the worst songs he has ever released, and 'Hey Diddle' can't rate much higher, for the finished song had remained safely locked in the archives since 1971. This clip first appeared on the *Wings Over The World* documentary, but this was the first time it had been made commercially available in its unedited form.

Wingspan data

Unusually, both LP and CD were issued on the same day, a sign that the vinyl record was making a comeback, at least in Europe. Parlophone issued the four-LP set with customised labels, printed inner sleeves, and a gatefold sleeve (two records in each pocket). The CD was issued with a 'limited' 3D slipcase. To promote the album, Parlophone issued an eight-song CD compilation (CD LRL 048), which featured McCartney introducing each song ('Band On The Run', 'My Love', 'Live And Let Die', 'Let 'Em In', 'Maybe I'm Amazed', 'Let Me Roll It', 'The Back Seat Of My Car', 'Waterfalls').

Capitol in the USA issued a ten-track *Wingspan Special Advance Sampler* CD (DPRO 7087 6 15951 2 5) without the introductions. They also issued a gold vinyl 7-inch jukebox single of 'Maybe I'm Amazed' / 'Band On The Run' (72438-58995-7-7A), complete with the spoken introductions. Special remixes of 'Let 'Em In', 'Silly Love Songs', 'Goodnight Tonight', 'Coming Up', and 'No More Lonely Nights' were also commissioned. Three mixes of 'Silly Love Songs' were issued in Japan (PCD-2458) and Germany (CDP-000587) as promotional CD singles, and in Italy as a 12-inch single (7243 880073 6 8). In Britain, EMI issued a 12-inch promotional single with 'Coming Up' / 'Silly Love Songs' (12-WINDJ-002).

GOOD ROCKIN' TONIGHT

THAT McCartney should choose to record a version of Presley's debut Sun single for this tribute album isn't surprising. He performed the song with The Quarry Men a few years after its original release and it remained part of The Beatles' repertoire well into the 1960s – the group recorded it for BBC radio in 1963. He returned to the song in 1987, recording a version for his *Choba B CCCP* album. Written by Arthur Crudup, 'That's All Right Mama' propelled Presley into the big-time. Yet, ironically, Elvis didn't have a national hit with the song; that distinction was reserved for Marty Robbins.

Guitarist Scotty Moore had lent his distinctive sound to the original recording, and he joined McCartney for this reworking. Drummer D J Fontana, who played on many of Presley's hit records, added his talents to the recording too.

GOOD ROCKIN' TONIGHT (THE LEGACY OF SUN RECORDS)
VARIOUS ARTISTS
PAUL McCARTNEY 'That's Alright Mama'.
US RELEASE October 16 2001; London-Sire 31165-2; failed to chart.

• **'That's All Right Mama'** (Crudup)
Paul McCartney (vocals, bass), Scotty Moore (guitar), D J Fontana (drums, backing vocals).
Recorded at Sear Sound Studios, New York City, NY, USA.
Produced by Ahmet Ertegun

'FROM A LOVER TO A FRIEND'

IF THERE'S one thing that drives McCartney it's writing songs. And if there's one thing above all else that impels his writing, it's a desire to explore the nature of relationships. 'From A Lover To A Friend' found him exploring his flowering romance with a new love, Heather Mills. They married on June 11 2002 at Castle Leslie in Glaslough, County Monaghan in Ireland.

As his love affair with Mills developed, McCartney found himself considering his actions, and the song may be his way of asking for absolution. "I had all these questions," he explained, "like, 'Oh my gosh, I've had a wife for 30 years. Is this allowed?' I think like most guys who go through that, [I felt] quite a degree of guilt."

Yet exactly whom he is addressing in this ménage à trois – himself, Heather, or Linda – is ambiguous. If the song was an attempt to solicit approval for his new relationship, McCartney suggested it was purely "subconscious". He remained unsure of the song's real meaning long after it was written, and revealed that the lyrics were simply strung together without much thought. "I kind of like it when you can string some words together and not quite know the meaning," he said. Ambiguity lies at the heart of this epistle. Its evocation of doubt manifests itself as a paradox or conundrum, with McCartney attempting to work his way through the puzzle. For this is a quest for forgiveness not solely from a third party but also for his own self-doubt.

The musical support was constructed from various unfinished fragments that McCartney reviewed at his own Hog-Hill studio, and then he got his engineer to edit them together. He said: "I liked this bit and I liked that bit, and we just stitched together a couple of bits which weren't meant to go together, but they just felt like they would go together." He also revealed that his home demo had captured a certain "intimate" vocal quality, which he tried to recapture when he recorded the song in the studio.

Recorded at Henson studio in Los Angeles, with session

players recommended by producer David Kahne, 'From A Lover To A Friend' finds McCartney once again exploring his passion for recording live in the studio with a small band. As he had with *Run Devil Run*, he sketched out the songs for the other musicians before recording them. This benefits 'From A Lover' as their unfamiliarity with the song echoes its tone and theme perfectly.

Besides David Kahne's original mix, two additional remixes were issued. The first removed most of the original backing in favour of orchestral samples to highlight McCartney's vocal; the second is essentially an instrumental with the vocal placed very low in Kahne's atmospheric mix.

'Riding Into Jaipur' recounts a trip McCartney and Heather took to India in January 2001. However, the melody predates their meeting and the holiday to India; he wrote it while on holiday with Linda in the Maldives. McCartney had a small Martin travel guitar, given to him by Linda, which had its own distinctive sound. "[It] seems to have a bit of a sound on certain frets, like a sitar," he recalled. The song remained unfinished until he added a lyric while in India. "I took the train to Jaipur," he said, "It was a very exotic overnight journey, and I did some words that were in the same vein as that original melody. So those two things came together." It was also recorded in LA, although here McCartney used a few Indian instruments and sampled loops to create a sonic souvenir of his journey through the country. But that's really all it is: if *Standing Stone* was a novel and 'Hey Jude' a short story, then 'Riding Into Jaipur' is little more than a postcard.

On the morning of September 11 2001, McCartney and Heather Mills were aboard an aircraft waiting to leave New York City for home. But before the plane could take off, all flights from the USA were cancelled. Terrorists had crashed two passenger aircraft into the twin towers of the World Trade Center, which, from his window, McCartney could see ablaze. Desperate to help in some way, he reasoned that the best thing he could do was to write a song to raise people's spirits. Influenced by these events and the heroic actions of the New York Fire Department, he wrote 'Freedom'.

Before those horrific events, he had been planning to launch his new album with a large-scale concert in Moscow. But, persuaded by film producer and director Harvey Weinstein, he put that idea on hold and applied all his efforts to a charity event, the Concert For New York, broadcast live on US television and on the internet. On the day of the concert, McCartney was involved in a car crash, but, despite some back pain, he continued with the rehearsals (extracts of which were made available on his website) and the concert.

He debuted 'Freedom' at the event, and the resulting live recording was enhanced at Quad Studios with Eric Clapton adding guitar. A simple but impassioned song about a right we all take for granted, its feeling of spontaneity, its repetitive chorus, and the closing applause evoke memories of the peace anthem that John Lennon wrote some 30 years earlier. A heartfelt statement of belief and solidarity, 'Freedom' was intended for New

'FROM A LOVER TO A FRIEND' / 'RIDING INTO JAIPUR'
PAUL McCARTNEY
UK RELEASE October 29 2001; Parlophone R 6567 released November 5 2001; CD single CDR 6567 'From A Lover To A Friend', 'From A Lover To A Friend' (David Kahne Remix 1), 'From A Lover To A Friend' (David Kahne Remix 2); CD single CDRS 6567 'Freedom', 'From A Lover To A Friend', 'From A Lover To A Friend' (David Kahne Remix 2) released November 5 2001; cassette single TCR 6567 'From A Lover To A Friend', 'Riding Into Jaipur', 'From A Lover To A Friend' (David Kahne Remix 2) released November 5 2001; download www.paulmccartney.com; chart high No.45.

'FROM A LOVER TO A FRIEND', 'FROM A LOVER TO A FRIEND (DAVID KAHNE REMIX 1)', 'FROM A LOVER TO A FRIEND' (DAVID KAHNE REMIX 2)
PAUL McCARTNEY
US RELEASE October 29 2001; Capitol 8-77671-2 (withdrawn).

'FREEDOM', 'FROM A LOVER TO A FRIEND', 'FROM A LOVER TO A FRIEND' (DAVID KAHNE REMIX 2)
PAUL McCARTNEY
US RELEASE November 13 2001; Capitol 8-77671-2; failed to chart.

'FREEDOM', 'FROM A LOVER TO A FRIEND'
PAUL McCARTNEY
US RELEASE November 14 2001; Capitol 7243 5 50291 2 6; 7-inch Capitol 50291-7-1 released September 2002; failed to chart.

- **'From A Lover To A Friend'** (McCartney)
Paul McCartney (vocals, bass, piano), Rusty Anderson (12-string guitar), Abe Laboriel Jr (drums), Gabe Dixon (piano).
Recorded at Henson Recording Studio, Los Angeles, CA, USA.
Produced by David Kahne and Paul McCartney.
- **'Riding Into Jaipur'** (McCartney)
Paul McCartney (vocals, acoustic guitar, bass), Rusty Anderson (12-string guitar, tambura), Abe Laboriel Jnr (Roland Handsonic electronic percussion with African drums), Gabe Dixon (piano), David Kahne (synth).
Recorded at Henson Recording Studio, Los Angeles, CA, USA.
Produced by David Kahne and Paul McCartney.
- **'Freedom'** (McCartney)
Paul McCartney (vocals, acoustic guitar), Rusty Anderson (guitars, backing vocals), Abe Laboriel Jr (drums, backing vocals), Gabe Dixon (keyboards, backing vocals), Eric Clapton (guitar).
Recorded live at Madison Square Garden and at Quad Studios, New York City, NY, USA.
Produced by David Kahne and Paul McCartney.

Yorkers and the world, and in a concise, understated way conveys similar ideals and passions as Lennon's earlier plea for love, peace, and harmony.

'From A Lover To A Friend' data

Parlophone issued the single on 7-inch, cassette, and two different CDs. It was also available as a digital download from McCartney's website. Promotional copies of the CD (DR002) were issued on October 1 2001 in white card sleeves with the title and a facsimile of McCartney's signature printed in black on the front cover.

In the USA, 'From A Lover To A Friend' was issued by Capitol and quickly withdrawn. Promotional copies of the CD single (DPRO 6 15992 2) were issued with a white gatefold sleeve with a facsimile signature in grey on the front cover. When McCartney announced that all profits would be donated to charity, Capitol rush-released the single (8-77671-2) with a track listing identical to the British CD single (CDR 6567). Issued with a three-quarter-inch circular black sticker stating that the royalties were going to New York Sept. 11 charities, 25,000 copies of the CD single were manufactured. Capitol shipped about 12,000 before issuing a return order and destroying its remaining stock. However, a small but unknown number had already been sold by retailers.

Capitol then issued 'Freedom' on November 14 2001. Promotional copies of the new A-side had been issued to radio stations a few weeks earlier. Two versions of the promotional single (DPRO 6 16903 2) were issued with a 2:36 edit and album version. Both have similar artwork, but one has the title printed on the front cover in upper case and the other in lower case. The commercial CD single (7243 5 50291 2 6) replaced the original A-side with 'Freedom' but retained the two David Kahne remixes of 'From A Lover To A Friend'.

Almost a year later, in September 2002, Capitol issued a 7-inch jukebox single (72435-50291-7-1). Issued with generic purple labels, it featured an edit of 'Freedom' backed with 'From A Lover To A Friend'.

'From A Lover To A Friend' entered the British charts at number 45, dipping to 64 the following week, and then out. In a desperate attempt to extend its chart life, 'Freedom' was vigorously promoted – McCartney appeared on two primetime UK television shows in one day, November 23, and another two days later – yet despite the artist's high profile, it spent only two weeks in British the charts.

DRIVING RAIN

McCARTNEY spent much of the 1980s attempting to erase imperfections from his increasingly polished recordings. All too often this left his records sounding immaculate but soulless. However, he began to dilute this perfectionism when he recorded *Off The Ground* with his then touring band, the first time he had recorded with a group since *Back To The Egg* in 1979. He'd returned to a simpler way of working to try to capture feel over perfection; now he was embracing the rough edges he'd once avoided.

Throughout the 1990s he refined this way of recording, making a string of albums that are among the best he's released. *Driving Rain*, recorded at Henson in Los Angeles, is cut from the same cloth and finds McCartney at the height of his powers.

David Kahne was chosen as producer from several suggested by McCartney's New York office, because, he explained, Kahne was producing music that was "a little bit adventurous but not too pop". Like everyone else involved with the album, Kahne had no idea of what McCartney wanted to record. "It was all very spontaneous," he said. "There were no rehearsals. He just brought the songs in and we started playing them. Basically, he'd show us a song on the acoustic guitar and we'd learn it."

McCartney described the experience as a "voyage into the unknown" that indulged his passion for creativity and freed him from the responsibilities of having to produce something conventional. "All of us were having to think on our feet, and that process led us into something different from what we normally do."

McCartney arrived at Henson in February 2001 and established a routine of set hours, usually recording from 11:30am to 6:30 pm. Working with a small band of session players he had never met before, he recorded 18 songs in two weeks. Most of the album's basic tracks were recorded on analogue tape machines and then transferred to digital equipment for overdubbing. McCartney then took a break from recording, returning to LA in June to record another four songs and mix the album.

Driving Rain could have been a record full of maudlin songs about loss, but although McCartney does explore the process of mourning, the album is not mournful. Like Lennon's *Double Fantasy*, it's about starting over. And just as Lennon found himself enjoying the process of becoming, so too does McCartney. But *Driving Rain* is more than an album about new beginnings. He doesn't reject the past out of hand, but considers how it has affected him.

If anything, *Driving Rain* is a considered response to his past and an intensely personal record of his resolve to accept it and begin again. This is McCartney baring his soul to the world, telling it like it is, and celebrating life.

Speaking after the release of the album, he revealed that his original plan had been to record a 'dance' album, but that after consideration he'd decided to make a more traditional rock record instead. The album certainly appealed to his long-term followers and received favourable reviews, but it didn't win him many new fans. *Driving Rain* reached Number 26 in the American album charts, before plummeting to 65; it fared even worse in Britain, where it reached Number 46 for one week only.

Its disappointing chart placing didn't reflect the quality of McCartney's music but the fickle nature of the charts, which were full of carefully manufactured pop groups designed to appeal to

DRIVING RAIN
PAUL McCARTNEY
CD 'Lonely Road', 'From A Lover To A Friend', 'She's Given Up Talking', 'Driving Rain', 'I Do', 'Tiny Bubble', 'Magic', 'Your Way', 'Spinning On An Axis', 'About You', 'Heather', 'Back In The Sunshine Again', 'Your Loving Flame', 'Riding Into Jaipur', 'Rinse The Raindrops', 'Freedom'.
UK RELEASE November 12 2001; CD Parlophone 535 5102; LP Parlophone 535 5101 released 17 December 2001; chart high No.46.
US RELEASE November 13 2001; CD Capitol CDP 535 5102; chart high No.26.

- **'Lonely Road'** (McCartney)
Paul McCartney (vocals, bass, guitars), Rusty Anderson (guitars, pedal steel guitar), Abe Laboriel Jr (drums, tambourine), Gabe Dixon (electric piano), David Kahne (organ).
- **'She's Given Up Talking'** (McCartney)
Paul McCartney (vocals, bass guitar, acoustic guitar, drums), Rusty Anderson (electric guitar), Abe Laboriel Jr (Roland Handsonic electronic percussion), Gabe Dixon (Hammond organ), David Kahne (electric guitar).
- **'Driving Rain'** (McCartney)
Paul McCartney (vocals, bass, acoustic guitar), Rusty Anderson (electric guitar), Abe Laboriel Jr (drums), Gabe Dixon (electric piano), David Kahne (synths).
- **'I Do'** (McCartney)
Paul McCartney (vocals, bass, acoustic guitar), Rusty Anderson (electric guitar), Abe Laboriel Jr (drums, tambourine), Gabe Dixon (piano), David Kahne (orchestral samples).
- **'Tiny Bubble'** (McCartney)
Paul McCartney (vocals, bass, guitars, Fender Rhodes electric piano), Rusty Anderson (guitars), Abe Laboriel Jr (drums), Gabe Dixon (organ).
- **'Magic' (McCartney)**
Paul McCartney (vocals, bass, guitars), Rusty Anderson (guitars), Abe Laboriel Jr (drums), Gabe Dixon (Fender Rhodes electric piano), David Kahne (synth).
- **'Your Way'** (McCartney)
Paul McCartney (vocals, guitars, drums, knee slaps), Rusty Anderson (bass, pedal steel, backing vocals), Abe Laboriel Jr (drums, electronic drums, backing vocals), Gabe Dixon (organ, backing vocals).
- **'Spinning On An Axis'** (Paul and James McCartney)
Paul McCartney (vocals, bass, guitars, percussion), James McCartney (percussion), Rusty Anderson (guitars, percussion), Abe Laboriel Jr (drums, Roland Handsonic, percussion), Gabe Dixon (percussion), David Kahne (Wurlitzer electric piano).
- **'About You'** (McCartney)
Paul McCartney (vocals, guitar), Rusty Anderson (bass, 12-string guitar), Abe Laboriel Jr (drums, percussion), Gabe Dixon (Wurlitzer electric piano, organ).
- **'Heather'** (McCartney)
Paul McCartney (vocals, bass, guitars, piano), Rusty Anderson (backing vocals), Abe Laboriel Jr (drums), Gabe Dixon (backing vocals), David Kahne (sampled strings), Ralph Morrison (violin).
- **'Back In The Sunshine Again'** (Paul and James McCartney)
Paul McCartney (vocals, bass, guitar), James McCartney (guitar), Rusty Anderson (guitar), Abe Laboriel Jr (drums), Gabe Dixon (piano).
- **'Your Loving Flame'** (McCartney)
Paul McCartney (vocals, bass, piano, tambourine), Rusty Anderson (guitars, backing vocals), Abe Laboriel Jr (drums, backing vocals), Gabe Dixon (organ, backing vocals), David Kahne (sampled orchestra), David Campbell, Matt Funes, Joel Derouin, Larry Corbett (string quartet).
- **'Rinse The Raindrops'** (McCartney)
Paul McCartney (vocals, bass guitar, guitars, piano), Rusty Anderson (guitars, backing vocals), Abe Laboriel Jr (drums, percussion, backing vocals), Gabe Dixon (keyboards, backing vocals).

All recorded at Henson Recording Studio, Los Angeles, CA, USA.
All produced by David Kahne.

the pre-teens rather than the mature fans of Paul McCartney. He wasn't the only major rock star from the 1960s finding it hard to sell records. Mick Jagger, who released his solo album *Goddess In The Doorway* a week after *Driving Rain*, sold only 11,000 copies in the first week of release, and *Driving Rain* did no better. With a growing number of established recording artists reduced to selling their records on the internet, McCartney is one of the lucky few who still has the backing of a global organisation like EMI. But even they found it hard promoting him to an audience who thinks that Beatles are nasty insects.

Driving Rain songs

Like *Run Devil Run*, *Driving Rain* is an album of mixed emotions. Encapsulating the plurality of feelings that McCartney dealt with in his emotional twilight-zone between relationships, the opening track, 'Lonely Road', finds its author reflecting on his feelings for two women he's found both inspirational and stabilising.

In considering his relationship with Linda, he found himself addressing thoughts of rejection and loss, which he thought might manifest themselves in the future. But this is no tearful song of self-pity. McCartney claimed it was "a defiant song against loneliness", which he wrote while on holiday in Goa in January 2001.

Musically, he evokes his unresolved feelings through contrasting vocals, although the organic backing suggests security and rootedness, which he thought he would find with Heather.

He got the idea for the next song, 'She's Given Up Talking', after chatting to a neighbour who revealed that a granddaughter had stopped talking at school. Not only would the child not speak to her teachers, she even refused to talk to her friends. But when she got home, she couldn't be stopped from talking.

Fascinated by the story, McCartney wrote 'She's Given Up Talking' while on holiday in Jamaica. Freud would, no doubt, have been equally transfixed by the tale, but let's not get too bogged down in psychobabble; 'She's Given Up Talking' is simply a catchy pop song, which its writer described as "a sort of strange little song. But when you know the real story behind it it's not really creepy". It remained unfinished until he reached the studio, because he claimed it gave him greater freedom.

McCartney wrote 'Driving Rain' after a day spent motoring with Heather along the Pacific Coast Highway. It's a jubilant account of the day's events, and McCartney recalled that it was written "in the evening. I was sitting at the piano and I just started writing something half-based on that day out". He called on his magpie instinct to help shape the opening line, which was inspired by troublesome security. "In the LA house we were staying in, they have an alarm system. [And] it always just used to say 'Something's open'. So I just used it. Sometimes I just steal things like that, just to get me going."

Although the song started life as a ballad, once McCartney got into the studio and began recording with a band, it developed into an up-tempo rocker that bounces along like a hyperactive-child on a space-hopper. Rarely has his euphoria been conveyed so effortlessly. Indeed, when he spoke about the album, he said: "I think if you're happy making a record, then it shows."

'I Do' was written in January 2001 while Paul and Heather were on holiday in Goa. Typical of McCartney's ballad style, it sounds like it could come from any of his previous solo albums. But does that mean it's timeless or generic? 'I Do' is the kind of song that once would have been inspired by Linda. As it is, Heather undoubtedly provided the inspiration for this romantic ballad. McCartney: "It was one of those 'if you only knew' songs, like just talking to someone; if you only knew, that it's OK from my side. It's like a communicative statement to someone – 'Whatever you think at any given time, remember this – I do.'"

McCartney said that before he recorded the song, he'd sing it in a lower register, but when he came to record it, to lift it in the second verse, he moved the melody up an octave. However, when he recorded his vocal, he caught his breath (at 0:46) before the octave leap, fluffing his delivery. Mistakes like this would usually be corrected with an overdub, but in this instance he kept the 'accident' as it seemed in keeping with the spirit of the project.

He wrote 'Tiny Bubble' on his Scottish farm, where he also recorded a demo. According to some reports, he was so pleased with the demo that much of it found its way onto the final master. But how much of his demo, if any, features on the track is unclear, particularly as he claimed that the band beefed it up a bit when he reached the studio. "It started a bit more ballady," he said, "but as happened with a few of the songs when you bring them to a band – with a drummer – they hip up a bit."

As with 'Mull Of Kintyre', he was moved to write the song by the beautiful countryside that surrounds his farm. But this is where comparisons end. While 'Mull Of Kintyre' was about a specific locale, 'Tiny Bubble' looks at the bigger picture. He said the song was "just a stream of consciousness, saying all the world's a tiny bubble". Quick to dismiss it as little more than automatic writing, he overlooked its greater meaning. Alluding to Earth's delicate environmental balance, his metaphor echoes more poetic observations on the subject, such as Gerard Manley Hopkins' *Binsey Poplars*. McCartney's lyric may not equal the poetry of Manley Hopkins, but it's obvious that both men share a love of nature and a concern for its protection, even if they are separated by over 100 years.

'Magic' was written towards the end of 1998, the year in which Linda died. As McCartney wrote the song in the wake of losing his wife of 30 years, one may have expected a mournful requiem. Indeed, in the weeks after her death, he found himself writing sad songs. But 'Magic' is a positive celebration that evokes powerful memories of the fateful night that Paul first met Linda. "It was the first night we heard 'Whiter Shade Of Pale'," said McCartney, "so you can tell how long ago that was. As she was leaving, I said to her, 'My name is Paul. What's yours?' And I thought, I can't believe I said that. Years later, I said to the kids: 'If I hadn't done that, you wouldn't be here.'"

Not for the first time, McCartney turned to music for comfort, and the act of writing 'Magic' marked a change in his grieving. "I realised I had turned a corner with that song, because I suddenly thought, 'I'm really proud to have known someone as beautiful as Linda for 30 years,' instead of thinking, 'Oh, we only had 30 years together.' Some people are together forever and don't have as good a relationship."

Borrowing from both 'Bip Bop' and 'Mother Nature's Son', McCartney wrote the country-flavoured 'Your Way' while on holiday in Jamaica. As the song alludes stylistically to the early years of Paul and Linda's relationship, it would be easy to speculate that this is a song about Linda. However, as the middle eight is written in the present rather than the past tense, it could just as easily be about Heather. To confuse things further, McCartney explained that the octave leap, which announces the chorus, may allude to "two sides of a personality singing to each other, like a man and a woman". Is this him examining his feminine side? Or is it a celebration of womanhood inspired by Linda and Heather? Whatever the song is about, its upbeat mood and celebratory lyric could only have been written by someone enjoying life and the journey through it.

'Spinning On An Axis' was the first song written by father and son to appear on a McCartney album, although not the first they had written together. It began, like so many of McCartney's songs, informally. Paul and James were in New Hampshire, watching the sun setting, and they began to talk about how it seemed that they were moving away from the sun rather than it from them.

According to McCartney, James was playing a riff on a

keyboard that inspired a 'parody rap' on the subject. This was captured on cassette, and the song was finished at a later date. Influenced by the celestial movements he had witnessed in the USA, McCartney developed his spontaneous rap to encompass themes that evoke notions of natural beauty and eternal recurrence – which could be read as metaphors of personal change and progress. Reflecting his positive state of mind, McCartney's lyric suggests that mankind's modernist agenda may be rewarded by peace of the soul. But like other songs on the album, it's the journey that's important, not the destination.

McCartney wrote 'About You' in Goa on a small guitar with its own built-in amplifier, which he often takes on holiday. Just as he had written songs in praise of Linda, he now offered thanks to Heather for helping him overcome the grief and pain of losing a loved one.

McCartney woke one morning and after breakfast began improvising at the piano. When Heather asked which Beatles song he was playing, he explained that it wasn't a Beatles song, but that he was making it up. Heather was so excited at witnessing the creative process that she insisted the music be recorded and found a Dictaphone onto which he recorded his demo. Later, she asked what the song was called. He told her it was called 'Heather'.

She can be forgiven for thinking that it predated their relationship, as McCartney's melody has a classic, timeless quality, of the kind that he appears to write almost effortlessly. His simple melodic statement eventually acquired an equally understated but intricately textured arrangement, which matures seductively before returning to its elemental form. Apart from a half-hearted lyric, 'Heather' has all the hallmarks of McCartney at his best, and if nothing else displays his talent for melodic invention and arrangement.

He began writing 'Back In The Sunshine Again' in Arizona in 1997 with his son James, who helped with the bridge and riff. At the time, Linda was fighting cancer, and McCartney must have found it hard to see any light at the end of the tunnel. Turning to music, he started to fashion a song about "leaving behind all our troubles and moving forward into the sunshine". He completed it in California just before starting work on the album.

A statement of intent, it maps his move away from the shadow cast by Linda's death and into the light of his new relationship with Heather. But if his lyric suggests deliverance from the pain, suffering, and soul-searching he'd experienced, the song's bluesy setting and his vocal, which appears burdened with emotional unease, suggests that he had yet to successfully cast off his despair. For 'Back In The Sunshine Again' is no glorious exhortation of the life-force but a song that finds its author in an emotional abeyance, caught between the warmth of the sun and the cool melancholia of the blues.

McCartney debuted 'Your Loving Flame' on British television's *Michael Parkinson Show* on December 3 1999, performing the song to his own piano accompaniment and with David Gilmour adding some guitar fills. Explaining that it was still very much a work-in-progress, he recalled that the song took shape while he was staying in the Carlisle Hotel in New York City. "I was on the 73rd floor, and it was a fantastic big suite with a plate-glass window overlooking Central Park. To the side, there was a black Steinway piano, so it was like walking into Cole Porter's life. So I thought: I've got to write a song if I get a chance. The next morning I wrote this one. It came very easily."

He wrote 'Your Loving Flame' at the start of his relationship with Heather, and like much of what he wrote for *Driving Rain* it finds him standing at an emotional crossroads, contemplating his future and wondering which direction to take. Inflamed by the thought of a new relationship, his emotions remain mixed and uncertain. Is this the right woman for him? And if it is, how can he understand her better? Like 'Maybe I'm Amazed', 'Your Loving Flame' finds McCartney struggling to come to terms with an emotional dilemma, which this time would affect not only him but also his children. He said: "I'd seen Heather, and I talked to the kids and said, 'How would you feel if I started getting feelings for another woman?' It was a hypothetical question. They said they wouldn't mind as long as I was happy and were really nice about it, and I needed them to say that. But even so, we still had to be sensitive, and [Heather and I] were a secret for a while."

Although McCartney was unable to resolve the potential consequence of his actions, 'Your Loving Flame' finds him delighting in the mood indigo. By the time he came to record the song in June 2001, it had matured considerably. The finished version is a model of simplicity, but it's important not to forget that at its heart rests a complex of emotions.

As the 1990s drew to a close, McCartney broadened his horizons and made public what he had been doing in private for years. Besides having his first art exhibition, he also published his first collection of poems. Few of his lyrics have started as poetry – 'All My Loving' is one of the few examples – but the words for 'Rinse The Raindrops' came to him as just that. But, as he explained, "I wasn't sure whether they were a poem or a song. I liked them and sort of wrote a rough melody for them in my head".

And that's how the song remained until he decided to record it toward the end of the first two-week recording session for the album. "We were in the studio one day," he recalled, "and I fancied doing something different with the guys. We'd come to the end of the prepared tunes, so I thought I'd do something crazy with this." After a quick rehearsal on acoustic guitar, he and the band jammed on the song for about half an hour. The resulting takes were then mixed and edited by Kahne, who produced the ten-minute version that appears on the album.

'Rinse The Raindrops' features one of the rawest vocals of McCartney's career. This, he explained, was due to having lost his voice while on holiday in India. When he was there, "a carpet salesman ripped me off. He told me that this carpet was the rarest thing ever, but when I got to the next town I found another 20 of them. So I rang him, and during the argument, and not helped by the weather, I started to lose my voice. The following day it went totally. I couldn't talk. So I came to LA with my voice in quite a rough shape, and [I] decided to do the easy songs first, just to get the tracks down. But then I ended up just letting loose on one track, this monster ten-minute song called 'Rinse The Raindrops', where I really ripped it – and it all came good."

Like 'Why Don't We Do It In The Road?', 'Rinse The Raindrops' is a raucous blues-based monolith that reveals its author's delight in jamming and his pleasure in exchanging ideas with other musicians.

Driving Rain data

Parlophone issued the album in the UK on CD with a screen-printed customised label and 12-page booklet. A month later, they issued a two-record set with customised labels, printed inner sleeves, and a gatefold sleeve.

In the USA, Capitol released the album on CD. To promote it they issued a *Driving Rain Sampler* (DPRO 6159952) in a custom card sleeve with a facsimile of McCartney's signature and the album title in black on the front.

'Lonely Road' was issued in a Dave Way remix as a promotional CD single (DPRO 6 16920 2) to coincide with McCartney's 2002 tour of America, as was 'Your Loving Flame' (DPRO 6 16914 2).

THE CONCERT FOR NEW YORK

THIS WAS the event staged to raise money for the families of the firefighters and police who lost their lives on September 11 2001 in the terrorist attacks on the USA. McCartney was the first artist approached by the organisers, and once his name was associated with the event others were quick to follow.

The concert, arranged at great speed, quickly grew into one of the biggest charity events since Live Aid. And like Live Aid, it was broadcast live to a huge audience. It was also filmed and recorded for release on CD and DVD.

As with Live Aid, artists played truncated sets, and McCartney delivered a brief six-song performance using the same musicians who backed him on *Driving Rain*. He played two songs from *Driving Rain* ('Lonely Road', 'From A Lover To A Friend'), three that were originally recorded by The Beatles ('I'm Down', 'Yesterday', 'Let It Be'), and his new song inspired by the terrorist attacks, 'Freedom'. Four songs from the set were released on this double CD of the concert.

McCartney opened his Beatles-era rocker 'I'm Down'. He'd begun writing it in late 1964 with the intention of coming up with something like Little Richard's 'Long Tall Sally', and recorded it with the group on June 14 1965 – the same day he recorded 'Yesterday'. Released as the B-side of 'Help!', 'I'm Down' closed almost all of The Beatles' concert appearances in 1965 and '66, although they continued to use the perennial 'Long Tall Sally' right up to their final gig at Candlestick Park in '66. McCartney chose to open the Concert For New York with 'I'm Down' because he thought it summarised the way he and many others felt about the events of September 11. It was the first time he'd performed the song in public as a solo artist.

THE CONCERT FOR NEW YORK
VARIOUS ARTISTS
PAUL McCARTNEY 'I'm Down', 'Yesterday', 'Let It Be', 'Freedom' (Finale).
UK RELEASE November 27 2001; Columbia/Sony Music 505445 2; failed to chart.
US RELEASE November 27 2001; Columbia/Sony Music 1C2K86270; SACD Multichannel Columbia/Sony Music 1C2S86270; failed to chart.

- **'I'm Down'** (Lennon, McCartney)

Paul McCartney (vocals, bass guitar), Rusty Anderson (guitars, backing vocals), Abe Laboriel Jr (drums, backing vocals), Gabe Dixon (keyboards, backing vocals).
Recorded live at Madison Square Garden, New York City, NY, USA.
Produced by Don DeVito, Chuck Plotkin, Bob Clearmountin, and Thom Cadley.

'FREEDOM'

TO PROMOTE *Driving Rain*, McCartney appeared on BBC Radio and performed a spontaneous version of 'Freedom'. Backed by the show's presenters, Mark Radcliffe and Mark Riley, this was his first music session for the BBC since June 1965. An unintended highlight of his promotional duties, it was later posted on the show's website

'FREEDOM'
PAUL McCARTNEY
Performed live on *Mark And Lard Show*, BBC Radio One, December 13 2001, posted on www.bbc.co.uk/radio1/markandlard/listen.shtml

- **'Freedom'** (McCartney)

Paul McCartney (vocals, acoustic guitar), Mark Radcliffe (drums), Chris Lee, (bass), Marc Riley (guitar).
Recorded at BBC Radio studios, Manchester, England.

VANILLA SKY

CAMERON Crowe, writer-director of *Vanilla Sky*, asked if McCartney could provide him with a song for the film's soundtrack, and McCartney duly obliged. He saw an early rough-cut of the film with Crowe and invited him back to Henson studio to hear what he'd been working on. Crowe said he wanted something folk-orientated and asked if he could write something specifically for the movie. A few days later, McCartney delivered the film's title song.

'Vanilla Sky' finds him contemplating life's rich emotional tapestry, and, like much of what appears on *Driving Rain*, there's a positive message behind its veil of ambivalence. An uncharacteristically lethargic melody, which hints at emotional rootedness, gives the song a compelling sense of restraint that is at odds with a lyric full of allusions to movement, flight, and escape.

Stylistically, it recalls the kind of 'folk' songs McCartney wrote while studying meditation in India in 1968, which he recorded for the *White Album* or later for *McCartney*. And like the best of what he recorded for those two albums, 'Vanilla Sky' has a plausible tension that undermines the fact that it was written to order.

Vanilla Sky data

It was nominated for a Grammy in the category Best Music, Original Song. To help promote the song and improve its chances of winning, a one-track promotional CD single of the title song was distributed to the voting panel and members of the media. This release, in a jewel case with full colour cover, was not issued with a catalogue number but can be identified by 'ECW-GKS-VANILLA SKY (2828-EC VANILLA SKY, GMI-CS)22856-1' inscribed in the area nearest the spindle hole.

A four-track promotional CD single (SP124W) was issued to radio stations in Spain. Issued in a slim line case with a cover similar to the commercial CD, it also featured Radiohead with 'Everything In Its Right Place', and R.E.M. with 'All The Right Friends' and 'Sweetness Follows'.

VANILLA SKY ORIGINAL SOUNDTRACK
VARIOUS ARTISTS
PAUL McCARTNEY 'Vanilla Sky'.
UK release February 4 2002; Warner Bros. 9362481092; failed to chart.
US release December 14 2001; Warner Bros. 9362481092; failed to chart

- **'Vanilla Sky'** **(McCartney)**

Paul McCartney (guitar, whistling, vocals), Rusty Anderson (guitar), unknown (flute).
Recorded at Henson Recording Studio, Los Angeles, CA, USA.
Produced by David Kahne.

PARTY AT THE PALACE

RECORDED at Buckingham Palace in London on June 3 2002, *Party At The Palace* formed part of the Queen Elizabeth II Golden Jubilee Celebration and featured some of Britain's leading musicians. McCartney closed the concert, performing 'Her Majesty', 'Blackbird', 'While My Guitar Gently Weeps' (with Eric Clapton), 'Sgt. Pepper's Lonely Hearts Club Band', 'The End', 'All You Need Is Love', 'Hey Jude', and 'I Saw Her Standing There' (not broadcast).

Whether it was nerves or lack of rehearsal time, he appeared nervous, and fluffed 'Blackbird' and the introduction to 'While My Guitar Gently Weeps'.

Speaking after the event, he confirmed that it was only when he walked on stage that the scale of the event finally hit home. "When I was singing, I just suddenly realised there were people in the Mall, all over Britain, and all over the world listening. That's a big audience!"

BBC engineers also marred his appearance by failing to turn on the appropriate microphones at the right time. Rod Stewart and Joe Cocker, who shared the first two verses of 'All You Need Is Love', were inaudible. But generally the sound quality and live mix was remarkably good. With Her Majesty having left the party and the concert officially over, McCartney gave a surprise reading of 'I Saw Her Standing There', which was just audible underneath the radio commentary.

PARTY AT THE PALACE
VARIOUS ARTISTS
PAUL McCARTNEY 'All You Need Is Love', 'Hey Jude'.
UK RELEASE June 24 2002; Virgin VTCDX463; compilation chart high No.10.
US RELEASE July 9 2002; Virgin VTCDX463; failed to chart.

- **'All You Need Is Love'** **(Lennon, McCartney)**

Paul McCartney (bass, vocals), Rod Stewart (vocals), Joe Cocker (vocals), Rusty Anderson (guitar), Brian Ray (guitar), Abe Laboriel Jr (drums), with Bryan Adams, Keith Airley, Atomic Kitten, Shirley Bassey, Tony Bennett, Blue, Emma Bunton, Eric Clapton, The Corrs, Phil Collins, Ray Cooper, Ray Davies, Dame Edna Everage, Tony Iommi, J'anna Jacoby, Elton John, Tom Jones, Ladysmith Black Mambazo, Annie Lennox, Ricky Martin, Ozzy Osbourne, Mark Andrew-Brydon, Brian May, Roger Taylor, Cliff Richard, S Club 7, Will Young, Ruby Wax, Brian Wilson, Steve Winwood (chorus).
Recorded live at Buckingham Palace, London, England.
Produced by Giles Martin.

'All You Need Is Love' had been chosen as the anthem for the BBC's Music Live events of 2002 and was performed simultaneously by numerous groups across Britain on June 3 as its culmination. Written by John Lennon, the song had originally formed Britain's contribution to the first global satellite television link-up, *Our World*, where it was performed by The Beatles. Its inclusive theme was obviously what the Palace and the BBC were looking for to evoke a notion of a culturally diverse cool Britannia. However, to drive the message home that this was a celebration of all things British, Michael Kamen's orchestral arrangement used the opening bars of the British national anthem, rather than the French anthem that George Martin had used for the original, and drew on the ad-libbed 'She Loves You' motif to give the song a more decisive ending.

BACK IN THE US

ALTHOUGH critics gave *Driving Rain* positive reviews, these did not translate into sales. The album spent only one week on the British album charts and didn't do much better in the USA. McCartney thought the album deserved better, and Capitol wanted to shift the small mountain of CDs that were rumoured to be sitting unsold in their warehouses. Although McCartney may have been persuaded to tour by his record company, he may also have been lured back by the money. He was paid $5,600,000 for two shows in Las Vegas, and the US leg of the tour eventually grossed $100 million.

Of course, he may have been tempted to tour by a genuine desire to get back on the road, and he certainly appeared to enjoy the experience. Whatever his reasons, having tested the water with a few benefit concerts, he was finally convinced that an American tour was the best way to promote his new album. It did the trick: repackaged in a new cover, *Driving Rain* was eventually certified gold (500,000 units) six months after its release.

McCartney's first tour in nine years was a resounding success, both critically and commercially. On the first leg of the tour, Driving USA, in April and May 2002, he played 27 concerts in 25 cities to around 407,000 people. Demand for tickets was so strong that many shows sold out within minutes of them going on sale. There were, however, some complaints about the expensive prices, which began at $50 and rose to $250, but McCartney defended the cost by referring to the prices asked by Madonna, Elton John, U2, and Barbra Streisand. One reason the tour didn't start in Europe was because the promoters could charge higher prices in America. However, ignoring Europe did little to promote *Driving Rain* in territories outside of North America, and it certainly upset one British EMI executive, who said: "It has sparked anger here, and it is sure to anger fans."

US fans were favoured with a 23-date second leg, Back In The US, booked for September and October 2002. This leg of the tour too failed to reach Europe, but he did visit Mexico and Japan in November. McCartney eventually toured in Europe, the Back In The World dates, from March to the beginning of June 2003.

McCartney and his band rehearsed for the tour at Sony Studios in Los Angeles, and some footage from these sessions was made available on his website. Although he was keen to use the same pool of musicians that had backed him on *Driving Rain*, he performed a number of songs entirely solo. Stripping them to the bone, McCartney delivered intimate readings of many songs never previously performed in concert. Although he was keen to play material from *Driving Rain*, his set was Beatle-heavy, and each concert featured tributes to his friends John Lennon and George Harrison.

Back In The US songs

'Hello Goodbye' began life as little more than an experiment in which McCartney and The Beatles' assistant Alistair Taylor played alternative notes on a harmonium. The lyrics developed in the same way, McCartney calling out a word and Taylor replying with its opposite, an early example of McCartney delighting in the thaumaturgic delights of improvisation. The song had a considerable amount of work lavished on it before it was finally issued as the 16th Beatles single.

McCartney opened his concerts and this album with a rocked-up reading 'Hello Goodbye'. He moves the song up a gear, making it tougher than the Fabs' version and transforming a brilliant psychedelic pop song into a top class rocker.

Originally issued by The Beatles on their *Sgt. Pepper's Lonely Hearts Club Band* album, 'Getting Better' was inspired by drummer Jimmy Nicol, who deputised for Ringo Starr on the group's 1964 tour of Europe and Australia. McCartney recalled that whenever Nicol was asked how he was getting on he would reply, "It's getting better." With this in mind, McCartney fashioned the song's melody and then asked Lennon to help with the lyric, which contains some of Lennon's typically dry responses to McCartney's sunny optimism.

Sticking close to the original arrangement, McCartney and band here give a remarkably authentic reading of this classic track. While none of the band can replicate Lennon's sardonic vocals, for a live recording this is remarkably close to the original.

McCartney recorded 'Mother Nature's Son' solo for The Beatles' *White Album*, having written the song in India. It's about the pleasures that McCartney found in the countryside, a theme he's revisited several times since. Percussion and brass were added to that original cut, but in concert and captured on this album he performed the song with just his acoustic guitar and Wix Wickens's accordion for accompaniment.

Originally part of the 'long medley' from *Abbey Road*, 'You Never Give Me Your Money' was McCartney's response to increased friction in group caused by business problems. Apple, which was haemorrhaging money at an alarming rate, was at the root of the trouble. In an attempt to bring the company under control, several British businessmen were interviewed, but none were deemed right for the job. McCartney then suggested his soon-to-be father-in-law,

BACK IN THE US
PAUL McCARTNEY
CD 1 'Hello Goodbye', 'Jet', 'All My Loving', 'Getting Better', 'Coming Up', 'Let Me Roll It', 'Lonely Road', 'Driving Rain', 'Your Loving Flame', 'Blackbird', 'Every Night', 'We Can Work It Out', 'Mother Nature's Son', 'Vanilla Sky', 'You Never Give Me Your Money', 'Carry That Weight', 'The Fool On The Hill', 'Here Today', 'Something'.
CD 2 'Eleanor Rigby', 'Here There And Everywhere', 'Band On The Run', 'Back In The USSR', 'Maybe I'm Amazed', 'C Moon', 'My Love', 'Can't Buy Me Love', 'Freedom', 'Live And Let Die', 'Let It Be', 'Hey Jude', 'The Long And Winding Road', 'Lady Madonna', 'I Saw Her Standing There', 'Yesterday', 'Sgt. Pepper', 'The End'.
US RELEASE November 26 2002; Capitol 5423182; chart high No.8 .

- **'Hello Goodbye'** (Lennon, McCartney)
Paul McCartney (bass, vocals), Rusty Anderson (guitar), Brian Ray (guitar), Paul 'Wix' Wickens (keyboards), Abe Laboriel Jr (drums).
- **'Getting Better'** (Lennon, McCartney)
Paul McCartney (guitar, vocals), Rusty Anderson (guitar), Brian Ray (bass), Paul 'Wix' Wickens (keyboards), Abe Laboriel Jr (drums).
- **'Mother Nature's Son'** (Lennon, McCartney)
Paul McCartney (guitar, vocals), Paul 'Wix' Wickens (accordion).
- **'You Never Give Me Your Money / Carry That Weight'** (Lennon, McCartney)
Paul McCartney (piano, vocals).
- **'Something'** (Harrison)
Paul McCartney (ukulele, vocals).

All recorded live at uncredited locations, USA.
All produced by David Kahne

who had considerable experience as a music business attorney. The other Beatles, particularly Lennon, were unhappy with this, and consequently McCartney's plan came to nothing.

Enter Allen Klein, who had been pursuing The Beatles since Brian Epstein's death. Klein convinced Lennon that he was just what they needed, and Harrison and Starr fell in with Lennon – and the rift widened. Even so, when it came to recording their swansong, Lennon, Harrison, and Starr accepted McCartney's idea for the 'long medley' as it allowed them to incorporate unfinished fragments that they had been unable to complete.

In its original form, 'You Never Give Me Your Money' evokes a sense of loss and longing for a more innocent time. Performed now, the song took on a cabaret feel, a consequence of McCartney's too jaunty delivery and a cavalier attitude to his own lyrics. When recorded for *Abbey Road* the song segued into 'Sun King', but for this tour McCartney incorporated another song from the 'long medley', 'Carry That Weight'.

In the early part of the new century, everyone knew that George Harrison was fighting a losing battle with cancer. Even so, when he died on November 29 2001 it still came as a shock. The world had lost another Beatle, but McCartney had lost another brother. By way of tribute, he performed 'Something' to remember his friend.

Harrison had written the song in 1968 while working on the *White Album*, and it was eventually recorded and issued on *Abbey Road* and as a single, the first and only time The Beatles issued a Harrison composition as an A-side.

For his concert reading, McCartney accompanied himself on a ukulele given to him by George. Harrison had grown very fond of the ukulele and often gave them to friends as gifts. McCartney had learnt how to play 'Something' on the instrument as a surprise for his friend and decided to perform the song as a tribute. Although the ukulele will forever be associated with the slapstick humour of another great Lancastrian, George Formby, it is the mark of a great song that it can be performed on any instrument and still have the ability to move an audience.

Back In The US data

Issued in the USA as a double CD, *Back In The US* sold 224,250 copies in the first week. As with *Run Devil Run*, Capitol issued an 'extra-value' item through the Best Buy chain of record shops. A one-track DVD-single of 'Matchbox' with customised label and full colour card sleeve was shrink-wrapped to copies of the CD. Additionally, Capitol produced a promotional CD (DPRO 7087 6 17584 2 9) that replicated Disc 2 of the commercial CD. A DVD of the tour was issued (also titled *Back In The US*) which bonus backstage material. When played on a computer, the DVD gave access to unique footage available through McCartney's website.

SECRET WEBSITE SHOW

THOSE who purchased the *Back In The US* DVD and had a computer to play it on could access a restricted area of McCartney's website that contained about 30 minutes of footage recorded at a soundcheck. Besides the usual rock'n'roll standards, McCartney and his musicians performed a couple of new songs and a band version of 'Celebration' from the orchestral *Standing Stone* album. The Secret Website Show has since been bootlegged on DVD.

Delivered up-tempo, 'Blackbird' was transformed into a light-hearted country hoe-down. While McCartney insists on authenticity when performing his songs in concert, when rehearsing or warming up at a soundcheck he is more than happy to play around with them. While few examples of reworked songs appear on his commercial releases, several have surfaced in radio or television broadcasts.

The Beatles recorded 'Honey Don't' in five takes on October

26 1964, featuring Ringo on vocals, and it was released on the group's fourth LP, *Beatles For Sale*. The song had been in the group's repertoire for some time and was usually sung by Lennon (and The Beatles recorded a version of the song for the BBC on September 3 1963 in Manchester with Lennon on lead vocals, later issued on *The Beatles At The BBC*). The song became a regular at McCartney soundchecks, and a version recorded at a soundcheck appeared on episode 11 of his *Oobu Joobu* radio series. As with other versions of the song, the take on the Website Show is a real fireball. given the number of times he's played it and his obvious delight in performing the song, it obviously remains high on his list of favourites.

'Secret Website Jam' is just that, a jam. McCartney introduces the band, and everyone takes a solo. That's all.

'India' was a new, atmospheric song that evokes the sights, sounds, and smells of that country. McCartney continued to perform the song at soundchecks during the Back In The World Tour, including the last date, in Liverpool. That both Lennon and McCartney should write songs titled 'India' shows the considerable impact the country had on them.

SECRET WEBSITE SHOW
PAUL McCARTNEY
WEBSITE-ONLY material available to purchasers of Back In The US DVD through www.paulmccartney.com, November 2002.

- **'Blackbird'** (Lennon, McCartney)
Paul McCartney (guitar), Rusty Anderson (guitar), Brian Ray (bass), Paul 'Wix' Wickens (accordion), Abe Laboriel Jr (drums).
- **'Honey Don't'** (Perkins)
Paul McCartney (guitar), Rusty Anderson (guitar), Brian Ray (bass), Paul 'Wix' Wickens (keyboards), Abe Laboriel Jr (drums).
- **'Celebration'** (McCartney)
Paul McCartney (piano), Rusty Anderson (guitar), Brian Ray (bass), Paul 'Wix' Wickens (keyboards), Abe Laboriel Jr (drums).
- **'Secret Website Jam'** (McCartney)
Paul McCartney (bass), Rusty Anderson (guitar), Brian Ray (guitar), Paul 'Wix' Wickens (keyboards), Abe Laboriel Jr (drums).
- **'India'** (McCartney)
Paul McCartney (bass), Rusty Anderson (guitar), Brian Ray (guitar), Paul 'Wix' Wickens (keyboards), Abe Laboriel Jr (drums).

All recorded live at uncredited location.
All produced by David Kahne.

'BAND ON THE RUN'

THE BBC commissioned McCartney to record a new version of 'Band On The Run', which they used to promote BBC Radio 2. Radically reworking the opening motif of the song's third movement, he incorporated an exotic range of sounds, produced using several avant-garde techniques. Random radio scans, the unusual application of piano strings scraped with a coin, and wine glasses were all used to create this new recording. The resulting song was used for both radio and television advertisements in edited and unedited versions. The new arrangement was also used on a few occasions during McCartney's European tour, where it was segued into a full band rendition of the song.

'BAND ON THE RUN'
PAUL McCARTNEY
BROADCAST piece to promote BBC Radio 2, late 2002.

- **'Band On The Run'** (McCartney)
Paul McCartney (all instruments).

Recording location unknown.
Produced by Paul McCartney.

BACK IN THE WORLD

IN MARCH 2003, *Back In The US* was issued in Britain and Europe. Well, almost. Because McCartney intended to alter the content of his European shows, he insisted on revising the track listing and re-titling the album *Back In The World*. Three songs recorded on the *Back In The US* leg of his American tour – 'Michelle', 'Let 'Em In', and 'She's Leaving Home' – appeared on the revised album, as did a new version of 'Hey Jude', recorded in Mexico. A new reading of 'Calico Skies', performed in Japan, was also included.

Rehearsals for the Back In The World tour took place at the London Arena, because it was closest to the size of venues they would be playing as they made his way across Europe. Although the European tour was considerably shorter than McCartney's US outing, the scale of the operation remained impressive. Forty trucks were required to transport the staging and equipment, and 116 crew members were employed to assemble it.

When Wings toured the world in 1976, McCartney had played a mere handful of songs written while he was a Beatle. With each tour, he increased the number of Beatles songs in his set. This time, he embraced his legacy and delivered heart-stopping performances of more than 20 Beatles songs. His attitude to performing these songs had changed dramatically. Whereas before he would have insisted on recreating the original arrangements note-for-note, this time he took a more liberal approach.

"I used to have a very, very strict view that The Beatles stuff was sacrosanct," he said. "It's slightly different this time, and that mainly came from the band. I didn't give the guys a brief. I didn't say to Rusty [Anderson] 'You must copy George's solo.' He just started playing a solo, and I thought: that's nice. I like what he plays and I like the idea that he varies it each night."

Previously, McCartney had insisted that the band play the same arrangement night after night. Anderson may have been allowed to vary his solos, but the performances remained as strictly choreographed as ever. However, there were a few surprises. A new arrangement of 'Band On The Run', based on a recording McCartney had made to promote BBC Radio 2, was performed at some shows, and when the band played in Spain he performed an a cappella version of 'Tres Conejos' from the *Liverpool Oratorio*.

'She's Leaving Home' is a perfect McCartney composition. The Beatles originally recorded the song for *Sgt. Peppers Lonely Hearts Club Band*, of course. McCartney had been inspired by a story he'd read in a daily newspaper and, assisted by Lennon, who helped with the chorus, fashioned one of the most moving songs of his career.

The original recording, made at Abbey Road on March 20 1967, featured just two Beatles – Paul and John. The rich orchestral backing was arranged by Mike Leander, and the finished recording was produced by George Martin.

McCartney performed it on this tour for the first time since it was recorded (the take on the album is from Mexico on November 3 2002) and the song required subtlety and restraint from his band. Although Lennon's absence is obvious, Anderson, Ray, and Laboriel make a good job of the backing vocals, and the combination of Anderson's nylon-strung acoustic guitar and Wickens's keyboard create a convincing replica of Leander's original arrangement.

BACK IN THE WORLD
PAUL McCARTNEY
CD 1 'Hello, Goodbye', 'Jet', 'All My Loving', 'Getting Better', 'Coming Up', 'Let Me Roll It', 'Lonely Road', 'Driving Rain', 'Your Loving Flame', 'Blackbird', 'Every Night', 'We Can Work It Out', 'Mother Nature's Son', 'You Never Give Me Your Money', 'Carry That Weight', 'The Fool On The Hill', 'Here Today', 'Something'.
CD 2 'Eleanor Rigby', 'Here There And Everywhere', 'Calico Skies', 'Michelle', 'Band On The Run', 'Back In The USSR', 'Maybe I'm Amazed', 'Let 'Em In', 'My Love', 'She's Leaving Home', 'Can't Buy Me Love', 'Live And Let Die', 'Let It Be', 'Hey Jude', 'The Long And Winding Road', 'Lady Madonna', 'I Saw Her Standing There', 'Yesterday', 'Sgt. Pepper', 'The End'.
UK RELEASE March 17 2003; Parlophone 5423182; chart high No.5.

• **'She's Leaving Home'** (Lennon, McCartney)
Paul McCartney (bass, vocals), Rusty Anderson (guitar), Brian Ray (guitar), Paul 'Wix' Wickens (keyboards), Abe Laboriel Jr (backing vocals).
Recorded live at Palacio de los Deportes, Mexico City, Mexico.
Produced by David Kahne.

HOPE
VARIOUS ARTISTS
PAUL McCARTNEY 'Calico Skies'.
UK RELEASE April 21 2003; WEA 5046658462; failed to chart.

• **'Calico Skies'** (McCartney)
Paul McCartney (guitar, vocals), Rusty Anderson (guitar), Brian Ray (bass), Paul 'Wix' Wickens (accordion), Abe Laboriel Jr (drums).
Recorded live at London Arena, London, England.
Produced by Paul 'Pab' Boothroyd.

Back In The World data

Parlophone issued the album with artwork based on the American version but with newly-designed customised labels. To promote the record, Parlophone issued a five-track CD (WORLD 002) in a gatefold sleeve with the same cover image as the commercial album but without the title.

HOPE

McCARTNEY donated this new reading of 'Calico Skies' to the War Child charity, who issued it on this CD to raise money for Iraqi children injured in the Second Gulf War. It was recorded at the London Arena on March 20 2003 during rehearsals for his European tour, but is not as good as the studio version.

THE IN-LAWS

IT TOOK over 30 years for McCartney to complete 'A Love For You'. Work on the song began in New York City in 1971, when McCartney, Hugh McCracken, and Denny Seiwell recorded the basic track while working on *Ram*. Some time later, McCartney added more electric guitar and Denny Laine and Linda added backing vocals and percussion.

By the mid 1970s, McCartney planned to issue the recording on his proposed *Cold Cuts* collection. Wings continued to add overdubs to songs destined for *Cold Cuts* until the album was abandoned in the early 1980s. Since then, several songs from the album have been issued as B-sides or, as is the case here, on soundtrack albums.

Before 'A Love For you' was issued on the *In-Laws* soundtrack, McCartney added more overdubs and altered the ending.

A two-track promotional CD single of 'A Love For You' was issued to publicise the album and film. (Consisting of a 4:01 edit and 4:44 album version, it was issued by the Bulletproof Recording Company in a jewel case with a printed rear inlay card.)

This different version of 'Live And Let Die' was recorded probably in August 1974 by Wings Mk.5 at Abbey Road while they shot the ultimately unreleased film, *One Hand Clapping*. Although Wings were there to film their rehearsals, some of the recordings they made, including 'Live And Let Die', were sweetened with overdubs.

THE IN-LAWS
VARIOUS ARTISTS
PAUL McCARTNEY 'A Love for You', 'Live And Let Die', 'I'm Carrying'.
UK RELEASE July 7 2003; Bulletproof/WSM 8122738862; failed to chart.
US RELEASE May 20 2003; Rhino R2 73886; failed to chart.

- **'A Love For You'** (McCartney)
Paul McCartney (bass, vocals), Linda McCartney (backing vocals), Hugh McCracken (guitar), Denny Laine (guitar, backing vocals), Denny Seiwell (drums), Laurence Juber (guitar), Steve Holly (percussion).
Recorded at A&R Studios and Columbia Studios, New York City, NY, USA.
Produced by Paul McCartney. Additional production and mixing by David Kahne.
- **'Live And Let Die'** (McCartney)
Paul McCartney (piano, vocals), Linda McCartney (keyboards, backing vocals), Denny Lane (bass), Jimmy McCulloch (guitar), Geoff Britton (drums), Del Newman (orchestral arranger, conductor).
Recorded at Abbey Road Studios, London, England.
Produced by Paul McCartney.

'WHOLE LIFE'

McCARTNEY recorded this at Abbey Road with his touring band and ex-Eurythmics man Dave Stewart, and donated it to the charity 46664 to help raise money to fight AIDS in Africa.

An up-tempo rocker, it restates much of what McCartney expressed with 'Simple As That', a song he'd given to an anti-drugs charity. This was his second attempt: he'd started work on the first version at Hog-Hill studio on May 19 1995, returning to add overdubs to it at Dave Stewart's Church studio in London on November 18 and 19. With the song finished, McCartney all but ignored it for eight years before dusting it off and re-recording it during one very productive session at Abbey Road on October 22 2003.

Like much of what McCartney recorded for his *Driving Rain* album, 'Whole Life' sounds rough and tough. Opening with a simple guitar riff, the band of young-ish Americas kick in with an overdriven guitar sound, over which McCartney delivers a gritty vocal. The lyric is typically optimistic and, in light of the AIDs epidemic sweeping Africa, reassuringly life-affirming.

The song was later issued on the 46664 *1 Year On* EP, made available on January 1 2005 through iTunes (and through the US iTunes site ten days later). The EP was issued on CD in Spain in an edition of 6,000. Issued in conjunction with Coca Cola, the 4-track EP was issued with a full colour screen-printed label.

'WHOLE LIFE'
PAUL McCARTNEY
DOWNLOAD www.46664.com, November 2003.

- **'Whole Life'** (McCartney)
Paul McCartney (bass, vocals), Dave Stewart (guitar), Rusty Anderson (guitar), Brian Ray (guitar), Abe Laboriel Jr (drums).
Recorded at Abbey Road Studios, London, England.
Produced by Paul McCartney.

CONCERT FOR GEORGE

THE TRIBUTE was staged one year after George Harrison's death, on November 29 2002, and was a star-studded event featuring many of his musician friends performing some of his best-loved songs.

The concert started with an Indian musical piece, 'Arpan', written by Harrison's friend Ravi Shankar. Next to appear were Monty Python, who bridged the gap between the serious part of the concert and the rock section. Eric Clapton then led the band through a set that spanned Harrison's career from The Beatles to the Traveling Wilburys.

Towards the end of the show, Ringo Starr took to the stage to perform 'Photograph' and 'Honey Don't'. Starr then introduced the other half of The Beatles' rhythm section, Paul McCartney. McCartney led the band through a faithful reading of 'For You Blue' followed by a reprise of his ukulele-based reading of 'Something'. This time he was accompanied by the house band, who joined him from the solo, taken by Eric Clapton. McCartney then sang 'All Things Must Pass' and rounded off the evening with a version of 'While My Guitar Gently Weeps'.

The concert was issued as a double CD and DVD. A four-track WSM-label promo CD-R acetate, which included 'While My Guitar Gently Weeps', was issued in the USA with custom printed disc and picture sleeve, with title and track-listing on the rear insert.

A SECRET HISTORY

PAUL McCartney may not be the first name you think of when considering influences on dance music. But his Fireman and Twin Freaks projects have led to a re-evaluation of his work in this genre.

A Secret History was a compilation that explored the roots of dance music, and it included a track from *McCartney II*, 'Temporary Secretary', to illustrate his influence. Speaking to the *NME* in November 2003, he said: "I'm really chuffed at the renewed interest in a track I made 23 years ago."

To promote the album, Parlophone issued a remix of 'Temporary Secretary', produced by Radio Slave, as a one-sided 12-inch single (TEMPSEC 01) in a limited edition of 500. Side one of the record has a black and sliver generic Parlophone label. Side two, which is blank, has a silver label with the drawing of McCartney and a secretary used for the original 12-inch sleeve. Each record was hand-numbered, and some came with an A4 press release. Not long after the record was issued, counterfeit copies began to appear. Counterfeits are identifiable by blurred printing and the B-side not having the hand-written number that appears on original pressings.

The July 2004 issue of *Uncut* magazine featured an extensive interview with McCartney and a CD, *Something For The Weekend* (UNCUT 2004 07). He selected the tracks for the CD, and they included three McCartney compositions: 'Spiral' from *Working Classical*, 'Calico Skies' from *Flaming Pie*, and the Radio Slave remix of 'Temporary Secretary'.

A SECRET HISTORY
VARIOUS ARTISTS
PAUL McCARTNEY 'Temporary Secretary'.
UK RELEASE November 17 2003; LP Regal 07243-594020-1-7; CD Regal REG 85 CD; failed to chart.

CONCERT FOR GEORGE
VARIOUS ARTISTS
PAUL McCARTNEY 'For You Blue', 'Something' (with Eric Clapton), 'All Things Must Pass', 'While My Guitar Gently Weeps' (with Eric Clapton).
UK/US RELEASE November 17 2003; Rhino 8122745462; failed to chart.

• **'For You Blue'** (Harrison)
Paul McCartney (guitar, vocals), Eric Clapton (guitar), Jeff Lynne (guitar), Albert Lee (guitar), Andy Fairweather-Low (guitar), Dhani Harrison (guitar), Gary Brooker (keyboards), Chris Stainton (keyboards), Billy Preston (keyboards), Dave Bronze (bass), Klaus Voormann (bass), Jim Capaldi (drums), Ringo Starr (drums), Jim Keltner (drums), Henry Spinetti (drums), Ray Cooper (percussion), Jim Horn (alto saxophone), Tom Scott (tenor saxophone), Marc Mann (electric guitar), Katie Kissoon (backing vocals), Tessa Niles (backing vocals). Recorded live at Royal Albert Hall, London, England. Produced by Jeff Lynne.
• **'Something'** (Harrison)
Paul McCartney (ukulele, vocals), rest as 'For You Blue'.
• **'All Things Must Pass'** (Harrison)
Personnel as 'For You Blue'.
• **'While My Guitar Gently Weeps'** (Harrison)
Paul McCartney (piano, backing vocals), Eric Clapton (guitar, vocals), rest as 'For You Blue'.

'HAPPY XMAS (WAR IS OVER)'

CHRISTMAS comes but once a year – and when it does there's often some Beatles-related product ready for release. In 2003 there was no Lennon reissue to tempt fans from their hard-earned cash. Instead, there was a new DVD, *Lennon Legend*, that updated the previous *John Lennon Collection*. Naturally, the CD of the same name was re-promoted, and the Lennon evergreen, 'Happy Xmas (War Is Over)', re-promoted for the umpteenth time to give both DVD and CD a little boost.

The single was issued as an enhanced CD and as a 7-inch. As with the original single, EMI pressed the record on green vinyl. However, this time the record was manufactured with black Parlophone labels with white print and backed with 'Imagine'.

The original picture cover was employed, but with minor differences: the rear now sported a barcode plus a reference to the *Lennon Legend* DVD and CD. The single was created using new masters and included an alternative version of 'Instant Karma!'.

The 2003 master features Lennon's live vocal from his *Top Of The Pops* TV appearance, known as the knitting version (in fact, Yoko is crocheting). It was also marginally longer than the original as it did not fade out. The enhanced CD single also featured an instrumental version of 'Imagine' – essentially the finished master without Lennon's vocal – to accompany a photo gallery.

'HAPPY XMAS (WAR IS OVER)' / 'IMAGINE'
JOHN LENNON & YOKO ONO/PLASTIC ONO BAND WITH THE HARLEM COMMUNITY CHOIR
UK RELEASE December 12 2003; Parlophone R 6627; CD Parlophone CDR 6627 'Happy Xmas (War Is Over)', 'Imagine', 'Instant Karma!', 'Imagine' (Instrumental Plus Photo Gallery); chart high No.33.

'TROPIC ISLAND HUM'

THIS was recorded in 1987 but remained unreleased while work continued on the animated film it accompanied. "I don't often write songs deliberately for children," said McCartney, "but we made this new film for kids and the film needed a song. As a songwriter, I'm always interested in trying to write music in different styles, so I took the challenge of trying to write another one for kids. I shouldn't imagine that too many of the Glastonbury bands would follow performing 'Helter Skelter' there with releasing a single for children by a cartoon squirrel, but it's ringing the changes like this which keeps me interested in the possibilities."

Similar in style to 'We All Stand Together', 'Tropic Island Hum' is infuriatingly catchy, with one of those simple tunes that, once heard, you can't stop humming. Neither deep nor particularly meaningful, it's a fun track for children – and had it featured in a Disney film, it might even be considered a classic of the genre.

'TROPIC ISLAND HUM' / 'WE ALL STAND TOGETHER'
PAUL McCARTNEY
UK RELEASE September 20 2004; Parlophone R 6649; CD single Parlophone CDR 6649; chart high No.21.

• **'Tropic Island Hum'** (McCartney)
Paul McCartney (piano, keyboards, upright bass, bass, bass, drums, vocals), Linda McCartney (backing vocals), Marion Montgomery (vocals), unknown (trumpet, trombone, flute), unknown (violin), London Community Gospel Choir.
Recorded at Hog-Hill Studio, East Sussex, England; orchestra recorded at AIR Studios, London, England.
Produced by George Martin.

'Tropic Island Hum' data

Parlophone issued 'Tropic Island Hum' as a CD and 7-inch single. The CD was issued with a jewel case and customised screen-printed label, and the 7-inch was pressed on yellow vinyl with customised labels and issued with a full-colour picture cover. Promotional copies of the CD single (CDRDJ 6649) were distributed about one month prior to the commercial release. Issued in a full-colour card sleeve, promotional copies of the single featured radio edits of A- and B-side. As EMI had closed its Swindon pressing plant in England, the CDs were manufactured in Europe.

ACOUSTIC

THIS new compilation of Lennon demos and live recordings was issued in Britain and the USA on November 2, but had appeared in Japan (TOPC-67483) on September 29 to coincide with a tribute concert there and was originally planned for Japanese consumption only. "I was just going to release *Acoustic* in Japan," Yoko Ono told the *Boston Globe*, "but then Capitol heard it and said, 'Can we release it here, too?'"

A Japanese-only release was never a feasible option, which Capitol, if not Ono, knew too well. Sales would have been lost to CDs imported from Japan or illegal downloads. With the music industry already suffering from a slump in sales, even an album with limited sales potential was worth issuing.

Of the 16 songs, nine had been previously issued on the *John Lennon Anthology*. The remaining seven had been available on bootlegs but were presented here in superior sound quality. Although some of the recordings were treated with noise reduction and reverb, the majority had been recorded on mono tape recorders and could not be remixed. Most of the songs on *Acoustic* were recorded as home demos and never intended for public consumption.

Unable to write musical notation, Lennon made home demos, and these were the foundations upon which the finished recordings would be based. "With the acoustic songs, first he would play them to me, then he would say, 'Yoko, let's record this,'" Ono recalled. "And he would set up the microphone in such a way that his voice and his guitar sound was very balanced. At first I wanted to collect some acoustic stuff on guitar and piano, but the piano tracks were not in good enough condition to put out. When he was banging the piano, he would put the microphone on top of the piano, so that you'd hear the piano much more than his voice. The balance was not good at all, so I could not rescue those songs. But with the guitar, he did a beautiful job of balancing the sound." Considering that most of Lennon's demo recordings were made on domestic cassette recorders, they sound remarkable.

Acoustic songs

Lennon recorded this demo of 'Well Well Well' on July 28 1970 while undergoing Primal Therapy in California. The tape was first aired on *The Lost Lennon Tapes* radio series, broadcast on August 14 1989, and later on the bootleg *The Dream Is Over*. It's a brief 1:17 take that lacks the power of the Plastic Ono Band version, but then this is only a demo and was never intended for public consumption. Interesting, but not essential.

The version of 'God' here also originates from the cassette of demo recordings that Lennon made that day in July 1970, revealing a work in progress. After a light-hearted introduction that echoes the rock'n'roll records of his youth, Lennon performs a version of the song lacking the closing "dream is over" verse. As with 'Well Well Well', this demo, along with three further takes, appeared on the *Dream Is Over* bootleg.

An alternative take of John's haunting lament for his mother, 'My Mummy's Dead', was issued commercially on this album for the first time. It too had appeared on *The Dream Is Over*. As this version was rejected by Lennon in favour of a superior take, it will come as no surprise that it's not quite as good as the version on *Plastic Ono Band*.

Lennon's acoustic home demo of 'Cold Turkey' sounds not unlike the kind of music being made by the then up-and-coming hippie duo Tyrannosaurus Rex. His vocalisations sound remarkably similar to those of the group's lead singer and future superstar Marc Bolan. While obviously influenced by Ono, Lennon would surely have been aware of Tyrannosaurus Rex. The duo was championed by British DJ John Peel on his *Perfumed Garden* radio show, and Lennon may have decided to adapt Bolan's vibrato for his demo recording. This version of the song has double-tracked guitars, as Lennon has added a second guitar part to his original take. The recording was first aired on *The Lost Lennon Tapes* broadcast on June 5 1989 and appeared on the bootleg *Gone From This Place*.

Lennon performs 'What you Got' on an un-amplified electric guitar rather than an acoustic model. This demo recording was first broadcast on the June 5 1989 edition of *The Lost Lennon Tapes*, although a longer, unedited version appeared on the bootleg *Listen To This*. The version presented on *Acoustic* has been edited and treated with noise reduction.

His demo recording of Dear Yoko was recorded while on holiday in Bermuda, and this version features an alternative introduction based on the song's chord structure. It also suffers from slight distortion, Lennon having set the input level too high while recording.

This was his second attempt at recording the song. Two months earlier, he'd taped several takes in front of a home video camera. Attempting the song again here, he recorded three takes, the first two breaking down and therefore incomplete. This version of 'Dear Yoko' was first aired on *The Lost Lennon Tapes* on August 12 1991.

Another acoustic-guitar version of 'Real Love' appears on *Acoustic*, the first having been issued on *Imagine: John Lennon, Music From The Motion Picture*. This is take 4 dating from June 1980 but does not improve on the previously issued versions. It was first broadcast on *The Lost Lennon Tapes* on June 12 1989 and was issued on the bootleg *Free As A Bird: The Dakota Beatles Demos*.

ACOUSTIC
JOHN LENNON
CD 'Working Class Hero', 'Love', 'Well Well Well', 'Look At Me', 'God', 'My Mummy's Dead', 'Cold Turkey', 'The Luck Of The Irish', 'John Sinclair' (Live), 'Woman Is The Nigger Of The World', 'What You Got', 'Watching The Wheels', 'Dear Yoko', 'Real Love', 'Imagine' (Live), 'It's Real'.
UK RELEASE November 1 2004; CD Parlophone 874 4282; failed to chart.
US RELEASE November 2 2004; CD Capitol 874 4282; chart high No.28.

- **'Well Well Well'** (Lennon)
John Lennon (vocals, acoustic guitar). Recorded at house on Nimes Road, Bel Air, CA, USA. Produced by Yoko Ono.
- **'God'** (Lennon)
John Lennon (vocals, acoustic guitar). Recorded at Bel Air, CA. Produced by Yoko Ono.
- **'My Mummy's Dead'** (Lennon)
John Lennon (vocals, acoustic guitar). Recorded at Bel Air, CA. Produced by Yoko Ono.
- **'Cold Turkey'** (Lennon)
John Lennon (vocals, acoustic guitar). Recorded at Tittenhurst Park, Sunninghill, near Ascot, England. Produced by Yoko Ono.
- **'What You Got'** (Lennon)
John Lennon (vocals, electric guitar). Recording location unknown. Produced by John Lennon.
- **'Dear Yoko'** (Lennon)
John Lennon (vocals, acoustic guitar). Recorded at home studio, Bermuda. Produced by Yoko Ono.
- **'Real Love'** (Lennon)
John Lennon (vocals, acoustic guitar).
Recorded at The Dakota, New York City, NY, USA.
Produced by John Lennon.

Acoustic data

The album was issued by Capitol on CD with an eight-page booklet and customised label that featured one of Lennon's drawings. To promote both *Acoustic* and the reissued *Rock'N'Roll*, Capitol issued a promotional CD, *John Lennon: Two Sides Of Lennon* (DPRO-70876), which featured a one-hour radio show based on a conversation between Yoko and Jody Denberg. They discuss both albums, with three songs from each highlighting the unique nature of each release.

INSPIRED BY GENIUS

INSPIRED BY GENIUS – THE MUSIC OF RAY CHARLES
VARIOUS ARTISTS
PAUL McCARTNEY 'Don't Let The Sun Catch You Crying'.
UK RELEASE June 4 2005; CD EMI 3305602; failed to chart.

THIS Ray Charles tribute album was issued by EMI and featured McCartney's live recording of 'Don't Let The Sun Catch You Crying' from his *Tripping The Live Fantastic* album.

'REALLY LOVE YOU'

ANOTHER remix project, another pseudonym. For this collaboration with remixer Roy Kerr it was presumably McCartney who chose the name – Twin Freaks – as it's the title of one of his paintings.

London-based DJ and producer Kerr, aka The Freelance Hellraiser, made his name producing mash-ups – a simple remix technique where the vocal from one song is overlaid on the instrumental track from another. His mash-up 'A Stroke Of Genius', which combined Christina Aguilera's 'Genie In A Bottle' with The Strokes' 'Hard To Explain', ensured that he become one of Britain's most sought-after remixers. In the summer of 2004, Kerr toured Europe with McCartney, opening each show with a 25-minute set of remixed McCartney tunes. This led to McCartney asking him to remix 12 songs for an album, also titled *Twin Freaks*.

'Really Love You' is a riff heavy mash-up of the track from *Flaming Pie*. The Freelance Hellraiser's remix is a real improvement on the original and transforms this impromptu jam into a hard-hitting dance track for the 21st century. 'Lalula' follows the same model – and this mix builds to an intense climax as the Hellraiser plays spot-the-sample – but it's not as successful as the A-side.

'REALLY LOVE YOU' / 'LALULA'
TWIN FREAKS
UK RELEASE June 6 2005; Graze GRAZE 012; failed to chart .

'Really Love You' data

The single was issued as a one-sided 12-inch in an edition of 2,000 copies, with the B-side etched with Paul's painting, *Twin Freaks*, in a PVC sleeve screen-printed with the title and artist's name. One-sided promo copies (GRAZE 010; 500 copies) were issued on May 16 2005 with a black label, with the Twin Freaks logo, in a PVC cover also printed with the Twin Freaks logo. A two-track CD single (GRAZE 013), which featured a radio edit of 'Really Love You', was issued in a white card sleeve. A second 12-inch promotional single, 'Rinse The Raindrops' / 'What's That You're Doing' (GRAZE 011; 200 copies), was also issued.

TWIN FREAKS

RELEASED one week after the 'Really Love You' remix single, *Twin Freaks* was issued as a two-record set by Parlophone/Graze Records. The vinyl edition was only issued in Europe; in other territories the album was available as a digital download only. The two-record set was issued in a gatefold sleeve with McCartney's painting, *Twin Freaks*, used for the front cover. One of the masked faces depicted in his painting was used for the customised record labels. Although the album was not released on CD commercially, promotional CDs were manufactured and distributed to the media. Issued with a plain sleeve, they incorrectly list 'Maybe I'm Amazed' as 'Baby I'm Amazed'. Counterfeit copies of the CD with artwork identical to the vinyl edition soon appeared on the black market.

A full-on freaky mash-up of McCartney's back catalogue, *Twin Freaks* is a little like McCartney's Fireman project, but this is anything but chill-out music. These 12 tracks are intense, sometimes dark, dance music – so turn up the bass, pump up the volume, and drive the neighbours mad.

TWIN FREAKS
TWIN FREAKS
SIDE 1 'Really Love You', 'Long Haired Lady' (Reprise), 'Rinse The Raindrops'.
SIDE 2 'Darkroom', 'Live And Let Die', 'Temporary Secretary'.
SIDE 3 'What's That You're Doing', 'Oh Woman, Oh Why', 'Mumbo'.
SIDE 4 'Lalula', 'Coming Up', 'Maybe I'm Amazed'.
UK RELEASE June 13 2005; LP Parlophone/Graze 311 3261; failed to chart.

'SGT. PEPPER'S LONELY HEARTS CLUB BAND'

LIVE 8 was conceived by Bob Geldof to raise awareness of the continuing crisis in Africa. The event, a follow-up to the Live Aid event that had taken place 20 years previously, was staged in major cities around the world. The London concert, which featured McCartney as opening and closing act, was held in Hyde Park. It was broadcast by the BBC and webcast by AOL.

McCartney was approached by Geldof, who suggested that it would be a good idea to open the concert with The Beatles' 'Sgt. Pepper's'. McCartney told Neil McCormick he played the event "with a little Irish band you may have heard of called U2, singing 'Sgt. Pepper's Lonely Hearts Club Band', a song made famous by another little band I used to play with. It was suggested to me by Bob and Bono, the mad Irish boys (God bless 'em) that it would be a good kick-off for the whole occasion. 'It was 20 years ago today ...' And it will be 20 years, almost to the day, that we all gathered together for Live Aid, and closed the show with Wembley Stadium singing another Beatles song, 'Let It Be'. It was a day that

'SGT. PEPPER'S LONELY HEARTS CLUB BAND', 'THE LONG AND WINDING ROAD'
PAUL McCARTNEY
DOWNLOAD www.7digital.com/downloads/live8, July 2005.

• **'Sgt. Pepper's Lonely Hearts Club Band'** (Lennon, McCartney)
Paul McCartney (guitar, vocals), Bono (vocals), The Edge (guitar), Adam Clayton (bass), Larry Mullen Jr (drums), unknown (horns).
• **'The Long And Winding Road'** (Lennon, McCartney)
Paul McCartney (piano, vocals), Rusty Anderson (guitar), Brian Ray (bass), Abe Laboriel Jr (drums).
Both recorded live at Hyde Park, London, England.
Both produced by Paul McCartney.

had huge impact, a landmark in our history, and I was very proud to be involved."

The performances of 'Sgt. Pepper's Lonely Hearts Club Band' and 'The Long And Winding Road' were made available to download, and they became the fastest-selling downloads ever at that time. They also entered the *Guinness Book Of Records* for being the quickest single put on sale. It was available online within 45 minutes and shot to the top of the download chart within hours of release.

'FINE LINE'

THE SECOND Paul McCartney single issued in Britain in as many months, 'Fine Line' found him back in pop mode after his brief partnership with the Freelance Hellraiser. An up-tempo, piano-driven pop song in the vein of 'Flaming Pie', it's packed with classic McCartney hallmarks mixed with new ideas that skew his usual template.

Recorded without a band – McCartney plays all the instruments – 'Fine Line' merges characteristically fluid melodies with an ELO-like orchestration. Beginning with a sparse setting of piano, bass, and drums, the arrangement is elaborated with acoustic guitars and the subtle use of a string section. The result is a light, airy pop song.

It's about choices, the importance of being true to oneself, and the consequences of such action. McCartney suggested that the song developed from the opening line. "You'll see some people just go 'waaaargh' and really think that's the way you do it, and sometimes it is just foolish and reckless, but they think that they're being courageous. That thought was what really started me off, and I just kind of followed on … that you've got to choose which of the two you're going to do. Be reckless or courageous."

'Fine Line' contains the words "chaos and creation", themes that have appeared in earlier McCartney work, such as *Standing Stone*. He is a great believer in what he sees as the 'magic' of songwriting. Improvisation, chaos, can often lead to the creation of something magical and beautiful. On this occasion, he was playing the song to his new producer, Nigel Godrich, and played an incorrect bass note. Godrich liked the accident and insisted that they keep it. Once again, the idea that wholeness and order can emerge from chaos was employed to fashion a song brimming with positive attitude and energy.

Two live-in-the-studio versions of 'Fine Line' were made available on the internet, both featuring McCartney's Paul's band. AOL Music featured 'Fine Line', 'Follow Me', and 'Let It Be', as part of their 'sessions' feature; the other, a recording made in Miami during rehearsals, was available on McCartney's site.

'Comfort Of Love' is a superb McCartney rocker with a strong melody and some of the grittiest guitar he has committed to record. It suggests that material possessions are transitory and insignificant; what matters is love. It's an eternal and universal message, that mankind needs to wake from its slumber, reject materialism, and embrace love. Only then will humanity transcend its troubles and obtain a state of grace.

One of the few songs he recorded with Nigel Godrich to feature musicians other than McCartney, 'Growing Up Falling Down' sounds positively alien. The song mixes the kind of aural experiments and tape-loops that McCartney usually reserves for his 'avant-garde' projects with a palate of extraordinary sounds. While elements of the piece evoke earlier works, such as 'Kreen-

'FINE LINE' / 'COMFORT OF LOVE'
PAUL McCARTNEY
UK RELEASE August 29 2005; Parlophone R 6673; CD single Parlophone CDR 6673 'Fine Line', 'Comfort In Love'; chart high No.20.
US RELEASE August 29 2005; Capitol C2 0946 3 34259 2 7; failed to chart.

• **'Fine Line'** (McCartney)
Paul McCartney (piano, spinet, bass, guitars, drums, percussion, vocals), Millennia Ensemble (strings). Recorded at RAK Studios and AIR Studios, London, England, and Ocean Way Recording, Los Angeles, CA, USA.
• **'Comfort Of Love'** (McCartney)
Paul McCartney (piano, Fender Rhodes electric piano, spinet, bass, guitars, drums, percussion, metronome, vocals). Recorded at RAK and AIR London. Mixed at Ocean Way Recording.
• **'Growing Up Falling Down'** (McCartney)
Paul McCartney (upright piano, classical guitar, bass, electric guitar, vocals), James Gadson (drums), Jason Falkner (classical guitar, grand piano), Pedra Eustache (duduk, didjeridu). Recorded at Ocean Way Recording.
All produced by Nigel Godrich.

Akore', the juxtaposition of tones, textures, and drones with a melody as soporific as a head-full of Quaalude creates a remarkable, atmospheric setting. McCartney's vocal is unlike any other he has delivered. It is a remarkable recording, too significant to be hidden on the B-side of a single. If nothing else, it proves what a remarkable talent McCartney is; as inventive and creative in the 21st century as when he first recorded in the 1960s.

'Fine Line' data

The single was premiered by AOL Music's *First Listen* show on July 26 2005 at 12:01 AM EST and was given another 'exclusive' airing on BBC Radio 2's *Terry Wogan Show* later the same day. It was posted on the official Paul McCartney website prior to release. All this one month before the single was available in the shops.

A one-track promotional CD single (CDRDJ 6673), issued in a card sleeve with screen-printed custom label, was issued to British radio stations and media on July 26. A similar one-track promotional CD single was issued in Mexico with a card sleeve (0946 336888 2 7) and in the USA in a jewel case (C2 0946 3 34259 2 7). One-track CD singles (perhaps unused promotional copies) were issued in America, where it retailed in some shops for 49 cents.

In Britain, commercial copies of the CD single (CDR 6673) were issued in a jewel case with two tracks, while in Holland it was issued as a three-track single with 'Growing Up Falling Down'. In Britain, 'Growing Up Falling Down' was issued as the B-side to a deluxe 7-inch single (R 6673) pressed on heavyweight vinyl with a customised label and issued in a thick card sleeve with a 35cm-square poster.

CHAOS AND CREATION IN THE BACK YARD

McCARTNEY'S recorded his 20th studio over a two-year period with producer Nigel Godrich. Sessions were divided between London and Los Angeles, with McCartney selecting to work in concentrated two-week blocks, separated by long breaks away from the project. Although Godrich produced the finished album, McCartney initially worked with David Kahne, who produced *Driving Rain*. Andrew Slater, chairman of Capitol records, recalls McCartney playing him 15 or 20 songs in the summer of 2004, eight of which Kahne produced. However, McCartney dropped Kahne in favour of Godrich. Best known for his work with Radiohead, Godrich is a Grammy Award-winning recording engineer and record producer who has also worked with Travis, Beck, U2, and R.E.M..

McCartney began recording with his touring band at RAK Studios in London. Intended as test sessions, these went well. As McCartney explained to *Billboard*: "First week, I came in with my live band, thinking that might be the way we'd go. But [Godrich] started to intimate toward the end of the week that he wanted, as he put it, to take me out of my safety zone, to do something different." Consequently the band were dropped, and instead Godrich encouraged McCartney to play most of the instruments himself. The producer wanted to make an organic sounding album, like those McCartney had made in the early 1970s.

Godrich: "I realised that it was better when it was just him. He's such a heavyweight, he needs people to spar with – and those people just don't exist. The best thing is to just keep him on his own, and then you get something more interesting."

As well as removing the safety zone, Godrich spoke his mind and rejected many of McCartney's ideas. This generated tension between artist and producer but made for a stronger, more consistent album. As McCartney recalled: "There were some tense moments making the album. Nigel wasn't sycophantic; he said from the off, 'I warn you, I know what I like.' There was some heated discussion. There's a song called 'Riding To Vanity Fair' where we got down to [snarls] 'I like it!', 'I don't like it!', 'Well, I like it!' But then I realised there's no point in charging him down like that; I should listen. We actually moved on to why he didn't like it – 'The first line's good, but after that …'. 'Oh, how about this then?'"

Godrich: "The third session, he came back and played me a song, and I was like, 'Fucking hell, that's so much better.' That was 'At The Mercy'. He said, 'I think I'm remembering how to do this!' Maybe he was expressing the concept of having to better what he's doing because someone was going to look at him and say, 'Not sure,' rather than just blindly taking everything that he proffers."

The album was issued on a wave of publicity that began before the record was even released. McCartney's public standing was higher than it had been for years. Appearances at Glastonbury in June 2004, where he debuted 'Follow Me', and at the Live 8 concert in July 2005 sustained his popularity and street-cred. In the USA, the album was supported by a three-month tour and a special edition of *Billboard* magazine. McCartney hit the interview trail, too, talking to print and radio journalists. Special programmes were recorded for the BBC, including a *Front Row* special and a 90-minute show for the *Sold On Song* series. In-store posters were distributed to record outlets, advertisements for the album placed in the media, and sponsorship deals struck with various corporations. Parlophone issued an interview disc (CHAOS 01) to promote the album.

Advance promotional copies of the CD were simply titled *Album* with the artist's name given as Pete Mitchell. The advance CDs carried a three-paragraph statement on the back cover warning against uploading the disc to a file-sharing service. The discs were printed with the name of the person and company to

CHAOS AND CREATION IN THE BACK YARD
PAUL McCARTNEY
CD 'Fine Line', 'How Kind Of You', 'Jenny Wren', 'At The Mercy', 'Friends To Go', 'English Tea', 'Too Much Rain', 'A Certain Softness', 'Riding To Vanity Fair', 'Follow Me', 'Promise To You Girl', 'This Never Happened Before', 'Anyway', 'She's So Beautiful'*, 'I've Only Got Two Hands' (hidden track). Track marked * appears only on Japanese edition.
UK RELEASE September 12 2005; CD, CD with DVD, Parlophone 337961 2 6; LP Parlophone 337 9581 released 3 October; chart high No.10.
US RELEASE September 13 2005; CD, CD with DVD, Capitol 338 2992; chart high No.6.

- **'How Kind Of You'** (McCartney)
Paul McCartney (guitars, bass, piano, flugelhorn, shaker, guiro, drums, loops, vocals), Nigel Godrich (loops, acoustic guitar).
Recorded at AIR Studios, London, England.
- **'Jenny Wren'** (McCartney)
Paul McCartney (acoustic guitar, floor tom, vocals), Pedro Eustache (duduk).
Recorded at Ocean Way Recording, Los Angeles, CA, USA.
- **'At The Mercy'** (McCartney)
Paul McCartney (piano, electric guitar, bass, cello, mass vibrachimes, tambourine, Hammond organ, vocals). Jason Falkner (electric guitar), James Gadson (drums), Millennia Ensemble (strings, brass).
Recorded at Ocean Way Recording; strings recorded at AIR London.
- **'Friends To Go'** (McCartney)
Paul McCartney (piano, guitars, bass, drums, tambourine on snare, flugelhorn, Melodica, shakers, vocals).
Recorded at AIR London.
- **'English Tea'** (McCartney)
Paul McCartney (piano, bass, bass drum, recorders, tubular bells, vocals), Millennia Ensemble (strings, brass).
Recorded at Ocean Way; strings at AIR London.
- **'Too Much Rain'** (McCartney)
Paul McCartney (piano, guitars, bass, autoharp, drums, maracas, vocals). Recorded at AIR London.
- **'A Certain Softness'** (McCartney)
Paul McCartney (classical guitar, bass, piano, harmonium, gong, cymbal, triangle, vocals), Jason Falkner (classical guitar), Joey Waronker (bass drum, bongos, shaker).
Recorded at Ocean Way.
- **'Riding To Vanity Fair'** (McCartney)
Paul McCartney (bass, guitars, toy glockenspiel, Wurlitzer electric piano, vocals), The Los Angeles Music Players (strings), James Gadson (drums).
Recorded at Ocean Way.
- **'Follow Me'** (McCartney)
Paul McCartney (bass, guitars, drums, percussion block, tambourine, vocals), Rusty Anderson (acoustic guitar), Brian Ray (acoustic guitar), Abe Laboriel Jnr (percussion block, tambourine), Millennia Ensemble (strings).
Recorded at RAK Studios, London.
- **'Promise To You Girl'** (McCartney)
Paul McCartney (pianos, bass, electric guitar, drums, Moog synth, tambourine, triangle, shaker, vocals).
Recorded at Ocean Way.
- **'This Never Happened Before'** (McCartney)
Paul McCartney (piano, bass, electric guitar, drums, vocals), Millennia Ensemble (strings).
Recorded at RAK.
- **'Anyway'** (McCartney)
Paul McCartney (pianos, bass, guitars, drums, Moog synth, harmonium, vocals), Millennia Ensemble (strings).
Recorded at RAK.
- **'She's So Beautiful'** (McCartney)
Paul McCartney (all instruments, vocals).
Recording location unknown.
- **'I've Only Got Two Hands'** (McCartney)
Paul McCartney (bass, piano, drums, guitar, Melodica, tape-loops).
Recording location unknown.
All produced by Nigel Godrich.

whom it was sent and with an additional warning that the disc was watermarked. These attempts to stop the album from appearing on the internet were only partially successful. It did find its way online, but only two days before its official release date.

Chaos And Creation In The Back Yard received glowing reviews. Almost everyone had something positive to say about the record, which no doubt helped sales.

It sold 357,000 copies in the USA in its first 12 weeks and was later certified a gold record. (Figures from *The New York Times* suggest that *Run Devil Run* and 2001's *Driving Rain* moved 232,000 and 400,0000 copies respectively). The album was nominated for two Grammys, as Album of the Year and Best Pop Vocal Album.

Chaos And Creation In The Back Yard songs

When McCartney brought 'How Kind Of You' to the studio he thought he would record it as a straight pop song. However, Godrich's influence ensured that the song changed considerably. McCartney described how the song changed its nature. "I put a harmonium in there, so it became sort of Indian, with this pop song sitting on top of it, and then brought in some drums about half way, and bass on a kind of 1960s kind of vibe, which reminds me of The Doors or somebody. But that changed quite a bit in the studio."

The obvious reference point is McCartney's late-2002 experimental reworking of 'Band On The Run' for BBC Radio Two. Again here, he used drones and loops to transform something that could have been run of the mill into a richly textured song.

Phil Sutcliffe of *Q* magazine suggested that 'How Kind Of You' may have been inspired by Linda's death. The line 'I won't forget how unafraid you were that long, dark night' appeared to him very personal. McCartney, however, said that "it wasn't in my mind" when he wrote it. He said he was inspired to write the song when he noticed the way some friends spoke. "I've got a couple of older posh English friends who, instead of saying 'that's very nice of you' or 'thanks a lot', they might say 'how kind of you'. So I just started with that phrase, and this whole idea 'how kind of you to think of me when I was out of sorts' ... So I was just imagining it from the point of view of somebody like that. It wasn't particularly about anything, just playing with that language thing and then trying to put the tune a bit more sort of rock'n'roll-pop, to set it against it. So it kind of wrote itself, that one, coming off the phrase 'how kind of you'." Although the inspiration stemmed from a bygone age in which manners and class mattered, 'How Kind Of You' managed to evoke a sense of longing for the past while remaining resolutely rooted in the 21st century.

Inspired by his composition 'Blackbird', McCartney wrote 'Jenny Wren' while in Los Angeles. Leaving the city behind, he drove to a canyon and began playing acoustic guitar. Recreating the two-part fingerpicking style that informed 'Blackbird', he fashioned a delicate ballad to accompany his earlier song.

Although he suggested that the song wasn't about anyone in particular, he did note that Jenny Wren was a character in Dickens' *Our Mutual Friend*, and that the character may have been lurking in his subconscious while he was writing the song. He also said that he may have been thinking about his favourite British bird, the wren. As with 'Blackbird', he gave the song a double meaning by leaving it to the listener to make up their own mind as to what it might be about. The result is an uplifting song of hope that sounds as fresh and original as the piece that inspired it.

'At The Mercy' was another song he wrote in Los Angeles between recording sessions, specifically for the album. By the time McCartney came to write it, he had been working with Godrich for some time and had got a feel for the kind of material that excited his producer. Improvising at the piano, McCartney stumbled on some unusual chords that he liked, and began to fit some equally spontaneous lyrics to his melody. He got the opening line, and then had to develop his lyric into something more meaningful. However, he only began to realise the significance of his lyric much later. When interviewed, he suggested that the song was about life's vicissitudes and humankind's ability to accept them with stoicism.

Like many songwriters, he often finds inspiration by imaging himself as someone else. When he wrote 'The Long And Winding Road', McCartney imagined himself as Ray Charles. On this occasion, George Harrison provided the inspiration. "I write songs by just picking up a guitar and sort of strumming," explained McCartney. "And on this particular one, I started off with this idea of: I've been waiting on the other side. And I didn't really know where I was going. I often don't. I've got a phrase, it pops into my head, and I just kind of explore it. And as I was getting this idea formed; I felt like the song was going in a very George Harrison direction. It wasn't like I was channelling him or anything, but I just ended up thinking: this song could have been written by George. And I saw someone the other day, and they said, 'That song, it sounds very like George to me.' And I said 'Good. You didn't hear the story where I tell that?' And he said, 'No, no, it just felt – I think it's the chords, it's the kind of song that George could have done.'"

Rock'n'roll may be as American as cheeseburgers and apple pie, but it can also be very English. In the 1960s, The Beatles, The Rolling Stones, The Who, The Kinks, and The Bonzo Dog Band mixed American influences with an English sensibility and fashioned something unique. The Bonzos, in particular, created a singularly English form of popular music that both celebrated and poked fun at the English and their foibles. Thirty years' later, McCartney wrote his own quintessentially English pop song that celebrated the English language and people.

'English Tea' recalls gentler times, perfect English lawns, cricket matches played on village greens, and that most idiosyncratic of English pleasures, high tea. "That's about living in England and listening to the way some English people speak and parodying that," McCartney told *The Observer*. "I love it, but I also find it funny. I mean, I say, 'Do you wanna cup of tea, la?' But somebody else will say, 'Would you care to take tea,' or, 'As a rule, we take tea at three,' or whatever. I kind of like that language. I went to a grammar school, and had a really good English teacher, and I love to read Dickens, so I love the English language. I even worked in the word 'peradventure'. [Sings in snooty voice:] 'Do you know the game croquet? Peradventure we might play.' It fell out of my head into the song, then afterwards I had to go to the dictionary, and go, 'Please, let there be a word peradventure!' And there it was." Sounding remarkably similar to the kind of songs that ex-Bonzos man Neil Innes writes when parodying the British, 'English Tea' is a wonderfully observant essay on Englishness.

Inspired by Charlie Chaplin's 'Smile', McCartney wrote his own feel-good song, 'Too Much Rain', that by his own admission borrowed heavily from Chaplin's original. He also admitted that Heather Mills had provided some inspiration. "I was thinking about some of the problems that my wife Heather has been through in life," he said. "So I had her in mind, and this ... Chaplin song. But I hoped then that if it worked out and became a nice song, it would translate to anyone who had problems – and, let's face it, there are plenty of people who have problems. I have people coming up to me on the street sometimes who say, 'Yeah, really, I was going through a terrible time, but that certain song really picked me up and saw me through it.' And I'm very proud of that."

McCartney wrote 'A Certain Softness' while on holiday in

Greece. With a Latin mood upon him, he decided to write the ultimate love song. "It's just sort of all the love songs that I've heard and the ones I love, cos I love a lot of old fashioned stuff, it's just so well-crafted. I have a lot of influences from before my time, before my dad's time even, you know? People like Fred Astaire, people like that I listen to and love, really. The craft behind it all. So sometimes all that just floods in and becomes a new song." Speaking to *The Miami Herald* about the song, he said: "I like love, so I like love songs. I like romance. I like to listen to songs that talk about that and that contain those kinds of feelings. I'm a great Nat King Cole fan ... I like to think of myself a bit in that tradition."

The most talked about song on the album, 'Riding To Vanity Fair', had many speculating that it was written about the ex-Beatles or Heather Mills. It's about rejection and resulted from personal experience. But for McCartney it had a universal resonance. "Most people during their lives encounter things like that. It can be someone at work. It can be someone in your family. It can be someone you know or whatever, where there's some kind of disappointment. You argue or someone rejects your friendship. I think that can happen quite often to people, no matter who you are. People say, 'It doesn't happen to you, does it?' It has in my life, obviously. On this album there were one or two like ['Vanity Fair'] where I thought, that's actually quite rich hunting-ground, to go into your emotional side and examine that kind of thing, rather than just ignoring it."

'Riding To Vanity Fair' went through a number of changes before McCartney and Godrich were satisfied. McCartney explained: "I had to try new melodies at the microphone until I found one. It was an embarrassing little process ... but in the end, after suffering that humiliation for too long – for me, I thought, 'OK, now that really is *much* better.'"

Besides reworking the melody, he also slowed the tempo, which he recognised changed its mood as well. "It was nice and dark and quite moody." Godrich had added some echo-type effects, "quite spooky", and McCartney finally agreed that all the extra effort had been worth it. "By the time we'd finished working with it, it was like: 'OK, we like this one now,' and it made its way back onto the album."

'Follow Me' was probably recorded in the early summer of 2004, as McCartney performed the song for the first time at the Glastonbury Festival on June 26 that year. Recorded with his touring band, it was inspired by an earlier composition, 'Let It Be'. McCartney explained that 'Follow Me', a song of hope that gives thanks for another's strength and support, was one of those songs that almost writes itself. "You know, sometimes you're feeling great about your life, not always, but you've been lucky. You're feeling great and, um, I actually had done something where I had sung 'Let It Be'. And I was thinking it's kind of nice having a song like that, because it's kind of quasi-religious but it's very uplifting, you know?"

Although the downbeat introduction of 'Follow Me' hints at melancholia, two brief passages lead the listener to the main body of the song, which is as big and bouncy as anything McCartney has written. The melodic motifs and opening statement both return at the end as optimistic rejoinders to his opening declaration.

The song developed around a two-part piano arrangement, which included a distinct bass melody. From here, McCartney developed what he described as a Motown feel. "I could hear the Motown guys, the Funk Brothers, putting a backing track to that," he said, referring to the Motown rhythm section that played on many of the company's hits, uncredited. "Anyway, so it just developed, went through that little Motown thing. Then I had this other little bit that is on the front of it. And that ends it as well. It's really two little songs put together, and then when we came to do it in the studio it was multi-layered, because it was just me ... but I think it sounds like a band in the end."

Whether or not McCartney intended to wear his influences on his sleeve with this album, they certainly appear more opaque than on previous releases. 'Jenny Wren' alludes to one of his earlier compositions; 'Anyway' draws its inspiration from Curtis Mayfield and Randy Newman; and 'This Never Happened Before' borrows from another great songwriter, Burt Bacharach. Returning to a much-explored theme, McCartney explained that 'This Never Happened Before' is a straight love song. "And I'm a lover not a fighter, as they say. ... It's always a big help if you get a nice little chord sequence, and the opening chords to the verse of that go a nice place. So they settle you down with your melody, and you feel like you're going somewhere. [It was] one of our very first things we did with Nigel at RAK, ... one of the things to see if we could sort of get it on, and I thought, 'This is good. We're going to go somewhere with this.'"

A classic McCartney ballad, 'Anyway' is an eloquent song about love. Although some speculated that it might be addressed to Heather Mills, McCartney was adamant that it was not about any anyone in particular. "It's about a lot of people. It's just a get-in-touch song. Give us a call, sort of thing."

With the song all but finished, he continued to hone the melody and arrangement. But it was only when he gave it an American feel that he considered it finished. "Why do you get these feelings? I don't know. But I was getting this feeling as if it was the deep South of America, like Charlestown, Savannah, something about the chords, I think. There was just something reminding me, almost sort of a Randy Newman kind of thing, [that] I thought I was doing. As always, it turns out nothing like him, but at the time I think I'm doing this thing, so that was going on."

'She's So Beautiful' was issued as a bonus track on the Japanese edition of *Chaos And Creation*, and McCartney wrote it for his daughter Beatrice. A beautiful piano ballad, it could have appeared on any of his albums from the previous 30 years. If you like your McCartney with a side order of sentimentality, then this is for you. If, however, you prefer his rockier or more experimental side, which Godrich successfully brought to the fore, then look elsewhere.

The surprise bonus track, 'I've Only Got Two Hands', was originally intended to open the album, but was used to close the record instead. "We just thought, how about opening the album with just something for nothing," said McCartney. "Let's just open it with like a little jam thing, a noise, just something to get your attention, then we'll go into the first song." He went into the studio with a few ideas, on piano and drums. "In the end, instead of choosing one of them for the beginning, we stuck three of them all together and put them at the end."

Godrich's production brought out the best in McCartney, resulting in an inspired and engaging album that built on 2001's *Driving Rain*. Like *Band On The Run* before it, *Chaos And Creation In The Back Yard* reveals that McCartney has lost none of his delight in composing and playing and that he's as gifted as ever.

Chaos And Creation In The Back Yard data

The CD was issued in standard and deluxe formats, with the deluxe version coming with an outer card sleeve and 50-minute DVD, which featured a 30-minute documentary on the making of the album, a studio performance video of 'Fine Line', a 12-minute animated film including three vocals-free instrumental tracks, and a five-minute menu featuring 'How Kind Of You'.

The vinyl edition was issued on heavyweight vinyl with customised labels similar to that used for the CD, a gatefold sleeve, and four fine-art prints by Brian Clarke.

In the USA, Capitol issued 'This Never Happened Before' as a two-track promotional CD single (DPRO-0946 6 49684 2 3). Issued in a jewel case with a printed inlay and a white screen-printed label with purple text, it featured a 3:13 edit and the album version.

WORKING CLASS HERO – THE DEFINITIVE LENNON
JOHN LENNON
CD 1 '(Just Like) Starting Over', 'Imagine', 'Watching The Wheels', 'Jealous Guy', 'Instant Karma! (We All Shine On)', 'Stand By Me', 'Working Class Hero', 'Power To The People', 'Oh My Love', 'Oh Yoko!', 'Nobody Loves You (When You're Down And Out)', 'Nobody Told Me', 'Bless You', 'Come Together', 'New York City', 'I'm Stepping Out', 'You Are Here', 'Borrowed Time', 'Happy Xmas (War Is Over)'.
CD 2 'Woman', 'Mind Games', 'Out The Blue', 'Whatever Gets You Thru The Night', 'Love', 'Mother', 'Beautiful Boy', 'Woman Is The Nigger Of The World', 'God', 'Scared', '#9 Dream', 'I'm Losing You', 'Isolation', 'Cold Turkey', 'Intuition', 'Gimme Some Truth', 'Give Peace A Chance', 'Real Love', 'Grow Old With Me'.
UK RELEASE October 3 2005; Parlophone 340 0802; chart high No.11.
US RELEASE October 4 2005; Capitol 094634039123; chart high No.135.

WORKING CLASS HERO

ISSUED a few days before what would have been Lennon's 65th birthday, this collection reworked earlier best-of compilations into the most comprehensive collection of Lennon's hit singles and key album tracks so far. Supervised by Yoko Ono, it was mastered from the latest digital remasters and issued on two CDs. The release of this compilation also saw the entire Lennon solo catalogue made available digitally through legitimate online music sites.

'JENNY WREN'

PARLOPHONE issued this single in the UK as a CD and 7-inch. Three new songs, all outtakes from *Chaos And Creation*, were issued across the two formats, and all four songs plus a live version of 'Jenny Wren' recorded during the *Chaos And Creation At Abbey Road* programme were available as digital downloads from the McCartney website.

'Summer Of '59' is a light-hearted recollection of a pre-fame summer from McCartney's youth. He explored the subject with greater success in *Liverpool Oratorio*, but this fails to convince because, like Lennon's early draft of 'In My Life', it's too literal.

In 'I Want You To Fly' McCartney examines the nature of relationships and stands at an emotional crossroads, contemplating his actions and the resulting emotional consequences. Freedom is experienced as a negative as well as positive sense, and the existential angst it engenders finds him musing on the nature of existence and rational thought. Musically, it's as powerful as anything recorded for the album.

'This Loving Game' finds McCartney bemoaning the fact that he occasionally experiences doubt and uncertainty in his relationships. Rejecting the advice of his peers, he acknowledges his weaknesses but restates the strength of his devotion, which, despite his hesitancy, remains unyielding.

'Jenny Wren' data

The deluxe 7-inch single was pressed on dark red vinyl and issued with customised labels, inner sleeve, and picture cover. CD1 was issued in a slim line CD case; CD2 in a standard jewel case with a

'JENNY WREN' / 'SUMMER OF '59'
PAUL MCCARTNEY
UK RELEASE November 21 2005; Parlophone R 6678; CD1 Parlophone CDR 6678 'Jenny Wren', 'Summer Of '59', 'I Want You To Fly', 'This Loving Game'; CD2 Parlophone 2CDRS 6678; download www.paulmccartney.com 'Jenny Wren', 'Summer Of '59', 'I Want You To Fly', 'This Loving Game', 'Jenny Wren' (Live At Abbey Road); chart high No.22.

- **'Summer Of '59'** (McCartney)
Paul McCartney (guitar, vocals). Recording location unknown.
- **'I Want You To Fly'** (McCartney)
Paul McCartney (bass, guitars, Fender Rhodes electric piano, piano, drums, EMS synth, vocals), Jason Falkner (electric guitar), James Gadson (drums). Recorded at Ocean Way Recording, Los Angeles, CA, USA.
- **'This Loving Game'** (McCartney)
Paul McCartney (bass, guitars, piano, harmonium, shakers, tambourine, vocals), James Gadson (drums). Recorded at Ocean Way.

All produced by Nigel Godrich.

poster. On October 3, Parlophone issued a two-track promotional CD single in a card sleeve (CDRDJ 6678) with a 2:08 edit plus full-length album version.

THE U.S. vs. JOHN LENNON

LENNON'S back catalogue is raided once again, this time for the soundtrack to the feature-length documentary film, *The U.S. vs John Lennon*. Co-written, directed, and produced by David Leaf and John Scheinfeld, the documentary sets out to explore the US government's attempts at silencing Lennon during the early 1970s. It also undertakes to draw parallels between the situation then and now in Iraq, and does so through archival film clips and music.

Some of Lennon's songs were remixed for the film to provide its score. "We were allowed to 'strip' lead vocals from Lennon's original recordings so that we could use his own instrumental work as the score for the movie," explained Leaf. "I think it's the first time that John's solo catalogue can be heard in this way."

However, only the instrumental version of 'How Do You Sleep' was issued on the album. Also included was the previously unreleased live recording of 'Attica State' from the John Sinclair Freedom Rally in Ann Arbor, Michigan.

(Parlophone and Capitol issued *The U.S. vs John Lennon* as a standard CD, with liner notes by Yoko Ono.)

ECCE COR MEUM

MCCARTNEY'S fourth classical album was more than eight years in the making. Following a visit to Magdalen College in Oxford, England with Linda in 1997, he was commissioned by Anthony Smith (later president of the College) to compose something "which could bc sung by young people the world over in the same way that Handel's Messiah is" and to celebrate the College's recently opened chapel.

"I was very excited by the idea," he said. "Linda and I went up there and stayed at the College. We went to the chapel; we heard the choir sing. Harmonically, it was all very interesting – I thought 'Wow!' It showed me the palette of where you could go."

He started writing the music for *Ecce Cor Meum*, planned as an oratorio in four movements, for choir and orchestra. Only later did he begin thinking about a subject for his text, which would be in English and Latin. He abandoned several ideas before inspiration struck while he was taking part in a concert of John Tavener's music in the Church of St. Ignatius Loyola in New York City.

"While I was waiting to do my bit," said McCartney, "I was looking around the church and I saw a statue, and underneath it was written 'Ecce Cor Meum.' I had done some Latin at school and I always had a fondness for it. So I worked it out. I believe it means 'Behold My Heart'."

He got off to a good start but soon found that he could not continue. "About a year or so into it, Linda passed away, which immediately held things up, and it went right on the back burner. Consequently I lost all momentum that I had gained in that first year and had to slowly start putting it back together.

"One of the ways that I did this was to just sort of write my sadness out. There is a lament in the middle called 'Interlude (Lament)' which was very specifically grieving over Linda. I

THE U.S. vs. JOHN LENNON
JOHN LENNON
CD 'Power To The People', 'Nobody Told Me', 'Working Class Hero', 'I Found Out', 'Bed Peace', 'The Ballad Of John & Yoko' (The Beatles), 'Give Peace A Chance', 'Love', 'Attica State' (Live, previously unreleased), 'Happy Xmas (War Is Over)', 'I Don't Wanna Be A Soldier Mama', 'Imagine', 'How Do You Sleep?' (Instrumental, previously unreleased), 'New York City', 'John Sinclair' (Live), 'Scared', 'God', 'Here We Go Again', 'Gimme Some Truth', 'Oh My Love', 'Instant Karma!'.
UK RELEASE September 26 2006; Parlophone 3749122; failed to chart.
US RELEASE September 26 2006; Capitol 74912-2; failed to chart.

remember playing it to someone and they started welling up – which was great, because I hadn't told them that it was anything to do with Linda, but something in the chords communicated itself to this person, who was listening to it for the very first time."

On November 10 2001 an early version of *Ecce Cor Meum* was performed by the Magdalen College Choir accompanied by a 23-piece orchestra. Conducted by Bill Ives at the Sheldonian Theatre in Oxford, it revealed several areas that needed revision.

McCartney said: "Eventually I made it all come together through correcting a lot of misapprehensions – a lot was learned before the Sheldonian performance, but a lot of it was learned afterwards.

"An experienced choral composer knows that children can't be given huge sustained passages; they don't have the energy and the stamina. At the Sheldonian, there was some quite hard stuff that I didn't realise, because I'd done it on the synthesizer – which has endless stamina – but during that first performance, the solo treble couldn't come on for the second half. I think I'd used him up in the first half.

"These are things that people either learn because they are taught them immediately at the first lesson, or you learn through the years. So it was good to go through the piece a lot of times, and we took out huge choral sections and gave them to the orchestra. If it had been a Beatles song I would have known how to do it. But this was a completely different ball game."

ECCE COR MEUM
PAUL McCARTNEY
CD 'Movement I: Spiritus', 'Movement II: Gratia', 'Interlude (Lament)', 'Movement III: Musica', 'Movement IV: Ecce Cor Meum'.
UK RELEASE September 25 2006; EMI Classics 0946 3 70424 2 7; Luxury Limited Edition EMI Classics 0946 3 70423 2 8; download 00946 3 70423 5 9; classical chart high No.2.
US RELEASE September 25 2006; Angel 70424-2; classical chart high No.2.

- **'Movement I: Spiritus'** (McCartney)
- **'Movement II: Gratia'** (McCartney)
- **'Interlude (Lament)'** (McCartney)
- **'Movement III: Musica'** (McCartney)
- **'Movement IV: Ecce Cor Meum'** (McCartney)

Kate Royal (soprano), The Boys Of King's College Choir Cambridge, The Boys Of Magdalen College Choir Oxford, The Academy Of St. Martin In The Fields, Gavin Greenaway (conductor).
Recorded at Abbey Road Studios, London, England.
Produced by John Fraser.

As with his previous classical works, McCartney employed some 'musical associates' to help with the score, but he insisted that all the notes were his. "They might say, 'That's too high for the horns,' so I'd listen to them and suggest the clarinets or oboes take the notes. They helped me arrange and notate, but the piece is totally mine."

He also insisted that the female soprano should sing without too much vibrato, which he thought old-fashioned. Singer Kate Royal said: "Paul heard my recent disc … and liked the reserved, clean sound I had. It's what made him approach me for *Ecce*. He wanted a natural sound; not an operatic warble."

Ecce Cor Meum has a spiritual rather than a religious tone that connects with people, regardless of their beliefs. The use of amateur choirs extends this egalitarian motif and ties in with McCartney's desire to touch as many people as possible with his music. Speaking to *Classic fm* magazine, he said: "I love working with choirs, because you realise the people who sing in them come from all walks of life. You can have a plumber next to a gynaecologist. You get this rich human mixture."

This is music for and by the people. It's an attempt to blur the boundaries between composer and performer – and while this kind of music is still seen as elitist or highbrow, it's a communal activity that brings people together.

The final version of *Ecce Cor Meum* was recorded at Abbey Road between March 13 and 17 in 2006.

Ecce Cor Meum data

EMI Classics (UK) and Angel (USA) issued *Ecce Cor Meum* as a standard and deluxe CD edition, with embossed cover and 60-page book. The album was also available as a digital download. Promotional copies of the CD were issued by EMI Classics in a card sleeve with an edit of 'Movement II: Gratia'.

REMEMBER

AND WOULD you like a John Lennon CD with your coffee, sir? Lennon's solo back catalogue is here revisited and newly compiled for Starbucks, the global coffee purveyors. Compiled by EMI-Capitol Special Markets division, *Remember* has 18 tracks that span his solo career. It was available exclusively from Starbucks coffee shops.

This isn't as odd as it may at first appear. Starbucks has become more than just about selling coffee. In 1999, the company bought Hear Music, an independent record retailer, and invested in new retail outlets that are music stores first and coffee-houses second. And they seem to have done OK.

When Ray Charles's *Genius Loves Company* CD went platinum in the USA, Starbucks were responsible for one third of its sales. With that kind of success, it made perfect sense for Capitol to compile this Lennon CD for sale exclusively through America's largest chain of coffee shops.

Drawing heavily on Lennon's first solo album, *Remember* mixes familiar versions of his music with alternative takes from the Lennon *Anthology* set. The inclusion of two spoken-word extracts is superfluous and does little to enhance the listening pleasure of what is otherwise a solid compilation.

Remember data

EMI Music Special Markets/Hear Music issued *Remember* with a tri-fold digi-pack cover, 12-page booklet, and screen-printed CD.

REMEMBER
JOHN LENNON
CD '#9 Dream', 'Instant Karma! (We All Shine On)', 'Working Class Hero', 'Hold On' (Anthology version), 'Watching The Wheels', 'Remember', 'God', 'Mother', 'Sean's Little Help' (from Anthology), 'Imagine', 'Steel And Glass', 'I'm Losing You' (Anthology version), 'Going Down On Love' (instructions only, from Anthology), 'Nobody Told Me', 'Isolation' (Anthology version), 'Nobody Loves You (When You're Down and Out)' (Anthology version), 'Jealous Guy', '(Just Like) Starting Over'.
US RELEASE January 03 2007; Capitol/Hear Music 71108-2-9; failed to chart.

LENNON COLLABORATIONS

Here we list John Lennon's contributions to the recorded work of other artists, as a producer and/or a musician.

YOKO ONO
Yoko Ono/Plastic Ono Band
Lennon co-produces with Ono, performs on all tracks except 'AOS'
Released December 17 1970
UK Apple SAPCOR17
US Apple SW3391

YOKO ONO
Fly
Lennon co-produces with Ono, performs on most tracks
Released December 3 1971
UK Apple SAPTU 101/2
US Apple SVBB-3380

DAVID PEEL & THE LOWER EAST SIDE
The Pope Smokes Dope
Lennon produces
Released April 1972
US Apple SW3391

DAVID PEEL & THE LOWER EAST SIDE
'F Is Not A Dirty Word' / 'The Ballad Of New York City' / 'John Lennon-Yoko Ono'
Lennon produces
Released April 1972
US Apple PRO-6498 / SPRO-6499

DAVID PEEL & THE LOWER EAST SIDE
'Hippy From New York City' / 'The Ballad Of New York City' / 'John Lennon-Yoko Ono'
Lennon produces
Released April 1972
US Apple SPRO-6545 / SPRO-6546

ELEPHANT'S MEMORY
Elephant's Memory
Lennon co-produces with Yoko Ono, performs on several tracks (with Ono)
Released September 1972
UK Apple SAPCOR22
US Apple SMAS 3389

ELEPHANT'S MEMORY
'Liberation Special' / 'Madness'
Lennon produces, performs
Released November 1972
US Apple 1854

ELEPHANT'S MEMORY
'Power Boogie' / 'Liberation Special'
Lennon produces, performs
Released December 1 1972
UK Apple APPLE45

MICK JAGGER
'Too Many Cooks'
Lennon produces
Unreleased

YOKO ONO
Approximately Infinite Universe
Lennon co-produces with Ono, plays guitar on 'Move On Fast', 'Is Winter Here To Stay'
Released February 16 1973
UK Apple SAPDO1001
US Apple SVBB-3399

YOKO ONO
Feeling The Space
Lennon performs on 'She Hits Back', 'Woman Power'
Released November 23 1973
UK Apple SAPCOR 26
US Apple SW-3412

RINGO STARR
Ringo
Lennon performs on 'I'm The Greatest'
Released November 23 1973
UK Apple PCTC 252
US Apple SWAL-3413

HARRY NILSSON
Pussy Cats
Lennon produces and arranges, performs on a few tracks
Released August 19 1974
UK RCA APL1-0570
US RCA CPL1-0570

RINGO STARR
Goodnight Vienna
Lennon performs on 'Goodnight Vienna', 'All By Myself', 'Only You (And You Alone)'
Released November 15 1974
UK Apple PCS 7168
US Apple SW-3417

ELTON JOHN
'Lucy In The Sky With Diamonds' / 'One Day At A Time'
Lennon performs on A-side
Released November 12 1974
UK DJM DJS340
Released November 18 1974
US MCA MCA 40344

DAVID BOWIE
Fame
Lennon performs on 'Across The Universe', 'Fame'
Released March 1975
UK RCA APL1 1006
US RCA 0998

DAVID BOWIE
'Fame' / 'Right'
Lennon performs on A-side
Released August 1975
UK RCA 2579
US RCA PB-10320

LORI BURTON
'Answer Me, My Love'
Lennon co-produces with Roy Cicala, performs
Released with Engelhardt *Beatles Undercover* book September 1998
CAN CGPINT8008

LORI BURTON AND PATRICK JUDE
'Let's Spend The Night Together'
Lennon co-produces with Roy Cicala, performs
Released with Engelhardt *Beatles Undercover* book September 1998
CAN CGPINT8008

DOG SOLDIER AND PATRICK JUDE
'Incantation'
Lennon co-produces with Roy Cicala
Released with Engelhardt *Beatles Undercover* book September 1998
CAN CGPINT8008

RINGO STARR
Ringo's Rotogravure
Lennon plays piano on 'A Dose Of Rock'n'Roll', performs on 'Cookin' (In The Kitchen Of Love)'
Released September 17 1976
UK Polydor 2302 040
US Atlantic 82417-2

YOKO ONO
'Walking On Thin Ice' / 'It Happened'
Lennon co-produces with Ono and Jack Douglas, performs
Released February 20 1981
UK Geffen K 79202
US Geffen 49683

McCARTNEY COLLABORATIONS

Here we list Paul McCartney's contributions to the recorded work of other artists, as producer and/or musician.

DONOVAN
'Mellow Yellow' / 'Preachin' Love'
McCartney background vocals on A-side
Released January 1967
UK Pye 7N 17267
US Epic 10098

MCGOUGH & MCGEAR
McGough & McGear
McCartney co-produces with Andy Roberts, performs on some tracks
Released May 17 1968
UK Parlophone PMC/PCS 7047

MARY HOPKIN
'Those Were The Days' / 'Turn Turn Turn'
McCartney produces, performs
Released August 30 1968
UK Apple APPLE 2
US Apple 1801

JACKIE LOMAX
'Sour Milk Sea' / 'The Eagle Laughs At You'
McCartney performs on A-side
Released August 30 1968
UK Apple APPLE 3
US Apple 1802

BLACK DYKE MILLS BAND
'Thingumybob' / 'Yellow Submarine'
McCartney produces
Released September 6 1968
UK Apple APPLE 4
US Apple 1800

BONZO DOG DOO-DAH BAND
'I'm The Urban Spaceman' / 'Canyons Of Your Mind'
McCartney produces (as Apollo C Vermouth) and performs on A-side
Released October 11 1968
UK Liberty LBF 15144
US Imperial 66345

MARY HOPKIN
Postcard
McCartney produces, plays bass, guitar
Released February 21 1969
UK Apple SAPCOR 5
US Apple ST-3351

JACKIE LOMAX
Is This What You Want?
McCartney performs on 'Sour Milk Sea'
Released March 21 1969
UK Apple SAPCOR 6
US Apple ST-3354

MARY HOPKIN
'Goodbye' / 'Sparrow'
McCartney produces, performs
Released March 28 1969
UK Apple APPLE 10
US Apple 1806

BADFINGER
'Come And Get It' / 'Rock Of All Ages'
McCartney produces, performs on A-side
Released December 5 1969
UK Apple APPLE 20
US Apple 1815

STEVE MILLER BAND
Brave New World
McCartney performs on 'My Dark Hour'
Released June 16 1969
UK Capitol EST-184
US Capitol SKAO-184

THE FOURMOST
'Rosetta'/ 'Just Like Before'
McCartney produces
Released February 21 1969
UK CBS 4041

JACKIE LOMAX
'How The Web Was Woven' / 'Thumbin' A Ride'
McCartney produces B-side
Released February 6 1970
UK Apple APPLE 23

JAMES TAYLOR
'Carolina In My Mind' / 'Something's Wrong'
McCartney produces
Released November 6 1970
UK Apple APPLE 32
US Apple 1805

CARLY SIMON
No Secrets
McCartney backing vocals (with Linda) on 'Night Owl'
Released November 3 1972
UK Elektra K 42127
US Elektra EKS 74082

RINGO STARR
Ringo
McCartney plays mouth sax solo on 'You're Sixteen (You're Beautiful And You're Mine)', piano, synthesiser, backing vocals on 'Six O'Clock'
Released November 23 1973
UK Apple PCTC 252
US Apple SWAL-3413

JAMES TAYLOR
Walking Man
McCartney backing vocals on 'Rock'n'Roll Is Music Now', 'Let It All Fall Down'
Released June 2 1974
UK Warner Bros. K 56402
US Warner Bros. W 2794

THORNTON, FRANDKIN AND UNGER AND THE BIG BAND
Pass On This Side
McCartney bass, backing vocals on 'God Bless California'
Released June 17 1974
US ESP ESP63019

SCAFFOLD
'Liverpool Lou' / 'Ten Years On After Strawberry Jam'
McCartney produces, plays Gizmo, bass, backing vocals
Released July 29 1974
US Warner Bros. 8001

ADAM FAITH
I Survive
McCartney plays synthesiser on 'Change', 'Never Say Goodbye', 'Goodbye', backing vocals on 'Star Song'
Released August 6 1974
UK Warner Bros. K 56054
US Warner Bros. BS 2791

ROD STEWART
Smiler
McCartney backing vocals on 'Mine For Me'
Released September 27 1974
UK Mercury 9104-001
US Mercury SRM-1-1017

PEGGY LEE
Let's Love
McCartney produces, plays piano on 'Let's Love'
Released October 1 1974
US Atlantic SD 18108

MIKE MCGEAR
McGear
McCartney produces, plays guitar, piano, bass, keyboards
Released July 4 1975
UK Warner Bros. K56051
Released October 14 1974
US Warner Bros. BS 2825
CD Rykodisc RCD10192 (features alternative version of Dance The Do)

PEGGY LEE
'Let's Love' / 'Always'
McCartney produces, plays piano on A-side
Released October 25 1974
UK Warner Bros. K 50064

MIKE MCGEAR
'Leave It' / 'Sweet Baby'
McCartney produces, plays keyboards, bass, backing vocals
Released October 28 1974
US Warner Bros. 8037

MIKE MCGEAR
'Sea Breezes' / 'Givin' Grease A Ride'
McCartney produces, plays keyboards, bass, backing vocals
Released February 7 1975
UK Warner Bros. K 16520

MIKE MCGEAR
'Dance The Do' / 'Norton'
McCartney produces, plays keyboards, bass, backing vocals
Released July 4 1975
UK Warner Bros. K 16573

RINGO STARR
Ringo's Rotogravure
McCartney performs on 'Pure Gold'
Released September 17 1976
UK Polydor 2302 040
US Atlantic 82417-2

ROY HARPER
Bullinamingvase
McCartney backing vocals on 'One Of Those Days In England (Parts 2-10)'
Released February 11 1977
UK Harvest SHSP 4060

DENNY LAINE
Holly Days
McCartney produces, plays drums, bass, guitar, backing vocals
Released May 6 1977
UK EMI EMA 781
Released May 19 1977
US Capitol 11588 ST
CD Magic 3930035, February 2001

GODLEY AND CREME
Freeze Frame
McCartney performs on 'Get Well Soon'
Released February 1979
UK Polydor POLD 5027
US Polydor PD-1-6257

GEORGE HARRISON
Somewhere In England
McCartney performs on 'All Those Years Ago'
Released June 5 1981
UK Dark Horse K56870
Released June 1 1981
US Dark Horse DHK 3492

DENNY LAINE
Japanese Tears
McCartney produces, plays bass, backing vocals on 'Send Me The Heart', 'I Would Only Smile', 'Weep For Love'
Released 1980
UK Scratch SCRL 5001
Released August 8 1983
US Takoma TAK 7103

RINGO STARR
Stop And Smell The Roses
McCartney produces and performs on 'Private Property', 'Attention', 'Sure To Fall'
Released November 20 1981
UK RCA LP 6022
US Boardwalk NB1 33246

LAURENCE JUBER
Standard Time
McCartney co-produces with Juber, Richard Niles, Chris Thomas and plays bass on 'Maisie'
Released July 9 1982
UK Breaking BREAK 1

THE EVERLY BROTHERS
'On The Wings Of A Nightingale' / **'Asleep'**
McCartney plays acoustic guitar on A-side
Released August 24 1984
UK Mercury MER 170

BAND AID
'Do They Know It's Christmas' / **'Feed The World'**
McCartney delivers spoken message on B-side
Released November 1984
UK Polygram FEED1

THE CROWD
'You'll Never Walk Alone' / **'Messages'**
McCartney delivers spoken message on B-side
Released May 20 1985
UK Spartan BRAD1

FERRY AID
'Let It Be' / **'The Gospel Jam Mix'**
McCartney vocal, piano dubbed from Beatles original
Released March 23 1987
UK CBS AID1

DUANE EDDY
'Rockestra Theme' / **'Blue City '**
McCartney produces and plays bass, backing vocals on A-side
Released September 21 1987
UK Capitol CL463
12-inch 12CL463 Rockestra Theme (Extended Version) / Rockestra Theme (7 Inch version) / Blue City

THE CRICKETS
'Tee Shirt' / **'Holly Would'**
McCartney produces and plays piano, backing vocals on A-side
Released September 5 1988
UK CBS TSH1

JOHNNY CASH
Water From The Wells Of Home
McCartney produces and plays bass, guitar, vocals on 'New Moon Over Jamaica'
Released May 9 1988
UK Mercury 834778-1
US Mercury 834 778

SPIRIT OF PLAY
'Children In Need' / **'Children In Need' (Instrumental)**
McCartney produces, plays bass
Released November 1988
UK Release KIDS1988

ELVIS COSTELLO
Spike
McCartney plays bass on 'Veronica', bass and backing vocals on 'This Town'
Released February 1989
UK Warner Bros. WX238
US Warner Bros. 925 848-1

EDDIE MURPHY
Love's Alright
McCartney vocals on 'Yeah'
Released March 1992
US Motown 374636354-2

10cc
Mirror Mirror
McCartney plays rhythm guitar on 'The One', strings, electric piano, frog and cricket sounds, percussion on 'Code Of Silence'
Released June 1995
UK Avex BOYCDO36

YOKO ONO
'Hiroshima Sky Is Always Blue'
McCartney vocals, upright bass (plus Linda on vocals, celeste, Heather McCartney on vocals, Stella McCartney on vocals, James McCartney on guitar).
Broadcast by NHK Japan, August 6 1995

THE SMOKIN' MOJO FILTERS
'Come Together' / **'A Minute's Silence'**
McCartney plays guitar, keyboards, backing vocals on B-side
Released December 4 1995
UK Go Discs GOD136

ALLEN GINSBERG
'The Ballad Of The Skeletons' (7:46) / **'The Ballad Of The Skeletons' (4:07)** / **'Amazing Grace'** / **'The Ballad Of The Skeletons' (Clean 7:46)**
McCartney plays guitar, organ, drums, percussion on 'The Ballad Of The Skeletons'
Released November 1996
US Mouth Almighty / Mercury 697 120 101-2

CARL PERKINS
Go Cat Go
McCartney co-produces with George Martin, plays keyboards, guitar, drums, bass, backing vocals on 'My Old Friend'
Released October 15 1996
US Dinosaur Entertainment 76401-84508-2

LINDA McCARTNEY
Wide Prairie
McCartney co-produces with various others, performs
Released May 5 1997
UK Parlophone CD 4979102, LP 4979101

LINDA McCARTNEY
'Wide Prairie' / **'Cow'**
McCartney produces, performs
Released November 9 1998
UK Parlophone RPD 6510 / CDR 6510

LINDA McCARTNEY
'The Light Comes From Within' / **'I Got Up'**
McCartney produces, performs
Released 1997
UK Parlophone RPD 6513 / CDR 6513

RINGO STARR
Vertical Man
McCartney plays bass, backing vocals on What In The World, backing vocals on 'I Was Walkin'', 'La De Da'
Released August 3 1998
UK Mercury 314 558 400-2
US Mercury 558 400

PETER KIRTLEY BAND
'Little Children' / **'Little Children Part 2'**
McCartney vocals on B-side
Released December 1998
UK Jubilee JUB001

HEATHER MILLS
'Voice', 'Paul McCartney's Mello Extension', 'Someone U Love Mix'
McCartney vocals
Released December 13 1999
UK CODA CODARCD004

SUPER FURRY ANIMALS
Rings Around The World
McCartney performs on 'Receptacle For The Respectable'
Released July 23 2001
UK/US Epic 502413 9

LINDSAY PAGANO
Love + Faith + Inspiration
McCartney accompanying vocal 'So Bad'
Released 18 December 2001
UK/US Warner Bros 9 47953-2

LULU
Together
McCartney co-vocals 'Inside Thing (Let 'Em In)'
Released May 2002
UK/US Mercury

RUSTY ANDERSON
Undressing Underwater
McCartney plays bass, backing vocals on 'Hurt Myself'
Released December 17 2003
UK Oxide OXI-001

BRIAN WILSON
Gettin' In Over My Head
McCartney performs on 'A Friend Like You'
Released June 22 2004
UK/US Rhino 812276471-2

STEVIE WONDER
A Time To Love
McCartney plays acoustic guitar, electric guitar on 'A Time To Love'
Released October 17 2005
UK/US Motown 9882094

TONY BENNETT
Duets / An American Classic
McCartney co-vocals on 'The Very Thought Of You'
Released October 30 2006
UK/US RPM/Sony 88697009012

GEORGE BENSON AND AL JARREAU
Givin' It Up
McCartney co-vocals on 'Bring It On Home To Me'
Released US October 24 2006 / UK November 13 2006
UK/US Concord 7223162

GEORGE MICHAEL
Twenty Five
McCartney co-vocals 'Heal The Pain'
Released November 13 2006
UK/US Sony 88697009012

LENNON DISCOGRAPHY

Over these pages we list John Lennon's album, CD, and single releases and promos issued in the UK, the USA, and Japan. Please note that release dates are shown in UK format: day, month, year.

UK LPs

Released	Title	Label/number
29.11.68	*Unfinished Music No. 1: Two Virgins*	Apple APCOR 2
29.11.68	*Unfinished Music No. 1: Two Virgins*	Apple SAPCOR 2
02.05.69	*Unfinished Music No. 2: Life With The Lions*	Zapple ZAPPLE 01
14.11.69	*The Wedding Album*	Apple SAPCOR 11
12.12.69	*Plastic Ono Band – Live Peace In Toronto 1969*	Apple CORE 2001
11.12.70	*John Lennon/Plastic Ono Band*	Apple PCS 7124
07.10.71	*Imagine*	Apple PAS 10004
00.06.72	*Imagine*	Apple Q4PAS 10004
15.09.72	*Sometime In New York City*	Apple PCSP 716
16.11.73	*Mind Games*	Apple PCS 7165
04.10.74	*Walls And Bridges*	Apple PCTC 253
21.02.75	*Rock'N'Roll*	Apple PCS 7169
24.10.75	*Shaved Fish*	Apple PCS 7173
17.11.80	*Double Fantasy*	Geffen K 99131
28.11.80	*Mind Games*	MFP MFP 50509
15.06.81	*John Lennon*	EMI/Apple JLB8
25.11.81	*Rock'N'Roll*	MFP MFP 50522
01.11.82	*The John Lennon Collection*	Parlophone EMTV 37
16.12.83	*Heart Play* – Unfinished Dialogue	Polydor 817 238-1
23.01.84	*Milk And Honey*	Polydor POLH 5
26.03.84	*Milk And Honey*	Polydor POLHP 5
02.07.84	*John Lennon/Plastic Ono Band*	EMI/FAME FA 41 3102 1
21.09.84	*Every Man Has A Woman*	Polydor POLH 13
24.02.86	*Live In New York City*	Parlophone PCS 7301
03.11.86	*Menlove Ave.*	Parlophone PCS 7308
10.10.88	*Imagine: John Lennon, Music From The Motion Picture*	Parlophone PCSP 722
00.00.89	*Double Fantasy*	Capitol EST 2083
17.02.96	*Rock'N'Roll*	EMI/Apple LPCENT 9
27.10.97	*Lennon Legend – The Very Best Of John Lennon*	Parlophone 8 21954 1
17.11.97	*Imagine*	EMI/Apple LPCENT 27
18.01.99	*Wonsaponatime*	Capitol 497 6391
22.03.99	*Walls And Bridges* millennium edition	EMI/Apple 4994641
14.02.00	*Imagine*	Apple5 24858 1

UK 8-TRACK CARTRIDGES

Released	Title	Label/number
11.12.70	*John Lennon/Plastic Ono Band*	Apple 8X-PCS 7124
00.11.71	*Imagine*	Apple 8X-PAS 10004
00.03.72	*Imagine*	Apple Q8-PAS 10004
15.09.72	*Sometime In New York City*	Apple 8X-PCSP 716
00.01.74	*Mind Games*	Apple 8X-PCS 7165
04.10.74	*Walls And Bridges*	Apple 8X-PCTC 253
21.02.75	*Rock'N'Roll*	Apple 8X-PCS 7169
24.10.75	*Shaved Fish*	Apple 8X-PCS 7173

UK CDs

Released	Title	Label/number
03.06.97	*Unfinished Music No. 1: Two Virgins*	RykodiscRCD10411
03.06.97	*Unfinished Music No. 2: Life With The Lions*	Rykodisc RCD10412
03.06.97	*The Wedding Album*	RykodiscRCD10413
01.05.95	*Plastic Ono Band – Live Peace In Toronto 1969*	Apple CDP 7 90428 2
04.04.88	*John Lennon/Plastic Ono Band*	Apple CDP 7 46770 2
18.05.87	*Imagine*	Apple CDP 7 46641 2
10.08.87	*Sometime In New York City*	Apple CDS 7 46782 8
03.08.87	*Mind Games*	Apple CDP 7 46769 2
20.07.87	*Walls And Bridges*	Apple CDP 7 46768 2
18.05.87	*Rock'N'Roll*	Apple CDP 7 46707 2
25.05.87	*Shaved Fish*	Apple CDP 7 46642 2
13.10.86	*Double Fantasy*	Geffen 299 131
23.10.89	*The John Lennon Collection*	Parlophone CD EMTV 37
23.01.84	*Milk And Honey*	Polydor 817 160-2
19.11.84	*Every Man Has A Woman*	Polydor 823 490-2
28.04.86	*Live In New York City*	Parlophone CDP 7 46196 2
13.04.87	*Menlove Ave.*	Parlophone CDP 7 46576 2
10.10.88	*Imagine: John Lennon, Music From The Motion Picture*	Parlophone CD PCSP 722
01.10.90	*Lennon*	Parlophone CDS 7 95220 2
14.10.96	*Rock And Roll Circus*	Mercury 526 771-2
27.10.97	*Lennon Legend – The Very Best Of John Lennon*	Parlophone 8 21954 2
02.11.98	*Anthology*	Capitol830 6142
03.11.98	*Wonsaponatime*	Capitol CDP 4 97639 2
14.02.00	*Imagine* remastered	Parlophone 524 8582
09.10.00	*John Lennon/Plastic Ono Band* remastered	Parlophone 528 7402
09.10.00	*Double Fantasy* remastered	Capitol 528 7392
08.10.01	*Milk And Honey* remastered	Parlophone 535 9592
07.10.02	*Mind Games* remastered	Parlophone 542 4252
27.10.03	*Lennon Legend – The Very Best Of John Lennon*	Parlophone 595 0672
13.09.04	*Milk And Honey / Double Fantasy*	Parlophone EBX23
27.09.04	*Rock'N'Roll* remastered	Parlophone 8743292
01.11.04	*Acoustic*	Parlophone 8744282
03.10.05	*Working Class Hero (The Definitive Lennon)*	Parlophone 340 0802
26.09.06	*The U.S. vs John Lennon*	Parlophone 3749122

UK 7-INCH SINGLES

Released	Title	Label/number
00.00.69	'Song For John', 'Let's Go On Flying', 'Snow Is Falling All The Time', 'Mum's Only Looking For Her Hand In The Snow', 'No Bed for Beatle John Radio Play'	Aspen Magazine
04.07.69	'Give Peace A Chance' / 'Remember Love'	Apple APPLE 13
24.10.69	'Cold Turkey' / 'Don't Worry Kyoko (Mummy's Only Looking For A Hand In The Snow)'	Apple APPLES 1001
05.12.69	'You Know My Name (Look Up The Number)' / 'What's The New Mary Jane' withdrawn	Apple APPLES 1002
06.02.70	'Instant Karma!' / 'Who Has Seen The Wind?'	Apple APPLES 1003
12.03.71	'Power To The People' / 'Open Your Box'	Apple R 5892
16.07.71	'God Save Us' / 'Do The Oz'	Apple APPLE 36
24.11.72	'Happy Xmas (War Is Over)' / 'Listen The Snow Is Falling'	Apple R 5970
05.12.72	'Woman Is The Nigger Of The World' / 'Sisters, O Sisters'	Apple R 5953*
16.11.73	'Mind Games' / 'Meat City'	Apple R 5994
04.10.74	'Whatever Gets You Thru The Night' / 'Beef Jerky'	Apple R 5998
24.01.75	'#9 Dream' / 'What You Got'	Apple R 6003
28.02.75	'Philadelphia Freedom' (Elton John Band) / 'I Saw Her Standing There' (Elton John Band featuring Lennon with Muscle Shoals Horns)	DJM DJS 354
18.04.75	'Stand By Me' / 'Move Over Ms. L'	Apple R 6005
24.10.75	'Imagine' / 'Working Class Hero'	Apple R 6009
24.10.80	'(Just Like) Starting Over' / 'Kiss Kiss Kiss'	Geffen K 79186
16.01.81	'Woman' / 'Beautiful Boys'	Geffen K 79195
13.03.81	'I Saw Her Standing There' / 'Whatever Gets You Thru The Night', 'Lucy In The Sky With Diamonds' (Elton John Band featuring Lennon with Muscle Shoals Horns)	DJM DJS 10965
27.03.81	'Watching The Wheels' / 'Yes, I'm Your Angel'	Geffen K79207
15.11.82	'Love' / 'Give Me Some Truth'	Parlophone R 6059
09.01.84	'Nobody Told Me' / 'O' Sanity'	Polydor POSP 700
16.03.84	'Borrowed Time' / 'Your Hands'	Polydor POSP 701
12.03.84	'Give Peace A Chance' / 'Cold Turkey'	Apple G45 2
15.07.84	'I'm Stepping Out' / 'Sleepless Night'	Polydor POSP 702
16.11.84	'Every Man Has A Woman Who Loves Him' / 'It's Alright'	Polydor POSP 712
18.11.85	'Jealous Guy' / 'Going Down On Love'	Parlophone R 6117
28.11.88	'Imagine' / 'Jealous Guy' / 'Happy Xmas (War Is Over)'	Parlophone R 6199
05.12.88	'Imagine' / 'Jealous Guy', 'Happy Xmas (War Is Over)'	Parlophone RP 6199
14.02.00	'Imagine' / 'Working Class Hero'	Parlophone R 6009
12.12.03	'Happy Xmas (War Is Over)' / 'Imagine'	Parlophone R 6627

UK 12-INCH SINGLES

Released	Title	Label/number
09.03.84	'Borrowed Time' / 'Your Hands', 'Never Say Goodbye'	Polydor POSPX 701
15.07.84	'I'm Stepping Out' / 'Sleepless Night', 'Loneliness'	Polydor POSPX 702
18.11.85	'Jealous Guy' / 'Going Down On Love', 'Oh Yoko!'	Parlophone 12 R 6117
28.11.88	'Imagine' / 'Jealous Guy', 'Happy Xmas (War Is Over)'	Parlophone 12 R 6199

UK CASSETTE SINGLES

Released	Title	Label/number
16.01.81	'Woman' / 'Beautiful Boys'	Geffen K 79195M
27.03.81	'Watching The Wheels' / 'Yes, I'm Your Angel'	Geffen K 79207M

UK CD SINGLES

Released	Title	Label/number
28.11.88	'Imagine', 'Jealous Guy', 'Happy Xmas (War Is Over)', 'Give Peace A Chance'	Parlophone CDR 6199
23.12.99	'Imagine', 'Happy Xmas (War Is Over)', 'Give Peace A Chance', 'Imagine' (Video)	Parlophone CDR 6534
12.12.03	'Happy Xmas (War Is Over)', 'Imagine', 'Instant Karma!', 'Imagine' (Instrumental/Photo Gallery)	Parlophone CDR 6627

UK 7-INCH SINGLE PROMOS

Released	Title	Label/number
05.12.69	'You Know My Name (Look Up The Number)' / 'What's The New Mary Jane' custom Apple labels	Apple APPLES 1002
05.12.72	'Woman Is The Nigger Of The World' / 'Sisters, O Sisters' white label test pressing	Apple R 5953
00.11.74	'Interview with Lennon by Bob Merger and Message to Salesmen'	EMI/Apple PSR 369
24.01.75	'#9 Dream' (Edit) / 'What You Got'	Apple R 6003
13.03.81	'I Saw Her Standing There' / 'Whatever Gets You Thru The Night', 'Lucy In The Sky With Diamonds' white label A-side 45rpm, B-side 33-1/3rpm	DJM DJS 10965
09.01.84	'Nobody Told Me' one-sided white label	Polydor POSP 70
09.03.84	'Borrowed Time' (Edit) / 'Your Hands'	Polydor PODJ 701

UK CD SINGLE PROMOS

Released	Title	Label/number
00.10.97	'Imagine'	Parlophone IMAGINE 001
00.12.97	'Happy Xmas (War Is Over)'	Parlophone IMAGINE 002
00.10.98	'I'm Losing You', 'Only You'	Capitol LENNON 001
00.12.97	'Happy Xmas (War Is Over)', 'Be-Bop-A-Lula'	Capitol LENNON 002
00.00.00	'Imagine', 'Happy Xmas (War Is Over)', 'Give Peace A Chance'	Parlophone CDRDJ6534

US LPs

Released	Title	Label/number
06.01.69	*Unfinished Music No. 1: Two Virgins*	Apple T 5001
26.05.69	*Unfinished Music No. 2: Life With The Lions*	Zapple ST 3357
20.10.69	*The Wedding Album*	Apple SMAX 3361
12.12.69	*Plastic Ono Band – Live Peace In Toronto 1969*	Apple SW 3362
11.12.70	*John Lennon/Plastic Ono Band*	Apple SW 3372
09.09.71	*Imagine*	Apple SW 3379
12.06.72	*Sometime In New York City*	Apple SVBB 3392
02.11.73	*Mind Games*	Apple SW 3414
26.09.74	*Walls And Bridges*	Apple SW 3416
17.02.75	*John Lennon Sings The Rock & Roll Hits: Roots*	Adam VIII A8018
17.02.75	*Rock'N'Roll*	Apple SK 3419
24.10.75	*Shaved Fish*	Apple SW 3421
17.11.80	*Double Fantasy*	Geffen GHS 2001
00.10.80	*Mind Games*	Capitol SN-16068
00.10.80	*Rock'N'Roll*	Capitol SN-16069
17.11.81	*Double Fantasy* corrected back cover, no 'CH' on label	Columbia House GHS 2001
00.00.81	*Double Fantasy*	RCA Music Service R 104689
00.00.82	*Double Fantasy*	Nautilus NR-47
00.00.82	*Double Fantasy* experimental sepia cover	Nautilus NR-47
08.11.82	*The John Lennon Collection*	Geffen GHSP 2023
08.11.82	*The John Lennon Collection* promo, Quiex II audiophile vinyl	Geffen GHSP 2023
05.12 .83	*Heart Play – Unfinished Dialogue*	Polydor 817 238-1 Y-1
23.01.84	*Milk And Honey*	Polydor 817 160-1 Y-1
17.09 .84	*Every Man Has A Woman*	Polydor 422-823 490-1 Y-1
00.00.84	*Reflections And Poetry*	Silhouette SM-10012
00.00.84	*Imagine*	MFSL 1-153
00.00.86	*Double Fantasy* corrected back cover, no 'CH' on black Geffen label	Columbia House GHS 2001
24.01.86	*Live In New York City*	Capitol SV-12451
24.01.86	*Live In New York City*	Columbia House SV-512451
24.01.86	*Live In New York City*	RCA Music Service R-144497
27.10.86	*Menlove Ave.*	Capitol SJ 12533
27.10.86	*Menlove Ave.*	BMG Direct Marketing R-144136
04.10.88	*Imagine: John Lennon, Music From The Motion Picture*	Capitol C1-90803
00.00.89	*Double Fantasy*	Columbia House/ Capitol C-1-591425
10.03.98	*Lennon Legend – The Very Best Of John Lennon*	Parlophone 8 21954 1
00.00.04	*Imagine*	MFSL 1-277
15.11.04	*John Lennon/Plastic Ono Band*	MFSL 1-280
00.00.05	*Mind Games*	MFSL 1-293
00.00.06	*Plastic Ono Band – Live Peace In Toronto 1969*	MFSL 1-283

US 8-TRACK CARTRIDGES

Released	Title	Label/number
06.01.69	*Unfinished Music No. 1: Two Virgins*	Apple TNM-85001
26.05.69	*Unfinished Music No. 2: Life With The Lions*	Zapple 8XT-3357
20.10.69	*The Wedding Album*	Apple 8AX-3361
12.12.69	*Plastic Ono Band – Live Peace In Toronto 1969*	Apple 8XT-3362
11.12.70	*John Lennon/Plastic Ono Band*	Apple 8XW-3372
09.09.71	*Imagine*	Apple 8XW-3379
09.09.71	*Imagine*	Apple Q8W-3379
12.06.72	*Sometime In New York City*	Apple 8XW-3393 and 8XW-3394
02.11.73	*Mind Games*	Apple 8XW-3414
26.09.74	*Walls And Bridges*	Apple 8XW-3416
26.09.74	*Walls And Bridges*	Apple Q8W-3416
17.02.75	*Rock'N'Roll*	Apple 8XK-3419
24.10.75	*Shaved Fish*	Apple 8XW-3421
17.11.80	*Double Fantasy*	Geffen GEF-W8-2001
17.11.80	*Double Fantasy*	Columbia Record Club W8-2001
17.11.80	*Double Fantasy*	RCA Record Club S-104689
08.11.82	*The John Lennon Collection*	Geffen GEF-L8-2023
24.01.86	*Live In New York City*	RCA Music Service S-144497

US REEL-TO-REEL TAPES

Released	Title	Label/number
12.12.69	*Plastic Ono Band – Live Peace In Toronto 1969*	Apple L-3362
11.12.70	*John Lennon/Plastic Ono Band*	Apple M-3372
09.09.71	*Imagine*	Apple L-3379

US CDs

Released	Title	Label/number
23.01.84	*Milk And Honey*	Polydor 817 160-2
19.11.84	*Every Man Has A Woman*	Polydor 823 490-2
18.05.87	*Imagine*	Apple CDP 7 46641 2
10.08.87	*Sometime In New York City*	Apple CDP 7 46782 / 3 8
03.08.87	*Mind Games*	Apple CDP 7 46769 2
20.07.87	*Walls And Bridges*	Apple CDP 7 46768 2
18.05.87	*Rock'N'Roll*	Apple CDP 7 46707 2
25.05.87	*Shaved Fish*	Apple CDP 7 466422
13.10.86	*Double Fantasy*	Geffen 2001-2
28.04.86	*Live In New York City*	Parlophone CDP 7 46196 2

Released	Title	Label/number
13.04.87	*Menlove Ave.*	Parlophone CDP 7 46576 2
04.04.88	*John Lennon/Plastic Ono Band*	Apple CDP 7 46770 2
10.10.88	*Imagine: John Lennon, Music From The Motion Picture*	Parlophone CDP 7 90803 2
23.10.89	*The John Lennon Collection*	Parlophone CDP 7 91516 2
01.10.90	*Lennon*	Parlophone CDS 7 95220 2
00.00.91	*Unfinished Music No. 1: Two Virgins*	Rock Classics SSI 9999
00.00.94	*Double Fantasy*	MFSL UDCD-1-590
01.05.95	*Plastic Ono Band – Live Peace In Toronto 1969*	Apple CDP 7 90428 2
14.10.96	*Rock And Roll Circus*	Mercury 526 771-2
03.06.97	*Unfinished Music No. 1: Two Virgins*	Rykodisc RCD10411
03.06 97	*Unfinished Music No. 2: Life With The Lions*	Rykodisc RCD10412
03.06.97	*The Wedding Album*	Rykodisc RCD10413
27.10.97	*Lennon Legend – The Very Best Of John Lennon*	Parlophone 8 21954 2
03.11.98	*Anthology*	Capitol C2 8 30614 2
03.11.98	*Wonsaponatime*	Capitol CDP 4 97639 2
11.04.00	*Imagine* remastered	Capitol CDP 5 24858 2
09.10.00	*John Lennon/Plastic Ono Band* remastered	Capitol 528 7402
09.10.00	*Double Fantasy* remastered	Capitol 528 7392
08.10.01	*Milk And Honey* remastered	Capitol 535 9592
07.10.02	*Mind Games* remastered	Capitol 542 4252
22.08.03	*Imagine* remastered Ultradisc II 24 kt. Gold	MFSL CMF759
20.01.04	*John Lennon/Plastic Ono Band* remastered Ultradisc II 24 kt. Gold	MFSL CMF760
02.11.04	*Rock'N'Roll* remastered	Capitol 542 4252
02.11.04	*Acoustic*	Capitol 744292
23.11.04	*Mind Games* remastered Ultradisc II 24 kt. Gold	MFSL UDCD 761
04.10.05	*Working Class Hero (The Definitive Lennon)*	Capitol 094634039123
08.11.05	*Plastic Ono Band – Live Peace In Toronto 1969*	MFSL UDCD 763
26.09.06	*The U.S. vs John Lennon*	Capitol 74912-2
03.01.07	*Remember*	Capitol/Hear Music 71108-2-9

US 7-INCH SINGLES

Released	Title	Label/number
00.00.69	'Song For John', 'Let's Go On Flying', 'Snow is Falling All The Time', 'Mum's Only Looking For Her Hand In The Snow', 'No Bed For Beatle John Radio Play'	Aspen Magazine
21.07.69	'Give Peace A Chance' / 'Remember Love'	Apple 1809
21.07.69	'Give Peace A Chance' / 'Remember Love'	Apple/Americom 1809P/M-435
20.10.69	'Cold Turkey' / 'Don't Worry Kyoko (Mummy's Only Looking For A Hand In The Snow)'	Apple 1813
20.02.70	'Instant Karma!' / 'Who Has Seen The Wind?'	Apple 1818
28.12.70	'Mother' / 'Why'	Apple 1827
22.03.71	'Power To The People' / 'Touch Me'	Apple 1830
07.07.71	'God Save Us' / 'Do The Oz'	Apple 1835
10.10.71	'Imagine' / 'It's So Hard'	Apple 1840
01.12.71	'Happy Xmas (War Is Over)' / 'Listen The Snow Is Falling'	Apple 1842
24.04.72	Woman Is The Nigger Of The World / Sisters, O Sisters	Apple 1848

Released	Title	Label/number
29.10.73	'Mind Games' / 'Meat City'	Apple 1868
23.09.74	'Whatever Gets You Thru The Night' / 'Beef Jerky'	Apple 1874
16.12.74	'#9 Dream' / 'What You Got'	Apple 1878
24.02.75	'Philadelphia Freedom' (Elton John Band) / 'I Saw Her Standing There' (Elton John Band featuring Lennon The Muscle Shoals Horns)	MCA MCA 40364
10.03.75	'Stand By Me' / 'Move Over Ms. L'	Apple 1881
04.04.77	'Stand By Me' / 'Woman Is The Nigger Of The World'	Capitol 6244
20.10.80	'(Just Like) Starting Over' / 'Kiss Kiss Kiss'	Geffen GEF 49604
12.01.81	'Woman' / 'Beautiful Boys'	Geffen GEF 49644
13.03.81	'Watching Tho Wheels' / 'Yes, I'm Your Angel'	Geffen GEF 49695
06.07.81	'(Just Like) Starting Over' / 'Woman'	Geffen GGEF 0408
09.11.81	'Watching The Wheels' / 'Beautiful Boy (Darling Boy)'	Geffen GGEF 0415
29.11.82	'Happy Xmas (War Is Over)' / 'Beautiful Boy (Darling Boy)'	Geffen GEF-7-29855
09.01.84	'Nobody Told Me' / 'O' Sanity'	Polydor 817 254-7
19.03.84	'I'm Stepping Out' / 'Sleepless Night'	Polydor 821-107-7
14.05.84	'Borrowed Time' / 'Your Hands'	Polydor 821-204-7
08.10.84	'Every Man Has A Woman Who Loves Him' / 'It's Alright'	Polydor 881 387-7
19.09.88	'Jealous Guy' / 'Give Peace A Chance'	Capitol B-44230
30.04.90	'Nobody Told Me' / 'I'm Stepping Out'	Polydor883927-7
00.10.92	'Imagine' / 'It's So Hard'	CEMA S7-57849
00.00.92	'Nobody Told Me' / 'I'm Steppin' Out'	Collectibles COL-4307
00.00.94	'Give Peace A Chance' / 'Remember Love'	CEMA S7-17783
00.00.94	'(Just Like) Starting Over' / 'Watching The Wheels' blue vinyl	CEMA 72438-58894-7
00.00.94	'Happy Xmas (War Is Over)' / 'Listen, The Snow Is Falling' green vinyl	CEMA S7-17644
00.00.94	'Woman' / 'Walking On Thin Ice' clear vinyl	CEMA 72438-58895-7

US 7-INCH SINGLE PROMOS

Released	Title	Label/number
	'The KYA Peace Talk'	KYA 1260
	'Instant Karma'! one-sided	Apple 1818
	'John Lennon on Ronnie Hawkins – The Short Rap / The Long Rap'	Cotillion PR-105
	'Mother' / 'Why'	Apple P-1827
	'Power To The People' / 'Touch Me'	Apple P-1830
	'God Save Us' / 'Do The Oz'	Apple P-1835
	'Imagine' / 'It's So Hard'	Apple P-1840
	'Happy Xmas (War Is Over)' / 'Listen, The Snow Is Falling' white label, black text 'NOT FOR SALE FOR RADIO STATION PLAY ONLY'	Apple S-45X-47663
	'Woman Is The Nigger Of The World' / 'Sisters, O Sisters'	Apple P-1848
	'Mind Games' mono/stereo	Apple P-1868
	'Whatever Gets You Thru The Night' mono/stereo	Apple P-1874
	'#9 Dream 'mono/stereo	Apple P-1878
	'What You Got' mono/stereo)	Apple P-1878
	'Stand By Me' mono/stereo	Apple P-1881
	'Ain't That A Shame' mono/stereo	Apple P-1883
	'Slippin' And Slidin' mono/stereo	Apple P-1883

Released	Title	Label/number
	'(Just Like) Starting Over' mono/stereo	Geffen GEF 49604
	'Watching The Wheels' mono/stereo	Geffen GEF 49695
	'Happy Xmas (War Is Over)' mono/stereo	Geffen GEF-7-29855
	'Nobody Told Me' / 'O' Sanity'	Polydor 817 254-7 DJ
	'I'm Stepping Out' 3:33/4:06	Polydor 821-107-7 DJ
	'Borrowed Time' / 'Borrowed Time'	Polydor 821-204-7 DJ
	'Every Man Has A Woman Who Loves Him' / 'Every Man Has A Woman Who Loves Him'	Polydor 881 387-7 DJ
	'Jealous Guy' / 'Jealous Guy'	Capitol P-B-44230
	'Every Man Has A Woman Who Loves Him' Lennon/Ono	Capitol 7PRO 6 15998 7

US 12-INCH SINGLE PROMOS

Released	Title	Label/number
	'(Just Like) Starting Over' / 'Kiss Kiss Kiss'	Geffen PRO-A-919
	'Happy Xmas (War Is Over)' / 'Beautiful Boy (Darling Boy)'	Geffen PRO-A-1079
	'Nobody Told Me' / 'O' Sanity'	Polydor PRO 250-1
	'Imagine' / 'Come Together'	Capitol SPRO-9585 / 6
	'Happy Xmas (War Is Over)' / 'Happy Xmas (War Is Over)' 2,000 hand-numbered for Central Virginia Foodbank	Capitol SPRO-9894
	'Rock And Roll People' / 'Rock And Roll People'	Capitol SPRO-9917
	'Happy Xmas (War Is Over)' / 'Listen, The Snow Is Falling' silver label, plastic sleeve, limited 1,500	Capitol SPRO-9929
	'Stand By Me' / 'Stand By Me'	Capitol SPRO-79453

US CD PROMOS

Released	Title	Label/number
	'Jealous Guy'	Capitol DPRO-79417
	Excerpts From John Lennon Anthology	Capitol DPRO-13507
	Starting Over conversation with Ono	Capitol DPRO-15670
	The Lennon/Ono Publishing Catalogue Sampler	EMI Music Publishing IFPIL433
	John Lennon: Two Sides Of Lennon	Capitol DPRO-70876

JAPANESE LPs

Released	Title	Label/number
	Life With The Lions Zapple logo	Zapple AP-8782
	Life With The Lions no Zapple logo	Zapple AP-8782
	Life With The Lions reissue	Zapple EAS-80701
	Wedding Album	Apple AP-9010
	Wedding Album	Odeon EAS-80702
	Live Peace In Toronto – 1969	Apple AP 8867
	Live Peace In Toronto – 1969	Odeon EAS-80703
	John Lennon/Plastic Ono Band	Apple AP-80174
	John Lennon/Plastic Ono Band	Odeon EAS-80704
	Imagine	Apple AP-80370
	Imagine quadraphonic	Apple EAZ 80006
	Imagine	Odeon EAS-80705
	Sometime In New York City	Apple EAP-93049
	Sometime In New York City	Odeon EAS-67110-11
	Mind Games	Apple EAP-80950
	Mind Games	Odeon EAS-80706
	Walls And Bridges	Apple EAS-80065
	Rock'N'Roll	Apple EAS-80175
	Shaved Fish	Apple EAS-80380
	Shaved Fish green vinyl	Odeon EAS-81457
	Double Fantasy with/without memorial OBI	Geffen P-10948J
	Double Fantasy	Geffen P-5909
	John Lennon 8-LP boxed set	Odeon EAS-67161-69
	Elton John & John Lennon Live! with poster/insert	King K28P-200
	The John Lennon Collection	Odeon EAS-91055
	Heart Play – Unfinished Dialogue	Polydor 20MM-9250
	Milk And Honey	Polydor 25MM-0260
	Milk And Honey Nice Price	Polydor 18MM 0609
	Every Man Has A Woman	Polydor P33P-26223
	Imagine O.S.T .	Odeon R P15-5690-91
	Live In New York City	Odeon ECS-9116
	Menlove Ave.	Odeon ECS-91197

JAPANESE CDs

Released	Title	Label/number
	Two Virgins	Rykodisc VACK 1125
	Life With The Lions	Rykodisc VACK 1126
	Wedding Album	Rykodisc VACK 1127
	Live Peace In Toronto – 1969 with '95 calendar	Odeon TOCP-8560
	Live Peace In Toronto – 1969	Odeon TOCP-65533
	John Lennon/Plastic Ono Band	Odeon CP32-5463
	John Lennon/Plastic Ono Band	Odeon TOCP-3122
	John Lennon/Plastic Ono Band Odeon Super Master	Odeon TOCP-6857
	Imagine	Odeon CP32-5451
	Imagine limited 24kt. Gold	Odeon CP43-5773
	Imagine	Odeon TOCP-67483
	Sometime In New York City	Odeon CP25-5466-67
	Sometime In New York City	Odeon TOCP-65523/24
	Mind Games	Odeon CP32-5464
	Mind Games	Odeon TOCP-3123
	Walls And Bridges	Odeon CP32-5465
	Walls And Bridges	Odeon TOCP-65526
	Rock'N'Roll	Odeon CP32-5452
	Rock'N'Roll	Odeon TOCP-65527
	Shaved Fish	Odeon CP32-5453
	Shaved Fish	Odeon TOCP-65525
	Double Fantasy	Geffen 32XD-447
	Double Fantasy	Geffen CP32-5750
	Milk And Honey	Polydor POCP-1884
	Milk And Honey	Odeon TOCP-65535
	John Lennon Collection	Odeon TOCP-53220
	John Lennon Collection promo	Odeon SPCD-1615
	Lennon 4-CD boxed set	Odeon TOCP-6281/84
	Imagine – O.S.T.	Odeon CP36-5690
	Imagine – O.S.T.	Odeon TOCP-65532
	Live In New York City	Odeon CP32-5126
	Live In New York City	Odeon TOCP-65530
	Menlove Ave.	Odeon TOCP-7615
	Menlove Ave.	Odeon TOCP-65531
	The Greatest 19-track compilation, embossed jewel case	Odeon TOCP-51056
	Imagine millennium edition	Odeon TOCP-65522
	John Lennon/Plastic Ono Band millennium edition	Odeon TOCP-65520
	Double Fantasy millennium edition	Odeon TOCP-65528
	Milk And Honey new century edition	Odeon TOCP-65535
	Milk And Honey promo sampler	Odeon PCD-2509
	Anthology	Odeon TOCP-65002-5
	Wonsaponatime	Odeon TOCP-65001
	Legend	Odeon TOCP-51110
	Mind Games remastered	Odeon TOCP-67075
	Rock'N'Roll millennium edition	OdeonTOCP-67500
	Acoustic with white guitar pick	Odeon TOCP-67483
	John Lennon/Plastic Ono Band remastered	Odeon TOCP-65520

JAPANESE 7-INCH SINGLES

Key GS = gatefold sleeve; SS = single-sheet sleeve; TS = trifold sleeve; LSI = lyric sheet insert; PS = pocket sleeve; 4 = ¥400 on sleeve; 5 = ¥500 on sleeve; 6 = ¥600 on sleeve; 7 = ¥700 on sleeve.

Released	Title	Label/number
	'Give Peace A Chance' / 'Remember Love' GS, 4 or 5, red or black vinyl	Apple AR-2324
	'Give Peace A Chance' / 'Remember Love' GS, 7	Odeon EAS-17120
	'Cold Turkey' / 'Don't Worry Kyoko (Mummy's Only Looking For A Hand In The Snow)' GS, 4 or 5, red or black vinyl	Apple AR-2399
	'Cold Turkey' / 'Don't Worry Kyoko (Mummy's Only Looking For A Hand In The Snow)' SS, 7	Odeon EAS-17121
	'Instant Karma!' / 'Who Has Seen The Wind?' GS, 4 or 5, red or black vinyl	Apple AR-2462
	'Instant Karma!' / 'Who Has Seen The Wind?' Odeon SS, 7	Odeon EAS-17122
	'Mother' / 'Why' SS, 4 or 5, red or black vinyl	Apple AR-2734
	'Mother' / 'Why' SS, 7	Odeon EAS-17123
	'Power To The People' / 'Open Your Box' GS, 4 or 5	Apple AR-2773
	'Power To The People' / 'Open Your Box' SS, 7	Odeon EAS-17124
	'Imagine' / 'It's So Hard' GS, 4 and 5, red or black vinyl	Apple AR-2929
	'Happy Xmas (War Is Over)' / 'Listen, The Snow Is Falling' SS, 4 or 5, red or black vinyl	Apple AR-2943
	'Happy Xmas (War Is Over)' / 'Listen, The Snow Is Falling' 7	Odeon EAS-17126
	'Woman Is The Nigger Of The World' / 'Sisters, O Sisters' TS, 1st issue, '1972 Apple Records Inc.'	Apple EAR-10082
	'Woman Is The Nigger Of The World' / 'Sisters, O Sisters' 2nd issue '1972 Gramophone Company Limited', 5	Apple EAR-10082
	'Woman Is The Nigger Of The World' / 'Sisters, O Sisters' SS, 7	Odeon EAS-17127
	'Mind Games' / 'Meat City' PS, LSI, 5, red or black vinyl	Apple EAR-10474
	'Mind Games' / 'Meat City' SS, 7	Odeon EAS-17128
	'Whatever Gets You Thru The Night' / 'Beef Jerky' SS, 5, red or black vinyl	Apple EAR-10650
	'Whatever Gets You Thru The Night' / 'Beef Jerky' SS, 7	Odeon EAS-17129
	'#9 Dream' / 'What You Got' SS, 5	Apple EAR-10700
	'#9 Dream' / 'What You Got' SS, 7	Odeon EAS-17130
	'Stand By Me' / 'Move Over Ms. L' SS, 5	Apple EAR-10750
	'Stand By Me' / 'Move Over Ms. L' SS, 7	Odeon EAS-17131
	'Be-Bop-A-Lula' / 'Ya Ya' SS, 5	Apple EAR-10827
	'Be-Bop-A-Lula' / 'Ya Ya' SS, 7	Odeon EAS-17132
	'Imagine' / 'Working Class Hero' PS, LSI, 5	Apple EAR-10880
	'Imagine' / 'Working Class Hero' PS, LSI, 7 or ¥659	Odeon EAS-17125
	'(Just Like) Starting Over' / 'Kiss Kiss Kiss' SS, 6	Geffen P-645W
	'Woman' / 'Beautiful Boys' SS, 7	Geffen P1502J
	'Watching The Wheels' / 'Yes, I'm Your Angel' SS, 7	Geffen P-1527J
	'Jealous Guy' / 'Going Down On Love' SS, 7	Odeon EAS-17133
	'Love' / 'Give Me Some Truth' PS, LSI, 7	Odeon EAS-17295
	'Nobody Told Me' / 'Your Hands' GS, 7	Polydor 7DM0100
	'I'm Stepping Out' / 'Sleepless Night' SS, 7	Polydor 7DM0107
	'Every Man Has A Woman Who Loves Him' / 'It's Alright' SS, 7	Polydor 7DM0128

JAPANESE CD SINGLES

Released	Title	Label/number
	'Beautiful Boy (Darling Boy)', 'Beautiful Boys' 3-inch	Capitol TODP-2360
	'(Just Like) Starting Over', 'Beautiful Boy (Darling Boy)' 3-inch	Capitol TODP-2544
	'Love', 'Stand By Me' 3-inch	Parlophone TOCP-51110
	'Love' 3-inch	EMI TODP-2555
	'Love' 5-inch	EMI PCD-2014

JAPANESE SINGLE PROMOS

Released	Title	Label/number
	John Lennon And Yoko Ono Interview 7-inch 33⅓rpm, limited 1,000	Toshiba/Apple 3ER-282
	John Lennon And Yoko Ono Interview same as above, reissued 1998 3-inch CD	BCDS-1046
	'I Saw Her Standing There', 'Lucy In The Sky With Diamonds' 7-inch live with Elton John	King 17DY-5611-1
	'Imagine', 'Come Together' 7-inch from *Live In New York City*	Toshiba/Capitol PRP-1163
	'Beautiful Boy (Darling Boy)' 3-inch CD plus cover by Japanese band Dreams Come True	Capitol PCD-0942
	'Love', 'Stand By Me' 5-inch CD from *Acoustic*	EMI PCD-3014

McCARTNEY DISCOGRAPHY

Over these pages we list Paul McCartney's album, CD, and single releases and promos issued in the UK, the USA, and Japan. V/A = Various Artists compilation. Please note that release dates are shown in UK format: day, month, year. Date entries with '00' etc mean precise date unknown.

Released	Title	Label/number

UK LPs

Released	Title	Label/number
06.01.67	*The Family Way*	Decca LK 4847/ SKL 4847
17.04.70	*McCartney*	Apple PCS 7102
21.05.71	*Ram*	Apple PAS 10003
15.11.71	*Wild Life*	Apple PCS 7142
03.05.73	*Red Rose Speedway*	Apple PCTC 251
06.07.73	*Live And Let Die O.S.T.*	United Artists UAS 29475
30.11.73	*Band On The Run*	Apple PAS 10007
30.05.75	*Venus And Mars*	Capitol PCTC 254
26.03.76	*Wings At The Speed Of Sound*	Capitol PAS 10010
10.12.76	*Wings Over America*	Capitol PCSP 720
29.04.77	*Thrillington*	EMI 2954
31.03.78	*London Town*	Parlophone PAS 10012
01.12.78	*Wings Greatest*	Parlophone PCTC 256
08.06.79	*Back To The Egg*	Parlophone PCTC 257
01.01.80	*The Summit* V/A includes Jet	NE 1067
16.05.80	*McCartney II*	Parlophone PCTC 258
23.2.81	*The McCartney Interview*	Parlophone CHAT1
03.04.81	*The Concerts For Kampuchea*	Atlantic K60153
08.03.82	*James Bond Greatest Hits* V/A inc 'Live And Live Die'	United Artists EMTV 007
26.4.82	*Tug Of War*	Parlophone PCTC 259
31.10.83	*Pipes Of Peace*	Parlophone PCTC 1652301
26.03.84	*Now II* V/A inc 'Pipes Of Peace'	NOW 2
02.04.84	*McCartney*	Apple FA 413100-1
02.04.84	*Wild Life*	Parlophone FA 416101-1
00.00.84	*Band On The Run*	Nimbus Supercut PAS 10007
22.10.84	*Give My Regards To Broad Street*	Parlophone PCTC 2
00.01.85	*Red Rose Speedway*	Parlophone ATAK 16
00.03.85	*Film Tracks: The Best Of British Film Music* V/A inc 'Honorary Consul'	London LPYEAR1
01.07.85	*Let's Beat It* V/A inc 'Say Say Say'	Epic EPC 26345
05.09.87	*Red Rose Speedway*	Fame FA 3191
18.11.85	*The Christmas Album* V/A inc 'Pipes Of Peace'	EMI NOX1
01.09.86	*Press To Play*	Parlophone PCSD 103
14.11.86	*Conspiracy Of Hope (For Amnesty International)* V/A inc 'Pipes Of Peace'	Mercury MERH 99
24.11.86	*It's A Live In World (The Anti-Heroin Project)* V/A inc 'Simple As That'	EMI AHP LP 1
05.10.87	*Red Rose Speedway*	Parlophone FA 1393
24.04.87	*Prince's Trust* V/A inc 'Get Back'	A&M AMA 3906
13.07.87	*Live And Let Die*	United Artists EMS1269
02.11.87	*All The Best*	Parlophone PMTV 1
05.06.89	*Flowers In The Dirt*	Parlophone PCSD 106
14.08.89	*Now 15* V/A inc 'My Brave Face', 'Ferry 'Cross The Mersey'	EMI NOW 15
06.11.89	*The 80s: The Album Of The Decade* V/A inc 'Ebony And Ivory'	EMI EMTV 48
13.11.89	*After The Hurricane* V/A inc 'Ebony And Ivory'	Chrysalis CHR 1750
27.11.89	*Flowers In The Dirt* (Special Edition)	Parlophone PCSDX 106
27.11.89	*It's Christmas* V/A inc 'Wonderful Christmastime'	EMTV 49
00.12.90	*The Royal Concert* V/A inc 'Get Back','I Saw Her Standing There'	Telstar 2TCD 2401
24.03.90	*The Last Temptation Of Elvis* V/A inc 'It's Now Or Never'	NME LP 038/039
06.08.90	*Knebworth – The Album* V/A inc 'Coming Up', 'Hey Jude'	Polydor 8439211
05.11.90	*Tripping The Live Fantastic*	Parlophone PCST 7346
13.05.91	*Unplugged – The Official Bootleg*	Parlophone PCSD 116
02.09.91	*Q: The Album* V/A inc 'Figure Of Eight'	Telstar STAR/TCD 2522
30.09.91	*Choba B CCCP*	Parlophone CDPCSD 117
07.10.91	*Paul McCartney's Liverpool Oratorio*	EMI Classics LPPAUL 1
01.06.92	*Earthrise: The Rainforest Album* V/A inc 'How Many People'	Polydor 515419
02.02.93	*Off The Ground*	Parlophone PCSD 125
00.10.93	*Now 1984* V/A inc 'No More Lonely Nights'	EMI NOW 84
08.11.93	*Paul Is Live*	Parlophone PCSD 147
15.11.93	*Strawberries Oceans Ships Forrest*	Parlophone PCSD 145
05.05.97	*Flaming Pie*	Parlophone PCSD 171
00.10.97	*Band On The Run*	Parlophone CENT 30
06.10.97	*Standing Stone*	EMI Classics EL 5564841
21.09.98	*Rushes*	Parlophone 4970551
22.03.99	*Band On The Run 25th Anniversary*	Parlophone 4994761
10.10.99	*Run Devil Run*	Parlophone 5223511
18.10.99	*Working Classical*	Parlophone 5568971
09.04.01	*Brand New Boots And Panties* V/A inc 'I'm Partial To Your Abracadabra'	East Central One NEWBOOTSLP2
07.05.01	*Wingspan – Hits and History*	Parlophone 5328501
12.11.01	*Driving Rain*	Parlophone 5355101
17.11.03	*A Secret History*	Regal 07243-594020-1-7
29.08.05	*Chaos And Creation in The Back Yard*	Parlophone 3383452
13.06.05	*Twin Freaks*	Graze 3113001

UK 8-TRACK CARTRIDGES

Released	Title	Label/number
17.04.70	*McCartney*	Apple 8X-PCS 7102
21.05.71	*Ram*	Apple 8X-PAS 10003
15.11.71	*Wild Life*	Apple 8X-PCS 7142
03.05.73	*Red Rose Speedway*	Apple 8X-PCTC 251
00.01.74	*Band On The Run*	Apple 8X-PAS 10007
30.05.75	*Venus And Mars*	Parlophone 8X-PCTC 2541
26.03.76	*Wings At The Speed Of Sound*	Parlophone 8X-PAS 10010
10.12.76	*Wings Over America*	Parlophone 8X-PCSP 720

UK REEL-TO-REEL TAPES

Released	Title	Label/number
17.04.70	*McCartney*	Apple TA-PMC 7102

UK CDs

Released	Title	Label/number
25.04.87	*McCartney*	Parlophone CDP7466112
25.04.87	*Ram*	Capitol CDP7466122
05.10.87	*Wild Life*	EMI/FAME CD-FA 3101
05.10.87	*Red Rose Speedway*	EMI/FAME CD-FA 3193
04.02.85	*Band On The Run*	Parlophone CDP7460552
19.10.87	*Venus and Mars*	EMI/FAME CD-FA 3213

Released	Title	Label/number
10.07.89	*Wings At The Speed Of Sound*	Parlophone CDP7481992
25.05.87	*Wings Over America*	Parlophone CDS7467158
21.04.87	*Original James Bond Themes* V/A inc 'Live And Let Die'	United Artists CDP 746079-2
29.08.89	*London Town*	EMI/FAME CD-FA 3223
04.02.85	*Wings Greatest*	Parlophone CDP7460562
18.09.89	*Back To The Egg*	Parlophone CDP74820022
05.10.87	*McCartney II*	EMI/FAME CD-FA3191
04.02.85	*Tug Of War*	Parlophone CDP7460572
29.02.84	*Pipes Of Peace*	Parlophone CDP7460182
22.10.84	*Give My Regards To Broad Street*	Parlophone CDP7460432
01.09.86	*Press To Play*	Parlophone CDP7462692
02.11.87	*All The Best*	Parlophone CDP7485072
05.11.90	*Tripping The Live Fantastic*	Parlophone CDPCST7346
26.11.90	*Tripping The Live Fantastic – Highlights*	Parlophone CDPCSD114
13.05.91	*Unplugged – The Official Bootleg*	Parlophone CDPCSD116
30.09.91	*Choba B CCCP*	Parlophone CDPCSD117
07.10.91	*Liverpool Oratorio*	EMI Classics CDPAUL1
05.10.92	*Liverpool Oratorio* – Highlights	EMI Classics 7 54642 2
02.02.93	*Off The Ground*	Parlophone CDPCSD125
15.11.93	*Paul Is Live*	Parlophone CDPCSD147
15.11.93	*Strawberries Oceans Ships Forest*	Parlophone CDPCSD145
01.05.95	*Ram*	Regal Zonophone 8 32145 2
00.12.96	*Jerry Maquire O.S.T.* V/A inc 'Momma Miss America'	Epic 486981-2
05.05.97	*Flaming Pie*	Parlophone CDPCSD171
06.10.97	*Standing Stone*	EMI Classics 5564842
00.12.97	*Music For Montserrat* V/A inc 'Hey Jude' (Live)	Eagle Rock ERECD 001
01.12.97	*Diana, Princess Of Wales: A Tribute* V/A inc 'Little Willow'	Sony Music 489333
13.04.98	*Twentieth Century Blues* V/A inc 'Room With A View'	EMI 494 6312
21.09.98	*Rushes*	Hydra/Parlophone 49705524
00.00.98	*Songs Of Elvis Costello* V/A inc 'My Brave Face'	Rhino R2 75273
15.03.99	*Band On The Run 25th Anniversary Edition*	Parlophone 4991762
04.10.99	*Run Devil Run*	Parlophone 5233042
18.10.99	*Working Classical*	EMI Classics 5568972
07.02.00	*A Garland For Linda*	EMI Classics 5569612
21.08.00	*Liverpool Sound Collage*	Hydra/Parlophone LSC01
07.05.01	*Wingspa n– Hits and History*	Parlophone 532 8676 2
12.11.01	*Driving Rain*	Parlophone 535 5102
27.11.01	*The Concert For New York* V/A inc 'I'm Down', 'Yesterday', 'Let It Be', 'Freedom'	Columbia 505445 2
04.02.02	*Vanilla Sky O.S.T.* V/A inc 'Vanilla Sky'	Warner Bros. 9362481092
10.06.02	*The Very Best Of MTV Unplugged* V/A inc 'Every Night'	Universal 583545-2
24.06.02	*Party At The Palace* V/A inc 'All You Need Is Love', 'Hey Jude'	Virgin VTCDX463
17.03.03	*Back In The World*	Parlophone 583005 2
21.04.03	*Hope* V/A inc 'Calico Skies' (New Version)	WEA 50466 5846 2
07.07.03	*The In-Laws O.S.T.* V/A inc 'A Love For You', 'Live And Let Die', 'I'm Carrying'	Rhino 8122738862
17.11.03	*Concert For George* V/A inc 'For You Blue', 'Something', 'All Things Must Pass', 'While My Guitar Gently Weeps'	Rhino 8122745462
17.11.03	*A Secret History* V/A inc 'Temporary Secretary'	Regal REG 85 CD
04.06.05	*Inspired By Genius – The Music Of Ray Charles* V/A inc 'Don't Let The Sun Catch You Crying'	EMI 3305602
29.08.05	*Chaos And Creation in The Back Yard*	Parlophone 337958 2 2
25.09.06	*Ecce Cor Meum*	EMI Classics 0946 3 70424 2 7
25.09.06	*Ecce Cor Meum* (Limited Edition)	EMI Classics 0946 3 70423 2 8

UK MID-PRICE REMASTERED CD REISSUES

Released	Title	Label/number
07.07.93	*McCartney*	Parlophone CDPMCOL1
07.07.93	*Ram*	Parlophone CDPMCOL2
07.07.93	*Wild Life*	Parlophone CDPMCOL3
07.07.93	*Red Rose Speedway*	Parlophone CDPMCOL4
07.07.93	*Band On The Run*	Parlophone CDPMCOL5
07.07.93	*Venus and Mars*	Parlophone CDPMCOL6
19.08.93	*Wings at The Speed Of Sound*	Parlophone CDPMCOL7
07.07.93	*London Town*	Parlophone CDPMCOL8
19.08.93	*Wings Greatest*	Parlophone CDPMCOL9
19.08.93	*Back To The Egg*	Parlophone CDPMCOL10
19.08.93	*McCartney II*	Parlophone CDPMCOL11
19.08.93	*Tug Of War*	Parlophone CDPMCOL12
19.08.93	*Pipes Of Peace*	Parlophone CDPMCOL13
19.08.93	*Give My Regards To Broad Street*	Parlophone CDPMCOL14
19.08.93	*Press To Play*	Parlophone CDPMCOL15
19.08.93	*Flowers In The Dirt*	Parlophone CDPMCOL16

UK 7-INCH SINGLES

Released	Title	Label/number
19.02.71	'Another Day' / 'Oh Woman Oh Why'	Apple R 5889
13.08.71	'The Back Seat Of My Car' / 'Heart Of The Country'	Apple R 5914
25.02.72	'Give Ireland Back To The Irish' / 'Give Ireland Back To The Irish' (Version)	Apple R 5963
05.05.72	'Mary Had A Little Lamb' / 'Little Woman Love'	Apple R 5949
01.12.72	'Hi, Hi, Hi' / 'C Moon'	Apple R 5973
23.03.73	'My Love' / 'The Mess'	Apple R 5985
01.06.73	'Live And Let Die' / 'I Lie Around'	Apple R 5987
26.10.73	'Helen Wheels' / 'Country Dreamer'	Apple R 5993
18.02.74	'Jet' / 'Let Me Roll It'	Apple R 5996
28.06.74	'Band On The Run' / 'Zoo Gang'	Apple R 5997
18.10.74	'Walking In The Park With Eloise' / 'Bridge Over The River Suite'	EMI EMI 2220
25.10.74	'Junior's Farm' / 'Sally G'	Apple R 5999
07.02.75	'Sally G' / 'Junior's Farm'	Apple R 5999
16.05.75	'Listen To What The Man Said' / 'Love In Song'	Capitol R 6006
05.09.75	'Letting Go' / 'You Gave Me The Answer'	Capitol R 6008
28.11.75	'Venus And Mars' / 'Rock Show', 'Magneto And Titanium Man'	Capitol R 6010
00.00.76	'Another Day' / 'Oh Woman Oh Why'	Capitol R 5889

Released	Title	Label/number
00.00.76	'The Back Seat Of My Car' / 'Heart Of The Country'	Capitol R 5914
00.00.76	'Give Ireland Back To The Irish' / 'Give Ireland Back To The Irish' (Version)	Capitol R 5963
00.00.76	'Mary Had A Little Lamb' / 'Little Woman Love'	Capitol R 5949
00.00.76	'Hi, Hi, Hi' / 'C Moon'	Capitol R 5973
00.00.76	'My Love' / 'The Mess'	Capitol R 5985
00.00.76	'Live And Let Die' / 'I Lie Around'	Capitol R 5987
00.00.76	'Helen Wheels' / 'Country Dreamer'	Capitol R 5993
00.00.76	'Jet' / 'Let Me Roll It'	Capitol R 5996
00.00.76	'Band On The Run' / 'Zoo Gang'	Capitol R 5997
30.04.76	'Silly Love Songs' / 'Cook Of The House'	Parlophone R 6014
23.07.76	'Let 'Em In' / 'Beware My Love'	Parlophone R 6015
04.02.77	'Maybe I'm Amazed' / 'Soily'	Parlophone R 6017
00.04.77	'Uncle Albert/Admiral Halsey' / 'Eat At Home'	Regal Zonophone 2594
11.11.77	'Mull Of Kintyre' / 'Girls' School'	Parlophone R 6018
23.03.78	'With A Little Luck' / 'Backwards Traveller/Cuff Link'	Parlophone R 6019
16.06.78	'I've Had Enough' / 'Deliver Your Children'	Parlophone R 6020
11.08.78	'London Town' / 'I'm Carrying'	Parlophone R 6021
23.03.79	'Goodnight Tonight' / 'Daytime Nightime Suffering'	Parlophone R 6023
01.06.79	'Old Siam Sir' / 'Spin It On'	Parlophone R 6026
10.08.79	'Getting Closer' / 'Baby's Request'	Parlophone R 6027
10.08.79	'Seaside Woman' / 'B Side To Seaside'	A&M AMS 7461
16.11.79	'Wonderful Christmastime' / 'Rudolph The Red Nosed Reggae'	Parlophone R 6029
11.04.80	'Coming Up' / 'Coming Up Live', 'Lunchbox/Odd Sox'	Parlophone R 6035
13.06.80	'Waterfalls' / 'Check My Machine'	Parlophone R 6037
18.07.80	'Seaside Woman' / 'B Side To Seaside'	A&M AMS 7548
01.03.82	'Walking In The Park With Eloise' / 'Bridge Over The River Suite'	EMI EMI 2220
29.03.82	'Ebony And Ivory' / 'Rainclouds'	Parlophone R 6054
21.06.82	'Take It Away' / 'I'll Give You A Ring'	Parlophone R 6056
20.09.82	'Tug Of War' / 'Get It'	Parlophone R 6057
29.10.82	'The Girl Is Mine' / 'Can't Get Outta The Rain'	Epic EPCA 2729
00.12.82	'The Girl Is Mine' / 'Can't Get Outta The Rain'	Epic EPCA 112729
00.06.83	'The Girl Is Mine' / 'Can't Get Outta The Rain'	Epic MJ 1-5
03.10 83	'Say Say Say' / 'Ode To A Koala Bear'	Parlophone R 6062
05.12.83	'Pipes Of Peace' / 'So Bad'	Parlophone R 6064
24.09.84	'No More Lonely Nights' / 'No More Lonely Nights'	Parlophone R 6080
12.11.84	'We All Stand Together' / 'We All Stand Together' (Humming Version)	Parlophone R 6080
03.12.84	'We All Stand Together' / 'We All Stand Together' (Humming Version)	Parlophone RP 6086
18.11.85	'Spies Like Us' / 'My Carnival'	Parlophone R 6118
09.12.85	'Spies Like Us' / 'My Carnival'	Parlophone RP 6118
07.07.86	'Seaside Woman' / 'B Side To Seaside'	EMI EMI 5572
14.07.86	'Press' / 'It's Not True'	Parlophone R 6133
27.10.86	'Pretty Little Head' / 'Write Away'	Parlophone R 6145
01.12.86	'Only Love Remains' / 'Tough On A Tight Rope'	Parlophone R 6148
24.04.87	'Long Tall Sally' / 'I Saw Her Standing There'	A&M FREE 21
16.11.87	'Once Upon A Long Ago' / 'Back On My Feet'	Parlophone R 6170
08.05.89	'My Brave Face' / 'Flying To My Home'	Parlophone R 6213
17.07.89	'This One' / 'The First Stone'	Parlophone R 6223
24.07.89	'This One' / 'The Long And Winding Road'	Parlophone RX 6223
13.11.89	'Figure Of Eight' / 'Ou Est Le Soleil?'	Parlophone R 6235
27.11.89	'Party Party' one-sided	Parlophone R 6238
29.01.90	'Put It There' / 'Mama's Little Girl'	Parlophone R 6246
08.10.90	'Birthday' / 'Good Day Sunshine'	Parlophone R 6271
26.11.90	'All My Trials' / 'C Moon'	Parlophone R 6278
28.12.92	'Hope Of Deliverance' / 'Long Leather Coat'	Parlophone R 6330
22.02.93	'C'Mon People' / 'I Can't Imagine'	Parlophone R 6338
28.04.97	'Young Boy' / 'Looking For You'	Parlophone RP 6462
07.07.97	'The World Tonight' / 'Used To Be Bad'	Parlophone RP 6472
15.12.97	'Beautiful Night' / 'Love Come Tumbling Down'	Parlophone RP 6489
25.11.99	'No Other Baby' / 'Brown Eyed Handsome Man', 'Fabulous'	Parlophone R 6257
06.12.99	'Run Devil Run' (boxed set as 7-inch singles)	Parlophone 5322291
05.11.01	'Freedom' / 'Riding Into Jaipur'	Parlophone R 6567
29.08.05	'Fine Line' / 'Growing Up Falling Down'	Parlophone R 6673
21.11.05	'Jenny Wren' / 'Summer of '59'	Parlophone R 6678

UK 12-INCH SINGLES

Released	Title	Label/number
23.03.79	'Goodnight Tonight' (Extended) / 'Daytime Nightime Suffering'	Parlophone 12Y R 6023
10.08.79	'Seaside Woman' / 'B Side To Seaside'	A&M AMSP 7461
18.07.80	'Seaside Woman' / 'B Side To Seasid'	A&M AMSP 7548
15.09.80	'Temporary Secretary' / 'Secret Friend'	Parlophone 12 R 6039
29.03.82	'Ebony And Ivory' / 'Rainclouds', 'Ebony And Ivory' (Solo Version)	Parlophone 12 R 6054
21.06.82	'Take It Away' / 'I'll Give You A Ring', 'Dress Me Up As A Robber'	Parlophone 12 R 6056
03.10.83	'Say Say Say' / 'Say Say Say' (Instrumental), 'Ode To A Koala Bear'	Parlophone 12 R 6062
24.09.84	'No More Lonely Nights' (Extended Version) / 'Silly Love Songs', 'No More Lonely Nights' (Ballad)	Parlophone 12 R 6080
08.10.84	'No More Lonely Nights' / 'No More Lonely Nights' (Dance Mix)	Parlophone 12 R 6080
08.10.84	'No More Lonely Nights' (Extended Version) / 'Silly Love Songs', 'No More Lonely Nights' (Ballad)	Parlophone 12 RP 6080
29.10.84	'No More Lonely Nights' (Extended Playout Version) / 'Silly Love Songs', 'No More Lonely Nights' (Ballad)	Parlophone 12 RA 6080
18.11.85	'Spies Like Us' (Party Mix), 'Spies Like Us' (Alternative Mix [Known To His Friends As Tom]) / 'My Carnival' (Party Mix), 'Spies Like Us' (DJ Version)	Parlophone 12 R 6118
02.12.85	'Spies Like Us' (Party Mix), 'Spies Like Us' (Alternative Mix [Known To His Friends As Tom]) / 'My Carnival' (Party Mix), 'Spies Like Us' (DJ Version)	Parlophone 12 RP 6118
07.07.86	'Seaside Woman' / 'B Side To Seaside'	EMI 12 EMI 5572
14.07.86	'Press', 'It's Not True' / 'Hanglide', 'Press' (Dubmix)	Parlophone 12 R 6133

Released	Title	Label/number
18.08.86	'Press' / 'It's Not True', 'Press' (Video Edit) 10-inch	Parlophone 10 R 6133
27.10.86	'Pretty Little Head' (Remix) / 'Angry' (Remix), 'Write Away'	Parlophone 12 R 6145
01.12.86	'Only Love Remains' (Remix) / 'Tough On A Tightrope' (Remix), 'Talk More Talk' (Remix)	Parlophone 12 R 6148
16.11.87	'Once Upon A Long Ago', 'Back On My Feet' / 'Midnight Special', 'Don't Get Around Much Anymore'	Parlophone 12 R 6170
30.11.87	'Once Upon A Long Ago' (Extended Version), 'Back On My Feet' / 'Lawdy MIss Clady', 'Kansas City'	Parlophone 12 RX 6170
08.05.89	'My Brave Face', 'Flying To My Home' / 'I'm Gonna Be A Wheel Someday', 'Ain't That A Shame'	Parlophone 12 R 6213
31.07.89	'This One', 'The First Stone' / 'Good Sign'	Parlophone 12 RX 6223
31.07.89	'This One', 'The First Stone' / 'I Wanna Cry', 'I'm In Love Again'	Parlophone 12 R 6223
13.11.89	'Figure Of Eight' / 'This One' (Club Lovejoys Mix)	Parlophone 12 R 6235
20.11.89	'Figure Of Eight', 'Ou Est Le Soleil?'/ etched B	Parlophone 12 RS 6235
27.11.89	'Figure Of Eight' / 'Ou Est Le Soleil?' (Remix), 'Ou Est Le Soleil?' (Tub Dub Mix)	Parlophone 12 RX 6235
29.01.90	'Put It There', 'Mama's Little Girl' / 'Same Time Next Year'	Parlophone 12 RS 6246
08.10.90	'Birthday', 'Good Day Sunshine' / 'P.S. Love Me Do', 'Let 'Em In'	Parlophone 12 R 6271
26.11.90	'All My Trials', 'C Moon' / 'Mull Of Kintyre', 'Put It There'	Parlophone 12 R 6278
15.01.93	'Deliverance' / 'Deliverance' (Dub Mix), 'Hope Of Deliverance'	Parlophone 12 R 6330
06.06.05	'Really Love You', 'Lalula' (one-sided 12-inch vinyl)	Graze GRAZE 012

UK CASSETTE SINGLES

Released	Title	Label/number
08.05.89	'My Brave Face', 'Flying To My Home'	Parlophone TCR 6213
17.07.89	'This One', 'The First Stone'	Parlophone TCR 6223
28.12.92	'Hope Of Deliverance', 'Long Leather Coat'	Parlophone TCR 6330
22.02.93	'C'Mon People', 'I Can't Imagine'	Parlophone TCR 6338
05.11.01	'Freedom', 'Riding Into Jaipur'	Parlophone TCR 6567

UK CD SINGLES

Released	Title	Label/number
16.11.87	'Once Upon A Long Ago', 'Back On My Feet', 'Don't Get Around Much Anymore', 'Kansas City'	Parlophone CDR 6170
08.05.89	'My Brave Face', 'Flying To My Home', 'I'm Gonna Be A Wheel Someday', 'Ain't That A Shame'	Parlophone CDR 6213
17.07.89	T'his One', 'The First Stone', 'I Wanna Cry', 'I'm In Love Again'	Parlophone CDR 6223
13.11.89	'Figure Of Eight', 'The Long And Winding Road', 'The Loveliest Thing'	Parlophone CDRS 6235
03.12.89	'Figure Of Eight', 'Rough Ride', 'Ou Est Le Soleil?'	Parlophone CD3R 6235
27.11.89	'Party Party' one-track CD	Parlophone CD3R 6238
29.01.90	'Put It There', 'Mama's Little Girl', 'Same Time Next Year'	Parlophone CDR 6246
08.10.90	'Birthday', 'Good Day Sunshine', 'P.S. Love Me Do', 'Let 'Em In'	Parlophone CDR 6271
26.11.90	'All My Trials', 'C Moon', 'Mull Of Kintyre', 'Put It There'	Parlophone CDR 6278
03.12.90	'All My Trials', 'C Moon', 'Strawberry Fields Medley'	Parlophone CDRX 6278
28.12.92	'Hope Of Deliverance', 'Long Leather Coat', 'Big Boys Bickering', 'Kicked Around No More'	Parlophone CDRS 6330
22.02.93	'C'Mon People', 'Deliverance', 'Deliverance' (Dub Mix)	Parlophone CDR 6338
22.02.93	C'Mon People', 'I Can't Imagine', 'Keep Coming Back For Love', 'Down To The River'	Parlophone CDRS 6338
28.04.97	'Young Boy', 'Looking For You', 'Oobu Joobu Part One'	Parlophone CDRS 6462
28.04.97	'Young Boy', 'Broomstick', 'Oobu Joobu Part Two'	Parlophone CDR 6462
07.07.97	'The World Tonight', 'Used To Be Bad', 'Oobu Joobu Part Three'	Parlophone CDRS 6472
07.07.97	'The World Tonight', 'Really Love You/ Oobu Joobu Part Four'	Parlophone CDR 6472
15.12.97	'Beautiful Night', 'Love Come Tumbling Down', 'Oobu Joobu Part Five'	Parlophone CDRS 6489
15.12.97	'Beautiful Night', 'Same Love', 'Oobu Joobu Part Six'	Parlophone CDR 6489
25.11.99	'No Other Baby', 'Brown Eyed Handsome Man', 'Fabulous'	Parlophone CDR 6527
25.11.99	'No Other Baby', 'Brown Eyed Handsome Man', 'Fabulous'	Parlophone CDRS 6257
29.10.01	'From A Lover To A Friend', 'From A Lover To A Friend' (Remix), 'From ALover To A Friend' (Remix)	Parlophone CDR 6567
05.11.01	'Freedom', 'From A Lover To A Friend', 'From A Lover To A Friend'	Parlophone CDRS 6567
29.08.05	'Fine Line', 'Comfort in Love', 'Growing Up Falling Down'	Parlophone CDRS 6673
29.08.05	'Fine Line', 'Comfort in Love'	Parlophone CDR 6673
21.11.05	'Jenny Wren', 'I Want You To Fly'	Parlophone CDR 6678
21.11.05	'Jenny Wren', 'I Want You To Fly', 'This Loving Game'	Parlophone CDRS 6678

UK 7-INCH SINGLE PROMOS

Released	Title	Label/number
28.06.74	'Band On The Run' (Edit) / 'Band OnThe Run' white label, black text	Apple R 5997
28.06.74	'Band On The Run' (Edit) / 'Band OnThe Run'	Apple R 5997
25.10.74	'Junior's Farm' / 'Sally G'	Apple R 5999
25.10.74	'Junior's Farm' / 'Sally G' white label, black text	Apple R 5999
25.10.74	'Junior's Farm' (Edit) / 'Sally G'	Apple R 5999
07.02.75	'Sally G' / 'Junior's Farm'	Apple R 5999
30.04.76	'Silly Love Songs' (Edit) / 'Silly Love Songs'	Parlophone R 6014
23.07.76	'Let 'Em In' (Edit) / 'Beware My Love'	Parlophone R 6015
11.11.77	'Mull Of Kintyre' (Edit) / 'Girls' School' (Edit)	Parlophone R 6018
23.03.78	'With A Little Luck' (Edit) / 'With A Little Luck'	Parlophone R 6019
13.06.80	'Waterfalls' (Edit) / 'Check My Machine'	Parlophone R 6037
15.09.80	'Temporary Secretary' one-sided	Parlophone R 6039
18.11.85	'Spies Like Us' (DJ Version) / 'My Carnival'	Parlophone RDJ 6118
08.05.89	'My Brave Face' / 'Flying To My Home'	Parlophone R 6213
08.10.90	'Birthday' / 'Good Day Sunshine'	Parlophone R 6271
26.11.90	'All My Trials' / 'C Moon'	Parlophone R 6278
07.04.97	'Young Boy' / 'Looking For You'	Parlophone RLH 6462
06.12.99	'Run Devil Run' / 'Blue Jean Bop'	Parlophone RDR003
02.10.00	'Free Now' one-sided	Hydra FREE002

UK 12-INCH SINGLE PROMOS

Released	Title	Label/number
08.10.84	'No More Lonely Nights' (Mole Mix) one-sided, plain white numbered sleeve, plain white inner sleeve	Parlophone 12 R 6080
24.09.84	'No More Lonely Nights' (Extended Version) / 'Silly Love Songs', 'No More Lonely Nights' (Ballad) blue 'Broad Street' label, black die-cut sleeve	Parlophone 12 R (DJ) 6080
00.07.89	'This One' (Love Mix)	Parlophone 12 RLOVE 6223
00.07.89	'Good Sign' / 'Good Sign' (Groove Mix)	Parlophone 12 GOOD1
00.11.89	'Ou Est Le Soleil?' (Remix), 'Ou Est Le Soleil?' (Tub Dub Mix) / 'Ou Est Le Soleil?' (Instrumental Remix)	Parlophone 12 SOL1
27.11.89	'Party Party' (Remix) / 'Party Party' (Remix)	Parlophone 12 RDJ 6238
24.03.90	'It's Now Or Never' 10-inch	NME NMEPRO101990
06.09.99	'Fluid' / 'Appletree Cinnabar Amber', 'Bison' (Long One)	Hydra HYPRO 12007
06.09.99	'Fluid' (Out Of Body And Mind), 'Bison' / 'Fluid' (Out Of Body), 'Fluid' (Out Of Body With Sitar Mix)	Hydra HYPRO 12008
28.12.92	'Deliverance' / 'Deliverance' (Dub Mix)	Parlophone 12 DELIVDJ 1
00.00.01	'Silly Love Songs' (Wings vs Loop Da Loop Mix) / 'Coming Up' (Linus Loves Mix)	Parlophone 12-WINDJ-002
00.00.04	'Temporary Secretary' (Re-edited By Radio Slave)	Parlophone TEMPSEC 01
16.05.05	'Really Love You' one-sided	Graze GRAZE 010
16.05.05	'Rinse The Raindrops' / 'What's That You're Doing'	Graze GRAZE 011

UK CD PROMOS

Released	Title	Label/number
08.05.89	'My Brave Face' one-track promo	Parlophone CD-PROMO-PM1
24.03.90	'It's Now Or Never', 'Viva Las Vegas' (Bruce Springsteen)	NME NMECDPRO1990
00.11.90	'Magical Mystery Tour', 'Biker Like An Icon', 'My Love', 'Paperback Writer', 'Live And Let Die'	Parlophone PMLIVE1
28.12.92	'Hope Of Deliverance', 'Long Leather Coat', 'Big Boys Bickering', 'Kicked Around No More'	Parlophone PMINT1
26.04.93	'Biker Like An Icon', 'Things We Said Today', 'Mean Woman Blues', 'Midnight Special'	Parlophone CDRDJ 6347
07.04.97	'Young Boy' one-track promo	Parlophone CDRDJ 6462
07.07.97	'The World Tonight' one-track promo	Parlophone CDRDJ 6472
00.09.97	'Celebration' card sleeve	EMI Classics PMC1
00.09.97	'Celebration' jewel case	EMI Classics PMC2
15.12.97	'Beautiful Night' one-track promo	Parlophone CDRDJ 6489
06.09.99	'Fluid', 'Appletree Cinnabar Amber', 'Bison' (Long One)	Hydra HYPROCD 12007
06.09.99	'Fluid' (Out Of Body And Mind), 'Bison', 'Fluid' (Out Of Body), 'Fluid' (Out Of Body With Sitar Mix)	Hydra HYPROCD 008
13.09.99	'A Leaf', 'Warm And Beautiful', 'Midwife', 'My Love'	EMI Classics PROMOWC
13.09.99	'Working Classical – Interview'	EMI Classics CDR (no number)
	Run Devil Run advance-listening CD	Parlophone CDLRL 019
13.09.99	'No Other Baby', 'Brown Eyed Handsome Man', 'Blue Jean Bop', 'Run Devil Run', 'Party'	Parlophone RDR001
13.09.99	'Run Devil Run', 'Blue Jean Bop'	Parlophone RDR002
10.10.99	'No Other Baby', 'Brown Eyed Handsome Man'	Parlophone RDR004
07.02.00	*A Garland For Linda* V/A inc 'Prayer For The Healing Of The Sick', 'Musica Dei Donum', 'Nova'	EMI Classics GARLAND1
02.10.00	'Free Now' one-track promo	Hydra FREECD002
00.05.01	'Band On The Run', 'My Love', 'Live And Let Die', 'Let 'Em In', 'Maybe I'm Amazed', 'Let Me Roll It', 'The Back Seat Of My Car', 'Waterfalls'	Parlophone CD LRL 048
00.03.01	'I'm Partial To Your Abracadabra'	East Central One NEWBOOTS 2 PRO
09.10.01	'From A Lover To A Friend'	Parlophone DR002
00.03.03	*Back In The World Sampler*	Parlophone WORLD 002
16.05.05	'Really Love You', 'Lalula'	Graze GRAZE 013
25.07.05	'Fine Line' one-track promo	Parlophone CDRDJ 6673
29.08.05	*Chaos And Creation in The Back Yard Interview Disc*	Parlophone CHAOS 1
03.10.05	'Jenny Wren' (Edit), 'Jenny Wren'	Parlophone CDRDJ 6678

US LPs

Released	Title	Label/number
24.04.67	*The Family Way*	London M 76007/ MS 82007
20.04.70	*McCartney* *	Apple STAO-3363
17.05.71	*Ram* mono promo in stereo cover	Apple MAS-3375
17.05.71	*Ram* *	Apple SMAS-3375
06.12.71	*Wild Life*	Apple SW 3386
30.04.73	*Red Rose Speedway*	Apple SMAL-3409
03.12.73	*Band On The Run*	Apple SO-3415
27.05.75	*Venus And Mars*	Capitol SMAS-11419
22.03.76	*Wings At The Speed Of Sound*	Capitol SW-11525
10.12.76	*Wings Over America*	Capitol SWCO-11593
10.12.76	*McCartney*	Capitol SMAS-3363
00.00.76	*Ram*	Capitol SMAS-3375
00.00.76	*Ram* black label	Capitol SMAS-3375
00.00.76	*Wild Life*	Capitol SW-3386
00.00.76	*Red Rose Speedway*	Capitol SMAL-3409
00.00.76	*Band On The Run* *	Capitol SO-3415
16.05.77	*Thrillington*	Capitol ST-11642
27.03.78	*London Town*	Capitol SW-11777
27.11.78	*Wings Greatest*	Capitol SOO-11905
00.12.78	*Band On The Run* (Picture Disc)	Capitol SEAX 11901
11.06.79	*Back To The Egg* *	Columbia FC- 36057
22.05.80	*McCartney*	Columbia FC-36511
26.05.80	*McCartney II* * with bonus single 'Coming Up' (Live)	Columbia FC-36511
22.05.80	*Ram*	Columbia FC-36479
22.05.80	*Wild Life*	Columbia FC-36480
22.05.80	*Red Rose Speedway*	Columbia FC-36481
22.05.80	*Band On The Run*	Columbia FC-36482
25.09.80	*Venus And Mars*	Columbia FC-36801
08.12.80	*The McCartney Interview* promo-only set	Columbia A2S 821
08.12.80	*The McCartney Interview*	Columbia PC-36987
30.03.81	*Concerts For The People Of Kampuchea* V/A inc six Wings tracks	Atlantic SD 2-7005
24.04.81	*Band On The Run* (Half Speed Master)	Columbia HC-46482
13.07.81	*Wings At The Speed Of Sound*	Columbia FC-37409
26.04.82	*Tug Of War*	Columbia TC-37462
00.00.82	*Wings Over America*	Columbia C3X37990
31.10.83	*Pipes Of Peace*	Columbia QC-39419
22.10.84	*Give My Regards To Broad Street*	Columbia SC-39613
25.08.86	*Press To Play*	Capitol PJAS-12475
14.11.86	*Conspiracy Of Hope (For Amnesty International)* V/A inc 'Pipes Of Peace'	Mercury 830588-1
11.05.87	*Prince's Trust Concert* V/A	A&M SP-3906
01.12.87	*All The Best*	Capitol CLW-48287
06.06.89	*Flowers In The Dirt*	Capitol C1-91653

Released	Title	Label/number
15.01.90	*Flowers In The Dirt* (Special Edition)	Capitol PCSDX 106
00.05.90	*After The Hurricane* V/A	Ultradisc UDCD-529
07.08.90	*Knebworth – The Album* V/A	Polydor 847 042-1
06.11.90	*Tripping The Live Fantastic*	Capitol C1-94778
26.11.90	*Tripping The Live Fantastic – Highlights*	Capitol C1-595379
27.05.97	*Flaming Pie*	Capitol C-1-8-56500-1

US 8-TRACK CARTRIDGES

Title	Label/number
McCartney	Apple 8XT 3363
Wild Life	Apple 8XW 3386
Red Rose Speedway	Apple 8XW 3409
Band On The Run	Apple 8XZ 3415
Band On The Run (Quadraphonic Mix)	Apple Q8W 3415
Venus And Mars	Capitol 8XT 11419
Venus And Mars (Quadraphonic Mix)	Capitol Q8W 11419
Wings At The Speed Of Sound	Capitol 8XW 11525
Wings Over America	Capitol 8X3C-11593
Thrillington	Capitol 8XT 11642
London Town	Capitol 8XW 11777
Wings Greatest	Capitol 8XOO 11905
Live And Let Die	United Artists EA-100
Back To The Egg	Columbia FCA 36057
McCartney II	Columbia FCA 36511
McCartney	Columbia JCA 36478
Ram	Columbia JCA 36479
Wildlife	Columbia JCA 36480
Red Rose Speedway	Columbia JCA 36481
Band On The Run	Columbia JCA 36482
Venus And Mars	Columbia JCA 36801
Wings At The Speed Of Sound	Columbia JCA 37409
Tug Of War	Columbia TCA 37462

US REEL-TO-REEL TAPES

Title	Label/number
The Family Way	London/Ampex LPL-70136
McCartney	Apple/Ampex L-3363
Ram	Apple/Ampex 3375
Live And Let Die	United Artists UST-100A

US CDs

Released	Title	Label/number
29.02.84	*Band On The Run*	Columbia CK 36482
29.02.84	*Venus And Mars*	ColumbiaCK 36801
29.02.84	*Wings Over America*	ColumbiaCK-37990/1
29.02.84	*Tug Of War*	ColumbiaCK 37462
29.02.84	*Pipes Of Peace*	ColumbiaCK 39149
22.10.84	*Give My Regards To Broad Street*	ColumbiaCK 39613
22.08.86	*Press To Play*	Capitol CDP 7 46269 2
01.12.86	*Wings Greatest*	Capitol CDP 7 46056 2
05.12.87	*All The Best*	Capitol CDP 7 48287 2
17.01.88	*McCartney*	Capitol CDP 7 46611 2
17.01.88	*Ram*	Capitol CDP 7 46612 2
17.01.88	*Wings Over America*	Capitol CDP 7 46715/6 2
17.01.88	*Tug Of War*	Capitol CDP 7 45057 2
00.11.88	*Red Rose Speedway*	Capitol CDM 7 52026 2
00.11.88	*Venus And Mars*	Capitol CDP 7 46984 2
00.11.88	*McCartney II*	Capitol CDM 7 52024 2
01.12.88	*Band On The Run*	Capitol CDP 7 46055 2
06.06.89	*Flowers In The Dirt*	Capitol CDP 7 91653 2
20.06.89	*Wild Life*	Capitol CDM 7 52017 2
20.06.89	*Speed Of Sound*	Capitol CDP 7 48199 2
20.06.89	*London Town*	Capitol CDP 7 48198 2
20.06.89	*Back To The Egg*	Capitol CDP 7 48200 2
20.06.89	*Pipes Of Peace*	Capitol CDP 7 46018 2
05.11.90	*Tripping The Live Fantastic*	Capitol CDP 7 94778 2
19.11.90	*Tripping The Light Fantastic – Highlights*	Capitol CDP 7 95379 2
04.06.91	*Unplugged*	Capitol CDP 7 96413 2
22.10.91	*Liverpool Oratorio*	Angel CDS 7 54371 2
29.10.91	*Choba CCCP*	Capitol CDP 7 97615 2
00.12.91	*Give My Regards To Broad Street*	Capitol CDP 7 46043 2
09.02.93	*Off The Ground*	Capitol CDP 7 80362 2
19.11.93	*Paul Is Live*	Capitol CDP 8 27704 2
22.02.94	*Strawberries Oceans Ships Forest*	Capitol CDP 8 27167 2
00.10.94	*Earthrise: The Rainforest Album* V/A inc 'How Many People'	Rhino R2718030
00.00.95	*Thrillington*	Regal Zonophone 7234 8 32145 2 5
27.05.97	*Flaming Pie*	Capitol 7243 8 56500 2 4
23.09.97	*Standing Stone*	EMI Classics 7243 5 56484 2 6
20.10.98	*Rushes*	Hydra 4970552
03.03.99	*Venus And Mars* DTS Surround Sound	DTS Entertainment MFI-4401
03.03.99	*Band On The Run* DTS Surround Sound	DTS Entertainment MFI-4403
15.03.99	*Band On The Run* 25th Anniversary Edition	Capitol 4991761
05.10.99	*Run Devil Run*	Capitol 7243 5 22351 2 4
16.11.99	*Twentieth Century Blues – The Songs Of Noel Coward* V/A inc 'Room With A View'	Ichiban KALA 6401
19.10.99	*Working Classical*	EMI Classics CDQ 5 56897 2
26.04.00	*A Garland For Linda* V/A inc 'Nova'	EMI Classics CDC 5 569621 2
26.09.00	*Liverpool Sound Collage*	Hydra 7243 528817 2 7
13.02.01	*Music Of Hope* V/A inc 'Nova'	Tim Janis Ensemble B000056PQV
07.05.01	*Wingspan – Hits and History*	Capitol CDP 5 32943 2
16.10.01	*Good Rockin' Tonight* V/A inc 'That's Alright Mama'	London-Sire 31165-2.
13.11.01	*Driving Rain*	Capitol CDP 535 5102
27.11.01	*The Concert For New York* V/A inc 'I'm Down', 'Yesterday', 'Let It Be', 'Freedom'	Columbia 1C2K86270
19.12.02	*The Concert For New York* SACD Multichannel	Columbia 1C2S86270
14.12.01	*Vanilla Sky O.S.T.* V/A inc 'Vanilla Sky'	Warner Bros. 9362481092
09.07.02	*Party At The Palace* V/A inc 'All You Need Is Love', 'Hey Jude'	Virgin 72438128332
26.11.02	*Back In The US*	Capitol 5 423180 2
26.11.02	*Back In The US* with DVD	Capitol 5 423180 2
21.04.03	*Hope* V/A inc 'Calico Skies' (New Version)	WEA 5046658462
20.05.03	*The In-Laws O.S.T.* V/A inc 'A Love For You', 'Live And Let Die', 'I'm Carrying'	Rhino R2 73886
17.10.03	*Concert For George* V/A inc 'For You Blue', 'Something', 'All Things Must Pass', 'While My Guitar Gently Weeps'	Rhino 8122745462
13.09.05	*Chaos And Creation in The Back Yard*	Capitol 338 2992
26.09.06	*Ecce Cor Meum*	Angel 70424-2 7
17.10.06	*Ecce Cor Meum* (Limited Edition)	Angel 70423-2 8

US DCC GOLD CDs

Released	Title	Label/number
1992	*McCartney*	DCC Compact Classics GZS-1029
1993	*Band On The Run*	DCC Compact Classics GZS-1030
1993	*Ram*	DCC Compact Classics GZS-1037
1994	*Venus And Mars*	DCC Compact Classics GZS-1067
1996	*Red Rose Speedway*	DCC Compact Classics GZS-1091
1996	*Wings At The Speed Of Sound*	DCC Compact Classics GZS-1096

US 7-INCH SINGLES

Released	Title	Label/number
22.02.71	'Another Day' / 'Oh Woman Oh Why'	Apple 1829
02.08.71	'Uncle Albert/Admiral Halsey' / 'Too Many People'	Apple 1837
28.02.72	'Give Ireland Back To The Irish' / 'Give Ireland Back To The Irish' (Version)	Apple 1847
29.05.72	'Mary Had A Little Lamb' / 'Little Woman Love'	Apple 1851
04.12.72	'Hi, Hi, Hi' / 'C Moon'	Apple 1857
09.04.73	'My Love' / 'The Mess'	Apple 1861
18.06.73	'Live And Let Die' / 'I Lie Around'	Apple 1863
12.11.73	'Helen Wheels' / 'Country Dreamer'	Apple 1869
28.01.74	'Jet' / 'Mamunia'	Apple 1871
18.02.74	'Jet' / 'Let Me Roll It'	Apple 1871
08.04.74	'Band On The Run' / 'Nineteen Hundred And Eighty Five'	Apple 1873
02.12.74	'Walking In The Park With Eloise' / 'Bridge Over The River Suite'	EMI 3977
04.11.74	'Junior's Farm' / 'Sally G'	Apple 1875
24.12.74	'Sally G' / 'Junior's Farm'	Apple 1875
26.05.75	'Listen To What The Man Said' / 'Love In Song'	Capitol 4091
29.09.75	'Letting Go' / 'You Gave Me The Answer'	Capitol 4145
27.10.75	'Venus And Mars/Rock Show', 'Magneto And Titanium Man'	Capitol 4175
01.04.76	'Silly Love Songs' / 'Cook Of The House'	Capitol 4256
01.04.76	'Silly Love Songs'/ 'Cook Of The House' black label	Capitol 4256
28.06.76	'Let 'Em I'n / 'Beware My Love'	Capitol 4293
28.06.76	'Let 'Em I'n / 'Beware My Love' black label	Capitol 4293
00.00.76	'Another Day' / 'Oh Woman Oh Why?' black label	Capitol 1829
00.00.76	'Uncle Albert/Admiral Halsey' / 'To Many People' black label	Capitol 1837
00.00.76	'Give Ireland Back To The Irish' / 'Give Ireland Back To The Irish' (Version) black label	Capitol 1847
00.00.76	'Mary Had A Little Lamb' / 'Little Woman Love' black label	Capitol 1851
00.00.76	'Hi, Hi, Hi' / 'C Moon' black label	Capitol 1857
00.00.76	'My Love' / 'The Mess' black label	Capitol 1861
00.00.76	'Live And Let Die' / 'I Lie Around' black label	Capitol 1863
00.00.76	'Helen Wheels' / 'Country Dreamer' black label	Capitol 1869
00.00.76	'Jet' / 'Let Me Roll It' black label	Capitol 1871
00.00.76	'Band On The Run' / 'Nineteen Hundred And Eighty Five' black label	Capitol 1873
07.02.77	'Maybe I'm Amazed' / 'Soily'	Capitol 4385
07.02.77	'Maybe I'm Amazed' / 'Soily' black label	Capitol 4385
31.05.77	'Seaside Woman' / 'B Side To Seaside'	Epic 8-50403
14.11.77	'Mull Of Kintyre' / 'Girls' School'	Capitol 4504
00.00.78	'Mull Of Kintyre' / 'Girls' School' purple label	Capitol 4504
20.03.78	'With A Little Luck' / 'Backwards Traveller/Cuff Link'	Capitol 4559
05.06.78	I''ve Had Enough' / 'Deliver Your Children'	Capitol 4594
14.08.78	'London Town' / 'I'm Carrying'	Capitol 4625
19.03.79	'Goodnight Tonight' / 'Daytime Nightime Suffering'	Columbia 3-10939
19.03.78	'Goodnight Tonight' / 'Daytime Nightime Suffering'	Columbia 23-10940

Released	Title	Label/number
04.06.79	'Getting Closer' / 'Spin It O'n	Columbia 3-11020
13.08.79	'Arrow Through Me' / 'Old Siam Sir'	Columbia 3-11070
26.11.79	'Wonderful Christmastime' / 'Rudolph The Red Nosed Reggae'	Columbia 3-11162
14.04.80	'Coming Up' / 'Coming Up' (Live At Glasgow), 'Lunchbox/ Odd Sox'	Columbia 1-11263
26.05.80	'Coming Up' (Live At Glasgow) one-sided	Columbia AE7 1204
22.07.80	'Waterfalls' / 'Check My Machine'	Columbia 1-11335
04.12.80	'Getting Closer' / 'Goodnight Tonight'	Columbia 13-33405
04.12.80	'My Love' / 'Maybe I'm Amazed'	Columbia 13-33407
04.12.80	'Uncle Albert/Admiral Halsey' / 'Jet'	Columbia 13-33408
04.12.80	'Band On The Run' / 'Helen Wheels'	Columbia 13-33409
12.06.81	'Silly Love Songs' / 'Cook Of The House'	Columbia 18-02171
29.03.82	'Ebony And Ivory' / 'Rainclouds'	Columbia 18-02860
21.06.82	'Take It Away' / 'I'll Give You A Ring'	Columbia 18-03018
13.09.82	'Tug Of War' / 'Get It'	Columbia 38-03235
25.10.82	'The Girl Is Mine' / 'Can't Get Out Of The Rain'	Epic 34-03288
25.10.82	'The Girl Is Mine' one-sided	Epic ENR-03372
26.11.79	'Wonderful Christmastime' / 'Rudolph The Red Nosed Reggae' stereo	Columbia 38-04127
03.10.83	'Say Say Say' / 'Ode To A Koala Bear'	Columbia 38-04168
05.12.83	'So Bad' / 'Pipes Of Peace'	Columbia 38-04296
08.10.84	'No More Lonely Night' (Ballad) / 'No More Lonely Nights' (Playout Version)	Columbia 38-04581
18.11.85	'Spies Like Us' / 'My Carnival'	Capitol B-5537
00.00.85	'Getting Closer' / 'Goodnight Tonight' grey label	Columbia 13-33405
00.00.85	'My Love' / 'Maybe I'm Amazed' grey label	Columbia 13-33407
00.00.85	U'ncle Albert/Admiral Halsey' / 'Jet' grey label	Columbia 13-33408
00.00.85	'Band On The Run' / 'Helen Wheels' grey label	Columbia 13-33409
14.07.86	'Press' / 'It's Not True'	Capitol B-5597
11.08.86	'Seaside Woman' / 'B Side To Seaside'	Capitol B-5608
03.11.86	'Stranglehold' / 'Angry'	Capitol B-5636
19.01.87	'Only Love Remains' / 'Tough On A Tightrope'	Capitol B-5672
08.05.89	'My Brave Face' / 'Flying To My Home'	Capitol B-44367
12.01.93	'Hope Of Deliverance' / 'Long Leather Coat'	Capitol S7-56946
06.04.93	'Biker Like An Icon' / 'Things We Said Today'	Capitol S7-17319
06.04.93	'Off The Ground' / 'Cosmically Conscious'	Capitol S7-17318
27.07.93	'C'Mon People' / 'Down To The River'	Capitol S7-17489
00.00.94	'Wonderful Christmastime' / 'Rudolph The Red Nosed Reggae'	Capitol S7-17643
23.11.99	'No Other Baby' / 'Try Not To Cry'	Capitol 72438-58823-7-1
21.05.01	'Maybe I'm Amazed' / 'Band On The Run'	Capitol 72438-58995-7-7A
29.10.01	'From A Lover To A Friend' / 'From A Lover To A Friend' (David Kahne Remix 1), 'From A Lover To A Friend' (David Kahne Remix 2)	Capitol 8-77671-2
00.08.02	'Your Loving Flame' (Remix) / 'Lonely Road' (Remix)	Capitol 72438 77730 7 3
00.09.02	'Freedom' (Radio Edit) / 'From A Lover To A Friend'	Capitol 72435-50291-7-1

US 12-INCH SINGLES

Released	Title	Label/number
12.04.82	'Ebony and Ivory' / 'Rainclouds', 'Ebony and Ivory' (Solo Version)	Columbia 44-02878
26.06.82	'Take It Away' / 'I'll Give You A Ring', 'Dress Me Up As A Robber'	Columbia 44-03019
10.10.83	'Say Say Say' / 'Say Say Say' (Instrumental), 'Ode To A Koala Bear'	Columbia 44-04169
08.10.84	'No More Lonely Night' (Extended Version) / 'Silly Love Songs', 'No More Lonely Nights' (Ballad)	Columbia 44-05077
08.10.84	'No More Lonely Night' (Extended Version) / 'Silly Love Songs', 'No More Lonely Nights' (Ballad)	Columbia 8C8 39927-S1
00.01.85	'No More Lonely Night' (Special Dance Mix) / 'Silly Love Songs', 'No More Lonely Nights' (Ballad)	Columbia 44-05077
18.11.85	'Spies Like Us' (Party Mix), 'Spies Like Us' (Alternative Mix [Known To His Friends As Tom])' / 'Spies Like Us' (DJ Version), 'My Carnival' (Party Mix)	Capitol V-15212
14.07.86	'Press', 'It's Not True' / 'Hanglide', 'Press' (Dubmix)	Capitol V-15212
11.08.86	'Seaside Woman' / 'B Side To Seaside'	Capitol V-15244
25.07.89	'Ou Est Le Soleil?' / 'Ou Est Le Soleil?' (Tub Dub Mix), 'Ou Est Le Soleil?' (Instrumental Mix)	Capitol V-15499

US CASSETTE SINGLES

Released	Title	Label/number
01.08.89	'This One', 'The First Stone'	Capitol 4JM44438
14.11.89	'Figure Of Eight', 'Ou Est Le Soleil?'	Capitol 4JM44489
01.05.90	'Put It There', 'Mama's Little Girl'	Capitol 4JM44570
16.10.90	'Birthday', 'Good Day Sunshine'	Capitol 4JM44645
12.10.93	'Hope Of Deliverance', 'Long Leather Coat'	Capitol 4KM07777
27.04.93	'Off The Ground', 'Cosmically Conscious'	Capitol 4KM-44924
06.05.97	'The World Tonight', 'Looking For You'	Capitol 4KM-8 58650 4

US CD SINGLES

Released	Title	Label/number
08.05.89	'My Brave Face', 'Flying To My Home', 'I'm Gonna Be A Wheel Someday', 'Ain't That A Shame'	Capitol CDP 7154682
23.01.93	'Hope Of Deliverance', 'Big Boys Bickering', 'Long Leather Coat', 'Kicked Around No More'	Capitol C2 7 15950 2
27.04.93	'Off The Ground', 'Cosmically Conscious', 'Style Style', 'Sweet Sweet Memories', 'Soggy Noodle'	Capitol 2 7 15966 2
20.07.93	'C'Mon People', 'I Can't Imagine', 'Keep Coming Back To Love', 'Down To The River'	Capitol C2 7 15988 2
06.05.97	'The World Tonight', 'Looking For You', 'Oobu Joobu Part One'	Capitol C2 8 58650 2
14.11.01	'Freedom', 'From A Lover To A Friend', 'From A Lover To A Friend'	Capitol 7243 5 50291 2 6
25.07.05	'Fine Line' one-track	Capitol C2 0946 3 34259 2 7

US 7-INCH SINGLE PROMOS

Released	Title	Label/number
	'Another Day' mono	Apple PRO-6193
	'Uncle Albert/Admiral Halsey' mono	Apple PRO-6278
	'Brung To You By'	Apple SPRO-6210
	'Hi, Hi, Hi' / 'C Moon'	Apple P-1857
	'My Love' mono/stereo	Apple P-1861
	'Live And Let Die' mono/stereo	Apple P-1863
	'Helen Wheels' mono/stereo	Apple PRO-6786
	'Country Dreamer' mono/stereo	Apple PRO-6787
	'Band On The Run' (Edit) mono	Apple PRO-6285
	'Band On The Run' (Edit) mono/stereo	Apple P-1873
	'Jet' mono/stereo	Apple P-1871
	'Jet' (Edit) mono	Apple PRO-6872
	'Helen Wheels'	Apple PRO-6786
	'Junior's Farm' mono/stereo	Apple P-1875
	'Junior's Farm' (Edit) stereo	Apple SPRO-8003
	'Junior's Farm' (Edit) mono	Apple PRO 6999
	'Sally G 'mono/stereo	Apple P-1875
	'Sally G 'mono	Apple PRO-8000
	'Listen To What The Man Said' mono	Capitol PRO-8138
	'Letting Go' mono	Capitol PRO-8225
	'Lotting Go' mono/stereo	Capitol PRO-4145
	'Venus And Mars/Rock Show'	Capitol PRO-8261
	'Venus And Mars/Rock Show'	Capitol P-4175
	'Let 'Em In'	Capitol P-4293
	'Let 'Em In' (Edit) mono	Capitol PRO-8423
	'Let 'Em In' (Edit) stereo	Capitol SPRO-8424
	'Silly Love Songs'	Capitol SPRO-8365
	'Seaside Woman' / 'B Side To Seaside' some red vinyl	Epic 8-50403
	'Seaside Woman' / 'B Side To Seaside'	Capitol P-B-5608
	'London Town' mono/stereo	Capitol P-4625
	'I've Had Enough'	Capitol PRO-8860
	'Mull Of Kintyre' (Edit)	Capitol SPRO-8746
	'Girls' School' (Edit)	Capitol SPRO-8747
	'Goodnight Tonight' mono	Columbia 3-10939
	'Getting Closer' mono/stereo	Columbia 3-11020
	'Say Say Say' (Edit)	Columbia 38-04168
	'Say Say Say'	Columbia 44-04169
	'Press' (Edit)	Capitol 7-PRO-9766
	'My Brave Face'	Capitol P-B-44367
	'Figure Of Eight' white label	Capitol 7PRO-79889
	'This One' / 'This One' white label	Capitol 7PRO-79700
	'Put It There' / 'Put It There'	Capitol 7PRO-79074
	'Seaside Woman' / 'B Side To Seaside'	Capitol P-B-5608

US CEMA JUKEBOX 7-INCH SINGLES

Released	Title	Label/number
12.01.93	'Hope Of Deliverance' / 'Long Leather Coat'	Capitol S7-56946
06.04.93	'Biker Like An Icon' / 'Things We Said Today'	Capitol S7-17319
06.04.93	'Off The Ground' / 'Cosmically Conscious'	Capitol S7-17318
27.07.93	'C'Mon People' / 'Down To The River'	Capitol S7-17489
00.00.94	'Wonderful Christmastime' / 'Rudolph The Red Nosed Reggae'	Capitol S7-17643
23.11.99	'No Other Baby' / 'Try Not To Cry'	Capitol 72438-58823-7-1
21.05.01	'Maybe I'm Amazed' / 'Band On The Run'	Capitol 72438-58995-7-7
00.08.02	'Your Loving Flame' (Remix) / 'Lonely Road' (Remix)	Capitol 72438 77730 7 3
00.09.02	'Freedom' (Radio Edit) / 'From A Lover To A Friend'	Capitol 72435-50291-7-1

US 12-INCH SINGLE PROMOS

Released	Title	Label/number
	'Maybe I'm Amazed' mono/stereo	Capitol PRO-8574/ SPRO-8577
	'Goodnight Tonight' long/short stereo	Columbia 23-10940
	'Coming Up' / 'Coming Up' (Live At Glasgow) red or white labels	Columbia AS 775
	'Every Night' (Live) / 'Lucille' (Live)	Atlantic FR 388
	'Seaside Woman' / 'B Side To Seaside'	Epic XSS 163106
	A Sample From Tug Of War	Columbia AS 1444
	'Say Say Say' (Edit)	Columbia AS 1758
	'No More Lonely Nights' (Ballad) same both sides	Columbia AS 1940

Released	Title	Label/number
	'No More Lonely Nights' (Special Dance Mix 6:53) / 'No More Lonely Nights' (Special Dance Edit 4:14)	Columbia AS 1990
	'Spies Like Us'	Capitol SPRO-9556
	'Press'	Capitol SPRO-9763
	'Angry'	Capitol SPRO-9797
	'Stranglehold' / 'Angry'	Capitol SPRO-9860
	'Pretty Little Head'	Capitol SPRO-9928
	'Ou Est Le Soleil?' (Dennis Muyet Edit 6:58)	Disconet Programme Service Vol. 11 Programme 9 MWDN 1109

US CD PROMOS

Released	Title	Label/number
	The New World Sampler, All The Best	Capitol DPRO-79671
	Paul McCartney Rocks	Capitol DPRO-79743
	'We Got Married'	Capitol DPRO-79979
	'Ou Est Le Soleil'	Capitol DPRO-79836
	'Party Party'	Capitol DPRO-79987
	'Off The Ground'	Capitol DPRO-79670
	'Off The Ground'	Capitol DPRO-79783
	'Off The Ground'	Capitol DPRO-79792
	'C'Mon People'	Capitol DPRO-79743
	Flaming Pie Advance CD	Capitol CDP 7243 8 56500 2 4
	Ecology	Best Buy 00031 27850
	Standing Stone Q&A	EMI Classic 7087 8 11861 2 3
	Band On The Run 25th Anniversary	Capitol DPRO 7087 6 13558 2 6
	Run Devil Run Full Album Promo	Capitol CDP 7243 5 22351 2 4-V
	'No Other Baby' (Edit) one-track promo	Capitol DPRO 7087 6 13851 2 0
	'Try Not To Cry' one-track promo	Capitol DPRO 7087 6 13852 2 9
	Best Buy Bonus Disc Paul McCartney The Interview	Capitol CDP 7243 5 23343 2 2
	Original Versions Of 4 Songs From Run Devil Run	Capitol DPRO 7087 6 15112 2 2
	Selections From A Garland For Linda	EMI CDSAMO08
	'Freedom' (with/without red & white horizontal CD stripes)	Capitol DPRO 7087 6 16903 2
	'Lonely Road' (Remix), 'Lonely Road'	Capitol DPRO 6 16920 2
	'Your Loving Flame', 'Your Loving Flame' (Remix)	Capitol DPRO 6 16914 2
	Driving Rain (Sampler) 'Lonely Road', 'From A Lover To A Friend', 'She's Given Up Talking', 'Your Way', 'I Do', 'Rinse The Raindrops'	Capitol DPRO-7087 6159952
	'That's All Right'	Sire PRO500055-2
	Vanilla Sky	Paramount no number
	Back In The US – Live 2002	MPL/Capitol CDR Acetate
	Talk In The US	Capitol CDR Acetate
	Back in the US In-Store Play	Capitol DPRO 7087 6 17584 2 9
	'Lonely Road' (Remix), 'Lonely Road'	Capitol DPRO 7087 6 16920 2 0
	'Your Loving Flame' (Remix) / 'Your Loving Flame'	Capitol DPRO 7087 6 16914 2 9
	'A Love For You'	Bulletproof CDR Acetate
	Classical McCartney	EMI Classics 7087 6 18659 2 9
	'Fine Line'	Capitol C2 0946 3 34259 2 7
	'Jenny Wren'	Capitol DPRO 0946 3 49375 2 8
	'Motor Of Love' (Lexus US Tour Promo)	Capitol CDP 0946 3 38299 2 3
	'Never Stop Doing What You Love' (Fidelity US Tour Promo)	Capitol 09463-46465-2-9
	'This Never Happened Before'	Capitol DPRO-0946 6 49684 2 3

MPL PROMOS

Released	Title	Label/number
	'We've Moved' 7-inch single	MPL1
	MPL's Treasury Of Songs – The Rock'n'Roll Classics	MPL CD 1-3
	MPL's Treasury Of Songs – The Standards	MPL CD 2-1/2-2
	MPL's Treasury Of Kidstuff	MPL KSMPL
	The Legendary Songs Of Carl Perkins	MPL20031
	Paul McCartney: Listen To What The Man Said	

JAPANESE LPs

Released	Title	Label/number
	McCartney	Apple AP-80377
	McCartney	Odeon EPS-80231
	Ram	Apple AP-80283
	Ram	Odeon EPS-80232
	Wild Life	Apple AP-80283
	Wild Life	Odeon EPS-80233
	Red Rose Speedway	Apple EAP80813
	Red Rose Speedway	Odeon EPS 80234
	Band On The Run	Apple EAP-80951 /
	Band On The Run	Odeon EPS-80235
	Band On The Run picture disc, lyric insert	Odeon EPS-90073
	Venus And Mars	Capitol EAP-80813
	Venus And Mars	Odeon EPS-80236
	Wings At The Speed Of Sound	Capitol EPS-80510
	Wings Over America	Capitol EPS-50001-3
	London Town	Capitol EPS-81000
	Wings Greatest	Odeon EPS-81150
	Back To The Egg	Odeon EPS-81200
	The McCartney Interview	Odeon EPS-27001
	Concerts For The People Of Kampuchea	Atlantic JPN P-5595/6A
	McCartney II	Odeon EPS-81324
	Tug Of War	Odeon EPS-81485
	Pipes Of Peace	Odeon EPS-91071
	Give My Regards To Broad Street	Odeon EPS-91094
	Press To Play	Odeon EPS-91180
	All The Best	Odeon RP15-5545/6

JAPANESE CDs

Released	Title	Label/number
	McCartney	Odeon TOCP-7851
	McCartney	Odeon TOCP-3124
	McCartney mini-LP sleeve	Odeon TOCP-65500
	Ram	Odeon TOCP-7852
	Ram	Odeon TOCP-3125
	Ram mini-LP sleeve	Odeon TOCP-65501
	Wild Life	Odeon TOCP-7853
	Wild Life	Odeon TOCP-65502
	Wild Life	Odeon TOCP-3126
	Wild Life mini-LP sleeve	Odeon TOCP-65502
	Red Rose Speedway	Odeon TOCP-7854
	Red Rose Speedway	Odeon TOCP-65503
	Red Rose Speedway	Odeon TOCP-3127
	Red Rose Speedway mini-LP sleeve	Odeon TOCP-65503
	Band On The Run	Odeon TOCP-7855
	Band On The Run	Odeon TOCP-65504
	Band On The Run	Odeon TOCP-3128
	Band On The Run mini-LP sleeve	Odeon TOCP-65504
	Venus And Mars	Odeon TOCP-7856

Released	Title	Label/number
	Venus And Mars	Odeon TOCP-3129
	Venus And Mars mini-LP sleeve	Odeon TOCP-65505
	Wings At The Speed Of Sound	Odeon TOCP-7857
	Wings At The Speed Of Sound	Odeon TOCP-3130
	Wings At The Speed Of Sound mini-LP sleeve	Odeon TOCP-65506
	Thrillington	Odeon TOCP-8600
	Wings Over America	Odeon TOCP-5986/7
	Wings Over America	Odeon TOCP-5986
	Wings Over America mini-LP sleeve	Odeon TOCP-65507/8/9
	London Town	Odeon TOCP-7858
	London Town	Odeon TOCP-3131
	London Town mini-LP sleeve	Odeon TOCP-65510
	Wings Greatest	Odeon TOCP-3132
	Back To The Egg	Odeon TOCP-7860
	Back To The Egg	Odeon TOCP-5990
	Back To The Egg	Odeon TOCP-3133
	Back To The Egg mini-LP sleeve	Odeon TOCP-65511
	McCartney II	Odeon TOCP-7861
	McCartney II	Odeon TOCP-65512
	McCartney II	Odeon TOCP-3134
	McCartney II mini-LP sleeve	Odeon TOCP-65512
	Tug Of War	Odeon TOCP-7862
	Tug Of War	Odeon CP35-3001
	Tug Of War	Odeon TOCP-3135
	Tug Of War mini-LP sleeve	Odeon TOCP-65513
	Pipes Of Peace	Odeon TOCP-7863
	Pipes Of Peace	Odeon TOCP-65514
	Pipes Of Peace	Odeon TOCP-3136
	Pipes Of Peace mini-LP sleeve	Odeon TOCP-65514
	Give My Regards To Broad Street	Odeon TOCP-7864
	Give My Regards To Broad Street	Odeon TOCP-3137
	Give My Regards To Broad Street mini-LP sleeve	Odeon TOCP-65515
	Press To Play	Odeon TOCP-7865
	Press To Play	Odeon CP32-5156
	Press To Play	Odeon TOCP-3138
	Press To Play mini-LP sleeve	Odeon TOCP-65516
	All The Best	Odeon TOCP-65517
	All The Best Gold CD	Odeon TOCP-6117
	Flowers In The Dirt Special Edition	Odeon TOCP-7866
	Flowers In The Dirt	Odeon TOCP-3139
	Tripping The Live Fantastic	Odeon TOCP-6451/52
	Tripping The Live Fantastic	Odeon TOCP-6481
	Tripping The Live Fantastic – Highlights	Odeon TOCP-6510
	Unplugged – The Official Bootleg	Odeon TOCP-6713
	Choba CCCP	Odeon TOCP-7865
	Choba CCCP	Odeon TOCP-6869
	Paul McCartney's Liverpool Oratorio	Odeon TOCE-7424-25
	Off The Ground	Odeon TOCP-6713
	Off The Ground with CD single	Odeon TOCP-7580
	Off The Ground	Odeon TOCP-3390
	Paul Is Live	Odeon TOCP-8071
	Strawberries Oceans Ships Forest	Odeon TOCP-8160
	Off The Ground (The Complete Works)	Odeon TOCP-8207
	Flaming Pie	Odeon TOCP-50200
	Band On The Run 25th Anniversary Edition	Odeon TOCP-8207-08
	The Greatest	Odeon TOCP-51055
	Wide Prairie (Linda McCartney)	Odeon TOCP 65065
	Standing Stone	Odeon TOCP-50300
	Rushes	Odeon TOCP-65018
	Wide Prairie	Odeon TOCP-65065
	Run Devil Run	Odeon TOCP-65269
	Working Classical	Odeon TOCP-65361
	Liverpool Sound Collage	Odeon TOCP-65599
	Wingspan – Hits & History	Odeon TOCP-65746-47
	Driving Rain	Odeon TOCP-65870
	Back In The US	Odeon TOCP-66110-11
	Back In The World	Odeon TOCP-66180-81
	Chaos And Creation in The Back Yard	Odeon TOCP-66460
	Chaos And Creation in The Back Yard	Odeon TOCP-66461
	Ecce Cor Meum	Toshiba EMI TOCP70099

JAPANESE SINGLES

Key GS = gatefold sleeve; SS = single-sheet sleeve; TS = trifold sleeve; LSI = lyric sheet insert; PS = pocket sleeve; 4 = ¥400 on sleeve; 5 = ¥500 on sleeve; 6 = ¥600 on sleeve; 7 = ¥700 on sleeve.

Released	Title	Label/number
	'The Family Way' / 'Theme For Jenny' GS, ¥370	London TOP-1177(S)
	'Another Day' / 'Oh Woman, Oh Why' GS, 4 or 5	Apple AR-2771
	'Another Day' / 'Oh Woman, Oh Why' GS, 5	Capitol EPR-10780
	'Another Day' / 'Oh Woman, Oh Why' GS, 7	Odeon EPS-17191
	'Eat At Home' / 'Smile Away' GS, 4 or 5	Apple AR-2879
	'Eat At Home' / 'Smile Away' GS, 5	Capitol EPR-10781
	'Eat At Home' / 'Smile Away' GS, 7	Odeon EPS-17192
	'Give Ireland Back To The Irish' / 'Give Ireland Back To The Irish' (Version) GS, 4 or 5	Apple EAR-10013
	'Give Ireland Back To The Irish' / 'Give Ireland Back To The Irish' (Version) GS, 5	Capitol EPR-10782
	'Give Ireland Back To The Irish' / 'Give Ireland Back To The Irish' (Version) GS, 7	Odeon EPS-17193
	'Mary Had A Little Lamb' / 'Little Woman Love' GS, 5	Apple EAR-10083
	'Mary Had A Little Lamb' / 'Little Woman Love' GS, 5	Capitol EPR-10783
	'Mary Had A Little Lamb' / 'Little Woman Love' GS, 7	Odeon EPS-17194
	'Hi Hi Hi' / 'C Moon' TS/GS, 5, red or black vinyl	Apple EAR-10241
	'Hi Hi Hi' / 'C Moon' GS, 5	Capitol EPR-10784
	'Hi Hi Hi' / 'C Moon' GS, 7	Odeon EPS-17195
	'My Love' / 'The Mess' GS, 5	Apple EAR-10350
	'My Love' / 'The Mess' GS, 5	Capitol EPR-10785
	'My Love' / 'The Mess' GS, 7	Odeon EPS-17196
	'Live And Let Die' / 'I Lie Around' GS, 5	Apple EAR-10401
	'Live And Let Die' / 'I Lie Around' GS, 5	Capitol EPR-10786
	'Live And Let Die' / 'I Lie Around' GS, 7	Odeon EPS-17197
	'Helen Wheels' / 'Country Dreamer' GS, 5	Apple EAR-10464
	'Helen Wheels' / 'Country Dreamer' GS, 5	Capitol EPR-10787
	'Helen Wheels' / 'Country Dreamer' GS, 7	Odeon EPS-17198
	'Jet' / 'Let Me Roll It' GS, 5	Apple EAR-10520
	'Jet' / 'Let Me Roll It' SS, 5	Capitol EPR-10788
	'Jet '/ 'Let Me Roll It' SS, 7	Odeon EPS-17199
	'Band On The Run' / 'Nineteen Hundred And Eighty Five' GS, 5	Apple EAR-10581
	'Band On The Run' / 'Nineteen Hundred And Eighty Five' GS, 5	Capitol EPR-10789
	'Band On The Run' / 'Nineteen Hundred And Eighty Five' GS, 7	Odeon EPS-17200
	'Junior's Farm' / 'Sally G' GS, 5	Apple EAR-10581
	'Junior's Farm' / 'Sally G' SS, 5	Capitol EPR-10790
	'Junior's Farm' / 'Sally G' SS, 7	Odeon EPS-17201
	'Walking In The Park With Eloise' / 'Bridge Over The River Suite'	Toshiba/EMI EMR-10706
	'Listen To What The Man Said' / 'Love In Song' PS, LSI, 5	Capitol EPR-10777
	'Listen To What The Man Said' /	Odeon EPS-17202

Released	Title	Label/number
	'Love In Song' PS, LSI, 7	
	'Letting Go' / 'You Gave Me The Answer' SS, 5	Capitol EPR-10863
	'Letting Go' / 'You Gave Me The Answer' SS, 7	Odeon EPS-17203
	'Venus And Mars/Rock Show' / 'Magneto And Titanium Man' SS, 5	Capitol EPR-10881
	'Venus And Mars/Rock Show' / 'Magneto And Titanium Man' SS, 7	Odeon EPS-17204
	'Silly Love Songs' / 'Cook Of The House' SS, 6	Capitol EPR-20020
	'Silly Love Songs' / 'Cook Of The House' SS, 6	Odeon EPR-20020
	'Let 'Em In' / 'Beware My Love' SS, 6	Capitol EPR-20070
	'Let 'Em In' / 'Beware My Love' SS, 6	Odeon EPR-20070
	'Maybe I'm Amazed' / 'Soily' SS, 6	Capitol EPR-20203
	'Mull Of Kintyre' / 'Girl's School' PS, LSI, 6	Capitol EPR-20370
	'With A Little Luck' / 'Backwards Traveller/Cuff Link' SS, 6	Capitol EPR-20430
	'With A Little Luck' / 'Backwards Traveller/Cuff Link' promo (DJ USE ONLY)	Capitol PRP-1038
	'I've Had Enough' / 'Deliver Your Children' SS, 6	Capitol EPR-20470
	'London Town' / 'I'm Carrying' SS, 6	Capitol EPR-20502
	'Goodnight Tonight' / 'Daytime Nightime Suffering' SS, 6	Odeon EPR-20572
	'Getting Closer' / 'Spin It On' SS, 6	Odeon EPR-20600
	'Wonderful Christmastime' / 'Rudolph The Red-Nosed Reggae' SS, 6	Odeon EPR-20644
	'Wonderful Christmastime' / 'Rudolph The Red-Nosed Reggae' SS, 7	Odeon EPS-17291
	'Arrow Through Me' / 'Old Siam Sir' SS, 6	Odeon EPR-20572
	'Coming Up' / 'Coming Up' (Live), 'Lunchbox/Odd Sox' PS, LSI, 6	Odeon EPR-20690
	'Waterfalls' / 'Check My Machine' PS, LSI, 7	Odeon EPS-17030
	'Seaside Woman' / 'B-Side To Seaside' GS, 7	ALFA/A&M AMP-707
	'Jet' / 'Hi Hi Hi' SS, 7	Odeon EPS-17153
	'Ebony And Ivory' / 'Rainclouds' PS, LSI, 7	Odeon EPS-17230
	'Ebony And Ivory' / 'Rainclouds' / 'Ebony And Ivory' (Solo Version) 12-inch	Odeon EPS10003
	'The Girl Is Mine' / 'Can't Get Outta The Rain' 7	Epic 07 5P-199
	'Say Say Say' / 'Ode To A Koala Bear' PS, 7	Odeon EPS-17401
	'So Bad' / 'Pipes Of Peace' SS, 7	Odeon EPS-17426
	'No More Lonely Nights' (Ballad) / 'No More Lonely Nights' (Playout Version) SS, 7	Odeon EPS-17483
	'Spies Like Us' / 'My Carnival' PS, 7	Odeon EPS-17595
	'Spies Like Us' / 'My Carnival' / 'Spies Like Us' (Party Mix) / 'Spies Like Us' (Alternative Mix Known To His Friends As Tom) / 'Spies Like Us' (DJ Version) / 'My Carnival' (Party Mix) 12-inch	Odeon S14-121

Released	Title	Label/number
	'Press' (Video Edit) / 'It's Not True' PS, 7	Odeon EPS-17648
	'Press' (Video Edit) / 'It's Not True'/ 'Press' (Video Soundtrack) / 'Press' (Dub Mix) / 'Hanglide' 12-inch	Odeon S14-148
	'Stranglehold' / 'Angry' (Remix) PS, 7	Odeon EPS-17678
	'Once Upon A Long Ago' / 'Back On My Feet' PS, 7	Odeon RP07-2011
	'Once Upon A Long Ago', 'Back On My Feet' 5-inch video-CD	Odeon CPV24-101
	'My Brave Face' / 'Flying To My Home' promo 7-inch	Odeon PRP-1384
	'My Brave Face', 'Flying To My Home', 'I'm Gonna Be A Wheel Someday', 'Ain't That A Shame' 3-inch CD (¥937)	Odeon XP10-2088
	'My Brave Face' / 'Flying To My Home' / 'I'm Gonna Be A Wheel Someday' / 'Ain't That A Shame' 12-inch (¥1,123)	Odeon XP12-2087
	'This One' / 'The First Stone' promo 7-inch	Odeon PRP-1413
	'This One', 'The First Stone', 'I Wanna Cry', 'I'm In Love Again' 3-inch CD, LSI, ¥1,123	Odeon XP12-2103
	'Put It There', 'Mama's Little Girl', 'Same Time Next Year' 3-inch CD (¥930)	Odeon TODP-2159
	'Birthday', 'Good Day Sunshine', 'P.S. Love Me Do', 'Let 'Em In' 3-inch CD (¥930)	Odeon TODP-2204
	'Birthday' 5-inch 1-track video	Odeon TOFF-7506.
	'The Long And Winding Road', 'C Moon', 'Mull Of Kintyre' 5-inch CD (¥1,200)	OdeonTOCP-6638
	'All My Trials', 'C Moon', 'Strawberry Fields Forever', 'Help!', 'Give Peace A Chance' 5-inch CD (¥1,200)	Odeon TOCP-6639
	'Hope Of Deliverance', 'Big Boys Bickering' 3-inch CD single (¥930)	Odeon TODP-2397
	'C'mon People', 'I Can't Imagine' 3-inch CD single (¥930)	Odeon TODP-2401
	'Off The Ground', 'Cosmically Conscious', 'Style Style', 'Sweet Sweet Memories' 5-inch CD (¥1,500)	Odeon TOCP-7942
	'A Leaf' 3-inch CD (¥1,000)	Toshiba/EMI Classics TODP2526
	'Young Boy', 'Looking For You' 5-inch CD (¥1,223)	Odeon TOCP-40040
	'The World Tonight', 'Young Boy' 5-inch CD (¥1,223)	Odeon TOCP-40073
	'Hello Goodbye' 1-track promo CD	Toshiba-EMI PM-0001
	'From A Lover To A Friend', 'From A Lover To A Friend', 'From A Lover To A Friend'	Toshiba-EMI TOCP-4015
	'Driving Rain' 1-track promo CD	Toshiba-EMI PCD-2532
	'Fine Line', 'Comfort Of Love', 'Growing Up Falling Down'	Toshiba-EMI TOCP-40183

This is a complete index of song and album titles. As in the rest of the book, songs are 'In Single Quotes', albums *In Italics*. Titles beginning with 'A...' or 'The...' are listed under the initial letter of the second word.

A

B

C

D

E

AUTHOR'S THANKS
For Rachel.
The author would like to thank the many people who have helped with this volume: EMI Archives, MSFL, Rykodisc Records, the Hard Rock Cafe Headquarters, the British Library Newspapers, Michelle at the Mark And Lard Show, Ron Clint at East Central One Records, and Herald Gernhardt, Mike Kovacich, and Steve Marinucci for the information posted on their web-sites. A big thank you to Nigel Osborne and all at Jawbone, and to Tony Bacon at Jawbone for his editorial work.

SOURCES
The author wishes to acknowledge here the various sources he used during the research and the writing of this book.

Books
Keith Badman *The Beatles After The Break-Up* (Omnibus 1999).
Keith Badman *The Beatles The Dream Is Over* (Omnibus 2001).
Richard Balls *Sex & Drugs & Rock'N'Roll: The Life Of Ian Dury* (Omnibus 2000).
BBC *The Lennon Tapes* (BBC 1981).
The Beatles *Anthology* (Weidenfeld 2000).
Johnny Black *Recording Sgt Pepper* (Tracks 1997).
John Blake *All You Needed Was Love* (Hamlyn 1983).
Peter Blake *About Collage* (Tate Gallery 2000).
Peter Brown & Steven Gaines *The Love You Make* (Pan 1975).
Tony Carr & Tony Tyler *The Beatles: An Illustrated Record* (New English Library 1991).
Alan Clayson *Ringo Starr: Straight Man Or Joker* (Sidgwick & Jackson 1990).
Alan Clayson *The Quiet One: A Life of George Harrison* (Sidgwick & Jackson 1995).
Clayson, Jungr & Johnson *Woman: The Incredible Life Of Yoko Ono* (Chrome Dreams 2004).
Ray Coleman *John Winston Lennon 1940-66* (Sidgwick & Jackson 1984).
Ray Coleman *John Ono Lennon 1967-80* (Sidgwick & Jackson 1984).
Ray Coleman *McCartney Yesterday & Today* (Boxtree 1984).
Ray Connolly *In The Sixties* (Pavilion 1976).
Philip Cowan *Behind The Beatles Songs* (Polytantric undated).
Cox & Lindsay *The Complete Beatles U.S. Price Guide* (Longman 1983).
Andy Davis *The Beatles Files* (Bramley 1995).
Paul Du Noyer *We All Shine On* (Carlton 1997).
Geoff Emerick and Howard Massey *Here, There And Everywhere* (Gotham 2006).
Kristopher Englehardt *Beatles Under Cover* (Collectors Guide 1986).
Kristopher Engelhardt *The Beatles Under Cover: Book & CD edition* (Collector's Guide 1998).
Mike Evans *The Art Of The Beatles* (Anthony Bond 1984).
Anthony Fawcett *One Day At A Time* (New English Library 1977).
Danny Fields *Linda McCartney: The Biography* (Little, Brown 1991).
Geoffrey Giuliano *Blackbird: The Life And Times Of Paul McCartney* (Dutton 1986).
Geoffrey Giuliano *The Beatles: A Celebration* (Sidgwick & Jackson 1982).
Geoffrey Giuliano *Tomorrow Never Knows* (Paper Tiger 1977).
Geoffrey & Brenda Giuliano *The Lost Beatles Interviews* (Virgin 1988).
Albert Goldman *The Lives Of John Lennon* (Morrow 1988)
Goldmine *The Beatles Digest* (Krause 2000).
Stefan Granados *Those Were The Days: An Unofficial History of The Beatles Apple Organisation* (Cherry Red 2002).
Jonathan Green *All Dressed Up: The Sixties and the Counterculture* (Pimlico 1992).
Jonathan Green *Days in The Life: Voices from the English Underground 1961-1971* (Pimlico 1994).
George Harrison *I Me Mine* (W H Allen 1994).
Tony Jasper *Paul McCartney And Wings* (Octopus 1977).
Jeffery Levy *Applelog, Fifth Edition* (Bagtwo 2006).
Mark Lewisohn *Complete Beatles Recording Sessions: The Official Story of the Abbey Road Years* (EMI 1988).
Mark Lewisohn *The Beatles Live* (Pavillon 1997).
Mark Lewisohn *The Complete Beatles Chronicle* (Pyramid 1989).
Mark Lewisohn *The Complete Beatles Recording Sessions* (Hamlyn 1977).
Mark Lewisohn (ed) *Wingspan* (Little, Brown 2002).
Ian MacDonald *Revolution In The Head* (Fourth Estate 1984).
Madinger & Easter *Eight Arms To Hold You* (44 1 Productions 2001).
George Martin *Summer Of Love: The Making Of Sgt Pepper* (Macmillan 1983).
Arthur Marwick *The Sixties* (OUP 1998).
Dan Matovina *Without You: The Tragic Story Of Badfinger* (Frances Glover 1997).
Paul McCartney *Paintings* (Little, Brown 1999).
Mike McGear *Thank You Very Much* (Arthur Baker 1981).
Miles *John Lennon In His Own Words* (Omnibus 1980).
Chrissie Lies *Yoko Ono: Have You Seen The Horizon Lately?* (Museum Of Modern Art Oxford 1997).
Miles *The Beatles In Their Own Words* (Putnam 1979).
Barry Miles *Paul McCartney: Many Years From Now* (Secker & Warburg 1999).
Alexandra Munroe & Jon Hendricks *Yes: Yoko Ono: Book & CD edition* (Harry N. Abrams 2000).
Jeremy Pascall *Paul McCartney And Wings* (Phoebus 1977).
Gareth Pawlowski *How They Became The Beatles* (Macdonald 1990).
Ian Peel *The Unknown Paul McCartney* (Reynolds & Hearn 2002).
George Perry (ed) *Paul McCartney's Broad Street* (Pavilion 1984).
Jo & Tim Rice *Guinness Book Of Hit Singles* (Guinness 1999).
Stephens & Stout (eds) *Art And The Sixties: This Was Tomorrow* (Tate 2004).
John Robertson *The Art & Music Of John Lennon* (Omnibus 1990).
Rolling Stone, Editors *The Ballad Of John And Yoko* (Rolling Stone 1982).
Nicholas Schaffner *The Beatles Forever* (McGraw Hill 1978).
David Sheff *The Playboy Interviews With John Lennon And Yoko Ono* (Berkley 1982).
Bruce Spizer *The Beatles On Apple Records* (Ninety-Eight 2003).
Bruce Spizer *The Beatles Solo On Apple Records* (Ninety-Eight 2005).
Neville Stannard *The Beatles The Long & Winding Road* – A History Of The Beatles On Record (Virgin 1982).
Neville Stannard *The Beatles Working Class Heroes Volume 2* (Avon 1984).
George Tremlett *The Paul McCartney Story* (Futura 1975).
Steve Turner *A Hard Day's Write* (Harper 1994).
Jann Wenner *Lennon Remembers* (Penguin 1973).

Newspapers, magazines, journals
Bassist; *Beat Instrumental*; *Beatles Monthly*; *Beatles Now*; *Beatles Unlimited*; *Beatlology Magazine*; *Billboard*; *The Boston Globe*; *British Beatles Fan Club Magazine*; *Classic fm Magazine*; *Club Sandwich: The Magazine of the Paul McCartney Fun Club*; *Creem*; *Crawdaddy*; *The Daily Mail*; *Disc & Music Echo*; *The Guardian*; *Guitar Player; Guitar World*; *Guitarist*; *Hotwired Inc.*; *The Independent*; *Insight*; *Instant Karma*; *Life*; *Maccazine: Dutch Paul McCartney Fanclub Magazine*; *Melody Maker*; *The Miami Herald*; *Music Week*; *Mojo* (including specials *1000 Days of Revolution*, *John Lennon Special*); *The Nashville Banner*; *New Musical Express*; *New Statesman*; *The Observer*; *OK*; *Oobu Joobu: A Track-By-Track Analysis Of His American Radio Show*, by Edward Eikelenboom, *Dutch Paul McCartney Fan Club*; *Paul McCartney FM*; *P.E.T.A. Animal Times*; *Playboy*; *Q* (including special *The Beatles, Band of The Century*); *Radio Times*; *Readers Digest*; *Record Collector*; *Record Mirror*; *Red Mole*; *Rocky Mountain News*; *Rolling Stone*; *The Scottish Daily Record*; *Sounds*; *The Tennessean*; *Time*; *The Times* (London); *TV Times*; *USA Today*; *USA Weekend*; *Vox*; *Woman's Own*; *Word*.

Websites
Christopher Brewer's McCartney recording sessions, rgo.simplenet.com/macca
Conference Archives, webcast.gatech.edu/papers/arch/Concannon.html
David Adcock's Paul McCartney page, www.geocities.com/SunsetStrip/Towers/6264/macca.html
Flaming Pie, www.flamingpie.com

Laurence Juber page, http://laurencejuber.com/juber/german.html
Linda McCartney Pro Cycling Team, www.lindamccartey-pct.co.uk
Macca Central, www.macca-central.com
Mix magazine, www.mixonline.com/
MPL, www.mplcommunications.com
MSN page, http://entertainment.msn.co.uk/music/paulmccartney/
Nitin Sawhney interview, www.undercover.com.au/idol/nitinsawhney.html
Notes From The Edge, www.nfte.org
Paul McCartney FAQ, www.macca-faq.com
Plugged 'Harald Gernhart's' Unofficial Paul McCartney page, cip2.e-technik.uni-erlangen.de:8080/hyplan/gernhard/macca/index.html
Rough Edge, www.roughedge.com
Standing Stone, www.standingstone97.com
Ubu Web: Sound, www.ubu.com/sound/index.html
Walls and Bridges story, http://johnlennonstory.homestead.com/johnlennonstory.html
Wingspan, www.paulmccartney.com

McCartney/Wings tour programmes

A Garland For Linda; Back In The World, 2003; Driving USA; Japan Tour 1980; Liverpool Oratorio; Music For Montserrat; New World Tour; UK Tour 1976; UK Tour 1979; Wings Over Europe; Working Classical; World Tour 1989/90; 04 Summer Tour.

McCartney press releases

Driving Rain; EMI Classics; Flowers In The Dirt; McCartney II; Pipes Of Peace; Press To Play; Run Devil Run; Standing Stone.

McCartney audio-visual sources

Band on The Run – The Story Of Wings Pt. 1 and 2, BBC Radio.
The Beatles Anthology, DVD Apple.
Desert Island Discs, BBC Radio.
Ecce Cor Meum, Classic FM podcast.
Flaming Pie Special, BBC Television.
Flaming Pie Radio Special, BBC Radio.
Interview on *Good Morning America*, May 2001.
Interview with Andy Peebles, 1980, BBC Radio.
Interview with Anthony Cherry, BBC Radio.
Interview with Bob Geldof, Triple M, Adelaide, Australia 1993.
Interview with Bob Harris, Knebworth, BBC Radio, 1990.
Interview with Chris Evans, *TFI Friday*, Channel 4, 1997.
Interview with David Wigg, March 1970, Polydor Records.
Interview with Jody Denberg, KGSR Texas, November 7 1999.
Interview with Johnny Vaughn, *The Big Breakfast*, Channel 4, 1999.
Interview with Jonathan Ross, *The Last Resort*, Channel 4, 1987.
Interview with Leslie Ash, *The Tube*, Channel 4, 1983.
Interview with Mark Lawson, *Front Row*, BBC Radio, May 2001.
Interview with Matt Lauer, *The Today Show*, NBC Television, July 1997.
Interview with Melvin Bragg, *The Making of Paul McCartney's Broad Street*, ITV, 1984.
Interview with Michael Parkinson, BBC Television, 1999.
Interview with Nicky Horne, Capital Radio, 1981.
Interview with Oprah Winfrey, Sky Television, 1997.
Interview with Richard Skinner, *McCartney*, BBC Television.
Interview with Selina Scott, BBC Breakfast News, BBC Television, 1986.
Interview with Terry Gross, *Fresh Air*, April 30 2001
Interview with Terry Wogan, BBC Television, 1987.
Jools Holland interview with Chas Jankel and Laurie Latham, BBC Radio, 2001.
Linda McCartney Landscapes, BBC Television.
McCartney On McCartney Pt. 1 – 8, BBC Radio.
Off The Ground Radio Special, Independent Radio.
Oobu Joobu radio programmes 1 to 17.
Paul McCartney and Wings *Rock Show*, PMI.
Paul McCartney *Get Back*, PMI
Paul McCartney: Ghosts From The Past, BBC Television.
Paul McCartney on *The Roxy*, ITV Television.
Paul McCartney *Once Upon A Video*, PMI.
Paul McCartney *Sold On Song*, BBC Television/Radio.
Paul McCartney *Standing Stone*, radio show.
Paul McCartney *Talk In The USA*, *Driving Rain* radio show.
Paul McCartney *Up Close*, BBC Television.
Press To Play radio special, BBC Radio.
Routes Of Rock, BBC Radio, 1999.
SFX Magazine, issues 11, 12, 1982.
Star Sound Extra, BBC Radio.
Top Of The Pops 2, McCartney Special, BBC Television.
Tug Of War radio special, BBC Radio.
Wingspan, DVD MPL.
Z is for Zapple, BBC 4 Television Archive Hour.

Lennon audio-visual sources

Apollo, Harlem, December 17 1971 (raw video footage).
Aquarius (raw video footage).
The Bed-In, EMI Video.
Eyewitness News (raw video footage).
Gimme Some Truth: The Making Of John Lennon's Imagine Album, EMI DVD.
In My Life: Lennon Remembered, BBC Radio.
Interview with Andy Peebles, BBC, December 6 1980.
Interview with Bob Harris, *The Old Grey Whistle Test*, BBC TV, April 28 1975.
Interview with Bob Miles, RKO, December 8 1980.
Interview with Capital Radio, 1975.
Interview with David Frost, *The David Frost Show*, June 14 1969 and December 16 1971 (raw video footage).
Interview with David Wigg, October 21 1969, Polydor Records.
Interview with Denis Elsas, WNEW FM, New York City, September 28 1974.
Interview with Dick Cavett, September 11 & 24 1971 and May 11 1972, DVD.
Interview with Elliot Mintz, KABC TV, November 1 1973.
Interview with Howard Cossel, *Monday Night Football*, ABC TV, December 9 1974.
Interview with Jann Wenner, December 8 1970, Rolling Stone podcast.
Interview with Mike Douglas, *The Mike Douglas Show*, February 14–18 1972.
Interview with Scott Muni, WNEW FM, Feburary 13 1975.
Interview with Tom Snyder, *The Tomorrow Show*, April 28 1975.
John Lennon – Imagine, The Film, EMI video.
John Lennon Live In New York City, EMI video.
Live at the Fillmore East with Frank Zappa (raw video footage).
Sweet Toronto, DVD.
Ten For Two (raw video footage).

PICTURE CREDITS

The jacket image was created by Balley Design Ltd from photographs by Harry Goodwin/Redfern's (Lennon) and Barry Peake/Rex Features (McCartney). Photographs used within the book were supplied by Redfern's, London, from the following photographers/collections: page 2, Max Scheler; page 6/7 Tom Hanley (Lennon), David Redfern (McCartney); page 26/27 Tom Hanley (Lennon), Jorgen Angel (McCartney); page 134/135 Rob Verhorst; page 196/197 Michel Linssen; page 246/247 Jim Sharpe.

"Madness is the first sign of dandruff." ***John Lennon, 1973***